WEST MÉXICO
FROM SEA TO SIERRA

WEST MÉXICO
FROM SEA TO SIERRA

A TRAVELER'S HANDBOOK
TO THE BAJA CALIFORNIA PENINSULA
& MEXICO'S WEST COAST

BY
CHARLES KULANDER

LA PAZ PUBLISHING
RAMONA, CALIFORNIA

WEST MÉXICO
FROM SEA TO SIERRA

Publishing History:
First Edition January 1992
Copyright 1992 © by Charles Kulander
Editor: Cris Featherweed
Maps & photos by author except as noted
Illustrations by Peter Jon Cole
Cover Photo: Barrel Cactus on Isla Catalana, hand-colored
Typesetting by Hunza Graphics
Typefaces: Times, Helvetica, Franklin Gothic #2, Lithos
Printed on Envirotech, an acid-free recycled paper
Printed by Bookcrafters, Inc.

Library of Congress Card Number 91-76304
ISBN 0-9629043-3-3

Printed in the United States of America
Published by: La Paz Publishing
              P.O. Box 1889
              Ramona, CA 92065
              (619) 789-8657

Library of Congress Cataloging-in-Publication Data

Kulander, Charles, 1953–
    West Mexico, From Sea to Sierra : a Traveler's Hand-
book to the Baja California Peninsula and Mexico's West
Coast / by Charles Kulander. — 1st ed.
        p.   cm.
    Includes bibliographical references and index.
    ISBN 0-9629043-3-3 (pbk.) : $16.95
    1. Mexico, Western—Description and travel—Guide-
books.
    I. Title
F1374.K85   1992   91-76304
917.2—dc20   CIP

The author and publisher have worked hard to make this book as accurate as possible, but in this country of contradictions, prices fluctuate, names change, and regulations are often re-invented on the spot. Errors inevitably appear. Therefore, both the publisher and author make no promises, offer no warranties, or accept any responsibility for injury, mishap or inconvenience incurred by any person using this book.

Table of Contents

10. *Sonora*

11. *Sinaloa & Barranca del Cobre*

12. *Nayarit*

Map Table

Photos

All photographs are by Charles Kulander, except for:
Bells of Misión San Javier, on page 142
by Jil Cole Kulander
Tarahumara, on page 242,
by Lillian Fisk, Courtesy San Diego Museum of Man
Cora in Native Dress, 1915, on page 267.
photographer unknown, Courtesy San Diego Musuem of Man.

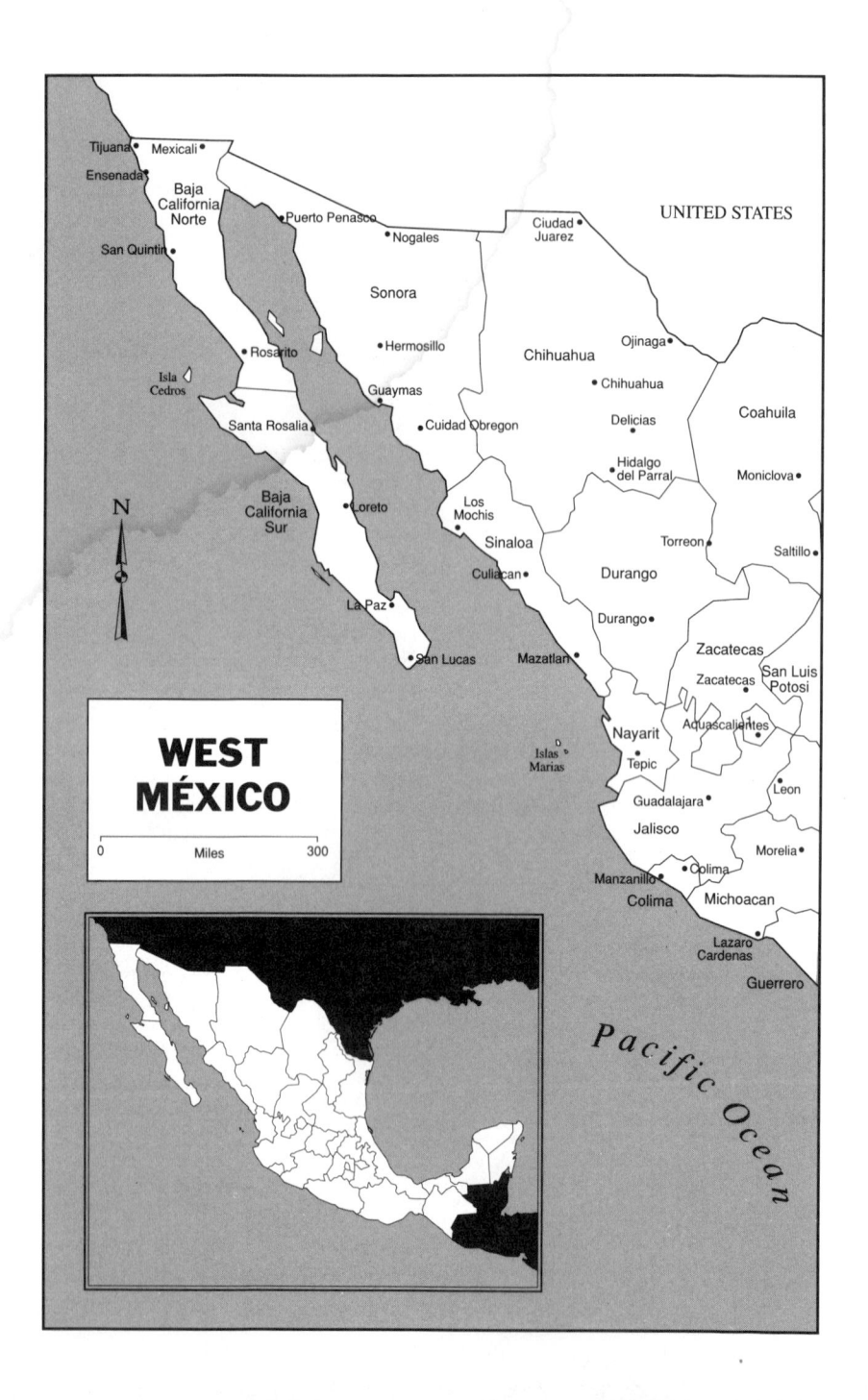

West México,
An Introduction

Western Mexico is not a land of contrasts. Sure, there are volcanoes and valleys, deserts and jungles, wealth and poverty. But the secret of Mexico lies not in the differences but in the sameness. Unlike the ethnic patchwork of the United States, a single *mestizo* culture dominates the country.

Mexico is the only true New World nation. Mexicans have more in keeping with the people who walked the land bridge across the Bering Strait than they do with those who sailed across the Atlantic. And though conquered by Europeans, the people of Mexico never cut their indigenous roots.

To cross the border from the United States to Mexico can be like going from the ordinary to the transcendent, from a world of fact to one of fiction. In Mexico, the mysteries of life stand closer to the surface of things. Death, religion, ceremonies, and fiestas seem more exuberant, loaded with color, emotion, and risk. The landscape is marked by miracles. Grass that hasn't been watered in 300 years grows in the shape of a cross in Tepic. In Barra de Navidad, you can see the crucifix that quelled a savage storm. Near Alamos, a miracle cactus. At the Basilica of Guadalupe, the face of the Virgin.

Time doesn't rush forward but moves slowly in circles. For even the most jaded traveler, Mexico is like a dream world, the subconscious of the North American continent.

There is more a gap than an actual boundary that separates our two countries, a kind of cultural canyon down which runs a river of prejudice and misunderstanding as real as the Río Grande. This cultural canyon is our true border, one that each traveler crosses sooner or later, and it can happen as easily in Los Angeles or Guadalajara as it can in Tijuana or Nogales. We cross this border when we stop seeing things through the eyes of our own culture, when we become what the Mexicans call *simpatico*, when we try to understand instead of judge.

Mexico and the United States are bound to each other by more than these political and cultural borders. Birds born in Mexico spend their summers in the United States. Gray whales are born in Mexico and feed in Alaska. The Rocky Mountains are cousin to the Sierra Madre. What once filled the Grand Canyon now carpets the Sea of Cortés. This natural world works to bring us together.

Western Mexico and the United States also share a common history. In fact, 150 years ago much of the American West belonged to Mexico. The legend of the Seven Cities of Cíbola, the myth of California, the imagined Straits of Anian brought the Spanish up from Mexico long before the first gringo crossed the Colorado. Their missions became our cities. They laid the foundation of the American West, which we filled in with the facts of our occupation. The American West is a marriage between two countries.

As Mexico has influenced the United States, we have left our imprint on their country. West Mexico bears the scars of our battles, the memories of our invasions, and the benefits of our business. Just as the Spanish founded cities in the United States, North Americans helped to lay down the city streets of Los Mochis, created vast agricultural colonies in Sinaloa and on the peninsula, brought in the railroad to Sonora, and mined for gold everywhere. Today, baseball is as popular as soccer. U.S. tourism supports entire cities. Our influence is inescapable. Consequently, when you travel around Western Mexico, it can seem both familiar and strange at the same time.

To travel in West Mexico is to learn not just about Mexico, but about our own country. Not just about Mexicans, but about ourselves.

1.

The History & Culture of West Mexico

HISTORY
The Conquest

Most colonists who settled in North America were seeking personal freedom in a new land. The Spanish came to conquer, to extend the realm. Drawn by dreams of gold and conquest, they poured into Mexico, searching for fortune, not salvation.

Greed provided a powerful impetus to explore. The Spaniards were wandering around Kansas almost a hundred years before the Pilgrims landed on the shores of Massachusetts.

The early conquerors were searching for chimerical cities of gold and islands of Amazons. These two 16th century myths were the driving force of the conquistadors' imagination, propelling them west and north into unknown lands.

The original explorers were Asian, migrants who walked the Bering Strait 18,000 to 20,000 years ago. Crossing from Asia to Alaska, they moved slowly down the continent. In Mexico, the earliest villages date to 3,000 BC, the earliest shards of pottery around 2,300 BC. As the more advanced tribes—the *Toltecs* and the *Nahoas*—moved down the west coast of Mexico, weaker tribes—the *Pericúes, Guaycura,* and *Cochimíes*—were forced down the barren Baja California peninsula, an atrophied limb of the continent that proved to be a geographical and cultural dead end.

By the time the Spaniards arrived, this coastal migration route down the west coast of Mexico had turned into a well traveled road connecting central Mexico to the Pueblo Indians of Arizona and the shores of California. Instead of migration, it was now used for trade. Turquoise from the American Southwest was traded for the parrot feathers of Nayarit. Corn for obsidian. Deerskin for gold.

The Spanish had nothing to trade but the threat of enslavement or death. After conquering the Aztec capital and subduing the surrounding tribes, their interest swung westward. Cortés' troops entered the native state of Colima in 1522, seeking a base from which to strike northwestward, their appetites whetted by indigenous tales of an island of Amazons.

Mythic Roots

History is littered with these imaginary islands. Legendary *Iemuria,* Plato's *Atlantis,* St. Brendan's *Land of Promise.* Herodotus wrote of islands and Amazons in the 5th century BC. The Chinese had their own version—an island called *Fusang,* populated by flat-chested females. Columbus believed in this myth, calling the island *Matenin*. It was the possibility of discovering *Matenin* that finally turned the ear of Ferdinand and Isabella.

Another medieval tale bearing on West Mexico dates back to 1150, when the Moors captured Spain. Seven bishops fled in boats, along with their followers, sailing west to an island called *Antilia*. Each bishop built a city. The Seven Cities of Antilia.

In 1510, Jacob Cromberger obtained the rights to publish and sell in newly conquered Mexico a big edition of *Sergas de Esplandian*, a book written to profit from this fascination with magical islands. It had to do with "an island, called California, very near the side of Terrestrial Paradise ...where black skinned women, Amazons, adorned with pearls and gold, were ruled by a great queen Califia." This book inflamed the imagination of the conquistadors, who, after the plunder of Tenochitlan, could no longer tell the difference between fact and fiction.

The *caciques* of newly conquered Colima told Cortés of an island that sounded the same as the fictional description of California. Cortés wrote to King Carlos about this island, called Ciguatan, that was "entirely populated by women, without any male ...they told me it is rich in pearls and gold. I will labor at making preparations to learn the truth." Two similar myths conjured a reality.

The First Explorations

From Colima, Cortés sent Francisco Cortés de Buenaventura north by land in 1524. Francisco Cortés followed native guides along a road through a series of towns until reaching Tepic, a place of perpetual spring-like weather at the base of a volcano. Not anxious to descend into the *tierra caliente* of the coastal lowlands of Sinaloa, he instead attempted to return to Colima by following the coast back from Tepic. Precipitous mountains defeated his plan. His greatest discovery was the road he walked on, the ancient

migration and trading route connecting the coastal lowlands with the central plateau, through the pass at Tepic.

Colima provided calm harbors at Manzanillo and Barra de Navidad, but it was a poor base for land expeditions, hemmed in by mountains. Tepic, with its mountain pass, was better situated. Before he could establish himself at Tepic, Cortés had to sail for Spain to defend himself from his enemies. He returned vindicated in 1530, with the right to rule any new land he conquered. But his arch rival, Nuño de Guzman, already had outflanked Cortés by establishing the Mexican northwest as his own fiefdom, which he named Nueva Galicia.

Guzman marched into the coastal lowlands of Nayarit and Sinaloa in 1530, also searching for this land of Amazons. The coastal plain was almost as populous then as the rural population of today. In a few short years, Guzman reduced this complex social organization to charcoal. Peaceful villagers who met him with open arms were given two choices: death or slavery.

Many fled. When Guzman came to the Río San Lorenzo south of Culiacán (the land of Ciguatan mentioned by the Colima caciques), he at first believed that he had actually entered the land of Amazons. He found only women and children. The men had already run for their lives.

Disillusioned with one myth, Guzman traded it for another. In 1530, he heard the story of a native who had accompanied his father to trade feathers for ornaments. They traveled 40 days to the north, finding seven cities where the streets were paved with silver. Seven cities, the mythical number!

An expedition of 400 Spaniards and thousands of natives began to march in 1531, searching for the seven cities. Inexplicably, they left the coastal route and attempted to cross the Sierra Madre, which they couldn't. Defeated by the geography, they remained to settle Culiacán, which Guzman turned into his center for slave trading.

Guzman continued to send out exploring

5

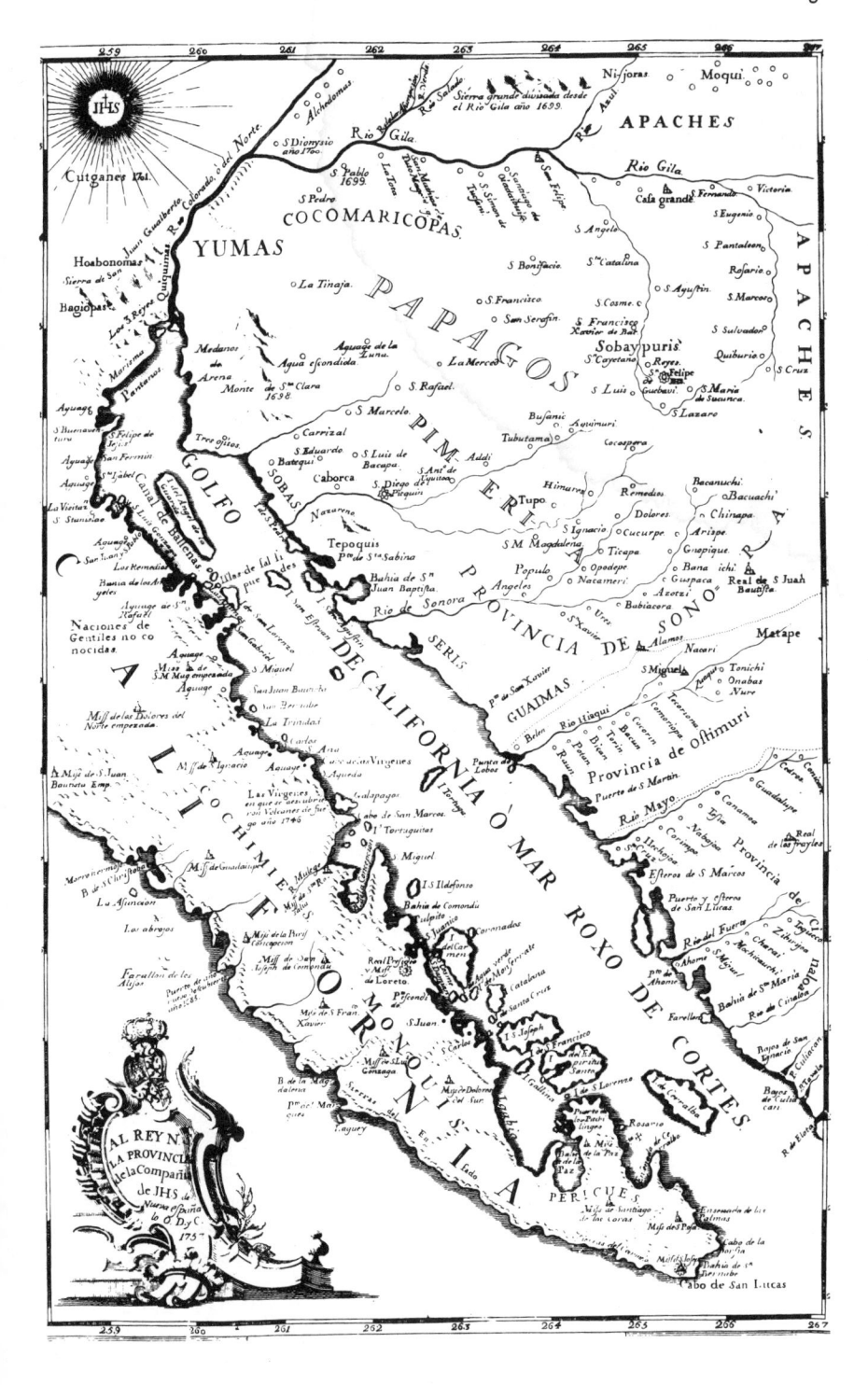

parties, as much to round up slaves as to look for evidence pointing to the seven cities made of gold.

Meanwhile, Cortés, blocked on the land route by Guzman to the north, sought by sea the queendom of Califia. In 1532, the year that the book *Sergas de Esplandian* was banned as inflammatory, Cortés sent Hurtado de Mendoza to search for this very island.

The first expedition ended in mutiny, as did another flotilla in 1534. But one of the mutinous ships landed at Bahia de La Paz, and brought back tales of pearls, supporting the myth of Califia.

Cortés himself sailed off in search of this island, which had already entwined itself with the name *California* in the imagination of the conquistadors.

Landing in Bahia de La Paz, Cortés learned first-hand of the peninsula's paucity. The few misshapen pearls and the primitive natives who lived like animals didn't justify the hardship. Dreams die hard. It wasn't until 23 colonists had starved to death in 1536 that the colony was abandoned.

Cabeza de Vaca

The same year the peninsula was abandoned, one of Guzman's slaving parties on the mainland encountered Cabeza de Vaca and his servant Esteban, survivors of an expedition that had been massacred along the coast of Texas. They had spent nine years wandering across the American Southwest, where no European had ever walked. They survived as shamans, going from tribe to tribe healing, praying, and preaching.

Reaching Arizona, they turned south along the well-traveled trading route into Sonora. After living for years among an indigenous people unsullied by European contact, Cabeza de Vaca and Esteban rejoined civilization in Culiacán, escorted into town by a band of slavers.

Horrified by the violence of the slave trade practiced by Guzman, Cabeza de Vaca protested vehemently in Mexico City and

was largely responsible for the end of the slave trade. But he also triggered a wave of Spanish intrusion into the untouched world of the northern indigenous tribes.

As he walked along the Río Sonora, the historic trading route between central Mexico and the high cultures of the Pueblos of New Mexico, he saw turquoise and stones he called emeralds but which were more likely of semi-precious nature. The traders told him these were brought down from mysterious cities in the north to be traded for skins and parrot feathers. These large pueblos of "many inhabitants and very large houses" were assumed by the Spanish to be the Seven Cities of Antiles—the Seven Cities of Gold.

Fray de Marcos

To gain more information on these seven cities, the new viceroy (king's representative) Mendoza sent Fray de Marcos de Niza on a secret expedition accompanied by Esteban, de Vaca's surviving companion. They left in 1539, following the trading route up through the Sonora Valley. The natives all pointed north to the great cities of a region they called Cíbola, most likely the pueblo towns of the Zuñi tribe of Arizona. Esteban traveled far ahead of Fray Marcos and was the first to see Cíbola. The chief warned him to go away, but Esteban, confident of his rapport with the natives, entered the town. After housing him for the night, the natives killed him in the morning.

Fray de Marcos heard of Esteban's murder. Before fleeing back to Culiacán, he claimed to have crept close enough to the city to verify its existence, a city "bigger than the city of Mexico." There is controversy as to whether Fray Marcos ever laid eyes on Cíbola, or if he was only trying to impress his superiors. If he actually did see the settlement, his eyes must have been clouded with fear.

Coronado

On his return, Fray Marcos' account was

proof of another gilded empire to the north, and a major expedition was outfitted for conquest. Cortés schemed to gain control of the expedition, but his failure on the peninsula tainted his reputation. Guzman was discredited for his cruelty. While Cortés pleaded with petitions, Coronado, a young upstart lieutenant, organized the expedition in Compostela and, with Fray Marcos de Niza at his side, left for Culiacán.

Coronado, given the official sanction, left Culiacán in 1540 along with 285 Spanish soldiers and close to 1,000 natives serving as guides, porters, and scouts. They traveled on the same trading route, which now became the *Camino Real*, the King's Road. It led through El Fuerte and Alamos, up past the Río Mayo, and through the Sonora Valley into what is now Arizona.

Coronado soon grew uneasy with Fray de Marcos, writing to Mendoza that "everything was the reverse of what Fray Marcos had told your lordship." Cíbola never glittered with gold, but was instead built of stone and adobe—highly cultured, multistoried but lacking in the one commodity on which the Spanish based their success: gold. On entering Cíbola, Fray de Marcos endured curses, insults, and jeers. For a second time he was forced to flee back to Mexico, this time by his own soldiers.

After the disappointment of not finding the Seven Cities of Gold, Coronado wandered about aimlessly as far as the plains of Kansas, looking to no avail for something worthy of conquest. After Coronado returned to Mexico, interest in further exploration in the northwest and the California peninsula evaporated. The dream of mythical islands and cities of gold submerged in a collective slumber.

El Camino Real

It took the Jesuits, and then the Franciscans to fill in the moral foundation of the initial conquest. They followed the route of the conquerors, constructing missions and visitas along the Camino Real on both the western coast and the peninsula. They sought souls with as much zeal as the conquistadors had searched for gold. Settlements, churches, presidios, and ranchos slowly took root in the wilderness, all strategically strung along the Camino Real. On the Baja California peninsula, a similar string of missions was slowly snaking north along a Camino Real of the church's own making.

The two Camino Reales, one following the river valleys through Sonora, the other threading the stony backbone of the Baja California peninsula, were the arteries that opened up the American West long before Lewis and Clark.

The myths that powered the exploration of the American West are of Hispanic heritage. We are linked to Mexico by this historical chain. The myths of California and the Seven Cities of Gold remain in our collective imagination. The land of Califia has become the California of today, a dream factory, still working its tarnished magic on anyone seeking a place "very near the side of Terrestrial Paradise." And the Seven Cities of Cíbola now have names: Tucson, Phoenix, Houston, Dallas, Los Angeles, San Fransisco, and San Diego. When their reflective glass towers are falsely gilded by a setting sun, they do seem to be made of gold, especially in the eyes of migrant Mexicans who come north every year in a centuries-old quest for greater wealth.

God, Gold, & Guns

As Coronado rode northward seeking golden cities, he was blinded to the mineral wealth that lay in its natural state. He camped in places that were later to become some of the world's richest silver mines.

These deposits of gold and silver were the catalyst for a violent history. As *gambusinos* (prospectors) explored the Sierra Madre, mining towns sprang up: Pánuco, Cópala, Cosalá, Alamos in the Sierra Madre, Santa Ana on the California peninsula.

Gold brought the settlers, God brought

the Jesuits. The priests settled the natives into missions and ranchos, protecting them as well as they could from forced labor in the mines. Many of the less sedentary tribes escaped domestication and continued to roam the mountains and deserts for the next 400 years.

The lands were settled, but never subdued. Spanish settlements and missions were devastated by raiding tribes. The Apaches and the Yaquis continued to kill settlers into the 1920s. The deserts and sierras provided sanctuary to many tribes, allowing them to resist *mestizaje*, the acculturation into Mexican society. The *Huichol* and *Cora*, the *Tarahumara*, the *Seri* and *Yaqui*, the *Mayo* still retain tribal ways.

Extinction

The rough terrain sheltered the indigenous people on the mainland from the European intrusion, but on the peninsula it exposed them. The few watering holes that could sustain life were preempted by the Jesuit and Franciscan missions and visitas. The *Guaycura* and *Pericú* tribes, gathered together under the influence of the church, were decimated by diseases they had never encountered on the peninsula: small pox, cholera, and syphilis. Supply ships from San Blas carried malarial mosquitoes. Soon the priests were ministering to empty pews. The extinction was so complete that by the early 1900s anthropologists could not find a single native in the southern half of the peninsula.

Independence

Sheltered from the rest of Mexico by its geography, West Mexico grew separate in spirit as well. Cut off from Mexico City by its mountains, Sinaloa, Sonora, and the peninsula were set up as an *Intendencia*, a self-governing district, rather than as a *Provincia* under the direct control of the viceroy, the King's appointed representative. During the War of Independence, which began in 1810, most people living in

this frontier were more concerned with defending themselves from Indian attack than in revolutionary rhetoric or in forging a new national identity. During the bloody eleven-year war to sever Mexico's allegiance to Spain, the battles raging inland made little impact on the daily life of the frontier. There were skirmishes but few battles.

The new nation-state of Mexico was fractured between those who believed in a regional federalism and those who called for a strong centralist government. Most who lived in West Mexico wanted a regional approach to government, and Guadalajara emerged as a counterbalance to the central power of Mexico City. Guadalajara was not dependent on the trade markets of the capital, and it was directly linked to commercial life at the ports of San Blas, Mazatlan, and Manzanillo. Mexico City was always viewed with mistrust.

Mexican-American War

As politicians debated and fought over the destiny of the new nation, the 30,000 *Norteamericanos* who had settled in the Texas province worried that a strongly centralist government would rob them of their regional autonomy. In 1836, the Texans rebelled and, after the massacre at the Alamo, were able to defeat General Santa Ana at San Jacinto Creek.

The Mexican government never recognized Santa Ana's capitulation. When the United States annexed Texas in 1845, war broke out. General Taylor rolled down from the north. Kearny swept through Texas and New Mexico. Fremont controlled California. As General Winfield Scott followed the route of Cortés from Veracruz to Mexico City, U.S. naval ships sailed for Mazatlán, Guaymas, and La Paz. There were some minor skirmishes in Mulege and San Jose del Cabo, but there were none of the fierce battles fought in central Mexico. Small bands of Mexican soldiers roamed the countryside, but they lacked the numbers to take

on U.S. forces.

When the war ended, the Treaty of Guadalupe Hidalgo ceded half of Mexico's territory to the United States, including everything north and west of the Río Grande, for which Mexico was paid $15 million. The Baja California peninsula, initially part of the ceded territory, was at the last moment returned to Mexico—to the chagrin of many of its leading citizens who had already pledged allegiance to the United States. They were evacuated with the troops and given compensation for their lost property. Many promptly returned back to La Paz to reclaim their holdings.

The independent spirit of western Mexico and the island-like isolation of the peninsula had always kept them at length from the central authority of Mexico City. But the very mountains and gulf which had insulated these regions from the political turmoil of Mexico now made them vulnerable to both foreign threats and influence. In the aftermath of war, the international boundary now lay at their front door, the mountains to their back.

Friend & Foe

The Mexican American War was "the most unjust war ever waged by a strong nation against a weaker one," to quote one U.S. general. It was a shameful theft of another nation's territory, which should have cast the U.S. as Mexico's mortal enemy. But the geography of the West welded our two cultures together in a way that transcended the enmity of war.

Because of its nearness, the U.S. replaced Europe as a center of culture. When they migrated, most Mexicans moved north instead of south. Thousands of miners walked the *Camino del Diablo* across the desert to California. Some credit Sonoran miners with teaching the '49ers how to mine for gold. During the Civil War, Mexico allowed the U.S. to use the Sea of Cortés to supply troops stationed in Arizona. Vast land tracts on both the peninsula and the mainland were granted to U.S. companies for colonization ventures. For much of West Mexico, the influence of the U.S. was as great as that of Mexico City.

Our shared geography inspired coopera-

legendary generals of the north, Obregón, De la Huerta, and Pancho Villa, who swept down on central Mexico, rebelling against the central authority of Porfirio Díaz. In asserting its own independence, West Mexico helped break his dictatorship and, in turn, the people gained a new nationalistic dimension to their regional character.

In the wake of the Mexican Revolution of 1910 (the first revolution of the 20th century), the men who guided the future of the new Mexican nation—Plutarco Calles, Abelardo Rodríguez, and Adolfo de la Huerta— all came from the northwest, the state of Sonora.

Today, West Mexico continues to struggle politically for control over its destiny, and in turn influences the nation. A politically conservative opposition party, *Accion Nacional* (PAN) battles pugnaciously for control of local government, and actually won the governorship of Baja California in July 1989, the first opposition party to do so since the revolution.

tion. It also encouraged armed invasion by American and French freebooters trying to take advantage of West Mexico's isolation from the central government. Count Boulbon landed in Guaymas in 1852, attempting to found a new nation-state. William Walker anchored off La Paz in 1853, proclaiming it part of his Republic of Sonora. Henry Crabb led 69 filibusters into Caborca in 1857. All three miscalculated the independent nature of the inhabitants. William Walker was hounded through the desert, barely escaping with his life. Boulbon was executed on the quay in Guaymas. Crabb's head was pickled in a jar of vinegar.

Nationalism & Regionalism

In Mexico, revolutions start in the north. Politically conservative, people here jump to defend their ideas, a quick-draw mentality evolved from their history. Shoot or be shot. And though settlers were not able to bring the hostile tribes into their society, they did incorporate the native's rebelliousness into their own lore of independence.

It is this propensity to defend their rights that helped ignite the Mexican Revolution. At Cananea, the first shouts of the Mexican Revolution were heard in protest over U.S. exploitation of the miners. And it was the

POWER & POLITICS

Since the Revolution of 1910, a single party has been able to consolidate one of the most unusual political systems in the world, a dictatorship in the guise of a democracy. But the token opposition parties have gained real power. These are the days of an emergent democracy, full of turmoil, struggle, fraud, and fighting. Unlike the United States, where the majority of citizens don't bother to go to the polls, in Mexico most people vote, even those that are dead.

Padding the vote with the names of the deceased or stealing the ballot box, traditional methods of insuring victory for the ruling Partido Revolucionario Institucional (PRI), are slowly giving way to accurate vote counts. Opposition parties are winning some political power locally, but PRI remains in control of central government.

Central Power

In Mexico City the president holds an imperial power, similar to an Aztec king. He goes on a largely ceremonial campaign trail, more a touring of the realm. At the end of his single six-year term, he chooses a successor, then retires quietly from the political area. Faces change, but the continuity of power remains.

The PRI constantly talks in revolutionary terms, robbing the opposition of rhetoric. It controls the media through a complicated apparatus of pay-offs, monopolies, rewards, and punishments, and even funds some of the opposition parties to provide the guise of democracy.

Cuauhtémoc Cárdenas

Times are changing. PRI, which consolidated power in the wake of the Mexican Revolution, grew complacent in the 1970s. In the '80s, the debt crisis led to decline in average wages and soaring inflation. In the 1988 election, the previously impregnable facade of the PRI cracked when Cuauhtémoc Cárdenas, son of the Mexican president who had nationalized the oil industry, bolted the party and challenged Salinas de Gortari for the presidency. Though Salinas won (helped in part by wide scale vote fraud), the opposition gained such power that PRI has since been forced to acknowledge losses in many local political contests as a way of relieving social pressure.

Cuauhtémoc Cárdenas draws support from the left wing, which is made up of a dozen feuding factions, such as the PPS, PCM, PST, PMT, PPM, and PSUM. Under his umbrella organization, called the *Partido de la Revolución Democrática* or PRD, he has been able to arrange this alphabet soup into a unified voice that speaks for the campesino, labor, the socialists, communists, and the indigenous. Support is strong in the countryside, where his name alone is enough to earn votes, reminding voters of his popular father as well as the last Aztecan king, the patriot martyr of Mexico.

The Conservatives

Counterbalancing PRD is *Acción Nacional* (PAN), made up largely of conservative businesspeople and an upwardly aspiring middle class. PAN was formed in 1939 of Catholics and old families whose fortunes had been affected by the Revolution. Their Catholic foundation has also given them surprising support among campesinos. PAN controls Baja California and many of the border towns, where emphasis is on economic empowerment rather than social justice.

The Struggle

Unlike a two-party system, the adept *priistas* (PRI) are able to play one side against the other in order to maintain their increasingly delicate fulcrum of power. This drama of unfolding democracy is taking place in every community in Mexico. Travelers in Mexico will no doubt run into political meetings, street assemblies, and protests. The flying flags define their stand. Red and black for the left wing, of blood and suffering. A celestial blue and white for the Panistas, conjuring up the image of God and divine right. Or the red, green and white of both PRI and the Mexican flag, which that party is trying so hard to keep one and the same.

WESTERN CULTURE

In Mexico, corn carries symbolic weight. According to many prehispanic legends, humans were born of corn. Most Mexicans eat corn tortillas, the traditional mainstay of indigenous culture. But in the northwest, inhabitants are more likely to eat flour tortillas, a more civilized foodstuff in their eyes. Wheat sets them apart from the corn-eating Indians, from the darker side of the *mestizo*. In the northwest, they dance to a variation of the polka imported by German settlers, eat carne asada instead of enchiladas, and wear cowboy hats instead of sombreros.

This independent stance in much of West Mexico contrasts to southern and central Mexico, which remains bound to traditions of the past. Though the people of western Mexico have been conditioned by their history and geography, and influenced by the pop culture of the United States, their character remains uniquely Mexican.

FATALISM

Mexicans were among the first people to measure time, yet they do not keep step to it. They invented the wheel, but never used it until forced by the Spanish. This discrepancy between insight and action runs like a chasm through their character, a dark canyon of fatalism.

We all will die, says the Mexican. Death is a fact, so life must also be predetermined.

If our lives are already set, the end so clearly in sight, then why burden ourselves with mundane routines, austere disciplines, and mindless industry? Life is a treacherous thing, and tomorrow it may rob you of the happiness you now have. Life is to be taken advantage of as the moment arises. Fiestas never end before the bottles are emptied. Politicians promise the world, even if they deliver little more than a handshake. A businessman will gouge for an immediate profit rather than invest for the long run. There is wisdom in all of this, but at the expense of productivity and the balance sheet. Northamericans may trust the bottom line, but Mexicans trust in death.

This is apparent during Día de los Muertos, the Day of the Dead. On November 1st and 2nd, cemeteries in Mexico blossom, as Mexicans spend the night next to family graves, drinking, praying, and talking to the dead. *Calaveras* are sung, songs that satirize the living as if they were already dead. Children eat candied skulls. Adults slice bread baked in the form of shrouded corpses. People seem at ease with death.

This familiarity with death stretches back to the Aztecs. Before the Spanish came, death was one of the gods, shaped like man but without flesh. Death was the god responsible for man's destiny in the universe.

Aztec religion was gloomy with fatalism. Their cosmos was always on the edge of dissolution, the natural cycles ready to wobble into oblivion at any moment. Only human sacrifice, the main religious rite, could keep the world from destruction. Only death could prolong life.

At the beginning of the 16th century, Moctezuma was awaiting the doom that his astrologers had divined from the stars. It arrived as predicted in the form of metal-clad Spaniards landing on the jungled coast of Veracruz, 600 men ready to conquer an empire. From that day, Mexican history has failed to run in any linear fashion easily captured by a time-line. Instead, it is like a substance forged of historical process, slowly taking shape over the centuries.

It is hard to tell whether an inherent fatalism has forged Mexican history or if history has forged this fatalism. The two seem interlocked, like a string of chromosomes.

THE MESTIZO

Eighty percent of Mexicans are *mestizos*, people of both Spanish and Indian blood. During the Colonial period, the *mestizo*

Spanish heritage. The mestizo character is forged of both unbending Spanish steel and malleable Indian gold, two dissimilar metals that can never be reconciled.

The effect of this dissonance in the national identity is best represented by three historical figures: Cuauhtémoc, Cortés, and Malinche.

Cuauhtémoc

Cuauhtémoc is considered the true Mexican patriot. He was the last king of the Aztecs, defiant and proud. When the final defense of Tenochtitlán crumbled, he was captured. When later threatened with revolt, Cortés had the Aztec king's feet anointed with oil and set afire. Cuauhtémoc endured his death with stoicism and dignity. His valor proved greater than the Spanish victory.

Mexican patriots have followed his example ever since. Morelos and Allende had their heads cut off. Morelos shot, after refusing a jailer's offer to escape. Iturbide executed. The Niños Héroes, jumping to their deaths rather than be taken prisoner by U.S. soldiers. Madero, murdered under police guard. Carranza, shot in his sleep by a friend. Zapata, Pancho Villa, Obregón, all of them assassinated.

Cortés

Opposite Cuauhtémoc, the conquered, is Cortés, the conqueror. He is despised in Mexican history as a raptor, bringing with him a wicked pestilence that ravaged the country. His victories, his courage, his steeled determination are given little credit. In Mexico, there are no statues of Cortés.

Malinche

These two seminal figures, Cortés and Cuauhtémoc, make up opposite sides of the Mexican psyche. The two are separated by a wide chasm of treachery, symbolized by Malinche. Malinche was the Indian mistress of Cortés, who supplied him with advice that proved crucial in the Conquest.

was treated as a bastard, excluded from the privileged white society of the Spanish *gachupines* and Mexican-born *creoles*. Likewise, they were forbidden to live with the Indians for fear they would stir rebellion. They found livelihood as rancheros, muleteers, miners. Some found shelter in the church clergy. But many, born out of wedlock, fathered by rape and the concubine, lived without home or job, an army of the dispossessed.

For three centuries Mexico remained under the rule of the hated *gachupines*. In 1808, Charles IV, the Spanish King, abdicated. Napoleon ruled Madrid. Spanish authority in Mexico grew weak. The *mestizo* rebelled against the diminishing Spanish rule.

After the bloody convolutions of the War of Independence in the 18th century, it took another century for the *mestizos* to gain firm control of the government. In the aftermath of the Mexican Revolution of 1910, a new national identity finally was forged— one that was thoroughly *mestizo* in both spirit and body.

Spanish Steel, Indian Gold

We often think of Mexicans as being "Spanish," but *mestizos* identify more with the Indians. Yet they are constantly at pain to resolve what they consider an illegitimate

Malinche betrayed the nation. Even today, a Mexican who covets foreign-made goods and takes on foreign affectations is called a *Malinchista*, a person who would sell out the nation.

Machismo

The historical drama played out between Cuauhetmoc, Cortés, and Malinche continues to be played out on a personal level. According to some cultural anthropologists, the *mestizo* is at war with himself, afflicted with both the Spanish obsession with honor and the Indians' humiliation of losing their women to the Spanish by force and treachery. Obsessive honor to defend a wounded masculinity. Add a fatalistic streak and the resulting *machismo* attains a particularly aggressive form that is evident in all facets of Mexican culture, from the bus driver who risks thirty lives on a blind curve, to drinking contests, to the saucy pursuit of women.

Some social anthropologists see a definite pattern in how women are both idolized and distrusted. The mother is adored in Mexico. Beyond reproach, she could never betray her family. But the wife, who is desired sexually, is demeaned not for what she is but for what she is capable of, namely treachery. Instead of waiting for her to betray him, the Mexican male strikes first, like Cortés, to conquer rather than be betrayed. He takes a mistress or sometimes a second family, called the *familia chica*. The resentful wife lavishes her tenderness on her son, who in turn holds her as the feminine ideal, beyond reproach. The vicious cycle continues through the generations.

The Mexican Mask

This distrust is much greater outside the family. The Mexican who opens himself to the outside world knows of the treacherous consequences illustrated so clearly by history. Any new experience promises the worst. The best defense has always been to isolate the outside world, the way the Indi-

ans shun contact with outsiders. Mexico's Nobel-prize winning poet Octavio Paz has written brilliantly about the Mexican mask, a kind of emotional armor which serves as a defense against a belligerent world. Cynicism abounds. *Ni modo* and *no importa* are two phrases you hear everywhere. It doesn't matter. It is not important.

What is important is to keep the world at bay through a number of elusive devices. Language is florid, poetic, and full of excessive courtesy. But it often has no more substance than does a smoke screen. The hospitality of the Mexican family is legendary among travelers, but when it comes down to the saying *mi casa es tu casa*, the truth is that few Mexican homes have doorbells.

While personal relationships outside of the family are no open door, creative expression pours out unhindered through open windows, allowing travelers to look into the heart of Mexican culture. Literary novelists like Carlos Fuentes and Ruben Dario carefully follow the convolutions of the Mexican psyche, threading them into masterful stories. Literary magazines crowd the bookstores. Artists have a gift of color and design that stretches back to their Indian heritage. The imagination flourishes in the tortured mental terrain. Everybody seems to play a guitar and sing. As one traveler said, "There are two things you will never hear in Mexico, 'I don't know how to sing,' and 'Watch out, your plate is too hot to touch.'"

Waitresses won't tell you that your plate is too hot to touch, because in Mexico people are used to taking care of themselves. This allows most travelers a tremendous feeling of individual freedom, the satisfaction of independence in a society free of restrictive prohibitions and lawsuits. Nobody will fine you for not wearing a seatbelt. It is your life, not theirs.

Some tourists are always tripping over the bumps and potholes in the sidewalks, knocking their heads on low awnings, getting shocked by exposed electrical wiring. Rather than traveling with open eyes, they cast blame on somebody else's carelessness instead of their own.

The danger, of course, is judging one culture by the norms of another. The difference between our two cultures is vast, the difference in maintenance standards being the least of it. In our society, we value the winners, whether in the economy, in politics, or in sports. In Mexico, valor is worth more than victory. Stoic fortitude in the face of adversity is valued more than any trophy.

We may be winners, but we are only fooling ourselves. In the end, Death will beat us all. The Mexican already knows this and, because of this, he is the wiser.

RELIGION

The Spanish had a tendency to name places after the saint's feast day on which they were first discovered. The cities and towns on the road map are a litany of Catholicism, a chanting of the saints' names: San José, San Lucas, San Felipe, San Javier, San Juan, San Carlos, San Pedro.

Every village and town is centered on the church. In the countryside, you will find chapels and altars in the most unlikely places, jammed in the trunks of trees or

chiseled out of rock. Crosses not only mark the spot where people are buried but, more importantly, the place where they died. Dangerous highway curves are  cropped with crosses. Crosses adorn the tops of half-completed buildings to ward off death, and on the peaks of hills to cherish it. This religiosity of the land overlies the Mexican terrain like a kind of metaphysical glazing, a varnish that glows of suffering and penance.

Catholicism

Mexico is 90 percent Catholic. The upper classes follow a more orthodox Roman Catholic doctrine, but the poorer people, and most of those in the countryside, practice a folk Catholicism, a mix of Christian and prehispanic beliefs.

Before Cortés, the Indians lived in an animistic world where jaguars and birds, the sun and moon, the wind and rain were guises for their governing gods. When the Spanish conquered the indigenous tribes, they also conquered their gods. Churches were built on top of temples.

The indigenous people were ready to accept a new religion—their defeat at the hands of the Spanish was also the defeat of their gods—but they could not grasp the Catholic concept of a single God; it was an abstraction that they could not see, touch, hear, or smell. Their belief in many gods was not abolished but instead transferred to the worship of saints, which were ordered into a new hierarchy of deities. A conceptual God overlooked it all, but the people prayed to the wooden, jewel-strung images of the saints.

The Virgin

On December 12, Mexicans celebrate a miracle that happened on this day in 1531,

Prehispanic Headress

an event that helped fuse the two religions. Outside Mexico City, a dark-skinned Virgin appeared before Juan Diego, a poor Indian. She told him to construct a church in her honor so that she could be near the Indians to protect them. The bishop did not believe him, so Juan Diego returned to the site. The apparition appeared again, ordering him to gather roses. The roses he carried in his cape left an impression on the cloth, the face of the Virgin herself. The Pope declared it a miracle, and today this Virgin is the patron saint of Mexico.

The Virgin appeared before Juan Diego atop the destroyed shrine to the Aztecan earth goddess, Tonantzín. The miracle was as much in the transference of belief, from earth goddess to Virgin, as in the event itself.

Patron Saints

Besides the Virgin, each village and town has its own patron saint. The icon, displayed in church and often in the home, is worshiped as if it were a divine being instead of a symbol. It can save crops from drought and insects, restore sanity, stop epidemics, solve personal problems. *Retablos*, tablets that are painted in thanksgiving to answered prayers, decorate many of the altars, a testament to the saint's power. Many of the saints have tormented faces, broken bodies. Crucifixions are far bloodier, more painful, than those found in most U.S. churches. Because the *campesinos* suffer so much, Christ must suffer even more in order to hold their faith.

Though faith is strong, regular church attendance is not as popular as would be expected. People go to church as the need arises, not as a practice. Much of this comes from suspicion of the church as an institution, a suspicion that reaches back for centuries.

Church & State

The first priests to arrive brought the indigenous people into the church, and did much to help them adapt to the new order. But those who came afterward were more eager to offer spiritual salvation to the Spanish, who in turn would will much of their wealth to the church. By the end of the 18th century, half of all Mexico belonged to the church.

By the end of the Mexican Revolution, the mestizo revolutionaries viewed the church as an oppressor. The new Constitution of 1917 barred the church from politics. Nine years later, President Calles enforced anti-church laws, which forbade priests from wearing their smocks in public, from teaching primary school, or from speaking out against the government. Even saying mass was considered a seditious act. In the 1930s, only 500 priests were left in the entire country. All churches and convents became government property, as they still are today. *Cristeros* (defenders of Christ) fought in a brief rebellion against government troops.

This schism of distrust still separates church and state. But these institutions have little to do with the true faith of the Mexicans, which you can see in every cross by the side of the road. From human sacrifice to the sacrifice of Jesus, from pyramid to basilica, the forms change, but the faith remains.

Bulls and Bravery

FIESTAS

Every city, town, and village in Mexico celebrates a few days in honor of the patron saint that guides its civic destiny. The high point of most celebrations is the firing of the *Castillo*, an intricate spindly tower powered by small cartridges of magnesium and black powder. The *castillo* will spin its wheels, shoot fearsome rockets into the crowd, spit flames, shower sparks, hiss, rumble, roar, and finally shoot into the heavens a brilliant spinning crown that almost disappears into the night only to come streaking back to earth aflame like a meteor.

Damage to life and property is inevitable, a great reason for its popularity.

Preceding this fiery masterwork, you can spend your time milling with the crowd while listening to the mariachis who stroll through the plaza. Walk on the balls of your feet, ready to jump when the *buscapies* (foot-searchers) start blasting around your ankles, ready to run when the *torito* (a bamboo rocket launcher carried on somebody's back), begins to head your way. And keep one eye on the children who will spring at you, deft as cats, to crack an

egg full of dye over your head that will color your hair red for days. Your tourist card is no safe conduct pass.

During the day, there are pedestrian pilgrimages from outlying ranchos. Sober litanies resound from the church. But most people crowd tightly into the cantinas and outdoor bars. The music never stops.

In the late afternoon, after the horse races and before the cockfights, a bullfight often takes place. In the smaller towns, the bulls are small and dangerous, the matadors clumsy and brave. Much less serious are the *jineteadas,* superb and often wild displays of horsemanship usually featuring a number of skinny bulls that are chased, lassoed, and brought to the ground, along with an occasional spectator.

While most fiestas are physically exuberant, and while you may feel like a conspicuous target, you will be treated with much courtesy and respect. Do not test this respect by photographing religiously sensitive moments. Likewise, be wary of the reeling drunks who will spend their last pesos to put you in a similar state. They will expect the same of you.

Despite hard economic times, no expense

Official Mexican Holidays

Jan. 1	*Año Nuevo* New Year's Day
Feb. 5	*Día de la Constitución* Constitution Day
March 21	Nationalization of the Oil Industry
May 1	*Primero de Mayo* Labor Day
May 5	*Cinco de Mayo* The battle of Pueblo
Sept. 16	*Dieciseis de Septiembre,* Mexican Independence Day
Oct. 12	*Día de la Raza,* known in other countries as Columbus Day
Nov.1	*Informe* the Presidential Address
Nov. 20	Anniversary of the Revolution
Dec. 12	Our Lady of Guadalupe
Dec. 25	*Navidad,* Christmas Day

is spared on these yearly fiestas, and there is much spending of money even in the poorest of villages. One Mexican author has described this extravagance as a means of attracting wealth of a different source, as an investment whose returns come back not as money but in the unmeasurable form of potency, life, and health. Like the gift or offering, the fiesta is one of the oldest of economic transactions.

To find out if there will be any fiestas during your trip, inquire on arrival at the local tourism office. Each town celebrates the major Mexican holidays of May 5, Sept. 15 and Dec. 12, as well as the three days preceding Ash Wednesday.

Note: you can predict fiestas yourself, as many towns were named by the Spanish after the saint's day of their discovery. Example: San Patricio, a small town near Manzanillo, holds its fiesta on the 17th of March, St. Patrick's Day.

RELIGIOUS HOLIDAYS

Navidad

Christmas isn't celebrated with the same gift-giving as in the United States, though this is changing. Most gift-giving takes place on *Día de los Reyes Magos*, the Day of the Wise Men, who came bearing gifts on January 6th. The nine evenings before Christmas are the *Posadas* (representing Mary & Joseph's search for an inn), when parties are held.

Carnival

Much like a European carnival, there are parades, floats, dancing in the streets, and boisterous crowds. In prehispanic times, the five extra days of the Aztecan year fell in February. The celebration of these five free days continued under the Spanish, the explosion of libido before the penitence of Holy Week. Carnival begins the weekend before Ash Wednesday. *Best places to watch Carnival are in the port towns: Ensenada, La Paz, Mazatlán, Veracruz.*

Holy Week

The religious cycle, begun with the exuberance of Carnival, ends with Lent. The week is celebrated with more reverence by the indigenous tribes, especially the Tarahumara, the Cora, and the Huichol, who have mixed folk Catholicism with the ancient symbolism of their spring festivities. Battles take place between the defenders and the destroyers of Christ, dressed as the Spanish and the Moors.

Día de los Muertos

The Aztecs used to celebrate their dead in August, the critical month for their farming. It was shifted by the Catholic church to November 1 (for dead children) and 2 (adults), which is when medieval Europe celebrated All Souls and All Saints Day. The dead have permission to visit the living during these two days. The graves at the *panteón* (cemetery) are decorated with flowers—marigolds are the flower of the dead—

incense, candles, photographs. This tradition is celebrated with more passion the farther south you travel.

ART

Mexican art was born in blood. Mesoamericans drew inspiration from their sacrificial view of the world. Seen today, their pyramids and artwork have a fierceness about them, an intensity of color and sense of design that transcends time and place. This powerful art has influenced the world, from the architecture of Frank Lloyd Wright to the gargoyles on Manhattan's Chrysler Building. Art Deco was inspired by prehispanic design.

This artistic vitality lost much of its energy after the conquest. European affectations diluted the aboriginal intensity, as most artists painted prim portraits, neoclassical figures, and provincial landscapes. Cut from its Mesoamerican roots, the art seemed to lose its life-force.

There was no major artistic movement until after the Mexican Revolution, when a new national identity demanded a new national art. This took the form of the mural movement in the 1920s, which borrowed from the fresco tradition of prehispanic times. Diego Rivera, José Orozco, and David Siqueiros were the most famous of the muralists. Painting for a largely illiterate audience, they were able to convey complex political themes by using murals. They all used a stylized realism to depict the history of revolution, from conquest to exploitation to revolt. Good (the natives) and Bad (foreigners) are easily recognized. This art form was preempted by the government, which subsidized the artists and incorporated their revolutionary images as part of their own political agenda. Today it is rare to enter any municipal building and not see intensely colored murals.

Modern Mexican art makes no claim to subtlety. In tune with its prehispanic roots, the paintings today are likely to be florescent with color, dramatic in design, exuberant in content—a sweep of country captured on canvas.

While artists paint from above, villagers create from below, producing enormous amounts of folk art that is perhaps a more natural expression of the Mexican psyche. Many of these crafts stretch back to prehispanic times, keeping the past alive. Products include pottery, ceramics, weaving and embroidery, gold and silversmithing.

DANCE

Many of the native songs and dances you see during fiesta days have been performed unchanged from prehispanic times, using the same kind of drums, flutes, and rattles (the Spanish introduced the stringed instruments). The Jesuit missionaries actually encouraged what they considered pagan dances as a way of bringing the natives into the arms of the catholic religion. These prehispanic dances are more mystical than religious, and the dancers sometimes jog themselves into a mystical stupor beyond our ken.

The missionaries also introduced their own dances as a way to educate the natives. The *Moros y Cristianos* (Moors and Christians), which is usually seen during the Semana Santa, recreates the war between the Moors and the Christians in the 14th century. The *Matachines*, another popular dance, originally came from a province north of Italy near the Austrian alps, where it is still danced with similar steps and costumes.

And the Indians created their own dances in the aftermath of the conquest, such as *Los Viejitos*, where young boys dress like old men, mocking the Spanish. They hobble about with canes, eventually breaking out into a lively dance. *Note: You can witness most of these dances during fiesta days, usually around the front doors of the church.*

CASA DE LA CULTURA

Most any city or town will have a Casa de la Cultura (House of Culture), which acts as a government-sponsored community center for the arts, with classes for everything from guitar to yoga to sculpture. Travelers are always welcome to drop in and scan the bulletin board for art films, gallery exhibits, music concerts, theater, and dance events.

ARCHITECTURE

In Mexico, the architecture tells the history of each city.

The earliest colonial architecture (1521-'80) was designed in a simple Spanish Romanesque style. Churches were built as basic basilicas, but the many flat surfaces were enlivened with medallions and pointed arches in the Plateresque style of restrained ornamentation.

Baroque

From 1580 to 1730, a Mexican Baroque style evolved, rebelling against restrained classical tastes. Baroque at this time was distinguished by two main architectural motifs: the Solomonic (twisted) column and the Corinthian capital.

From 1730 to 1780, the Baroque became even more profuse, as the structural elements soon became engulfed in a stone froth of foliage, statues, garlands, cherubs, and medallions, a style known as Churrigueresque. This excessive style was quickly embraced throughout Mexico, since the Indians relished this elaboration of design, which matched the complexity of their own pre-Conquest architecture. In a Churrigueresque church, dramatic murals covered the four walls of the sacristy, the naves were tiled with retablos, and statues of the saints reached out as if to touch the worshipers. The Church became a personal experience that tapped into pre-conquest emotions.

NeoClassical

From 1780 to 1919, the imaginative Churrigueresque gave way to the rationality of the Neoclassical, officially imported by the viceroyalty half a century after it emerged in Europe. After the War of Independence, the new national governments retained the neo-classical tradition, seeking to imitate European architecture, trying to prove it too numbered among the civilized nations of the world. During the Porfiriato, the indigenous people were disregarded by the government, as the *Scientíficos* (the rational, fair-skinned intellectuals who influenced government) looked to Europe for their heritage. Those in power felt a moral imperative to reject the vulgar baroque tastes of the masses in favor of a more rational, superior style. As a reflection of this, elaborate public buildings rose in a variety of Neoclassical styles, from Italianate Art Nouveau to Islamic Gothic, leading one critic to say "All that was worst in French municipal taste went in the public buildings during the age of Porfirio Díaz (1876-1910)."

The Mexican Revolution put a violent halt to such elitist pretensions. Mexico turned its back on Europe in favor of forging its own national identity, which today is in full bloom. No longer imitative, modern Mexican architects have returned to earlier roots, embracing an indigenous imagination. Bold colors. Conceptual treatments of volume and mass. Pyramidal structures. Use of indoor and outdoor light. Massive structures. Mexican engineers now lead the world in the use of concrete, just as their ancestors once led the world in cut stone.

CITY, TOWN & VILLAGE

Mexican towns appeared to D.H. Lawrence "as if they had been lowered from heaven in a napkin, and deposited, rather foreign, upon a wild plain." Most did not evolve naturally, but were created first on paper in the form of a corporate charter, a civic template laid down on a wild landscape. Strict regulations on the municipal layout were meant to enforce a subordination to a central power.

Plaza kiosk, the center of things

In the middle of the plaza in Mexico City once stood a *zócalo*, or pedestal, which was built for a statue of the Spanish monarch. The statue never arrived, and the name zócalo soon became slang for the central plaza. The zócalo today remains the social focus of almost every city in Mexico—a place of music, dancing, fiestas, resounding speeches, and public protest.

This social activity was chaperoned by the symbols of Spanish dominance. The church, the municipal palace, and the homes of royalty and crown officials all surrounded the zócalo.

Banks and hotels have taken the place of private residences, but church and state buildings continue to dominate the central plaza, exerting an authoritarian influence. The Spanish crown is gone, replaced by the national government, but the city continues to exert the will of a central power even though the players have changed. So have the street names, repeated throughout Mexico, named after revolutionary heroes and dates: Allende, Morelos, Zaragoza, Juárez, Obregón, 16 de Septiembre, 21 de Marzo. In Mexico, the city itself is a political design.

Note: Public Markets are generally within two to three blocks of the central plaza, as are the post and telegraph offices, and the cheaper hotels. Bus stations usually are situated on the fringe of town, though always connected by city bus.

Villages

The pattern of the smaller villages is more dispersed, having developed according to geography, defense, and access to a water source. Most still have a token central plaza with a bandstand, a town hall, a school house, a few stores selling mostly dry goods, a village well, and a church. *Note: village churches are often locked, but the side door is usually left open.*

Orientation

A system of reliable numbered street addresses to help people find their way has never developed in Mexico. Many addresses are numbered erratically, while many are simply labeled *s/n* , short for *sin numero* (without number). Others are called *domicilio conocido,* which means that everybody knows where it is.

Directions are often based on street names, not addresses. If a building is in the middle of the block on Morelos, the address will often be given as *Morelos entre Zaragoza y 5 de Mayo* (on Morelos between Zaragoza and 5 de Mayo). Or if it is on the corner, or close to the corner, it is called *Morelos esquina con Zaragoza* (on Morelos at the corner of Zaragoza), or simply Morelos y Zaragoza (at the intersection of Morelos and Zaragoza).

Most streets in Mexico are either *avenidas* (avenues) or *calles* (streets), which are abbreviated as "Ave." or "C." Main streets often have an abbreviated compass direc-tion: *Ote.* for *Oriente* (east), *Pte.* for *Poniente* (west), *Nte.* for Norte, and *Sur* (south). *Note: Streets often change name as they run through different areas of town.*

Directions

When asking directions, be aware that most Mexicans feel it is impolite to answer a question in a negative way." If they do not know, they will usually guess, since it is more important to send you cheerfully on your way than to disappoint you. Don't rely on one person's directions. Instead, keep asking as you go, homing in. And don't ask leading questions that can be answered yes or no, because the answer often will be an automatic yes. *Note: women are the best to ask about places within the neighborhood, men about locations farther afield.*

2.
Traveling in Mexico
Rules & Reality

PAPERWORK
Tourist Cards

To officially enter Mexico, you need a tourist card, which can be picked up for free at airline offices, travel agencies, Mexican consulates, and national tourist boards, or from places that sell car insurance. You can also pick them up at your Mexican port-of-entry. The *Oficina de Migración* (immigration office) is always close to the actual border crossing, and you should stop there anyway to get your card stamped and thus validated.

To validate your the tourist card, you must have both a photo I.D. (such as a driver's license) as well as something that identifies you as a citizen: an original or certified birth certificate, passport, naturalization papers, voter registration card, certificate of discharge from the armed forces, or even a sworn declaration properly notarized. A passport (even if expired) combines photo and proof, and is strongly recommended for travel in Mexico (especially when cashing traveler's checks).

Validation & Extensions

Be sure to get your tourist card stamped by *Migración*, either at the port-of-entry office at the border, or the international air-port in Tijuana. If you arrive on an international flight, your tourist card will be stamped when you deboard. Most cards are validated for 90 days, though if you say you are going to stay only for a week, they may only sign you in for 10 days. Give yourself leeway. Tourist cards are renewable for an additional 90 days for a total of 180 days, after which you must leave the country.

Don't wait until expiration before you renew it. Occasionally officials will want to see proof of financial solvency before granting a 90-day extension. A credit card often is enough of an illusion of prosperity to convince them of your worth. Migración officials are notoriously arbitrary. An extension can never be taken for granted.

If you should lose your tourist card, or if it should expire while you are in Mexico, you can usually arrange for a new one with a certain amount of persuasion ($10-$50). It pays to be unfailingly polite and humble in such situations, befitting your status as an illegal alien. Some veteran travelers carry several blank copies of tourist cards to help cope with just such emergencies.

Leaving the Country

You are supposed to turn over your tourist card to *Migración* when leaving the country. There is no enforcement of this on land routes, but if you are leaving by plane, you must surrender your tourist card at the airport when departing on an international flight, or at the Tijuana or Ciudad Juárez airport if you are flying just to the border. If your card is expired or lost, arrive at the airport in plenty of time to plead your case to the immigration officials. Their take-home pay depends on just such situations.

Final authority: Dirección General de Asuntos Migratorios of the Secretaría de Gobernación at Albañiles 19, corner Eduardo Molina, 11270 Mexico City, tel: 795-6685.

Border Visits

You are not required to have a tourist card for visits of less than 72 hours to border towns, including Ensenada, San Felipe, as well as Puerto Peñasco and El Golfo de Santa Clara farther inland. Of all the immigration offices along the border, the one in Ensenada is the most efficient, the best place to obtain or validate your card.

Children's Papers

Children should have their own tourist cards rather than have them tagged onto their parent's card (in case one parent has to leave). Travelers under age 18 will need two copies of a notarized letter signed by both parents, giving them permission to travel in Mexico; they must also carry a passport. Single parents traveling with minors need the other parent's notarized permission.

Pet Papers

By law, you are supposed to pick up an International Health Certificate from a U.S. veterinarian, along with a pet visa from a Mexican consulate, before entering Mexico. These are rarely asked for. Occasionally pet owners are asked for a small fee to let their pets enter Mexico. To bring a pet back into the U.S., you need to have a rabies certificate. *Caution: it is not uncommon in Mexico for city workers to throw poisoned meat on the street at night as a way of controlling the dog population.*

Car, Boat, & Motorcycle Papers

To bring a car or boat into mainland Mexico, you need a Temporary Importation Permit, which can be obtained once you are in Mexico. This permit is not necessary if you stay on the Baja California peninsula. If you cross over on the ferry you will need to obtain one in La Paz or Santa Rosalia. No charge, but you will need five items: proof of ownership, a registration card, unexpired license plates, a valid driver's license, and a tourist card. If the vehicle is not registered in your name, you will need a notarized affidavit from the owner, granting permission for you to drive it in Mexico, even if the owner is a bank or financial institution; in such cases, get a translation into Spanish to avoid problems. The import permit is valid until your tourist card expires.

Each vehicle, whether boat, motorcycle or car, must have an import permit, but one person cannot have more than *one* import permit. Often the rule is ignored. When not, another person in the party can be assigned the second import permit, but this too becomes a problem when that person is not the owner of the vehicle, or when there is no second person. These situations are almost always settled in the travelers' favor, with occasional contributions in appreciation of the official's interpretation of the law.

Final authority resides in Mexico City, at the Registro Federal de Automóviles of the Secretaría de Hacienda y Crédito Público situated at Calzada de Tlalpan 2775, Colonia El Reloj, Mexico City. *Note: you can obtain a Temporary Import Permit at Tijuana on a 24-hour basis.*

Boating & Fishing Papers

Anybody 16 years and older needs a fishing license in order to fish. Licenses are sold for the day, week, month, or year. Enforcement is rare, punishment severe—including loss of all your fishing gear, and possibly your boat as well, depending on the arresting officer's interpretation of the 24 articles that make up the fishing code. Fees and bag limits are in flux (currently 10 fish, 5 per species), seasonal prohibitions subject to change. *Note: though you may avoid enforcement of fishing regulations while in Mexico, you may be stopped by U.S. Customs when returning; they work with Mexican officials to enforce some regulations. Lobster, for example, cannot be brought into the United States out of season.*

Boat permits are needed for all motorized boats, and can be obtained for a small fee, along with the fishing papers, at the Mexico Department of Fisheries at 2550 5th Ave., Suite 101, San Diego, California, 92103-6622. Boating and fishing regulations seem to change with the tide. Contact the San Diego office for current fees and regulations: phone 619-233-7311 or fax 619-233-0344.

CB Radios

If you have a CB radio in your car, you will need a permit for it from the Mexican consulate before you leave for Mexico; no permits are issued in Mexico, and if you don't have one, your radio can be confiscated. Three channels are used in Mexico: #9 for emergencies, #10 for communication between tourists, #11 for directions and information.

THE BORDER

You are not allowed to bring flowers, fruit, plants, or magazines containing flagrant nudity to Mexico. Neither can you bring in new sporting or electronic goods (take off all price tags). Computers and anything else that is expensive and out-of-the-ordinary requires a special permit which you can get by writing to the Mexican Department of Tourism (see appendix) 90 days in advance of your trip; list the article's brand and serial number along with your passport number and other personal data.

Obtaining permission to bring a gun to Mexico is not even worth considering.

You are allowed to bring 110 lbs of clothing (132 lbs if flying), 12 rolls of film, 200 cigarettes, 50 books, 20 cassettes, and three liters of wine, among other things.

Rather than count your cigarettes or weigh your clothes, most Mexican custom officials will just wave you on across the border *unless your cargo looks excessive or commercial in purpose.* If so, you will be flagged over into the secondary check area, where you will most likely be charged a minor sum and allowed to move on. This sum often can be bargained down, but only in a friendly way. If you get mad, you will find yourself hopelessly entangled in a costly bureaucratic web.

Advice: when dealing with the aduana, those who struggle most, suffer most.

CROSSING THE BORDER, WHEN & WHERE

Tijuana: 24 hours
Otay Mesa: 6 a.m. to 10 p.m.
Tecate: 6 a m to 12 p.m.
Mexicali: 24 hours
Algodones: 6 a.m. to 8 p.m.
San Luis: 24 hours
Sonoyta: 6 a.m. to 12 p.m.

Nogales: 24 hours.
Nogales—Mariposa entrance:
6 a.m.-8p.m.
Nogales —foot entrance:
10 a.m. to 6 p.m.
Sasabe: 8 a.m.to 8 p.m.
Agua Prieta: 24 hours

RETURNING TO THE U.S.

When asked to declare what you are bringing back from Mexico, be honest. Some Customs officials can tell by the dilation of your eyes whether you are telling the truth. A hidden mango will cost you $50. That extra liter of tequila will become your contribution to the government (confiscated liquor is handed over to the U.S. Embassy for their cocktail parties). If you have spent much time in Mexico, you will likely be directed into a secondary area, where trained dogs nose around your car while inspectors ferret through your belongings.

U.S. Customs allows you to bring in $400 worth of goods duty-free from Mexico, for personal, not commercial, use. On the next $1000 worth of goods, you must pay 10% duty. Any amount over $1400 is assessed at the individual rate for the item according to the government's tariff schedule. A family of four can bring in $1600 worth of goods duty-free on one declaration. For a complete list of what you can and cannot bring into Mexico, write: "Know Before You Go," U.S. Customs Service, P.O. Box 7407, Washington DC 20044.

Tactic: ask the customs inspector to group items with the highest tariff under the allowances, and assess the additional duty on lower-tariff items.

Canadian citizens are usually allowed into the U.S. without paying duty, since they will have to pay duty at the Canadian border. Canadians are allowed $300 worth of Mexican goods. Anything above this limit is taxed at 20 percent. For more information, write: Canadian Department of External Affairs, Ottawa, Ontario K1A 0G2.

THE LAW

The first article of the political constitution of Mexico grants foreign travelers the same rights and responsibilities it guarantees its citizens. A nice gesture, even if this concession is negated by article 33, which states that undesirable aliens can be deported without appeal and for any reason. Other articles prohibit foreigners from working (except under special permit), owning land (except through bank trusts), and voting (never).

The law is more a web of words than a code of conduct. Foreign travelers are advised to stay clear of the entire indecipherable process. There are few legal avenues available for compensation or redress. It is usually better to just accept your fate as a lesson learned, and move on.

Mexican law is based on the Napoleonic Code. You are guilty until proven innocent. Like original sin, all of us are a little bit guilty, even if we didn't do anything wrong. Once you invoke the judicial process, it is hard to predict which way the wheels of justice will spin.

If in need of legal assistance, call the *Secretaría de Turismo* (Tourism Secretariat) offices or the 24-hour "Hot Line" Emergency Telephone Service they maintain within Mexico (dial 91-5-250-0123 or 250-0151). They will provide initial counsel, but only as long as it pertains to hotels, car rental agencies, tourist guides, or other traveler services.

If a mechanic ripped you off, or if a store refuses to take back defective merchandise, you may want to contact the *Procuraduría Federal del Consumidor* (Federal Consumer's Protection Office), which maintains offices in all state capitols, as well as in Ensenada and Tijuana. This authority is responsible for making sure that products and services comply with their obligations.

Both the Tourism Secretariat and the Procuraduría move at a glacial pace. The entire procedure of complaint-and-redress usually lasts longer than your tourist card. Whatever actions you undertake should be not for your own compensation but for the next traveler coming down the road.

If you are the victim of a more serious

crime, you either go to the police or the *Agente del Ministerio Público* (Public Prosecutor), who will be found at the *Procuraduría General de Justicia* (Attorney General's office). They will take your report and investigate. Most offenses such as theft, injury, and rape are regulated by state law. Drug laws are federal.

Precautions

It is safer to travel in Mexico than in the United States as long as simple precautions are taken. Don't sleep alongside the road in your car. Strip yourself of gold watches and other emblems of conspicuous consumption before heading into the remote countryside. If you stumble onto patches of illegal agriculture, turn and leave. Don't hide valuables in your hotel room; use the security box in the lobby. And make sure the wind wings of your car are impossible to open from the outside (the Achilles' heel of automobiles, as far as car theft in Mexico goes).

Don't trample on the local customs. In Indian villages, treat your camera with the same sensitivity as if it were a gun, just don't point and shoot. Drinking beer while walking down the street will draw at least a rebuke, maybe more, from the cops. Prostitution is legal, but nudity on the beach is a crime. Is possession of marijuana worth the risk of seven years in a Mexican penitentiary? Use judgement in giving strangers a ride; there are numerous drug checkpoints along the west coast of Mexico. If your hitchhiker is carrying *mota* (marijuana), you may find yourself signing the registration of your car over to the authorities.

Drug Checkpoints

Drug-and-gun checkpoints ocassionally are set up along Hwy. 1 on the Baja California peninsula, and along Highways 2, 15, and 200 on the west coast of Mexico. Those that are operated by the military are fairly routine, usually no more than a quick look in your glove compartment. Searches are more thorough for northbound cars, especially near the border.

These checkpoints are often manned by plainsclothed *judiciales federales*, who act with more authority and arrogance than the military. They are liable to spend up to half an hour on your car, taking air samples from your tires, and tapping all the hollow spaces with a rubber mallet. *Note: body searches are extremely rare. If anybody wants to search your pockets, something may be amiss. Immediately pull your pockets inside-out to avoid the possibility of planting.*

Arrested

If you are arrested, you have certain rights, which may or may not be granted. Foreigners have no special privileges, though by international treaty you are allowed to contact the U.S. consular agent (see appendix), though it may be wiser to phone the U.S. Embassy. You can be jailed for up to three days (72 hours) without being charged. According to the Mexican Constitution, you cannot be held incommunicado (artículo 20, fracción II), and you must be advised of the crime or charges (artículo 19, párrafo primero). It is your right to ask for a translation of all documents into English.

Bail can be obtained before the District

Attorney if the felony is a traffic accident, as long as damages are fully guaranteed or covered and there is no evidence of drugs or alcohol. Unfortunately, in other cases bail is not granted to foreigners since it is easy to skip the country.

In Mexico, judges, not juries, decide all cases. Most Americans in jail simply admit guilt and try to get out on a prisoner exchange program with the United States rather than prolong their stay in what can be a lengthy appeals process. *Note: Most Americans in prison are there for crimes involving drugs, a federal offense in Mexico. Seven years in a penitentiary for possession (up to a kilo of marijuana), up to 15 years for trafficking (a kilo or more). If caught with less than 100 grams (3.5 ounces), you will probably be fined and deported.*

Who's Who

The most numerous are the *Policía de Tránsito* (transit police), usually dressed in blue or khaki, and standing around major intersections. They are more likely to carry whistles than guns, and, if on foot, are often ignored by any cars they attempt to pull over. The armed and uniformed *Policía Federal de Caminos* (Federal Highway Police) patrol the highways between towns, and will stop to help if you are parked on the side of the road, hood up. Of all the police in Mexico, they are considered the least corrupt. Conversely, the *Policía Judicial Federal* are one of the most feared. They prefer designer clothes and four-wheel drive Broncos, usually with U.S. plates. Other than at highway drug checkpoints, few travelers will come into contact with them.

Police

Police in Mexico depend on what they can make on the streets for their livelihood. More like freelance taxi drivers, they often must use their minimal salaries for maintaining their vehicles, repairing their uniforms, and buying bullets for their guns. Occassionally a policeman will ask for gas money before pursuing a crime. Consequently, it often isn't worth the time to report a theft, unless you need a police statement for an insurance claim. Even if your things are recovered, it can take three days of filling out forms to get them back.

3.
Money, Shopping, Food & Health

Pesos & Dollars

The dollar has been the stronger currency. Exchange rates change daily. Consequently, it is best to keep most money in dollars, converting to pesos sparingly. Once you have pesos, it is expensive to convert back to dollars.

Lana (wool) is Mexican slang for money, similar to our use of "dough" or "bread."

Traveler's Checks

The best traveler's checks to buy are from companies that have refund offices in Mexico. Both American Express and Thomas Cook maintain service centers in Mexico. So does Bank of America, though its office in Mexico City is geared for corporate accounts.

Don't buy traveler's checks denominated in German marks or Canadian dollars. These are difficult to cash, especially in stores. Record the check numbers; traveler's checks are not easily replaced in Mexico, especially if you are far from a service center or if you lack check numbers. Also, their reputation has been tarnished by a growing number of counterfeited checks. Consequently, merchants and bankers are wary of cashing large checks. It's best to buy your checks in smaller denominations

($20 and $50). Not only are they easier to cash, but you can use them at restaurants and stores on most minimum purchases, saving you from spending your day at the bank.

Caution: Mexicans practice their typically florid signatures until they are as exact as a thumbprint. Bank managers expect the same from you. Your two signatures on a traveler check must look the same or you stand a good chance of having your checks invalidated.

Credit Cards

Credit cards are actually a more convenient way to obtain funds in Mexico.

When you use your credit card in Mexico, you are billed in dollars at no more than 1.4 of 1% above the wholesale exchange rate. And when using a credit card in Mexico, the exchange rate to dollars isn't set until your bill drifts into a regional processing center, a period during which the exchange rate will undoubtedly slide in your favor.

You can also get cash advances easily using either Visa at any Bancomer bank, or American Express at one of their service centers (in Hermosillo, Mazatlán, Puerto Vallarta, Guadalajara). You will be stuck with a minor finance charge, which averages about the same as the sales commission and retail mark-up of traveler's checks. Only other disadvantage is that occasionally merchants try to impose a surcharge on your credit card, illegal but commonly condoned. Most common cards in order of their popularity: Visa, American Express, Mastercard, Diners Club, Carte Blanche.

Automatic Teller Machines

A growing number of ATM machines are to be found in Mexico, usually at Banamex banks. These are linked to Plus and Cirrus systems in the U.S. But the international operation is not yet reliable. Try them but don't rely on them.

Personal checks

Personal checks are extremely hard to cash in Mexico, unless you can find a resident friend who can deposit it into their bank account, using their balance as collateral. Hotels affiliated with an international chain sometimes will cash your personal checks if you are a guest. If you have an American Express card, you can cash a personal check at one of their service centers. If you plan on spending a long period of time in one place, you can open your own account, though you will generally have to post a $500 minimum balance. Personal checks drawn on a U.S. bank take from ten to 14 days to clear.

Banks

The air conditioning is usually cool, the tellers icy, the pace of transactions glacial. Even the simplest transactions take time for the money to be counted and the necessary forms filled out, stamped, approved, transferred, and honored. Bring a book.

Most banks open 8:30 a.m. (Monday-Friday) though it is usually best to go around 9:00 a.m. since some banks won't exchange pesos for dollars until a phone call from Mexico City verifies the day's exchange rate. Banks traditionally close around 1:00 or 1:30 p.m., though many now stay open later.

Avoid banks on Mondays and Fridays or the 1st and 15th, when government employees cash their checks. Also, plan ahead of holidays to get money; some banks actually run out of cash around Christmas and Easter.

You will only receive pesos at a Mexican bank even though your checks are denominated in dollars.

Tip: when cashing traveler's checks, ask at the first desk you encounter as to where you should go to get it authorized (autorizado). Usually you will be directed straight to a bank officer whose signature is necessary to cash the check, saving you from having to stand in line first.

Sending Money

There are various ways to shift money to Mexico, none of them particularly fast.

One. The quickest is to send money through American Express, if your are near one of their regional offices (Hermosillo, Mazatlán, Puerto Vallarta, Guadalajara). **Two.** Funds can be cabled by telex from a bank in the U.S. or Canada to either a Banamex or Bancomer bank in Mexico. This can be accomplished in two to five days. You must pay the cost of the cable, plus a commission, usually around $20 to $30. If you have plenty of time, you may opt for a bank draft. You still pay the commission, but you save a few dollars having it sent as registered air mail. **Three.** You can send money through Western Union to a telegraph office or hotel in Mexico. This takes from three to ten days, as your money takes a circuitous route through Mexico City. Delays are common, and even if the Mexican telegraph office receives the money order, they may not have the cash on hand to pay you, especially in the smaller towns. **Four.** An international money order can be sent via registered mail, often a slow process with a sad ending. Few banks or *casas de cambio* will honor it. Locate a place to cash it before having one sent.

Exchanging money

Merchants often offer exchange rates higher than what you get at the bank. Hotels traditionally provide the worst exchange rates, only because unquestioning guests are willing to pay for the convenience. *Casas de Cambio* usually offer exchange rates competitive with banks, though banks often pay a slightly better rate for traveler's checks.

Generally, the closer you are to the border, the better the exchange rate. The best exchange rates can often be found at the Casas de Cambio on the U.S. side of the border. *Caution: many bordertown exchange houses advertise no commission, but only for those buying dollars, not pesos.*

SHOPPING

IMPUESTOS

Most products are subject to the *impuesto al valor agregado*, a value added tax better known as IVA: 6% on food, 15% on most consumer goods, which includes restaurants, bars and hotels, 20% on deluxe goods. IVA is traditionally included in the price, though sometimes it is added on as a surprise. If you are buying unprocessed food items, or from market food stands or street and beach vendors, you are exempt from the tax. *Note: whenever you are charged the tax, ask for a nota (receipt). If they won't give you a receipt, you won't have to pay the tax.*

Prices & Bargaining

The overriding business philosophy is based on short term gain at the expense of long term growth. Low demand inspires even higher prices. Quantity discounts are rarely given. Customers often are treated as if they were seeking favors instead of purchases. If you break it, you buy it. If you buy it, you may find it impossible to return.

Bargaining is expected in all shops where items are not price-tagged. Even the fixed prices in some shops are usually no more than a signal that the absentee owner doesn't trust employees to bargain on their own. As a rough estimate, most travelers are able to shave about 25% off the original asking price. Offer half of the original price, and when the price seems stuck, ask *"¿es lo menos?"* (Is that the least?)

Shop when the stores just open, or right before they close. Some merchants are superstitious concerning the first and last sale of a day and will accept a lower price as a way of insuring their luck to come. They will take your money, and say *"que tenga buena mano,"* (May you have a good or lucky hand). Offer to pay cash instead of using a credit card which costs the store a four to six percent service charge. Merchants also prefer cash for reasons of tax evasion. Other strategies: feign disinterest, point out imperfections, ask for greater discounts on second purchases.

Many shoppers visit a government-operated FONART *(Tiendas Artesanales del Fomento Nacional de Artesanías)* store to get an idea of art and craft prices. Villagers who used to make crafts spontaneously now churn their work out full-time, selling to FONART at the minimum wage scale. Consequently, some of the FONART work shows a kind of artistic sacrifice to mass production. But the prices set a kind of highwater mark for the buying public.

Note: avoiding the merchant by going directly to the source does not necessarily save money. In fact, some villagers trick travelers into buying their imperfect seconds.

Consumer Caution

Fabrics touted as pure wool often aren't. Sometimes just the fringe is wool, the rest cotton or synthetic. Look for the shine of acrylic. Smell for the genuine aroma of lanolin. One sure test is to burn the warp thread with a match, which the vendor may not approve of. Wool burns, synthetics melt. If the fabric feels oily, and if twigs are woven into the warp, the wool has been poorly prepared. Burro hair is often added for extra body; it grows scratchier with age.

Bleeding colors can ruin the finest weave. If you dip a corner of the fabric or yarn into water, and squeeze the excess onto a paper towel or napkin, it should leave no trace of color.

Authentic silver jewelry, even earings, will have the numbers .925 stamped on its surface, proof that it contains at least .925 parts of pure silver and not more than .075 of alloy (usually copper to give it strength). The stamp alone is not proof you are getting genuine silver. *Alpaca,* a poor man's silver, is similar in appearance, and occasionally sold as silver; normally it retails for 30% to 50% less.

Handmade silver jewelry is usually sold at a standard kilo-price. Machine made pieces, or those considered seconds, are tagged at a lower kilo price. If buying quality silver, check that its surfaces are free of etches and flaws. Marks that happen during buffing should be almost invisible.

When buying jewelry, avoid gems, which may be counterfeit. Amethysts and opals are about the only semi-precious stones mined in quantity in Mexico. Ground-up soda bottles can look like opals, and a few pearls have turned out to be machine-grade ball bearings.

Beware of red clayware. Beanpots and *cazuelas* made of raw red lead oxide (unfritted lead) are not safe to use as containers for acidic liquids like salad dressing or orange juice. Acid picks up the lead from these low-fired glazes. In fact any glazed pottery, especially the green-colored kind, should be used with caution in the kitchen (Indians traditionally hand rubbed their pottery; glazing was a Spanish introduction).

Make sure any copperware you buy is not copper-painted iron.

When buying hand-decorated stoneware, pass your hand over the surface. You can't feel the design if the piece is cheap china. The glaze on more expensive and harder Tlaquepaque stoneware stands out in relief.

Likewise, when buying quality lacquerware, run your fingers over the surface to make sure the design is *encrustado* (encrusted). Trays and platters decorated with flashy flowers are usually *aplicado* (applied), a much cheaper finish. Drop a bit of water on the surface. On fine laquerware, the water runs freely. On cheaper varnished or painted surfaces, the water drags on the surface.

When buying hammocks, check their length and string count. Make sure the length is long enough for you to stretch out in; many hammocks are made to a shorter Indian size. A matrimonial hammock that holds two people or more should have a minimum of 100 pairs of strings at each end. Single hammocks should have a minimum of 50.

Finally, you can own pre-Columbian artifacts while staying in the country, but it is illegal to leave the country with them. *Note: By some estimations, more pre-Columbian artifacts are being manufactured now than during the reign of the Quetzalcoatl.*

Shipping

If you arrange for a store to ship your purchase to the United States, you will be liable for duty, unless it is a present to a friend or relative and costs less the $50. You can arrange for shipping to Tijuana, Mexicali, or Ciudad Juárez, then transport it yourself across the border. Shippers can be found in any city, are relatively cheap, though trucks may take up to two weeks to reach the border.

FOOD
Provisioning

Since the easing of import restrictions, it is much easier to find familiar foodstuffs from the U.S. on Mexican grocery shelves. At least in the larger towns and cities. In the countryside, grocery stores are more austere, often stocking only the basics: onion, rice, chile, canned tomatos and sardines, pasta noodles, tortillas and corn, perhaps some fresh meat.

Though markets are colorful places to shop, if you go first to the *supermercado* (supermarket) you can get an accurate idea of prices. Food prices in the market tend to fluctuate according to your perceived wealth. Bring your own bag, and watch your language. *Chile* is slang for penis, and when you say "*tiene huevos* (do you have eggs), you are actually asking "You got balls?" Ask for *blanquillos* instead, or say *"hay huevos"*.

The cheapest grocery stores are *Conasupos*, government outlet stores that sell subsidized staples. The *Sedena* stores run by the military, and the *ISSTE* stores run by the social security administration, are also substantially cheaper than the regular supermarkets, and are open to the public.

Shop sparingly. In Mexico, the milk goes bad quicker, the tortillas turn hard and the produce mushy.

Buy seafood cautiously. Fish shouldn't smell too fishy. The gills should be bright red. You can often buy shrimp and fish direct from the boats at the dock, but since most belong to *cooperativas* (cooperatives), this practice is technically illegal.

Mexico recycles containers, and you will save considerably by buying your beer in returnable bottles from the *cervecería* and your soft drinks direct from the distributor. Five-gallon glass or plastic *garrafones* (jugs) can be filled at the *purificadora de agua* (water plant) for less than the one-gallon jugs in most supermarkets. Bring your own egg cartons. Most eggs are sold loose.

Eating Out

Breakfast prices are often the same, whether you eat in a shack or a carpeted restaurant, so it pays to be discerning.

The main meal is served between 1:00 and 4:00 p.m. Though you can order *a la carte*, your best savings is to order the *comida corrida*, Mexico's version of fast food. These meals are typically advertised on a chalkboard, and usually includes a soft

Tortilla Press and Dough

drink, tortillas, a choice of soup, the main course and dessert.

The *cena* (dinner), can be anything from another full course meal to a light snack of tacos, usually served from 8 to 10:30 p.m.

Budget meals

Restaurant prices are generally lower the closer you are to the market. At the market, you will find the cheapest meals at the *fondas,* or food counters.

Street vendors are not to be overlooked, despite the misconception that they guarantee stomach upset. Most street vendors are meticulous about cleanliness, which is why most stands are staffed by two employees: one cooks, the other handles money. They break down and clean their equipment every day, and they prepare food under your direct scrutiny, unlike restaurants that hide their sometimes slovenly kitchens in back.

Restaurant Tips

A bill rarely will be brought to your table until you request it. This is a gracious national characteristic that often is a cul-

tural backfire; many gringos wait impatiently for the bill which never comes until they pound the table. Don't ask that the bill be broken down for members of a party going dutch; figure it out yourself later. Tipping is commonplace—15% in better establishments, 10% in others.

Rough calculation: *tip the amount of the tax on your food bill (this saves you from tipping on the tax as well); in places where you aren't taxed, it often is not customary to leave tips.*

The restaurant menu is often more a list of what has been served on occasion in the past rather than what is being offered today. Rather than spend time puzzling over the menu, ask *"Que hay?"* (what is there?).

You can smell bad fish or oysters, except when smothered in sauce. Lobster tails should be white instead of gray. If you order a beer or soft drink, and are asked *¿al tiempo?*, they are not the asking you for the time but whether you want your drink served at room temperature (which many Mexicans prefer). Order *sopa de arroz* and you will get a plate of rice, not soup. Ask how *picante* (hot) a meal is. If your mouth is afire, don't drink water; it just spreads the heat around in your mouth. Use milk or a mouthful of salt to kill the burn.

Café

Coffee usually is a cup of hot water and a spoon of Nescafe. Ask if they have *café de grano* or *café americano* if you want brewed coffee. If you want a bit of cream with coffee, order *cafe con crema*, not *cafe con leche*, which is a drink of equal parts milk and coffee. *Café de olla* is an aromatic brew of coffee laced with cinnamon and sometimes sugar. If you want coffee without sugar, be sure to specify *café sin azucar*, otherwise your coffee may arrive already mixed into a syrup with sugar. Except in American-style coffeeshops, most coffee is sold per cup.

HEALTH & HAZARDS
Intestinal Disorders

All travelers worry about *tourista* while in Mexico. The main culprit is E. coli, a bacteria that grows like seaweed in our digestive tracts. There are different varieties of *E. coli*. When the Mexican strain is introduced into your digestive tract, it multiplies quickly, and your body rebels. *Result: upset stomach, diarrhea, and nausea for the one to three days it takes for your bacteria to come to a new equilibrium.*

Moderation

If you allow the new bacteria to venture into your digestive tracts in a moderate way, you can usually avoid a massive upset. Unfortunately, most people indulge in drink an food when crossing the border, which is why this malady often appears about three days after arrival. Avoid too much alcohol or sun; both dehydrate your body, lowering your resistance. Instead, drink lots of non-alcoholic fluids.

H-2-Uh-Oh

Potable water in Mexico is often contaminated with bacteria. This is especially true in villages, where most water comes from *ojos* (springs), *pozos* (wells), *ciénagas* (seeps), *ríos* (rivers), or even *arroyos* (ditches). Always drink water that has been treated. Politely refuse water that comes from suspect sources or even from the tap (especially during the summer rainy season).

Don't go by appearances. If the cap from the water bottle in your hotel room doesn't pop off under a slight pressure, the bottles may have been re-filled with tap water.

1. Boil the water (the most effective).

2. Add *yodo* (iodine), which you can buy at any *farmacia* (buy an eyedropper at the same time). About five to seven drops per quart. Let stand for half an hour.

3. Add liquid bleach: two drops of 6% liquid chlorine bleach (standard Clorox) per quart of water. Double the drops if the water is dirty or cloudy.

4. Add water purification tablets, such as Halazone (the most expensive solution).

Carbonated water is the safest; its slightly acidic nature inhibits bacterial growth. You can buy purified water at a store or water plant (only a few cents a gallon when you have your own five-gallon *garrafón*), or treat the water in one of four ways:

You can obtain similar tablets in most Mexican farmacias. Ask for *pastillas para purificar agua* (water purification tablets).

Note: to lighten the taste of treated water, add a pinch of salt and aerate by pouring it from one container to another.

Other Precautions

Treat vegetables and unpeelable fruit with bleached or iodinized water by soaking for 10 minutes. Use straws instead of lips to drink from dirty or wet bottles. Be wary of cheese products in rural areas (Chihuahua cheese is almost always made of pasteurized cream). Lime juice and garlic are used liberally in Mexico. Both have antibacterial qualities.

Rinse dishes with purified water. Occasionally let them soak in bleach.

Mexican law states that all ice cubes must be made of purified water. Block ice is not restricted. Microbes responsible for intestinal distress can survive freezing. Of the ten percent that survive thawing in an ice cube, most respond favorably to club soda, are uncomfortable in cola, start to die in scotch and soda, and are decimated by tequila. If you must have ice, even if of dubious origin, then the stiffer the drink the less risk of gastric illness (from microbes).

Germs survive on skin or inanimate objects much longer than you would suspect. Fifteen percent of all Mexican peso notes carry diarrhea-causing bacteria. Just washing your hands frequently lowers your risk of exposure.

Prevention

According to scientists, chewing two Pepto-Bismol tablets four times a day helps to prevent traveler's diarrhea. But you have to be willing to live with the possible nontoxic side effects: a darkening of the tongue and a barely detectable ringing of the ears. The Pepto-Bismol regimen should not be tried for more than three weeks. A more natural variation of this treatment is the taking of Pepsin tablets, sold in most health food stores, and to eat plenty of papaya.

Cure

If you feel yourself coming down with tourista, drink plenty of purified water (flavored with lime) to keep from becoming dehydrated. *Té de Manzanilla* (chamomile tea) is a natural stomach soother, as are the traditional native cures: green bananas and papaya.

Continued symptoms may mean it is time to use stronger chemicals to kill the bacteria in your system. Most common drugs are *Donamycina P.G.* or *Bentimycin.* These lower the colony count of the E. coli bacteria so your immune system can adapt to the new bacteria. *Diodoquin, Mexaform,* and *Streptomagnum* are also popular. If you a running a fever (as well for the bathroom), you may be offered *Septra* or *Bactrium*; don't take these if you are allergic to sulpha drugs.

Lomatil remains one of the most popular drugs for traveler's diarrhea, though medical opinion is shifting away from its use. Like all diarrhea suppressants, this potent over-the-counter drug is not a cure. Instead, this morphine derivative paralyzes your stomach, benumbing all bowel movements. It contains opium, which makes you sleepy, as well as belladonna, which gives you a slight nausea (so you don't become a

---

TWO-GLASS GULP FOR DIARRHEAL DISEASE

In the first glass:
8 ounces of orange juice, or other fruit juice (for the potassium)
1/2 teaspoon of honey or corn syrup (glucose is necessary for the absorption of the essential salts)
1 pinch of table salt (for sodium and chloride).
In the second glass:
8 oz. of carbonated water or boiled water
1/4 teaspoon of baking soda (for sodium bicarbonate).
Drink alternately from each glass, supplementing the formula with carbonated beverages, boiled water or hot tea. Avoid solid foods and milk until you are fully recovered.

Courtesy of the U.S. Health Service

Lomatil addict). Its use may keep you from the bathroom, but it prolongs your illness. Use only when conditions require it, such as a 12-hour bus ride. In the same league as Lomatil are *Paregórico* and *Entero-Vioformo*. *Kaopectate* is also a diarrhea suppressant, but uses pectin (glue) instead of opium.

Self-Help

If you feel you are suffering from an unknown intestinal ailment, you can test yourself by taking a stool sample in one of your film canisters to any of the numerous *laboratorios biológicos*. For a token charge these laboratorios will test your stool for signs of bacteria, giardia, amoebas, or worms. Repeat the test at least three times. You can usually take the results straight to a farmacia and have them prescribe the correct antidote.

Farmacias

Farmacias (pharmacies) in Mexico are graded *primera*, *segunda* and *tercera*. Only *farmacias de primera* feature a registered pharmacist. Many people use their free advice instead of the doctor's. You can even receive injections here (insist on disposable needles).

Stick to *farmacias de primero*. Employees in the lower-rung stores are often ignorant of the dangers and side effects of what they sell, including many drugs banned in the United States.

Most antibiotics and other powerful drugs, such as Retin A and steroids, are routinely sold over the counter. Mood-enhancing drugs such as Valium do need a prescription, though codeine-laced cough syrup still can be bought off the shelf.

Prices for drugs are extremely low, controlled by the government. Look for the tiny type that says *Precio Máximo al Público*. *Note: always check the shelf life of the drugs you buy. Antibiotics or vaccines are affected by high temperatures, and should be kept in a refrigerator, not on the shelf.*

Best Medical Guide

An indispensable aid for the off-road traveler is "Donde No Hay Doctor" (Where There is No Doctor), written by David Werner and published by the non-profit Hesperian Society in both Spanish and English. It is a complete self-help medical guide for anyone traveling or living in Mexico, covering all situations from dysentery to bewitchment; its appendix is a vast encyclopaedia of pharmacology, offering recommendations, dosages, and possible side effects. Leave this book as a gift to someone who needs it. Order through your nearest bookstore, or send $13 to: The Hesperian Foundation, Box 1692, Palo Alto, CA 94302.

Health Care in Mexico

The better doctors are aware of local and common illnesses, and rely strongly on antibiotics, though most major cities have doctors who specialize in acupuncture or holistic treatments. Most charge low fees of about $15 to $20 for a consultation. Lab work is less expensive than in the United States.

Even cheaper than doctors in private practice are those in hospitals. For help, go to the emergency ward of the nearest hospital. Public hospitals should be avoided, as hygiene and medical standards are compromised by an unending stream of impoverished and ailing people. Military hospitals are more expensive, but usually have better facilities, more competent doctors. Privately funded medical clinics bridge the gap between doctors in private practice, and hospitals. Most have a laboratory on the premises for quick diagnosis.

Insurance

Find out if your insurance covers you while

in Mexico. Read the miniscule print. Unless you find specific wording that excludes medical expenses incurred outside the U.S., the insurance company must provide coverage. Most major insurance companies will cover your costs on short term or regular basis (Medicare is a notable exception). You still must pay cash while in Mexico, keeping receipts for filing an out-of-country claim with your insurance company.

If you don't carry insurance, AAA offers a temporary plan for travelers to Mexico.

Evacuation

For major emergencies, there are a number of reputable air evacuation services that transport critically ill travelers.

Air-Evac International, 8665 Gibbs Drive, Ste. 202, San Diego, CA 92123; tel. 619-292-5557, 619-278-3822.

Critical Air Medicine, Inc., 4141 Kearney Villa Rd., San Diego, CA 92123; tel. 619-571-8944.

Life Flight, 1203 Ross Sterling Herman Hospital, Texas Medical Center, Houston, TX 77030; tel. 800-392-4357, 713-797-3590.

Schafer's Ambulance, 4627 Beverly, Los Angeles, CA 90004; tel. 213-469-1473.

Inoculations

No immunizations are required for traveling in Mexico, but some are suggested. If you are heading into southern Mexico, phone the Center for Disease Control in Atlanta for the latest advisories concerning disease and inoculation: 404-329-3311. In Canada, the Travel Information Offices of Health and Welfare provide a similar service, though the data is not as current.

Malaria

If you plan on spending considerable time in lowland tropical areas (below 3,000 feet elevation), you risk contracting malaria, especially during the rainy season. You might consider a regimen of chloroquine phosphate, starting treatment one week before trip, and continuing it for six weeks after. See your doctor for dosage. The *anopheles* mosquito bites mostly during the dusk and dawn hours. Malaria is spreading throughout the world, but so far, the chloroquine-resistant strains have not been found in Mexico. *Note: don't use the new drugs for chloroquine-resistant strains of malaria; otherwise, Mexican mosquitoes might develop a resistance to it.*

Mosquitoes

There are a number of ways to combat mosquitoes short of slathering yourself with poison.

The most effective way is the least plausible. Don't breathe. The carbon dioxide you exhale activates mosquitoes from the resting state. They then fly at random until they enter this plume of humid breath, following it to its source. If you have higher skin temperatures and moisture-transpiration rates, you'll attract more mosquitoes than the person next to you.

The trick is to throw them off the scent. Some people disguise their odors by ingesting huge quantities of vitamin B1 or brewer's yeast, which seems to work. Others burn coconut husks or mosquito coils at their feet and hide in the smoke. Mosquitoes like to hang out around bushes, which dark clothing resembles. A white shirt is the best disguise, blue the worst color.

Avoid camping amid vegetation. Windy campsites are generally free of mosquitoes. Keep a campfire smoking during the dawn and dusk hours when mosquitoes are most apt to appear. *Mosquiteros* (mosquito netting) are designed to fit over a bed or hammock and can be bought at most markets in tropical Mexico (harder to find in northern Mexico and on the peninsula).

Repellants

There are numerous repellants made of natural extracts, the most effective being those made of pennyroil and citronella (check your health food store).

Avon's Skin-so-Soft enjoys an underground reputation as an insect repellant. According to the Letterman Army Institute of Research, standard *diethyl-toluamide*-based repellents on the market outperfom Skin-So-Soft 30 times over.

These DEET-based repellants (Off, Cutter) are the most effective, but they can irritate mucous membranes as well as cause behavioral changes in the very old and very young. It's also a solvent for many plastics (you'll stick to the vinyl seat of your car). Many people consider these a minor irritation compared to the risk of malaria or dengue. Apply repellant liberally to clothes, cautiously to skin.

Note: once bitten, don't scratch. Push down on your bites instead, so you don't break skin and increase the chance of infection. Mexicans often use lime juice to lessen the itch. You can buy Caladryl or Andatol lotion at the farmacia to reduce itching.

Other Bugs

Pulgas (Fleas): use repellent. They bite, but don't make a habitat of your body.

Garrapatas (Ticks): check your body after hikes through the bush. Touch their body with the head of a just-burnt match, or smother with Vaseline, and they will let go.

Piojos (Lice): the reason for all those shaven heads you see in the countryside. Instead, buy a special shampoo at the farmacia.

Chinches (Bedbugs): turn off all the lights in your room, wait for a few minutes, then check for chinches with a flashlight. Best prevention: bring your own bedroll.

Jejenes (biting gnats): a powerful and almost invisible force of nature; best measure is to flee.

Gorgojos (weevils); a common and harmless occupant of corn or meal that has been stored too long.

Gusanos (Worms): Hookworm is transmitted ground-up in Mexican villages. Wear shoes. Check your stool now and then for evidence of pinworms or tapeworms.

Note: if swallowed, the worm at the bottom of a mescal bottle will pass through your system intact. Don't mistake it for something that was alive inside you.

Scorpions

There are two kinds of scorpions: lethal and non-lethal. Non-lethal scorpions usually stay on the ground. Lethal scorpions defy gravity and are are often found clinging on the underside of things. Like firewood.

If bitten, lie down and, if possible, apply ice to bite. Bites from non-lethal scorpions tend to be localized at the site, while bites from lethal scorpions are systemic and *do not* swell. Take aspirin or antihistamines if needed, but avoid opiates such as codeine or darvon, as well as dairy products, cigarettes, and alcohol. Most bites are no more severe than a yellowjacket sting. An *antialacrán* (anti-scorpion) shot should be considered for children under four, those of advanced age, or if the pain or difficulty in breathing seems severe. Make sure whoever is administering the anti-alarán also has adrenaline in case of a bad reaction.

Snakes

You should take the same snake precautions in West Mexico as you would in the United States. Eyes open. Walk in clear areas. Go around instead of over. Collect firewood gingerly. Rattlesnakes usually are denned in the winter, appearing mostly in the hotter months, when they are active at night. Other snakes, such as *fer de lances*, pit vipers, and water moccasins pose a very slight hazard, as they are rarely seen.

Less than one percent of all poisonous snakebites are fatal.

Jellyfish

All sorts of remedies for jellyfish stings have been used with some degree of success: Windex, papaya juice, diluted ammonia. The most popular remedy is warm urine. Victims often forget about the sting in horror of the cure.

For more serious cases, don't rub or let the skin dry out (or use fresh water), as this discharges even more stingers into the skin. Instead, saturate the area for ten minutes with a mixture of baking soda or meat tenderizer mixed with water. Then pour more baking soda or tenderizer over the area (or use dry sand), and scrape the mixture off the skin; this lifts off the remaining stingers.

Stingrays

Stingray wounds on the extremities are never fatal. Intense throbbing pain is the overriding symptom, followed by redness and swelling. Clean the wound with saltwater and remove any debris left by the stinger. Immerse the wound for 30 to 60 minutes in water as hot as the patient can stand (if on the body, use hot moist compresses); the pain should subside almost immediately. Watch for signs of shock.

Wounds from other fish with venomous spines, such as the scorpionfish and sculpin, respond equally well to the same hot water treatment.

Sharks

Due to overfishing, sharks are rarely seen close to shore. Shark attack is not a worry in the water, though if you should sight their dorsals you may want to stay on the beach.

Sea Urchins

Stepping on a sea urchin is only half as painful as the after effects. The spines are hard to dig out and cause inflammation. Applying lime juice or vinegar four times a day helps dissolve the spines.

Sunburn

If you think you have had too much sun, immediately take two aspirin and continue to do so every four hours. Keep up the aspirin regimen for two days (aspirin retards the production of skin enzymes that cause much of the redness and burning).

If redness already has appeared—generally three to six hours after exposure—it may be too late to save your skin from feeling like scorched paper. In which case taking aspirin may still reduce and shorten the time of discomfort. Also drink plenty of liquids and apply aloe vera or papaya on your skin. *Note: if taking antibiotics, your skin will be more prone to sunburn.*

Miracle Cure

Most stings and venom from sea animals or insects are protein poisons, and can be broken down rapidly by applying heat, as hot as can be tolerated. Another destroyer of protein poison is *ablandador de carne* (meat tenderizer) containing papaina (not plain MSG). If mixed with water to a paste and appled to stings from jellyfish, fire coral, and insects, it substantially relieves the pain.

4.
Communication, Transportation, & Lodging

COMMUNICATIONS
Mail

The Mexican mail system is dependable for letters, risky for packages. Mail takes an average of ten days, give or take five, to travel to the United States or Canada. Delays of up to three weeks are not uncommon. Mail coming *from* the United States and Canada moves at a similar pace. Always send letters *correo aéreo* (air mail). Never drop letters in the *buzón* (mailbox), as mail is not picked up every day. Send your mail either at the post office or from a major hotel. Don't mail a letter in any city without an international airport. You should not send anything of value. Mail must measure less than 40 by 60 centimeters (15 1/2 by 23 1/2 inches).

Sending a package is always risky, more so when sent from the United States or Canada. Any package or bulky envelope will be opened by the aduana for inspection and clumsily resealed. Missing contents are common.

If you have an important package or letter, send it via registered mail. If time is more important than cost, you can send your material via the Mexican postal system's new express service or through Federal Express (U.S. 800-238-5355) or DHL (U.S.

800-225-5345), both of which maintain offices in Mexico.

When receiving a package in Mexico, you will most likely have to pay duty on it. Sending a package from Mexico often involves a trip to the *aduana* (customs).

The abbreviation A/C before a name stands for *al cuidado de* (in care of).

Lista de Correo

Most travelers depend on the *lista de correo* to receive mail. Arriving mail is posted daily at the post office on a typewritten sheet, the names listed in alphabetical order. To pick up mail, you must have identification (or a permission slip to pick it up in someone else's name). After ten days, the mail is returned to sender. If you are leaving town before your mail arrives, you can fill out a change of address card and ask to have it forwarded to another town. Another way to avoid the ten-day limit on mail is to write on the letter *favor de retener hasta llegada* (Please hold until arrival). *Caution: when checking the lista de correo, look for your name alphabetized under first, last or middle name (In Mexico, paternal last names are put in the middle, between the first name and maternal last name).*

If you have American Express checks or a credit card, you can have mail sent to an American Express Service Center (see appendix). They will hold it for 30 days.

TELEPHONES

Dialing to Mexico is cheaper than dialing from Mexico. From Mexico, it is less expensive to phone home collect instead of to direct dial. *Note: in Mexico, you answer the phone "Bueno," not "Hola".*

Calling Collect

Within Mexico, the cheapest way to call home is to call from a phone booth. Dial 09 for the international English-speaking operator. Be patient. If you can't get through, phone 02, the Spanish-speaking operator, and ask to be connected to the international operator. Only calls made *por cobrar* (collect calls) can be made at phone booths. They will ask you for a name. Avoid the higher surcharge for person-to-person by saying "con quien conteste" (whoever answers), in which case you will be billed at cheaper station-to-station rates. *Lowest rates: weekends, or after 11 p.m.*

Caseta de Larga Distancia

Every city and town has a *caseta de larga distancia* or phone service, usually found at the bus or train station, but more likely inside a farmacia. Most have private phone booths, worth the nominal service charge for making collect phone calls. *Note: if your collect call does not go through, you may still be billed a token charge.*

You can also dial direct nationally and internationally and pay at the caseta, an expensive proposition. Most hotels provide the same service (it's just a matter of getting hold of the international operator), but their service charges vary from charity to piracy.

Phoning from the United States

Phoning from the U.S., you first dial 011, which is the International Access Code,

---

Direct dialing from Mexico

When phoning from a private phone, you can call direct to anywhere in the world by prefacing your call with a two-digit *lada*, which routes your call to the proper switchboard.

91: for station to station calls direct within Mexico, dial 91, then the Mexican area code and phone number.

92: for person-to-person calls within Mexico, dial as if it were 91, and operator will intervene.

95: for station-to-station calls direct to the U.S. and Canada (except Alaska and Hawaii).

96: same as for lada 95, but for person-to-person calls.

98: for station-to-station calls to the rest of the world, via satellite. Be sure to use the country code found in phone book.

99: same as for lada 98, but for person-to-person calls.

Two-digit numbers beginning with "0" connect you with an operator:

01: long-distance information.

02: for placing long-distance calls within Mexico.

04: for local information.

09: for international operator.

---

followed by the Country Code, which is 52, the particular three-digit City Code, and then the phone number (see appendix for city code numbers).

TELEGRAPHS

Telegrams are a cheap way to send messages within Mexico.

There are three classes: *carta nocturna* (cheapest), *ordinario* (most common), *urgente* (most expensive). Ordinarios are sent out anytime during the day, while urgentes are immediately punched in. *Cartas nocturnas*, cabled during the night, arrive the next day.

Incoming international telegrams arrive at the *Oficina de Telégrafos* (usually situated near the post office), where they are posted on a *lista de telegramas*, or they can be directed to the post office, hotels or private residences. Telegraphs cannot be sent collect.

TRANSPORTATION BY CAR
Rules of the Game

To drive safely in Mexico is to pay more attention to the road than to rules. Stop signs really mean "yield" and traffic lanes are often ignored, due to potholes and the anarchist tendencies of most drivers.

There are a few genteel codes of conduct which keeps traffic in check. As in yachting, there is an overlap rule. Once a passing vehicle overlaps you, it assumes the right-of-way. This is why a passing bus will start easing back into your lane though you are still abreast with its rear wheels, forcing you to hit the brakes or go off the road.

Drivers communicate in Mexico with lights. On a narrow bridge, oncoming drivers who blink their headlights first have right-of-way, unless the other vehicle is bigger, in which case the "might-is-right" rule prevails. Headlights are also blinked when there is danger up ahead. If the truck in front of you signals with the left blinker, it usually means that it is clear for you to pass (though the driver's interpretation of safe passing may differ from yours). On the other hand, the truck may be signaling a left hand turn, which, if misinterpreted, could lead to a collision. To confuse matters even more, many trucks turn on their left blinkers as a way for oncoming traffic to judge clearance.

Mexican roads are more of a challenge

than a comfort. Grades are steeper, curves tighter, lanes narrower. Most are built on raised roadbeds, with no shoulders to pull off on (to go off the road often means rolling upside down). Small rocks on the road fly up under the wheels of trucks like rifleshot, breaking windshields. Larger rocks are set on the road as a warning of a larger obstruction ahead, usually a disabled truck; after repairs, these rocks are often left behind on the roadway. Road crews often rely on your car to act as a steamroller on fresh asphalt. Rain, oil and soot tend to pool on the flat roadbed, causing a loss of traction.

You have to be eternally vigilant to avoid the *baches* (potholes). Domestic animals prefer to graze along the edges of the pavement, and constantly threaten to step into your path. You skirt fatalistic bicyclists coming home from the fields in the early darkness (since there are few shoulders, they ride on the road).

Most arroyos are not culverted, and you drop into these *vados* like a carnival ride. As you emerge on the other side of the vado, what you thought was the dim single beam of a motorcycle turns into an 18-wheeled cyclops whose passing jet stream sucks you into the oncoming traffic. To compensate, you pull hard on the wheel, and nearly run off the narrow road. The approaching village offers refuge from the night, but without warning you suddenly slam into a *tope,* a curb-like bump in the road that knocks your head against the roof. You recover at the point where the federal pavement suddenly turns into the rutted dirt track of the town. Three blocks later, oncoming traffic is honking at you. The road, without warning, has turned into a one-way street. Chagrined, you turn off onto the first street you see, which is too narrow to do anything but follow wherever it goes. In a matter of minutes, you have gone from a federal highway to being lost in a strange town whose narrow streets were made for mules, not Chevrolets.

Car Preparation

You don't need a superbly outfitted car to travel in Mexico. Older pre-1976 Detroit models, gutless Volkswagen vans, and wheezy Renaults can be the most adaptable to Mexican road conditions. Roadstop mechanics know nothing of computer chips, let alone fuel injection. Older cars accept the inevitable dents and dings without devaluation, parts can be scavenged easily, insurance is cheaper, and their motors run well on leaded *Nova*.

Unleaded gas (*MagnaSin*, the green pumps) can be hard to find off the major highways; cars built after 1976 will destroy their catalytic converters if they run on leaded gas. It is illegal to remove your converter in the United States unless you first get an exemption from the Environmental Protection Agency. U.S. auto repair shops sell a pollution control tester which bypasses the converter. Mexican mechanics can also bypass the converter for a nominal charge.

Besides the standard emergency tools and parts, you should bring along a tire gauge. Most gauges don't work, others are calibrated in kilograms (kilo-to-pound conversion charts don't work for air pressure). To deter theft, install a hood lock to keep your battery in place, and perhaps an anti-theft cutoff between your coil and distributor. Tires should come on 14", 15", 16" or 17" rims; tires in half-inch sizes can be hard to find in Mexico.

Change your oil more frequently the farther south you drive. Humidity causes condensation, which can reduce motor oil to an emulsion after 45 days. If you are going to be spending time on the coast, consider getting a *soplete de diesel* (diesel oil sprayed onto the bottom of your car) at an underbody service station to prevent rusting.

Gasoline

Mexican gasoline is of lower octane, and occasionally mixed with water and other impurities. Unleaded *MagnaSin* comes from the green pump, leaded *Nova* from the blue pump (Mexicans make a pun of the name; *no va* means "it doesn't go"). If your car needs high octane, bring plenty of gas additive; the Mexican variety isn't very effective. To avoid low-octane pinging, retard your spark and adjust the carburetor. Add a liter of cane alcohol or a dollop of diesel to your tank periodically to burn off accumulated water. Install an in-line fuel filter.

Gas Stations

Gas stations are generally situated at the outskirts of towns and, except on major routes, rarely stay open all night. Except for some backyard entrepreneurs, all gas is distributed through Pemex stations.

For some gas station attendants, tricking the driver is an honorable (and lucrative) pursuit. Most common tactic is to start pumping without tripping the register back to zero. *Prevention: install a locking gas cap, which allows you time to make sure the pumps are zeroed.*

Another tactic is for the attendant to use a pump with a broken price register, confident that you will not take the time to calculate a total from the liters shown. *Note: In this case, the appearance of a hand calculator usually keeps things honest. Also, label your gas tank with its capacity in liters, so you can prove that the 65 liters showing on the pump could not fit into your 10-gallon tank.*

Always count your change, and check your gas gauge before leaving. If you asked for a full tank and your gauge registers 3/4 full, you probably have been tricked, despite your precautions. Motorists who ask for a set sum (*écheme 10 mil pesos, por favor*) are less likely to be tricked than those who ask for a full tank (*llénelo, por favor*).

Mexican service station attendants do not check fluids and tires unless requested, for which a tip is expected. Windshields are usually given over to children who will slap a wet, dirty rag onto your windshield to gain your attention. *Note: If you have a late-model car, bring along a large funnel; some older gas nozzles won't fit into tiny orifices.*

Green Angels & Car Repair

If your car should break down, try to find a shoulder to pull out on. Failing that, set out flares or put rocks in the roadway, a universal sign of trouble ahead (red Tecate beer cans, found in a plentiful supply along most roadways, make excellent reflectors). Raise your hood and stay with your car. If you must leave, hire a guard to watch your vehicle. Like the scavenger law at sea, an empty car is considered abandoned.

The repair trucks of the Green Angels patrol all major routes at a leisurely 45 m.p.h., passing each point twice a day (each truck patrols about 120 miles). Each truck is supposed to carry two English-speaking mechanics, who will help to fix your car. Labor is free, though you must pay for parts or gasoline. They offer 15-miles' free towing but do not work at night or in or around towns or cities. Most trucks communicate via radiotelephone and can be dispatched to you if you can get to a phone. The 24-hour hotline number is 905-250-0123. *Note: if your car is ailing, consider driving in escort with a Green Angel.*

Night Driving

Traditionally, night driving is advised against. Many trucks, buses, and cars drive with dysfunctional lights. There are more drunk drivers. Cows are harder to see. At night it is hard to judge the shoulder of the road, especially since many roads lack center lines.

But night driving, if risky, does have its rewards: less traffic (most truck drivers sleep during the night), more wildlife, and moonlit nights. *Night driving tactic: drive behind a big truck and let them run interference.*

Offroad Driving

The single dirt road shown on the map is often a tangle of roads leading to the same destination. When one route gets too sandy or rough, a new road branches off. Roads that split usually come back together again. Follow your intuition as much as the map.

All cars going offroad should have a tire pump, a folding shovel, and a tow rope.

Rough roads take their toll. Check your underbody beforehand so you know where the low points are. If you puncture a gas tank, you can seal it with a bar of soap.

Don't carry your spare underneath the car, or you may have no way of getting to it if you are caught in soft terrain. Bring plenty of gas; mileage on dirt roads can be half of what you normally get on a paved road.

When driving through sand, don't hesitate or you will sink. Avoid downshifting if you can. Its best to lug your engine so the tires don't spin. Once stuck, digging out is a tiresome chore. Let the air out of your tires down to 10 psi (as long as you have a pump). Wet the sand with buckets of water. Throw branches or rocks under the jacked-up tire for additional traction.

Speed Limits

Though rarely enforced, the posted maximum speed limit ranges from 110k to 80k per hour (about 68 to 50 m.p.h.) on the highway, 40k to 30k per hour in towns and villages, (about 18 to 25 m.p.h.). *Caution: watch out for slow moving trucks and cars on the freeway. Many ranchers are accustomed to driving the same speed on the highway as on a dirt road.*

Infractions

Traffic laws are erratically enforced. As a way of forcing you to pay *mordida* or a fine, police may remove your license plate—which should be fastened in a way to prevent this—or take your driver's license; some travelers carry a sacrificial driver's license, since a duplicate often costs less than mordida or the fine. If the violation is bogus, stand your ground and refuse to pay mordida; by being willing tọ go to the station to protest your innocence, you will most likely be sent on your way. If the violation is real, paying mordida will circumvent the need to go to the station to pay the fine. Often an officer seeking mordida will tell you the fine is much greater than it really is.

Insurance

Car insurance rates are set by the Mexican government, so there is little need to shop around other than for the free road logs and other amenities that distinguish the various car insurance companies along the border. Coverage can be bought by the day, month or on an annual basis. If you plan on parking at the beach for a month, you can save money by insuring your car just for the days you actually will be traveling. If you return early from Mexico, you can ask for a refund. If staying a month or more, a year's coverage is often cheapest, especially if bought through special interest clubs, such as *Vagabundos del Mar* or *Mexico West Travel Club*. Yearly rates are surprisingly low, not because there are fewer accidents, but because insurance claims are for physical damage only; in Mexico, there are no millionaire whiplash victims. *Remember: if towing a trailer, your car insurance will be invalid unless the trailer (and whatever is on it) is also insured.*

All policies include a deductible for collision. Personal property is not covered unless considered a permanent part of the car. Vandalism is not covered, nor is partial theft; the entire car has to be stolen in order for insurance to pay off. Insurance is cancelled if you drive drunk, an unlicensed driver is behind the wheel, or if damage comes from driving over rough or unpaved roads. Neither will conventional coverage pay off if you run into government property, such as a streetlight. You need special *juridical* insurance for this. *Note: be sure you receive a list of adjusters in Mexico when you buy your policy, and leave it in the glove compartment.*

Accidents

As far as collisions are concerned, liability is determined by a simple formula: *el que pega, paga* (he who hits, pays). All people involved in a serious accident, even witnesses, are held in custody until guilt is determined. Some people, especially if guilty, flee an accident before the police arrive.

If involved in a minor accident, try to

work it out with the driver before the police complicate the situation. Most Mexicans don't carry insurance or have the money to repair your car; minor dings should be accepted as one of the wages of driving in Mexico. If you are at fault, offer to drive to the nearest car repair shop, get an estimate, and pay off.

Your insurance really comes into play if involved in a major accident. Never admit guilt or otherwise incriminate yourself. Sometimes the police assign guilt to both parties on a percentage. You can be 10% guilty. Get in immediate contact with the nearest adjusters and let them work to secure your release. Even if you have insurance, your car may be impounded until the adjuster settles all damages.

RENTAL CARS

Like insurance, the rental price of cars is controlled by the government and varies little among rental agencies in any one area. Most major U.S. car rental companies have affiliates in Mexico: *Avis, Budget, Dollar, Hertz, National.*

Prices are higher than in the U.S., and it may be cheaper to rent a taxi after you factor in the additional costs of air conditioning, automatic transmission, insurance premiums, extra kilometer charges, drop off fee, gas refill, and tax. Renters need a valid driver's license, credit card, and must be over 25 years of age.

Only Mexican-made cars can be rented: Volkswagen, Nissan, Ford, Chrysler, or General Motors.

Note: Air conditioned cars with automatic shift are in short supply and should be reserved in advance from the U.S. It is not uncommon to be given a different car than the one reserved. Take it, but refuse to pay extra for it. Before leaving the rental yard, count the hub caps, and make sure you have a jack and spare tire.

BY BUS

Most Mexicans travel by bus. Even on remote roads, buses normally pass every couple of hours. Just stand by the side of the road and wave them down. First class and express buses will stop·anywhere to drop off passengers but usually accept riders only at designated stops. Second-class buses will stop every hundred yards if necessary.

Bus Stations

Bus stations in villages and towns are usually on or near the central plaza. Most larger cities are served by *central camioneras* (central bus stations), usually situated on the periphery of town and linked by *colectivas* or private taxis to city center. In cities, all bus lines must operate out of these central camioneras; tariffs are set by the SCT, the Transportation Secretariat. These bus stations are like air terminals, with post offices, bathrooms, banks, telegraph offices, food, and newspaper stalls. All central camioneras have *guarderías* or *paqueterías*, luggage rooms where you can store your bags during layovers.

Grupo Tres Estrellas de Oro has the lock on western Mexico. Under its corporate umbrella are the ubiquitous *Tres Estrellas de Oro* (the best first class bus line in West Mexico); the mediocre *ABC*, which runs

buses down the Baja California peninsula; *Transportes del Pacífico*, which operates down the Pacific Coast from Tijuana and Nogales to Mexico City; *Auto Transportes Aguila* (older buses prone to breakdown), which rolls down the Baja peninsula; and *Tres Estrellas del Norte*, which runs along the border route (Ensenada, Mexicali, Tijuana).

Tickets & Seat Selection

Bus tickets are cheap, about a dollar an hour. They are valid only for a specific route and time. If you miss the bus, only by persuasive argument can you use your ticket on the next bus. Unpaid reservations are not accepted, but you can often buy your tickets at the station a few days early to insure a seat. Otherwise you have to show up and take your chances. During peak travel times (weekends, Easter), you may have to spend hours at the station waiting for a seat.

When you buy your ticket, request a seat assignment, otherwise you may end up in the back row next to the toilet stall. Ask to see the seating plan, then pick the scenic side of the bus. *Note: Front row seats can be terrifying for first time bus riders, with little room to stretch your legs.*

Unless you are traveling heavy, carry all your luggage aboard with you; bags stored below stand a greater chance of being lost or damaged.

Always try to catch a bus from its originating station in order to insure a seat. If you board a bus that already is in transit (called *camiones de paso*), seats will not be sold until the bus arrives and the number of empty seats are counted. You often can board a full bus if you are willing to stand until a seat opens up.

Note: Always keep your receipt. If injured, or if your baggage is lost, you have no legal footing without a receipt. If you are not issued a receipt after boarding a first class camión de paso, your fare is probably going directly into the driver's pocket.

The Ride

Bus rides are a cacophony of crying babies, loud stereos, cold drafts of air, clouds of cigarette smoke, and the push and sway of a speeding bus. You may be frightened by the risks the driver takes with your life, but accidents are few. Buses are more likely to *cause* accidents than actually be in them.

Before boarding a bus, constipate yourself with Bimbo bread, and avoid coffee, beer, and other diuretics unless you are sure

Cheap Comforts

Clip-on reading light: many hotel rooms lack reading lights; those on buses are often broken.

Heating element: boil your water for health and coffee.

Walkman: as much to block out sound as to enjoy it, indispensable on long bus rides.

Cigarette lighter: in Mexico; book matches are sold, not given away.

Flashlight: power outages are never convenient.

Sunglasses: Aviator Ray Bans are a status symbol of Mexico's aspiring middle class.

Wash n' dry towelettes: a cool respite from the grime of travel.

Insect Repellant: to avoid itching and disease.

Compass: align it to your city street maps for a quick orientation.

Hand calculator: its appearance is enough to keep transactions honest.

Small chain and lock: so you won't have to lug your baggage everywhere.

the bus has a working toilet.

Even express buses stop three times a day for meals, usually at crowded, fly-ridden restaurants with marginal bathrooms. The driver calls out how many minutes until departure—usually long enough to make a dash for a grocery store or nearby taco stand.

Overhead reading lights are often not aligned with seats and many bulbs are burned out, so you should bring a flashlight for reading. Other valuable equipment: inflatable pillow, Walkman headphones, a gallon of water, toilet paper, and a good book to read.

City Buses

Routes of city buses can be hard to decipher, but every city has a standard route that travelers can use to get from hotel to city center to beach: the Sábalo route in Mazatlán, the Pitillal route in Puerto Vallarta, the San Carlos-Guaymas run. Most city buses will stop if you wave them down, though some brake only at designated areas. Drivers make change and issue tickets. To get off the bus, shout "Baja," and the driver will stop at the first convenient spot. Avoid morning and evening rush hours, when passengers jam the stairwell and pickpockets work the crowd.

BY AIR

Air travel has improved from the days when Aeroméxico was called Errorméxico, thanks to the government's turning over its control to private enterprise in the wake of a disastrous bankruptcy. Rates are straightforward, with little of the chaos of U.S. airlines. As a general guide, excursion fares are about 90% of regular fares, with three-day minimum/21-day maximum stays. Weekend flights are often more expensive than weekday flights.

Some U.S. airlines (Alaska, Continental,

U.S. Toll Free Numbers	
Aeroméxico:	800-237-6639
Mexicana	800-531-7921
AeroCalifornia	800-258-3311
Alaska Airlines	800-426-0333
Continental	800-231-0856

etc.) also fly to major tourist destinations in West Mexico. Traditionally, flights leaving from Tijuana have been cheaper than those leaving from Los Angeles or San Diego, but international airlines have dulled Tijuana's competitive edge. Some charter flights are available at lower prices, but this industry does not flourish on the west coast like it does in Cancún.

Obscure locations such as Guererro Negro are serviced by regional airlines that harken back to the days of Lindberg; they use older but reliable aircraft, like the old DC-3 gooney birds. Fares on these regional airlines are reasonable, but don't expect to buy flight insurance.

On Mexican airlines, if you make changes or cancellations within 24 hours of a scheduled flight time, you are charged a penalty. Miss your flight on an international route, and you will be responsible for 50% of ticket price (cancellation fees for domestic no-shows have been eliminated on Mexicana). If bumped, there is no "denied boarding" compensation. There usually are no seating assignments, so passengers scramble to secure a seat.

The two major airlines in Mexico are Mexicana and AeroMéxico, both now under private ownership though they still must get government approval for fare changes. Mexicana has the older aircraft, a contributing cause to its reputation for arriving late. AeroMéxico has fewer but more modern planes, and strives harder to keep to its arrival time, occasionally leaving before their scheduled departure time.

Note: each time you leave on a domestic or international flight in Mexico, you must pay a departure tax in pesos.

回回回回回回回回

BY TRAIN

An American pacing back and forth along the rails complains to the ticket agent, "The train is already an hour late." The agent says, "Tranquilo, gringo, your ticket is good for three days."

Trains are slower than buses, and harder on the senses; the weak air conditioning, lack of food and water, and long delays can exasperate travelers looking only for transportation. But the clackety-clack romance of rail travel usually overcomes these discomforts.

Tickets

Unlike bus travel, train sleepers and first class reserved seats should be booked in advance. Don't just ask for *primera clase*, which may be an inferior seat; ask for *primera especial*. If you want a sleeper, ask for a *primera dormitorio* or *primera de Pullman* (curtained-off bunk beds), *camarín* (tiny private room), or *alcoba* (private room with bathroom). Second class seats should be avoided except by the very poor or the very curious. Train cars can range from 1930s Pullman to second-hand Amtrak.

Tickets can be bought from *Mexico by Rail* in Laredo, TX (tel. 800-228-3225) or from Romero's Mexico Service in Newport Beach, CA (tel. 714-548-8931). Tickets at both are marked up 20% to 30%. Advantage is that tickets can be bought on your credit card. Disadvantage is the greater chance of a mix-up than if you buy your ticket direct from the station.

You can write or phone the train stations direct to make a reservation. If you want to stop along the route, you can either reserve the ticket from the border to your layover spot and purchase the second ticket as soon as you get off the train, or pay a surcharge of about 15% for a stopover privilege. You can also just hop aboard the train as it is leaving, but you will probably lack a seat

and will have to pay an extra 25 percent surcharge.

Children under five ride for free; 5-12 years pay half fare, older kids, full price.

Routes

All lines fall under the government-owned umbrella company of *Ferrocarriles Nacionales de México*. The rail routes in West Mexico are operated by the *Ferrocarril del Pacifico* (the Pacific coast route), the *Nacional de Mexico* (from Manzanillo to Guadalajara), and the *Chihuahua Pacífico* (the Copper Canyon route), which is the only route that cannot be made quicker on a bus.

The Pacific Route leaves from both Mexicali and Nogales in the early morning, joining at Benjamin Hill (where the trains stop for about 40 minutes). Journey ends at Guadalajara, a trip of 1,700-miles (average speed: 36 mph).

The Copper Canyon Route leaves at the break of dawn from both Chihuahua and Los Mochis, a 420-mile route which takes 12 to 15 hours to traverse.

The Manzanillo-Guadalajara route departs from Manzanillo daily at 1 p.m., arriving in Guadalajara at 8 p.m.; the Manzanillo-bound train leaves Guadalajara every morning at 9 a.m., arriving at 4 p.m.

Note: if you are traveling from Guadalajara to Mexico City, consider the renovated overnight train, El Tapatío, which has both sleepers and chair cars.

Train Tips

Bring the essentials: food, toilet paper, flashlight, and water (take a couple of gallons already frozen; it will be the only thing cold on these un-air-conditioned trains). If you can't feed your stomach, you can at least feed your mind; bring lots of books. Never stray farther from the train than you can sprint in 10 seconds.

HOTELS

All Mexican hotels are rated by the government and given one to five stars, each with its own price ceiling. In this book, hotels are roughly graded into three categories: budget ($), moderate ($$), and expensive ($$$). In choosing a hotel, always ask to see the room first. All room rates are posted in the lobby. Also look for a book on the counter called *Surgencias y Quejas*, a book where guests write their comments and complaints.

Budget ($)

The budget hotels, which rank from one to two stars, usually cost from $7 to $20. These hotels are to be found around the public market and *zócalo*, and near the bus station, convenient for those who don't need a garage. Many of these hotels call themselves *pensiones, posadas,* and, the cheapest, *casas de huespedes.* You can usually expect a few insects, stained sheets, uncomfortable beds, ceiling fans, and bare light bulbs. The "C" and "F" on the faucets are more likely to mean Cold and Freezing than *Caliente* and *Frio*. Sometimes these budget hotels are former colonial mansions or convents, which add an historic character. Always ask if the price at these cheaper hotels includes meals, which you may be paying for unawares.

Note: if you have to park your car on the street overnight, pay the beat cop or hotel velador (night watchman) two dollars to keep an eye on it for you.

Youth hostels are usually in obscure locations. Age limit is 27, but parents with children are also allowed (Get card from American Youth Hostels, 1332 I Street NW, Ste. 800, Washington DC 20005; tel. 202-783-6161).

Moderate ($$)

Moderately priced hotels, which rank from three to four stars, cost from $20 to $50.

These hotels usually are in the older resort areas of town, or near the *zócalo*. Often, these are the luxury hotels of yesteryear, and some still offer a glimmer of their former selves. They often provide the best hotel value, offering hot water, a garage, maybe a café or restaurant, perhaps a pool and television, and usually a choice of ceiling fan or air conditioning.

Air conditioned rooms are more expensive and often not worth it, since the a.c. usually makes more noise than cool air. A *ventilador* (fan) is quieter and, especially in the tropics, the humidified breeze can be just as cool, and keeps the mosquitoes at bay.

Many moderate-priced motels are found along the main highways leading into town. *Caution: motels on the fringes of town and surrounded by walls are trysting sites.*

Expensive ($$$)

Expensive hotels and motels cost from $50 up, and are usually on the outskirts of town or on the beach. At most resort cities, the farther away from city center, the more expensive. Expect air conditioning, TV, perhaps a carpet, rarely a bathtub, maybe a servi-bar. Travelers rarely find worthwhile peso value here. These places attract mostly tourists on prearranged travel packages, or business travelers on expense accounts. They often ask for a major credit card when registering (don't forget to reclaim the imprint if paying your bill with cash). Some of these resorts are sightseeing attractions. You don't have to stay in them to use their facilities.

Reservations

Reservations are rarely needed, except at coastal resorts during holidays. Even then if you show up at the front desk around check-out time, you usually will luck into a room.

If you do make a reservation, remember that cancellations must be made at least two days before the reservation date if you expect to see a refund.

Overbooking can be a problem at the beach resorts. If a hotel refuses to honor your reservation, ask them to get you into another hotel or complain to the local tourism office. Always get a confirmation number if you make reservations.

Discounts

Always ask if tax (6% to 15%) is included in the rate quoted. If business is slow, explore the possibility for a discount by asking *¿no hay cuartos mas barato?* (aren't there any cheaper rooms). If you are staying for more than a few days, ask about a long-stay discount. Look for weekend discounts in the bigger cities which depend on business travelers. If you are a member of Mexico West Travel Club, you can get a 10% discount at some hotels. Card-carrying members of the American Automobile Association can often get 10% discounts at hotels that give this same discount to members of the AMA, the Mexican Automobile Association.

CAMPING

Unlike the U.S., no laws prohibit travelers from sleeping wherever they choose (except near military posts). Many primitive beaches are leased out as concessions to the *ejidos,* who charge a slight fee—enough to pay for garbage haulout but not enough to keep them from perpetual poverty.

There is no shortage of trailer parks in Mexico, ranging from deluxe operations that cost more than some hotels to concrete slabs set in the desert.

There are still plenty of free beach camping sites, more so on the peninsula than on the mainland.

Away from the coastline, many travelers will find a sound sleep in the countryside, in soccer fields, atop microwave stations, even in the middle of the zócalo in small villages.

Beachfront restaurants often don't mind travelers slinging a hammock on the premises.

There are some places where it is not prudent to camp: under coconut trees (thump), around Manzanillo trees (sap and fruit are poisonous), alongside the highway (an invitation for thieves), in an arroyo (flash floods), near stagnant fresh water (mosquitoes), or near any long highway grade where trucks are common (the *escapes* or compression release valves will blast you from your sleep).

Mexico has its own camping club, with an informative newsletter: Club Monarca de Acampadores (Apartado Postal 31-750, 45050 Guadalajara, Jalisco, México).

Etiquette: always ask for permission to camp from any nearby rancho. Not only is it polite, but it will alleviate any fears they might have about you. In return, they will assure you of the safety of sleeping there.

Useful Paraphernalia: a small length of garden hose, for filling water bottles and sun showers.

COOKING FUELS

Don't cut living trees for their branches; it is illegal. You can always buy firewood from local ranchers as a way of contributing to the local economy. Mesquite *carbón*, which is sold around the market, makes an excellent charcoal.

White gas is difficult to find. *Tractolina*, a low grade diesel fuel that billows black smoke, substitutes as kerosene and is easiest found on the blackmarket (just ask around); it is usually siphoned from rusty barrels hidden in the back of a private home.

Propane is the most practical fuel, known in Mexico as *gas;* every city of size has a *planta de gas* on the outskirts of town.

Note: avoid overfilling by marking the capacity of your tank in kilograms (convert pounds to kilos by dividing tank poundage by 2.2).

5.
Crossing the Sea of Cortés, Weather and Waves

BY AIR

On the Baja California peninsula, the only airports where you can catch a plane to the other side of the Sea of Cortés are at Tijuana, La Paz, and San Jose del Cabo. Flights go to Puerto Vallarta, Guadalajara, Guaymas, Culiacán, and Mazatlán. You can only fly on one of the national airlines: *AeroCalifornia, Aeroméxico, Mexicana* or *Noroeste.*

BY SEA

The only places you can cross the Gulf by sea are Santa Rosalia and La Paz on the peninsula, and Mazatlán, Topolobampo, and Guaymas on the mainland. The Santa Rosalia-Guaymas run, and the La Paz-Topolobampo take eight hours. The longest run is between La Paz and Mazatlán, a 16-hour crossing.

The Sematur ferries that make the crossing are mostly aging Danish ships, kept in marginal operating condition: the *Azteca, Coromuel, Puerto Vallarta, Benito Juárez,* and the smaller *Guaycura* and *Loreto* (two others have sunk). The larger ferries on the Mazatlán route have cafeterias, restaurants, TV video rooms, safe deposit boxes, even discos. The crossing is usually calm, warm, and bright with stars.

The ferries that run to Guaymas and Topolobampo are the warhorses, more for truckers than for travelers (don't expect them to be childproofed). But they are certainly endurable for the short eight-hour crossings.

Tickets

You can choose between four kinds of tickets: *salon, turista, cabina,* and *cabina especial.*

Salon tickets are like bus seats and cannot be reserved. The salon is noisy and uncomfortable. Many people buy these tickets just to get onboard, then sleep out on the deck, under the stars, a common practice.

Turista tickets, which must be reserved, are for a small two- or four-bedded cabin with a wash basin but no toilet; you must share the often dysfunctional toilets and showers with everybody else.

Important: *when buying a turista ticket, plead for a cabin with a window; the ticket agent knows which ones these are (though they may feign ignorance). Cabins on the inside are dark as night, and hot as a sauna if the air conditioning should falter (which it usually does).*

Cabinas are the most comfortable, all with

Gulf Ferry

windows, showers, toilets, and usually enough room for a table and couch. The Cabina Especial has bedrooms and a larger sitting area.

Children under two travel free. Children under 12 pay half fare.

Crossing with Vehicles

If you are bringing a car across, you need to first get a temporary import permit, which can be picked up in Santa Rosalía or La Paz (if you are on the mainland, you will already have one). Vehicles longer than five meters, or those with trailers, pay 25 to 30% more than smaller cars. *Note: when boarding, try not to be one of the last ones on. Last one on is the last one off, that is, if you can survive the carbon monoxide.*

Reservations

Always make reservations ahead of time to insure space. In Mexico, you can call toll free to their central reservations office in Mazatlán (tel. 91-800-696-96) or phone direct to the city office where you are departing (see city sections). *Note: if you*

don't have a reservation and there is no room, ask to be put on the lista de espera, *a stand-by list similar to that used by the airlines. Tickets not sold by 2 p.m. on the*

FERRY SCHEDULE

Guaymas to Santa Rosalia:
T, Th, Sat, Sn, departs 10 a.m.
Phone: (622)-2-33-90
Fax: (622)-2-33-93
Santa Rosalia to Guaymas:
T, Th, Sat. Sn, departs 11 p.m..
Phone: (685) 2-00-14
Topolobampo to La Paz:
Daily except Tuesday, departs 10 a.m.
Phone: (686) 2-01-41
Fax: (686) 2-00-35
La Paz to Topolobampo:
Daily except Friday, departs 8 p.m.
Phone: 682-5-38-33
Fax: (682) 2-52-58
Mazatlán to La Paz:
Daily, departs at 5 p.m.
Phone: (678) 4-11-98
Fax: (678) 1-52-35
La Paz to Mazatlán:
Daily, departs at 5 p.m.

day of departure are then given to those on this list. If there is no space for your vehicle and you are desperate, consider paying a trucker to put it on an empty flatbed trailer and chain the axles down. You can drive it on and off of loading docks at La Paz and Mazatlán.

Baja Express

A jet boat service operates out of La Paz to Topolobampo, making the trip in 3 1/2 hours. The hydrofoil leaves the Muelle Fiscal (the main pier) in La Paz every day at 10 a.m. and is scheduled to return the same evening. Routes and schedules are subject to change.

The catamaran carries 315 passengers on two levels, the cheaper lower level and the more expensive upper level with an open bar and leather seats. It is fairly expensive (about the price of a *cabina* on the Sematur ferry), sleek, and certainly fast; its first charter was shuttling refugees out of Beirut. *Note: don't rely on the scheduling. The boat remains tied to the dock during rough seas.*

THE SEA OF CORTÉS

Not quite lake, not quite ocean. On a calm day, the Gulf is as flat as a pane of glass. Under the calm surface, reefs and shoals lie unmarked by surf. Tidal currents that run like rivers consume your gas and pull you off course. Should the wind blow, this placid surface immediately rears up in vertical walls of water that can broach the ablest of small craft. Despite appearances, the Gulf has a nervous temperament.

The shoreline is not to be trusted either. Most of the nautical charts were surveyed in the 19th century and are of too large a scale for accurate coastal navigation (if you can find a pre-1945 edition of *Sailing Directions*, they provide much more information than today's anemic H.O. Pub. 153,

Lighthouse keeper

which is written for tankers, not small boats). Along the coast, unreliable lighthouses are mostly unmanned. The solar panels are used by frigatebirds and osprey as nesting sites. Workmen service these remote beacons just twice a year.

The best navigational aid along this coastline is your own vision. Dark blue reefs and light-green shoals. Polarized sunglasses help.

Even your vision can be deceived at times. The clarity of the atmosphere compresses distances and lures skippers far from port. A dry gas tank is the leading disabler of outboards.

If you should fetch up disabled on a deserted shore, an AAA road map will prove more valuable in pointing out the nearest road than any navigational chart. Unless it is over the nearest rise, the best advice is to stay put; you will likely be rescued by a passing *panga* (never leave port without gallons of water). If you need immediate help, keep to the coast in search of the nearest fish camp or rancho; both are usually situated in the lee of major headlands.

The VHF radio is a practical safety item, but a mirror remains the best device to attract the attention of the numerous fishing pangas that you will see working offshore.

If you are in the upper Gulf, consult your tide tables before anchoring or you might waken to find your boat careened under a full moon; tides of twenty feet are common.

Be on the lookout for renegade reefs. Low declining headlands or rocky outcroppings suggest offlying reefs, while bold cliffs or steep beaches often indicate deeper water.

Take the prevailing winds into account when planning a trip. Travel south in winter, north in summer.

WEST MEXICO WEATHER
Winter

In Mexico, winter winds generally blow down the southeast slant of the coastline, drawn onshore in some places by the local sea breezes. In the Sea of Cortés, high pressure to the north induces predominantly north winds.

The farther south you travel, the warmer and more benign becomes the weather. Up in the northern Sierra Madre, snow can fly at the upper elevations. Farther south, around Guadalajara, the weather remains a perpetual spring.

Equipatas

The southern half of the Baja California peninsula is occasionally struck by the same Pacific storms that lash the California coast. But these stray winter cyclones, called *equipatas*, follow a much more southerly course, generally developing aloft and then working their way down slowly to the surface. For a few days, their light frontal winds and heavy rains pump in large amounts of maritime tropical air from the southwest. Although they arrive as a surprise to travelers who think they have escaped the wet grip of winter, *Equipatas* are seldom dangerous, and their rain-laden clouds come as a blessing to the sunburnt peninsula.

Where the peninsular divide is low or narrow, these equipatas spread across to the Sea of Cortés as well, covering it with a low grey ceiling of clouds. The wind usually has little substance; if it roars at all, it is with the authority of a paper lion.

The frequency and strength of these *equipatas* decrease with the latitude. By late spring, as the Aleutian low gradually weakens and the Pacific high again dominates the North Pacific, these cyclonic intrusions soon come to a halt.

El Norte

More dangerous than the *Equipatas* is the strong north wind that funnels down the Sea of Cortés. It arrives suddenly, with little warning other than a line of whitecaps on the horizon. Gale force is not uncommon, though it generally stays in the 18 to 35 mph range. Greybeard seas and dry winds. They blow wildly for days on end and never seem to quit.

This wind plays on your nerves, perhaps due in part to the atmospheric ions that create depression, like the Mistral winds of France, or the Santa Anas of California.

Northers have more in common with Santa Anas than just atmospheric ions. Both originate from a dome of cold high pressure that often forms over the four corners area of the plateau states. A cold wind falls off the top of this dome and drains into the Gulf, attracted by the lower pressure farther south.

Note: Some Mexican shrimpboaters say Northers blow during the full moon, but a pocket radio can better predict their occurrence. Listen to a Los Angeles radio station, such as KNX (AM 1070). If the weather broadcaster is predicting Santa Anas for Southern California, it is likely El Norte will strike.

SPRING

The late spring months in Mexico bring the

Chubasco

most pleasant weather. Along the west coast of Baja, winds often blow steadily over 20 knots due to a strong clockwise circulation of air around the strengthening Pacific high, which reaches its greatest development during August. This anti-cyclone acts as a barrier to storms carried eastward by the westerlies. The rest of the Mexican coast basks in the northwest trades that brush softly against the coast, encouraged by an onshore breeze that rushes in to replace the warmer air rising inland. When temperatures fall at night, these winds are often reversed by a light offshore zephyr. Mornings are often as calm as if you were indoors. In the Sierra Madre, the days grow warmer.

As the brilliant sun of late spring and early summer starts to warm up the waters of the Gulf, strong, offshore westerly winds frequently blow off the mountainous east coast of Baja California. At night, the high mountain slopes cool rapidly, chilling the surrounding air. This cold, dense air falls down the steep slopes and funnels through arroyos—gaining velocity—to blast out at sea level. These gusty winds occur late at night and often during the dawn hours, and can cartwheel your dome tent right into the sea. *Prediction: many Mexicans living along Baja's east coast believe that if the sea breeze dies at night and you can hear thunder in the mountains, these winds will soon come tumbling down.*

SUMMER & FALL

The first hot breaths of summer are felt by the end of May. The doldrum belt moves northward, rains begin to fall along the lower coast of the mainland, and the first tropical cyclone of the season may already be terrorizing the coast. Sea breezes reverse themselves. Southwesterly coastal breezes are common along the mainland, while southeasterly winds make an appearance in the Gulf of California, moving farther north month by month. By late summer they usually blow along the entire length of the Gulf.

Chubascos

Airmass thunderstorms raging over the Sierra Madre illuminate the night skies like a strobe, visible from the peninsula. Of more concern are the coastal thunderstorms which occur almost daily at some points along the mainland. These *chubascos* form most often in July, August, September, and occasionally in October. Along the mainland, they often build over the coastal mountains between noon and 4 p.m.. In the late afternoon, the southwesterly sea breeze veers ENE as these storms tend to break into violent squalls, complete with lightning, rain, and strong winds. They last for as long as four hours.

Along the Baja California peninsula, thunderstorms often form along the eastern slopes of the coastal mountain ranges on hot, balmy days. The prevailing southeasterly wind pushes humid air up the steep slopes of these mountains. It rises to meet with the upper level moisture that has been carried westward by a limb of the Bermuda high centered over the Gulf of Mexico. If there is no strong wind to break up the vertical current, these cells of rising air grow into imposing anvil-shaped cumulonimbus. Although they usually let loose their thunder and rain over the mountains, coastal stretches are sometimes struck by stiff winds and heavy rains.

Some chubascos, called *Toros*, form over the water, particularly in late summer and most frequently at night when the surface water temperature does not fall as much as the night air's. Once these storms break, they move about dangerously at will; their winds can attain hurricane strength for short durations. *Weatherwise: The shark fishermen of San Evaristo say that when the offshore wind howls at night, it is a sign that no Toros will form. These offshore winds probably disrupt the rising air necessary to form a thunderstorm.*

Often times, the circulation of a tropical storm up to 300 miles away will draw humid moist air across the spine of the peninsula, forming huge tracts of menacing cumulonimbus. Though capable of fitful squalls and blasts of rain, the real danger comes from the tropical cyclones that generate these thunderstorms.

HURRICANES

Hurricanes are the result of a basic inequality in the distribution of heat. In the polar regions, most of the sun's heat is radiated back out to space, while in the tropics most heat from the sun is absorbed. A hurricane attempts to rectify this imbalance by transferring heat northward. It acts as a simple heat engine, fueled by warm moist air drawn from a tropical sea and given an initial spin by the earth's rotation. Once spun into life, it builds up muscle and then makes an erratic four- to five-day dash for the higher latitudes. Hurricanes in Mexico generally dissipate before reaching as far north as San Diego.

Generally speaking, storm tracks during mid-season run to the northwest. But in May and June, and especially in September and October, these hurricanes are more dangerous, since they tend to recurve to the northeast, towards land.

From late May to November, these warm waters breed up to 30 tropical cyclones of storm strength, with approximately 12 maturing into hurricanes above 64 knots.

The hurricane's leading edge comes from the southeast and contains the strongest, most violent winds to strike the coast of Mexico. Coastal residents call these southeast winds *El Cordonazo de San Francisco*, the Lash of St. Francis. It is traditionally believed to hit between the 1st and 5th of October, during the feast days of St. Francis. It often does, but not for religious reasons. The beginning of October is the dangerous peak of the hurricane season, a time when cyclones reel across the Pacific like drunks in search of a fight. Not until the end of November does the sobering influence of winter halt most tropical storm activity.

Weatherwise: often in the summer, residents along the mainland coast will complain of bochorno, a sullen intense heat that arises when the sea breeze shuts down. This is usually the first indication that a tropical storm or hurricane is nearby. If a long, thick swell begins to slam on the beach you can be sure of it. The storm will lie in the direction of these swells. As the wind starts to pick up, add 115 degrees to its direction and you will have a rough second fix on the cyclone.

6.
MAPS
& OTHER MISCELLANY

MAPS

Mapmaking is a relatively new science in Mexico. Most contain errors. Some roads jump from the drafting table to the map without ever being built, while others that have been built have yet to be noted. Try to carry at least two different maps in order to cross reference your routes.

It is easier to obtain a map of Mexico in the United States than in Mexico.

General Road Maps

The Mexican government publishes the *Carta Turistica*, a small scale (1:1,000,000) road map that shows major, secondary, and dirt roads. Three maps, *Noroeste, Norte,* and *Occidente*, cover all of west Mexico to Guerrero. Much of this information is out of date, and you should supplement it with either the AAA map of Mexico, or better yet, the *Atlas de Carreteras*, published by Pemex. This atlas is the most current road map, with mileage posted in kilometers and miles. The advantage of this atlas are the little orange gas pumps showing the location of Pemex gas stations across the country; it also contains street maps of all major cities, showing hotels. You can find this map at most bookstores or newsstands in Mexico, or by special order to the San Diego Map Center (tel. 714-291-3830).

Another map publisher in Mexico, the Guia Roji (República de Colombia No. 23, México, D.F.), prints city, state, and national maps, but these are not as up-to-date as the Pemex atlas.

Topographic Maps

Topographic maps are published by the *Instituto Nacional de Estadística Geografía E Información* (INEGI). The entire country is covered in a series of 1:1,000,000 scale maps that include roads set against a topographic background; this is often used as a road map, but the roads don't list mileages. The maps named Tijuana, La Paz, Chihuahua, and Guadalajara cover the entire west coast of Mexico as far as the Golfo de Tehuantepec. They also publish larger scale maps (1:500,000, 1:250,000 & 1:50,000) that show paths and tracks as well as roads.

INEGI offers an assortment of maps: geologic, geographic, demographic. They have offices in Hermosillo (Carretera a Bahía Kino Km. 0.5), Guadalajara (Jalisco y Avenida Alcade No. 788, Esquina Jesús García, Sector Hidalgo), and in Mexicali (Pasaje Oaxaca No. 566-3rd floor, 21000 Mexicali, Baja California).

A collection of INEGI topographic maps

(1:50,000) covering the Baja California peninsula have been collected in book form, the *Baja Topographic Atlas Directory* (published by Topography International) with running mileage, and other travel information added, a fine compilation for off-road travel on the peninsula.

Note: most college libraries stock INEGI maps. You can photocopy just those sections you plan to explore.

Aeronautical Charts

Even if you don't have a plane, the large-scale (1:1,000,000) aeronautical charts published by the U.S. Department of Commerce complement the Mexican topo maps; these Operation Navigation Charts are defined by shaded 1,000 foot contours. Four of these maps cover Mexico: Northwest Mexico (ONC H-22), Northern Mexico (ONC-H-23), Central Mexico (ONC J-24) and Southern Mexico (ONC J-25). These maps can be ordered from the Dept. of Commerce through the National Oceanic and Atmospheric Administration, Riverdale, MD 20840, through the National Ocean Survey, Washington DC, 20235, or through the Aeronautical Chart and Information Center, US Air Force, St. Louis, MO 63118. *Note: an aviation dealer at the local airport often stocks or can order these maps.*

Nautical Charts

Most of the nautical charts published by the NOAA were surveyed in the 19th century and are of too small a scale for accurate coastal navigation. Except for long navigations, most boaters would do better with a topographic map and a Coast Pilot, a book describing the coastline, mile by mile. The earlier editions of the Coast Pilot (before 1940) offer a more detailed coastal description, but are found only in used bookstores or at the library.

Map Source

The *San Diego Map Centre* offers the widest selection of maps and books covering Mexico (except nautical charts). They will send you a catalog listing a wide assortment of Mexico maps, along with ordering information. Write or phone: 2611 University Avenue, San Diego, CA 92104; tel. 714-291-3830.

PHOTOGRAPHY

You are allowed to bring 12 rolls of film into Mexico, a rule rarely enforced. If you prefer a brand other than Kodak, bring a lot. Kodak is the only film easily found in Mexico (transparencies and black and white can be scarce). Kodak has standardized its production worldwide. The film made in Mexico is the same you buy in Los Angeles.

It still pays to be cautious. Check the film's expiration date and the condition of the box. If the price tag obscures the expiration date, it may have been placed there on purpose. Though the expiration date may be valid, it may have been sitting in a sun-struck display window. Check for faded colors.

Keep your film and camera out of the sun, off the dashboard. In more tropical regions of Mexico, fungus may grow on the film surface. To prevent this, keep your rolls in aluminum screw top cans instead of the plastic ones (or wrap them in aluminum foil). Keep a small package of silicate in with your camera. Develop the film as soon as possible to avoid heat damage.

Dust instead of fungus is the biggest problem in desert areas. An enema syringe from the local drug store is the most efficient instrument for delivering a stream of air at high pressure.

Security X-ray machines are stronger in Mexico and can fog your film, especially if it is of high ASA. *Trick: instead of setting your film on the conveyor belt, carry it through the gate. When the metal detector buzzes, hand it to the inspector, who usu-*

ally hand-inspects buzzed items, thus avoiding the X-rays.

GIFTS & BARTER

Postcards, toys, stickers, decals, buttons, ballpoint pens, and clothes make fine gifts to locals. Children's clothing and fish hooks are useful in bartering for fresh seafood. Skin magazines and cheap liquor also work, but while the fisherman may be satisfied, his family is left out of the exchange.

LAUNDRY

Laundromats are overpriced and hard to find. Those found often operate more like a dry cleaner; you hand your clothes over and come back when they are done, often the next day. It is much cheaper to have your clothes washed by hand. Ask in town or go to the river and follow the soap suds upstream; most will be glad for some indepen-dent income. Your clothes will be pounded clean, though perhaps at the cost of a few buttons.

Note: If you are beach camping, and washing your own clothes, use Jabón de Coco, *the best saltwater soap.*

TIME ZONES

The state of Baja California Norte is on Pacific Standard Time, as well as Daylight Savings Time from early April to late October. Baja California Sur, Sonora, and Sinaloa are on Mountain Standard Time. The rest of the west coast of Mexico stays on Central Standard Time.

ELECTRICITY

You can use the same 110 volt appliances in Mexico. The electric current is standardized to 110 volts, 60 cycles AC, same as in the United States.

Conch Diver on Isla San Francisco

7.

Baja California Peninsula, The Root of the Dream

The Baja California peninsula is the root of California. Here, in the southern half of the peninsula, the Spanish first settled. Only then did they start moving slowly north through wide deserts and contrary seas, always searching for something more. After three centuries, a single California stretched from Cabo San Lucas to north of San Francisco.

California was first born of fiction, a 15th century story about the mythic island realm of Califia, populated by Amazons and rich in pearls. The first explorers came here expecting an island of available women and easy wealth. Instead they landed on a thorny, arid peninsula inhabited by stone age Indians.

These indigenous tribes were among the poorest on the continent. Like those in Tierra del Fuego, the tribes of the southern peninsula—the *Guaycura, Pericú,* and *Cochimí*—had been pushed down by more powerful tribes, surviving in a kind of cultural equilibrium to the harsh climate. They lacked pottery, fishing lines, boats even. They would thumb through their feces for undigested seeds that could be re-eaten, the second harvest. The missionaries recounted a story of how the Indians would tie a string around a piece of meat, swallow it, enjoy a brief digestion, then pull it up from their stomach to pass on to the next.

But those who sailed across the gulf refused to acknowledge the harsh reality, a peculiarity that has run throughout the peninsula's history. This long desert land has always been like a mirage, where people are more likely to follow maps of their own making instead of the terrain in front of them. Deserts always seem to inspire this kind of inner vision, a place of prophets and madmen.

On the peninsula, these dreams often stumbled over the terrain.

Cortés, the conqueror of México, was the force behind the Spain's discovery of California, sending out three expeditions in search of new lands. The first to arrive, a band of mutineers in 1533, was massacred, but a few survivors returned with tales of pearls.

Cortés himself sailed here in 1535, seeking the wealth of Califia. He set up a colony at La Paz. This time he didn't burn his ships to keep his men from deserting like he did 16 years earlier at Veracruz. Within two years, the colony was abandoned, starved out. The conquistadors had no appetite for second harvests.

Fifty-nine years later, Vizcaíno also

founded a colony at La Paz. Leaving the settlers, he set off to search for pearls. He returned empty-handed only to find them in a rebellious mood. The colony was burned to the ground—accidentally—but it was the excuse the colonists were looking for. La Paz was again abandoned.

Pearling expeditions were launched to the gulf in 1615, 1627, and 1628. Most ended in lawsuits and disaster.

In 1683, the Jesuits Atondo and Kino attempted another colony near Loreto, this one lasting less than two years.

They tried once more, a new site in La Paz, but they were forced to flee after firing a cannon at a group of natives they had invited to a feast.

Father Salvatierra gained the first secure foothold on the peninsula, building a mission settlement in Loreto in 1697. Through tenacity and faith, the missionaries effort expanded throughout the peninsula, despite rebellions, drought, and lack of supplies. But as the missions spread the word of civilization, they also carried the bacillus of infection. Most Indians found that death and salvation walked hand in hand. By the 19th century, most of the more remote missions were abandoned for lack of natives.

The peninsula has always been seen as an opportunity, a great emptiness inviting man's presence. William Walker, the American freebooter, invaded the peninsula to create his own empire. Foreign colonists came by invitation of the dictator Porfirio Díaz to work what many Mexicans considered a wasteland. The English in San Quintín, the Americans in Los Planes, Bahía Magdalena, and Mulegé. All ended in disillusionment and labor lost.

People are always trying to find a use for the peninsula. It was proposed as a refuge for the Apaches, as a homeland for the Jews, and even today rumors abound of its being the 51st state of the Union, or the new Hong Kong after Chinese annexation of that island in 1997.

Though the peninsula's future is at best chimerical, its past is a visible reminder that this land is unforgiving: forgotten historic sites, empty concrete buildings, adobe walls melting in the sun, abandoned ranchos, dry wells. But instead of suggesting failure, these ruins tell the story of human endurance, imagination, and vision. In the harsh light of the desert, only shadows remain, but they still measure the optimism of the human spirit. The story of fortitude in the face of futility is a common one here.

Natural History

The kind of fortitude shown by the people who live in the peninsular desert is also demanded of the plant and animal life here, much of it found nowhere else in the world. The flora and fauna survive only by creatively adapting to this waterless environment: rattleless rattlesnakes, black jack rabbits, boojum trees, hundreds of grotesque plant forms, 2700 plant species. Nature has gone off on an evolutionary tangent, insulated from continental influences.

In many cases, nature not only survive, but thrives. The offshore islands are the continent's richest nursery of seabirds. The air hums with insects. After a rain, flowers carpet the desert. The peninsula has been set aside from the continent as a timepiece of the natural world, much of it unblemished by man.

A Once and Future Island

This peninsula broke away from the Mexican mainland 25 million years ago, torn by the Pacific tectonic plate. This plate is grinding north a few centimeters every year, carrying the peninsula with it. One day in the geologic future, the peninsula will be an island off the coast of California.

Though still a peninsula, it is this island-like quality that adds to the mystique of the place. Even the European cartographers drew California as an island for 200 years after it was proven to be a peninsula.

The effects of this geographic isolation

have not imprinted only on the flora and fauna. It is also seen in the independence and peacefulness of the people who now live here, at least those away from the border areas. Many of the customs and traditions of mainland Mexico are absent, but so are many of the severe social problems such as land distribution, indigenous rights, urban pollution, and overcrowding.

The *Baja Californianos* have become relatively self-sufficient, relying for years on their own imagination and endurance. The desert is full of ranchos with quixotic names, like *Rancho Esperanza, Rancho El Imposible, Rancho Progreso.* Impossible, Hope, Progress.

In many cases, hope has triumphed, impossibility overcome. Progress, because it is so hard won, is rarely questioned.

The result is development not always in the best interests of nature, such as at Ciudad Constitución, where miles of desert continue to be uprooted for crop land, though the water supplies are diminishing. Or Cabo San Lucas, where a chunk of the Southern California Dream has come home to its roots, bringing with it the ills of overdevelopment it seeks to escape.

Fernando Jordon, a famous Mexican journalist, called the peninsula *El Otro Mexico.* It also can be called *La Otra California—* the other California, the first California. And though people tend to think that the greater Los Angeles basin is the epicenter of the California Dream, it actually finds its historic source on this peninsula, which slowly moves toward becoming the island it once was and will be again.

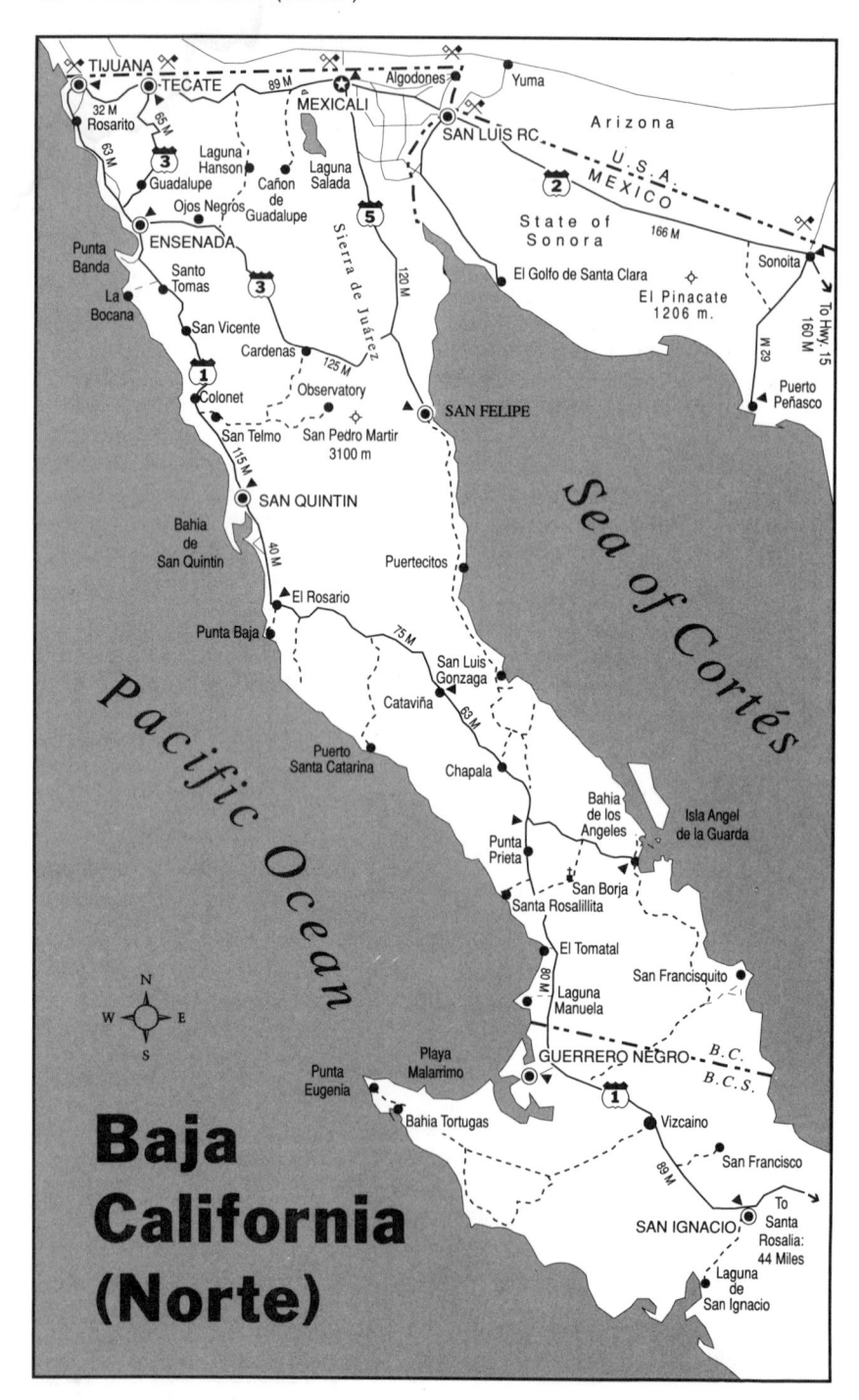

Baja California (Norte)

8.
Baja California Norte

TIJUANA

Tijuana is a sudden, garish introduction to Mexico. What we see is as much a reflection of ourselves as of Mexico: the show bars, the plaster statues of Elvis, the velvet paintings. These are a mirror of our own culture, given a Latin interpretation. And the gold embroidered sombreros, the bandoleroed waiters, the mock village shopping bazaars are for American consumption, images of Mexico without substance.

Tijuana is full of these cross-cultural flourishes. Some critics think Tijuana is no more representative of Mexico than the zebra-painted burros on Av. Revolución are of real zebras.

Though it is farther away from Mexico City than any other town in the republic, it is actually one of the most Mexican in its own peculiar way. Not only are all the crafts of Mexico sold here, but the people who make them have migrated here as well. Tijuana is Mexico in microcosm. You can eat at a Michoacan restaurant, buy earings from a Taxco silversmith, and listen to *jarocha* music from Veracruz. There are drawbacks, of course. The weaver from Oaxaca, stripped of the dignity of his village environment, seems sadly displaced, like an animal taken from the wild and put on display. Some call Tijuana a zoo.

But then zoos are for people who don't have the time or inclination to travel. Tijuana serves its purpose. This is the world's largest border crossing. Average stay is less than a day.

This gateway is also the world's largest illegal border crossing. The chain link fence between the two countries is rent with gaping holes. Every night, hundreds of immigrants hop through these holes and jog towards the lights of San Ysidro. This flimsy fence—the Tortilla Curtain—is an important international safety valve. Not only does it release the social pressure of rising unemployment in Mexico, but it also supplies the U.S. with the cheap, uncomplaining labor force that it has relied on since the days of the short-handled hoe.

The border was surveyed in 1848, after the Mexican-American War. It immediately changed this agricultural valley into a border town, a refuge for outlaws like Juan Mendoza, who terrorized this area for ten years. The area was finally domesticated when the Mexican government set up a customs house here to capture revenue.

Soon there were two settlements, Tijuana on the Mexican side, Tía Juana (Aunt Jane) on the U.S. side. In 1908, Tía Juana changed its name to San Ysidro (after the patron saint of Madrid), ending the confusion. Most gringos still call Tijuana "Tía Juana", or simply TJ, which has a derogatory ring. The early Indians who lived here called this place *Ti-uan* (near-the-water). The first foreigners arriving in 1769 commented on the tight-fisted trading of the Indians. Six weeks later, Father Serra stopped here too, but decided not to stay. He thought the Indians were too insolent.

At the turn of the century, only 240 people lived here. There was a school, an adobe church, one curio store, and the Tía Juana Hot Springs Hotel at Agua Caliente. The cemetery grew as fast as the town.

In 1911, Mexican socialist revolutionaries and American Wobblies (International Workers of the World) stormed the town, attempting to establish the beginnings of a socialist revolution in Mexico. It lasted all of a month before Mexican army troops forced them across the border to the safety of an American jail, much to the enjoyment of the tourist crowds who watched from the security of San Ysidro. June 22nd, the day of the victory, is still celebrated as a local holiday.

Another invasion occurred right after the U.S. Congress passed the Volstead Act in 1920. Prohibition turned Tijuana's Av. Revolución into a gauntlet of bars, clubs and illicit pleasures. Gambling at Agua Caliente attracted the Hollywood elite. It was a grand slide for 10 years until President Cárdenas outlawed gambling in 1935. Despite the repeal of prohibition, Tijuana held on to its shady reputation, especially during World War II.

Seamy show bars still exist, but mostly as relics in a rapidly changing city. Young women find greater opportunity to work in one of the growing number of *maquiladoras* (bonded assembly plants), where they can earn $1.25 an hour in a country where the daily wage is about $5.

The poverty is unsettling, but the brash shantytowns blossoming on the eastern mesas are built in the hopeful spirit of the frontier. You can still buy switchblades and steroids on Av. Revolución, but locals prefer the modern shopping mall. Like the twin towers of the Fiesta Americana that rise up like a tuning fork over the skyline, this city is vibrating to a higher pitch.

TRAVELING ABOUT
By Taxi
Push through the two turnstiles into Mexico and you are soon faced with one of the largest taxi fleets in world. Steel yourself. The farther you walk down the gauntlet of insistent *taxistas*, the more the prices will drop. State what you are willing to pay (about $5-$7 to bus station, a bit more to the airport, $2-$4 to downtown or Cultural Center), and keep walking until your price is met. Your ace in the hole: the bus stop is just beyond.

By Bus
Just beyond the taxi fleet at the border is a bus stop where you can catch the *Central Camionera* bus to the airport or bus station, passing through some of the poorer slums of Tijuana. Buses run from the border to Av. Revolución, but the one-mile trek over the Río Tijuana pedestrian bridge is almost as fast. From Av. Revolución, you can catch buses back to the border at Calle 2 between Revolución and Constitución.

By Rental Car
You can rent cars at the airport or at offices of the major companies: *Avis* on Blvd. Agua Caliente 3310-1 (tel. 86-40-04), 4), *Budget* on Paseo de los Héroes Z.P. 77 (tel. 84-02-53), *Dollar* on Blvd. Sanchez Taboada 37-C (tel. 84-06-78), *Hertz* at the Hotel Palacio Azteca 86-43-71. *Note: Dollar is one of the few rental companies that allows their cars rented in the U.S. to cross the border into Mexico.*

BEARINGS
Tijuana is divided into four main areas: **Avenida Revolución** is the traditional tour-

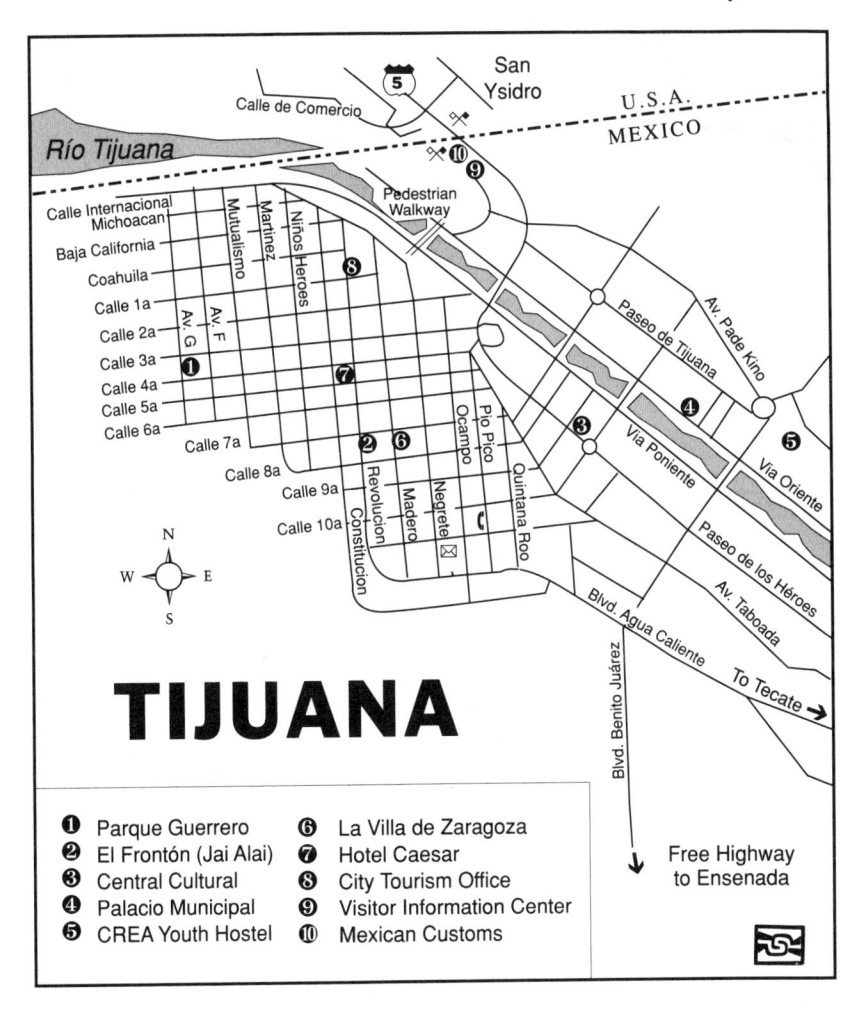

TIJUANA

❶ Parque Guerrero
❷ El Frontón (Jai Alai)
❸ Central Cultural
❹ Palacio Municipal
❺ CREA Youth Hostel
❻ La Villa de Zaragoza
❼ Hotel Caesar
❽ City Tourism Office
❾ Visitor Information Center
❿ Mexican Customs

↓ Free Highway to Ensenada

ist zone, reached easily by foot from the border; sleazy below Calle 2 (Benito Juárez), respectable and even fashionable above Calle 2.

Av. Revolución runs into **Blvd. Agua Caliente**, a four-lane thoroughfare leading to the bullring, race track, country club, the best hotels, and eventually on to Tecate.

Paralleling Blvd. Agua Caliente, but nearer the Río Tijuana is the newer **Paseo de los Héroes**, a modern Tijuana of broad boulevards, shopping centers and the Cultural Center.

Playas de Tijuana, two miles away on the coast, is mostly a place of residences and cancer-cure institutes; the polluted beachfront is ignored by most.

TRAVEL INFORMATION

Just past the main border gate is the Visitor Information Center, which stays open until 10 p.m. weeknights, 11 p.m. on Friday nights, 8 p.m. on Sundays. Staff is helpful. Armed with maps and markers, they will trace out a walking route, give advice on taxi fares, etc. Another tourism kiosk is on Av. Revolución, between Calles 3 & 4. The Tijuana Chamber of Commerce operates an information office on the corner of Av. Revolución at Calle 1 (also known as Calle Comercio). You can also call 83-1405 or 83-1310 for city information. The State Tourism Office (tel. 84-2173) is found in the Government Center, Via Oriente 1-208, along the Río Tijuana. For information from the U.S., phone the Tijuana Baja Information Center: 800-522-1516, or the Mexican consulate in San Diego at 619-231-8423.

PLACES
Av. Revolución

This main avenue and environs continue to be Tijuana's main pull, with its five *pasajes* (shopping alleys), duty-free perfume shops, crafts stores, and show bars (most tucked away in the notorious Zona Norte, west of Av. Revolución, north of Calle 2). The two authentic mercados are at Calle 6 and Negrete, and on Niños Héroes between Calles 1 & 2. Two respites from the commercialism of Av. Revo-lución are the **Catedral de Nuestra Señora de Guadalupe** (Av. Constitución and Calle 2), typical of the modern Mexican church, and **Parque Teniente Miguel Guerrero** (six blocks west of Av. Revoución, on Av. F, between Calles 3 & 4), where you might catch a Sunday music concert. This is a bit of traditional Mexico, with its shady laurel trees and central kiosk. Opposite the park is the **Catedral de San Francisco**. The park's **Monumento de los Heroés de 1911** is probably the only monu-

ment in Mexico dedicated to Porfirio Díaz' anti-revolutionary troops, who pushed the American and Mexican socialist forces back across the border.

El Frontón Palacio de Jai Alai

The most historic building on Av. Revolución is the Frontón (Av. Revolución & Calle 7), where they play jai alai every evening at 8 p.m. except Thursday. For a modest admission, you can watch men with wicker scoops sling a rubber ball wrapped in goatskin at up to 150 m.p.h., enough to kill a spectator if it weren't for the wire barricade. The game is played against three walls, a cross between lacrosse and handball. All betting is pari-mutuel, the easiest being a straight bet on whatever color of armband your chosen team is wearing. The Basques of Spain are considered the originators of the game, though some claim it was created by the Aztecs and imported to Spain after the conquest.

Caliente Race Track

This track hearkens back to Tijuana's more raucous past, even though most of it is a modern re-creation rebuilt after a 1971 fire. One dollar gets you into the grandstand, double that for the clubhouse, a bit more for entrance to the Turf Club. Thoroughbred racing runs noon to 5 p.m. Saturdays and Sundays. Greyhounds run nightly (except Tuesday), and onweekday afternoons. You can also bet on foreign races. The race track is situated a few miles from downtown, along Av. Agua Caliente.

Plazas de Toros

Tijuana's two *plazas de toros* (bullrings) alternately share the season, which runs from May to September. The more impressive ring is the Plaza de Toros Monumental (in Playas de Tijuana), the second largest bullring in the world. The other ring is El Toreo, on Av. Agua Caliente halfway between Av. Revolución and the Agua Caliente Race Track. The world's top matadors fight at both, though some prefer not to. These are the only bullrings in Mexico where many in the audience routinely leave during the performance, jolted by the blood. Though tickets can be bought at Ticketron, don't assume that bullfights are an entertainment. *Note: for those who have never been to a bullfight, expect to be confronted by complex and conflicting emotions, of life, death, art, and courage.* All bullfights begin at 4 p.m.

Central Cultural Tijuana

This federally funded cultural complex was built for both foreigners and Mexicans. For foreigners, to promote the country; for Mexicans, to combat the influence of U.S. culture, which might weaken Tijuana's political ties to Mexico City. The fear was realized, as the state is now in the hands of the opposition party, PAN. But the show goes on. This complex encompasses a performing arts center, bookstore, cafeteria, art gallery, and the best museum on the peninsula, encompassing history, indigenous ethnology, and regional exhibits.

In a separate circular building, there are a few regional archaeological pieces on display near the entrance to the Omnimax theater, where a film, *Pueblo del Sol*, takes you on a dizzy tour of Mexico. The film is projected on an aluminum dome, the sound coming from pin-point holes in the screen. Second features are whatever happens to be floating around the Omnimax circuit (only 25 of these theaters in the world). Hours of showing can vary, so you should phone first (tel. 1-706-684-1111 or 1132) for current price and time. Complex is situated in Zona Río Tijuana, on Paseo de los Héroes at Av. Independencia, about a mile from the border. *Note: stop at the border tourist office for dollar-*

off coupons. The Spanish version is half the price of the English version.

Playas de Tijuana

The beach lies three miles west of Tijuana, a long run of sand fronted by storm damaged buildings. Recreation value is nil, due to extreme pollution and its for illegal border crossings; U.S. Border Patrol helicopters sweeping across the beach add to the apocalyptic atmosphere. The only tourist draw is the Plaza de Toros Monumental. Directly behind the bullring is a 12 ft. obelisk marking the international boundary, hemmed by a cyclone fence. Moving the obelisk is about the only crime for which you can be prosecuted by both nations. The rest of the neighborhood is made up of a few aprés-bullfight restaurants, a tract of suburban homes, and private medical clinics specializing in things they couldn't get away with in the United States. Only one road goes in or out of Playas de Tijuana, departing Hwy. 1D just before reaching the first tollgate.

SPENDING THE NIGHT
Budget

Hotels under $20 are too sleazy for most travelers, though they can be found in the downtown area. Many are used as a staging area by those about to cross the border under cover of darkness. A notable exception is the CREA Youth Hostel, situated off Av. Padre Kino, just past Calle 16. Its dormitory beds adjoin a park-like sports complex, and it is on the bus route to the Central Camionera or to city center.

Moderate

Hotels around Av. Revolución have benefited from the area's moral renovation, and they offer some interesting rooms. The Moorish-influenced **Hotel Caesar** (tel. 85-1606), on Av. Revolución & Calle 5, is a paean to bullfighting, with exhibits in the lobby, including tails and ears cut by famous matadors who used to stay here in the

BORDER BASICS
U.S. To Mexico

San Diego Trolley leaves for San Ysidro every 15 minutes from the Santa Fe Depot in San Diego, or from a new railhead in El Cajon; you can jump on at any stop. It takes about 45 minutes from San Diego to the border. Hours of operation: 5 a.m. to 1 a.m. (trains run every 30 minutes after 7:30 p.m.).

More expensive than taking a trolley and a cab are the two private bus lines. **Mexicoach** (tel. 619-232-5040) runs international buses from the Amtrak station in San Diego to behind the Frontón Jai Alai in Tijuana; a few of their buses also stop at the Central Cultural. To return to San Diego, just show up at Av. Madero, between Calles 3 & 4; you should call for times, but no reservations are needed. **Greyhound** (tel. 619-239-3266 or 800-237-8211) also provides service every 90 minutes between the Los Angeles, San Diego, and Tijuana bus stations. *Note: returning buses are granted a special lane to avoid traffic delays.*

Mexico to U.S.

On a busy day, the wait can be up to two hours. Cars and tempers overheat as people jockey for position. Avoid Monday mornings, when Customs has the fewest officers on duty. The easternmost lanes are traditionally faster, since these are used by commuters who exit the freeway once they are across the border; they have ID and are rarely hung up by Customs. Don't get caught in a false lane, as it is very hard to merge back into a moving lane once you are stalled. Tune the radio to 690 AM. Border crossing times at San Ysidro and Otay Mesa are reported every 15 minutes; it is often quicker to drive the 20 minutes to Otay Mesa. At San Ysidro, the border is actually where the line of metal discs begin to separate the traffic lanes.

old days (and still do, claims management). Rooms are a funky mishmash of furnishings. The Caeser salad was allegedly created in the hotel's restaurant. Cheaper but not as historic is the **Hotel Nelson** (tel. 85-43-03), also on Av. Revolución, a cheap sleep with a plain coffeeshop. Slightly more expensive is the **Hotel La Villa de Zaragoza**, Av. Madero 1120, conveniently situated right behind the Jai Alai Palace; the clean rooms have TV, a.c., and heating.

Hotels out along Agua Caliente Blvd are more expensive, except for the **Motel Padre Kino** (tel. 86-42-08) on Blvd. Agua Caliente 3; clean, cheap, and strategically situated within short walking distance from the Hipódromo (racetrack). The gaudy **Palacio Azteca** (tel. 86-42-08), two blocks south of Blvd. Agua Caliente on old Hwy 1., is something of a backwater now that traffic patterns have changed.

In the Playas de Tijuana area, the **Jardines del Mar** (tel. 80-10-62) on Av. Del Pacífico No. 109, is three blocks from the bullring, next to a Chinese restaurant; clean and boring but with unobstructed ocean views.

Deluxe

The top dollar **Fiesta Americana** (tel. 81-70-00) on Blvd. Agua Caliente 4500 rises above the competition, a glass-faced 24-story tower marbled and mirrored òn the inside; rooms on south side look out on golf course, while north-facing rooms take in the slums.

Less expensive is **El Conquistador** (tel. 81-79-55) at Blvd. Agua Caliente 1777, a colonial-style motel surrounded by noisy traffic; bring earplugs for the pool and whirlpool. But rooms are big, furniture massive.

Just down Agua Caliente is the **Paraíso Radisson Tijuana** (tel. 81-72-00), a long block from the Caliente Race Track. More spirited than stylish, atmosphere is upbeat, and pool, sauna, and whirlpool help make this best choice here for the rates.

The **Lucerna Hotel** (tel. 84-01-15) on

10902 Paseo de los Héroes two blocks off Blvd. Agua Caliente, has a reputation for respectability. A decent choice for its pool courtyard, but rooms are starting to look ragged.

ARRIVING-DEPARTING
By Air
The Tijuana International Airport (tel. 83-27-00) lies six miles to the east of the main border crossing but a short two miles from the Otay Mesa border crossing. For those afoot, taxis run from both border crossings. Mexicoach departs from the San Diego Amtrak station to the airport, but the rates are more than double what it would cost taking the trolley to the border and then hiring a private taxi. Three Mexican airlines operate here: *AeroMexico* (tel. 85-44-01), *Mexicana* (tel. 81-75-72) and *AeroCalifornia* (tel. 84-21-00). To get from airport to border, take government-regulated taxis (buy a ticket from the kiosk; rates are posted). They drop you off a short walk from the border.

By Bus
The Central Camionera is about four miles ($5-$8 taxi ride) from the main border crossing, near where Blvd. Lázaro Cárdenas crosses the Río Tijuana. At the border bus-stop beyond the taxis, catch any bus named *Buenavista* or *Central Camionera*. The bus terminal offers frequent express departures with destinations to Ensenada (1.5 hours), La Paz (24 hours), Mazatlan (24 hours), Guadalajara (36 hours), and Mexico City (46 hours), with stops at all intermediate points. The three main bus lines are the *Tres Estrellas de Oro* (recommended; tel. 86-91-86), *Transportes del Pacífico* (tel. 85-49-81) and *Transportes Norte de Sonora* (tel. 86-90-26).

By Car
If driving straight to Ensenada via the toll road, keep to your left after crossing the San Ysidro border, then turn counterclockwise on the overpass, which will disgorge you onto Calle 3. Drive to the first stoplight, turn right, and you will end up on Calle Internacional. This street runs west along the border fence for four miles to an intersection at Smuggler's Gulch; straight ahead on the Libramiento Sur will put you on the free road to Ensenada. Turn right for the quicker, more scenic toll road to Ensenada.

Tijuana Addendum
If you encounter any legal problems in Tijuana or Baja California, phone the *Procuraduría de Protección al Turista* in the Government Center (tel. 84-21-81); they will help you with legal disputes. For more immediate action, the Tijuana Police can be reached at tel. 85-70-90.

The U.S. Consulate (tel. 86-00-01 to 00-05) is situated behind the Tijuana Country Club, at Calle Tapachula No. 96, Colonia Hipódromo. *Note: circumvent the long line of Mexicans seeking visas; go through the north door, and go directly upstairs, where they deal with U.S. citizens.*

The Canadian Consulate is at German Gedovius 5-202.

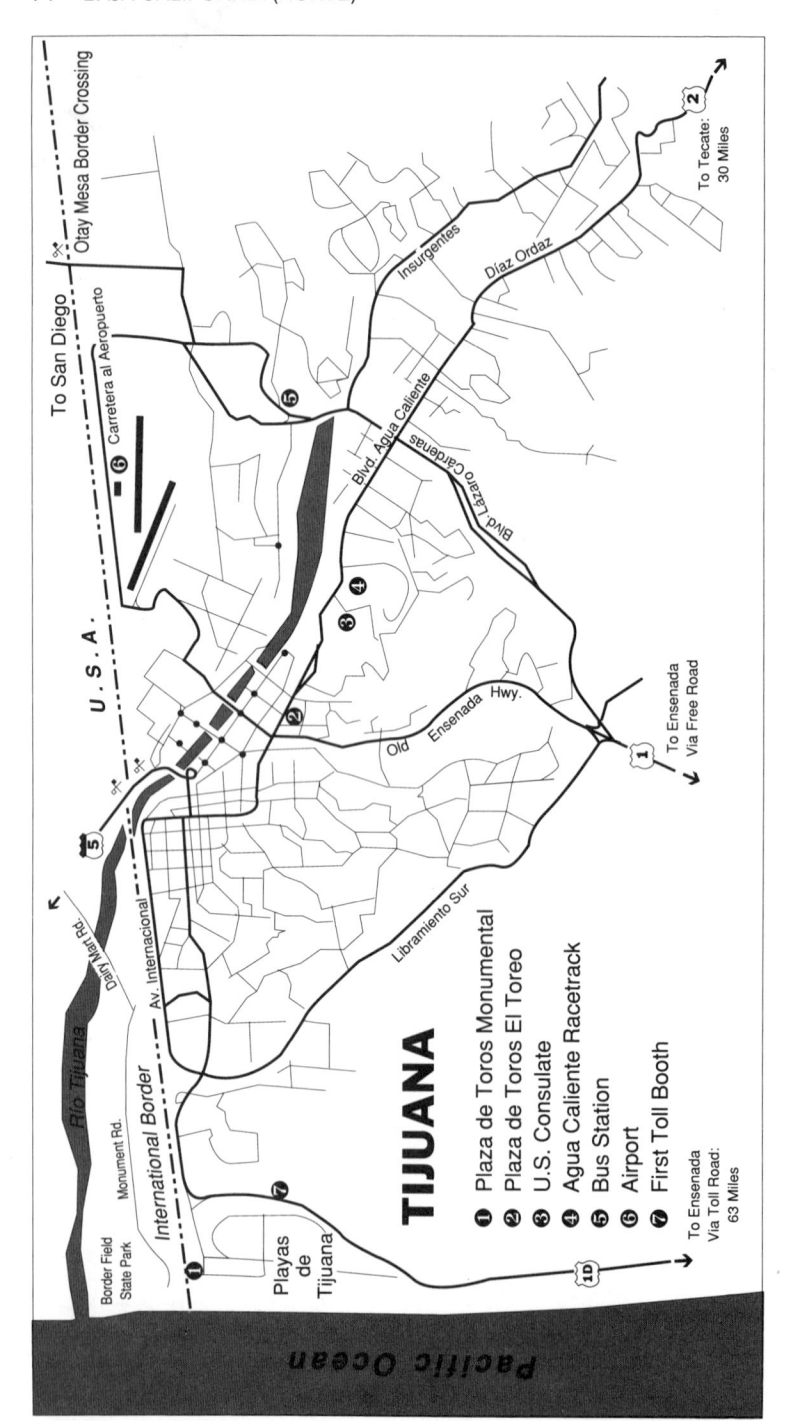

TIJUANA TO TECATE

The road from Tijuana to Tecate runs 30 miles through arid borderland. Leave Tijuana by following Agua Caliente Blvd. to the east. Within ten miles you cross **Presa Rodríguez**, a dam built in 1935 to hold back the Río de las Palmas for Tijuana's water supply. These drought years, plus a burgeoning population, have forced Tijuana to pipe water from La Misión to the south and Río Colorado to the east. After passing through **El Florido** (17 miles from Tijuana), and **El Carricito** (21 miles), you come to **Rancho La Puerta** ($$$; tel. 654-1160), 2.5 miles before Tecate. This famous vegetarian health spa, opened by Professor Szekely in 1940 in a remodeled stable, now sprawls on 125 acres. People come here to reduce stress as well as weight. This is no fat farm. In fact, guests who are too fat aren't even allowed. Guests are expected to stay the week. Overnighters are accepted when there are vacancies. You can stop in for a vegie meal and to walk the herb-laden grounds.

TECATE

Many people think of Tecate more as a product than a place. No race tracks here, no bullring or jai alai palace, no tourists except those who drive the twisty 30-mile road down from El Cajon. The border crossing shuts down at midnight.

After Colonel Cantú bought the town site for $20,000 at the turn of the century, this agricultural valley started to develop, spurred by a railway built through town. Today, a few international *maquiladoras* (assembly plants) are set up to take advantage of the cheap wages. The *Nacional Cafetalera* plant roasts coffee beans from Chiapas and Veracruz.

But the dominate feature of this valley remains the metal silo hops of the *Cervecería Cuauhtémoc*, makers of Tecate beer. Alberto Aldrete built the brewery in 1943 alongside the Río Tecate, tapping into a clean reservoir of spring water and turning it into one of Mexico's most famous beers. To differentiate the town from the beer, townspeople sometimes write the town's name "TKT," letters that sound the same as name (in Spanish).

The Kiliwa tribe who roamed this valley were probably the first to call it *Tecate*, meaning "where the sun passes." Others claims it evolved from Valle de Zacate, the name of a nearby valley.

After the Mexican American War ended, U.S. ranchers were accused of sneaking across the new border to cut firewood here. Some even claim Tecate comes from the English words "to cut."

This is a tenuous claim. Not only was the name in place before the Mexican-American War, but this boulder-strewn valley must have been a poor provider of firewood. The dusty town blends in well to the rocky, treeless foothills of the Sierra Juárez in which it is nestled. Despite its scorched look, Tecate's elevation of 1500 feet helps temper the blasts of summer.

There really isn't much to keep a traveler from traveling. A beer plant tour, poke around a few shops, splash your hands in the fountain, and sit in the shade of the *zócalo*. A pastry from the panadería, a cup of coffee, and press on.

Travel Information

The State Office of Tourism (tel. 4-10-95) is on the corner on the southeast side of the park, but it's more convenient to get the same information from the kiosk on your right as soon as you cross the border.

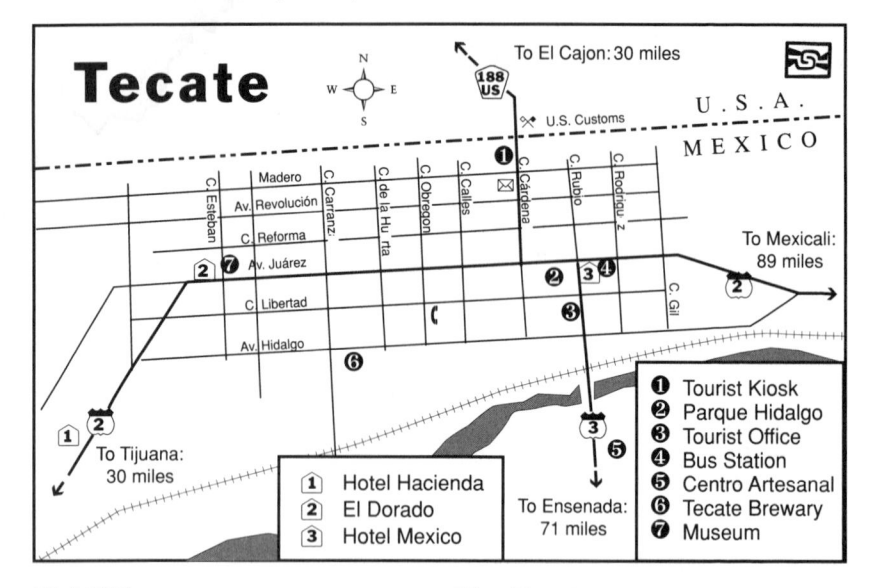

PLACES

Parque Hidalgo

When government funding allows, Saturday evening band concerts often are held here during summer.

Cervecería Cuauhtémoc

In Tecate, instead of making an industry of tourism, tourism is made of its industry. Tour the beer factory from 8 a.m. to noon on the first three Saturdays of every month. Phone to see if tours are given at other times: tel. 4-12-02 or contact the State tourism office in town (see above). The factory is on Av. Hidalgo between Calle Lázaro Cárdenas and Calle Alvaro Obregón, the largest buildings in town.

Centro Artesanal

A government-sponsored FONART store sells national crafts at regulated prices. Shop is about a mile south of Mex. 2 on highway to Ensenada.

Museo Municipal

A museum of regional art and archaeology is situated a mile west of Parque Hidalgo, on Av. Benito Juárez between Calle Santana and Calle Esteban.

Pico Tecate

Pico Tecate, the 4,000 ft. peak which straddles the border here (that's a TV relay station on the mountain), is better known as Kuchamá, considered by Native Americans to be one of the holiest sites on the continent. To remove a stone or take a plant is to risk death.

This mountain is where the spirit of Kuchamá was incarnated as a powerful shaman who lived on the southern slope and taught peace to the warring tribes. It is now considered as place of healing, and many shamans have been cremated here, their ashes scattered near the mountaintop altar, a flat rock slab. Halfway up the mountain are petroglyphs of whales and dolphins. According to Florence Shipek, an anthropologist who has written extensively about the mountain, "In some mystical way, the spirit of God and of Kuuchamaa remains inside the mountain, calling to individuals with special innate abilities for healing and for good."

The Border

Border hours are 7 a.m. to 12 p.m. There is rarely any wait here. With enough pleading, tourist cards and car permits can be obtained from the *Migración* and *Aduana* offices at the border.

Events

The Tecate-Ensenada bicycle race, purportedly the largest in the world, leaves from here. On December 12, Día de la Virgen de Guadalupe is celebrated, as is the grape harvest, usually the first Sunday in July. Saturday is the traditional market day. *Note: the August running of the bulls has been cancelled; the spectators proved to be wilder than the bulls.*

Places to Sleep

Tecate's high hotel rates are due to isolation more than quality. **Motel El Dorado** ($$; tel. 4-11-02), on Av. Juárez less than a mile west of the Parque Hidalgo, is comfortable enough with its TV and a.c., but basically is a drab motel. **Hotel Hacienda** ($$; tel. 4-12-50), half a mile further to the west on the same road, is more of the same, though livelier with a disco bar. **Hotel México**, also on Ave. Benito Juárez at No. 230, is about the only budget hotel in town.

ARRIVING-DEPARTING
By Car

Tecate is 70 miles north of Ensenada via Highway 3, 30 miles east of Tijuana, and 89 miles west of Mexicali via Hwy. 1.

By Bus

You can catch buses to Ensenada, Tijuana and Mexicali from the station (tel. 4-12-21) at Benito Juárez and Calle Rodríguez, a block from the park.

TECATE TO ENSENADA

Highway 3 leaves Tecate from Parque Hidalgo and travels 65 miles before hitting the coast at El Sauzal, five miles north of Ensenada. The first 17 miles to **Valle Las Palmas** curves through dry, treeless hills, as cracked and corrugated as the asphalt on the highway. Valle Las Palmas offers little more than a restaurant and gas station. 13 miles beyond is **El Testerazo**, where wood carvers put out animal shapes along the roadside. Another 15 miles brings you to **Valle de Guadalupe**, carpeted with vineyards. These grapes are fed into the Domecq winery that stands by the roadside (no tastings). Two miles beyond, the highway bears left, and a road forks left to Guadalupe.

Guadalupe

Some homes in Guadalupe have pitched roofs to keep off a snow that never falls. Some have their backs turned to the streets. A few still have bathhouses.

In 1905, a Russian religious sect, the Malakans (Milk Drinkers) founded a farming colony here, as far as they could get from Czar and Russian Orthodox repression. They brought their traditions with them. The 100 original families stayed through the Mexican Revolution, but the agrarian reform begun by Cárdenas stripped them of much land and most migrated to Los Angeles. Today, the only things written in Cyrillic are the headstones in the cemetery west of town.

The Milk Drinkers settled on the site of a Dominican mission (1834-1840), which was abandoned after Indians murdered three people here. Some claim the ruins of the mission can be seen on a small hill east of the main street.

From Guadalupe, Hwy. 3 winds out of the hills for 18 miles to its junction with Hwy. 1 at El Sauzal, 5 miles north of Ensenada. There is a place to camp between Guadalupe and El Sauzal, at *Rancho María Teresa*, 14 miles before reaching El Sauzal.

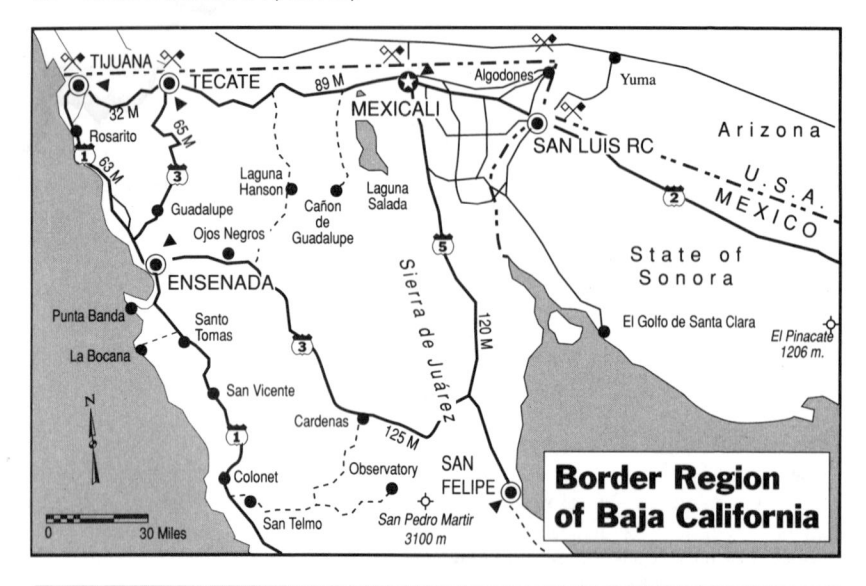

TECATE TO MEXICALI

Highway 2 from Tecate to Mexicali travels 89 extremely diverse miles, from pinyon to desert. The highway has turnoffs to Rancho Verónica (21 miles from Tecate), Laguna Hanson (39 miles), Cañon de Guadalupe (67 miles), and Playa Laguna Salada (69 miles) before reaching Mexicali.

RANCHO VERONICA

This backcountry resort of 5,000 acres is owned by a matador, Sr. Bustamante, and summer guests at the hotel can practice capework in its bullring. Pool and tennis courts are on premises, as well as both a primitive campground and one with full hook-ups. To get there, turn off 20 miles from Tecate at the sign for Santa Verónica at El Hongo (otherwise known as Colonia L. Eccheverría). Follow road for seven miles to resort.

LAGUNA HANSON

At the K72 marker, 38 miles from Tecate, begins a 38-mile lrough dirt road that climbs

the sierras to a lake at the *Parque Nacional Constitución de 1857*. This shallow, rocky lake is ringed with pines. Depending on the rainfall, it can be anything from a kilometer-long lake to a marsh. A smoother 22-mile-long dirt road to the lake leaves from Hwy. 3 between Ensenada and San Felipe (see Ensendad to San Felipe section).

LA RUMOROSA

This small town, the halfway mark between Tecate and Mexicali (about 40 miles from either), is up on a 4,000 ft. mountain plateau spotted with pines, the summer retreat of the former president General Rodríguez. After Rodríguez left office, the retreat was turned into a sanitarium for tubercular patients, and then a mental hospital. According to rumor, dead patients were thrown into a canyon behind the hospital to be eaten by vultures and coyotes. The name of the canyon remains, *El Pudridero* (the rotting place). But everything else at this altitude seems cleansed by the mountain-crisp air of the Sierra Juárez, a relief from the oven-like temperatures found at the bottom of the Cantú Grade.

CANTÚ GRADE

Two miles east of La Rumorosa, the highway drops down the north end of the Sierra de Juárez. The only paved road to cross this mountain range, it drops 4,000 feet to the desert floor, 15 miles of hairpin curves and steep grades. Beyond the rusted wrecks that decorate the roadside, you can see the shimmering of Laguna Salada, and the shadows of the Cocopah Mountains, covered with sand blown down from the Yuma Desert. To the north the Imperial Valley, to the east Valle de Mexicali.

CANYON OASIS & HOT SPRINGS

Before Hwy. 2 reaches Laguna Salada, a dirt road turns off 66 miles from Tecate, 2.5 miles west of the gas station at Playa Laguna Salada. This road follows the western edge of the Laguna, reaching Rancho La Poderosa about 17 miles in. The first canyon, **Cantú Palms**, is about 1.5 miles from here. You will be able to see the palms; there are water seeps, but no stream. Petrogylphs and bedrock metates can be sighted in the canyon.

By staying on the main road and continuing for 26.5 miles from Hwy. 5, you will reach a fork; bear right for another 7.6 miles and you will reach the campground at **Cañón de Guadalupe**, a cleft in the Sierra Juárez where hot mineral water spurts up. This water is channeled into a pool, and individual rock-paved hot tubs at the campground. Scattered in the canyon are metates and some petroglyphs. Rare blue fan palms grow among the more common *Washingtonia filifera*. A trail runs two miles upstream to the Pool of the Virgin, now filled with sand. The road is suitable for bravely driven passenger cars.

LAGUNA SALADA

This shallow lake lies below sea level and once was part of the Sea of Cortés. Legend claims that an early Spanish ship carrying a treasure of pearls sailed into this laguna and grounded in the shallow water—the ship was abandoned, the pearls lost.

Similar to the Salton sink, it is slowly filling in with fresh water spilled over from the Río Colorado. There is a cafe and camping area on the beach, half a mile off Hwy. 2, at Playa Laguna Salada; this is the last campground before Mexicali 15 miles down the road.

MEXICALI

State capital. World's biggest cotton gin. Largest city on the peninsula. Quite an accomplishment considering that one hundred years ago this was a waterless desert. Average rainfall here is three inches a year. The water this city depends on for its survival comes entirely from the United States. No other city in Mexico is so dependent on the U.S. for its very existence. Its fate hinges on the wording of a treaty that allows for at least 1.5 million acres of water from the Colorado River every year. The growing thirst of Los Angeles threatens Mexicali. Without this water, Mexicali would return to the desert.

Not only does Mexicali depend on water, but it sells most of its commerce and agriculture to the United States, or ships it overseas from San Diego or Los Angeles (Mexico City is 2,000 miles away by truck). Consequently, our two economies are as interlinked as its name, Mexi-Cali. The International Border Commission came up with that one.

Before irrigation, Mexicali was a desert owned by the American-owned Colorado Land Company. A few men made a little money running livestock across its sandy wastes. But in 1902, the Imperial Canal brought in river water, and soon vast fields of long-staple cotton were planted. Thousands of Chinese immigrants came to work the fields.

In 1919, in the xenophobic wake of the Mexican Revolution, these Chinese immigrants were stripped of their rights (a cruel act, but Mexico was following the U.S. example of the Chinese Exclusion Act of 1882, which was the first U.S. law denying naturalization to members of a specific ethnic group). The Chinese influence remains in the many Asian restaurants and import shops of Mexicali.

In 1937, President Lázaro Cárdenas annulled the foreign land concession to the Colorado Land Company and later divided it into *ejidos*, collective farms.

The town of Mexicali was born of necessity as a terminus and supply point for these new agricultural lands. But the large amounts of capital invested in the city's growth came not from agriculture but in the form of graft payments to the government, made by the opium refiners, houses of prostitution, and gambling casinos.

These illicit businesses have since been rooted out of Mexicali (though a large number of bars remain). As you drive through, it is hard not to be impressed by the strong economic look of this city, surrounded by more than 500,000 acres of farmland and bolstered by a growing industrial base. One result of this activity hangs in the evening sky of Mexicali, a dusty haze blown from the tilled fields and smokestacks, which colors the sunset sky the deepest hues of red, and at times closes in over the city, the veil of progress.

Bearings

There are two main thoroughfares that lead out to the junction of Highways 2 and 5. Av. Francisco Madero runs parallel to the border through an older commercial area of curio stores, tawdry bars, and residences to Calzada Sierra, where a right turn will take you out through a more prosperous area where most of the better hotels and restaurants are situated. At the main *glorieta* (traffic circle), bear around on Calzada Juárez, which takes you out to the highway junction.

An easier way to navigate the city is to take the five-mile long Calzada López Mateos, which runs past a newer industrial area, the state theater, railway and bus stations, and new government buildings, before hitting the highway junction.

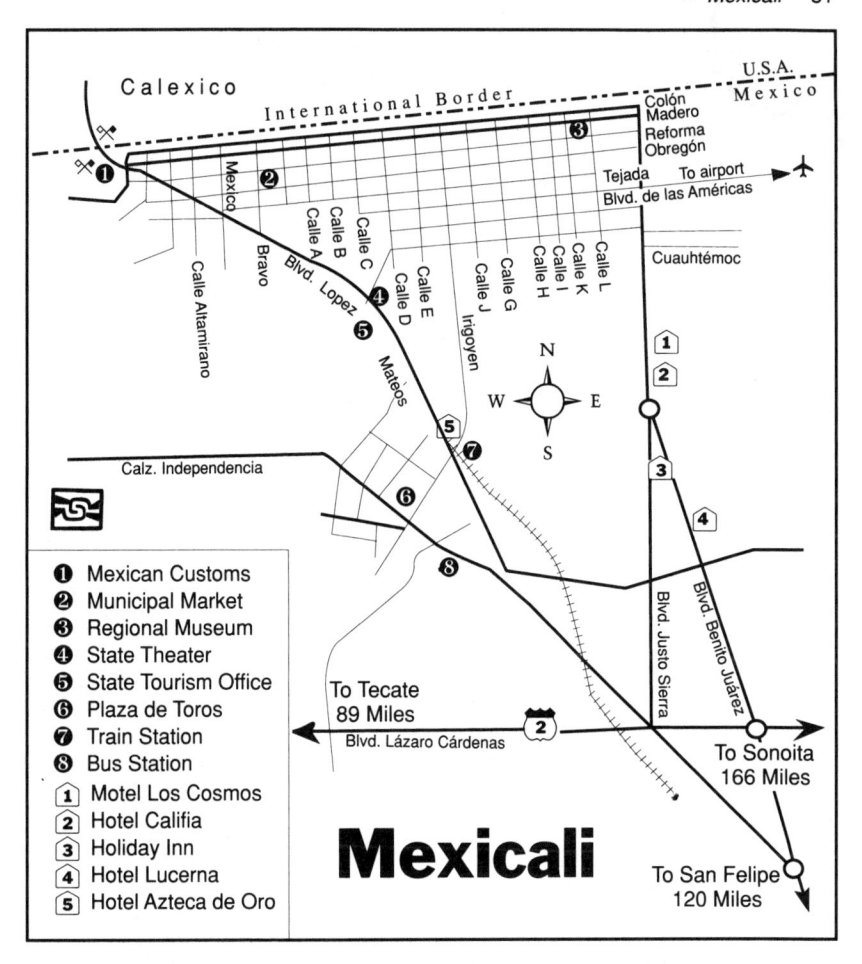

Mexicali

- ❶ Mexican Customs
- ❷ Municipal Market
- ❸ Regional Museum
- ❹ State Theater
- ❺ State Tourism Office
- ❻ Plaza de Toros
- ❼ Train Station
- ❽ Bus Station
- ① Motel Los Cosmos
- ② Hotel Califia
- ③ Holiday Inn
- ④ Hotel Lucerna
- ⑤ Hotel Azteca de Oro

Note: Mexicali is notorious for its lack of visible street signs.

Travel Information

Mexicali maintains a tourism office at Calzada López Mateos and Calle Camelias, just beyond the state theater. The state office is at Calle del Comercio 204, between Av. Reforma and Obregón, about seven blocks from the border.

The Border

You can cross the border 24 hours a day. Tourist cards and car permits can be picked up at the Aduana and Mígracion offices at the border crossing.

TRAVELING ABOUT
By Bus & Taxi

If you need to get to the train or bus station, you can catch a taxi at the border or walk two blocks to Calle Altamirano, where you can grab a *Centro Cívico* bus to the train station or a *Central Camionera* bus to the bus station; both stations are about 2.5 miles from the border.

PLACES
Museo Regional

The Museo Regional de la Universidad Autónoma de Baja California (tel. 2-57-15), at Calles Reforma and "L," is a small multi-chambered museum where you can see exhibits on the local geology, some bones, and other exhibits of regional interest. Closed Sunday and Monday.

Plaza de Toros Califia

The bullring is in the Centro Cívico area, near bus and rail stations, on Av. Califia, two blocks from Blvd. López Mateos. Matadors fight every other Sunday from October to May. Get the more expensive *sombra* (shade) seats; the sun here can be searing.

Events

Mexicali celebrates its founding in 1903 with a 17-day **Fiestas del Sol**, Oct. 9-26. Industrial exhibits, cultural events, art showings. Inquire at the city tourism office for scheduled events.

Mexicali Addendum

You can usually score a better exchange rate in Calexico than in Mexicali. Compare prices along Calexico's Imperial Ave., the main boulevard that leads to the border crossing.

On crossing the border, the first thing you see is El Caliente Betting Center on Calle Melgar. Just beyond, you are met by a rash of neon nightclubs and curio shops on Calle Melgar and Av. Reforma, not a very gentle district.

From the border it is an easy seven-block walk to the **Mercado Municipal**, on Av. Obregón and Calle de Comercio.

The neoclassical **Casa de la Cultura** and shady **Parque Chapultepec** on Av. Madero at Calle Altamirano evoke an earlier Mexicali.

El Teatro del Estado on Blvd. López Mateos (about 1.5 miles from border), showcases national talent—theater, dance, and music.

During the winter, Las Aguilas play baseball (Mexico's Pacific League) at the **Estadio de Beisbol** off Calzada Justo Serra, on Av. Cuauhtémoc. Mexican-styled rodeos take place on occasional Sundays; the **Lienzo de Charro** is about 3.5 miles east of Calzado Justo Serra.

For some shade and water, try **Lago Xochimilco**, where there is a small zoo.

If you are really strapped for ideas, the city tourism department can send you on an **industrial tour** of town.

ARRIVING & DEPARTING

By Air

The airport terminal is 12 miles east of town, a $10 taxi ride there, $6 *colectivo* ride back. Only Mexicana and a local airline, AeroNoreste, fly out of this small airport.

By Bus

The *Central Camionera* (tel. 7-24-51) is on Av. Independencia near Calzada López Mateos in the Centro Cívico area; city buses run from the near the border on Calle Altamirano to the bus station and back. Two bus lines dominate: *Tres Estrellas de Oro* (tel. 7-24-10) and *Norte de Sonora*. Buses leave frequently for San Felipe, Tijuana, and east through Sonora to Mazatlán, Guadalajara, and Mexico. In Calexico, the Greyhound bus station is on the main drag at 901 Imperial Ave.

By Train

The *Estación de Ferrocarril* (tel. 7-24-44, 7-21-01) is at Calle Ulises Irigoyen, just north of the intersection of Aves. Independencia and Mateos. Two trains leave every morning for Guadalajara, with intermediate stops down the coast, including Puerto Peñasco, Hermosillo, Mazatlán, and Tepic. The first train, the #2 Del Pacífico, leaves at 9:20 a.m., arriving in Guadalajara 36 hours later. This train is equipped with a dining car and sleeping compartments.

The second train, the #4, leaves at 9:50 a.m., and takes 42 hours. On this slower train, you sleep in your seat. Schedules change, so you should phone for latest time and fare information. From the United States, phone 011-52-65—57-2101. You can buy your ticket early in the morning before 8:30 a.m. Reservations can be made by writing Reservaciones, Estación de Ferrocarril, P.O. Box 231, Calexico, CA 92231.

PLACES TO SLEEP
Budget Hotels
Like most bordertowns, the cheap budget hotels have dubious reputations.

Moderate
It can be cheaper to stay on the U.S. side of the border than to book into most of the motels on the Mexican side. The old **Hotel San Alberta** in Calexico, a few blocks from the border, is the old standby. As soon as you cross the border bear left, and you will see two respectable if somewhat noisy hotels, the **Hotel Del Norte** (tel: 2-81-01) on Calle Melgar 205 at Madero and, two blocks down Madero, the **Hotel Plaza** (tel. 2-97-57). Better accommodations can be found along Blvds. Benito Juárez and Justo Serra, the major hotel zone.

Modest rooms with cable TV and thin walls can be found at **Los Cosmos** (tel. 8-12-55) on Justo Sierra 1493, next to the Hotel Califia, and **La Siesta** (tel. 4-11-00) on Justo Sierra 899. For those catching the morning train, the **Motel Azteca de Oro** at C. de la Industria 600 stands by the rail station.

Expensive
The three best hotels are clustered together. The **Hotel Califia** on Calzada Justo Serra 1495 is the newest but plainest of the three, a convention hotel. The **Holiday Inn** (tel. 6-13-00) on Blvd. Juárez 2220 shares top honors with the nearby **Lucerna Hotel** (tel.4-10-00) on Blvd. Juárez 2151. The formula-like HI is more comfortable, but the wandering grounds and mix of rooms give the Lucerna more character.

MEXICALI TO SAN FELIPE via Hwy. 5

The 120-mile highway from Mexicali to San Felipe passes mud volcanos, indigenous settlements, edges a sluggish river, and crosses a parched desert.

MUD VOLCANOS
Twenty miles from Mexicali, near the dead volcanic cone of Cerro Prieto, you can see steam rising from the ground, a ten-square-mile area of mud spatter cones where water and gas are forced to the surface. These sulfurous mud volcanos—the volcano lake described by early explorers—have mostly been taken over by the Cerro Prieto Geothermal Plant, where wells are turning this energy into electricity. But you can still see a few of the mud volcanos if you are willing to walk. *Access: At 20 miles from Mexicali, turn east on the paved road to Nayarit (Hwy. 18). Three miles past Nayarit, turn left at the T-intersection until coming to Delta, then parallel the railroad tracks to the Geothermal Plant. Park and walk.*

RIO HARDY
This river, an offshoot of the Colorado, actually has more water than the mother river. Because this area is subject to drastic flooding during rainy years (Morelos Dam does not have that much capacity), many of the old resorts have been drowned. The various *campos* that still exist are mostly ramshackle shantytowns that pass for resorts, appealing mostly to those fishing for bass and catfish. The highway edges the reedy shore (about 37 miles south of Mexicali) at Campo Hardy. A mile south is **El Mayor**, a small settlement of Cúcapa Indians, a tribe indigenous to the Lower Colorado Delta. Six miles further south,

you roll across the flats of the Laguna Salada, where you will see water or mirages depending on the snowpack in the Rockies.

DESIERTO DE LOS CHINOS

Hwy. 5 crosses the driest desert in Sonora 50 miles from Mexicali. This area is parched by the rain-blocking Sierra Juárez that rises up like a wall to the east. During summer, the mercury often hits 120F here.

The desert bears a tragic name. In 1902, 42 Chinese, desperate to work in the new cotton fields of Mexicali, tried to walk there from San Felipe, some of them barefoot. The first well near Cerro El Chinero they couldn't find. The second, at Tres Pozos, was dry. Only five Chinese survived the walk to Río Hardy.

Thirty-one miles before reaching San Felipe, Hwy. 5 intersects with Hwy. 3 to Ensenada 125 miles to the northwest (see Ensenada to San Felipe section).

SAN FELIPE & BEYOND

The pair of giant arches that stand at the entrance to San Felipe speak of vision. It's easy to have grand visions here. The eastern escarpment of the Sierra de San Pedro Martir rises up to 10,000 ft. behind the town. A beryl sea stretches endlessly on the horizon. In the dry air, distances compress. Things seem closer than they really are. Just like this town's hoped-for future.

This town has high hopes of following the blazing fortune of Cancún, a high-volume tourist factory. But the region lacks the languid monotony of the tropics. This is an area of extremes, of searing summers, and blustery, cold winters. When the 22 ft. tide of a full moon reveals half a mile of bare beach, it's like somebody pulled the plug on the ocean.

Behavior can be a bit extreme also. San Felipe has the reputation of a party town, close enough for a weekend trip to blow off some smoke. Dune buggies and ATVs scream through the desert unhindered by off-road regulations or noise ordinances. Spring breakers don't have to worry about getting carded at the liquor store. A frontier feeling of anything goes prevails.

The town itself stands close to the sea, a colorful, tacky arrangement of curio shops, restaurants, and bars—nothing too sleazy or risque, just good fun. Though there is an uneven arrangement of hotels in town, most people camp out in an RV park or in one of the countless beachfront *campos* that flank both sides of the town for miles.

San Felipe was named by Father Consag in 1746 and was used 50 years later as a port to supply the Dominican Misión San Pedro de Verona nearby. But the water gave out, both here and at the mission. In 1876, San Felipe was again developed, this time in hopes that it would support the gold mines up at Real del Castillo.

Ensenada became the port San Felipe wanted to be.

San Felipe eventually did become a port during WWII, when shrimp boats found both fertile grounds and a fine anchorage. In their wake came sport fishers, who battled the giant *totoava*. The totoava are now an official endangered species. But tourists have grown in number. Tourism officials claim 600,000 visitors a year. The visitors come in waves. Most visit on weekends and holidays, during Spring Break and summer. At other times, San Felipe can look unnaturally empty and exposed, like these beaches at low tide.

Bearings

Calzada Chetumal enters town, ending at Av. Mar de Cortés, a one-way southbound

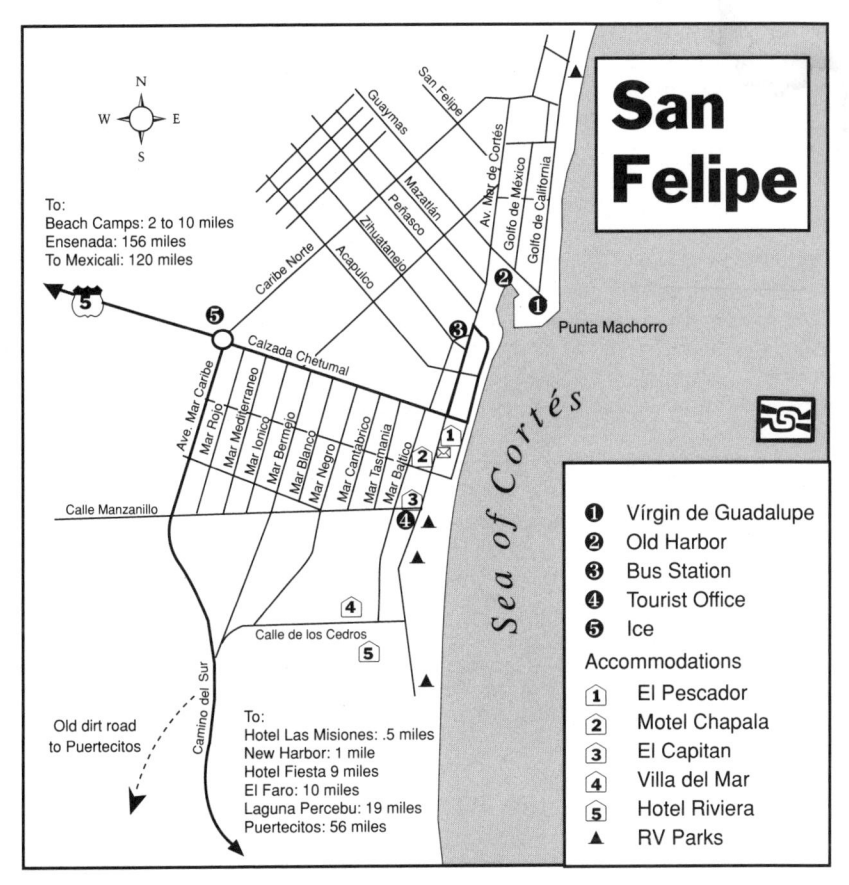

San Felipe

To:
Beach Camps: 2 to 10 miles
Ensenada: 156 miles
To Mexicali: 120 miles

Punta Machorro

Sea of Cortés

❶ Vírgin de Guadalupe
❷ Old Harbor
❸ Bus Station
❹ Tourist Office
❺ Ice
Accommodations
① El Pescador
② Motel Chapala
③ El Capitan
④ Villa del Mar
⑤ Hotel Riviera
▲ RV Parks

Calle Manzanillo

Old dirt road
to Puertecitos

Calle de los Cedros

To:
Hotel Las Misiones: .5 miles
New Harbor: 1 mile
Hotel Fiesta 9 miles
El Faro: 10 miles
Laguna Percebu: 19 miles
Puertecitos: 56 miles

---

street on which most hotels, RV parks, curio shops, and restaurants are situated. Paseo de Cortés runs one-way northbound along the malecón and beach, and is given over mostly to taco and fish stands. Ten blocks from the gulf, Av. Camino del Sur heads south to a newer area of condos and residences, and the Hotel Misiones.

Travel Information
A tourist office (tel. 7-11-55) is situated by the El Capitán Motel, at the corner of Av. Mar de Cortés and Calle Manzanillo.

PLACES
La Virgin de Guadalupe
For a post card view of San Felipe, the old boatyard, and a long stretch of coastline,

climb up the Cerro de la Virgin, a promontory just off the north end of town. There are reputed to be hot springs down by the old ice house at its base.

Beaches
The beaches of San Felipe can be as much as half a mile wide when the tide rolls out. Don't expect much in the way of snorkeling or diving—too much tidal turbulence. Because of the miles of beach both north and south of town, you should be able to stake out some tranquility, even if most of the coast is divided into privately run campos, which can range from primitive camps to permanent RV dwellings. If you are sensitive to noise, choose a campo that isn't inundated with off-road vehicles and mo-

torcycles. Don't expect too much weekend tranquility. People have been known to water ski behind dune buggies here.

Playa El Faro, south of town, is a fairly secluded beach marked by the lighthouse on the bluff above. The further from San Felipe, the quieter the beaches.

Roca Consag

From the beach, on a clear day you can see a 286 foot pinnacle rising from the sea 18 miles from shore, 35 miles south of the Río Colorado. This unique sedimentary rock was named after Padre Consag, who in 1742 made an epic voyage in a sailing canoe to the mouth of the Río Colorado, finally proving that this gulf was not the fabled Straits of Anian but a geographical dead end. Actually, these triangular rocks were first named *Los Diamantes* (the Diamonds) by Ulloa in 1539 because of their white surfaces, indicative of how the Spanish explorers imagined wealth even when staring at guano.

Entertainment

There is nothing of much cultural or historical interest in town. Most people shop, drink, eat, and catch some sun, buy a sombrero or ironwood sculpture, set off fireworks, play volleyball at Rockodile, wade in the gulf, take photos of the shrimp fleet, and generally just amble about town.

Events

San Felipe celebrates June 1st, *Día de la Marina Nacional* with a carnival.

ARRIVING & DEPARTING
By Bus

Buses leave every few hours for Mexicali—less frequently to Ensenada via Hwy. 3—from the station on Av. Mar de Cortés (tel: 7-10-39).

PLACES TO SLEEP
Budget Hotels

The cheapest hotels in San Felipe are clus-tered downtown. The **Motel Capitán** (tel. 7-13-03) on Av. Mar de Cortés 298 and **Motel Chapala** (tel. 7-12-40) on Av. Mar de Cortés 142 are both drab motels with little to offer besides location. At least the **Motel El Pescador** (tel. 7-10-44) across the street faces the beach and an occasional sea breeze.

Moderate

Hotel Riviera (tel. 7-11-85) is perched on a rise looking out over town; though not on beach, its pool is a respite from summer sun. The **Motel Villa del Mar** on Av. de los Cedros Sur also has a pool.

Expensive

Hotel Las Misiones (tel. U.S. 800-336-5454; 1-706-5767-1280) the old Castel San Felipe, is the top pick here, on the beach a mile to the south. Big palapa, pool, and tennis court. Another eight miles to the south is the **Hotel Fiesta** (tel. 4-03-93), on a bluff that gives gulf views from all of the rooms.

Camping

The in-town trailer parks offer full hook-ups and amenities that escalate with the rates. A particularly luxurious RV park is **El Faro**, near the lighthouse 11 miles south of town. Dozens of primitive campos stretch for miles both north and south: Playa Blanca, Pete's Camp, Campo Peewee, Campo Pai Pai, Pops, Campo Los Amigos, etc.

Note: These primitive camps cost from $4 to $12; bring your own water.

San Felipe Addendum

No problem getting money here; there are three banks in town.

Post Office is on Av. Mar de Cortés and Calzada Chetumal.

To fish (your best chance is during winter and spring) you first need a license, which you can get at the Fishing Cooperative at the end of Calle Zihuatanejo, along the waterfront.

[decorative border pattern]

THE SOUTHERN LOOP SAN FELIPE TO HWY. 1

From San Felipe, a paved road runs 56 miles to Puertecitos. But the asphalt surface is severely potholed and has turned into rough washboard in many places. From Puertecitos, an unpaved road parallels the coast south for 50 miles before veering inland another 37 miles until it joins Hwy. 1 just north of the dry lake bed of Laguna Chapala. Only sturdy cars should attempt the trip.

Laguna Percebu

At 19 miles from San Felipe, a dirt road runs 2.5 miles down to a long narrow *estero*, where the tides regularly uncover acres of sand and shells. You can camp on the sand next to a small settlement and cafe. Between 26 and 36 miles from San Felipe, the road veers closer to shore and you will find numerous spur roads that run down to the beaches, many of which are in the throes of development.

PUERTECITOS

Puertecitos is much like Cholla Bay on the other side of the Gulf, a haphazard American settlement of aging trailers, plywood shacks, and more substantial vacation homes built on leased land. Like much of this coastline, stolen street and highway signs from the U.S. adorn most homes, erasing the sense of being in Mexico; beneath the humor, the signs seem like an unconscious attempt at annexation, which is how some Mexicans see it.

For those continuing south, there is a Pemex gas station here, as well as a modest Posada here with a dozen rooms for rent, which seem an unnecessary indulgence given the clean beaches you can sleep on (for a minor charge) just to the north of Puertecitos.

Puertecitos Hot Springs

The bay here is extremely shallow, bare sand at extreme low tide. But the great natural attraction here is the **hot springs**, which well up among the surf-smoothed rocks at the high tide line. You can sit in various pools of different temperatures, just below the frothing surf and watch the moon rise from the gulf. *Note: the hot springs are found not in the bay, but on the north side of the northern point.*

SOUTH OF PUERTECITOS

From Puertecitos, an unpaved road continues south, bypassing the feared *cuestas* (30% grades) that before blocked this section of coast. The road passes the **Huerfanito** fish camp at 18.5 miles, named after a solitary islet offshore. At 40 miles from Puertecitos, a spur road runs down to **Punta Bufeo**, where there are a few rental cabins, a cafe, and a long beach. Another 5.5 miles brings you to the **Papa Fernandez Resort** at Bahía Willard, which also has rental cabins and rooms. The mile-long turnoff to **Bahía San Luis Gonzaga** (where there is a small gringo community) is situated another four miles south, (49.5 miles from Puertecitos). From here, the road veers inland 37 miles to Hwy. 1 at Laguna Chapala.

Panga at rest

TIJUANA TO ENSENADA

From Tijuana to Ensenada, you have two choices: to pay or not to pay. The 65-mile toll road is quick, multi-laned, and scenic. The free road is a bit longer, narrow, tends to wander away from the coast, but allows you greater freedom to stop. The three tollgates on Hwy. 1D are at Playas de Tijuana (El Monumental), Rosarito, and San Miguel.

San Antonio del Mar

Off Hwy. 1D, at km 22 (7.6 miles from first toll booth), there is an offramp to a KOA trailer park perched high on a hill, the closest camping spot to Tijuana. This place is more inspirational than practical; you have a grand view of the Coronado Islands offshore, but the beach on the other side of the highway is a very long walk away.

Rosarito

Just 12 miles south of Tijuana, this area of curio shops, liquor stores, hotels, and restaurants is a weekend resort for Southern Californians and is as much an extension of San Diego as a part of Mexico. Actually it once *was* a part of San Diego. The boundary separating Alta and Baja California was drawn from Rosarito to the mouth of the Río Colorado in 1788. Only after the Mexican-American War was the boundary moved up to Tijuana. Three casinos operated here during gambling's heyday in Mexico, but the Rosarito Beach Hotel is the only vestige of this time.

Rosarito south to Descano is popular with surfers and sailboarders. *Note: the bus depot is across from the hotel; local buses depart for Ensenada and Tijuana every 30 minutes.*

El Descanso

At El Descanso, huge sand dunes rise up on the coast, where you can camp among the dune buggies. Off the Cantamar exit, a third of a mile east of the highway on a hill north of Rio Descanso, is the site of Misión Descanso, founded in 1814 by the Dominicans, one of the last missions built in Baja. The white chapel that can be seen from the highway has since been built on the site, with nothing remaining of the original mission except, it is claimed, the old wood altar.

La Misión

From La Misión south, you come to a less developed area of coastline where you can still find camp sites on the coastal bluffs. If you take the free road south and follow it inland for a mile east of the bridge crossing over the Río Guadalupe, you will come to La Misión school. Surrounded by a fence in the schoolyard are the adobe ruins of the Misión de San Miguel Arcángel de la Frontera.

At the La Misión exit, the Plaza del Mar Archeological Garden (part of a resort complex) displays replicas of some of Mexico's prehispanic ruins, including an ersatz pyramid. A modest museum displays smaller artifacts.

El Sauzal

Abelardo Rodriguez, an interim president of Mexico, was the force behind El Sauzal. He planted the olive trees up on the hills (where he himself is now planted) to use their oil for canning fish. A breakwater was constructed to shelter the fishing boats. The cannery, first built to process explosives and then fertilizer, now churns out cans of tuna and albacore.

Caution: beware of camping to close to El Sauzal; the smell from the cannery can carry far on the wind.

ENSENADA

Vizcaíno sailed into this bay on Nov. 1, 1602, the Day of the Dead. He named it Ensenada de Todos los Santos, now secularized to just plain Ensenada (small bay). Except for the tending of cattle, not much happened for 250 years; even the missionaries walked by without building a church. It was gold, not God that brought about the town. Ambrosio Castillo discovered yellow nuggets in nearby Valle de San Rafael in 1872, triggering a gold rush. Ensenada quickly became a supply center with all the illicit side-effects of sudden wealth. In 1882, Ensenada was named capital of the territory. By 1889, the gold fields were exhausted. The population of 1,375 was mostly disillusioned miners.

Ensenada cast about for a new calling, selling out briefly as headquarters of an American and then British land company holding title to vast land tracts in the south (see San Quintín). After the turn of the century, Ensenada lost the capital seat to Mexicali. The land charters were annulled by the Mexican Revolution in 1915. Ensenada was left to fend for itself.

During the 1930s, the town took advantage of being the closest foreign port to California, developing not only as a harbor for shipping Mexicali farm products, but for the smuggling of bootleg liquor also. Hotel Riviera del Pacífico opened in the early 1930s with a grand casino and a well stocked bar. For a brief time Ensenada flirted with the idea of emulating Havana, playing to Southern California's repressed libido. Then came two crippling edicts: the U.S. legalized alcohol, and the Mexican government outlawed gambling.

Ensenada has since learned to stand on its own regional legs, building on a less glamorous but more reliable fishing and shipping industry, giving it a steady footing from which to promote tourism.

Since the beaches are polluted, and a cantina left over from frontier days is about the only historical site worth visiting, Ensenada relies on events instead of attractions. Numerous special events attract waves of U.S. tourists that inundate the city: Mardi Gras and Cinco de Mayo celebrations, the world's largest international yacht race, bicycle and powerboat races, small plane rallies, seafood festivals, dog shows and chili-cook-offs. Go midweek to avoid crowds, make reservations for weekends.

BEARINGS

The central tourist area lies on and between two main thoroughfares: Av. López Mateos (aka First St.) and Blvd. Costera (aka Blvd. Lázaro Cárdenas), which runs along the waterfront. A clutch of commercial hotels anchor the newer eastern end of Av. López Mateos, which gains character and loses respectability as it runs west, ending appropriately enough near Hussong's Cantina and the city jail. Most of the newer restaurants and bars have spread out along Blvd. Costera, beyond the radius of casual strollers. If you're striking inland, the streets running parallel to the ocean are numbered in sequence: primero, segunda, tercero, cuarto, etc. Five blocks inland you hit the congested traffic of Av. Juárez, the main business artery of Ensenada.

TRAVEL INFORMATION

The State Tourism Office (Av. López Mateos 13-B; Tel: 676-22-22) is full of coupons for free margaritas. The Tourist & Convention Bureau, run by the city, has an information post on the northern end of Blvd. Cárdenas and Av. Gastélum (tel. 8-24-11). *Peso Saver: Parking meters, which sprout everywhere in Ensenada, require*

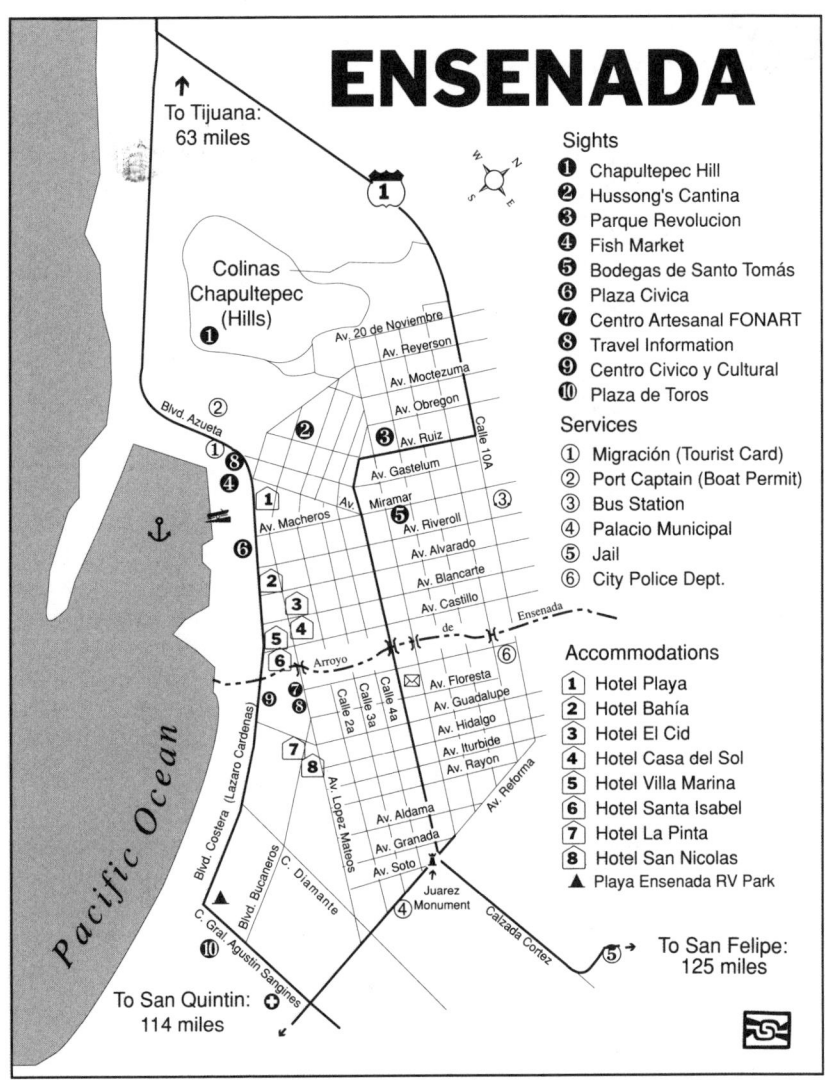

ENSENADA

↑ To Tijuana:
63 miles

Colinas
Chapultepec
(Hills)

Sights
❶ Chapultepec Hill
❷ Hussong's Cantina
❸ Parque Revolucion
❹ Fish Market
❺ Bodegas de Santo Tomás
❻ Plaza Civica
❼ Centro Artesanal FONART
❽ Travel Information
❾ Centro Civico y Cultural
❿ Plaza de Toros

Services
① Migración (Tourist Card)
② Port Captain (Boat Permit)
③ Bus Station
④ Palacio Municipal
⑤ Jail
⑥ City Police Dept.

Accommodations
1 Hotel Playa
2 Hotel Bahía
3 Hotel El Cid
4 Hotel Casa del Sol
5 Hotel Villa Marina
6 Hotel Santa Isabel
7 Hotel La Pinta
8 Hotel San Nicolas
▲ Playa Ensenada RV Park

To San Felipe:
125 miles

To San Quintin: ⊙
114 miles

Pacific Ocean

Mexican coins; purchase a parking permit here for one dollar, good for 48 hours of unlimited parking.

TRAVELING ABOUT
By Rental Car

It isn't worth renting a car in Ensenada unless you want to escape town, and even then a trip to Punta Banda 15 miles away is cheaper in a taxi or bus (summer only). The three car rental agencies are conveniently located side-by-side on Alvarado St., between Av. Mateos and the Costera.

A less expensive alternative is to rent a moped at the corner of Macheros & Blvd. Costera. *Calandrias* (horse-drawn buggies) wait for riders on the same corner.

By Bus

The bus system avoids the tourist district and is almost indecipherable to a tourist. Best avoided.

PLACES

Bodegas de Santo Tomás

This is Mexico's largest winery, founded in 1888 in the mission valley of Santo Tomás, then moved here in 1934, at Miramar 666, between Calles 6 & 7. Fifteen-minute, bilingual tours of the bottling room, and the giant redwood and oak casks in the bodegas (storerooms) are followed by a trip to the wine tasting room, the highwater mark on this $1.50 tour (discount coupons at tourist info booths). Some surprisingly good cabernet, chardonnay, and pinot noir is produced here. Wine is handled rudely after it leaves the winery. Consequently it is best to buy direct at the winery, where bottles can be bought at less-than-retail prices. Open Mon.-Sat. at 11 a.m., 1 p..m., 3 p.m.; tel: 8-25-09; 4-08-36. Best time to visit: August and September, when the wine is brought in for crushing.

Chapultepec Hill

For aerial views of Ensenada, follow Av. Segunda up to El Mirador (The Lookout). If

---

Polluted Waters

Bacteria levels at some Ensenada beaches are 50 times higher than the limit at which American beaches would be closed to the public. Few warnings are posted. Most polluted waters are in the city harbor and stretch from El Sauzal a few miles north to a creek known as Arroyo del Gallo, half a mile south of the harbor. This creek is the main sewage discharge point, emitting a mixture of raw sewage and industrial waste. Fish processing plants also dump their waste directly into the sewer system. The coast's southern areas, beginning at the El Ciprés military base about five miles south of the harbor and down to Estero Punta Banda, are relatively free of contamination. *Note: Highest levels of bacteria concentration are in summer.*

---

your brakes are weak, it's best not to begin the ascent. Near the summit, the road is badly decomposed. Despite its touting as an attraction in the tourist brochures, not many people bother to reach the summit.

Hussong's

Opened in 1892, the boisterousness of frontier Ensenada is still bouncing off the walls here, which is why it is now an historic point of interest. One result is that women are welcome. Extremely welcome, yet still respected. This gives them the opportunity to witness the flavor of that male institution: a Mexican cantina. Weekend nights can be standing room only.

Centro Social Cívico y Cultural de Ensenada

This Spanish Mediterranean palace facing the Costera was the infamous Riviera del Pacífico, a grand casino managed by the boxer Jack Dempsey (actually he was little more than a public relations figurehead). Now it is relegated to wedding receptions and the staging of occasional cultural events. Travelers are welcome to walk around. Best features include a 30 ft. relief map illuminating the missions of California, occasional art exhibits, bathrooms and a sometimes-open bar where you can sit with the ghosts of Erroll Flynn and Harlow.

Parque Revolución

This traditional green park set back three blocks from Av. Mateos offers a shady respite from the tourist rush, and a well kept playground where you can unleash the kids.

Plaza Cívica

If you wonder where the drum and bugle wake-up call is coming from, walk over to the Plaza Cívica on Av. Cárdenas. The Naval Base holds flag ceremonies at sunrise and sunset, under the gaze of the 12 foot-high gilded busts of three Mexican patriots: Juárez, Hidalgo and Carranza. These mammoth heads may look prepos-

terous, but the tradition of oversized *cabezas* (heads) stretches directly back to the pre-hispanic Olmecs in the state of Tabasco, whose monolithic stone cabezas, like those of Easter Island, still amaze archaeologists.

Organized Tours

The basic city-and-countryside tour makes the rounds to the Bodegas de Santo Tomás, Riviera del Pacífico, Chapultepec hills, and out to La Bufadora on Punta Banda. Viajes Guaycura, next to Best Western Cortés Hotel at Av. López Mateos No. 1089, makes the 3 1/2 hour trip (tel. 8-37-18/8-16-41).

Harbor Sightseeing

The rainbow-streaked waters of the inner harbor are unusually calm due to oily pollution, which makes for easy gliding in a *panga* (skiff) to view the freighters moored to the quay, ships abuilding on the weighs, giant tuna seiners in for repair, fishing boats unloading catch. Pangas for hire can be found south of the sportfishing dock.

Fishing

Ensenada advertises itself as the yellowtail capital of the world and pulls in a thriving charter fishing business. Yellowtail are most abundant from June to September, along with albacore, barracuda, bonita, white sea bass, and halibut. Winter months are much slower, the weather more erratic. Most reliable operators are located in the sportfishing dock area just south of the fish market. Day trips leave around 7:30 a.m. and head for Punta Banda, San Miguel, or out to Islas de Todos Santos, returning around 3 p.m..

Horseback Riding

You can gallop (horse willing) on the beach for $8 to $12 an hour. Cheapest horses are at Hermosa Beach; better mounts and a wider beach are found six miles south, between El Estero Hotel and El Faro Trailer Park.

El Caliente Race Book

For those who would rather bet on horses than ride them, the El Caliente Race Book is behind the FONART Store just off Av. Mateos. Devoid of atmosphere, only for those intimate with the Daily Racing Form.

Plaza de Toros

The new bullring on Sangines is bolted together like scaffolding. No specific season, only when promoter decides to stage an event. Not the best place to watch your first bullfight; many matadors do not consider Ensenada *muy aficionada*.

Shopping

Main shopping district is found on both sides of Av. Mateos, a bonanza for even disinterested shoppers. There are no real indigenous crafts here. As in Tijuana, most everything is brought from the interior, resulting in a familiar bordertown melange of authentic art and hastily made curios, choice crafts and cherry bombs, supple leather jackets and mop-cloth pullovers. Unlike Tijuana, the hawking is less shrill, the pace more leisurely. Most goods are tagged lower than in Tijuana, and still have enough leeway for friendly bargaining. Many experienced buyers consider Ensenada the best shopping town on the peninsula. Go to Centro Artesanal FONART at Av. López Mateos 744, next to the State Tourist Office to get the government line on art-and-craft prices to use as a point-of-reference. *Peso Saver: though the dollar is the preferred currency of most store owners, their exchange rate usually favors paying in pesos.*

Entertainments

Most nightlife is pedestrian and follows a geographical pattern, moving from south to north, and back again. From the hotel zone on the southern end of Av. Mateos, groups move slowly up Av. Mateos, stopping to check out a bar here, a disco there. Some drop down to the waterfront, while others continue down Av. Mateos. Most eventually reach Hussong's for the midnight hour. Then the flow makes its way back down Av. Mateos under the baleful eye of the beat cops. When reaching Calle Miramar, most continue on to their beds, while the imprudent may be drawn west into a netherland of

skin shows and cheap bars, perhaps finding themselves in the *Política Alegre, El Gallo del Oro*, or *Los Tres Ases*, places that make Hussong's look like the Rotary Club. *Tip: don't walk any street in Mexico with an open beer in your hand. It's against the law.*

SPENDING THE NIGHT

Because of the event-driven nature of the tourist economy, hotel rates are pushed high by a flood of weekenders. When this tide of weekenders recedes, rates often remain at the highwater mark even when the hotels lay empty, a distressing situation for budget travelers in on weekdays.

Budget Hotels

Hotel Plaza (Av. Mateos 540; tel: 8-27-15), though growing more arthritic with the years, remains the top budget pick, more for its on-the-strip location than what it offers, which is little more than bare rooms and limber beds. **Motel Pancho** (211 Av. Alvarado) is a good second choice to the Plaza, and motorists rank it higher for its at-door parking; rooms are worn, but the rates are welcome. Rooms are a bit cheaper at the **49 Motel** (Miramar No. 695; tel: 4-03-08), which is as prosaic as its name, set around a bare two-story motel court between the Costera and Av. Mateos. Other budget choices farther out of town include the **Hotel America** (Av. Mateos y Espinosa No. 1309; tel: 6-13-33), which is across from the FONART building south of the arroyo, and the **Flamingo Motel** (Av. Mateos 1797 and Rayon), which has a pool in recompense for its distant location.

Caution: centrally located, yes, but the budget hotels on Calle Miramar should be avoided; they often rent by the hour.

Moderate & Deluxe

The old veteran, **Hotel Bahía**, (Blvd. Costera and Alvarado: tel. 8-21-03) works hard at hiding its scars; steady maintenance allows it to compete with the newer commercial upstarts, helped in part by its on-strip location, moderate cafe, and its slightly lower rates; best rooms are the 16 garden units on first floor. **El Cid Motor Hotel** (933 Lopez MaTeos; tel. 8-24-01) stands out from the commercial clutch with its eccentric rooms, equipped with wet bars and mini-fridges, mirrored beds, and, in the front units, sliding glass doors to balconies overlooking the main drag. The **Travelodge** (Av. Mateos and Blancarte 130; tel. 8-16-01/37-01) provides the most predictably comfortable address downtown, its practical motel configuration camouflaged by an impressive modern colonial styling. Next door, the **Casa del Sol**, a Best Western (Av. Mateos No. 1001 at Av. Blancarte), is one step behind the pace, and priced accordingly; 40 years old, it nonetheless offers all the perks (cable TV, free coffee, secured parking). Butted up against the Casa del Sol is a clone, the **Cortez Motor Hotel** (Av. Mateos No. 1089; tel. 8-23-07), also a Best Western; dated in furnishings, it does keep neat rooms and offers rapid service, secure parking, and a trim restaurant with Italian specialties. Farther from downtown but still within pedestrian striking distance are two perennial favorites: **La Pinta** (Bucaneros & Floresta aves.; tel. 6-26-01/02), a Mexican version of a commercial chain hotel, and the more flamboyant and expensive **San Nicolás** (Av. Mateos at Guadalupe; tel.6-19-01 to 3), a place of wandering hallways, a huge pool, overblown Aztec motifs, and a sunken nightclub under a lighted waterfall. The 12-story **Villa Marina** (Av. Mateos & Av. Castillo; tel. 8-33-21; 8-33-51) provides the vantage point from its miniature balconies, but service tends to fall flat in this under-occupied tower. The **Motel Villa Fontana** (Ave Mateos and Av. Blancarte; tel. 8-34-34) keeps to an historic style of peaked ceilings and bay windows; during midweek, these are about the best-value rooms in Ensenada.

Camping

The only camping spot in central Ensenada is the **Campo Playa Ensenada RV Park** (tel. 6-29-18), one mile south of downtown, across the street from the waterfront. There is an area for pitching tents as well. Palm trees soften the urban atmosphere.

Rancho Todos Santos Trailer Park, farther south, is close to the beach, but most sites are taken up by permanent guests and an offshore wind can waft an offal smell from fish canneries nearby.

ARRIVING-DEPARTING
By Car

When arriving on the outskirts of town from the north, do not continue inland on Highway 1 or you will be swallowed up in chaotic stop-and-go traffic. Instead, hug the ocean, which will lead around the harbor and directly into the main tourist district. When coming from the south, turn left towards the ocean on Sangines to avoid this same central downtown area.

By Bus

The bus terminal is on Riveroll between Calle 10 and Calle 11, a long but not daunting 11-block walk to the tourist district and waterfront. Buses from Tijuana, Mexicali, and points south arrive and depart continuously.

By Plane

Flights on a DC-3 to Isla Cedros and Bahía Tortuga can be made from the El Ciprés military airport situated along Hwy. 1, 3.7 miles south of the intersection at Calle General Sanginés. Currently, flights leave Mondays and Fridays at 10 a.m., weather permitting. Phone *Omega Aeroservicios* at tel. 6-60-76 to verify schedule.

ENSENADA ADDENDUM

The immigration office is at Av. Virgilio Uribe & Av. Gastélum (see map), open 7 days a week. *Note: if you have not obtained a tourist card yet, this is the easiest place to get one, conveniently situated on main boulevard leading into town. Get your tourist* cards validated here as well. The staff is efficient, and doors stay open until 8 p.m., later if any ships are due in.

Police Station is at Calle 9 and Av. Espinosa (tel. 6-24-21; 6-26-96; 6-44-44). *Note: any type of fine can be paid immediately at the Tourist Information Center. Ask the arresting officer to take you there and an authorized cashier will issue a receipt,* at least during the day from 9 a.m. to 7 p.m., Sun 9 a.m. to 2 p.m. After hours, you must follow the officer to the police department or, more expensively, settle it on the spot.

The Procuraduría de Protección al Turista (Tourist Protection) is situated next door to the State Tourist Office at Av. Mateos 13-B (tel. 6-36-86).

ENSENADA TO SAN FELIPE via Hwys. 3 & 5

Highway 3 leaves Ensenada from Calzada Cortés and travels southeast for 125 lonely miles to its junction with Hwy. 5, 31 miles north of San Felipe. From Ensenada, you trudge up a steep 13-mile grade, pass through dry coastal hills and mountain valleys, and then descend precipitously to Desierto de los Chinos, sea to sea.

Agua Caliente

Situated at the top of the grade, about 16 miles from Ensenada, is a dirt road to the south, which descends 5.5 miles to a rustic hotel, whose best feature is the tepid hot springs that have been piped into two swimming pools. Rooms are spartan and unkept, but you can camp here as well. The hotel sometimes closes down winter. *Rancheros* say a trail continues down the Cañón Agua Caliente for some five miles to San Carlos, where another hot springs resort, San Carlos, once operated. The road in from Hwy. 1 to San Carlos has been storm-damaged.

Valle de Ojos Negros

Hwy. 3 descends to this farming valley, 25 miles from Ensenada. The town of Ojos Negros is easily and justifiably missed, as it lies two miles off the highway. Until its expropriation in the 1930s, Ojos Negros was owned by gringos, who based the million-acre Circle Bar Ranch here; some old buildings of this era still remain.

Laguna Hanson

Twelve miles beyond the turnoff to Ojos Negros, there is a signed turnoff for **Laguna Hanson**, which is the centerpiece of the **Parque Nacional Constitución de 1857**. This dirt road travels 23 miles to Laguna Hanson, which also can be reached from Hwy. 2 near Rumorosa, a rougher, longer route.

You can camp among the pines by the lake's edge, which fluctuates according to the rainfall. Declared a national park in 1962, this mountain plateau is home to mule deer, bobcat, mountain lions, and gray foxes, and is also a way station for migrating birds. The Parry pines here, a four-leafed pinyon pine, are found only in this region, along with oak and Jeffery pine, manzanita and chamise. Adeptly driven passenger cars can usually make the trip in summer. *Warning: snow can fall at this altitude.*

Valle La Trinidad

At 76 miles from Ensenada, the highway drops into another valley, a flat, straight respite before the road winds down to the dry desert plains of the gulf. Halfway between Valle La Trinidad and Ojos Negros (58 miles from Ensenada), a dirt road leaves the highway at Llano Colorado for Santa Catarina, a settlement of indigenous Paipais. This was the site of the Dominicans' last mission, which the Paipais burned down in revolt; you can still see the mounds, as well as the cemetery where the martyred missionaries lie.

Crucero La Trinidad

Highway 3 deadends at Hwy. 5 at this barren junction, 31 miles from San Felipe.

ENSENADA TO SAN QUINTIN via Hwy. 1

Hwy. 1 travels 114 miles to San Quintin, winding through coastal foothills, cleaving through vast vineyards, and finally straightening out as it enters the broad agricultural plains of the San Quintin Valley.

Playa Hermosa

Though the sand dunes are inviting, the ocean is too polluted for swimming. The surrounding junkyards on Ensenada's southern fringe mock the name of this once-lovely beach. Only notable attractions here are the Cueva de Leones restaurant and the **Hermosa Beach RV Park**, a brave venture in this forlorn area. Directly offshore you can see Islas Todos Santos. To reach Playa Hermosa, drive south on Hwy. 1 to Av. Las Palmas; turn left to the ocean.

Islas Todos Santos

These two waterless rocky islets lie almost nine miles from Ensenada, and are used as a rookery for seagulls, pelicans, and cormorants (birds nest from February to May). Visited mostly by fishermen and surfers who charter boats from the Ensenada waterfront (about $100 for a day trip in a 22 ft. panga). A fish camp is established most of the year in a cove at the south end of the larger southern island; most visitors camp on a flat area overlooking a cove on the north end. *Note: Camping on the smaller northern island is prohibited, though there is a lighthouse keeper who lives here (radio contact with Ensenada).*

San Carlos Hot Springs

Sulfuric mineral baths can be found at the end of an 11-mile road that winds up the San Carlos Arroyo; turnoff for the arroyo is 6.5 miles south of Ensenada (from the intersection of Sanguines and Hwy. 1). The dirt road is unmarked. Severe storms destroyed the resort here many years ago, and the road, which threads back and forth across a shallow stream, is in very rough shape. From the abandoned resort, there is supposedly a trail rising to a waterfall, and beyond to connect with the better known Agua Caliente Hot Springs, reached via Hwy. 3.

Playa El Faro

Five miles south of Ensenada, a gentle surf rolls onto this wide beach (turn-off at sign for Estero Beach Hotel). It is less polluted and more attractive than Playa Hermosa. Primitive camping is pleasant in a secure sandy lot facing the beach ($). There are salty showers in the permanent trailer park village which backs the camping lot, a kind of rusty museum of art deco vintage trailers. Restaurant operates in season. Horses can be rented on the beach for about $10 an hour.

The beach ends at the shores of a large

estero, next to the **Estero Beach Hotel** ($$$). This resort combines 1960ish functionalism with a Mayan motif, and the tranquil public areas are worth a stroll, at least to see the ersatz museum full of reproductions of Mayan, Zapotec, Aztec and Olmec artifacts (the exhibits behind glass are genuine). Hotel also has tennis courts, and a trailer park on the inner bay. *Note: no tents allowed.*

Estero Punta Banda

The broad estero is protected by a 2.5 mile finger of land embracing a vast tract of marshlands teeming with wildlife. Many migratory birds, including the light-footed clapper rail and the California least tern depend on these marshlands. These same species once thrived in California's coastal lagoons; they have been forced south to this estero due to overdevelopment.

Same story is being threatening here. The 800-acre Baja Beach and Tennis Club is under construction along the estuary's western shore. Since this is being built on *ejido* land, legal difficulties have slowed the pace, giving environmentalists time to organize.

Dunes here provide a unique flora and fauna that form a defense against storms. If the channel is dredged as planned, these shallow zones necessary for the nourishment of this delicate eco-system will be lost—one of the last esteros left for these birds.

Punta Banda

This bold southern point of Todos Santos Bay reaches far out into the Pacific, catching a cold current of water that brings in marine life usually found in central and northern California. Sheer rock walls fringed by russet-colored kelp drop deep into the blue water.

A long beach stretches along the eastern base of the point, 8 miles west of Hwy. 1. Here, at **La Jolla Beach** (where there is a trailer park) a geologic fault plunges into the water. *Note: If you scoop holes in the sand, hot mineral water will seep in, creating a natural hot tub on the beach.*

This same paved road runs along the east side of the point, ending 14 miles from Hwy. 1 at **La Bufadora**, a free natural attraction (though you may be hit for a parking fee). Each ocean swell compresses air inside of a crevice; as the swell recedes, the air bursts free, shooting water 100 feet into the air, then falling back as rain on your head. More impressive than the sight is the sound, a deep unearthly roar. Near the blowhole is a gauntlet of overpriced stalls selling sea schlock: conch shells, firecrackers, and lock-jawed shark heads. There are several restaurants here serving fresh lobster dinners cheaper than you can find in Ensenada.

Divers can find calm water entry a few hundred yards south at **Bahía Papalote**, where there is an underwater arch and wall. A dive shop here offers air fills and daily rentals. *Caution: for obvious reasons, don't swim anywhere near the blowhole.*

At the head of Bahía Papalote is the **Toscano Ranch**, where tame deer and peacock wander among the colony of home sites Sr. Toscano is leasing. A trail leads around the bluffs to **Caleta Puerto Escondido**.

Best primitive camping is on the flat bluff above Bahía Papalote. More private sites can be found atop Punta Banda at the ejidal campgrounds; views are great, but the descent to a rocky surf-whipped coastline is treacherous. More facilities can be found back at the La Jolla Beach Camp, where the beachfront camping area has yet to be usurped by permanent motorhomes. This is a popular spot with catamaran sailors for its steady wind and mild surf.

Note: the bus runs hourly from the Ensenada bus terminal to La Bufadora during summer and Easter vacations.

MANDEADERO

This farming community, 8.5 miles south of Ensenada, tills the fertile Valle de

Mandeadero for its sustenance. On Wednesdays, a huge market stretches for half a mile along the road, selling everything from chile strings to dome tents. On the south end of town is an immigration checkpoint, usually dormant but sporadically springing to life. Technically, you can't travel beyond this point without a validated tourist card.

EJIDO URUAPAN

This ejido, 12 miles south of Mandeadero, operates a small campground in a grove of scrub oak alongside the highway, near a shallow creek. If you follow the dirt road two miles to the east, crossing to the north side of the creek bed, you will come to the **hot springs**, the ejido's main source of hot water. There are three private bathing stalls next to the laundry boards. The *nacimiento* (source) of the springs is in a nearby muddy vale. Not particularly appealing.

SANTO TOMÁS

In 1791, the Dominicans founded a mission in this broad valley. They planted a vineyard here too, ostensibly to make altar wine. Little did they suspect that within 200 years, their mission would become a melted hump of adobe, while their vineyards would carpet the fertile valleys of northern Baja California. Most vineyards were re-planted in the 1960s with European varietal grapes (Cabernet Sauvignon, Pinot Noir, Merlot, etc.). Currently, the oldest vineyards are found around Rancho Los Dolores, which is on north side of the arroyo, off the highway in a Eucalyptus grove. Here is a crumbling wall section preserved under a shelter, often mistaken for the old mission but actually the ruins of the first Santo Tomás winery built in 1888; nearby is a pool of spring water, what is left of an old *balneario*.

The slumped walls of the original mission can still be seen in a field near several tall fan palms a few steps north of the olive orchard of El Palomar Trailer Park. Two years after this mission was abandoned (the last mission forced to close due to the 1848

church secularization order of the Mexican Government), Santo Tomás was named capital of this area. The seat was shifted to Ensenada when gold was discovered near there.

Besides a restaurant, store and gas station, there is a clean but overpriced 10-room motel. The trailer park is an oasis of olive trees, featuring two tennis courts, two pools, and childern's play area.

LA BOCANA

Just north of Santo Tomás, a dirt road branches off the highway, traveling 15 miles to La Bocana, a small village at the mouth of Río Santo Tomás. You can camp next to the beach, near the freshwater lagoon. Rustic cabins and boats can be rented through the Gomez family (Read "God and Mr. Gomez," Reader's Digest Press, New York, NY, by Jack Smith, columnist for the LA. Times). Small boats can be launched from the river's mouth. The road continues north two miles along the coast to Puerto Santo Tomás, a small storm-protected cove used as a port by the missionaries to ship out wine casks. The ruins of the original Misión Santo Tomás, built in 1791, lie inland. Fishermen living here take advantage of both the port and the rich sealife in the bay, caused by an upwelling of cold water brought up by the California current as it brushes by the point. Water is 10 to 12 degrees colder here than farther north.

SAN ISIDRO

South of Santo Tomás 17 miles is a paved side road to Erendira, an *ejido* eleven miles away where gas and basic supplies can be bought. A dirt road continues two miles to the beach and another half mile to Puerto Isidro. You can rent simple oceanside cabins at Castro's Fishing Camp. Fishing trips can also be arranged (tel. 6-28-97; P.O. Box 974, Ensenada). Notice the emphasis of fishing; there are few sandy spots along this rocky coast.

SAN VICENTE

What's left of the Misión San Vicente Ferrar lies less than half a mile off the highway just south of the Km-88 marker. Founded by Dominicans in 1780, it was the largest of their missions and later was the headquarters for a garrison of troops. No bucolic mission life here. Yuma Indians scorched the area with constant attacks. Smallpox decimated the converts. Father Sales lamented how he had to whip the Indians constantly to keep them at their tasks. By 1867, all was lost. The only things to show for the suffering are the crumbling walls under a thatched shelter, and a silent cemetery above. The town of San Vicente lies nearby, south of the Río San Isidro whose waters irrigate the vineyards of this valley.

TROUT

An unusual species of rainbow trout, the Nelson Rainbow Trout *(Salmo Nelsonii)* is found in these mountain streams. Originally they existed only below El Salto Falls in Arroyo San Antonio. In 1929, Charles Utt, a California philanthropist, in conjunction with the Melings, carried these fish in aerated leather bags to other streams. Trout up to 12 inches are now found in Arroyo San Antonio, San Rafael, La Grulla and San Pedro Martir rivers, with smaller ones in Arroyo La Zanza. Scientists have yet to figure out how the trout first arrived in this isolated mountain pocket, whether the missionaries brought them (the only other specimens used to exist in Spain) or whether they are a mutated steelhead that climbed up from the Pacific.

SAN ANTONIO DEL MAR

Broad dunes and berms line this mile of sandy beach, which acts as a soft catch basin for flotsam and jetsam brought down on the currents. Beachcombing is often rewarded on this lee shore. Unfortunately the dune area at times turns into a big sandbox for the off-road vehicle set. This beach is reached by leaving Hwy. 1 at Colonet (23 miles S of San Vicente), and rolling down a broad coastal plain for seven miles on a dirt road. Primitive campsites can be found.

PARQUE NACIONAL SIERRA DE SAN PEDRO MARTIR

Less than eight miles south of Colonet is the signed turn-off for a graded road to the national park and observatory 63 miles away. Situated on a ridge over 9,000 feet high, this is Baja's Darien, where you can see both the Gulf and the Pacific. Nearby looms El Picacho del Diablo, the tallest peak on the peninsula at 10,498 feet. You must walk the last mile to the observatory; short tours are occassionally allowed. A nominal fee is charged at the national park entrance, 14 miles before reaching the observatory. Pine and fir forests sprout among the boulders, and the high hilly terrain is occasionally flattened by meadows and cut by streams. The park is best visited from May to July. Winter storms can dump snow at this altitude, closing down the road.

Halfway between Hwy. 1 and the *observatorio* is **Meling Ranch**, where organized pack trips into the high country can be arranged in the spring and summer. This historic ranch is still run by the families that pioneered the region in the early 1900. Though the ranch was destroyed during the Mexican Revolution, it was quickly rebuilt and today is a working cattle ranch whose country hospitality has engendered a popular guesthouse and stream-fed swimming pool. For information, phone: U.S. 619-758-2719, or write: P.O. Box 1326, Ensenada, BC, Mexico.

PACIFIC BEACHES

Access roads to the sand and pebble beaches of the Pacific leave the highway at kilometer markers K 142 and K 150, reaching the shore in about six miles.

MISION SANTO DOMINGO

A side road runs east at K 169 to Santo Domingo five miles inland, where stand the adobe walls of a mission founded by the Dominicans in 1775, and abandoned 110 years later; close by is the old cemetery and a stone dam built by the Indians.

COLONIA GUERRERO

This swiftly growing agricultural community clings to the highway and offers little of non-commercial interest, but an isolated sand and cobble beach can be reached by way of a confusing three-mile-long network of dirt roads that lace down the Arroyo de Santo Domingo; Mexicans often picnic here, hoeing for clams under the rocks at low tide.

Just off the highway, two popular trailer parks lie half a mile from each other; **Mesón Don Pepe** (tel. 6-22-16), closest to the highway, is the more colorful, with its historical-funk restaurant and grassy areas where you can pitch a tent. Others may prefer the orderliness of **Posada Don Diego**, which is set farther back from the traffic and provides live music in its cafeteria for the RV caravans that are likely to be tethered here. **Motel Sanchez** ($) along the highway offers large clean rooms under pine beam ceilings, but the **Motel Chávez** ($$) in San Quintín farther down the highway provides a more comfortable accommodation.

SAN QUINTIN

San Quintín is hard to define. Town, bay, and beach are all called San Quintín.

The Town

The Valle de San Quintín centers on a vibrant agricultural town, called Lázaro Cárdenas. This community doesn't revolve around the traditional zócalo. Its allegiance is to the harvest and its shipping to the U.S. via the transpeninsular highway, along which this town stretches. There isn't much scenic value to its storefront facade.

Surrounding the town are green fields. Most of what is picked ends up in the U.S., and most farms are controlled by U.S. interests.

From June to October, up to 50,000 migrant workers live here, grouped in 27 agricultural camps, the poverty of some you can see by the side of the road. Different tribes keep to different camps. Though there are *Zapotecos, Triquis, Nahuas,* and *Tarascos,* the majority of them are *Mixtec* from drought-stricken Oaxaca. They travel thousands of miles just to earn the minimum wage, about $5 a day. The pesticide, the long hours, the low wages, the shacks they live in are an indication of how desperate life is in their native lands farther south. Whole families migrate. Some stay all year,

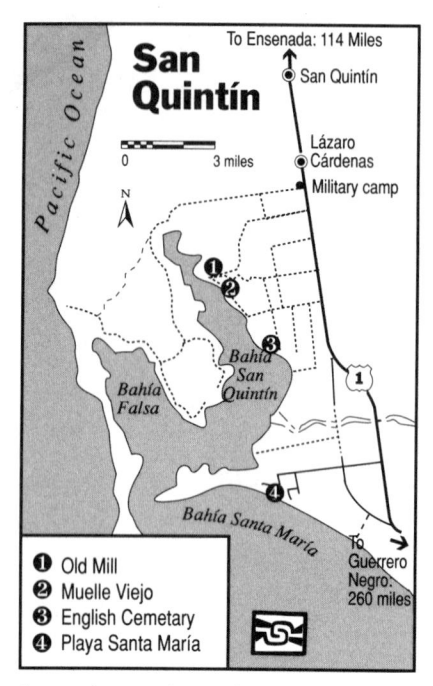

San Quintín

To Ensenada: 114 Miles

San Quintín

Pacific Ocean

0 — 3 miles

N

Lázaro Cárdenas

Military camp

Bahía San Quintín

Bahía Falsa

Bahía Santa María

To Guerrero Negro: 260 miles

❶ Old Mill
❷ Muelle Viejo
❸ English Cemetary
❹ Playa Santa María

becoming what the others call *Oaxacalifornianos.*

They bring with them many of the traditions of southern Mexico. Look for the colorful *huipiles* of the women, their babies swathed in *rebozos* (shawls). They sell their bright, woven crafts on the street, or at the Pemex gas station.

Strung along this highway are three hotels catering to sleepy motorists: **Motel Chávez** ($$), **Hotel Romo** ($$) and **Motel Uruapan** ($). The Uruapan is the cheapest, but for a few dollars more, Chavez is the superior pick. The newer, similarly priced **Hotel Romo** is conveniently situated next to the bus station, but rooms are cramped in size.

The Bay

Behind the storefront prosperity of Lázaro Cárdenas lies an older San Quintín, situated along the shallow bay two miles to the west. Little remains today of the community, except some graves on a lonely knoll surrounded by marsh, pilings from an old pier, rusting mill machinery, and three hotels of waning popularity. Lined with tidal flats

and backed by stark volcanic cones, this bay was first used in the 1800s to ship contraband. In 1890, the Lower California Development Company was granted a charter during the *Porfiriato* to develop a farming colony here. Two years later, 200 English and American colonists arrived. They built post and telegraph offices, dug wells, imported irrigating equipment, built a flour mill, laid tracks for a railway, and built a dyke to breach the bay. Then they waited. From 1892 to 1896, no rain fell. The enterprise was abandoned. In 1918, President Carranza made it official by cancelling the charter.

The bay today is good for birdwatching, searching out Anglo names on weathered wooden tombstones, and fishing from pangas rented at Puerto Molino Viejo.

There are three bayside motels: **Molino Viejo** ($$; PO Box 90, San Quintín), **Ernesto's** ($$; 2319 S. Corning, Los Angeles, CA; 213-870-5074) and **Muelle Viejo**, also called **Hotel San Carlos** ($$). Of the three, Molino Viejo has the most potential with its harbor, the historical pieces of the old mill saved from the scrap iron buyer, and the kitchenettes in the otherwise rustic rooms; the place is held together by habit. Ernesto's next door is a poor second, its bare unkept rooms overpriced. Three miles away, San Carlos Hotel (Muelle Viejo) has the only rooms built with a decent bay view; there is not much else to do here, as the shore is too shallow to launch boats. Nearby are the pilings of the old pier, and two miles south lies the old English cemetery, still in use.

The road to the Molino Viejo and Ernesto's leaves the highway 1.4 miles south of the military camp in Lázaro Cárdenas; 1.8 miles beyond is another road to the bayshore, this one leading to Muelle Viejo; both should be signed.

The Beach

South of the bay is yet another San Quintín, where a gentle children's surf pummels the

English Graveyard

flat sand beaches. Sand dollars and pismo clams litter the beach, and a long dune field provides romantic nooks. The turnoff for this beach, more properly called Playa Santa María, lies eight miles south of the military camp at San Quintín; a paved road runs 3.2 miles to the beach.

La Pinta Hotel ($$$), an almost-luxury resort, has a splashy courtyard and big room terrazas overlooking the beach; only drawback is a slight flooding problem when the sea (pushed by winter storms) invades the kitchen, a perennial problem. The **Cielito Lindo Motel** ($$) is about half the price of the La Pinta, and is set back more prudently from the shore. Consequently, its 12 rooms, big and bare, lack views. Restaurant and lounge are a local hangout, often blooming on Saturday nights. The hotel exercises desultory control over the nearby trailer park at ocean's edge, where overnighters often leave before the collection man makes his rounds. Not surprisingly, management does not put much effort into keeping the premises functional. Free beach camping can be had in the vicinity. *Note: Check the* *tides for the April to August full moon grunion runs here.*

ISLA SAN MARTIN

This circular volcanic island, a mile in diameter and topped by a crater, lies 10 miles NW of the entrance to San Quintín, an 1-1/2 hour voyage in calm seas. Lava tubes through which you can walk burrow into the hillside on the north and west sides. An easy trail circles the island, passing through fields of spring wildflowers and past a colony of elephant seals (be careful not to disturb them, they often injure themselves in a terrified rush to the surf). There is a fish camp at the SE end of the island, where there is an unnatural looking harbor (Hassler's Cove) formed by a long boulder point (legend calls it the work of pirates, constructed while they waited for galleons to pass). Cabrillo anchored here on his historic voyage up the California coastline. Nearby is a shallow lagoon, home to harbor seals. To reach the island, you can charter a panga from Molino Viejo.

SAN QUINTÍN TO LAGUNA CHAPALA

Hwy. 1 from San Quintín to Laguna Chapala, a distance of 150 miles, first runs through agricultural fields, then fringes the Pacific shore, winds over badlands, and finally turns inland, entering the mystical Central Desert, for many the true beginning of the peninsula.

SOUTHERN BEACHES

The beaches south of San Quintín vary from sand to rock, backed mostly by bluffs that grow in height the farther south you travel. The highway closely parallels the coast. A score of dirt roads run a short half mile to the isolated shore. South of San Quintín 9.5 miles is **Playa Pabellón**, where there is a trailer park, **Honey's Camp**, 200 yards behind a duney beach. The beach is rockier five miles south, at **El Socorro** ($), where there is a salty well, toilets and cold showers. About six miles south of here, six different arroyos break to the sea, offering secluded camping.

EL ROSARIO

Most travelers make a hard left at El Rosario (28 miles south of Santa María), continuing inland towards the central desert, unaware that they are passing through not El Rosario, but Rosario de Arriba. An older Rosario, called Rosario Abajo, is located across the arroyo, a mile and a half away. Many of the buildings here date from the 1800s. Of particular note is a bell, inscribed "Santa Rosa 1788," which hangs in a small church near some old adobe mission ruins now used as a bike jump by village children. It used to ring the Indians to service back in mission days.

Father Vicente Mora chose this valley the Indians called Viñadaco as the site of the Domincan's first mission after taking over the peninsula from the Fransicans in 1772. Their first attempt, a mission built near Rosario de Arriba in 1774, was abandoned when the water gave out 28 years later. They moved downstream to build another at Rosario del Abajo, but in 1832 it too was abandoned. Eight quiet years passed till Carlos Espinosa, in reward for some soldiering, obtained a land grant here. A mestizo community slowly grew, and for a while it was the seat of military government in the northern area, positioned to fend off any possible U.S. invasion.

Besides tonging the bell, you can partake of history by visiting the **Museo** (two old wagons stand at the entrance) opposite the "Espinosa" Pemex station, which is around the corner from the Casa Espinosa, one of Baja's legendary restaurants run by the same pioneer family. This town was the jumping-off spot for south-bound travelers before the asphalt was laid, the last outpost of civilization before the desert. For those too tired to continue, **Hotel El Rosario** ($) offers a bed, color TV and hot water. *Note: To get to Rosario del Abajo, turn west at the 90 degree turn in the highway, take the left fork to cross the arroyo, then bear right after one mile and continue to the village.*

THE PETRIFIED FOREST

Eighty million years ago, dinosaurs grazed in the humid jungles of Baja California, before it was geologically ripped from the Mexican mainland. In the badlands behind the beach near Rosario, the petrified bones of a the largest seagoing duck-billed dinosaur ever found were excavated, along with some of the oldest mammal remains to be dug from the west coast of this hemisphere (the Los Angeles Country Museum of Natural History carted away ten tons of bones

for reconstruction). You can still make out fossilized palms and other trees, and there is always the chance you might stumble on some paleontological prize in this area of bald eroded mesas. To reach the petrified forest, go the bend in Hwy. 1 at Rosario. Turn west, but instead of crossing the arroyo to go to Rosario del Abajo (see above) bear right and stay on north side of the arroyo. Beyond the fish cannery, bear right again; this road will take you through the badlands, eventually reaching a cobble beach 4.5 miles away, where you can search through the rocks for whitened bits of petrified wood and bones that have been washed down from the hills.

BOOJUM MAGIC

From Rosario, the highway cuts inland, crosses a wide arroyo by bridge, and then rises up into the low hills of the magical Central Desert. Cardons, relatives of the great Arizona Saguaro, march down the hillsides like a surrendering army, arms upraised. Ocotillos, their whiplike branches tipped with blood-red blossoms, look as if they have been frozen in an act of self-flagellation. From the swollen trunks of the Elephant Trees, you can peel off a parchment so fine you can write on it with a pen. All of these desert plants represent nature at its most imaginative, surviving in an area where three inches of rain is considered a wet year.

The most unique plant growing in this dry wonderland is the boojum, a weird plant usually described as an inverted twiggy carrot, first seen about eight miles south of Rosario. Growing to 50 feet, it is an unmistakable sight. Called the *milapa* by the Indians, it was christened the *cirio* (wax candle) by Father Fernando Consag in 1751; the cream-colored flowers made it look like the altar candles he carried with him. The Jesuit Clavijero listed it in his History of California under the chapter "Noxious and Grotesque Plants." Two centuries later, in 1863, a botanist gave it its western name,

Idria columnaris, awarding it its own genus (nearest relative is the ocotillo). When botonist Godfrey Sykes sighted his first Idria columnaris in 1922, his first words were "Ho, ho, a boojum, definitely a boojum," inadvertently giving it the name most North Americans now call it (the boojum is a mythical creature in Lewis Carroll's *Hunting of the Snark*).

You will only find these plants within a latitude of 200 miles, from the southern end of the Sierra San Pedro Martir to the Tres Virgenes region, on Isla Guarda del Angel, and in a small area around Puerto Libertad in Sonora. Transplanted specimens can grow outside these strictly drawn boundaries, but will not reproduce. Their growth rate is as little as one inch a year. Their age is measured in centuries, not decades. As you pass through boojum country, notice how they seem to grow in different groups of the same height, with no in-between sizes, a noticeable generation gap. Years can pass before some unknown local event triggers another wave of boojum births, which is why they grow nowhere else. Just one of the many mysteries of this central desert.

Note: The missionaries complained of headaches when using boojum trees as firewood.

SAN FERNANDO DE VELICATA

The Franciscan order was not too ambitious in Baja California when taking over from the Jesuits, and acted mostly in a custodial fashion. But at San Fernando de Velicata, you can see what is left of their single attempt at building a mission in the desert. These ruins were originally laid in part by the hands of Padre Junípero Serra, who later went on to build the foundations of modern California. Currently he is a candidate for beatification by the Vatican (his bone fragments have been packaged and authenticated in Rome and are now available in various mountings for donations ranging from $25-$250; contact the Roman Catholic Church). The mission actually was a successful operation until most of the Indians were killed off by an epidemic that lasted four years (1777-80). The mission was abandoned in 1818, and since then has been melting in the sun. A more interesting historical statement might be the **Indian petroglyphs** chipped into a canyon wall half a mile NW of the mission. The mission ruins lie 3.2 miles west of Hwy. 1; turn off at the Km 114 marker, 37.5 miles south of Rosario.

EL MÁRMOL

Its name is a misnomer, since it was onyx, not marble, that was mined from the quarry, abandoned since 1958. The only structure left standing is its most heralded attraction: the world's only schoolhouse built of onyx, now roofless. Other remnants include an onyx cistern, a cemetery, and blocks of stacked onyx. The arrival of plastics technology put an end to the quarry and village. But in this age of imitation, nature continues to produce; a jeep and foot trail continues a long four miles to El Volcán, where an active soda spring with occasional gysers is creating a new generation of onyx. El Mármol is reached via nine dusty miles east of Hwy. 1; the turnoff is just south of Café Tres Enriques, 56 miles south of El Rosario.

CATAVIÑA

Two miles beyond the turnoff to El Mármol, along a dirt road that parallels the highway, there is a shrine to La Virgen, where there are some trees that shouldn't be growing here except that they were planted and watered years ago by faithful travelers passing by. Even if La Virgen is not good for a few pesos, the vegetation is worth a dollop from your canteen as a way of paying homage to this special area called Las Vírgines.

From here begins the national park, a natural rock garden which looks artfully arranged by a higher hand. Boojums sprout from the piles of boulders that seem to have

Arroyo El Palmarito, Cataviña

been dropped from the sky. In the sandy arroyos, bluish fronds from rare blue fan palms (*Erythea armata*) shiver in the slightest breeze. A shimmering stream runs shallow over the rocks and disappears in the sand. Indian paintings color some of the rocks, and numerous petroglyph sites and even rock alignments arranged by the Indians can be found by focused hikers. Above all is the quiet of the central desert, the moan of wind, the call of birds. Few travelers are immune to the spell, and it is well worth the time to spend a night here when passing through.

There are only two hotels. **La Pinta Cataviña** ($$$) is the luxury address here. Though the tennis court and two murky pools are a surprise, so are the high rates posted in the lobby. Maintenance is always a problem in this isolated location, and the air conditioning can shut down at the most inappropriate times. Its barrel-vaulted restaurant is its best feature, a welcome respite from the highway. You can sleep in the bunkhouse at **Rancho Santa Inés** ($) for less than the room tax at La Pinta; the one-

mile road to the ranch turns off Hwy. 1 a mile south of La Pinta Hotel. Campers can park at the ranch for a token charge, and those just passing through can eat at the outdoor counter here, or make a donation for a shower.

There is an RV park at Cataviña, but few will appreciate the humor of its cyclone fence in this vast unpeopled desert. Best primitive camping site is two miles north of La Pinta Hotel, where a dirt road drops off the east side of the highway to the edge of an arroyo.

INDIAN CAVE

Two miles north of La Pinta Hotel, a large arroyo (*El Palmarito*) crosses Hwy. 1. Walking east up the arroyo, you can make out a small sign perched on the far hillside that splits the arroyo. This sign marks the location of an **Indian Cave** richly painted with polychromatic designs. Though the cave's purpose is unknown, it still works its magic on anyone willing to sit in its dark recess, surrounded by the symbols of a lost culture.

MISSIONS LOST & FOUND

From Santa Inés, a 14-mile dirt road (possibly navigable by four-wheel drive but best walked) leads to a spring oasis, croaking with frogs, where you will find the foundations of **Misión de Santa Maria de los Angeles** still standing. Short-lived, it was founded by Padre Arnés in 1767, one year before all the Jesuits were exiled to Europe. A chapel was built here by the Franciscans in 1768, but the site was completely abandoned one year later.

According to a legend scorned by most historians, another mission site, called **Santa Isabel**, lies somewhere near Misión Santa María. During their 70-year tenure of the peninsula, the Jesuits were thought to have gained a fortune in pearls, gold and silver (in truth, they lived in poverty). When they heard rumors of their forthcoming expulsion, they gathered the wealth of all their missions, sequestering it in a deep gorge, a site they called Santa Isabel. They closed off the entrance to the gorge by landslide. There have actually been serious expeditions seeking this lost mission.

LAGUNA CHAPALA

This lake bed has no exit to the sea. Little need for one, since rarely does water gather here. Sand blown from this dry lakebed has built into dunes on the south end, leaving the lake's dry surface of sun-cracked red clay hard enough to drive on. The highway skirts the edge of the lake bed at Rancho Nueva Chapala.

On the north edge of Laguna Chapala, 33 miles south of Cataviña, a washboard road runs 38 miles to Bahía de San Luís Gonzaga and on to Puertecitos (87 miles away) and San Felipe (143 miles). See Puertecitos section for more detail.

SIDE TRIP TO MISIÓN SAN BORJA & BAHÍA DE LOS ANGELES

Thirty miles south of Laguna Chapala, a 42-mile long paved road runs to Bahía de los Angeles. This narrow road winds through the sierras, skirts a dry lake bed, and drops down through a bare landscape to the Gulf, passing a turn-off to Misión San Borja.

MISIÓN SAN BORJA

The Grand Duchess in Spain, Señora María Borja (of the infamous Borgia family) donated money for a new mission under one strange condition: that it be built in a remote and inaccessible location, which is the one great truth about this abandoned mission. If you don't have 4WD or high clearance, you best stay on the pavement. Founded in 1759 by the Jesuits at the spring of Adac (water still pools behind the church), it wasn't until 1801 that this graceful Moorish-styled building with a vaulted roof and carved portals was erected by the Dominicans. By 1818, it lay abandoned, its belltower never completed since there were no Indians left to call to service.

Considered the third most impressive mission on the peninsula after San Javier and San Ignacio, it is still used occasionally by passing priests for the benefit of the few families that live here. On October 10th there is a fiesta which draws together the local rancheros.

The signed dirt road leaves the road to Bahía de los Angeles at the 40K marker (24 miles from Hwy. 1) and runs about 22 miles to the mission. An alternate route (same distance, better road) leaves Hwy. 1 at Rosarito, 32 miles south of the Bahía de los Angeles turnoff.

ROCK ART

Though the dirt road to Misión San Borja may be too ambitious for casual travelers, you can reach an admirable rock art site a third of the way in, a destination in itself. Take the signed entrance to San Borja at the 40K marker of the road to Bahía de los Angeles. At 1.8 miles you will come to a Y in the road, marked by a white post. Turn left. After passing through a *cardonal* (cardon forest), at 6.3 miles you will reach the pictographs. Look for them at the bottom of some steep cliffs to the northeast of the road. These paintings are geometric rather than anthropomorphic like ones found farther south on the peninsula.

BAHÍA DE LOS ANGELES

Bahía de los Angeles is a nude beauty. The landscape is bald of vegetation. The setting sun brings out the true geologic colors of the earth: red swaths of volcanic stone, grey ash piles, the burnt umber of a distant ridge, bleached guano-covered rocks, the variegated hues of the offshore islands, and the mineral blue of this deep bay. The only natural burst of greenery is on a hillside behind the Casa Díaz, marking a spring (where you can fill your water jugs).

In 1746, when the Jesuit missionary Padre Fernando Consag first explored the bay, he was drawn in by this same "verdue of the herbs growing near the springs." On landing, he was attacked by a tribe of Indians. He was offended not so much by the violence, but by the "total nakedness of the girls," and he prayed that "by the light of faith they will come to see the turpitude of such nudity."

The Indians were later clothed and moved 15 miles inland to the new mission at San Borja, where by 1811 only 200 of the 3,000 survived. In 1880, an American company moved into the vacuum, searching for silver at **Los Flores**, ten miles from the present town, mining two million dollars worth of ore before the Revolution of 1910 brought a sudden end to their endeavor. Attention

turned to the sea, and a fishing village slowly evolved, mostly focusing on shark livers (sold for its vitamin E) and the harpooning of green turtles.

In the 1940s, history came a circle when a group of disenchanted office workers, fleeing the "turpitude" of Mexico City, came to this barren bay to found a nudist colony. They settled near Punta Gringa, and set up an outpost on waterless Smith Island. The utopian colony was short-lived under this blistering sun.

Synthetic vitamins put an end to the shark-fishing. The turtles were slaughtered to the point of diminishing returns.

Enter Antero Díaz. He sized up the tourist potential of this bay, and almost singlehandedly built the air strip and fishing resort that today stands as the kingpin of this modest community that clings to the shore of the bay. Though vestiges of this history can still be glimpsed, most people visit Bahía de los Angeles to fish, to camp, and to soak in the raw natural history of this bay.

Caguama

PLACES
Museo de Naturaleza y Cultura.
Built on goodwill and donations, this small museum behind the main square provides a crash course on the natural and human history of the bay, with the hope that you will be less likely to go out and inadvertently tramp on the delicate eco-system. Whalebones are on display. Cochimi Indian artifacts. A shell collection. Mining paraphernalia. Photo exhibits. If lucky, you can catch the slide show on the ecology of the area. The museum opens only for a few hours in the afternoon, but even if its closed you can look at the mine shaft replica and ball mill outside, and memorize the names of plants in the botanic garden.

Campo Archeleone
Twenty years the turtle fishery supported the village. Now Green Turtles are an endangered species, illegal to catch or sell, but this doesn't stop their clandestine slaughter. *Caguama* (turtle) is sold openly in many grocery stores in Mexico. Antonio Reséndiz of the Institute of Pesca and his wife Beatrice Jiménez have dedicated themselves to saving the turtles. Helped in part

by organizations such as Greenpeace and the Sea Turtle Center, and using their own meager salaries complemented by donations, they have built three turtle pens on land donated by the local ejido.

They now care for 34 turtles: loggerheads, green sea turtles, extremely rare hawkbills, two Atlantic turtles from Scripps and two Pacific turtles. By researching growth rates and learning how to take care of these terrapins in captivity, they hope to create a raise-and-release program that will help re-populate the species. They once cared for 44 turtles, until some misguided gringos decided to re-populate the species on their own, releasing ten of the turtles in a midnight raid on the pens. Like a dog biting its tail, the eco-guerillas, thinking the turtles were awaiting slaughter, unknowingly destroyed years of research.

You are welcome to visit the turtle pens, and even more welcome to pitch some money into the donation box. Camping is possible in a forlorn trailer park not ten yards from the pens, near Punta Arena.

Punta Gringa
The north end of Bahía de los Angeles is protected by a hook of land called Punta Gringa, which faces numerous islets offshore, fringed by pebble beaches and backed by a boggy marsh alive with long-legged waterbirds. Along the shore is a fish camp that boils sea cucumbers brought in by divers for export to Hong Kong. Just beyond is a fine bayside campsite, worth the seven-mile drive to get here. Two roads run from the village to the point, one a whoop-de-do affair that humps along the shoreline passing several fine camping sites, the other flat and washboardy, running inland straight to the point. Since this is all ejido land, you usually will have to pay a minimum fee for primitive camping along this shore.

Las Flores
About 10 miles south of the village lie the remains of Las Flores mine, abandoned in

1912. Ore was carried from the mines by a 2.5 mile wire tramway, and then by seven miles of narrow-gauge railway to the smelter at Las Flores. Little remains besides some dangerous mine shafts, a smelter, and a boiler. The locomotive and many artifacts are now in the Museo de la Naturaleza y Cultura.

BAHÍA SAN FRANCISQUITO

A graded dirt road continues past the ruins of Las Flores to Bahía San Francisquito, 82 miles from Bahía de los Angeles, a smoother approach than the alternate 75-mile long road that passes through El Arco. Primitive camping spots along the way can be found at **Bahía de los Animas**. There is a rustic accommodation at San Francisquito, the Punta San Francisquito Resort where there are a score of modest cabins, with a restaurant, common bathroom and airstrip. If you don't like the cots, you can camp on the beach and use their public facilities.

Fishing & Diving

Though the water is too cold for billfish or dorado, there are numerous smaller species for the taking. April to October is the most productive time if you can take the heat: sierra, cabrilla, roosterfish, grouper, yellowtail, and corvina. Late summer is best for dorado, October the peak month for yellowtail. Samuel Díaz, next door to Casa Díaz, sets the rate standard for boat rentals here. Boats can also be contracted at Guillermo's. A cheaper price can sometimes be negotiated out at Punta Gringa, which is closer to best fishing grounds.

Divers should be self-sufficient, as compressors in town are not reliable. Most interesting diving is along offshore islands, as the shoreline is uniformly bare and boring. There are launch ramps at Guillermo's and Casa Díaz.

Warning: during the winter and spring, water in the bay can be too cool for swimming or snorkeling without a wetsuit (though winter water temperatures rarely drop be-low 60F). Water is clearer, tides not as great as the upper Gulf, but powerful tidal currents race around the islands offshore. Dives should be done during slack tide, or with somebody following you with a boat.

PLACES TO SLEEP
Hotels

Accommodations, all of which are set back from the shore, are rustic and often plagued with maintenance problems, electrical outages, and water shortages. Electricity usually shuts down by 10 p.m.

Casa Díaz ($$; PO Box 579, Ensenada) is the pioneer resort here, a simple operation of 15 stone cabins that open onto common verandas, set back 100 yards from shore behind the Pemex station. Besides a small grocery store, there is a family-style restaurant that may or may not be open. Some prefer the more expensive **Villa Vitta** ($$; tel: 619-298-4958 in San Diego), which would be a fine resort in Loreto or La Paz, but is a bit too ambitious for this austere area: the pool might be empty, the air conditioning dysfunctional, the restaurant closed depending on the occupancy level. Appropriately named **Mini-Hotel** ($), run by owners of Las Hamacas restaurant, offers three large but basic sleeping rooms with views out over trailer park to bay.

Camping

With so much camping space around, to sleep in a walled-in cubicle seems ironic. Of the three trailer parks in the village, **Guillermo's** is the most popular, with the result that overnighters have been crowded off the beachfront by long term renters; some hook-ups are available. **Casa Díaz Trailer Park** is set back from shore. Its bay views are obstructed by vacation homes, but it offers full hook-ups. **La Playa Trailer Park**, run by Villa Vitta Motel, offers the only in-village trailer park with beachfront sites free of permanent campers. There is a marginally maintained trailer park a mile north of town, next to the turtle pens at

Campo Archeleone. Camping can be found in most any clearing by the sea between the village and Punta Gringa (where a few trailer parks are springing up), but you will most likely be charged a minimal access fee by the ejido or a concessionaire.

BAHÍA ADDENDUM

Have your flashlight handy by 10 p.m., when the town blacks out. Food supplies are best brought in. Selection is scanty and usually comes in cans.

No banks. Be sure to bring all the money you are going to use in cash, and in pesos. Don't expect to use a credit card, since there are no phones to verify your account.

The gas station is frequently out of Nova (no MagnaSin), so make sure you have enough to get you out to the nearest reliable gas station: Cataviña going north (105 miles), or Guerrero Negro going south (121 miles). The gas station at Punta Prieta is not so reliable.

You can leave outgoing mail in the care of the Pemex gas station, which will hand it off to those driving to Ensenada, a tenuous but usually reliable system.

Incoming mail can be received on arrangement through the Díaz post office box in Ensenada.

Summers can be blistering hot (100F during the day, 80F at night). During winter, the bay occasionally is swept by northers or by winds that drop out of the canyons at gale force, blowing camping equipment into the bay.

THE MIDRIFF

This middle part of the gulf, called the Midriff, is girded by islands which pinch the strong tidal currents, causing eddies and surface upwellings which bring up cold water from below, making the surface temperatures off Bahía de los Angeles the coldest in the gulf. This agitation injects oxygen into the water, acting like a fertilizer for the growth of immense populations of microscopic plants and animals, the first rung of a prolific food chain that has important hemispheric consequences. Sardines proliferate in these plankton-rich waters. Besides supporting large numbers of gamefish, they also maintain the bird populations. (If sardines are scarce one year, the birds lay fewer eggs. By counting birds, biologists can gauge the number of sardines).

These cold waters and bare offshore islands are a giant nursery ground for whole populations of migratory birds, whales, and fish, making this a prime sighting ground for naturalists, and an area crucial to the survival of many wild species.

You might see huge finback whales, humpbacks, sperms, brydes, and an occasional blue whale, the world's largest animal. Leaping dolphins are a common sight. On the islands in the bay alone, there are over 152 species of birds. Binoculars and a copy of Peterson's Birds of North America should be standard issue.

There are many islands in the midriff, all

SAVE THE TURTLES

The non-profit SEA TURTLE CENTER, in conjunction with Antonio Reséndiz, has become involved in conservation programs in the Midriff area, and especially in the islands of Bahía de los Angeles. In order to combat anticipated environmental dangers resulting from tourism and unregulated fishing activities, STC is working to monitor bird populations, identify problems and develop recommendations to lesson the impact of tourism. They welcome all the help they can get. Contact: STC; Nevada Center, PO Box 634, Nevada City, CA 95959.

unique. For example, four-mile long **Isla San Esteban** is home to an estimated 4,500 rare blotched chuckwalla lizards. Their numbers have dwindled, mostly due to agents of the exotic pet trade (lizards are easy to smuggle). The United States has listed them as endangered wildlife, but they are still not protected internationally.

Isla San Pedro Martír was mined for guano at the turn of the century, and the collectors actually built terraces for the nesting birds as a way to increase production, causing later explorers to feel they had discovered some ancient Mayan civilization. This island is a breeding ground for blue-footed and brown boobies.

The 42-mile island that reclines on the horizon off Bahía de los Angeles is **Isla Angel de la Guarda**, the second largest in the gulf (Tiburón is the largest). It has always been uninhabited (except by an over-abundance of rattlesnakes). Padre Linck was one of the first to explore it in 1765 after some Indians sighted fires on the island. He found no Indians, no footprints, no water. The mysterious fires have since been explained by historians as St. Elmo's Fire, supposedly a common occurance on gulf islands in clear cool weather.

ISLA LA RAZA
Of all the islands of the midriff, the most interesting is **Isla La Raza,** about 40 miles from Bahía de los Angeles. Though comprising only 140 rocky acres, it is the only known breeding ground of the elegant tern, as well as 95 percent of the world's population of Heermann's Gulls (they range from Guatemala to Vancouver Island). One person tramping across this island during the April-May breeding season can provoke a whole colony to rise in the air, leaving eggs and chicks exposed to predator birds. Some birds, such as the elegant tern, can be safely observed only from a distance of 100 meters.

Biologists live on Raza (declared a wildlife preserve in 1964) from March to July to study and protect the birds from egg collectors and other unwanted intruders, and you need to hail them from a boat in order to gain permission to land here (inquire for current regulations at Bahía de los Angeles). Trips can be arranged from either Bahía de los Angeles or San Francisquito.

Best time to visit: after the first of May when the eggs have hatched; it takes about two months after hatching before the baby gulls take to the air.

Isla Raza once was considered a sacred burial ground of the Seri Indians, and legend has it that a monument was erected for each tribal death. Egg collectors noticed that the ground bared by the gathering of rocks for monuments attracted even more bird nests. Over the years, this stacking of stones covered the entire island. This is one of the more plausible explanations for the mysterious stone piles. Another theory is that guano collectors stacked the stones so it would be easier to scrape up the natural fertilizer that these birds produce in copious amounts (as at Isla Martír).

LAGUNA CHAPALA TO GUERRERO NEGRO

From Laguna Chapala, Hwy. 1 runs 71 miles to Guerrero Negro, winding out of the mountains, and running three to ten miles inland from the coast, offering easy access to Pacific beaches.

BAHIA SANTA ROSALILLITA

This broad bay is famed for the legendary mile-long ride on a surfboard (not to be confused with San Blas in the state of Nayarit, which makes a similar claim). Consequently, this point break is mostly visited by surfers and sailboarders, who are about the only ones who appreciate the afternoon northwesterlies. South of the fishing cooperative (no supplies available), you can pitch camp on the bluffs or head north to sleep among the sand dunes. Road to the bay is 39 miles south of the Bahía de los Angeles turn-off, at K38. The ten-mile graded dirt road to the coast is car-safe.

EL TOMATAL & MILLER'S LANDING

The closest Pacific beach access from Hwy. 1 between El Rosario and Todos Santos 790 miles to the south is at El Tomatal (8.6 miles south of Santa Rosalillita), where there is a broad sandy beach just three miles off the pavement. A camp site can be made on the flats next to a bearded grove of date palms along a brackish lagoon, but you may have to share space with idling trucks awaiting shipment from the fish camp located a quarter mile south along this beach. For complete isolation, backtrack 0.2 miles from the beach, and turn south onto the dirt road that heads along the coast. Follow your instincts for two miles and you will arrive at Miller's Landing, once one of the loading sites for the onyx mine at El Mármol. All that is left are a few yellow-crusted blocks of onyx, mute testimony of labor lost.

LAGUNA MANUELA

This saltwater estuary lies in the southern shadow of Morro Santo Domingo, which protects it from unruly waves. Previously called Santo Domingo Landing, it was a supply point for the Calmalli mines during the early 1900s. No supplies today, though you can buy fresh oysters from the oyster farm and lobster from the fishermen. The bay curves off for 12 miles to the south, and the rocky point is home to a seal rookery. This area is visited mainly by fishermen cruising the eelgrass beds and casting out over the sandbars; there is little area for camping and the high tides of winter and early spring can flood the area. Turn-off from Hwy. 1 just north of the K96 marker, and take the flat washboard road seven miles to the lagoon.

SARAFAN DUNES

Baja's Sahara lies two miles off the highway, 2.5 miles north of the giant steel eagle that marks the state boundary. Unanchored by vegetation and bordered to the west by Laguna Guerrero Negro, this vast virgin dune area moves about like a living thing, blown by Pacific breezes that will quickly erase your footprints, leaving you disoriented as you wander its 16 square miles of vales and valleys. Bring a compass and canteen.

PARALELO 28

Latitude 28 is the dividing line between the states of Baja California and Baja California Sur, marked by a 140 foot monument, an abstract eagle of heroic proportions, wings raised, talons down. The stadium, cultural center, and school around it have been abandoned to the elements, a fitting tribute to the desolation of the Vizcaino desert.

El Solitario, Agua Verde

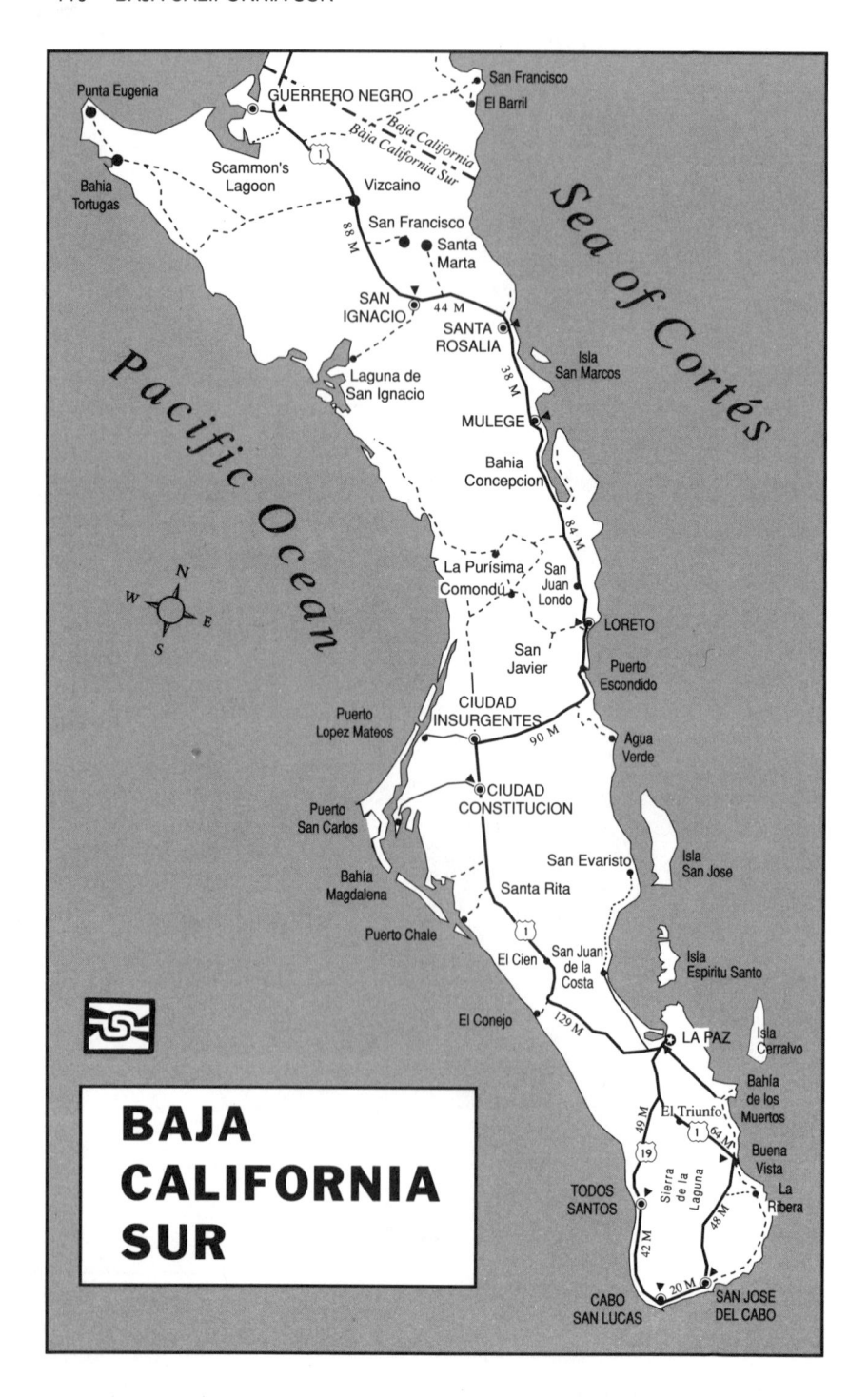

Punta Eugenia

GUERRERO NEGRO

San Francisco
El Barril

Baja California
Baja California Sur

Scammon's Lagoon

Bahia Tortugas

Vizcaino

San Francisco

Santa Marta

88 M

SAN IGNACIO

44 M

SANTA ROSALIA

Isla San Marcos

Laguna de San Ignacio

38 M

MULEGE

Sea of Cortés

Bahia Concepcion

84 M

Pacific Ocean

La Purísima
Comondú

San Juan Londo

N
W   E
S

LORETO

San Javier

Puerto Escondido

Puerto Lopez Mateos

CIUDAD INSURGENTES

90 M

Agua Verde

Puerto San Carlos

CIUDAD CONSTITUCION

San Evaristo

Isla San Jose

Bahía Magdalena

Santa Rita

Isla Espiritu Santo

Puerto Chale

1

San Juan de la Costa

El Cien

El Conejo

129 M

LA PAZ

Isla Cerralvo

Bahía de los Muertos

El Triunfo

49 M

1   64 M

19

Buena Vista

TODOS SANTOS

Sierra de la Laguna

48 M

La Ribera

42 M

20 M

CABO SAN LUCAS

SAN JOSE DEL CABO

BAJA CALIFORNIA SUR

9.
Baja California Sur

GUERRERO NEGRO

Guerrero Negro is a bleak, windswept place of horizontal lines, as elemental as the shallow lagoon to which it owes its existence. A growing string of cinderblock restaurants, hotels, auto repair shops, gas stations, and supermarkets cling to both sides of the long road leading into the older company town, rarely entered by most travelers; this is where the municipal buildings, post office and local stores are located.

Guerrero Negro may not be pretty, but it is a functional stop for travelers in need of auto repair, gas, a bed, medical attention, money, or a meal. It also offers a cool respite from the overheated temperatures of the Vizcaíno Desert inland. Despite its utilitarian charms, few linger longer than it takes to fill a gas tank, missing out on the natural resources seen in the nearby lagoons: the world's most productive salt flats, as well as its largest nursery for grey whales (see Scammon's Lagoon).

PLACES
Salt tours

If you find yourself in town on a Monday, Wednesday, or Friday morning by 9 a.m., you can find out where half the world's salt comes from. You will be chauffeured in a company car through the entire process. You start at the evaporative ponds south of town (you can catch a glimpse of these on your left as you enter town). High salinity, low rainfall, strong wind, and lack of storms all contribute to a rapid evaporation rate, leaving the pure salt extract to be dredged and dumped onto monstrous trucks. The salt is taken to the quays west of town, put on barges and towed out to Isla Cedros, where it is stored and then shipped on larger vessels, mostly to Mitsubishi (majority partner) in Japan but about a third goes to the U.S. and Canada for pulp and paper manufacturers. The one-hour tours leave from offices at the western end of the business district at 10 a.m., but you must sign in at least a half an hour before. ***Warning:*** *many south-bound travelers forget to reset their watches, missing the tour by an hour.*

Puerto Viejo

From the front of the salt company gate, a wide road hard-coated with salt and gypsum runs eight miles on a high levee, past miles of marsh that make for great winter birding, reaching Laguna Guerrero Negro (not to be confused with Scammon's). There is an abandoned salt-loading port here,

OSPREY

The huge, crudely built nests seen perched atop the tallest *cardones*, or abandoned signposts, belong to the Osprey (Pandion haliaetus), a fishing bird of prey that inhabits much of the coastline of the Baja California peninsula. These permanent residents nest between February and May, normally laying two eggs. If you should enter their territory, you will hear a series of sharp calls. If you persist in approaching the nest, the Osprey may take flight, abandoning the nest. If there are eggs or young chicks, the sudden and excessive cold or heat may kill them. These birds are slow breeders and are already endangered by the pollutants that accumulate in the fish they eat, resulting in eggshell thinning. The loss of a single clutch affects the entire population.

where osprey come to roost in the ruins. Beyond the lighthouse, swift currents race by rusty pilings, where you can sit with a pair of binoculars and watch grey whales from late December to late March. Mario Rueda often runs a 30 ft. barge on whale-watching tours here during February and March, and can be contacted through the Malarrimo Restaurant (before booking, inquire first on the number of whales in this lagoon; it varies greatly depending on how shallow the entrance channel is). Even without whales, the bracing wind, the distant dune fields, virgin marshes, exotic birds, level ground, and a pier to fish from make this a good overnight camp site. *Beachcombing Tip: The beach that stretches between Laguna Guerrero Negro and Scammon's rivals the more famous but less accessible Malarimmo Beach farther south for flotsam and jetsam.*

Arriving & Departing
By Bus

Buses pass through Guerrero Negro hourly both north and south, stopping at the new bus stop at town entrance.

By Car

If you are driving to La Paz, this is the halfway mark.

By Plane

You can catch a DC-3 to Isla Cedros and Bahía Tortuga from the airfield next to the turnoff to Puerto Viejo. Aérolinea California (tel. 7-00-57/55) operates these gooney birds, with inexpensive flights leaving daily at 11 a.m., except on Sundays and Wednesdays. Flights depart from Isla Cedros to Guerrero Negro at 3 p.m.

PLACES TO SLEEP
Hotels

La Pinta Guerrero Negro ($$$), next to the eagle monument three miles from town, is built in the La Pinta courtyard mold, minus the pool. Its isolated location and relatively high rates keep the occupancy down to ghostly levels. Hotel suffers from perennial maintenance problems, and service often falls flat. The best lodging value in town is **Motel El Morro** ($$; PO Box 6, Guerrero Negro); the reading lights are a nice gesture compared to the naked bulbs of its in-town competitors, and it offers the most secure parking lot for those loaded with equipment. Nearby **Dunas Motel** ($) is just that, the rooms often full of gritty sand blown in from its interior parking lot. But it is the second choice here, its clean if worn rooms more comfortable than the cell-like cubicles at the similarly priced

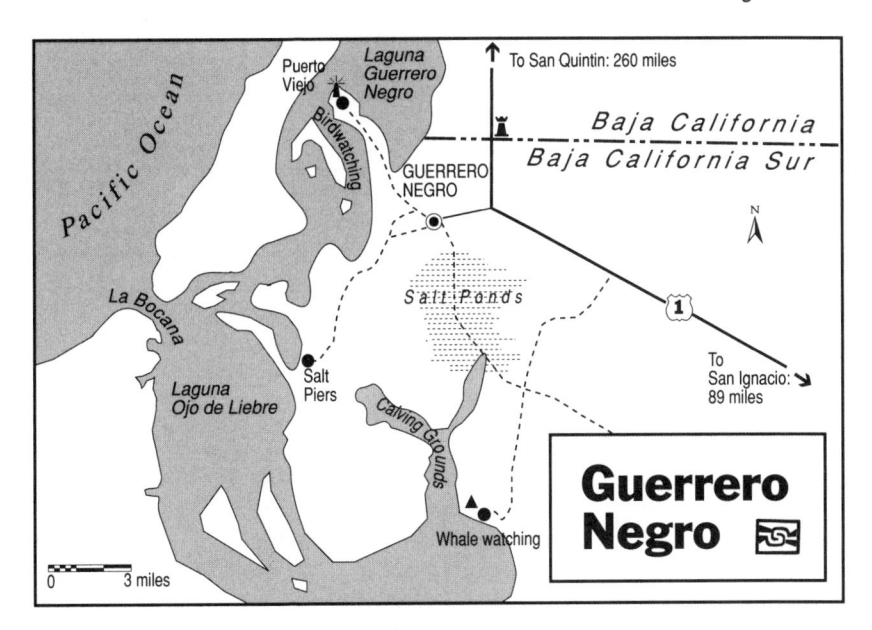

The map shows:
- To San Quintin: 260 miles
- Puerto Viejo
- Laguna Guerrero Negro
- Pacific Ocean
- Birdwatching
- GUERRERO NEGRO
- Baja California / Baja California Sur
- La Bocana
- Salt Ponds
- Laguna Ojo de Liebre
- Salt Piers
- Calving Grounds
- To San Ignacio: 89 miles
- Whale watching
- **Guerrero Negro**
- 0   3 miles

San Ignacio Hotel ($) down the street. For rock bottom lodgings, pass by the **Hotel Gámez** in favor of the **Cuartos de Smith-Sanchez** in the older section of town on Calle Juan de la Barrera. Rooms here have showers, toilets, and are jammed tight with beds; "drunks and scandals are not tolerated in rooms."

Camping

There is a popular trailer court behind the **Malarrimo Restaurant**, with about 14 sites, some with hook-ups, but those who don't want to enter town can pull into **Benito Juárez Trailer Park** next to La Pinta Hotel, where there are 60 mostly empty spaces, with full hook-ups for a dollar more. Free camping can be found out at Puerto Viejo.

ISLA DE CEDROS

On a clear day, you can see Isla de Cedros from Guerrero Negro, a 20-mile long island named for the pine trees on its peaks. The village on its SW flank is reached by an hour-long flight from Guerrero Negro and a long taxi ride into town. Casual travelers

are an oddity in this hardworking village of saltworkers and fishermen (the young but arthritic-looking fishermen you might see suffer from the bends, diving too deep for too long in their search for abalone). Near the airfield, Japanese freighters dock to load the mountains of salt. Besides a modest hostelry, there is a cannery, immigration office (don't forget your tourist card), stores, and homes. Two miles north along the shore is a historic spring first used by the Manila galleons and later by 19th century whalers. From the village, trails cross the island; you might see the endemic species of mule deer. Elephant seals live on the rocky north end.

Arriving & Departing

Except for chartering a boat from Punta Eugenia, Bahía Tortuga, or Guerrero Negro, the only way to get to Isla Cedros is by plane from either Guerrero Negro (leaves daily except Wed. and Sun. at 11 a.m.: phone *Aérolinea California* at 7-00-57/55 in Guerrero Negro) or Ensenada (leaves Tuesdays, Fridays at 10 a.m.; phone Omega Aeroservicios in Ensenada at 6-60-76).

GUERRERO NEGRO TO SAN IGNACIO

THE VIZCAINO DESERT

From Guerrero Negro to San Ignacio, the highway runs 89 miles with the wind at its back, blowing in strongly from the Pacific. This stark desert is flat and bare, the plants widely spaced. Though the wind carries high humidity, little moisture actually drops on this dry region. Ball moss, *Tillandsia recurvata*, thrives, as it obtains moisture directly from the air, but other species struggle to survive. The most successful plant to grow here is the *Yucca valida*, or datillo, which looks like a Joshua tree, characteristically tilting east with the wind.

In the midst of the desert, 22 miles from Guerrero Negro, the desert is furrowed and green, irrigated with water trapped by a groundwater barrier, thanks to a transpeninsular fault crossing the peninsula near the highway. At Ejido Vizcaíno, deep wells bring up enough water to support a bustling farming community growing red and yellow spices. Where there is water, the desert proves as rich as an Iowa cornfield.

SCAMMON'S LAGOON

Otherwise known as Laguna Ojo de Liebre, this is the world's largest nursery for the gray whale. The 16 mile sandy access road leaves Hwy. 1 at 5.5 miles east of the junction to Guerrero Negro, at the K208 marker. On the shores of the lagoon, the camping sites are primitive and unsheltered from an often cold wind; the local ejido collects a small camping fee. Mornings and evenings seem to be the best time for sightings from shore. Bring binoculars, or else hire a panga and go out to the isthmus. It is illegal to launch your own boat into the lagoon if it has an engine. If the whalewatching is slack, you can always turn your binoculars to the great variety of wintering waterbirds that stalk the tidal flats. Beware when driving in this area not to stray onto the salt operations.

Whalewatching Tip: Scammon's is not the best place to watch whales, especially if you don't have a boat (most whale action is far from shore). Better spots include Laguna San Ignacio and Bahía Magdalena, the latter where you can still launch a boat without permission.

Gray Whales

The most primitive of living baleen whales (Eschrichtius gibbosus), the gray whales filter their food through long plates of baleen in shallow water, characteristically feeding on their right side, sanding one side of their heads clean. The rest of their bodies are blotchy with barnacles, scars, and parasites, making them appear gray, hence their name. Up to 50 foot in length, they swim leisurely and surface frequently, buoyed by great reserves of fat, making them prime candidates for a harpoon (up to 50 barrels of oil can be rendered from one whale).

When Captain Scammon first discovered the nursery in 1856, he rapidly decimated the herd. Whaling in confined shallow waters was much easier than in open ocean; by attacking the calves, they could lure the cows to their longboats. By 1890, there weren't many cows left, and for the next 40 years only 30 gray whales were taken. Their extinction was assumed. After a brief, mad flurry of whaling in the 1930s, an international agreement in 1938 saved the last 100 or so remaining grays. They have since proven resilient; grays have grow in number by 10 to 11 percent each year. Now there are as many as 18,000 grays cruising the Baja coastline, their estimated pre-whaling population.

The grays arrive at Scammon's in early January after a 5,000 mile migration, the longest for any mammal. The first to arrive are pregnant females (gestation takes about 13 months). Many of the bulls, calf-less cows, and juveniles spend their time outside of the lagoons or near the entrances. Calves, born tail first, weigh 2,000 pounds and measure 12 feet at birth. Sucking on fat-rich mother's milk, calves grow so quickly they are hard to tell from their mothers as they leave the lagoons in March or April, though they will stick by their mother's side for at least a year. The herds reach the Bering Sea in May or June.

Breaching: Launching out of the water, a whale will twist and fall on top of its head, often repeated two or three times. They are either shaking off parasites, or jumping for the fun of it.

Spyhopping: Whale rises up, its 4-inch eye above the water, often repeated. Reason: to clean their baleen plates, or perhaps to just look around.

Surface Swimming and Fluke Dive: Whales will often swim at 3 to 5 m.p.h., surfacing every 30 seconds. After three to five breaths, they often dive deeper, showing their massive tail fluke, and staying under for a few minutes.

Note: though you can't see births, which happen underwater, you can spot their occurrence by great flocks of gulls gathering to eat the afterbirth.

MALARRIMO

This is the most famous beachcombing spot on the west coast of North America, reaching out to grab whatever flotsam and jetsam has been circulating around the Pacific. People have found everything from ancient shipwrecks to human skeletons. But it is very hard to reach and should only be attempted in high clearance vehicles, preferably 4WD. For information on the easiest way to get there, inquire at Malarrimo Restauant in Guerrero Negro.

BAHÍA TORTUGAS

From Ejido Vizcaíno, 43 miles from Guerrero Negro, a graded dirt road runs to Bahía Tortugas, a deep protected bay halfway down the length of the peninsula. While the town itself is not worth the 111 dusty miles it takes to get there, the bay is a strategic R&R stop for yachts cruising up and down the coast, an excellent spot to grab a berth as crew. The road is fairly well traveled by fishermen, and you should be able to swing a ride from Ejido Vizcaíno. Best times of year to catch a ride: early winter for boats going south (a downhill slide), spring for boats going north (a tough, bumpy trip).

EL ARCO

This gold mining town, two miles north of the state boundary and reached by a 25-mile once-paved road, was developed by an American company in the 1920s, but a miner's strike put an end to the enterprise. The town has since been slowly evaporating, especially now that the highway has been re-routed around it. It is not really worth the detour unless you are a rockhound, or are on your way to Bahía San Francisquito, 75 miles from Hwy. 1 (a better road runs down from Bahía de los Angeles).

SAN IGNACIO

San Ignacio is about water, shade, and coolness. Whether coming up from the scorched, volcanic wasteland or across the bleak Vizcaíno desert, you will find refuge in this green arroyo, a genuine oasis among the basaltic outcroppings. A wild forest of more than 80,000 date palms traces its roots to seedlings planted by the Jesuits in 1756. Freshwater pools, ringed with tules and oozy with mud, resound with mysterious plops and splashes, the call of birds. The zócalo is dark under a canopy of ancient Indian laurel trees. Across the street, inside the mission, you can sit in complete silence, separated from the heat by four-foot-thick walls of lava rock.

The people who live here also seem cool, yet polite. You may think you are getting the cold shoulder, but it is really more a question of manners. The culture here is Castillian, brought by the early Spanish settlers and soldiers. The people are polite in a stiff-spined way. These courtly manners—the limp handshake, the soft voice—have only been accentuated by the isolation and quiet of these mountains. The same families have lived in this region for generations; the phone book is full of Arces and Villavicencios, families whose chromosomes are linked to the Spanish soldiers Juan de Arce and José Villavicencio who accompanied the missionaries here.

It is this feeling of contentedness with place that makes this oasis so appealing. It also makes it frustrating for travelers seeking a restaurant or a hotel. Facilities are few. Tourism is not sought, because that would mean change, and change sounds suspiciously like something that would disturb this town's historic slumber.

PLACES
Misión San Ignacio

Though the mission was originally established by the Jesuits in 1728 and named after San Ignacio de Loyola, the founder of the Society of Jesus, credit for its final construction goes to the Dominican Padre Gómez, who finished it in 1786, using the original plans. Built of hand-hewn basalt, its gracefully vaulted roof shelters a baroque altar leafed in gold, the most elaborate and best preserved of the peninsula's missions. Though founded when 5,000 Indians were living at this place they called Kadacaamán (Arroyo of the Swamp Grass), at its completion, only a couple hundred Indians remained.

Swimming Holes

The springs of San Ignacio make for great swimming. The closest swimming hole is where the road to town crosses the river, but the best spot, complete with watersnakes, is at La Candelaria Trailer Park; a small day use fee is charged if the owner happens to be around.

Zócalo

Most business is taken care of by parking at the zócalo, where you can visit the church, take on water from a spigot, make a phone call at the telephone office, mail a letter, go to the bank, pick up groceries, or grab a bite to eat before heading back out of town.

Events

The Date Harvest festival in held the end of July. There is no systematic cultivation of dates. They are picked whenever the ripen. *Tip: don't eat these dates in the dark.*

Arriving, Departing

San Ignacio is situated one mile off the highway. Unfortunately, the bus no longer enters town, instead letting passengers off at the Pemex gas station, which means it's either a $2 taxi ride or a pleasant half hour walk into town.

Misión San Ignacio

PLACES TO SLEEP
Hotels

A grim picture if you don't have a sleeping bag. There are only 34 hotel rooms, 28 at the pricey yet attractive **Hotel La Pinta** ($$$) located on the fringe of town with its own chlorinated pool, and six more at the spartan **La Posada Motel** ($$), three blocks back from the zócalo. La Pinta gets mostly tired overnighters, while La Posada harbors mainly expedition-type people getting ready to go out on cave-painting trips organized by the owner of the motel, Oscar Fisher.

Camping

The ejido-run **San Ignacio Trailer Park** lies behind the Pemex station along the highway, but this location hardly seems worth the convenience of hook-ups, when for the same price you can camp in a primitive palm grove at the edge of a freshwater pool at **La Candelaria**; bring bug spray. Several other primitive RV camps open and close sporadically.

San Ignacio Addendum

The modest **Loncheria Chalita** facing the square offers the quickest and cheapest Mexican meal. A more expensive alternative is **Restaurant Tato**, a small shack of a restaurant, one of those hideaway places you think you are the first to discover, only to find an entire wall plastered with business cards ranging from IBM account executives to International Harvestor salesmen. The only substantial restaurant is in the cool brick vault of **La Pinta Hotel.** Look for the roadstop **Quichule** (don't dare come in without a shirt on) on the west side by the fruit inspection post.

BACKCOUNTRY SIDETRIPS
Whales at Laguna San Ignacio

This Pacific lagoon, two to four miles wide, is home to the so-called "friendly whales," and is a better place to view gray whales than at Scammon's, since they usually swim much closer to shore. Panga drivers can be hired so the whales can get a better look at you. Though controversy rages as to whether these whales are being friendly or just using you to scratch their parasites, this is the bay where you can come closest to touching one. The trip from San Ignacio to Laguna San Ignacio takes about 2 hours to cover the 46 miles of sedan-safe dirt road. Once there, try to set up as close to Punta Prieta as possible, where a whale camp is usually set up. *Tip: If you lack wheels, go to the operating base of **Cooperativa Laguna de San Ignacio**, opposite the La Pinta Hotel. They run trucks back and forth daily, and you can usually arrange a ride with the dispatcher.*

Cave Paintings in the Sierras

Two improved roads have opened up access to some of the most striking cave paintings on the peninsula. At the K118 marker about 28 miles west of San Ignacio, a serpentine road rises 23 miles up the Arroyo de San Pablo, reaching the small village of **San Francisco** (motorhomes have

made the trip). A mile before you get to the village, just off the road on the eastern edge of a ridge, there is a sign for **Cueva Ratón.** A large overhang displays an array of deer, rabbit, sheep, men, and a curious black mountain lion. Go first into the village to arrange for a guide; it is against the law to visit to the paintings without one.

Another dirt road leaves the highway at K59, 9 miles east of San Ignacio, for **Rancho Santa Marta**, 28 miles away. Here you can arrange for a guide to take you to see **Cueva Palmarito**, a two-hour hike on an old section of El Camino Real, the mission trail. Beside depictions of large deer and a mountain lion, this 150 ft. mural emphasizes a collection of human figures with headdresses, and red figures that appear to be wearing black pants (which the missionaries seized on as proof that a more virtuous, less naked people once lived in these mountains). It must have been a virtuous time indeed; animals are similarly clothed.

Three-day mule expeditions to even more spectacular sites can be taken from San Francisco or Santa Marta. You can arrange them yourself at these villages, or use Oscar Fisher, owner of the La Posada Motel in San Ignacio, as point man. He charges for transportation to the villages, and arranges for guides and mules. Bring your own food (and food for the guides). Baja Expeditions organizes week-long treks into these mountains; phone 800-843-6967 for catalog. **Best Resource:** The Cave Paintings of Baja California, by Harry Crosby, Copely Books, La Jolla CA, 1984.

SAN IGNACIO TO SANTA ROSALÍA

The 45 miles between San Ignacio and Santa Rosalía take you from the Central Desert to the gulf, a sudden drop in both altitude and attitidue.

TRES VÍRGENES

East of San Ignacio 25 miles, the landscape turns igneous, as the highway cuts through black lava flows (the missionaries wrote of an eruption in 1746). To the north you can see a stark group of volcanos, the Tres Vírgenes (the Three Virgins), the tallest rising over 6,000 feet. The sight is primevally spellbinding, but don't gaze too hypnotically, for the highway drops suddenly and steeply down the Cuesta de las Vírgenes. About the time you start worrying about your brake fluid, it drops yet steeper down the infamous Cuesta del Infiernillo. As you fall down to sea level, temperatures rise.

This sunbaked terrain, bare of vegetation but rich in minerals, seems purgatorial, a place to galvanize your spirit before reaching the shores of the Sea of Cortés, which shines on the horizon like a pool of quicksilver. *Tip: plan to go up these grades in the early morning or late evening if your engine is prone to overheating.*

PLAYA SANTA MARÍA

Where the highway hits the shore, 4.5 miles north of Santa Rosalía, a dirt road leaves the pavement, traveling north to a pier where *yeso* (gypsum) is loaded onto ships. Before reaching the pier, 2.8 miles from the highway, there is a stony beach called Santa María, with some primitive campsites; this is no match for the calcium-white beaches farther south, though they are the most private to be found near Santa Rosalía.

SANTA ROSALÍA

Santa Rosalía is the antithesis of a mission oasis: built of imported wood instead of local stone, for money instead of God, by foreigners instead of Mexicans, in an area dry of water and bare of shade. The town bears an unmistakable Gallic stamp, arrogant in its physical layout, a company town designed in Paris.

As a way to check a growing American presence on the peninsula, Porfirio Díaz granted the French a concession to mine the copper here in 1884, giving them mineral rights and control over 2,000 square miles (including the people who happened to be living there as well).

Sixteen years before, Rosas Villavicencio had found little balls (*boleos*) of copper carbonate. Local merchants lacked the money to mine the ore. The French had the money, and *Comagnie du Boleo*, financed by the Rothschild banking interests, was formed. A smelter was built, tracks laid, water brought in 10 miles by pipe. Company ranches were built to supply food to the 8,000 Yaqui Indians brought in to work mines called *Purgatorio* and *Soledad*.

The French overseers built their own little island of provincial charm atop the northern mesa, while the Mexican government and garrison were sequestered on the southern mesa. Below, where the grime from the smelter tended to settle, the Yaqui laborers lived in a streamlined town of standardized housing, each unit with an identical floor plan, the boards hammered on horizontally. The harbor, built in 1905 from slag (the fused by-product of the smelter) sheltered one of the largest fleets of square-riggers in the world, bringing in coke from Hamburg to fuel the smelter, carrying the copper bars back to Europe or to Tacoma, Washington.

Mining activities ceased in 1953. Two years later, a Mexican company started up three of the eight furnaces of the smelter, but recently the mining operation has stopped altogether. The soot is gone, though the threat to re-open the mines still hangs over this town. Most residents prefer the foundry to remain closed.

The social segregation has since broken down, slag dumped offshore has washed up to color the beaches as black as those in Hawaii, the shade trees have filled in, and the distinctive French colonial architecture has gained a kind of decadent beauty. Santa Rosalía may yet emerge like a Cinderella from the slag heaps of its history.

PLACES

Templo Santa Bárbara

This church is also known as the Eiffel church after the famous architect who designed it in 1884 (he also designed the interior armature of the Statue of Liberty). It was first exhibited in 1889 next to the Eiffel Tower; its graceful lines won awards for architectural beauty, while the Eiffel Tower was considered a "disgraceful skeleton."

Originally intended to ward off the termites of Central Africa, it was instead sent in 1895 to Santa Rosalía, where it took two years to figure out how to rivet the flat galvanized iron sheets together again.

French Bakery

Instead of waiting in the ever-present line at the Panadería El Boleo for a bag full of *bolillos* (small bread loafs), ask to go in back, where you can view the huge ceiling pulleys and brick-fired ovens that were originally imported from France in the 19th century.

Mesa Francesa

The grand homes of the French officials atop the north mesa are decaying with age,

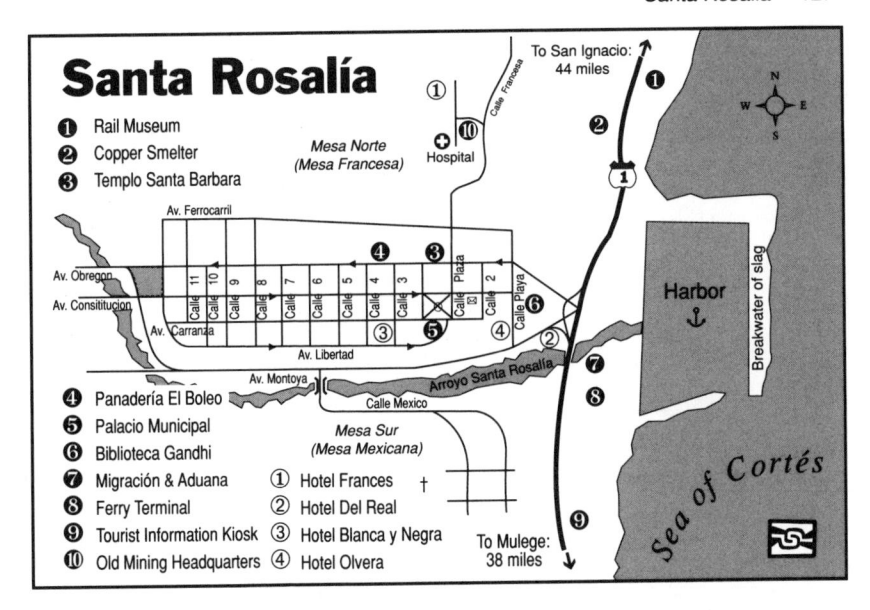

Santa Rosalía

① Rail Museum
② Copper Smelter
③ Templo Santa Barbara

④ Panadería El Boleo
⑤ Palacio Municipal
⑥ Biblioteca Gandhi
⑦ Migración & Aduana
⑧ Ferry Terminal
⑨ Tourist Information Kiosk
⑩ Old Mining Headquarters

① Hotel Frances
② Hotel Del Real
③ Hotel Blanca y Negra
④ Hotel Olvera

Mesa Norte
(Mesa Francesa)
Hospital

To San Ignacio:
44 miles

Av. Ferrocarril
Av. Obregon
Av. Consititucion
Av. Carranza
Av. Libertad
Av. Montoya
Calle Mexico
Arroyo Santa Rosalia

Mesa Sur
(Mesa Mexicana)

To Mulege:
38 miles

Harbor

Breakwater of slag

Sea of Cortés

which makes their tropical French colonial appearance even more haunting. Besides the company headquarters, built in 1893, the restored **Hotel Francés** is worth a quick tour to see its ore collection and to leaf through an 1892 company ledger that lists in elegant scroll the assets of an entire town as if it were a small village store.

Walking About

The **Mahatma Gandhi library** (former kindergarten at the foot of town) has an historic photo collection lining its walls, dating from its squarerigger days, as does the elegant **Palacio Municipal** facing the central park. The old smelter is closed to the public, but its conveyer system which crosses the highway next to the harbor is an ingenious contraption. You can walk out on the **harbor breakwater**, built of pure slag, sit on the rusty locomotives and narrow gauge cars that line the side of the highway (the so-called **Industrial Museum**), or look into some of the shafts of what once comprised a network of 370 miles of underground tunnels. The **Hotel Central** looks like a paragraph from a Somerset Maugham novel, and in fact was the rendezvous of a

dozen German ship captains whose coke-bearing clipper ships were anchored offshore awaiting the end of WW I. At war's end, the crews had all moved ashore, and the ships were confiscated and sold to a U.S. shipping concern for hauling Pacific coast lumber. The **cemetery** atop the southern mesa is of cosmopolitan character with its sprinkling of French and German headstones.

ARRIVING & DEPARTING
By Bus

The bus pulls in to the terminal restaurant half a mile south of town and doesn't stay long enough for you to quick-tour the town. So it's either jump off here and take a chance on getting a seat on the next bus out, or pass on this chapter of Baja history. *Tip: it isn't too hard to reserve a seat, since some routes begin and end here.*

By Ferry

The Santa Rosalía-Guaymas route provides the shortest crossing of the gulf, about 8 hours. The ferry leaves at 11 p.m. for Guaymas on Sunday, Tuesday, Friday, and Sunday, arriving at 7 a.m. On these same days, the ferry leaves from Guaymas at 10 a.m., arriving at Santa Rosalía at 7 p.m. Try to make you reservations in advance (phone: 685-5-82-62). Even if you have a reservation, get to the ticket office early to buy your ticket, and if you have a vehicle, to obtain your temporary import permit next door at the Oficina de Migración. Then you can kill time exploring the town. *Note: the schedules in winter, particularly in November and December, are occasionally disrupted by strong northerly winds.*

PLACES TO SLEEP
Hotels
No hotel better represents the French essence of Santa Rosalía than **Hotel Francés** ($; tel. 2-08-29), the old company hotel high up on the north mesa. The pool is most likely empty, but the rooms preserve the period look with paneled wainscotting and padded paisley walls, as do the lobby and restaurant (which may or may not be open). Only place with a reliable pool is **Motel El Morro**, ($$; tel. 2-04-14), which stretches out along a coastal bluff, giving most rooms a bluewater view. Besides the typical motel comforts of rabbit-ear TVs and air conditioning, the cocktail lounge and restaurant are locally popular.

The other budget hotels are situated in the oven-like arroyo bottom of downtown, lack air conditioning, and are not worth the slight savings over the cooler Hotel Frances up on the mesa. Of these, **Hotel Del Real** ($; tel. 2-00-68) across from the train monument at entrance to town, the **Hotel Blanca y Negra** on Av. Sarabia ($; tel: 2-00-80; not all rooms have fans), and **Hotel Olveraz** ($) on Plaza #14, are the three better picks. Formerly a business travelers hotel, the **Hotel Central** has taken on the slouchy atmosphere of the billiards hall on its bottom floor, best seen from the outside.

Camping
The closest camping beach north is at **Playa Santa Maria**, though you can free camp along the beach just south of Motel El Morro. On the southern skirt of town is **Las Palmas Trailer Park**, a quarter mile back from the beach. Heading south, the nearest waterside trailer park is at San Lucas, 9.5 miles away.

SANTA ROSALIA ADDENDUM
The weather can be oppressively hot summers; average temperature from June to September is 87 degrees.

The legacy of the French did not extend to cooking, and no single restaurant has gained an enviable reputation. For waterfront atmosphere, try **Restaurant Selene** near the ferry terminal. **Hotel Frances** is good for at least a course of history if the food falters (phone first to see if they are open).

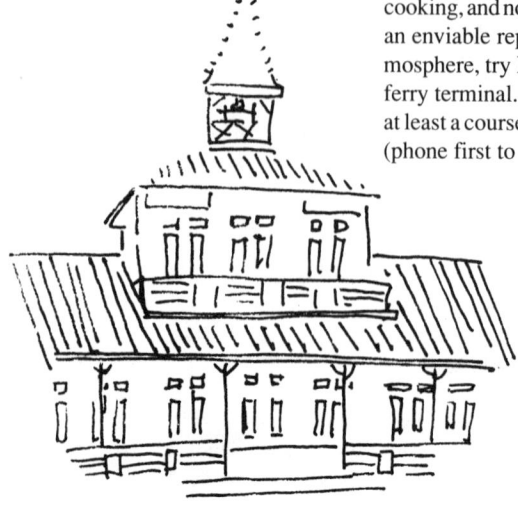

SANTA ROSALÍA TO MULEGE

The 38 miles between Santa Rosalía and Mulegé is a desert rich with petroglyphs, cave paintings, mission ruins, shady villages, and sunstruck beaches.

SANTA AGUEDA

The water you drink in Santa Rosalía comes from the springs of this old Indian ranchería, once called Guajandeví, until it became a visiting station of the Mulegé mission during 1720s. Abundant water has turned this small village into a garden of fruit, date, and palm trees (this was where Rosas Villavicencio stumbled across those copper boleos, selling all his mineral rights for a quick 16 pesos). Santa Agueda is eight graded miles off the highway; the road treads another 20 miles beyond Santa Agueda (high clearance vehicles only) to a rancho at La Candelaria run by the Villavicencios, where there are impressive cave paintings of antlered deer.

SAN LUCAS

The muddy bottom of this two-mile long shallow lagoon fringed with date palms is thick with clams. The Indian middens that line the shore in back of the beach are the largest on the peninsula. At the lagoon's north end, you can usually pull into a waterfront site at the trim **San Lucas RV Park**, where there is a small seasonal cafe and full hook-ups. The south side of the lagoon is more Mexican, where you can camp in a scraggly stand of date palms, next to fish camp and near a small cantina where soldiers from the nearby "Tactical Strike Force" pass their hours drinking slowly from amber-colored bottles. Don't bother looking for the Wildlife Refuge advertised on the highway; as one fisherman explained, since the area is a refuge for wildlife, everything is easy to catch.

PETROGLYPH FIELD

Near the K179 marker of Hwy. 1, between San Lucas and San Bruno, a side road heads inland up El Pollo arroyo over a track of grapefruit-sized rocks. Unless you have high clearance, you will have to walk the 1.3 miles in, till you come to a stone fence. Follow the fence up the western hillside and you will be surrounded by the petroglyphs of a lost culture. Like braille, you can read ancient stories by lightly running your fingers over the hundreds of fish, starfish, animals, abstract designs, and sexual organs, all artfully chipped into this vast boulder field. *Doubletake: rock art protectors say the oil on your hands is destructive to the stone.*

SAN BRUNO

The site of a 19th century land swindle, the village has since turned to the sea, the houses often strung with the dried carcasses of *calamar* (squid) and *pulpo* (octopus) that twirl in the wind. You can beach-camp by the dunes at the **Costa Sirena Trailer Park**, half a mile off the highway (signed); no electricity but you are welcome to stoke the furnace if you want a hot shower. Offshore, the south end of Isla San Marcos looks as white as chalk, one of the earth's richest deposits of gypsum, some of it so pure the missionaries cut pieces to use as windows for the Mulegé mission. You can arrange for a day trip to the mines and village on the island from San Bruno or at the harbor at Santa Rosalia, 15 miles to the north.

ARROYO MAGDALENA

A side road trends west from the highway, 17 miles south of Santa Rosalía, passing some Dominican ruins and the quiet village of San José de Magdalena at nine miles. The rough road eventually halts at a mule trail 32 miles from the highway, which winds up to the remains of **Misión Nuestra Señora de Guadalupe**, where there is an aqueduct several miles long, partly cut into the rocks.

CUEVA SAN BORJITAS

An extensively documented cave painting site lies 20 hard miles west of Hwy One, 14 miles north of Mulegé near the turn-off to Punta Chivato. Described by the missionaries and photographed as early as the 1890s by Leon Diguet, this rock grotto indented in an arroyo cliff (Arroyo San Baltazar), is painted with more than 80 recognizable bicolored figures, many stuck with arrows, possibly a battle scene. To the rear of the cave are brightly colored deer, fish, and rabbit. Scores of petroglyphs, mostly vulvas, are chipped into the the softer side walls. Guided tours can be arranged from Mulegé, or you can tackle it yourself in a high-clearance truck or van. *Note: Since the grotto faces west, time your trip to arrive in the afternoon, when the figures come alive in the sun's glow.*

The Cave Painters

These cave paintings, restricted mainly to arroyos and canyons that cut through the Sierras, radiate mystery. Who made them? Why? Of what? And when?

The painters crushed bright volcanic rocks (white from solidified volcanic ash, brick red from crushed lava), adding some mysterious binder (the old masters of Europe used urine) that has allowed their art to withstand centuries of weathering. Since metallic oxides were used instead of organic material, carbon and amino acid dating have proven useless.

In 1971, Harry Crosby discovered a strange painting in the Arroyo del Parral of the Sierra de San Francisco, a crescent moon backed by sun-like object, which matched a similar depiction in two rock art sites in northern Arizona. Astronomers have calculated that on July 5, 1054, there was a brilliant conjunction of crescent moon and supernova (the birth of the Crab Nebula) visible only in Western North America, a spectacular event most likely recorded on these rocks, a kind of astronomical postmark. Most experts place the age of the paintings at between 500 A.D. to 1500 A.D.

When the missionaries first arrived in the 1600s, the Cochimí Indians believed that those who painted the rocks were not their ancestors but of a different race altogether; some tribes claimed these people to be giants who had come down from the north. Who painted them, and what has happened to their culture is a mystery; they left no buildings, no pottery, no sign of their passing other than these images. Throughout the sierras, all appear to be painted to some

Cueva San Borjitas

☆ A 20-minute hike on foot trail

20.5m

← 17.6m

← Fence 17.0m

Rancho ☐ ← 15.7m
San Borjitas

Fence 12.6m

← 9.7m

← 7.5m

5.3m

← 6.3m
═ Fence

← 3.0m

0.0m

Hwy. 1

To Mulegé | To Santa Rosalía
14 miles | 25 miles

↓ To Punta Chivato

Caution: Map not drawn to scale

code, not as individual expression. All the human figures, for example, hold their arms up, as in praise, or surrender. And for what reason did they paint? For hunting success? Healing rituals? Fertility rites? The pursuit of magic? Religious worship? Whatever message behind their creation, these paintings remain preternaturally mysterious, meant to invoke higher powers.

PUNTA CHIVATO

This point of land, reached via 16 miles of severe washboard from Palo Verde, offers colorful snorkeling, primitive campsites, an RV park ($$), and prolific shelling on a beach west of the phoenix-like Punta Chivato Hotel, which now gets better reviews than the original Borrego de Oro. This self-contained hotel offers 30 rooms equipped with fireplaces, a lounge and dining room, and boat rentals ($$$; P.O. 18, Mulegé, tel: 3-01-88; US: 54 Fairway Loop, Eugene OR 503-683-3423.) Turn-off from Hwy. 1 is at Palo Verde, 13 miles north of Mulegé. *Warning: no free beach camping is found at Punta Chivato.*

MULEGÉ

On Oct. 1, 1874, during the height of the Mexican-American War, the USS Dale entered the estuary of Mulegé, capturing a ship. The next day, 60 U.S. soldiers landed and fought a pitched day-long battle against the Mexicans in the shadow of *El Sombrerito*, the tall hat-shaped hill that stands guard at the entrance to the river. The marines were forced to retire at the end of the day, unsuccessful in their attempt to carry the fight up the river to the village.

This river is actually an estuary, decidedly salty and governed by the tides, which runs two miles upstream to a dam. The dam is a kind of anti-dam, built to keep the saltwater from tainting the freshwater behind it. This freshwater comes not from a river but from rainfall making its way down through the porous lava rock of Guajadenu Peak and emerging as a spring to feed this entrapment. The Cochimi named this place Mulegé, "the place where water comes from a ravine."

The Jesuits found this ravine to be a fine place for a mission, building a small chapel called Santa Rosalía de Mulegé in 1705; a more substantial mission was erected in 1766 by the Jesuit Father Escalante, but rainfall streaming down the arroyo in 1770 undercut the original construction. Three years later, the Dominicans re-invested in the mission, which was repaired and remodeled several times, evolving a fortress-like appearance projected more against the elements than against the local Indians, who, in 1782, numbered less than a hundred.

The mission was finally abandoned in 1828. Mainland mestizos filled the void, laying out a small village alongside the estuary. For the next 150 years, this town slumbered in the shade, rarely troubled by the outside world (except for the bizarre appearance of the U.S. Marines).

This oasis village is shaded by a verdant forest of date palms and mangroves that appear out of the arid brown hills like some vision of the South Pacific—the Bali Hai of Baja. The pleasant lethargy of this town has been carefully cultivated by an increasing number of semi-permanent Americans who have built elaborate refugee camps along the estuary jungle.

Even today, Mulegé refuses to be taken by frontal assault. The streets are too narrow for unwieldy Winnebagos to come barreling into town, the estuary too shallow to enter by anything but a skiff. Fishing and diving are certainly attractions, the few historic sights in town are worth visiting, but the real lure of Mulegé is its sense of sanctuary, best sought by walking about town very slowly, enjoying the shadows.

PLACES
Río Mulegé
This estuary is lined by two roads that parallel its length for two miles to the gulf, both fine walks. The northern road is wild with mangrove, and ends at El Sombrerito. The southern road is tamer, more a pedestrian walkway than a road; it passes through a shangri-la of palms, docks, restaurants, vacation homes, and trailer parks—an American counterpart to the Mexican town across the river. Warm springs are reputed to bubble up from smooth rocks near the Hacienda Hotel (a warm spot to bathe). The legendary giant snook lurk in the forked roots of the mangroves, though nobody ever seems to catch them.

Mision Santa Rosalía de Mulegé
This fourth mission founded by the Jesuits was one of the last to be constructed before their forced expulsion from the New World. Its two naves are built of thick stone walls and support a white barrel-vaulted roof, an austere place stripped of much historic adornment. Behind the church, a pathway leads up to a more meditative spot, *el mirador* (the lookout), a lava rock promontory overlooking a sea of wild date palms surrounding the river. Another path leads down to the dam which keeps the saltwater at bay.

La Cananea
Often mistaken for the mission, this is one of the most graceful-looking jails in Mexico.

Constructed just after the turn-of-the-century, the territorial prison is perched above the town, easily seen from the highway that was its downfall.

Ahead of its time, the jail operated on the honor system, the prisoners let out to work in the village during the day, summoned back each evening by guards blowing through conch shells. If a prisoner escaped, another was set out to catch him. But with the paving of the transpeninsular highway, the trust system broke down, and the prison closed (though it is still occasionally used as an overnight lock-up). You may be able to enter the gates and walk the quadrangle of graffiti-scarred cubicles if it's not locked. An elderly caretaker who may unofficially ask for a few pesos was once an inmate here, evidently a very happy one; he still lives here.

El Sombrerito
The hat-shaped hill at the harbor mouth is topped by a lighthouse which can be reached up a path and stairs. The pebbly beach just north is federal, which means you can camp the night here if you wish.

Fishing & Diving
Fishing is best November to March for yellowtail, sierra, and cabrilla. Dorado provide the best catch from May to October. Pangas can be rented through the hotels in Mulegé.

Diving is best in Mulegé at Punta Prieta, near the lighthouse at Sombrerito, depending on the visibility. Much better diving can be found offshore at the Santa Inés Islands and in the waters just north of Punta

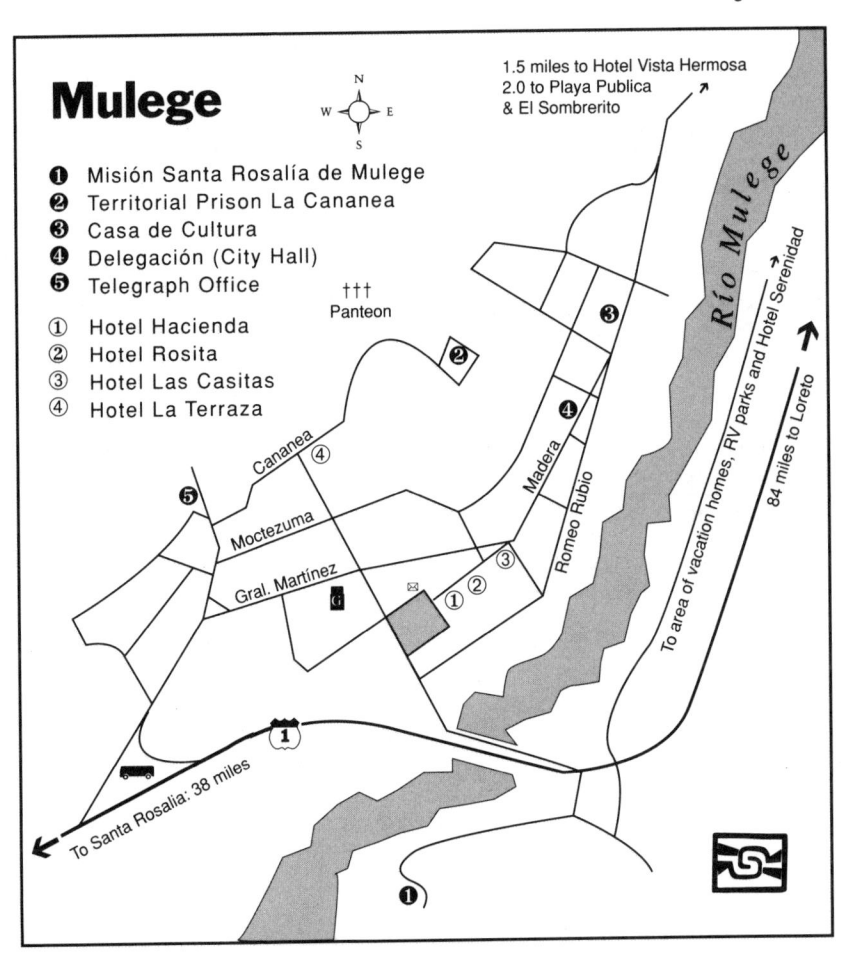

Mulege

N W—◇—E S

1.5 miles to Hotel Vista Hermosa
2.0 to Playa Publica
& El Sombrerito

❶ Misión Santa Rosalía de Mulege
❷ Territorial Prison La Cananea
❸ Casa de Cultura
❹ Delegación (City Hall)
❺ Telegraph Office

††† Panteon

① Hotel Hacienda
② Hotel Rosita
③ Hotel Las Casitas
④ Hotel La Terraza

Río Mulege

To area of vacation homes, RV parks and Hotel Serenidad

84 miles to Loreto

Cananea

Moctezuma

Gral. Martínez

Madera

Romeo Rubio

To Santa Rosalia: 38 miles

Concepción. The only full-fledged dive operators, Mulegé Divers (Calle Madero 45) offer certification courses.

PLACES TO SLEEP
Budget Hotels

More than 200 years old and facing the main plaza, the 17-room **Hotel Hacienda** is perfectly situated as the local character hotel; its thick walls and heavily timbered roofs support a decadent air of dissolution, and its big interior courtyard speaks of grander days (the pool in back is a modern afterthought). Take your pick: ancient front rooms with fireplaces, big second floor rooms with ceiling fans, or poolside rooms in back with air conditioning, all priced the same. Two blocks away are the two *casas de huespedes*: **Manuelita**, half the price of the Hacienda, and **Nachita**, cheaper still for its common bathrooms.

Moderate

Of the two moderate picks in town, **Las Casitas** (PO Box 3, Mulegé; tel: 3-00-19) is the more stylish choice. Once the home of a minor Mexican poet, Alan Gorosave, it offers an excellent location, eight simple air conditioned rooms facing a landscaped patio walkway, and an outdoor dining patio that draws people in off the street. If you want solitude with your air conditioning, you might do better at **Terrazas** (tel. 3-00-09) on Calle Zaragoza, which is perched on a short hillside overlooking town; unfortunately most of the 35 low-ceilinged rooms lack any kind of view and tend to be buggy.

Expensive

Hotel Serenidad (tel. 3-01-11) and **Hotel Vista Hermosa** (tel. 3-03-33) are on opposite sides of the estero, away from town. Both were originally built as fly-in resorts. Serenidad enjoys a timeworn look, while the Vista suffers from it. Pig roasts are held on Saturdays, Mexican Nights on Wednesdays at the Serenidad, a local tradition. Its rooms, named instead of numbered, are done in old California style, with fireplaces and verandas. The 21 rooms at the Vista Hermosa cling to a 1960ish commercial motel look, and the scraggly grounds offer little to contemplate.

Camping

Though you can camp on the public beach at El Sombrerito, most people prefer the security of the trailer parks on the southside of the estero. **Hotel Serenidad** offers the most civilized operation, nine sites behind the hotel; not much view within its walled compound, but you get the full run of the hotel's facilities. The more expensive **Maria Isabel Trailer Park**, just up the estero, is known for its tiled pool and La Chingadera bakery, which puts out American-style pastries and pizza; its 30 sites have access to the estero. **Pancho's Trailer Park**, next down the line, is the cheapest of the trailer parks, but offers little besides an electrical outlet and water tap. Biggest and smoothest operation is **La Huerta Saucedo Trailer Park**, also known as **The Orchard**; they still offer a few estero-front sites for overnighters, as well as a boat ramp and tent camping area.

Mulegé Addendum

Shopping in Mulegé is limited, but some small curio stores and gift shops are blending into the street scene, selling mostly typical Mexican arts and crafts imported from the mainland.

Nightlife is mostly focused on a group of local mariachis who make a circuit of the hotels, playing Wednesdays at Serenidad's Noche Mexicana, Thursdays at La Terraza, skipping over to Las Casitas on Fridays, then back over to Serenidad for the pig roast on Saturdays (phone hotels to confirm schedule).

Granny's Goodies, under the bridge, is the local information center for English-speakers, a combination coffee stop/bakery/book exchange/lonely hearts club/rumor mill where information and advice are freely dispensed—otherwise known as Radio Mulegé.

Best breakfast place is La Jungla Bambú, on the south side of the estero amidst trailer park row.

Water from the pipes is supposed to be potable, but most residents boil or filter it. An elaborate purification system has been installed at the Jorge del Río Trailer Park, where you can buy it by the gallon. Bring a container.

Don't count on much fresh fish in restaurants despite all the fishing boats; fishermen earn more money selling their catch for export.

Note: Buses going either north or south can be stopped by flagging it at the highway stop. If you are going to La Paz or Tijuana, it's best to buy your ticket in Loreto or Santa Rosalía, the only places where you can get a seat assignment.

MULEGÉ TO LORETO

From Mulegé, Hwy. 1 runs near shore for the first 37 miles, almost skimming the waters of Bahía Conception, before turning inland and winding another 47 miles to Loreto. Many travelers never reach Loreto, waylaid by the beauty of Bahía Concepción.

BAHÍA CONCEPCIÓN

When Don Francisco Lucenilla, a pearling captain, visited this 25-mile long bay in 1668, he reported seeing white-skinned Indians who lived on desert fruits and oysters. These Indians were soon lured into the Mulegé mission and Christianized by Padre Basaldúa. He also was responsible for constructing the trail along the bay's west shore in 1705 which the highway follows today.

The western side of the bay is etched with biological beaches, made entirely of seashells, ground down to a calcium-white powdered sand that contrasts brightly with the limpid shallow waters. This tame bay is a miniature version of the Gulf, and thus a good introduction to the Sea of Cortés. Its waters are calmer and more protected than the open gulf, its sand littered with sea buttons and olive shells.

There isn't any potable water or grocery store along the length of the bay, so you need to fill up in Mulegé or Loreto (trucks selling produce and supplies sometime roll through the campgrounds). Since there are no local buses, hitchhiking (or stopping for hitchhikers), is part of the local etiquette. Minimal fees are charged at all beaches for primitive camping. This bay offers variety: windsurf, hike, watch birds, fish, snorkel, search for petroglyphs, soak in the hot springs, contemplate your good fortune.

Warning: during the late spring and early summer months, a bloom of seaweed often clouds the visibility in the bay, making the water look as green as an unkept swimming pool. Snorkeling is limited, but for good reason. This is the birth phase of the marine cycle, when fish lay their eggs, and entire schools of baby fish dart through the primeval soup, hidden from their enemies.

BEACHES OF BAHÍA CONCEPCION
Playa Punta Arena

The closest beach to the mouth of the bay, it is rich in sealife, one reason why an itinerant fish camp is often set up here, surrounded by endless piles of discarded scallop shells. You can camp farther south at **Cabañas Punta Arena**, a palapa-shrouded camping area with pit toilets. A crosswind blows strong here, making this a

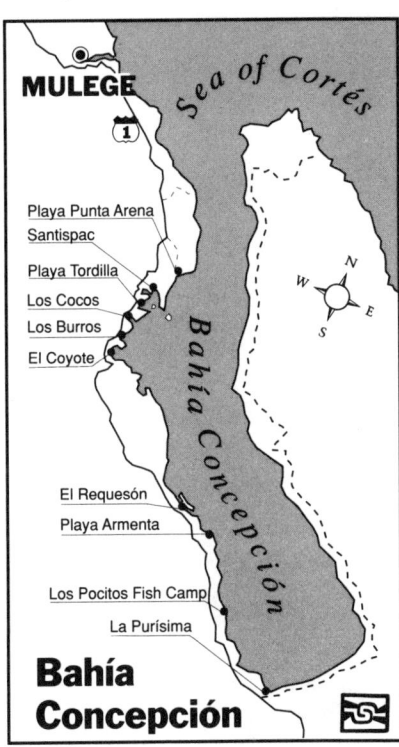

MULEGE — *Sea of Cortés*

Playa Punta Arena
Santispac
Playa Tordilla
Los Cocos
Los Burros
El Coyote

El Requesón
Playa Armenta

Los Pocitos Fish Camp
La Purísima

Bahía Concepción

Bahía Concepción

popular sailboarding beach. Since it is also the hardest beach to reach, 2.3 miles off the highway on a bumpy road, the crowds are thinner. An old coastal foot trail, perhaps dating to the missionaries, connects with Santispac, the next beach south.

Santispac

Two and a half miles south of the turn-off to Playa Punta Arena, this flat beach can look like an RV trade show during the winter, displaying the latest in solar panels, ATVs, portable satellite dishes, water stills and advanced toilet technology. The beach is well fertilized by two decades of dump hoses. A few open-air restaurants serve inexpensive meals, including the venerable **Ana's** with its Sunday bakery. The presence of a local naval detachment keeps non-military revelry in check. Yachts perennially anchored offshore complete the panorama. If you want to partially escape the cheek-to-jowl atmosphere, camp towards the southern end of the beach. *Note: on a cool night, it is soothing to immerse yourself in one of the two hot springs hidden behind the mangrove lagoon.*

Playa Tordiilla

A mile and a half south of Santispac, this beach has been privatized by **Posada Concepción**, a trailer park that has mutated

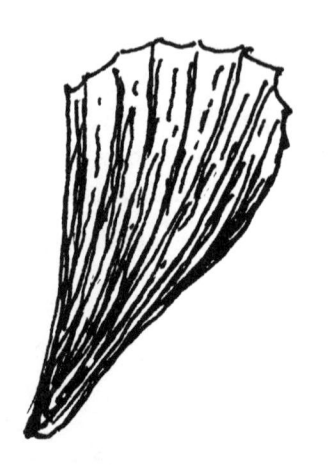

over the years into a semi-permanent mini-village. A few overnight sites in back are still rented though, and provide an excellent value if you are interested in playing tennis, soaking in the natural hot springs, plugging into some electricity, or showering in what the owner calls "the cleanest bathrooms in Baja". Primitive camping is available farther down this same beach, at Playa Escondido.

Playa Los Cocos

Backed by a mangrove lagoon, this beach boasts sand as powdery as any, but the highway skirts by at a spot where trucks like to blast open their *escapes* (compression releases). This beach works best at catching the overflow when the other playas are filling up. A more private beach can be reached on the other side of the northern rocks.

Bahía Los Burros

Two miles south of Playa Tordilla, this popular camping beach is in full view of the highway. It is equipped with palapas, pit toilets, and trash barrels. A crashed airplane lies offshore 200 yards in about 10 feet of water, an interesting spot for snorkelers. *Petroglyphs: on the NE corner of the bay, opposite an abandoned roadside water tank there is a short arroyo of tumbled rocks, scored with hundreds of petroglyphs, some which you can see from the highway.*

El Coyote

Less than a mile south of Bahía Burro, this is the southernmost of the Bahía Coyote camping spots. This beach offers the only shade trees and freshwater well (for showering, not drinking) found along the bay, one of the most idyllic spots on Bahía Concepción. At the far south end of the beach, a trail runs to an undeveloped hot springs at water's edge. *Caution: the half mile access road to this beach can flood at high tide, so watch out during new or full moons.*

Coyote Cave Painting

Just south of El Coyote, at the K106 marker, a dirt road drops immediately down to the arroyo bottom, where you can see some faint Indian paintings of fish and turtle in a large-mouthed cave.

El Requesón

Nine miles south of El Coyote, this beach is connected by an umbilicus of sand (a *tombolo*) to what technically is an island offshore, as least when this isthmus disappears at high tide. Fine camping under palapa shelters, with firepits and pit toilets.

Playa Armenta

This beach can't be seen from its turnoff (between the K91 & 90 markers, 1.2 miles south of El Requesón). Since it faces north, it is more exposed to the prevailing winter wind and waves, which makes it one of the least crowded beaches on the bay.

The Bay's East Coast

Separated from the gulf by a long mountainous mini-peninsula, the bay's east coast offers lots of lonely beach exploration if you have a trustworthy high clearance vehicle. Disadvantages: this is the windward side, so you are open to occasionally unruly northerly breezes, the roads are rough, and there are few sandy beaches. Advantages: no crowded shoreline or late-night generator noise, fine shelling, solitude.

From the southern reach of Bahía Concepción, Hwy. 1 travels 38 miles to Loreto, passing two historic sites.

SAN JUAN LONDO

This green "glen of Loreto" was used by the first Kino expedition in 1683 to raise cattle, then by Father Salvatierra in 1699 to minister to the Indians. The ruins left a chapel built in 1705 may not be as impressive as the great restored missions, but the thick rock wall curving gracefully up to a long forgotten roof, and the limestone ornamentation that lies in rubble around the walls are historically haunting, a feeling echoed by the faded plastic wreaths of the cemetery around it. From the signed Hwy. 1 turnoff, 18 miles north of Loreto, the ruins are little more than half a mile from highway, near a tall stand of palms.

SAN BRUNO

In 1683, Padre Kino and Admiral Atondo began the first colony of California in a small valley near the gulf shore, building "the Real in triangular form, with a stone cannon at each corner." Though the 200 colonists endured almost two years—during which time Kino made his famous walk to the Pacific, and during which time little rain fell—the colony was abandoned. The ruins are 6.8 miles east of Hwy 1 at the Km 21 marker, 12.6 miles N of Loreto, and then another mile by trail. Ask the ranchers to help direct you, since there is controversy as to which pile of rocks constitutes the authentic ruins.

LORETO

The house where the the Virgin Mary was born was carried by angels from the Holy Land to Dalmatia, to keep it away from the Turks, and then to Recanati, Italy, where they set it down in a grove of Lauretum. A chapel, called Loreto, was built of wood from this venerated grove. Thus the name Loreto came to be cherished (Mussolini hung by his heels in Milan's Piazza Loreto).

When Padre Salvatierra set across the Gulf in 1697 to begin the first permanent settlement in the Californias, he carried a wooden Madonna, Our Lady of Loreto, whose powers he invoked to stay alive during a storm, and again to quell a mutiny when the crew found out they were going to harvest souls, not pearls. And again, when stumped for a location to begin the colony, "Inasmuch we were beset with difficulties on every side, we chose the Madonna as our patroness. In order to secure her assistance, we decided to cast lots in her name. The slip of paper drawn out bore the name of San Dionisis." San Dionisis became the site of Loreto.

The mission took root, becoming the trunk from which exploration and civilization branched out in all directions. For 132 years, Loreto was capitol of California. When the Jesuits were expelled in 1768, the mission was turned over to the Franciscans. Fray Junípero Serra left from here five years later with a loaf of bread and a block of cheese on his way to civilize Alta California.

Drawing lots is chancy business. The chosen site of Loreto was at the mouth of the steep Arroyo de las Parras, which after heavy rains turns into a raging torrent of water. In 1830, this raging torrent carried away the capitol of California. These inundations later appeared with devilish regularity. Kicked over by an earthquake in 1877, Loreto fell to a heap of ruins, while Alta California, its glittering progeny, declared her sovereignty.

The damaged church managed to survive. The arroyo was channeled, and a malecón (seawall) built to stem the ocean's steady advance. As if fate were attempting to rectify itself, the priest won a lottery, which allowed him to repair the collapsed bell tower, and, with the money left over, to install a town clock.

Then Mayan crude was discovered off Yucatan, foreign loans poured into Mexico, and an abundance of money was ceremoniously pumped into Loreto to turn it into another Cancún. This only served to inflate her sense of place along this sleepy coast. When the bubble burst, Loreto was left with only a vision and grand but empty boulevards laced with powerlines.

The town, now committed to tourism, has slowly gained style on its own. No longer a fishing village, its zócalo has been closed to traffic, outdoor cafes, and chic gift shops have opened, and the main artery has turned into a pedestrian walkway. Still a small town, it's easy to walk around, taking in the sights, which are few. Nightlife is nil but you'll find warm pockets of conversation in the hotel bars. It's all window dressing for most travelers who come primarily to fish, dive, explore the five islands offshore, and enjoy the raw wonder of this coast.

Traveling About

The reason most people want a rental car in Loreto is to take side trips, such as to Primer Agua or San Javier (which car rental companies prohibit). For shuttling up and down the coast, a taxi usually is cheaper; and the municipal bus, which runs down the coast as far as Liguí, cheaper still, though fickle where schedules are concerned.

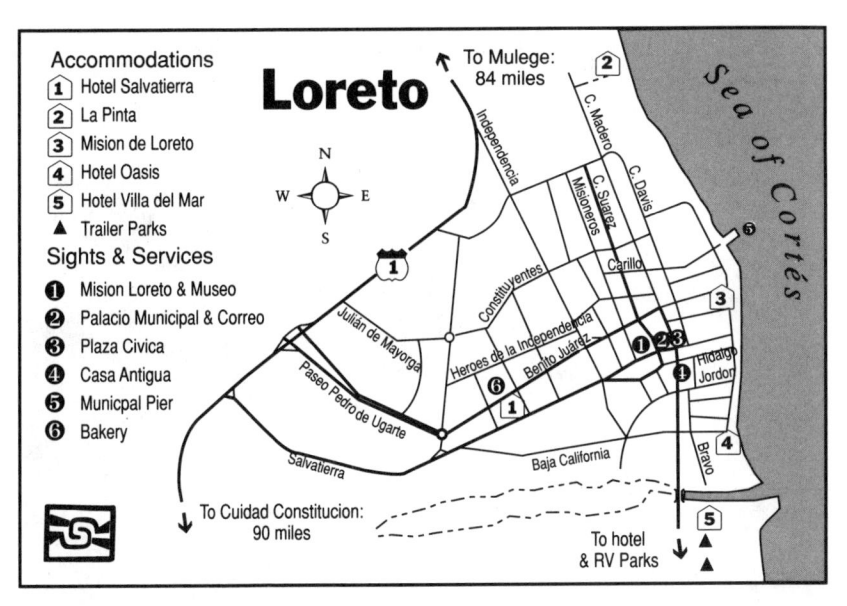

PLACES
Misión Loreto

Constructed from 1742 to 1752, this mission has weathered many natural and ecclesiastical storms. You can still see the original Roman brick worked into the wall at irregular intervals, donated by Roman patrons and brought over as ballast. Its Spanish-Italian architecture comprises a central nave with choir loft and separate wings for the sacristy, chapel, and baptistry: pine pews, thick walls, blue and gold altar. At one time 86 oil paintings by Murillo and Cabrera hung on the walls, and Our Lady of Loreto was swathed in opalescent pearls. Now only a few damaged paintings by unknown Old Masters adorn the church, and the pearls gone. But the Madonna still has a subtle, enigmatic smile on her face.

Museo de la Misión

As much a showcase of 18th century ranchero life as of the missionaries, this museum offers much more than saddles and swords. Set around the mission quadrangle, its tranquil landscaped grounds re-create a California pastoral atmosphere. The entrance fee is token, and the church surely doesn't recoup much from the bookstore, where cultural pamphlets and anthropological tomes are sold, few having anything to do with Baja California. Open 9 a.m.-4 p.m., closed Monday and Tuesday.

Casa Antigua

Few buildings survived the natural catastrophes of the 19th century, but you can see one that endured, thanks to its stout stone structure. Next to the Playa Blanca Restaurant on Calle Madero, a plaque on its front reads "en este lugar se firmo el acto de adhesión de la Baja California a la República Federal el 11 de Agosto 1824," where Baja California formally joined the newly formed nation of Mexico. Don't go in uninvited; it's a private home.

Malecón

The new breakwater, topped by a sidewalk, runs along the gulf-front, built as a dike-like defence against the sea (the waterfront sometimes floods at high tides). At the far north end, the malecón ends at a pier which is a barometer of the fishing; if it's crowded during the winter, the yellowtail are probably running.

Loreto Plaza

Fishing & Diving

These waters are prolific with sportfish, depending on what migratory species happen to be passing through. During the winter, its yellowtail, sierra, amberjack. In summer, you might get red snapper, grouper, yellowfin tuna, but most boats patrol for dorado. Hotels can arrange charters, though you can do it cheapest yourself by going down to fishing cooperatives just north of the pier.

Loreto is one of the first areas south of Santa Rosalia where the diving is excellent. The water visibility clears to 60 to 80 feet during the summer from April to November, but can decrease to 30 to 50 feet December to March; spring algae blooms can choke visibility down to ten feet. Beach diving can be boring, but free diving off any of the promontories (Nópolo, Juncalito) is varied and deep. Best tank diving is off the north end of Isla Carmen. The only dive facility is five miles south of town, on the premises of Hotel El Presidente.

Events

Loreto celebrates its Fiesta Patronal on September 8, with sports competitions, cultural events, popular dances, and a regional fair.

PLACES TO SLEEP
Budget Hotels

The 18 unpretentious air conditioned rooms at the **Motel Salvatierra** (tel: 3-00-21) is about the least expensive budget property here, but it's a long hot hike to town center and cheap places to eat. The zócalo is even farther from the next cheapest accommodation, **Hotel Villa del Mar** (Francisco I. Madero, Col. Zaragoza, Loreto BCS 23880: tel: 3-03-99), which has all the attributes of a resort, though its bunk-bedded rooms are small; in the bathrooms, you can't sit on the toilet and close the door at the same time. But the generous pool area, moderately priced cafeteria and long beach compensate, making it worth the jump in price over the Salvatierra.

Moderate

Next step up the price ladder is the **Misión de Loreto** (#1 López Mateo Blvd.; tel: 3-

00-48), across the street from the malecón. Its dark rooms are more comfortable, done in austere colonial style; its two bars are jovial, the restaurant palatable, and the pool with its palm tree island the high note. Of the other two beach resorts, **La Pinta** (tel: 3-00-25) is a decent choice, its rooms divided between villas and less-expensive haciendas, which are spread out along the weedy sand, but it's a mile-long trudge to town center. Best value in Loreto is the older, less commercial **Hotel Oasis** (PO Box No. 17, Loreto, BCS; tel: 3-00-12); its old California-style rooms open to a common veranda strung with hammocks; you can hire pangas, play tennis, and the restaurant is very capable.

Deluxe

El Presidente Stouffer (Mision de Loreto S/N; tel: 3-07-00) lies isolated, six miles south of town facing a skimpy stretch of imported sand, the most deluxe hotel between Ensenada and La Paz.

Camping

There are two trailer parks that sit side-by-side south of town, **Las Palmas Trailer Park**, shady with palms, and **Ejido Loreto RV Park**. Free camping is found south of Loreto, at Notri, Juncalito and Liguí.

ARRIVING & DEPARTING
By Bus

Even if just passing through, the bus usually stops for a half-hour food stop at the Don Luis restaurant, more than enough time to visit the mission a block away, peak through the museum, and make a loop of the zócalo. You usually don't have to wait more than three hours to catch a bus going in either direction, to La Paz or Tijuana.

By Air

The airport is a few miles south of town. The cheapest way to get to Loreto from the airport is to take the *colectivo*. A taxi is about four times the cost of a single ticket.

Loreto Addendum

Despite its size, there is only one bank in town, Bancomer (tel: 3-03-15). Don't try to cash your traveler's checks on a Monday morning.

There are any number of island tours, the most popular to Coronado Island, a five-hour trip with lunch on the beach; departures usually leave from the town pier at 9:30 a.m.

The two cheapest places to eat with any character are at **La Casita** and under the umbrellaed tables of **Cafe Olé** next door, two hip-pocket restaurants within view of the Municipal building; **Playa Blanca** on the next corner is a cut above in price, quality, and elevation, its open-air second-floor a fine observatory for watching the street life below.

The bus station restaurant, **Don Luis**, is now in its third re-incarnation, still attentively managed by the Don himself.

BACKCOUNTRY SIDE TRIP
San Javier

From a turn-off just south of Loreto, a dirt road follows the original El Camino Real, winding 24 miles into the steep Sierras, to the site of the Jesuits' most impressive

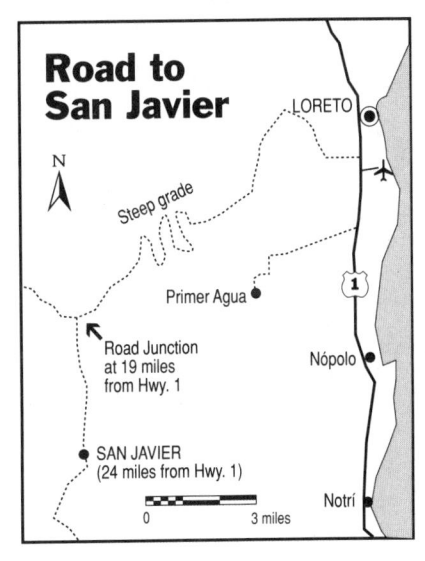

Road to
San Javier

N

Steep grade

Primer Agua

Road Junction
at 19 miles
from Hwy. 1

SAN JAVIER
(24 miles from Hwy. 1)

LORETO

Nópolo

Notrí

0   3 miles

Bells of Misión San Javier

faded figures are painted on the rocks (follow stream for about 60 yards from the road). At 12 miles, you will pass **Rancho Las Parras**, an historic rancho. After crossing the divide (1,750 ft.) at 14 miles, it is an easy roll into San Javier, a small village (about 300 souls) laid out in deference to the mission, which stands at the head of the street.

The second link in the mission chain (founded 1699, but church dates to 1758), Misión San Javier is designed in simple Moorish-style, laid out like a Greek Cross with arched roof, two small lateral chapels, a baptistry, and a gilded altar containing a statue of St. Francis brought by mule from Mexico City. The vestry contains the threadbare vestments worn by Fathers Salvatierra and Piccolo. For a tip, the keeper will open the spiral staircase to the bell tower, where hang three bells, dated 1761 and 1803. The road can be driven in a sedan but only if you are a cautious risk-taker. *Note: this village comes alive during the first week in December (Dec. 3 is St. Francis Day), with pilgrimages from the surrounding backcountry.*

accomplishment, the Misión San Javier. This arid climate and isolated canyon have preserved the mission as if in a vacuum. Eight miles from the turn-off are the **Cuevas Pintadas** (Painted Caves), where eight

ISLANDS IN THE BLUE

Just off Loreto are five unique islands, a mini-galápogas offering a glimpse at the way nature has evolved, largely without man's help.

Isla Monserrate

This island lies 7-1/2 miles north of Agua Verde and about 16 miles to the SE of Puerto Escondido. Unlike most of the Gulf islands, Monserrate presents a gentle, low-lying appearance, rising just 740 feet. From a distance at sea, you can make out the distinct terraces of gently dipping limestone; they lie in contrast to the underlying red and brown volcanic rocks. Except after the rains, the island appears brown, dry, and deeply eroded. Although today there is no dependable source of water, Indians inhabited the island until 1717; where they drank from nobody knows. The south end of the island provides calm protection from northerly winds, a little over half a mile NW of the lightower, where the red volcanic bluffs give way to light sandstone. The north end of the island has one of the most beautiful beaches to be found in the Gulf, bordered by sandstone bluffs and sand dunes.

Isla Catalana

This island has gained renown in scientific

circles for two reasons: the largest barrel cactus in the world, and rattle-less rattlesnakes. In 1952, one of these snakes was found on the island. Scientists scoffed until nine more snakes were captured two years later. Now they are considered a new species, *Crotalus catalinesis*. Though they lack rattles, they are still venomous. The barrel cacti are found throughout the island in giant phallic forests. There are reported to be two springs of freshwater on the island, with palm trees surrounding one of them. Most landings are made on the southeast end of the island, where there is a lightower; fishing boats are frequently anchored here, and there are trails that run off to the western beaces. The island is twelve miles east of Isla Monserrate

Isla Carmen

The Indians who lived near Loreto lacked any cohesive theology, but they did believe that when they died, their souls flew off to Isla Carmen. The Jesuit missionaries put a stop to such blasphemy, but the notion of heaven-on-Carmen still persists.

At Bahía Salinas, on the east side of Carmen, in the sunken crater of an ancient volcano, there is one of the largest salt deposits in Mexico, first mined by the missionaries. Until recently, when operations ceased, 150 villagers worked the salt beds.

Less than two miles south of the NW tip of the island is Puerto Balandra. A shipwreck lies ashore, the skeleton of a salt transporter caught in a southeaster in 1959. Ashore, a narrow footpath passes the adobe ruins of an old supply ranch and continues up the wooded arroyo to the salt flats on the other side.

On the north end of the island, Puerto La Lancha offers deep diving, while 3/4 miles to the NE at Arroyo Blanco, chalk white cliffs fall down into the water, sculpted cleanly into grottos and underwater caves. From Puerto La Lancha, a road runs to the abandoned salt village at Bahía Salinas. Isla Carmen is five to eight miles offshore.

Barrel Cactus on Isla Catalana

Isla Danzante

When Ortega discovered Puerto Escondido, the Indians celebrated his arrival by dancing and playing flutes. In their honor, he named the bay Bahía de los Danzantes, Dancers' Bay. Somewhere in the rush of history, the small slag of an island two miles offshore was instead given the name. Not that the name doesn't apply. The abundance of cholla and cactus and the steep hills makes you literally dance from rock to rock, balancing to keep from getting punctured. The western shore provides an excellent landing. *Note: A recently discovered species of scorpion infests the sargasso that washes up on the beaches here.*

Isla Coronado

Six and a half miles north of Loreto, Isla Coronado is a volcanic peak, possibly as young as 2,000 years (some of the flows are still bare of vegetation from a geologically recent eruption). Easy landing is made on the NW side of the long spit that extends of its western side.

LORETO TO CIUDAD CONSTITUCIÓN

Hwy. 1 runs 90 miles from Loreto to Ciudad Constitución. For the first 20 miles, the road parallels the coast in the shadow of the steep escarpment of the Sierra de las Gigantas, a raw stadium of rock facing the Gulf. After Liguí, the highway scales the escarpment, then follows the wide Arroyo Huatamote which drains onto the flat Magdalena Plain. The road runs straight and narrow for the last 30 miles.

PRIMER AGUA

From a signed turn-off 3-1/2 miles south of Loreto, a four-mile graded dirt road goes inland to a historic oasis where a stream of water spurts from the rocks. Indians drank here, the missionaries planted a garden here, a thriving plantation in the 1860s shipped schooner-loads of oranges to San Francisco from here. Now the water is channeled through a thick grove of mango trees into a rustic quasi-natural pool, green with pond algae, an idyllic place to picnic and swim. Before you drive up there, you must buy tickets first from either the Fonatur office in Nópolo or at El Presidente, which organizes fish and clam bakes here. Admission is a steep $5, and children pay full price, which helps to keep this shady refuge as empty as the desert around it.

NÓPOLO

Fonatur has reworked Nópolo into an ambitious development centering on El Presidente Hotel and a separate posh tennis center (Blvd. Misión de San Ignacio; tel: 3-04-08). Don't be fooled by the sand in front of the hotel, it's brought in by truck and raked out to cover the natural pebbly shore. There are not many sandy beaches along this part of the coast. The volcanic rocks are not coarse enough to break down into sand grains. Those that are sandy are mostly biological beaches, ground from shells. But you can drive a mile past the hotel to the sandiest beach in the area, a tidal sandspit that connects the 75 foot Nópolo Rock with the shore. The natural eco-system here has been uprooted by tourism, the mangroves cut back, the dunes raked out for a golf course. But the waters around the point still abound with sea life. Camping may be possible here, depending on the pace of development.

NOTRI

A mile beyond Nópolo, you can camp on a sand and pebble beach with fine views of Isla Carmen. The diving is boring over a flat bottom, and there are no facilities other than shade provided by a wild stand of palms. Can be noisy at night, since the highway runs close by.

JUNCALITO

Thirteen and a half miles south of Puerto Escondido, this crescent bay, also known by its Indian name *Chuenque* (Place of Amaranth), is the most popular camping spot along this coast. You can set up right at the high tide line. The sandy beach runs to a dune field, and you can drive towards it as far as you dare. Offshore, a tilted rock island, Juncalito, guards the bay, and a trail runs south to a hidden cove of Puerto Escondido. Juncalito was once the site of an Indian ranchería, and if you walk back towards the old rancho, you may stumble across ancient stone foundations, purportedly the ruins of a Jesuit visiting station.

PUERTO ESCONDIDIO

This unique harbor, almost completely landlocked, offers in microcosm the ecology of the Gulf. Except for surf-battered reef, every marine environment is found: sand bot-

Puerto Escondido

tom, stone and mud shores, boulders, broken rock, coral, racing tide, quiet shallow areas, even cement seawalls. This diversity allows for an assorted birdlife: herons, egrets, curlews, oystercatchers, godwits, grebes, willets, frigates, pelicans, even bats.

And there's mystery too. When Francisco Ortega entered this bay in 1633, he sailed in from the northeast, where since the 1800s two stone dikes (the "windows") have breached the bay. Some historians claim the Jesuits constructed these windows to better protect the bay, but geologists insist these rocks are a "tombolo" (like the one at El Requesón), heaped up in precise form by some forgotten weather convulsion. Now the tide's ebb and flow is constricted to a narrow entrance channel on the south side, an excellent place to float with a face mask, watching the sealife enter and leave the bay: turtles, sea lions, and even occasional pilot whales may be seen gliding in with the currents.

The bay's lake-like configuration makes this the gulf's best hurricane hole, to which hundreds of yachts flock every summer. Since Puerto Escondido is in the throes of development (disrupting its fragile ecology), camping along the bay has been prohibited. The elaborate Tripuí RV Park (PO Box 100 Loreto 23880: tel.: 3-08-18; 3-08-28) half a mile inland offers the only alternative: besides some RV sites, there are a few modest motel rooms ($$), swimming pool, tennis court, restaurant, tent sites and hook-ups. *Note: walk up the arroyo on inland side of the turnoff to Puerto Escondido, and you will reach some tinajas, rock pools of fresh water.*

LIGUÍ & ENSENADA BLANCA

Two beaches can be reached 20.8 miles south of Loreto by turning off at the village of Liguí. One road heads south for two miles to **Ensenada Blanca**, a fishing village, where a white sand beach stretches south with the kind of grace found only in a French Curve. Shallow bay, warm water. The road continues beyond the village to primitive camping sites along the shore. A footpath travels 22 miles to Agua Verde.

The other road heads directly for the more modest **Playa Liguí** a mile away, a public beach. Along the way, about 250 yards up from the beach in a stand of mesquite, you can see the foundation stones of **San Juan Bautista de Liguí**, built by children in 1705; since the older Indians could not be bribed to work, Father Ugarte got the children to labor by making a game of it (prizes for the most bricks made, jumping barefeet on mud to make the adobe). But attacks by belligerent Pericú Indians, lack of water, and a plague ended this mission after 16 years.

AGUA VERDE

In 1596, a Spanish pearler gave this place its name. Easy to see why. The sandy beaches scalloped into the coast reflect every hue of green. About 100 people live in the wide palmy arroyo that empties out into Bahía Agua Verde, which is guarded by a huge rock pinnacle offshore. Life is simple: fishing and raising goats. Only the most basic supplies can be bought. Bring your own water; the wells are brackish and unsafe. A footpath winds south to Bahía Santa Marta, three miles away, a pleasant hike through wild arroyos. *Pictographs: another trail heads west, past a cemetery, to a cave a mile away (about 150 yards from beach), where 53 ochre-colored handprints are painted on the wall, the signature of the Guaycura Indians who lived here.*

The road to Agua Verde turns off the highway at the K64 marker, 38 miles south of Loreto. The 25-mile road is steep but graded, narrow in places, and cramped by hairpin turns. Once at Agua Verde, there are not many places to camp (a minor fee) along the shore without leaving your car.

MAGDALENA PLAIN

The Magdalena Plain is a sloping desert, edged by the steep escarpments of the Gigantas to the east and by the lagoons and sand dunes of the Pacific coast to the west. The soils nurture a variety of cacti: *cardón, creeping devil, cholla, cereus, pitahaya agria* and *pitahaya dulce.* Underlying this desert is a vast water reservoir, laid down during the Pliestocene. Deep wells have tapped into this dinosaur water, replacing the fatigue-green desert with bright leafy fields of chlorophyll-rich food plants. But the water is not being replenished, and this desert will one day be reclaimed by nature.

CIUDAD CONSTITUCIÓN & BAHÍA MAGDALENA

Like smaller Ciudad Insurgentes 15 miles to the north, this new bustling agricultural community, the second largest in the state, revolves around the sowing and harvesting of cotton, wheat, alfalfa, and other vegetables. Little attention is given to the tourist, who most likely will roll through town, stopping only for the traffic lights (the only ones between Ensenada and La Paz). There are few sightseeing attractions, other than the Farmer's Market on Sundays, or watching the crop dusters skim the fields or maybe strolling the aisles of **Mercado America** for its collection of utilitarian kitchen implements and home-made knives.

Though there's not much to do for leisure, if you need to accomplish something practical, you'll come to love this city with its banks, ice house, laundry, car repair, gas stations, propane plant, phone office, supermarkets, and hotels. It's also the gateway to the vast but little-known Bahía Magdalena (see below).

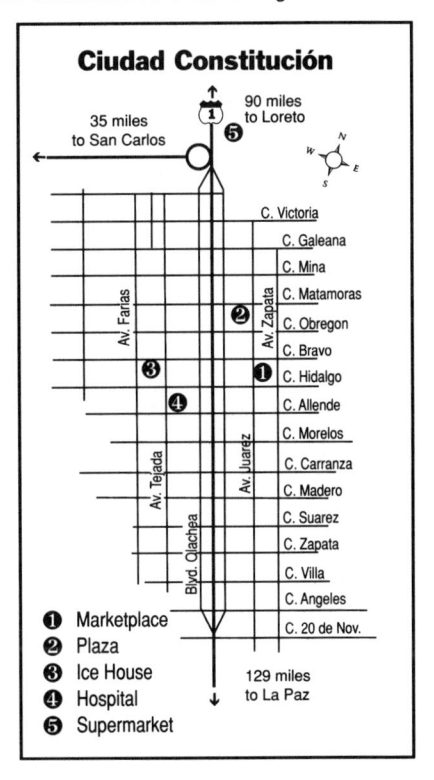

Ciudad Constitución

- ❶ Marketplace
- ❷ Plaza
- ❸ Ice House
- ❹ Hospital
- ❺ Supermarket

Hotels

Hotel Conchita ($; Hidalgo y Olachea; tel. 2-02-66) and **Hotel Casino** ($; Olachea St.; tel: 2-07-54) are the two bottom budget choices, the latter preferred for its courtyard parking and quieter location two blocks off the thoroughfare; don't expect much more than that. The two top-end choices are about a third more expensive, but still in budget category. The **Maribel** ($; Olachea y Victoria 156; tel: 2-01-55) is a business traveler's hotel, clean but a little garish with its matted shag rugs and flocked wallpaper; rooms with color TV cost $5 more and sell out first (not much entertainment in town). The centrally located **Hotel Conquistador** (Nícolas Bravo 161; tel: 2-15-55) offers the best rooms in town.

Camping

You can camp among alfalfa fields (they keep the dust down) at **Campestre La Pila Trailer Park**, a working farm that doubles as a country club. Besides full hook-ups, there is a bucolic pool and grassy picnic area. Though per-person camping fees are expensive, you can stop for a swim for a dollar. Less than a mile west of Hwy. 1, south end of town.

BAHÍA MAGDALENA

This grand deepwater bay, the largest on the peninsula, is rarely visited by travelers though it is easily reached from Ciudad Constitución; there is only one place that could be called a hotel and camping sites are often choked out by the mangroves that fringe the shoreline. Many of the beaches reached by car are occupied by fish camps and piles of decaying clam shells. It takes a boat to gain the most from the bay, whether you are whalewatching, fishing, or camp-

ing among the sand dunes of the western shore. The bay is a nursery for sea and birdlife. The water teems with sardines, herring, and gamefish. The shores are embroidered with mangrove thickets, boggy with salt marshes, and stretched with blinding fields of white sand. Gray whales give birth in the shallow lagoons that run like a labyrinth through its 80 square miles of waterways.

Historical Dry Run

In 1863, U.S. capitalists received a grant from the Mexican government for the use of two-thirds of the peninsula. This grant would be rescinded if they could not colonize it with 200 families within five years. The group chose Magdalena Bay as the site for their city of Cortés. They flooded California with propaganda: "Homes for the poor, health for the rich." Soil of "pure black mold." Instead, the gullible colonists found an impenetrable waterless desert. They begged passage back to California.

The operation foundered. Then a passing ship captain noticed the ball moss, called *orchilla*, which was being harvested profitably in the Galápagos for its red dye. He told the concessionaires of this possible market. They went to New York and rounded up 265 colonists, mostly penniless street bums, contracting with them to pick orchilla. Once on the shores of the bay, these colonists were treated like slaves, forced to sleep on the ground without blankets, and made to pay for their meager rations with what they picked during the day. Fifty died in four months. The Mexican government didn't recognize the orchilla pickers as colonists. The land grant was rescinded.

But U.S. attention remained focused on the bay. In 1908, the Great White Fleet sailed into Bahía Magdalena for a month of target practice. Secretary of State Root wanted to buy the strategic bay or lease it like Guantánamo Bay in Cuba. William Randolph Hearst decided the U.S. needed this harbor, and found his pretext when a Japanese company became interested in beginning a fish cannery here. In 1912, the Hearst press insisted there were already 20,000 Japanese at the bay (a figure that jumped a few months later to 75,000), most of them soldiers. But a four-man investigative team sent down by the Los Angeles Examiner found only two Japanese—fishermen, not samauri. So they made up a story that 100,000 Japanese were on their way. The U.S. Senate looked at the evidence and found the story wanting for facts, but they were sufficiently alarmed by all the public hysteria to pass the Lodge Resolution, which extended the prohibitions of the Monroe Doctrine to all non-American powers, even private corporations. If the U.S. couldn't own the bay, at least they could keep all other outsiders away with the threat of war.

Bahía Magdalena provided a kind of historical dry run. The Japanese eventually did attack Pearl Harbor. The plains of Magdalena are now as verdant as Iowa. Ciudad Constitución, its telephone lines heavy with ball moss, is what the city of Cortés could have become, and even today, yellow journalism influences our lawmaking.

Access
There are three main access points to the bay accessible to cars: Puerto López Mateos, San Carlos, and Puerto Chale.

Puerto López Mateos
From Ciudad Insurgentes, a paved road runs 25 miles west to Puerto López Mateos, where there is a fishing village and cannery. On the north side of town, past the cannery, a *cooperativa* is set up for whalewatching from 22' pangas; this is one of the best places to see gray whales on the peninsula. The narrow channel constricts their movements. On good days, the channel erupts like a geyser field. You can hire a panga to take you across the channel to the sand

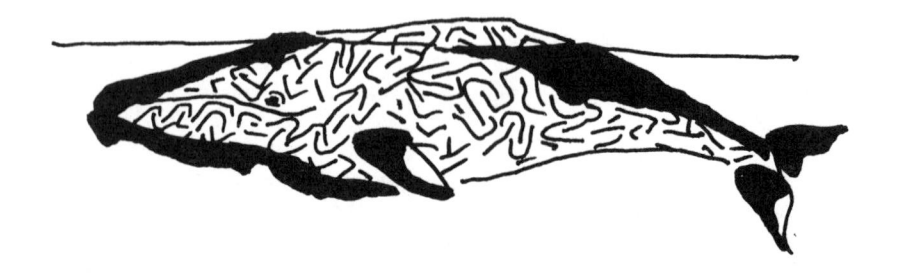

dunes, the best campsite around; deserted Pacific beaches can be reached by hiking west through the dunes for half an hour.

San Carlos

San Carlos, the largest settlement on the bay, lies 35 miles from Ciudad Constitución via paved road (turn at the traffic circle north of town). A shipping point for the area's agriculture, its pier, which extends 200 yards over shallow water, is usually lined with trucks. The village is no tourist attraction, but there is a primitive camping site on the beach a mile east of town. *Warning: occasional drafts from the nearby cannery combining with the odors of low tide can create a bracing essence-of-marine smell.* **Las Palapas** ($) languishes nearby; its 14 rustic cabins are fitted with showers and single beds, the only hotel accommodations on the bay, if you can find the manager. Pangas can be hired at a nearby inlet for whalewatching, beach-combing on the Pacific beaches on other side of bay, or fishing. Nearby beaches popular with locals include Playas de San Buto, La Herradura, El Chisguete, Curris, Banderitas, and the popular Curva de San Carlos at the entrance to town.

Puerto Chale

This small village is laid out on a small muddy estero on the southern end of the bay, 14 miles on a graded road off Hwy. 1, 33 miles south of Ciudad Constitución. There is little use for this port except as entry to the bay. You can launch or hire a boat here for exploring the southern part of the bay and Magdalena Island offshore. There are no stores or supplies, only water from a solar distillation plant (it makes up to 275 gallons a day). Camping is possible a few hundred feet from shore, within sight of the few homes here. Reason most people come here: snook, pompano, perch, corvina, snapper, and pargo.

CIUDAD CONSTITUCIÓN TO LA PAZ

The 129-mile stretch between Ciudad Constitución and La Paz can seem interminable. As Hwy. 1 runs down the middle of the peninsula, there are few access roads to the beaches. But the desert is clean, wide, and open to explore.

EL CONEJO

This desolate coastline can be reached nine miles on a dirt road, leaving Hwy. 1 near the K80 marker, 48 miles north of La Paz. Biggest users of this rocky beach are surfers.

SAN JUAN DE LA COSTA

Ten miles before reaching La Paz, a paved road runs 25 miles from the Hwy 1 turnoff to a a small village and phosphorus mine, where the earth is scraped, dried, leached with saltwater, and loaded onto ships to be spread elsewhere as fertilizer. Interesting as industry goes, but the true attractions lie beyond. After leaving San Juan, this road turns to graded dirt and passes through a sedimentary fantasy land of green, purple, and pink rocks. Spur roads lead down to solitary camping beaches, most seasonally occupied by fishermen. The washboard road continues to follow the old mission trail, going inland around **Monte Mechudo**, deteriorating the closer it gets to **San Evaristo**, a fishing village 45 miles from the highway; you'll need high clearance for the last 14 miles, which are steep.

Cabeza Mechuda

This steep coastal bluff lies near the the dome-shaped Monte Mechudo, a southern pinnacle of the Sierra de la Gigantas, easily seen on a clear day from La Paz. The waters around this point were once rich in pearl oysters. At the end of every season, the divers offered the last pearl to the Virgin of Loreto. One year, after the ritual pearl had been taken, a diver jumped into the water for more. His companions warned him that they already had the Virgin's pearl. "One for Satan then," he said. He dove,

never to reappear. Cabeza Mechudo became "taboo" for divers, and people say you can still see him, his hair growing long over the years, undulating with the currents, and in his hand, an enormous pearl. He holds it out to you, but it's not his to give. It belongs to the Devil, as anybody who reaches for it will discover.

LA PAZ

La Paz confuses people. Situated on the shores of a bay within a bay within a gulf, this city twists your sense of direction. Travelers are surprised to see the sun set in the "east." Paceños call it "Ciudad de Ilusión."

People walk to their own inner compasses, see only what they want to see. Always have. The early explorers each saw something different here, be it empire or a fortune of pearls or saved souls. All failed.

First discovered by a band of mutineers, it was officially introduced to Spain on May 3, 1535 by Hernándo Cortés himself, who landed expecting to find an island of Amazons and pearls. His disillusioned colony lasted less than a year. Sixty years later, Vizcaíno named this place La Paz, because of the gentleness of the Guaycuras, but his colony accidently burned down after a few months. Then came Father Kino and Atondo y Antillón, who, after firing a cannon into the feast to which they had invited the Guaycura chiefs, were forced to leave. Padres Ugarte and Bravo arrived in 1720 and founded the first mission, but the wary Indians rebelled 14 years later, forcing the Jesuits to escape in canoes to Isla

Espíritu Santo.

It wasn't until the War of Independence that settlers arrived in number, fleeing to this place called La Paz. In 1830, La Paz became the new capital of the territory. But not for long. In 1847, the 7th Regiment of the New York Volunteers occupied the town for the duration of the Mexican-American War. Six years later, William Walker, the filibusterer, stormed ashore and for two days took control of the Municipal Palace, proclaiming himself President of Baja California before he was forced to leave. Then came the insurrection of Juárez, the revolt of Díaz, and the upheaval of the Mexican Revolution, which La Paz rode out with characteristic aplomb, an island unmoved by the stormy seas around it.

By all accounts, La Paz should be a poor town (the pearl oysters disappeared during the 1940s). Instead, it has the highest per capita income of any city in Mexico. La Paz gives the illusion of moving impressively forward, even during rough economic times. As one paceña said, "we are all encased in a crystal here, removed from the Mexican realities of poverty and political struggle". Apart from its isolated geography, nobody

La Paz

Bahía de la Paz

El Manglito

To Pichilingue
14 miles

Alvaro Obregón

Morelos

Félix Ortega

Isabela la Catolica

5 de Mayo

Bravo

5 de Febrero

Jalisco

Colima

Abasolo

N
W — E
S

To Ciudad
Constitución
129 Miles

Whale's Tail
Monument

To Bahía de los Muertos
Signed "Los Planes"
36 Miles

To Cabo San Lucas
122 Miles via Hwy. 1
91 Miles via Hwy. 19

❶ Hotel La Posada
❷ Hotel Gran Baja
❸ Bus Station
❹ Hotel Los Arcos
❺ Museo Antropológico
❻ El Teatro
❼ Palacio de Gobierno
❽ CREA Youth Hostel

really understands why, but nobody questions too deeply either. La Paz is to enjoy, not dissect.

The saving grace for La Paz is its lack of a decent beach. There are no pink jeeps here. No parasailing. No time-share vendors hawking free breakfasts. Even the pearls come from Japan. There's really not much for a traveler to do but fall into the day-to-day lifestyle of the place. If you come here without expectations, it's hard to leave. In fact, the more time you spend in La Paz, the more disorienting and strange it becomes. And the stranger it becomes, the more at home you feel. This is the conundrum of La Paz, Ciudad de Ilusión.

Bearings

This city of 200,000 is laid out along a narrow declining tableland between the bay and the nearby Sierra de las Cacachilas. The old town center of disjointed streets is built at the mouth of an arroyo, up which runs up 16 de Septiembre. The rest of the city is designed to a more navigable grid.

Traveling About

Taxis are priced fairly. Most bus routes radiate from the Municipal Market at Av. Revolución and Degollado, moving through the city and out to the *colonias*. The bus most often used by travelers is the Pichilingue bus, which leaves from the corner of Independencia and the malecón (the bayfront) every hour to the ferry terminal 14 miles away, passing by the beaches of Caimancito, Tesoro and Pichilingue.

PLACES
Malecón

The malecón kiosk at the foot of 16 de Septiembre has usurped Plaza Constitución as the city's social center. This seaside promenade provides an aesthetic fringe to the city—shaded by palms, fitted with benches for sunset watching (La Paz is famous for its flambé sunsets), and offering one of the finest jogging courses in Mexico, running along four miles of shoreline.

El Teatro de la Ciudad

Nine blocks back from the bay on the corner of Navarro and Altamirano is a monolithic cultural complex encompassing a 1,000-seat theater, art gallery (9 a.m.-8 p.m.), modest library, historical archives (1740 to present), and an elaborate children's playground. For a modest price, you can catch a concert, dance, or play; even if you don't speak Spanish, you'll enjoy the spectacle (and the air conditioning). Check posters in town or phone for theater schedule: tel: 5-02-94.

Museo Antropológico

This cubistic three-story block, on 5 de Mayo and Altamirano, does a clean job of packaging the natural and human history of the lower peninsula with paintings, fossils, artifacts, and an occasional art exhibit. It's definitely worth the nine-block walk up from the malecón. The Ágora de La Paz next door is the best bookstore in La Paz for local history and Mexican literature. Open Tue.-Sat. 9 a.m.-6 p.m.; tel: 2-01-62.

Palacio Municipal

Art exhibits frequently are held in the courtyard, where there is also a city mural by Francisco Merino, worth a look if you are passing by.

Casa de Gobierno

On Madero and Cinco de Mayo, facing Plaza Constitución, is a recreation of the original government building, built in 1982 despite what the dates on its facade would lead you to believe. Inside is a permanent display of oil paintings that reenact scenes of La Paz history in storybook fashion. **Biblioteca de las Californias** (tel. 2-26-40), in the same building, is stocked with English and Spanish-language history books on the three Californias (Sur, Norte, & Alta), which you are welcome to read.

Catedral Nuestra Señora del Pilar de La Paz

Built in 1861, it derives from the original mission that most likely occupied the top of the hill on the corner of Zaragoza and Degollado. Now it faces Plaza Constitución on Revolución but holds little historic or architectural interest.

Fishing & Diving

Fishing is not as productive as at Loreto, Buena Vista, or Cabo San Lucas. The main fishing grounds lie more than 15 miles away; travel time cuts into fishing time and prices are on the high side. You have a chance for black marlin July to November, sailfish May to November, but some of the best action is for dorado, from June to December. Winters can be slow.

Diving is poor near La Paz, but the quality increases the farther you travel from the city. Snorkelers must go beyond Pichilingue for deep clear water, though beginners may enjoy the shallow water around Caimancito. Snorkeling excursions on the Tío Eduardo can be arranged at travel ag-encies along the malecón for a day trip to Bahía Balandra, or the sea lion colony at Isla Espíritu Santa. Best dive spots: the wreck of the Salvatierra, the sea lion colony (during the spring, while mating and giving birth, the sea lions can be aggressive), and El Bajo, where you can swim with hundreds of hammerhead sharks (scalloped hammerheads, a docile species).

La Paz Waterfront

Best visibility: late summer, early fall, as much as 100 feet.

Boating

La Paz has three marinas and a highly organized floating village. Activities are often staged, such as dinghy races, but most effort is put into La Paz Race Week at Isla Espíritu Santo, usually in April. It's fairly easy to find a ride to the island from among the hundred participating yachts. La Paz is also a strategic place for finding a berth to points south (or north). Scan the bulletin board of the Marina de La Paz for any crew notices, or place your own.

Events

On May 1st, Día de la Marina is celebrated with sports contests, naval maneuvers, and music. This celebration bridges into the May 3rd festival honoring the founding of La Paz, when the landing of Cortés is re-enacted. Carnival, the week before Holy Week, is celebrated vigorously, with music, games, booths, and parades. Buy a bag of confetti-filled eggs and retaliate.

La Paz Addendum

Given the economy of the desert, things grow slowly here. It often takes years for a menu to mature. Consequently, the best restaurants are not hideaways, they are institutions. Most popular are the Terraza de la Perla, next to the Hotel Perla, and LaPazlapa, at the end of the malecón. Best tacos: Tacos Hery, on 5 de Febrero. Vegetarian food: El Quinto Sol, one block from Plaza Constitución on Independencia, look for the wild paint job.

La Paz historically is a trade center, and not many products are made here that would interest travelers, except for maybe Damiana, a local shrub made into a tea and liqueur famous for its aphrodisiac powers (available in all liquor stores). Though technically a duty-free zone, prices for imported goods are generally higher than in the U.S. Weaver Fortunato Silva has his shop set up across from the Conasupo on the road out of town, producing inexpensive cotton blankets on his looms (a tourist attraction).

Best live music is at Las Varitas, a saw-dust-floored peña where once a year a musical homage is paid to John Lennon, otherwise pop, rock, and progressive music.

Best hospital for travelers is Hospital Militar on Madero and República: tel: 2-34-66.

ARRIVING & DEPARTING
By Air

The only way to get from airport to city six miles away is by *colectivo*. *Timesaver: fall in with tourists when boarding a colectivo, not locals; otherwise you may waste an hour driving all over the city dropping others off first, instead of going straight to the hotel zone.*

By Bus

It's too far to walk from the Central Camionera (Jalisco y H. de la Independencia: tel: 2-42-70) to town; taxis line up across the street for the honor, but city buses also pass by here frequently on their way to the mercado, a block from the budget hotel district. For departures, Tres Estrellas de Oro buses leave about four times daily for Tijuana and Cabo San Lucas. Second-class bus lines also leave in both directions more frequently. Second class buses also leave for Cabo San Lucas from Autotransportes La Paz at Degollado and Gmo. Prieto (tel: 2-21-57), and from Autotransportes Aguila at Independéncia and the malecón.

By Ferry

Ferries leave from Pichilingue, 14 miles from downtown La Paz, but your work takes place in-town. First make a reservation. You can call in advance: call 011-52-682-5-38-33 from the U.S., 5-38-33 locally, or send a fax from the U.S.: 011-52-682-2-50-05. If you have a vehicle, you need to go to the government building fronting the Muelle Fiscal, the main pier downtown; take your current registration and validated tourist card. A decal will be affixed to your windshield and a temporary import permit issued. Then you must go to the ferry office on the corner of 5 de Mayo and Ramirez (tel. 5-38-33/5-46-66) to confirm your reservation. You pay for your ticket there or at the ferry terminal at Pichilingue.

Turista cabins have a sink but no toilet. Cabinas have sink, toilet, and shower. Cabinas especiales are larger but fitted the same. Salon tickets (bus-type seating) can't be reserved, so you queue up as early in the morning as you can to insure a seat.

If you don't have a reservation, ask to be placed on the *lista de espera* (waiting list). Reserved cabins not confirmed by 2 p.m. the day before departure are sold at 3 p.m. to those on this list. *Note: if you are on foot, take the bus that leaves for Pichilingue from the station on the malecón at Independencia; allow 45 minutes for the trip.*

The Mazatlán ferry leaves every day at 5 p.m., weather permitting; it arrives in Mazatlán at 9 a.m. The Topolobampo ferry leaves at 8 p.m. every night except Friday and arrives 6 a.m., early enough to catch the train up to the Barranca del Cobre if you are lucky.

A jet boat service leaves the main pier for Topolobampo, and may soon be operating new routes to Mazatlán and Puerto Vallarta (or just as likely be out of business).

ACCOMMODATIONS
Budget Hotels

La Paz is rich in budget hotels, making the 20-block haul inland to the **CREA Youth Hostel** (Hwy. 1 Sur and 5 de Febrero; tel: 2-26-15) unnecessary. **El Convento**, a former monastery, and **Pensión California**, whose eclectic inner courtyard is the poor man's Louvre, are recommended for their austere monkish rooms, among the cheapest in La Paz. For a few dollars more, **Hotel Posada de San Miguel**, noticeable by its Puebla-style tiled facade, and **Hotel Yeneka**, with its rusty Model A on display, also show some worthy regional character for the rates. The **Hotel Lorimar** (Bravo y Mutualismo:

tel: 2-67-26) makes up for what it lacks in style with air conditioning, a restaurant, and the nearest budget location to the malecón. Other budget hotels abound, but none as appealing as these.

Moderate

Hotel La Perla (Av. Alvaro Obregón 1570 tel: 2-07-77) is the traditional choice in this category on the malecón, and certainly the liveliest due to its terraza restaurant, second floor nightclub, and new pool terrace with views out over the bay. Its air conditioned rooms aren't much, but neither are the rates. If rooms are sold out here, then walk back a block to the **Plaza Real**, which looks like an adjunct to La Perla. **Gardenias Hotel** (tel: 2-30-88) is a favorite of Mexican business travelers, a quiet place on the north side, a long walk from town center. **San Bernadino** (Abasolo 436 between 5 de Febrero y Cuauhtémoc, tel: 2-92-10/ 2-92-20) and **Hotel Bermejo** (5 de Febrero Tel: 2-50-99) on the south side of town offer semi-secure parking and air conditioning, but their locations are a long hike to town center.

Expensive

No hotel in La Paz hits five stars, so rooms here cost half of those in Los Cabos. There are six hotels in this class, each with its own character. **Hotel La Posada de Englebert** (as in Humperdink, a part owner) is on the southern end of town (Nueva Reforma and Playa Sur, tel: 2-40-11; 2-06-63): small operation, big rooms. The 25 Spanish Mediterranean villas are equipped with fireplaces and set back for quiet from the pool, restaurant, and palapa bar, all of which look out on a sandy beachfront. Just down the beach, the **Hotel Gran Baja** provides poetic contrast, the tallest structure in the state, built of raw concrete. It offers the most panoramic views but has always rung hollow of spirit, and suffers endemic service problems. A nice blend between the traditional and the ruthlessly commercial is the **Hotel**

Los Arcos (tel: 2-27-44), the only in-town hotel in its category, right on the malecón. Servi-bars and cable TV. It's worth the extra $2 for bayview units. For more seclusion, try **Las Cabañas** across the street, part of Los Arcos but operated separately. **El Palmira**, hidden in a palm grove on the northern outskirts of town, across the road from the malecón, is mainly oriented to Mexican conventioneers, which doesn't mean you won't be happy here, just out-of-place. **La Concha Beach Resort** (K 5 Carretera a Pichilingue, tel: 2-65-44), three miles north of La Paz on road to Pichilingue, originally was a trainee hotel for the old El Presidente chain, given a facelift and now positioned as a luxury resort here; its best feature is that it's located on the only swimming beach in La Paz. Worst feature: small rooms.

Camping

There is an oversupply of trailer parks in La Paz. **El Cardón Trailer Park** (Hwy. 1 North; tel: 2-12-61; 2-00-78), on the southside of town, once the finish line of the Baja 1000, remains the traditional choice. **El Carrizal**, off Hwy. 1 Sur, on road to Los Planes, is the largest trailer park, but usually lies empty of guests, giving it a bankrupt appearance. **Los Aripez** (Km. 15 in El Centenario) is the smallest, on the muddy back bay seven miles from La Paz, the only one without a pool; best for those who want be near the water, but not in it; great for birdwatching. **La Paz Trailer Park** (Brecha California No. 120, P.O. Box 482, Tel: 2-44-80; 2-99-38) near Hotel La Posada, is the most popular here, due to its satellite TV, pool, whirlpool, and tennis court.

You can free camp on the beaches north of La Paz, the farther away the better.

BEACHES AND ISLANDS OF LA PAZ

El Mogote

This long 7-mile sandspit opposite La Paz is best reached by boat across the mile-wide channel. Dolphin are common in the currents that stream off El Mogote. Once past the mangrove, you can hike across to its broad outer beach, which acts as a cul-de-sac for flotsam. Shelling is also excellent here, with many strombs and augers at low tide. On the sandy dunes grows the ciruelo (Crytocarpa edulis), whose wild plums ripen in late summer and fall. *Local legend: if you eat one of these plums, you will never leave La Paz.*

El Comitán

This is the back bay beach of Ensenada de los Aripes, more a tidal mudflat than a sandy beach; bring binoculars instead of a bathing suit.

Coromuel

This is the carnival beach of La Paz, a traditional summer Sunday spot with a restaurant, palapas and toilets, and defunct waterslide. Coromuel is named for one of the great winds of the world, a local southerly summer breeze that brushes across from the Pacific like a broom, sweeping away the late afternoon heat. It blows all night and disappears with the morning. Local legend claims that the wind was named for Cromwell, an English pirate who would sally forth each evening from La Paz, his sails bellied by this predictable breeze. No pirate by that name is known to history, but there was a merchant boat called Cromwell.

Playa Caimancito

This beach is named for a rock 50 yards offshore that resembles a lurking alligator. The water is shallow, but some interesting snorkeling can be found around the rock and elsewhere. On one end of the beach is La Concha Hotel. Swim in the clear water of an incoming tide, not in the ebb, which flushes out the inner bay. And don't swim around the north point to the next beach; the palatial residence above is the governor's house, and the fidgety guards don't appreciate guests who come by sea.

Playa del Tesoro

This small sand beach is wedged between two rocky points, the perfect baby's beach for its shallow calm and generally clear water. Restaurant overlooks the palapas on the beach. Beach was named for a small chest of silver and coin accidently unearthed while the paved road to the ferry terminal was being laid.

Pichilingue

This ferry port was named after a Dutch port, Vlissingen. Some believe the name Pichilingue came from the pidgin Spanish of the Indians, who called the pirates *pecho lenguas*, the chest-throated men.

Many of these pirates sailed from Vlissingen in the 16th and 17th century. The Spanish called the Dutch port *Flejingas, Flexilingas,* and *Frechilengues.* By 1588, the "F" closed into a "P," becoming *Pechilingues*, which then turned into *Pichilingue.* In the beginning of the 17th century, Pichilingue became synonymous with Dutch pirates as well as the Dutch port. When Spilbergen beat his way into the Pacific with his Dutch fleet, they were known as *pichilingues*, as was a ragged band of pirates whose *modus operandi* was to capture some local head official and hold him for a ransom, a ransom the villagers rarely had motive to pay. The *pichilingues* sailed into this bay in 1688 and found "an

Old Coaling Station, Pichilingue

excellent port, sheltered from all winds . . . a fine place to career ships, with wood and fresh water." When they left, the name stayed.

According to some, they left more than a name. In 1863, Manuel C. Rojo, a citizen of La Paz, wrote that the local Rev. Don Carlon had received a map from a bishop of France about a buried treasure of 11,000,000 pesos at Pichilingue, declared by a certain sinner on his deathbed. They found the bones of the fourteen dead men who went with the treasure, but no treasure. It's supposed to be on Isla San Juan Nepomuceno, which is why you will see strange excavations in the hard desert crust near the ruins of an old U.S. coaling station.

The United States acquired this base in 1866, a time of Indian warfare. Its purpose was to supply troops stationed at Yuma and above, via the Gulf and Colorado River. Close to 2,000 tons of coal were kept here, and the two piers, built of Washington pine, still remain, though in ruins. If you swim off the pier, you will see a giant anchor, and farther on, if the water is clear, what is left of a copper-sheathed hull, an old sailing ship.

Behind the coaling ruins, an extensive salt pan has been diked off. Ortega mentioned these salt flats 350 years ago, and the first colonists of Santa Cruz probably made use of the naturally produced salt.

There is still controversy as to where Cortés founded Santa Cruz, the first European colony in California (1535). Many historians believe it was at Pichilingue, along the eastern shore of the harbor. Vizcaíno, landing there in 1596, named the bay Puerto Marquez in honor of Cortés, for he found ruins he believed were left by the colonists who had forsaken the site after a year of hardship. It is possible that Cortés strode this beach, ceremoniously striking the bushes with his sword, claiming what was to become a ferry terminal in the name of King Charles of Spain.

Playa Pichilingue, just north of the ferry terminal, is a wide swath of sand backed by palapa restaurants.

Puerto Balandra

Reached by a four-mile dirt road that continues past Playa Pichilingue, this bay is

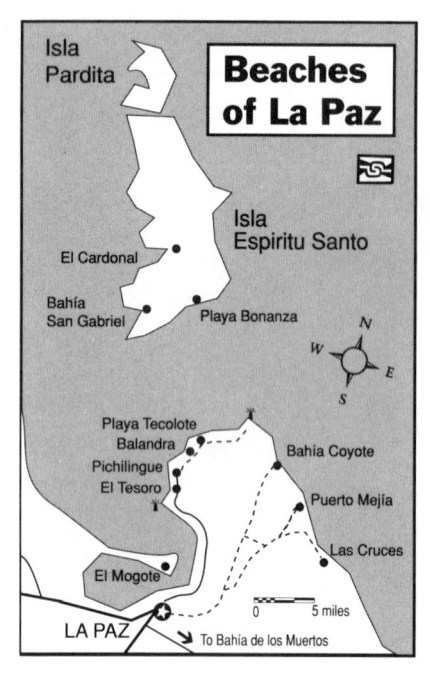

Playa Tecolote

A mile beyond Puerto Balandra, this beach is actually more crowded on weekends, since you can drive right up to this straight sandy run of primitive beach. For more privacy, especially if camping, you can follow the road all the way to the lighthouse at Punta Coyote, three miles away. In between are numerous spur roads dropping down to lonesome channel beaches facing Isla Espíritu Santo, three miles offshore.

THE EASTERN BEACHES

A dirt road departs from the end of 5 de Mayo, heading north four miles before splitting to three different beaches that range from primitive to exclusive. The left fork continues 8.5 miles to **El Coyote**, a clutch of ranches 1.5 miles back from a broad pebbly bay.

The right fork takes you six miles to another split in the road. Bearing left again will take you to **Puerto Mejia**, a private development. You can park at the head of the road and walk in on public access to a small crescent beach pinched by rocks on either side (high clearance). The right fork goes to **Las Cruces**, a road barely navigable by high-clearance vehicles; if you make it, don't expect a warm welcome—the road is kept that way on purpose. Rancho Las Cruces began as a port serving the needs of the pearlers who worked Isla Cerralvo. During the 1930s, when the pearl oysters disappeared, so did the village. In 1950, the abandoned site was developed by an ex-president of Mexico (Rodriguez) with the help of some deep wells that brought back the drought-stricken fruit trees now coloring this coast green. The hotel was converted into a private club in 1962. Bing Cosby had a house here. The villa with the guitar-shaped pool belonged to Dezi Arnez.

The three crosses that crown the top of the bluff near the small boat harbor commemorate the first landing of Hernán Cortés on the peninsula, an honor more likely belonging to Los Frailes to the south.

scalloped with five white sand beaches—among the most stunning along this coastline. Except for the shallow beach where you park, all other beaches must be reached on foot or by boat. The bay can be waded across at its lower end to reach the beaches on the southside. On Balandra's middle beach lies the famous logo of La Paz, fallen on its side. Attempts to re-erect this unique mushroom rock have failed, yet it lives on in the tourist and post card industry. Diving along the outlying points is excellent. Brightly colored parrot fish, cabrilla, chameleon-like cornetfish, stingrays, and moray eels swarm in the unnaturally warm water, along with thick schools of sergeant majors and goatfish (which, when eaten in quantity, can have an hallucinogenic effect).

A small inlet to the east leads into Laguna Azul, which is as rich in birdlife as the bay is in fishlife. *Warning: burglarproof your car (lock your hood if possible) before hiking to one of the more remote beaches here.*

BAHÍA DE LOS MUERTOS

This is a sandy bay of clear water and cloudy history. Leaving La Paz from the signed turnoff from Hwy. 1 Sur, the paved road humps over the Sierra de las Cacachilas, then drops in a straight line to the farming community of Los Planes below, then six dirt miles more to Los Muertos, a total of 36 miles from La Paz. A popular primitive camping site on sandy bluffs overlooks a calm anchorage. Pangas can be rented. Tropical fish darting around the rocks beyond the quay are dizzy with color. The rock mole and abandoned warehouse on NE side of cove were built in 1924 for the shipment of ore from the nearby mines of El Triunfo.

Just back from the beach, you'll see some wooden crosses that hint at its name, Bay of the Dead. In 1885, a Chinese ship stricken with yellow fever was refused entrance to La Paz. Drifting helplessly, the crew managed to put into this bay, where, one by one, all 18 soon died. The fishermen buried their bodies here above the high tide line, under rocks to keep the coyotes from digging them up, and marked them with crosses.

Twenty-two years earlier, a land swindle brought American farmers to colonize this area. Upon landing at this bay, they tried unsuccessfully to farm the desert. Most walked to La Paz or to the mines at El Triunfo, some dying of hunger or thirst along the way.

These deaths were not the first. Maps as early as 1777 use the place-name "Los Muertos" for this area, alluding to some prior tragedy lost to history.

CUEVAS DE LEONES

Almost two miles before reaching Los Muertos, a road splits left to **Hotel Arenas**, an isolated hotel overlooking the Cerralvo Channel; its rack rates are high, but most clients are in on economical fishing packages arranged in the States (CA: 800-352-4334; 800-423-4785). The hotel borders **Cuevas de Leones**, where a long range of bluffs drop into an underwater boulderscape teeming with fish. To the north, the Punta Arena de la Ventana lighthouse stands sentinel over a nine-mile long sweep of sand to the east; the camping is excellent, remote and shadeless.

SOUTHERN ISLANDS
Isla Cerralvo

Five miles north of Punta Arena de la Ventana lies a narrow granite ridge called Isla Cerralvo, the southernmost of the gulf's islands. There are only two good landings on ths island, along the western shore. You can land in a small bight immediately NW of the Punta Vieja lightower near the south end of the island. Excellent shelling in this remote spot: cowries, helmuts, cones, sea buttons, and olives. The other landing is 4.5 miles from the northern extremity of the island, where there is a small sand and gravel beach. *Caution: the Cerralvo channel separating the island from the peninsula is four to seven miles wide, and is known for its strong currents which can kick up a nasty sea when a wind blows hard against the tide.*

ISLA ESPIRITU SANTO & ISLA PARTIDA

These are the most accessible of the gulf islands, 18 miles north of La Paz. Together they look like a pair of weathered hands, knuckled with rounded hills and mesas, their long fingers reaching gently westward into the sea. Between these fingers of land nestle soft coral sand beaches backed by arroyos carved with Indian caves, shaded by wild fig and small mesquite, and popu-

Los Candeleros, Isla Espiritu Santo

lated by a mysterious species of black jack-rabbits, found nowhere else in the world (jackrabbits are universally gray or brown; black has no survival value, an interesting riddle to evolutionists).

You can charter a panga from La Paz to take a trip out to the island for camping excursions. **Playa Bonanza** along the SW side of the island is the longest stretch of beach here, a popular day excursion from La Paz. At the SE end of the island, **Bahía San Gabriel** has a nice run of beach; to one side are the masonary ruins of an intricate canal built in the 1900s for pearl oyster cultivation. The dyke and waterways were vandalized during the Mexican Revolution and have lain in ruin ever since. **Los Candeleros** lies to the north and is easily recognized by the large rock offshore which divides the cove in two. Up the northern arroyo is a freshwater well, constructed by the pearling enterprises at the turn of the century. Fine snorkeling is found around the offshore rock. **La Partida** is where the sand umbilical connecting the two islands is cut by a shallow tidal stream, navigable by shallow draft boats. A flotilla of yachts often anchors here, site of the yearly Sail Week. Just north of La Partida, on **Isla Partida**, is a narrow cove called **El Cardoncito**, where there is another well; a bucket and 15 feet of line are needed to draw water. At the northern end of Isla Partida, a spacious indentation encompasses four white sand beaches; silent Indian caves littered with oyster shells overlook one of the anchorages (up to 250 Indians once lived on the island; evidence of their occupation is everywhere). At the north end of the island is **Los Islotes**, a sea lion rookery.

Volcanic Layering, Isla Espiritu Santo

THE CAPE REGION, GULF AND PACIFIC ROUTES

Like an island onto itself (which it once was), the Cape Region hugs the steep granitic slopes of the Sierra de la Victoria, separated from the rest of the peninsula by the flat pass that runs from La Paz to the Pacific. Oak and piñon woodlands crown its 6,000 foot peaks. A tropical thorn forest slopes down to the shore. Much of the fauna and flora is endemic in this unique biosphere.

Most travelers keep to the shore, which has three different personalities. The broad beaches of the Pacific shore are wracked with surf. The Sea of Cortés laps gently on its eastern shore. In between, the southern Cape beaches are a beguiling hybrid, a mingling of two seas, the wildness of the Pacific tempered by the more constrained gulf.

When driving south, you must decide which way to turn at the junction of Hwy. 1 and 19. Hwy. 1, the Gulf Route, winds through historic mining towns, briefly touches the Sea of Cortés, and then heads to San José del Cabo, a distance of 114 miles. The quicker Hwy. 19 races across a desert plain to Todos Santos, then parallels Pacific beaches down to Cabo San Lucas, a distance of 91 miles.

THE PACIFIC ROUTE
LA PAZ TO CABO SAN LUCAS

TODOS SANTOS

This small oasis is a green pocket amid the dry folds of the desert, separated from the Pacific by a mile of lush fields and reedy freshwater lagoons. Century-old brick and adobe buildings, some abandoned, others renovated, line the narrow streets that surround the square. The desert heat is cooled by Pacific breezes that clatter through the fronds. Lethargy hangs over the shady town.

This verdant meseta was discovered by Padre Bravo in 1724. Crops were planted to supply the mission at La Paz. In 1734, a mission was built up the arroyo from the present town, but that same year the Pericú rose in rebellion, and it was hastily abandoned (no ruins remain). The current church, first built in 1840, was remodeled after it was wrecked in a 1941 hurricane.

Mestizos settled in during the 19th century, planting mostly sugar cane. If you walk around town, you can still see remnants of the *trapiches* where the sugar was pressed from the cane, boiled in vats, and formed into *panocha*, a black sugar molded into cones.

This is a pedestrian's town and only by walking can you appreciate the somno-

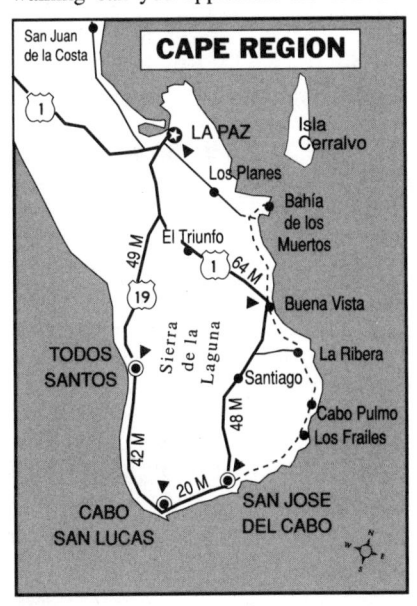

lence of this place. There is a small museum at the Casa de la Cultura, where you see the red-painted bones of the second-burial, a unique custom of peninsular Indians. A path wanders through the planted fields, from Todos Santos to the beach one mile away.

Note: the Fiesta Patronal de Nuestra Señora del Pilar is celebrated on October 12, though festivities begin on October 3.

PLACES TO SLEEP

Hotel California ($$; tel: 4-00-02), next to the Pemex station, is the only mainstream hotel in town, complete with pool, restaurant, and bar. Besides the El Molino Trailer Park in town, there is another campground at El Pedrito four miles south. Free camping at beaches to the north and south.

LA LAGUNA

This mountain meadow was once a freshwater lake. It now has dried to grass and is surrounded by stands of pinyon pine and oak. You can get there only by walking or on mule-back, steeply climbing up from Las Burreras, a rancho where horses or mules can be hired. The trail takes from 8 to 10 hours to the meadow, a favorite trek of La Paz students. The trail continues down the other side to San Dionisio near Santiago, where guides also can be found.

BEACHES OF TODOS SANTOS

North of Todos Santos, a long unbroken stretch of sand is hit with a heavy surf. A dirt road leaves town, passing past Cañada Honda, an old sugar plantation, reaching Estero del Batequi at 5.5 miles; a palm grove is on the beach. Just beyond is La Pastora, where there is a camping meadow.

South of Todos Santos, the shoreline is divided by bold promontories punctuating the long runs of beach. But they also create complicated currents and rip tides that demand cautious swimming. For the most part, you can camp free on these beaches, which are remote yet easily reached by car.

PUNTA LOBOS

Just north of the Km. 54 marker, a dirt road runs down to the beach at Punta Lobos. The fishermen launch and land their boats through the surf here, a great spectator sport. The boats usually come in between 2 and 3 p.m. A lighthouse stands close by the beach. The 700 ft. bluff is named for a colony of *lobos del mar* (sea lions) that live here. A tough trail goes over the bluff to a rocky cove known as Puerto Campechano. Free camping.

PLAYA SAN PEDRITO

This place has all the plus-marks of paradise, with just enough negatives to let you know you're not dreaming: a half-mile long beach flecked with feldspar (hot on the feet), a forest of Washingtonia fan palms and coconut trees (beware of falling coconuts), a placid freshwater lagoon (the mosquitoes are vicious) and a beryl sea crashing with surf (watch out for rip currents). Turnoff at Km. 57 is four miles south of Todos Santos, opposite a biological station along the highway where a botanical desert garden is open to the public (free).

PLAYA SAN PEDRO

This long sandy beach nestles against the rocky head of Punta San Pedro. Waves peal off the point, making this place popular with surfers. Head farther down the beach for swimming or body surfing; the shallow rocky areas near the point bristle with sea urchins. The **San Pedrito Trailer Park** offers hook-ups near the beach, but not near enough for most campers, who camp closer to the waves, paying a lesser fee to use the showers, pool, and restaurant facilities. The beach is reached by a signed two-mile graded road from the highway, near the K 59 marker. Just beyond the turn-off, you will pass through **El Pescadero**, a small agricultural village set back from the sea. Along the highway on the north side of this community is an organic farm where you can buy pesticide-free produce.

LOS CERRITOS

Two miles south of Pescadero, and two miles from the highway at Km. 64, this beach offers the most protected water you'll find along this coast. The wide flat beach sheltered by Punta Pescadero breaks the big swells down into little wavelets, ideal for children. Farther offshore, the thick breakers usually make for good body and board surfing. An ejido trailer park here is back in operation after its destruction by a tropical storm. Most people opt for free camping in the dunes behind the beach.

PUNTA GASPARINO

This 75 ft. bluff marks the southern end of Playa Los Cerritos, seven miles south of El Pescadero. For the next 17 miles, the highway roughly parallels the coast, with dirt roads taking off at every opportunity to the desolate beaches of this undeveloped southern coast. If you want solitude and wild beauty, it doesn't come closer to the highway than this.

THE GULF ROUTE
LA PAZ TO SAN JOSE DEL CABO

EL TRIUNFO

This ghost town, 31 miles from La Paz, heard its last trumpet call more than a century ago, when 10,000 miners, mostly Yaqui Indians under American management, worked seven different mines here, bringing gold and silver ore down to the largest stamp mill south of California's mother lode. Now it's a ghost town, though a few people eke a living weaving palm frond baskets or reprocessing the old tailings with arsenic (which has gotten into the water supply). A walking tour of the town takes you past the municipal building with its courtyard stage and jail cells, past the facades of its eroding buildings, over a Roman brick bridge to the abandoned mill, and through the U.S. cemetery, which com-

El Triunfo Gold Mine

prises a dozen above-ground crypts apparently bored into (local legend is that when the Americans left, they couldn't take any gold with them, so they hid it somewhere). The Mexican cemetery on the other side of the highway tells the grim story of the mines: the average age of death was about 25 years.

SAN ANTONIO

San Antonio was founded in 1756 as a rival mining center to Santa Ana five miles away, which no longer exists. Consequently, this town became the first non-Indian community in the Californias (in the early years, local Indians were not allowed to work in the mines). But it already has seen its heyday, serving as capital of California for two years after the ruin of Loreto (1828). The town was soon overshadowed by the prospering mines of El Triunfo five miles away. Now it's reached a quiet equilibrium of about 800 people, a tranquil town of palm, adobe, and cobblestone. The zócalo is a place to sit and view Baja California as it was 100 years ago. The unique bunker-style church next to the plaza was originally built in 1825 but has since been remodeled.

SAN BARTOLO

Water springs forth naturally here, turning this dramatic arroyo into a leafy garden. Mangos, figs, oranges, guava, bananas, avocados. Sweet syrup taken from the fields of sugar cane are used to bind these fruits in many ways; outdoor fruit stands along the highway sell the renowned candied fruits, *jaleas, atés,* and *mermeladas.* In the early summer, the sweet smell of ripening fruits is overpowering. San Bartolo is 53 miles south of La Paz. *Tip: if you want to fill up on water, take the road that drops down to the arroyo bottom; it leads to a spring that pours forth water.*

ENSENADA DE LAS PALMAS

The highway touches the gulf at Ensenada de las Palmas, a slight indentation of the coastline. There are two communities, **Los Barriles** and **Buena Vista**, but development has blurred the distinction between the two. The wide bay is popular mainly with two special interest groups: fishers and boardsailers. The idea of catching but not killing marlin first took hold here, through a marlin tagging and releasing program conducted under the auspices of Woodes Hole. The prolific fishing is due in part to the 100-fathom line which runs less than a mile offshore, bringing the big ones in close. Marlins and sailfish are caught from June to December. Yellowtail pass through from January to June, with striped marlin, dolphin, and tuna hooked all year.

The shoreline configuration also provides good crosswind conditions and a safe lee shore for sailboarding. World championships have been held here. Los Barriles has developed as the sailboarding center, Buena Vista as the sportfishing headquarters.

PLACES TO SLEEP
Hotels

Hotels along the bay are stripped down versions of the more luxuriant hotels of the Cape, less expensive, more intent on sport than glamor. In Los Barriles, **Hotel Palmas de Cortés** ($$$; PO Box 1284 Canoga Park, CA 91304; tel: 800-222-5717) and the less expensive **Playa Hermosa Hotel** ($$; c/o Vela Travel, 125 University Ave. Ste. 40, Palo Alto, CA; tel: 800-223-5443; 415-322-0613) have both evolved as sailboard centers to complement their panga fishing fleets. In Buena Vista, the **Hotel Rancho Buena Vista** ($$$; PO Box 673, Monrovia, CA 91016; tel: 818-303-1517) is the traditional fishing resort here. The newer **Club Spa Buena Vista** ($$$; PO Box 218, Placentia CA 92670; tel: 714-524-6656) lacks the historic patina of Rancho Buena Vista, but is just as comfortable, more so if you like natural hot springs, which are pumped into sterile-looking tiled bathing rooms and into the more attractive pool outside. The fishing fleets of both bob offshore. South of Buena Vista, there is a small but unique palapa-styled hotel **Rancho Leonero** (PO Box 2573, Canoga Park, CA 91306; tel: 818-703-0930), a beachfront hideaway on the coastal dirt road to La Ribera.

Camping

There are no budget hotel rooms here, but there are two beaches where you can camp for free: a rocky one ("North Shore") favored by sailboarders, three miles north of the village of **Los Barriles**, and a sandier one closer to the highway, next to the Hotel Palmas de Cortés. **Playa de Oro RV Resort** ($$; 3106 Capa Drive, Hacienda Heights, CA 91745; tel: 818-336-7494) is on the beach, though a bit rocky; it's far enough from hotel noise for privacy. **Marin Verdugo's RV Park** (PO Box 477, La Paz, BCS), next to the Hotel Play Hermosa, often requires reservations, though there is usually room to stake out a tent. **La Capilla RV Park** is on the sandy southern shore of the bay, more private and isolated but often filled with long term renters.

Shark Fins

PUNTA PESCADERO

This headland is reached from Los Barriles, on a nine-mile dirt road that clings to the bluff along the north shore of Ensenada de las Palmas. On the point is **Hotel Punta Pescadero**, (PO Box 1044, Los Altos, CA 94022; tel: 415-948-5505), which has its own panga fleet and a scuba compressor (guests only). The caves both north and south of the hotel were Indian burial sites, a good area to search for petroglyphs. The road continues north along the coast, past Rancho Los Alamos, eventually linking with the road to Los Muertos, at least for those with 4WD.

SANTIAGO

This town is divided in two by a river bed, 12 miles south of Buena Vista and 1.5 miles west of Hwy. 1. You enter *Loma Norte* first, past quiet buildings surrounding the plaza. The Santiago church is on *Loma Sur*; no trace of the original mission survives, razed during the Pericú Indian rebellion of 1734. The small shady **Hotel El Palomar** is a fine place for book reading. There are few attractions here besides the town's overall tranquil atmosphere. Biggest draw is the state's only zoo, a mile out of town on the road to Miraflores. The caged animals range from bobcats to coyotes. Horses run for money during a three-day festival every year in July, when this town explodes with music and drink. Santiago is a staging area for guided expeditions into the Sierra de la Laguna, most leaving from San Dionisio, a rancho 14 miles into the sierras.

The **Agua Caliente Hot Springs** can be reached by taking an alternate 10-mile dirt road linking Santiago with Miraflores farther south. At 6.5 miles you reach Agua Caliente, then take the spur road that runs to **El Chorro**, a dam filled from hot springs.

TROPIC OF CANCER

This northern boundary of the tropics is marked by a six-foot high sphere along the highway, two miles south of Santiago. Stand here at high noon during the summer equinox, you will have lost your shadow.

MIRAFLORES

This town, 1.5 miles off the highway, 6.5 miles south of the Tropic of Cancer, is known for its local leather industry, which produces crude but long-lasting items, such as belts that could be mistaken for razor strops. Don't overlook the by-products, like the bleached cowheads, nor the wallets and belts made from rattlesnake skin. A tannery is on your left as you enter town. As in Santiago, guides and horses can be contracted to help you up into the woody highlands of the sierras. This town celebrates the festival of the Virgin Mary on Dec. 10 to 12 with horse races and craft exhibits.

THE EAST CAPE LOOP

At Las Cuevas, eight miles south of Buena Vista, a side road departs from Hwy. 1, travels 63 miles through a coastal fantasy of green water and white beaches, then returns to paved reality at San José del Cabo. This graded dirt road is easily navigated by most cars, though washboarding can be severe. Bring more than enough gas and supplies; most people stay longer than planned.

The dirt road begins at **La Ribera**, reached eight paved miles off Hwy. 1. After passing through town, take the road that turns right and passes the Pemex gas station (last chance). In one mile you come to a fork; bearing left will take you out to **Hotel Punta Colorado** (PO Box 2573 Canoga Park, CA 91306 213-703-1002). Keep to the right and continue on 6.3 miles to the turnoff to **Punta Arena** (a slight road to the north of the ranch house). Punta Arena is a long low sandy point punctuated by a tall black and white striped lighthouse. A contingent of marines live here, and you should go through the formality of asking them for permission to park or camp. The undeveloped beaches of Punta Arena, strewn with polished shells and beach junk, stretch for miles. Just south of Punta Arena is **El Rincón**, a small exclusive hotel (Reservations: c/o Casa de Sierra Nevada, Hospicio 35, Box 226, San Miguel de Allende, Gto.), but you can camp just south of the hotel.

For 9.5 miles, the road undulates with the coast, most of which has been developed, till reaching the green waters of Cabo Pulmo.

CABO PULMO

In years past, this palm-draped village was the southern boundary of the pearl oyster, which the villagers harvested until the oyster's mysterious disappearance in the 1940s. Now most money comes in from travelers and seasonal snowbirds who camp along the edge of the bay. A minimal fee is charged for beach camping, enough to cover costs of carting away the garbage. Tito's restaurant in Pulmo sets the stage for the social scene here, but the big draw is the Polynesian-like beauty of the shore, and the coral reef growing here, the only full-size living reef in the Gulf.

Coral is not a plant or mineral. It's an animal, related to the jellyfish. Actually, they are millions of animals that sharing common digestive tubes. They build their limestone skeletons by extracting calcium from seawater (the Jesuits collected coral to use as mortar for their missions). As coral grows, the outer edges of the colony do most of the feeding, while the lower members are eventually smothered, leaving a bare skeleton. Because coral is limited to a shallow depth, the outer edge becomes abrupt as it extends outward from land towards deeper water. As pieces of coral break off of the formation, they often form a talus at the base of the reef, full of nooks and crannies for reef-dwelling fish. Cabo Pulmo is designated as an Underwater Ecological Refuge. Scientists are concerned about large-scale bleaching of this reef (when coral dies it turns white), and think the cause lies in cold water temperatures. This is the northernmost coral reef on the west coast of North America, existing at the edge of its tolerance.

The Castro brothers, for a fee, take divers out to the reef in pangas, but you can also swim there. In fact, the inner reef begins in a few feet of water at the foot of the village.

LOS FRAILES

Beyond Cabo Pulmo, the road travels 4.5 miles to Los Frailes. The first time "California" appeared on the map, it was as a place-name for this placid, sand-rimmed bay. Before Cortés arrived, "California" was a fictional island in a popular book of the time, the "Sergas de Esplandían." This island stood "very near the side of Terrestrial Paradise . . . where black-skinned women, Amazons, adorned with pearls and gold, were ruled by a great queen Califia." The conquistadors expected to find this dream-like island. Instead their landfall was this barren bay. The name jumped ashore anyway, stepping from fiction to fact.

Just as Lake Victoria was the mysterious source of the Nile, this bay lies hidden at the headstream of the California Dream. From here, the name "California" had real terrain to work with. It spread across the peninsula like wildfire. The name was too legendary, too loaded with mythical and emotional import to be contained by this lone promontory. And when the name "California" went on to greater things, this imposing headland was left as an orphan, taking on various names before adopting the offhanded name of its nearest kin, a few rocks set close offshore—Los Frailes.

The California Dream has since migrated to the Greater Los Angeles Basin, a civic example of how our worst nightmare is often a dream come true. Now, the California Dream has come home to roost in all its glory, as imperious U.S. developers are busy remaking the tip of the peninsula into their own image of what a revenue-producing paradise should look like.

This particular terrestrial paradise now has a fence around it, under development, but you can still visit the beach where there is a public well with good water (the fish camp has been evicted).

On the SW side of the bay, an underwater canyon cuts down to 900 fathoms, carved eons ago when the lower end of the peninsula was at a higher elevation than it is today; you can swim in this deep blue abyss, letting your imagination play with the large shadows that circle about. If you want to camp, you'll have to continue south, where big yawning arroyos break out on the shore, laying down thick beds of sand: **Boca de Salado** (6.7 miles from Los Frailes), **Boca de Tule** (5.5 miles farther south) and **Boca de Vinoramas** (another 5.5 miles south). Five miles south of Vinoramas, 13 miles north of San José del Cabo, is **Shipwreck**, where a Mexican freighter lies stranded on the beach, a popular summer surfing spot. The road finally enters San José del Cabo, passing first the lighthouse and then a stream where you can stop to wash the dust off your face before rejoining civilization.

LOS CABOS

Los Cabos is a marketing term to describe both Cabo San Lucas and San José del Cabo. There is little to be gained from lumping them together other than the economics of shared advertising. Cabo San Lucas is full of unbridled enthusiasm, wild and whimsical, while San José del Cabo is more restrained, traditional in outlook, the seat of government. One has broken free of the past, the other leans on it.

SAN JOSÉ DEL CABO

Unlike Cabo San Lucas, where new buildings seem to leap off the drawing board, the beauty of San José del Cabo is in its century-old architecture and sense of history. The church with its tiled fresco depicting the martyrdom of Father Taramal faces the shady zócalo, the town's social pivot, where a bronze bust of José Antonio Mijares gazes down the boulevard carrying his name, now lined with attractive restaurants and bars thronged with North Americans. Lying one mile inland from the sea, this traditionally conservative town of 30,000 has recently undergone a facelift, courtesy of Fonatur: sidewalks have been turned into promenades, shade trees planted, the neo-Colonial buildings renovated.

The hotel zone along the beach is now thriving in an area where the first mission was abandoned the same year it was founded in 1730, next to a large freshwater lagoon. Swarms of mosquitoes (now largely abated) forced the missionaries inland. When soldiers came to put down the Pericú rebellion (which resulted in the death of Taramal), they inadvertently brought along malarial mosquitoes. Epidemics in 1742, 1744, and 1748 swept through the Pericú, killing most. When Father Taraval attempted to restore the mission near the original lagoon site, there were too few Indians to minister to.

This lagoon also attracted commerce, as galleons, privateers, coastal schooners, and whalers would anchor offshore to take on water and food. A town eventually grew, catering to this commerce; it was large enough to warrant U.S. occupation during the the Mexican-American War. Twenty U.S. marines occupied the town (or at least the mission outbuilding they were trapped in for two months). Leading an unsuccessful charge to dislodge the invaders, Lt. Mijares was killed by a cannonball. The next day, the Mexicans retreated, mistaking two whaling ships that had come for water for American warships. Today, the town profits from foreign invaders, most of whom miss the irony of a street name they are strolling down.

Not many travelers stay in town. Most prefer an oceanview room down on the Costa Azul. This new tourist zone is a model development along the lines of Ixtapa or a budding Cancún, somewhat bland in its master plan approach, but impressive in execution. Of the 13 hotel slots, five are already built. This two-mile hotel zone is backed by a nine-hole golf course, around which condominiums are sprouting, and ends at the freshwater lagoon from which this town originally grew.

Traveling About

Since it's a mile between the beaches and town, a walk can be invigorating or debilitating depending on the heat. Taxis constantly make the three-minute jaunt.

PLACES
Beaches

The Costa Azul is notorious for steep, sudden waves. Many hotels post signs warning guests against swimming. Even for strong swimmers, the waves can be challenging. Protected water laps in the lee of Punta Palmilla (the northern end of Costa Azul).

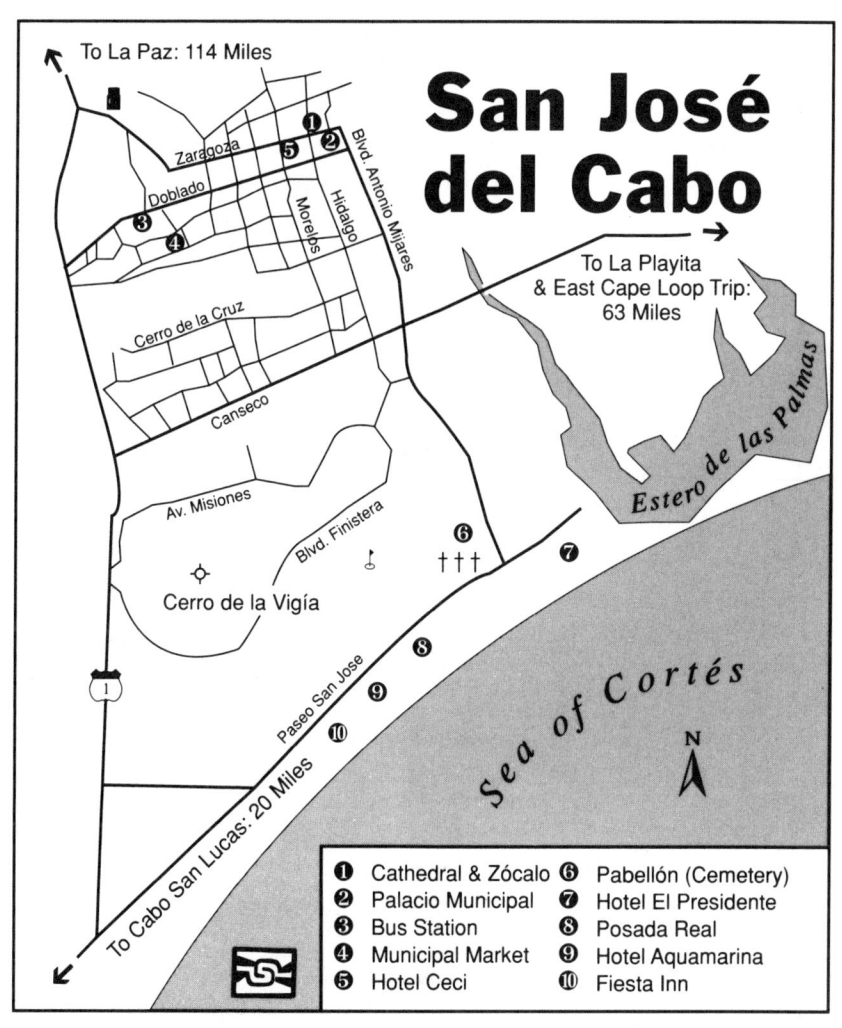

To La Paz: 114 Miles

San José del Cabo

To La Playita
& East Cape Loop Trip:
63 Miles

Estero *de las Palmas*

Sea of Cortés

N

Cerro de la Vigía

❶ Cathedral & Zócalo **❻** Pabellón (Cemetery)
❷ Palacio Municipal **❼** Hotel El Presidente
❸ Bus Station **❽** Posada Real
❹ Municipal Market **❾** Hotel Aquamarina
❺ Hotel Ceci **❿** Fiesta Inn

A mile northeast of the freshwater lagoon, a tongue of the San José submarine canyon touches shore at La Playa, where pangas are launched through the surf. This is also a good place to swim, since the waves are smaller here than elsewhere.

Estero de las Palmas

The freshwater lagoon is best reached by walking through the lobby of the El Presidente, out past the pool, and then doubling back along the beach. The setting could be the Amazon, with its towering palms, reedy islands, and winter flocks of exotic birds (70 species at last count). Pay $5 to the dockmaster and take your pick of craft tied to the pier.

The water comes from a 19-mile long underground river. For three centuries, the early explorers would risk capsizing in the surf so they could fill their casks here, the only reliable watering hole on the lower peninsula. The sandy berm separates sea from lagoon and acts as a filter through which the freshwater percolates into the sea. When summer rains flood the lagoon, a hole is cut into the berm, letting the freshwater pour into the sea.

Pabellón Municipal

The municipal cemetery next to the golf course and main boulevard is camouflaged by a wall of bougainvillea, which hides the ancient graves and tombs of this town's early missionaries, politicians, and soldiers, including Lt. Mijares. The caretakers welcome visitors and the grounds are both tranquil and colorful, the sweet, decaying smell coming not from the graves but from the wilted flowers that adorn this forest of crosses and crypts. *Best time to visit: after Nov. 2, Día de los Muertos, when all the graves are decorated.*

Nuestra Señora de San José

This church wasn't built until 1940, but the gruesome tile mosaic on its front depicts the 1733 Pericú rebellion. The Jesuits had punished a Pericú chief for polygamy, a common practice among the Indians. This sparked a general uprising, in which the Indians dragged Father Tamaral out of the mission while he was saying mass, and decapitated him using knives that he originally had given to them as presents. Epidemics and soldiers later extinguished the entire tribe.

San José del Cabo Addendum

Fishing is excellent all year for striped marlin, roosterfish, wahoo, and dorado, while black marlin are caught from September to December. Prime fishing grounds are at Gorda Banks, especially for wahoo. Fishing can be arranged through the hotels or, cheaper yet, directly on the beach at La Playita, where two cooperativas are set up.

Naturalists have a chance to view whale sharks at Gorda Banks—the largest of all living fish, some to 50 foot in length.

Shopping in town is a quick affair, a perusal of the few curio and gift stores that import crafts from the mainland.

Nightlife does not flourish in town. In fact you'll be hard put to find a dance floor. Most people head to Cabo San Lucas or retire to whatever their hotels are offering.

If you're not staying in a hotel, about the only place to make a phone call is at the public telephone office on Calle Doblado next to bus station.

The post office is in the Municipal building on Plaza Mijares.

PLACES TO SLEEP

Beachfront hotels are expensive. In-town hotels are cheap, with little middle ground between the two.

Budget Hotels

Choices are limited to three one-star hotels in town. **Hotel Ceci** (tel. 2-00-51) is near the center of town, at 22 Zaragoza, half a block from the Bancomer. **Hotel Colli** (tel. 2-00-52), on Av. Hidalgo, is also a convenient pick. The **Hotel Pagamar** on Obregón rounds out the choice, though there is the rock bottom **Casa de Huespedes Central** on Zaragoza. The Brisa del Mar Trailer Park has ten rooms for rent.

Moderate & Expensive

The cheapest hotel on the beach is the **Aquamarina Comfort Inn** ($$; tel. 2-03-06); its architecture looks more like low-cost housing than a resort. A better pick is the new four-star **Fiesta Inn** ($$$; tel: 2-07-01) next to it, which has an all-inclusive price system, or the 3-star **Best Western Posada Real** ($$$; tel: 2-01-55), which is a bland version of the more expensive five-star **El Presidente** ($$$$; tel: 2-02-11). The first hotel venture here, the Presidente still offers the most of everything (pool bar, disco) and its location next to the lagoon and beach is bracing. But rate hikes have launched it into the price bracket of the more deluxe Cape hotels.

Camping

The only free camping in San José del Cabo is on the beach at Pueblo La Playa 1.5 miles away, but you will have little luck sleeping in, since the fishermen launch their boats with the sunrise. The well-equipped **Brisa del Mar Trailer Park** on the Costa Azul is the ony developed trailer park in Los Cabos actually on the beach.

ARRIVING & DEPARTING
By Plane
The International Airport servicing Los Cabos is situated nine miles from San José del Cabo, 29 miles from Cabo San Lucas. Yellow taxis and vans cover the route at official prices. The Mexicana ticket office in town is at Blvd. Mijares and Zaragoza, San José del Cabo; tel: 2-02-30.

By Bus
The terminal is downtown on Calle Doblado. Buses depart to either Cabo San Lucas or La Paz, with departures about every 90 minutes.

CAPE BEACHES
The 20 miles of shoreline between San José del Cabo and Cabo San Lucas have been lost to developers. New hotels are being built on old camping grounds. You can still find solitude by driving down unmarked dirt roads, though you are more likely to run into a security fence. Most campers have retired to trailer parks, or camp at crowded **Barco Varado** (Shipwreck). The three luxury hotels that stand on the rocky headlands—Palmilla, Cabo San Lucas, Twin Dolphin—are rated among the most scenic in the world. Even if you don't spend the night in one, you can still soak up enough of their beauty to justify a round of drinks.

PLAYA PALMILLA
This beach, in the lee of Punta Palmilla, is a calm spot on this coast, the surf broken up by a reef that runs into the blue water, a fine snorkeling spot. A small diving shop rents snorkeling gear and other watersports equipment, and fills dive tanks. When you've finished with the water, walk into the expensive **Hotel Palmilla** ($$$; tel: 2-05-82) on the point, a Spanish-Moorish fantasy hotel fringed in surf. Sip $6 Margaritas on the terrace, then do battle on the chessboard with life-size pieces.

PLAYA CHILENO
This is a public beach 10 miles east of Cabo San Lucas, with a big lot where you can park, a soft stretch of sand to lie on, and a rocky reef swarming with tropical fish to swim through. A watersports concession rents watersports and dive equipment here.

On the promontory nearby is the traditional favorite of old money, the **Hotel Cabo San Lucas** ($$$: tel:3-01-23), its grounds bathed in palm trees; units range from simple studios to huge villas on the beach, set around small pool, two tennis courts, putting green, and restaurant with a cliffside al fresco terrace. A popular surfing break curls off the point below the hotel.

On the east side of the hotel is one of the last old ranchos left on this coast, once an important navigational mark, now a relic surviving in the shadow of the hotel.

BAHÍA SANTA MARÍA
This horseshoe cove is headed by a crescent of sand beach that slopes into water as clear as tequila. Schools of tame fish dart around you demanding handouts. Farther offshore, along the bouldered bottom, giant iridescent parrot fish illuminate the blue backdrop. King Angelfish flutter like the flags of some African nation.

A trail leads up the western promontory for views of the surf-whipped coast.

The **Hotel Twin Dolphin** ($$$: tel: 3-01-40; U.S.: 800-421-8925) next to the cove has a modern lean design that is harmonious with the desert around it. Its walls are painted with 17 reproductions of peninsular cave paintings; these are linked by an educational walking tour. Hotel also offers a botanical walk that winds through the nearby desert. The pool area looks like a fashion shoot (this place is a decompression chamber for Hollywood celebrities).

To get to Bahía Santa Maria, you can turn off half a mile west of the Km. 13 marker and drive as far as the electronic gate, then walk in. *Tip: It's easier to park at the Hotel Twin Dolphin and take the short trail that leaves from behind the hotel, a public walkway the hotel does not care to advertise.*

BARCO VARADO

Otherwise known as Shipwreck, this beach is the last primitive camping area left, though its days seem to be numbered. The beach takes its name from the rusting hulk of a Japanese fishing boat that sits on the beach, thrown up in 1966 by a chubasco. Around it the shore is pocked with tidepools. A long beach sweeps west towards the lighthouse at Cabeza Ballena (Whale Head), an area offering more private camping if you can find the right access road. Immediately west of the shipwreck, a fleet of aluminium boats is pulled onto the calm beach, above which is the main camping area; it is usually crowded here. The unmarked access road is 1.1 miles west of the entrance to the Hotel Twin Dolphin.

CABO SAN LUCAS

Land's End. Can't go any farther. And since all the restlessness that brought everybody down here in the first place has no more forward momentum, this energy tends to ball up, creating the spirit of Cabo San Lucas much in the same way that Key West generates its energy from the Florida peninsula. A plethora of restaurants and bars tap into this current, and the entire town seems constructed for the traveler's pleasure, be it drinking, eating, or romancing.

The town is surrounded by a landscape of white sand beaches, tawny hills, and huge granitic batholiths that stand knee-deep in some of the bluest water in the world, thanks to an underwater canyon that winds right up into the bay. Offshore are anchored glossy yachts and sportfishers, dwarfed by the ubiquitous cruise ship. If you are seeking the soul of Mexico, you'd best retreat. If you want a good time—cost be damned— you have arrived.

History has left little mark on this town. The Indians who first lived here had no permanent structures, no water containers other than animal bladders, no hooks or line to catch fish with. Their insular environment held them in evolutionary limbo until the Spanish arrived. Though discovered in 1541, the Spanish did not settle this bay, making it a safe refuge for pirates who awaited the yearly Philippine galleons to pass. Both Thomas Cavendish in 1587, and Woodes Rogers in 1709 captured treasure-laden ships.

Ranchers moved here in the late 18th century, and ships began to call at Cabo to pick up supplies and water, especially the U.S. whaling ships. As the whales diminished, so did the town. At the turn of this century, only 12 families remained, most earning a wage stripping the bark from *palo blanco* trees, and shipping it to San Francisco to be used in the tanning of leather. In 1917, a floating cannery was brought down from San Diego, and a new industry began. In 1941, a hurricane demolished the town, which was prudently rebuilt a mile back from shore (a lesson forgotten by the new hotels and condos that have been constructed by water's edge).

Then California marlin fishers discovered that they could catch the big glamor fish down here long after the season ended each November up north. The marlin attracted people with lots of money, for whom

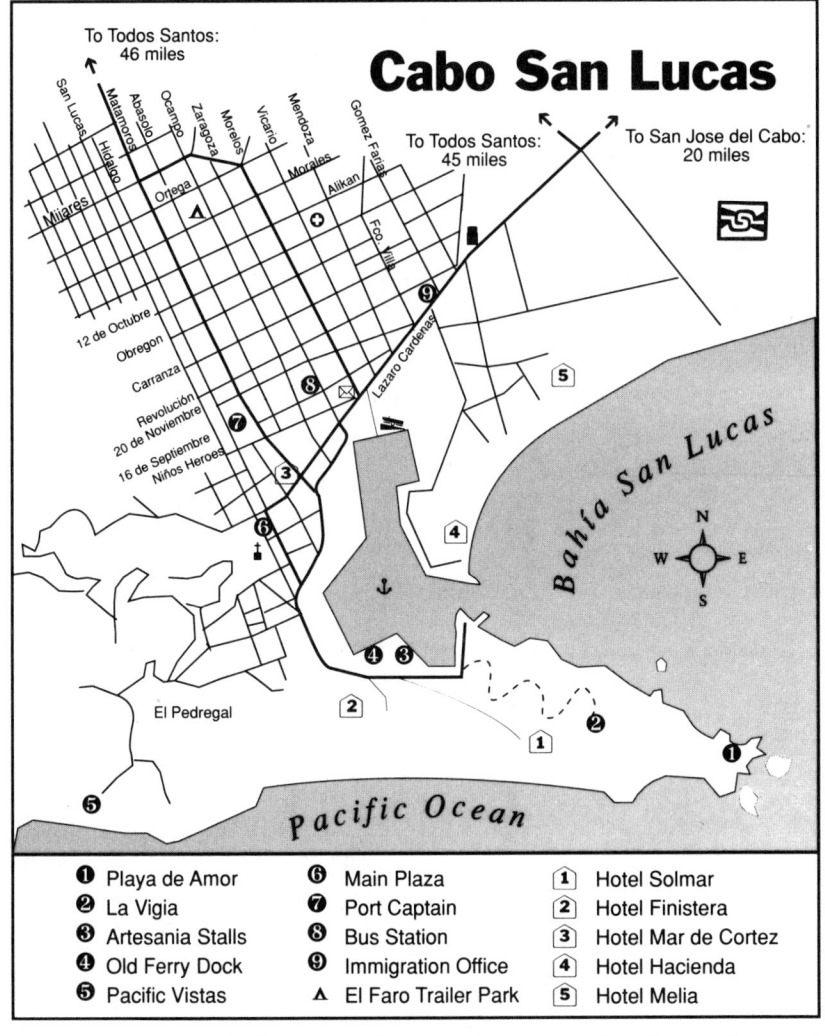

Cabo San Lucas

To Todos Santos:
46 miles

To Todos Santos:
45 miles

To San Jose del Cabo:
20 miles

Bahía San Lucas

El Pedregal

Pacific Ocean

❶ Playa de Amor	❻ Main Plaza	① Hotel Solmar
❷ La Vigia	❼ Port Captain	② Hotel Finistera
❸ Artesania Stalls	❽ Bus Station	③ Hotel Mar de Cortez
❹ Old Ferry Dock	❾ Immigration Office	④ Hotel Hacienda
❺ Pacific Vistas	▲ El Faro Trailer Park	⑤ Hotel Melia

luxurious hotels were built in the early 1960s. From this foundation, Cabo has built itself a freewheeling tourist economy that still caters to the high end of the market. Construction seems to go up overnight, like a Hollywood set, which some people complain this town resembles. Others enjoy the romantic veneer. Cabo itself is hard to define, other than as the sum of its tourists,

Traveling About

Since the town is situated a mile back from the beachfront hotels, most people take taxis between the two. Cars can be rented through the major hotels. A breezier alternative are mopeds, which rent by the hour or for the day at **Chubascos** (tel:3-04-04; VHF 13), at 22 Blvd. de la Marina or at the Melia Hotel. They also rent bicycles.

PLACES
La Vigía

This 500 foot hill flanks the bay. Pirates as well as Spaniards kept lookouts posted on its peak. At the turn of the century, people seeking passage had to climb up here and

California's Birthstone

burn a signal fire to hail passing ships. Now on its top is a sailor's altar, a cross with a crucified Christ, the sadness of his face weathered by the wind and rain into an expression of howling grief. The view from up here is as inspiring as the altar is holy. Offshore, the warm salt-laden Sea of Cortés meets the colder bluer Pacific Ocean, the mingling of two seas.

Straight ahead, La Vigía tumbles down to form Los Frailes and the famous arch. Off to the west you can see Cabo Falso. The true southern end of the peninsula is neither here nor there. Land's End is the innocuous rocky outcropping between the two, the birthstone of California.

The trailhead to the top of La Vigía is behind the old cannery on the southside of the harbor.

Playa de Amor

This small stretch of beach is nestled into the cape formation near the famous arch. Since this beach is easily reached by boat as well as by walking around from the Hotel Solmar, don't expect to find the kind of privacy its name alludes to. You can rent a panga to take you out, then give them a certain time to return to pick you up. *Tip: don't pay in advance.*

El Arco

This arch is a poetic punctuation to the peninsula, an inspired piece of natural artwork that you shouldn't miss. Unless it is an extremely low tide, the only way to get a close look is to rent a panga. An experienced driver will weave among the huge pinnacles offshore, skate across heaving swells, bring you right up to the sea lions, and play the surf like a dancer—in addition to letting you view the arch. On the way back, ask to land for a picnic and swim at Playa de Amor; boat tours leave from the sportfishing pier.

Glass-bottom boats also depart from the sportfishing pier for short coastal tours along the rocks and past the sea lion colony. *Tip: before buying a ticket, take a look at the glass to be sure it's clean enough to see through.*

Centro Cultural

This is a small park built around a small knoll which has been terraced over and commemorated with various monuments to the Mexican flag and ecology. The buildings below house the post office and library, and there is a children's playground and basketball court here.

Fishing

The marlin grounds are close by, from eight to 20 miles out, though every year people catch big marlin less than a mile from shore. Besides the hotel fleets, there are 65 registered pangas also available through most any hotel. If you want a good overview of current prices, walk down to the sportfishing pier where the various fleets have set up stands, a buyer's market. The Pisces Fleet (Plaza Cabo San Lucas on Madero off Marina Blvd.; tel: 3-05-88) strongly advocate releasing marlin. *Tip: watch the boats come in, marlin flags flying. Blue triangular flags indicate number of billfish caught, red ones with white "T," the number released.*

Diving

Even in winter, the surface water temperatures are as high 85 degrees, 65-75 deeper down. Biggest attraction is the enormous canyon which pours sandfalls beginning about 85 feet down. Snorkeling trips, organized through the hotels, go out to Pelican rock, while dive trips head to the sandfalls below Pelican rock, off Neptune's Finger or around the Pinnacle. *Caution: if diving or snorkeling around the pinnacles in November and December, be wary of the sea lions; this is their mating season.*

Faro Viejo

The old lighthouse stands sentinel on a windswept, sandy bluff three miles from town. The wind over the years sandblasted the smooth lens to a glaze, reducing its candlepower to a useless glow. The site was abandoned in 1962. The glass blew out long ago and now lies in frosty shards on the sand below. All that remains of the lens station are the rusty studs of the turret, framing the vast Pacific in a perfect picture of desolation. The sand has covered the final approach of the road, which means you will have to hike the last half mile. *Tip: you can go on a $25 three-hour horseback ride to the lighthouse and avoid the sandy trudge. Inquire at Ramon's Horses (or through Hacienda Hotel).*

Boating

This port is busier than any other port in Mexico, since the bay is a navigational touchstone for boats on their way to Honolulu, Tahiti, Galápagos, Easter Island, Costa Rica, and even Cape Horn. If you are interested in a major lifestyle change, you might find a berth. Best place to look is the bulletin board at the Taquería San Lucas, or put a message out on the Cabo Net.

Cabo Net

Every morning at 8 a.m. (except Sundays), the English-language Cabo Net brings you the weather, news, gossip, and community announcements via channel 22 on the VHF. No longer restricted to boats, most businesses and many private homes now use the VHF radio instead of the telephone. Even the police, fire department, and doctors rely on it. You can use the public VHF radios at Taquería San Lucas, Las Palmas, or Kan Kun.

Cabo San Lucas Addendum

Hotel-hopping is a popular self-designed tour activity that seems to go hand-in-hand with scooter rentals.

City tours leaving from the sportfishing pier are designed for cruise passengers anxious to get back to the ship.

Booze Cruises leave late afternoons on two-hour trips.

Horse rental can be arranged through Hotel Hacienda: $10 an hour.

Cabo San Lucas has innumerable restaurants and bars; two of the wildest are El Squid Roe, a Carlos & Charlie's operation, and Cabo Wabo, owned by rocker Van Halen.

For budget food, go to the outdoor Taquería San Lucas for cheap breakfasts and dinners. For barbecue ribs, it's the Faro Viejo Trailer Park Restaurant. At the Giggling Marlin, marlin fishermen work out their guilt by hanging themselves upside down on the fish scales by the bar.

PLACES TO SLEEP

Hotels in Cabo San Lucas post high prices, and some have a ten percent service charge, in addition to the 15% tax on posted rates.

Budget

The cheapest place to sleep in Cabo is the communal hostel, the **CREA Albuergue**, but its location far inland defeats the purpose if you blow your money on taxis to get you to the beach and back. The cheapest lodging right in town is the **Dos Mares** (Emiliano Zapata s/n; tel: 3-03-30); the wheezy air conditioning is appreciated, but little else.

Moderate

The only moderately priced choice here is the venerable **Hotel Mar de Cortés** (tel: 3-00-32; US: 408-373-3206). Rooms in the older back section are cheapest. This functional operation, half a mile from the water, suffers few pretensions and offers the basics: air conditioning, a large courtyard with two pools, and a cafeteria-style restaurant. If you don't mind foam beds on concrete platforms, and you want to save some money cooking in your own kitchen, then check the four apartment units at **Pirate's Cove Inn** (tel: 302-68) set back a few yards from the beach between the Melia and Hacienda Hotels.

Expensive

The **Finisterra Hotel** (tel: 3-01-00) is impressive on the surface but stumbles in spirit. Best features are the Whalewatcher Bar and the spectacular views; while the views are breathtaking, so are the 200 steps down to the beach. On the beach below is **Hotel Solmar** (tel: 3-00-22; US: 213-459-3336), the southernmost hotel in California, simply designed in clean whitewashed style; social focus is on the swim-up bar. The crashing shorebreak is too intimidating for casual swimming. On the sand bluff on other side of harbor, the more expensive **Hacienda Hotel** (tel: 3-01-22; US: 800421-0777; CA: 800-282-4809) is well orchestrated; age has added a warm tenor to its operation, yet it still hits the lively high notes and remains the local social center here with its Saturday night barbecues and lively bar (watch out for unposted prices). The new **Hotel Melia** (tel: 3-10-00: US: 305-854-0990; 1-800-33MELIA), just down beach, eschews the low-profile high-class image in favor of a commercial-formula approach, complete with a two-tiered

pool area where you can swim across one pool, shoot down the waterslide, and paddle over to a sunken pool bar. Standardized luxury is the key here, yet it still remains brash and bald of regional tradition. Three miles out of town is **Calinda Cabo Baja** (tel. 3-00-44; US: 800-221-2222), dramatically strung along a high bluff with great ocean views from its restaurant and cliffside pools and whirlpools. But most rooms lack views, and the beach is a ten-minute walk away.

Camping

Since encroaching development has limited primitive camping sites, trailer parks have flourished. None of them, though, are on the beach. Most line Hwy. 1 at entry to town. One of the most popular is **El Faro Viejo Trailer Park** (Abasolo & Morales), which is nowhere near the old lighthouse, but instead is many blocks inland. Its offbeat location gives it an inverse appeal, as if it doesn't *need* to be on the beach (Keith Richards of the Rolling Stones was married here). Other operations along the highway include **El Arco Trailer Park**, **Cabo Cielo RV Park**, **San Vicente RV Park** (tel: 30-07-12), and **Vagabundos del Mar Trailer Park**, (tel: 3-05-11-95). You can still find free camping on the beach west of Cabo San Lucas by taking some of the spur roads that run off the main track to Faro Viejo.

ARRIVING & DEPARTING
By Bus

The bus station, on the corner of Calle Zaragoza and 16 de Septiembre, sends out buses to San José del Cabo and La Paz about every two hours.

By Air

Being that the international airport is a long 29 miles away, it's best to share a taxi ride there. If you are traveling light and cheap, take a bus, and ask to be dropped at the turnoff to the airport, then walk the one mile to the tarmac.

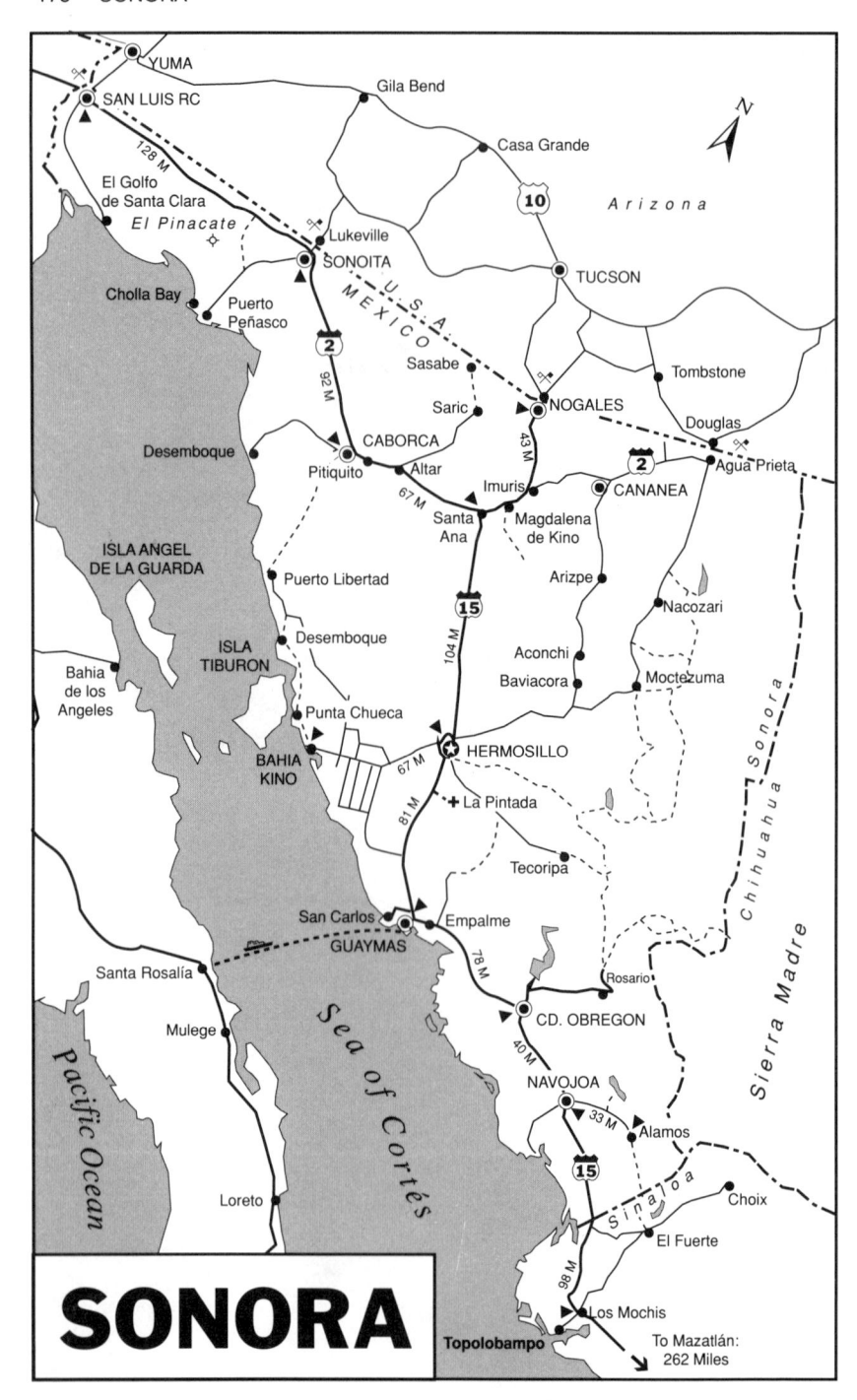

SONORA

10.
SONORA

The two arms of the Sierra Madre cradle Mexico's high central plateau. Primeval seas laid down the gentle eastern range, but the impregnable peaks of the Sierra Madre Occidental were thrown up by volcanic upheaval. This western range, 800 miles long, shields Sonora and Sinaloa from the rest of Mexico. No paved roads cross the northern Sierra. Its rugged range of mountain peaks soar 10,000 feet, a landscape sheered by deep canyons cut into soft volcanic rock. Though the Sierra Madre does not occupy much of Sonora and Sinaloa, its presence is always felt, both in the rivers it sends down to water the lowlands and in the personality of its inhabitants, people as tough as the terrain.

Along the Baja California peninsula, the desert is closely embraced by the sea on both sides, as if on display. But in Sonora, the surrounding desert is raw, wide, and wild. Along the head of the Gulf of California lies the lowest, hottest, driest terrain in Mexico. In this vast landscape of endless sand dunes, volcanic craters, and desert plains beats the heart of the Sonoran desert.

Between Nogales and Hermosillo, numerous mountain ranges give way to lower plains, called *bajadas*. The *Gran Llano*, a vast flat plain, lies north of Hermosillo.

The hilly area south to Guaymas is the Sonoran Desert's southeasternmost penetration. Stands of mesquite and cacti soon give way to the fertile bottomlands that surround the rivers winding down from the Sierra Madre: Yaqui, Mayo, Fuerte, Sinaloa, Humaya, and Culiacan. This change from desert to tropical is first noticed along the banks of the rivers of northern Sinaloa.

The seashore along the gulf also varies in character from north to south. From the mouth of the Río Colorado to Kino Bay, the shoreline is generally sandy, scorched, and shadeless. But from Bahía Kino south to below Mazatlán, large shallow bays indent the coastline. This coast is largely composed of uninhabited barrier beaches separated from the mainland by seasonal swamps edged with dense thickets of mangrove, impenetrable except by shallow draft boats. For this reason, the highway and railroad do not run along the coast but instead travel a few miles inland, along the skirt of the Sierra Madre.

MEXICALI TO SONOITA

Hwy 2 runs 166 miles from San Luis RC to Sonoita, a road that travels through the vast Desierto de Altar, one of the most wild, barren stretches of road in Mexico, a track that parallels the infamous *Camino del Diablo* (Devil's Road) of the 19th century.

ALGODONES

This alternative border crossing lies 18 miles north of San Luis RC (this jag in the international border is a quirk of the 1854 Gadsen Purchase). Once a station stop on the stagecoach that ran between Yuma and San Diego, this crossing is now used by the eastbound traveler trying to jump from U.S. Hwy. 8 to Mex. 2 without having to spend the five extra miles driving through Yuma. The border is open from 6 a.m. to 8 p.m. *Note: eastbound travelers heading towards Hermosillo will save 100 miles by taking Mexican Hwy. 2 instead of staying on the U.S. side and entering Mexico from Nogales.*

SAN LUIS RC

RC stands for Río Colorado, which no longer streams through town. But the dry river bed still marks the state line between Sonora and Baja California Norte as well as the change between Mountain and Pacific time. This city of 150,000 was first settled by boat. In 1917, Captain Calles sailed up the river under orders to found a farming colony. It wasn't until the 1937 land grants (free land) that the town blossomed.

The highway runs through the center of thids border town. You'll find little of importance here except its convenience as a port-of-entry, unless you pass through during the Fería de Algodón, Sept. 24 to Oct. 4.

The town draws most of its business from nearby Yuma and its military establishments. Cheap curio shops cluster around the border crossing. Two miles south of town, at the end of Calle 26, is a depressing *zona de tolerancia* (red light zone) where the nightclubs look more like jails. There are five motels in town, modest alternatives to those in Yuma, 23 miles to the north.

Note: no tourist card or import permit is required if you are traveling to El Golfo, Sonoita, Puerto Peñasco, or west to San Felipe or Mexicali.

RÍO COLORADO

The Colorado River drains much of the Rocky Mountains, as well as a third of the Sonoran Desert. Once it was much larger; early explorers navigated up from the Gulf, bucking tremendous currents. Now you can walk across the riverbed without getting your feet wet. Every gallon has been measured, analyzed, and negotiated.

In 1902 came the first effort to divert water for irrigation. In 1944, a treaty guaranteed Mexico 1,500,000 acre-feet of water annually, necessary for the budding fields in the Mexicali district. Mexico constructed the Morelos diversion dam above San Luis RC, assuring a steady flow. But in 1961, a new American irrigation system was leaching saltwater out of the soil and dumping it back into the Río Colorado above the Morelos Dam. Salt concentrations rose so high they threatened the Mexicali Valley with permanent damage. The Mexicans let the water run straight to the gulf, demanding both virgin water and compensation for lost crops. The U.S. replied that the treaty contained no water quality assurances, and, after all, the water originated entirely in the U.S. Demonstrations erupted in Mexico, as the left wing organized protests against Yankee Imperialism. The U.S. responded to the political pressure by paying for a 13-mile canal to divert the salty water to a point below the

Morelos Dam, where it could flow directly into the Sea of Cortés.

Before 1935, when the Hoover Dam breached the Colorado River, the Colorado delta was a positive estuarine system. Since man's demand for water has superceded the Nature's, water from the Río Colorado ends up irrigating thousands of acres of otherwise desert land and spills out of taps as far away as Tijuana and Los Angeles. The Colorado River delta, formerly as rich as the Nile, is now a negative estuarine system. The brackish environment is hypersaline. The delta has been salted into sterility.

EL GOLFO DE SANTA CLARA
A Side Trip from San Luis RC

Some of the highest tides in the world sweep the beaches of El Golfo. This small fishing village is reached by a 70-mile paved road from San Luis RC down the east side of the Río Colorado. Because of the slight seaward slope, big tidal swings (up to 25 feet) can leave a wide 30-mile stretch of muddy beaches strewn with shells (depending on the tide, El Golfo first is on the shoreline, then eight hours later is a mile inland). In the muddly flats north of town you can dig for large butter clams. Don't expect tequila-clear seas: strong tidal currents stir the water, clouding visibility. *Caution: more than a few stuck vehicles have been drowned by the tide. Cars here charateristically drive on almost flat tires to avoid getting trapped in the sand (not much pavement here). Selling compressed air is a backyard business.*

Behind town is an area noted for petrified wood brought down by the Colorado River many millions of years ago; ask in town for directions. During Easter and on Día de la Marina (June 1), the town attracts many Mexicans from the border towns. There is a new government-financed trailer park here, as well a couple modest motels.

EL PINACATE

This extinct volcano dominates the horizon, 17 miles south of Mex. 2, 94 miles from San Luis RC. The Parque del Gran Desierto del Pinacate surrounding the volcano is one of the most unique desert environments in the world, a lava flow 45 miles long and 30 miles wide.

Two cone-shaped peaks (what's left of the rim) crown its top at 4,000 feet, *Los Picos del Pinacate.*

Pinacate is named after a black stink bug whose tracks you'll probably see treading the sand. The Pápagos simply called the peak, *Tjuktóak*—Black (tjuk) Mountain (Tóak). According to the Pápagos who lived here, at one time the mountains rose much higher than they do today, so high that the sun would set soon after rising. Iitoi (Elder Brother) decided to lengthen the day by lowering the mountain. He built fires on the two peaks. The mountain was made lower and the day longer, but wind blew ashes everywhere, covering the ground with black volcanic dust.

This grainy volcanic dust, called *morusa*, blankets large areas, giving the terrain an otherworldly quality (NASA trained its moonwalkers here).

Two roads flank the volcano, giving easy access to the 2,000 craters, cinder cones, and calderas. This igneous landscape, with its vast sahuaro fields, orange and umber cones, and black lava plains, is a protected habitat for the endangered Sonoran Antelope and Bighorn Sheep. You can camp anywhere.

Access: The dirt road (K63) to the NW side of the volcano leads to some craters as well as Pápago Tanks, the only surface water found in the park. A vast dune field advancing from the gulf forces the road to double back to the highway. The more-traveled dirt road to the east of the volcano (turnoff 4.7 miles past Los Vidrios at the Km. 51 marker) connects with paved Hwy. 8 after 23 to 29 miles (depending on route), a slow but scenic shortcut to Puerto Peñasco for eastbound travelers. This route saves 30 miles; don't be discouraged by the rough rock section just beyond the morusa quarry three miles in. It soon smooths out.

Don't miss the signed side road to El Elegante (13 miles from Hwy 2); this gaping caldera is a giant natural excavation of the earth's crust, so deep it is dizzying.

Warning: Because of the vast emptiness here, and its closeness to the border, Pinacate has been used on occasion for smuggling. Don't go blundering into strange campsites.

SONOITA

Sonoita, 60 miles from Santa Ana, 166 from Mexicali, was the halfway point on the desert trail from Yuma to Caborca, the infamous Camino del Diablo, a route used by missionaries, early explorers, and gold seekers. Much of the actual trail runs along the international boundary, now used by the U.S. border patrol. There are many unmarked graves in this desert, people whose water ran out before they reached the Sonoita meadow, the only dependable watering spot found along this 225-mile stretch.

The Pápagos named this site, "place where the corn grows," which it did quite well in this fertile valley of the Sonoita River. Kino established a cattle ranch here in 1699, and two years later founded the northwesternmost mission in Sonora, San Marcelo del Sonoydag. Fifty years later, the Seris murdered Father Ruhen, and the mission was abandoned and forgotten. You can see the adobe slump of the mission, as well as a monument to Father Ruhen, 1.3 miles upstream from the town, which clusters around the junction of Hwys. 2 and 8.

Sonoita lacks the sordid atmosphere of a border town, since its historic importance has been as a station-stop, not a border crossing. In fact, it lies two miles from the international boundary (open 8 a.m. to midnight.). The four hotels ($$) are all situated along Hwy. 2. Excelsior Motel is about the best of the lot. *Caution: slow down when passing through town; Sonoita is a notorious speed trap.*

SONOITA TO PUERTO PEÑASCO, A Side Trip to the Gulf

From Sonoita, Hwy. 8 runs 62 miles to Puerto Peñasco, passing through flat plains and desert, an easy drive to the gulf.

SAND DUNES

At the Km 73+ sign on Hwy. 8 is a dirt road turnoff that tracts for six miles before miring in the sand, an inland sea of dunes, blown in from the Gulf. These dunes stretch for eight miles, from the sea to the flanks of Pinacate. This vast dune field was much feared by the early explorers and Indians. Even Father Kino, the indefatigable explorer, was forced to follow his tracks back to firm ground; it's easy to lose your orientation here, so bring a compass.

PUERTO PEÑASCO

While Japan menaced the Pacific coast in the early 1940s, the U.S. Army Corps. of Engineers was paving the 62-mile long road from Lukeville to Puerto Peñasco as part of a defense network for California, an escape route. Today its purpose is being put to the test, as recreational vehicles escape across the border en masse to its sandy beaches and free-wheeling atmosphere.

Like San Felipe across the gulf, Puerto Peñasco is a party town, as much a frame of mind as a destination. The shrimp fleet still anchors the old part of town to its own reality, but most attention centers on catering to the tourists who stay along the beaches north and south of town; there is no shortage of curio shops and cold beer. Bahía Cholla, seven miles north, is a U.S. resort community built on a cleft in the coast.

PLACES
Puerto Viejo
This is where Puerto Peñasco first took root, on the rocky promontory separating the wide Bahía de Adair from Bahía San Jorge. The small harbor sheltered by the point is packed tight with shrimp boats, and the fish stalls that fringe the malecón offer the best variety of fresh seafood in town.

Playa Miramar
This slim beach south of the old town stretches a few miles south to a wealthy enclave of beach homes. In between is a long run of full service trailer parks, mainly a roost for snowbirds.

Playa Hermosa & Playa Bonita
These are two names for the same wide, flat run of beach, which begins north of the harbor and stretches all the way to Sandy Beach. No camping is permitted on these municipal beaches, though there is a plush RV park above them, the Playa Bonita.

Sandy Beach
This beach lacks a Spanish name, a concession to the foreign presence here, a beachhead of American motorhomes camped at water's edge. Though facing a vast sandy beach, the common interest here focuses on off-road vehicles. Since these machines are prohibited from driving on the beach, they run back and forth behind the campers, throwing up a cloud of perpetual dust, or careen around the northern dunes, buzzing like mad bees. A convention hall-sized bar, the Reef, sits at one end of the beach while offshore rocks at the other end provide decent snorkeling when tidal currents don't stir up the water too much. This is as close to free camping as you'll find in Puerto Peñasco, one-fourth the cost of the full service RV parks in town (showers cost extra). **Access:** Take the washboard road to Cholla Bay for 4.5 miles, turn right at sign and follow another third of a mile to beach.

Tip: buy firewood by the railroad tracks on road to Cholla Bay; these beaches are bare of wood.

Bahía Cholla
Pioneered by American retirees in the 1950s, this resort sits on a rocky knoll at the southern end of Bahía de Adair, a community of mainly Arizona sports people attracted by its beauty, fishing, freedom of space, and inexpensive land leases. These cheap leases have engendered a booming shantytown which thrives on its honky tonk atmosphere, with most action taking place at the infamous J.J.'s Cantina.

Unless you have an address here, Bahía Cholla holds little of interest, except for charter fishing, walking the long empty beaches at low tide, or snorkeling over the rocks off Pelican Point at the SW end of the bay (when visibility allows). An abundance of shells can be found near Cerro Prieto and the Oyster Farm to the north, if you have four-wheel drive. Horses can be rented at the entrance to Bahía Cholla. For current inside information on fishing, boat launching, fishing licenses, contact Cholla Bay Sportsmen's Club, 4922 West Hubbell, Phoenix, AZ 85035; local headquarters is at J.J.'s Cantina. **Access:** turn north off of Hwy. 8 before entering Puerto Peñasco, and travel 6.5 miles on sandy road.

Sunset Watching
On clear-air days, look across the Gulf at sunset and you might see the faint outline of 10,154-foot Picacho del Diablo, the highest peak on the Baja California peninsula, often capped with snow October to May.

Events
Like most coastal cities, the big fiesta is Día de la Marina, celebrated on June 1st.

Puerto Peñasco Addendum
Travelers to Puerto Peñasco don't need tourist cards.

The tides present a great natural phenomena here, with 24-foot ranges not uncommon, but water visibility near shore is often clouded by these same tidal currents. For accurate tidal charts to the upper Gulf, write to Tide Calendar, Printing & Reproduction, University of Arizona, Tucson, AZ, 85721 and ask for their mail order procedure (or just send $9).

Places to Sleep
Hotels
Hotels in Puerto Peñasco are solidly middle class, like their clientele. **Motel Señorial** ($$; tel. 3-20-65), three blocks back from the beach is one of the most popular, but is pinched for space. For six dollars more, the **Hotel Viña del Mar** ($$$; tel. 3-36-00), overlooking a rocky beach, is the only hotel to offer the amenities of a full facility resort, complete with disco and hot tub (hotel often suffers from lack of water). Other reliable choices include the **Costa Mar**

across from the Viña del Mar, the **Granada del Mar** ($$; tel. tel. 3-27-42) and **Manny's Beach Club Inn** ($$; tel. 3-36-05; AZ: 602-387-6921). The **Motel Mar y Sol** ($$: tel. 3-31-90) on highway leading into town is in an inconvenient location.

In Bahía de Cholla, other than five landlocked bungalows, the only choice is **Vista del Mar**, ($$; tel. 3-43-73), offering excellent gulf views from the long balcony.

Camping
There is no shortage of trailer parks in Puerto Peñasco, most of which are situated on the southern end of town. Primitive camping is found at Sandy Beach.

ARRIVING & DEPARTING
By Car
Travelers coming from California can follow Mex. 2 to Sonoita, but U.S. 8 to Gila Bend is faster; from Gila Bend, take 85 south through Ajo and Lukeville.

By Bus
Three buses leave daily for Tijuana and Sonoita. You must buy your tickets at the bus terminal next to Pemex gas station on Blvd. Juárez at Calle Cárdenas (schedule information: tel. 3-20-19).

By Train
Ferrocarril del Pacífico trains pass through Puerto Peñasco daily on their way to Mexicali or Guadalajara; phone 3-26-10 for schedule information. Station is on Calle Serdán and Calle Ferrocarril.

PUERTO PEÑASCO SOUTH
Despite what many maps show, the 85-mile road (Hwy. 37) from Puerto Peñasco to Caborca (bypassing Hwy. 2) is not fully paved, and one short sandy stretch blocks most but four-wheel drive traffic. *Note: though this route bypasses the immigration check-point at San Emeterio on Hwy. 2, there is an immigration substation set up along this road. No papers, no pass.*

SONOITA TO CABORCA via HWY. 2

From Sonoita, Hwy. 2 travels 93 miles to Caborca, through the heart of the Sonoran Desert, still following the original El Camino del Diablo, the road that brought Mexicans up to the gold fields in Califonia.

CHECKPOINT

San Emeterio lies less than six miles from Sonoita, an immigration and customs checkpoint. To pass this point, your tourist card and car import permit must be in order; sometimes they will issue them here, if you don't already have them. Otherwise you will be sent back to the border.

SONORAN DESERT

Hwy. 2 tracks through the epicenter of the hottest, driest desert in North America. The Sonoran Desert hangs like a horseshoe around the head of the gulf, more than 400 miles across and 850 miles long. The desert's dry air, free of moisture-bearing haze, lets you see for more than 60 miles. Sierras ride on the horizon like distant ships on a desert sea—basin and range country.

The stark mountain ranges give way to *bajadas*, or alluvial fans, that slope to the flat basins between each range. The bajadas and basins are scored with *arroyos*, dry washes which fill with a tumultuous runoff during sudden rainstorms (it is ironic that many people drown in the desert). These arroyos often wind out onto a dry lake, or sink, where the water evaporates, leaving behind a salty crust where few plants grow. Creosote and burro weed cover the dry plains, while along the arroyos you'll find mesquite, smoke trees, ironwood, and palo verdes. In the upper elevations grow ocotillos and cacti. The great saguaro, a cousin of the peninsular cardón, will first be spotted east of the Colorado River. Unlike other biospheres, no single plant family domi-

nates the desert, making for this diverse arrangement.

Plants of the Sonoran Desert have evolved in one of the harshest environments on the continent, demanding from nature an evolutionary imagination without parallel. Sahuaros pollinated by bats. Palo verdes wearing cholorphyll-green skin. Oil-impregnated creosote bushes that can easily survive a year without water. Barrel cacti storing water like a camel.

Unlike more temperate regions, there is no luxuriant plant life to lay down a soft bed of humus. Nothing to cover the naked geology of dune, rock, lava, and granite. Age is counted by millenium, not by year. In the desert, you are on geologic time, in which a human life span is just a blink, to be remembered only as a trace of calcium in some sedimentary layer. But hiking among these desert plants offers solace. The plants don't tower over you, but grow to human scale. Some, such as the sahuaro, even grow to human form. It is easy to empathize with these plants and admire their fortitude. Their endurance is a triumph in the face of harsh circumstance, relying on nothing but their own hereditary imagination and a few drops of rain.

CABORCA

This dusty agricultural town, 92 miles from Sonoita, was founded as a mission by Padre Kino in 1693, an ill-fated endeavor. The first resident missionary, Father Saeta, was killed the following year by rebel Pimas. A second Pima uprising in 1751 took the lives of Father Tello and 11 converts.

In 1857, Henry Crabb, a Yankee freebooter, traveled down the Camino del Diablo, accompanied by 69 gringos intent on colonizing the valley. Mexican volunteers met Crabb's force with gunfire, but, overpowered, took refuge in the mission church. Crabb's men failed to blow down the church door with dynamite and soon found themselves besieged in the nearby convent, under attack by Mexican reinforcements. They surrendered on word that they would be led safely across the border. Instead all except a 16-year-old boy were executed against a wall 200 yards from the church. Crabb's head was pickled in a jar of vinegar. When a scout for a second group of 20 *Norteamericanos* later asked for the whereabouts of Mr. Crabb, he was handed the jar (the second group also was stood against the wall and shot). His head now lies somewhere in the desert, thrown out when the preservative failed during a victory march to Ures. For three days around April 6th, this town exuberantly celebrates the battle and beheading of Crabb, not the most appropriate fiesta day for visiting gringos. A more innocuous cotton fair is celebrated Nov. 18-20.

Moderately expensive American-style motels are strung along the highway. About the best of them, convenient to the highway is **Motel El Camino** ($$).

Misión Padre Kino

Built in 1809, the church is similar to the famous Mission San Xavier del Blac in Arizona. It is a well-preserved example of late Mexican baroque, though the apse, two sacristies, and much of the main dome were completely renovated after flood damage (mission is perched on the bank of the Río Asunción). But the church is no longer hallowed ground. Services are no longer held. Instead the church has become a federal monument to Crabb's massacre. Its facade remains scarred with bullet holes, its back with graffiti, while inside a small museum gathers dust behind locked doors. The mission is situated in Caborca Viejo a mile east of Obregón, the main boulevard leading into town. Follow signs for Misión Padre Kino.

CABORCA TO DESEMBOQUE
A Side Trip to the Gulf

A paved 63-mile long highway connects Caborca to Desemboque, a fishing village.

La Proveedora

A 500 meter-hill, known as La Proveedora, six miles west of Caborca on the southside of the paved road to Desemboque, is the most prolific petroglyph site in the region. Walking along its base, you'll spot hundreds of drawings cut into granite: turtles, deer, lizards, astronomical figures, abstract labyrinths and even some full scale human figures. Most are found on the southern backside of the hill, near ground level. The majority are situated along the base of the hill; few are more than 90 feet up.

Desemboque

About 63 miles from Caborca on a paved road, this small and scraggly beach village of fishermen offers few facilities (do not confuse with El Desemboque, the Seri village farther south). On summer weekends, it is a seaside retreat for people living in Caborca. *Note: some maps show a paved Hwy. 37 continuing north to connect with Puerto Peñasco, but the unpaved road remains impassable except for four-wheel drive vehicles.*

CABORCA TO SANTA ANA Via Hwy. 2

From Caborca to Santa Ana, a distance of 67 miles, Hwy. 2 travels through a desert land of Biblical severity, where the early Spanish missionaries tested their faith against the elements and the Indians.

PITIQUITO

In the 1960s, miraculous figures began to appear on the interior of the Iglesia San Diego del Pitiquito as a cleaning woman was scrubbing the walls. Hidden under years of whitewashing, colorful frescos were revealed: a giant skull, a pair of scales, Adam and Eve, a winged figure holding a snake, a bird's head. Though these paintings are still visible, their origin remains hidden in historical fog.

The barrel vault of this church, built by the Franciscans in 1786, offers a cool respite from desert heat. You can sit under the gaze of an ominous 10-foot human skeleton in faint black outline, under which is the motto "Mene Tekel Pheres." According to the Book of Daniel, these same words appeared miraculously on a wall once before, during King Belshazzar's feast, a warning that "God has numbered the days of your kingdom." That night Belshazzar was slain.

On a hill, the church is easily seen from the highway, facing west towards where the center of town once was situated. The original mission remains lost to history, but it probably stood on this site, since according to historians, Jesuits liked to build on hills, while the Franciscans usually chose sites along riverbanks. The only other attraction in this small town is Pieles Pitic, two blocks from the church, where leather clothes such as beaded Indian vests and black mini-skirts are manufactured, available from a showroom. Pitiquito celebrates November 12 in honor of San Diego. Pitiquito is seven miles east of Caborca.

ALTAR

This town of 6,000, 14 miles east of Pitiquito, came into being after the second Pima uprising, which took the life of Father Tello in Caborca. This is one of the few towns in the region that began as a military, not missionary, settlement; no colonial architecture has survived the constant Indian warfare. The town celebrates the Feria del Algodón from October 8 to 16, and the Virgin of Guadalupe on Dec. 12.

Altar River Route, a Side Trip

Altar is the turnoff for a sidetrip on a paved road that follows the mission towns north along the Altar River. This is one of the six river routes that the early Jesuits followed to create their network of missions which have grown into the small towns and villages of northern Sonora. The other river routes follow the Río Asunción, Río Magdalena, Río San Miguel, Río Sonora, and Río Moctezuma.

Oquitoa, seven miles from Altar, is the first village you approach. On the east side of road, its church was built in 1730 to a cruciform plan, with a narrow nave typical of the earliest churches. The church at **San Francisco de Atil** also was built in 1730, but only the walls remain (center of town). Twenty-nine miles from Altar, the mission at **Tubutama** is one of the most impressive colonial sites in Sonora. Built in 1783, this structure, designed in a Latin cross with barrel vaulting, is situated broadside to the zócalo to better fend off Indian attack it has been suggested (Kino's first mission was destroyed within four years of its founding by an Indian rebellion in 1695 and again during the Pima revolt in 1751). The current structure is the latest reincarnation of five previous churches built here, and much of the construction is grafted onto previous structures, as seen in the crooked dome and arch. More relics and religious paintings are preserved here than in any other mission in Sonora. The paved road continues on to **Saric,** where all that's left of the

original church is a mound of adobe.

Mission resource: The Southwestern Mission Research Center publishes bimonthly newsletters on the latest research and history on the area. For information on membership, write to the Arizona Historical Society, 949 E. Second St., Tucson, Arizona, 85719.

LAS TRINCHERAS

Thirteen miles off Hwy. 2 (signed turn-off about 15 miles east of Altar), a dirt road leads to the rail station of Las Trincheras. Its name derives from a series of 20 terraces that run up the north side of the adjacent mountain, rising to a height of 400 feet. These ancient Indian works are often wondered about, since they weren't of any value as fortification or agriculture sites (ruled out by archeological studies). As with any unknown, speculation is that they were of a religious nature. There are other similar trincheras to be found in Sonora, but none that rank in scale with these impressive terraces.

SANTA ANA

This junction town where Hwys. 2 and 15 meet holds little of interest, except during the regional fair in honor of Santa Ana, which takes place July 16 to 25 when Yaqui Indians perform their dances. This town has been destroyed several times by Pima, Seri and Apache Indians, and few vestiges of the past remain. **Motel Elba** ($) is situated at the junction next to bus station.

NOGALES

Like two halves of a walnut from which these two cities take their name, Nogales lies on either side of the international boundary. Though separated by government, together they form an economic whole, their fortunes linked to the international ebb and flow of goods and services.

Nogales was founded on trade. One of the first buildings was the customs office in 1880, built to anticipation the Nogales-Guaymas railway which showed up two years later. John T., Brichwood's saloon best summed up the symbiotic nature of Nogales in the 19th century; built on the international boundary, customers could evade the laws of either country simply by walking to the other side of the bar.

From 1910 to 1920, Nogales was the most important city in Sonora, an axis of transportation and money. To control northwestern Mexico, one had to control Nogales. Alvaro Obregón, Plutarco Calles, and even Pancho Villa have alternately taken the city by arms, much to the fear and delight of spectators on the other side of the border.

Much tamer these days, Nogales is a city pinched between hills, its commercial district limited to a long, narrow run of shops near the border, the typical border town melange of off-track betting, curio stores, and tacky bars. There are few points-of-interest, other than La Caverna restaurant, set in a cave which, used as a jail, kept Geronimo behind bars (legend claims he escaped). Also worth a look if you're waiting for a bus or rail connection is the old customs house and the Sacred Heart church. From May 3 to 5, both sides of the border celebrate an annual flower festival blends into Cinco de Mayo festivities.

Border Notes

US 89 runs straight to the border. Migración and the Aduana (open 24 hours) are just to your right as you cross the line. A tourist information office is also located in this building.

Alternative crossing: If you are towing a trailer or driving an unwieldy vehicle, or simply wish to avoid the hectic traffic, the easiest way to cross the border is via the newer border crossing. Turn off the Tucson Highway (U.S. 89) onto Mariposa (U.S. 189). After you pass under the Hwy. 19 overpass, follow this road for three miles to the new border crossing. This road connects with Hwy. 15 four miles from the border, avoiding most city traffic.

Note: Nine miles beyond this junction is an immigration and customs checkpoint.

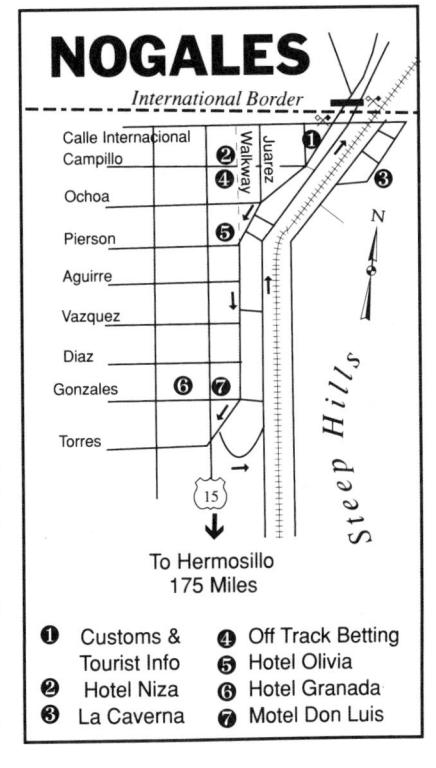

NOGALES

International Border

Calle Internacional
Campillo
Ochoa
Pierson
Aguirre
Vazquez
Diaz
Gonzales
Torres

Walkway
Juarez

N

Steep Hills

15

To Hermosillo
175 Miles

❶ Customs & Tourist Info
❷ Hotel Niza
❸ La Caverna
❹ Off Track Betting
❺ Hotel Olivia
❻ Hotel Granada
❼ Motel Don Luis

Places to Sleep

Recommended hotels are the new **Holiday Inn, the Marquis ded Cima, Hotel Olivia** ($$; tel. 2-22-00) and **Hotel Granada** ($$; tel. 2-29-11). Other reputable choices are **Motel Don Luis**, in the center of town and **Hotel Fray Marcos de Niza** (tel. 2-16-51), next to the off-track betting center.

ARRIVING & DEPARTING

By Bus

The station is located close to the border crossing, on Juárez, a walkable distance with luggage. Buses leave at all hours for points south. On the U.S. side of the border, a Greyhound bus station is situated near U.S. Customs.

By Train

The train station is on the outskirts of town, best reached by taxi. Two trains leave daily for Guadalajara. Only the first class train should be considered. The "Del Pacífico" leaves Nogales at 2 p.m., stops in Mazatlán at 6:30 a.m., and arrives at Guadalajara at 5 p.m., a 27-hour trip. This train is equipped with both a dining car and sleeping compartments.

NOGALES TO HERMOSILLO Via Hwy. 15

The 170-mile drive on Hwy. 15 from Nogales to Hermosillo passes through an interesting Sonora riverine landscape before dropping onto the numbing expanse of the *Gran Llano* (Great Plain), a flat plain that stretches to Hermosillo. The four-laned highway makes for quick if uninteresting travel.

IMURIS

Forty-three miles south of Nogales, this junction town is where Hwy. 2 breaks east from Hwy. 15 to Ciudad Juárez. Most people zoom right on through. Though founded around the Misión de San José de los Hímeres, established by Kino in 1687, nothing remains of the colonial period except a black Christ hanging in the church sacristy (turn down the street marked by the statue of Kino on horseback). Statues of a dark-skinned Christ were popular with converts, who preferred not to worship a white figure. But these black-skinned Christs are rare, and for some obscure reason often associated with spring waters—in this case, mineral baths, which are found past the plaza on a dirt road. The bus station is alongside Hwy. 15, next to Kino statue.

SAN IGNACIO DE CABORICA

This, the second mission founded by Kino, is an outstanding example what beauty the missionaries wrought from the desert. Almost identical to what Cocóspera once was like, this blinding white building dates from 1720, though first built in 1693. In the sacristy, behind bars, is a small exhibit of Jesuit artifacts and brocade vestments, heavy crosses, and the original retablo, with its ionic spirals and ancient oil paintings. For a more hands-on approach, ask the caretaker to unlock the tower. Its *caracol* (seashell) staircase is the only original construction that escaped later rebuilding, an enduring design copied from nature. The rough hewn mesquite beams wind up to the roof, where you can walk out and rap the bronze bells held up by a tangle of steel chain. Their giant cracks come from occasional falls to the ground. Church and village are easily accessible, two miles off Hwy. 15, 2.3 miles north of Magdalena, 11.5 miles south of Imuris.

MAGDALENA

The largest city on the Magdalena River, it also is the most festive. Attention centers

Caracol Staircase, Misión San Ignacio

on a big shady zócalo, ringed by stores selling amulets and other religious curiosities, and fronted by a church where lies the image of San Francisco Javier, highly revered by Indian tribes in both the United States and Mexico (particularly the Seri, Mayo, Pápago, Pima and Yaqui tribes). The yearly celebration begins the eve of September 22 and concludes on Oct. 4, when thousands of indigenous pilgrims throng the plaza. This is one of the best opportunities to hear the chant of native songs, and witness dances such as Los Matachines, Las Pascolas, and El Venado. On December 3rd, there is another celebration in honor of San Francisco Javier.

Motel Kino and Trailer Park provides about the best lodging here; it is situated across from the dirt road that travels 37 miles to Tubatama.

PADRE KINO

Another celebration taking place in Magdalena, from May 20 to 28, pays homage to Father Kino. Born in 1645 in the Italian Alps, he died in Magdalena on March 15, 1711, having come that night to dedicate a new chapel. Sleuthing archaeologists found his grave in 1966. You can see his remains in a modern glass-paneled tomb in the zócalo, his gray bones finally at rest (his breastbone is stained by the crucifix he wore).

This obstinate Italian Jesuit was a thorn in the thumb of his superiors, who could not control Kino's desire to add to God's empire. In 24 years, he expanded the frontier to include 25 missions, made the first two Jesuit expeditions into Baja California, brought seven tribes into the church, discovered the Gila River, and introduced wheat, grapes and apricot, citrus, peach, fig, pear and pomegranate trees to these river valleys.

While he will always be remembered for his legendary work in Sonora and Arizona, his passion focused on California. In fact, while assigned to the Pimería Alta (Pima and Apache land), he was ridiculed by his superiors for trying to construct a supply ship for California. He built it in Caborca, 60 miles from the nearest place it could possibly float.

While preaching in the Sonoran desert, he came across some Indians carrying blue shells, which he immediately recognized as those found along California's Pacific Shore (Kino had made the first land excursion across the Baja California peninsula to the Pacific in 1684). Since no Indians had boats capable of crossing the gulf, these shells had to have traveled by land, hence he deduced that California must be a peninsula, not an island. These abalone shells, which circulated all over Mexico as proof of his theory, were responsible for redrawing the maps of European cartographers, finally closing the fabled Straits of Anian.

Kino later made two expeditions across the waterless desert to the head of the Gulf, to physically prove his greatest discovery. He never did finish his ship in the desert, perhaps knowing he could always walk to California.

TO HERMOSILLO

From Santa Ana to Hermosillo 104 miles away, the four-lane road passes through a flat featureless plain, El Gran Llano. Sparsely settled, most towns (which predate the highway) cling to the railway that runs close nearby: Estación Llano, Benjamin Hill, Querobi, Carbo, and Pesquiera.

Of these, the only interesting stop might be Benjamin Hill, 27 miles south of Santa Ana, one mile off the highway. This town is the rail junction for tracks running to Nogales and Mexicali. A steam locomotive stands on display in front of the station, next to the modest **Hotel Morelos** ($). Benjamin Hill was a Mexican general involved in the Revolution of 1910 (on the winning side).

A more interesting way to travel to Hermosillo is on the **Río Sonora Route**, through Cananea and down the Río Sonora.

░░░░░░░░░░░░░░░░░░░░░░░░░░░░

RUTA RÍO SONORA,
An Alternate Route to Hermosillo

Though 60 miles longer than taking Hwy. 15 to Hermosillo, the Río Sonora route offers more for the traveler: revolutionary towns, mission ruins, hot springs, and an enchanting Sonoran riverine landscape. From Imuris (43 miles south of Nogales on Hwy. 15), take Hwy. 2 east for 52 miles to Cananea, then drive south following the Río Sonora along Hwy. 118. Total distance from Imuris to Hermosillo is 230 miles.

COCÓSPERA

Midway between Imuris and Cananea (about 25 miles from both) lie the ruins of the most important mission founded by Father Kino in 1689 (as late as the 19th century, it still was considered headquarters for the Pimería Alta). Unfortunately, the Cocóspera valley was along the Apache's favorite east-west raiding route. They sacked and burned the church and village many times. These are actually the ruins of a later Franciscan church, built within the adobe walls of the original Jesuit mission, one church inside the other.

Our Lady of Pilar Santiago de Cocóspera now is supported in its old age by a crutch of scaffolding to keep its facade from falling. The roof has already collapsed, but the stone buttresses and thick walls remain, and you can still see much of the scalloped moulding and other plaster detail work around the altar. The village surrounding the mission has disappeared, but potsherds dating to 1700 continually turn up in the soil. The ruins stand guard on a bluff overlooking the highway, about half a mile to the east of the current village.

CANANEA

This turn-of-the-century mining town (52 miles from the junction of Hwys. 15 and 2 at Imuris) takes its biblical name from these sunburnt hills, which contain one of the largest deposits of copper in the world. It is also known as the birthplace of the Mexican Revolution.

At the turn of the century, the dictator Porfirio Díaz invited an American, Col. William Greene, to mine these hills at little cost. Greene employed 6,000 Mexicans, mostly *campesinos* and Yaqui Indians dispossessed from lands farther south. He also employed about 600 Americans, who received double the wage for the same work. In 1906, led by the Flores Magon brothers, the Unión Liberal Humanidad was founded to force a better deal from Greene. Five pesos for eight hours. Green refused. On May 31st, the strike broke. When 2,000 miners rioted, looting the pawnshops of rifles, Greene gathered a gang of Pinkertons,

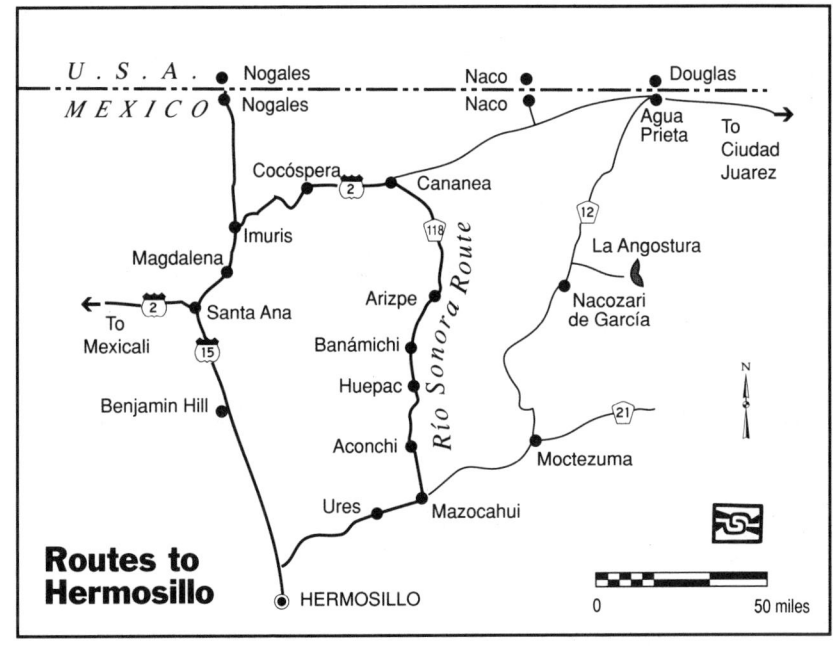

Routes to Hermosillo

Map labels: U.S.A., MEXICO, Nogales, Nogales, Naco, Naco, Douglas, Agua Prieta, To Ciudad Juarez, Cocóspera, Cananea, La Angostura, Imuris, Magdalena, Arizpe, Nacozari de García, To Mexicali, Santa Ana, Banámichi, Benjamin Hill, Huepac, Aconchi, Moctezuma, Ures, Mazocahui, HERMOSILLO, Río Sonora Route, 0 50 miles

company goons, and reinforcements from Ft. Huachuca across the border. This renegade army rode into Cananea, calling themselves the Arizona Rangers. Striking miners were lynched, shot, impressed into the Mexican Army, and sent to the penal colony on Islas Tres Marías.

Though defeated, these Mexicans miners forged a new identity for the nation, that of an independent working class. These miners became the first proletariat, largely as the result of one gringo's refusal to pay an equal wage for equal labor. The strike at Cananea was the first shout of rebellion that five years later erupted in the Mexican Revolution.

The martyrs of 1906, as they are called, are memorialized by a monument on the main road leading into town. The town itself looks much as it did in the early 1900s, a mineral town with corrugated tin roofs. Big trucks grind through the city, carrying copper concentrates for exportation through Guaymas and Nogales. The open pit mine, Cobre Grande, dominates the town and is fronted by an amalgam of old brick buildings, the offices for the copper mine. Between the town center on one mesa and the mine on another stretches a busy boulevard, the main artery of town.

PLACES
Cárcel de Cananea

Me aprehendieron los gendarmes
al estilo americano,
Como un hombre de delito
todos con pistola en mano.

La cárcel de Cananea
está situada en una mesa,
y en ella fui procesado
por causa de mi torpeza.

A Mexican *Corrido* (Folk Song)

This jail was built in 1903 with money loaned by Greene, a man with foresight. The cells, which once held striking miners waiting for execution, now display the history of that turbulent time. This jail (now called Museo de la Lucha Obrera), is famous throughout Mexico (the jail in Mulegé, B.C.S. is a replica) and worth the detour off the highway (signage is in Spanish).

Cobre Grande

Mine tours can be arranged at the company offices at the mine gate. This is the 10th largest copper mine in the world, producing 45 percent of Mexico's copper output.

Casa de Greene

Three blocks from the jail, there is a manorial residence, appropriately trimmed in green paint. Though Greene crushed the strike, he lost the mine to the Anaconda Copper Company in 1919, along with this house (the mine has since been nationalized). Across the street is an assortment of mining equipment lying in front of the *Centro Cultural,* next to another huge mansion, the *Casa de Huespedes,* which once housed American mining executives.

GRINGO

Gringo is a word that can be either affectionate or derogatory. Its origins are as vague as its meaning. Some experts claim it was first used during the American invasion of Mexico in 1847. General Winfield Scott's troops wore green uniforms. The Mexicans shouted "Green Go (Home)" as a way of protest. Others claim that the name came from a song the U.S. troops always seemed to be singing, which began "Green grow the rushes." Then there are those who believe that the word gringo actually came about in Cananea, as striking miners chanted in the streets: Greene Go, Greene Go. Whether it came out of color, song, or politics, it has shed much of its original derisive quality. It is one of those words that take on meaning only through its intonation. In either case, take no offense.

Events

Cananea celebrates the Día de la Santa Cruz, May 3 to 5, preceded by a particularly exuberant May 1st Labor Day. Called Fiesta de las Flores, there are regional dances, parades, and, strangely enough in the gritty town, contests of floral arrangements.

Places to Sleep

Take your pick: **Hotel Central** ($), near the Union Hall, with views of the mine, or **Hotel Alameda** ($), one block from the Cárcel de Cananea. Outside of town is the cleaner, less colorful **Motel Valle del Cobre** ($$), on the highway one kilometer east of the monument.

CANANEA TO HERMOSILLO

A mile east of Cananea on Hwy. 2, you turn south on Sonora Hwy. 118 to Arizpe and Ures, a road that takes 197 miles to reach Hermosillo. This road follows the course of the Río Sonora, a route explored by Coronado on his way to the Río Grande in 1540. It was along this same path that the missionaries made their first incursion into this wild land 100 years later. This is the heart of rural Sonora, a landscape of dried corn stalks and red garlands of chile, tall cottonwood trees, melted adobe ruins, and colonial towns, all linked by a shimmering river that winds through arid hills.

These original mission villages are set above the flood plain along the river's edge, and are surrounded by patchwork fields of chiles, melons and tobacco irrigated by the same canal-and-ditch system used by the Pima and Opata Indians that lived here before the missionaries arrived. Surrounding the irrigated tracts are *temporales,* agricultural fields that depend on seasonal rains.

Caution: there are half a dozen river fordings between Cananea and Arizpe, impassable during rains. During autumn and spring, the Río Sonora is frequently dry both above and below Huepac. Flooding is frequent during the summer, but winter rains are more severe.

ARIZPE

At the junction of the Sonora and Bacanuche rivers, 68 miles south of Cananea, lies a small town whose quiet colonial character has been preserved by its isolation. Once it was the center of all things. In 1788, administrators headquartered here controlled the destinies of California, Baja California, Arizona, Sonora, New Mexico, and Texas. The Church of Nuestra Señora de la Asunción, whose baptismal records start in 1648, was once the largest in Sonora. Its fortress-like construction, built to withstand Indian attack as well as time, still stands. Two blocks from the zócalo, it's easy to spot.

Inside the nave of the church, in a glass-topped sarcophogus, you'll find the bones of Juan Bautista de Anza, dead since 1788 yet still dressed in full uniform. De Anza cut the trail to California. In the winter of 1775, he led 240 settlers 1,200 miles north to San Francisco, where he founded a mission and presidio. The U.S Congress has given national historic trail status to the Juan Bautista de Anza route.

Like the bones of De Anza, Arizpe is a ghost of its former importance, though it remains the closest colonial town south of the border. It does come alive with dances and music on Oct. 4th, the day of St. Francis of Assisi.

SAN LORENZO DE HUÉPAC

Misión de San Lorenzo was built in the 18th century by Jesuits, though the town was actually founded in 1679. Its simple facade is hung with three bells, but the corbelled ceiling of its interior is more extravagant. An old-fashioned flour mill is the only other attraction here. Huépac is situated 32 miles south of Arizpe.

AGUA CALIENTE HOT SPRINGS

This is the most unique camping spot in northern Sonora, at the foot of the Sierra Aconchi. Hot water gushes from the ground at 130 degrees, and is directed into a series of aqueducts that lead to pools of varying temperatures. Farther back is a shady camping area, which, when the daytrippers leave, offers you private midnight swims in steaming pools of spring water.

From a turnoff 3.8 miles south of Huépac, a paved road runs for a mile through the village of San Felipe, then changes to dirt for another six miles to Agua Caliente. A shorter (3.5 miles) but more difficult approach can be made from Aconchi; you ford three water crossings along the way.

ACONCHI

This small village is laureled with red chile strings, a tradition. (strings cost about $5, and can be brought into the U.S.). The mission, San Pedro Aconchi, was built by the Franciscans in the 18th century. Their coat of arms is carved over the entry. Inside hangs a unique Black Christ similar to the one in Imuris. As in Imuris and other localities where Black Christs are found, mineral springs are nearby. Aconchi is six miles south of Huépac.

Chile

BAVIÁCORA

Though this town was founded in 1639, little remains of its colonial days. The church was clumsily redesigned in a pseudo-Moorish style, with an onion dome. This style is mimicked with more elán by a newer cathedral that stands to its side. A modest motel ($) lies just north of town, along the highway; it's clean, but keep an eye out for the giant centipedes. Baviácora is eight miles south of Aconchi.

MAZOCAHUI

Founded in late 17th century, Mazocahui today is of little distinction except that it marks the turnoff for Moctezuma, Nacozari, and the border town of Agua Prieta. Mazocahui is 13 miles south of Baviácora.

URES

Another town once powerful, now forgotten. Ures was twice the capital of Sonora (1838-42 and 1847-76), and most of the town has changed little from that time. The old Misión San Miguel stands to one side of the zócalo, while a few blocks away on Zaragoza is the house of Gen. Ignacio Pesqueira (an ex-governor of the previous century), next to the old Jesuit cemetery. On the edge of town is the Nápoles Hacienda, a pre-revolutionary mansion. But locals are apt to point you to two sights that bear little on the town's history. One is the *carroza*, a 19th-century horse-drawn funeral hearse built in New York and kept on exhibit in the Ayuntamiento facing the zócalo. The other is a series of four 19th

---

MAZOCAHUI TO AGUA PRIETA
Loop Trip Back to Border

From Mazocahui, a paved road (Sonora Hwy. 20) travels 40 miles east to Moctezuma, where the road intersects Sonora Hwy. 12, which runs north 116 miles to the border town of Agua Prieta.

Seventy-six miles south of Agua Prieta (46 miles north of Moctezuma), you pass through **Nacozari de García**, a town almost erased from the map in 1907, saved only by an act of unadulterated heroism. When a train of dynamite caught fire at the station, Jesús García drove the train out of town, sacrificing his life for the town's. The town changed its name in his honor. For one year, the women in town dressed in black. Monuments were dedicated to his memory not just in Mexico, but in Cuba, Guatemala, England, and Germany. The memorial in Nacozari de García is a single 30 foot column; the bronze plaque at its base bears a striking resemblance to Jesus Christ, his namesake. Beneath his face is the coat of arms of the Republic of Mexico.

A few miles north of Nacozari, a 20-mile dirt road runs to **Lago Angostura**, known for its bass fishing.

Hwy. 12 ends at **Agua Prieta**, where you can cross over to Douglas, Arizona, or loop back to Cananea, 100 miles away on Hwy. 2.

Agua Prieta was named after a water hole, which was discovered when the border between the U.S. and Mexico was laid out in 1855. But it takes its fame from the Plan de Agua Prieta, a document whereby the generals of Sonora rebelled against Venustiano Carranza, giving presidential power to Adolpho de la Huerta. It was signed on April 23, 1920, at the Edificio de la Aduana, close to the safety of the international border. This quiet town celebrates a lively Día de Independencia on Sept. 16. The Grito ("Viva México" three times) is shouted on the evening of the 15th. *Note: the border is open 24 hours.*

century bronze statues of Grecian figures standing in the zócalo, cast in New York by J.W. Fiske.

Ures likes to calls itself "La Olvidada Atenas," the forgotten Athens. In 1812, its college offered courses in German, French, Italian, Greek, and English. But the world has distanced itself from this quiet pueblo which now slumbers through the years, except for the festival days of San Miguel Arcángel (Sept. 29) and San Juan (June 24). Ures is 23 miles south of Mazocahui.

GUADALUPE

As Aconchi is to chili strings, Guadalupe is to sugar cane. Stalks are sold roadside, and there is a modern sugar mill here. Look for *piloncillo*, a brown sugar candy made here. Guadalupe is situated 3.5 miles south of Ures, and 38 miles north of Hermosillo.

HERMOSILLO

Hermosillo doesn't take its name from the Spanish adjective "hermosa" but from a hero in the fight for Mexican Independence, José María González de Hermosillo. Still, the controversy rages as to whether Hermosillo deserves its name. Some argue that the city is colorless, that it has no endearing qualities, no regional dress, no great sights, and that the only handicraft here is the making of Ford pick-ups. Others disagree, seeing beauty in its many large parks, broad boulevards, wedding cake cathedrals, and flowering orange trees.

Its original name was a Pima word, Pitic, which had to do with the confluence of the Sonora and San Miguel Rivers. A small mission was built for Seri Indians forcibly displaced from their homes on Isla Tiburón. The Seris lived on the south bank (today still called Villa del Seri), the Spaniards on the north bank (the plush residential area still called Pitic). In 1828, Pitic changed its name to Hermosillo and two years later became the capital of Sonora, which it remains.

Due to its location along the river route, the city grew rich on trade. Goods imported from Guaymas passed through town on their way to northern Sonora and New Mexico. In return came a steady stream of gold, copper, silver, and wheat. Hermosillo became a city of merchants.

John Ross Browne labeled Hermosillo in the 19th century "one of the most beautiful cities in the northern part of Mexico, if not the whole continent of America." Unfortunately, no colonial structures have survived the city's rush towards anything modern, which usually means anything from the United States: franchise restaurants, full-service motels, parking meters, and 7-11-style convenience stores. But if beauty has to do with comfort and convenience, then Hermosillo is the most stunning city in Sonora.

Bearings

Hwy. 15 enters Hermosillo from the east, turns into a broad tree-lined boulevard which goes through four name changes, and emerges on city's south side. Blvd. Transversal provides the axis, a major artery that eventually turns into Hwy. 16 heading to Bahía Kino. The city is circled by the Periferico, a less scenic loop avoiding city traffic, used mosty by truck drivers.

Traveling About

Bus stops in the city are posted with maps explaining the different routes.

Tourist Information

The tourist office, located in the Palacio de Gobierno facing Plaza Zaragoza, offers folders and maps for Hermosillo and the state of Sonora in general.

Hermosillo from Cerro de Campana

PLACES
Abelardo Rodríguez Museum

This is the most accessible sight for passing travelers, on the corner of the main intersection of town (Transversal and Hwy. 15). This tall building, unmistakable for its soaring arches and Stalinesque severity, contains a 50,000 volume library, auditorium, art gallery, and small museum. The museum's most famous exhibit is a petrified man, found in 1959 in a cave near Yécora (in southeast Sonora), surrounded by cave paintings, tools, and weapons. The Yécora mummy possibly dates back 12,000 years, and certainly predates the Seri, Pima, and Opata cultures of this area. Across the street is the University of Sonora.

Museo de Sonora

Mexico may be a prisoner of its history, but history itself has been imprisoned here. Built in 1907, this building was used as the state penitentiary until 1979. You must walk through its narrow cell doors to see the exhibits. Set against the eastern slope of

Cerro de la Campana, this museum offers a walk through of the regional history, geology, and culture. The exhibits are well-done, and include many artifacts, most signed in English. Closed Mondays and Tuesdays.

Cerro de Campana

Westward a few blocks from the highway, *Cerro de Campana* (Bell Hill) looms over Hermosillo. The hill is bell-shaped, but some say its name actually comes from the crystalized carbonate of lime of which it is made. When struck by a hammer, it rings. Some have gone so far as to say the name Sonora comes from the sonorous sound. Actually the state name comes from Cabeza de Vaca's attempt to teach the natives something about Catholicism. They didn't pick up much except the word, Señora, which soon became the name of one of the first Spanish encampments in the region, a base camp for early explorers.

A steep narrow road winds up to the top, where there is an overview of the city, a flat green expanse marked by the spires of the church at Plaza Zaragoza.

Plaza Zaragoza

The central zócalo is bookended by the Catedral de la Asunción and the Palacio Municipal, a neo-classical timepiece. The palacio is worth a look inside for its two-story Moorish-arched patio and murals by Enrique Estrada and Teresa Morán. But it is the overall whiteness that makes the greatest impression. The wrought iron kiosk and park benches, the cathedral, the palace, even the tree trunks, are all painted blinding white, a harmony of architecture and color, church and state. Scarlet orioles and cowbirds add song to the picture.

Capilla de San Antonio

The oldest structure in a modern town. Already a ruin, it was built in 1841 on the site of a previous Franciscan chapel of 1773. The brick ribs reinforcing the barrel

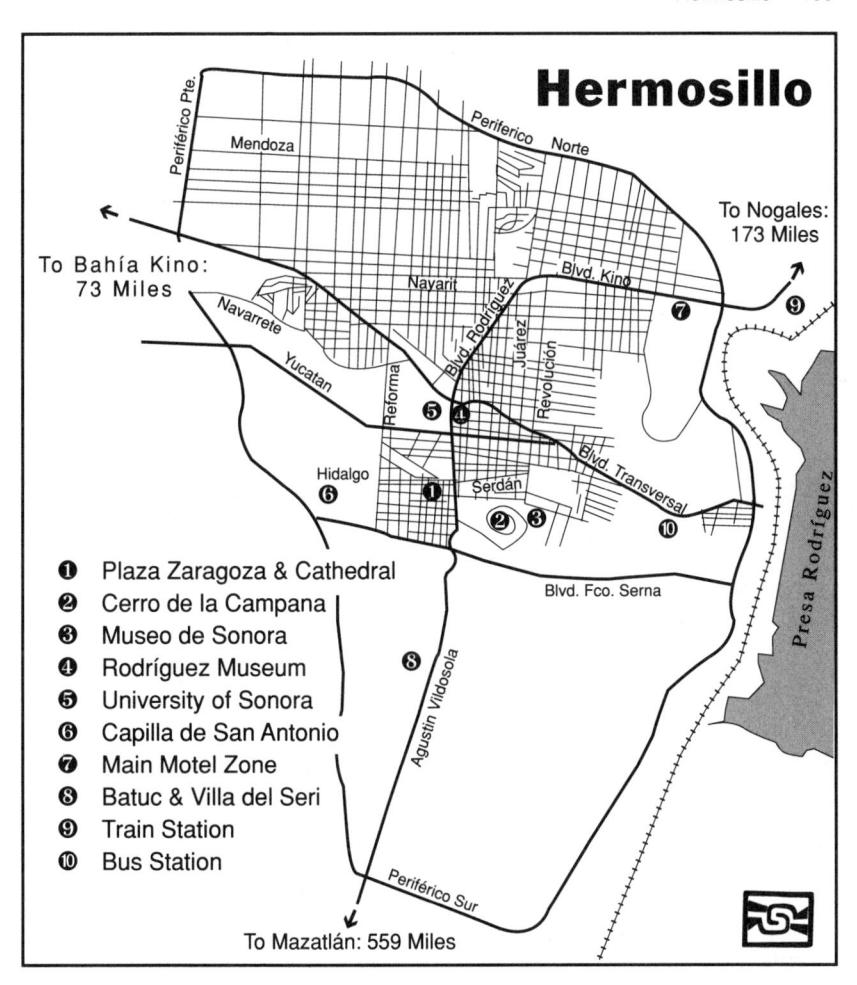

Hermosillo

To Nogales:
173 Miles

To Bahía Kino:
73 Miles

Periférico Pte.
Mendoza
Periférico Norte
Nayarit
Blvd. Kino
Navarrete
Yucatan
Blvd. Rodríguez
Juárez
Revolución
Reforma
Hidalgo
Serdán
Blvd. Transversal
Blvd. Fco. Serna
Agustin Vildosola
Periférico Sur
Presa Rodríguez

❶ Plaza Zaragoza & Cathedral
❷ Cerro de la Campana
❸ Museo de Sonora
❹ Rodríguez Museum
❺ University of Sonora
❻ Capilla de San Antonio
❼ Main Motel Zone
❽ Batuc & Villa del Seri
❾ Train Station
❿ Bus Station

To Mazatlán: 559 Miles

vaulting still stand, but the original roof has long fallen. The facade is interesting for its unusual columns, pinched in the middle. From Plaza Zaragoza, follow Calle Hidalgo about six blocks past Reforma (where it turns into a two-way street). Hidalgo deadends at the chapel site.

Batuc

This monument is symbolic of how Sonora treats the past with respect, yet does not let it interfere with the future. The facade of the mission San Francisco Xavier de Batuc (1758) was removed from its original location along the Río Moctezuma, now deep under the waters of El Novillo Dam. It was reassembled on the west side of Highway 15, just south of the dry bed of the Río Sonora at Plaza de los Tres Pueblos, where it serves as a monument to the displaced inhabitants of Batuc and two other towns which disappeared underwater in 1967.

The limestone facade is the most elaborately carved of the early Jesuit buildings in Sonora, and is easily seen from Hwy. 15 as you pass through town. If you turn west at the plaza you enter **Villa de Seri**, the oldest colonía in Hermosillo. In 1844, 384 Seris were forcibly transported here from Isla Tiburón; many escaped back to the island.

No full-blooded Seris live here now. The Villa is centered on Parque Xochimilco, the plaza facing the church, three blocks from the highway. The Fería de San Juan is held here on June 24, with music and dancing.

Centro Ecológico de Sonora

This park offers a spectacular crash course on desert ecology, originally modeled after the Arizona Desert Museum near Tucson. On its expansive natural grounds you can spy grey wolves, bighorn sheep, and other endangered species, along with coral snakes, scorpions, exotic birds, and all manner of marsupials, reptiles, amphibians, and secretive desert dwellers in their natural Sonoran desert environment.

There are also aquariums, aviaries, a giant tropical greenhouse, an area for exotic African animals, a sea lion pond, and an audiovisual room with educational films. The pathway which winds through the desert hills takes from one to three hours to walk (very few shortcuts), depending on the degree of interest and heat (lots of shaded shelters, drinking fountains). Labels are in English, but descriptions are in Spanish only. Park is just off Hwy. 15 to Guaymas, on the southern outskirts of Hermosillo. Open Wed. to Sun, 8 a.m. to 6 p.m. (closes 5 p.m. winters).

Events

Fiesta de la Vendimia, a grape harvest celebration, is celebrated in July. The Feria Comercial is held from June 21 to 26. Yaqui dances can be seen during Semana Santa (Easter Week) in Barrio El Coloso.

Hermosillo Addendum

Both the post and telegraph offices are in the same building, on Rosales and Serdán.

The American Express office is at Monterrey and Rosales.

There is a U.S. Consulate in Hermosillo, at Blvd. Miguel Hidalgo 15; phone 3-89-22 to 25.

PLACES TO SLEEP
Hotels

The fanciest, most expensive motels line Hwy. 15 at the northern entrance to the city, attracting those whose need for sleep after a six-hour shoot from the border overcomes frugal instincts. Motels **Valle Grande** ($$; tel: 4-45-70), **Bugambilia, El Encanto** ($$; tel: 4-47-30) and the **Gandara** ($$; tel: 4-44-14) all provide American-style amenities expected of its American-style rates, as does the **Holiday Inn**.

In the center of town are the older but more inexpensive city hotels. Hermosillo's grande dame remains the **San Alberto** ($$; tel: 2-18-00), a big downtown hotel centerpiece, on Hwy. 15 a few blocks from Plaza Zaragoza. Also near the Plaza, close to the base of Cerro de la Campana, is **Hotel Kino** ($), a more modest yet equally clean accommodation.

There is quite a gap between these and the budget rooms on Calle Sonora, which are dives. **Posada Macbeth** implies the tragedy of its rooms, while the **Sonia** and **Colonial** are likewise best for locals sleeping off benders at the nearby bar.

ARRIVING & DEPARTING
By Bus

Buses leave hourly from the main terminal on Blvd. Transversal 400, one mile from downtown (tel. 3-33-73); Tres Estrellas de Oro (tel. 3-24-16) is the major line here. Buses to Bahía Kino depart from Transportes de la Costa de Hermosillo on Ave. Plutarco Elías Calles 99 (tel. 2-21-94), or you can catch them on their way out of town along Blvd. Transversal.

By Train

The Ferrocarril del Pacífico terminal is just off Hwy. 15, less than two miles north of downtown. Train south leaves evenings, northbound in the mornings. There is a ticket office at Blvd. Transversal and Calle Manuel González; tel: 3-87-01 for fare and schedule information.

HERMOSILLO TO PUERTO DE LA LIBERTAD & BAHÍA KINO

From Hermosillo, Blvd. Transversal turns into Hwy. 16, passing after seven miles the Domecq and Vergel Wineries, makers of brandy. The paved highway runs straight through fields of grapes, mesquite grasslands, sugar cane, and forests of cacti. Fifty-five miles from Hermosillo, there is a turn-off to **Puerto de la Libertad** (107 miles) and **Desemboque** (121 miles). This paved side road passes through cultivated fields on the east side of the Sierra del Seri.

DESEMBOQUE

Thirty miles before reaching Puerto de la Libertad, a graded turnoff leaves Pozo Coy-ote to **Desemboque del Seri** (14 miles), the principal Seri Indian village, famous for its ironwood carvings (fabric, digital watches, wood files are good trade items). This road, often in poor condition, continues south 40 miles to Punta Chueca, another 16 miles to Bahía Kino.

Four miles south of Libertad is a turnoff west to a **Boojum Forest**, a unique stand of cirios found nowhere else in the world except on the peninsula and these few coastal stretches in Sonora.

PUERTO DE LA LIBERTAD

This is the site of a giant thermo-electric plant on the coast, reached by a 107-mile long paved road, which turns off from Hwy. 16 (Hermosillo-Kino highway), 55 miles from Hermosillo. Puerto Libertad was once an Indian settlement, gathered around one of only five water holes between here and Bahía Kino (called Xpano Hax "sea-in-water," since the freshwater flows out of the sand below the high tide line). Now fresh water is generated along with the electricity.

During the 19th century, high duties and taxes encouraged smuggling along this coast (to dock at Guaymas, foreign ships had to pay a lighthouse tax, even though there was no lighthouse). To stem illegal trade, the government established Puerto Libertad as an alternative trading port in 1859, but it was rarely used except by the U.S. government to supply calvary troops in Arizona during the Civil War. American interests also were involved here during World War I. In 1917, a clandestine radio station was built here by the Germans (Mexico was neutral) so they could receive spy reports from the U.S. and warn their ships in the Pacific. Unable to send a full squadron of

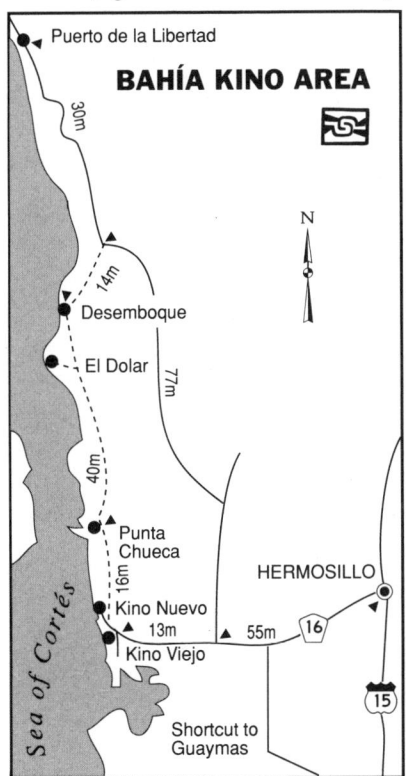

BAHÍA KINO AREA

Puerto de la Libertad

30m

14m

N

Desemboque

El Dolar

77m

40m

Punta Chueca

16m

HERMOSILLO

Kino Nuevo

13m   55m   16

Kino Viejo

15

Sea of Cortés

Shortcut to Guaymas

Beach at Kino Nuevo

soldiers across the international boundary, the U.S. government hired an American prospector who found and destroyed the radio transmitter. There are secluded camping beaches north and south of Puerto Libertad, a town of little interest to most travelers, except as a place to purchase gasoline. A rough dirt road continues up to Caborca, 79 miles to the northeast. *Note: Puerto Libertad can be reached by bus from Hermosillo.*

BAHÍA KINO

This long sandy bay is divided into two parts: Kino Nuevo and Kino Viejo. The two Kinos complement each other like night and day. The authenticity of Kino Viejo, the fishing village, is balanced by the quiet dreaminess of Nuevo Kino, the resort. One wakes you to all your senses, the other lulls you into a dream state.

The highway arrives first at Kino Viejo, a ramshackle town of dirt roads, fish markets, and backyard artisan shops. A few restaurants and a burgeoning number of curio stores draw tourists from Kino Nuevo, where there is a dearth of dining. The iron-wood carvers congregate mainly on the road to the beach 100 yards past the Pemex station. These ironwood carvers imitate and expound on the original designs of the Seris, using power tools to produce them quicker, in greater numbers, and at a much lower price. Though smoother in form, they lack the aboriginal crudeness of the handmade Seri carvings. Some would make better paperweights than art objects.

If you stay on the paved road, it becomes Blvd. Mar de Cortés, an impressive strip of big-investment vacation homes interspersed with sections of public beach, where flowering dunes drop down to shell-strewn beaches shaded with palapas. The limpid water is calm in winter, mildly surfy in summer, protected by Isla Tiburón close offshore. Elsewhere on the horizon ride a fleet of islands: Alcatraz, Turner, San Pedro Mártir. On a clear day, you can see the Baja California peninsula, sixty miles away.

PLACES
Museo de los Seris

In Kino Nuevo, along the northern reach of Blvd. Mar de Cortés, is a small museum dedicated to the Seri culture, documenting their history and crafts, with maps and samples of their best handiwork: ironwood carvings, necklaces, and baskets woven so tight they hold water. Visiting this place is a good first stop for anybody driving up the coast to the Seri village at Punta Chueca.

Fishing

For inside information, drop by the Club Deportiva Bahía Kino, situated in a white Quonset hut one block from beach behind Kino Bay Trailer Park, or write: Apartado Postal 84, Bahía Kino, Sonora Mexico 83340). Pangas can be rented off the beach in Kino Viejo or through organized charter rentals in Kino Nuevo.

Kino Addendum

There two inexpensive seafood restaurants in Kino Viejo, the Marlin and the Palapa.

There is a bank (Bancomer) in Kino Nuevo, on Calle Yavaros.

There is no tourist office, but you can pick up travel information at the Club Deportiva Bahía Kino in Kino Nuevo.

PLACES TO SLEEP

In Bahía Kino, there are many trailer parks, some free camping space, and few hotels.

Hotels

Only full service hotel is **Posada del Mar** ($$; tel. 2-01-55), on the south end of Kino Nuevo, across the street from ocean. The **Kino Bay Motel & Trailer Park** ($$; tel: 2-01-40) rents 13 modest kitchenette units, also across street from the beach. The only hotel actually sitting on beach sand is the **Santa Gemma** ($$$; tel: 2-00-26); its 14 split-level bungalows are big enough for families.

Cheapest rooms in Bahía Kino are just outside of Kino Viejo at the **Islandia Trailer Park**; the four bungalows are beach-rustic, with bare kitchens and separate sleeping areas.

Camping

Kino Nuevo is rich with trailer parks, the largest being the **Kino Bay Trailer Park**. Only three parks are beachside: **Caverna del Seri** at the northern end of Blvd. Mar de Cortés, **Santa Gemma** ($$$), and **Islandia Marina** ($) outside of Kino Viejo.

Along the beach to the estero mouth (fine shelling here), about a mile south of Kino Viejo, there are few level car camping sites but plenty of room for tents. Camping in Nuevo Kino is suburban, with RVs frequently pulling into the beach lots between homes, while tents are pegged to the public palapas.

You can find the most solitude at Red Rock, about three miles north of Kino Nuevo, if you can negotiate the steep hill that lies between; follow the dirt road after the pavement ends at the north end of Kino Nuevo.

From the airport, a graded road runs 17 miles north to Punta Chueca. This is Seri land, and they may charge you to camp on their beaches, reached by exploring the spur roads that run down from the graded road. *Warning: some of the tracks leaving the graded road turn into sand traps.*

Arriving & Departing

The best place to catch a bus to Hermosillo is at the Pemex station outside Kino Viejo. Local buses run between Kino Viejo and Nuevo; just flag them down. If returning to Hermosillo for the night, be careful not to miss the last bus; they leave about every two hours, the last one out usually departing around 5:30 p.m.

Seri Woman

THE SERI

Offshore, 45 minutes by boat from Bahía Kino, lies Isla Tíburon, the largest island in Mexico and the the ancestral home of the Seri. One of the most independent and primitive Indians in Mexico, the Seri acquired a fierce reputation in the 19th century, including that of being cannibals, neither proved by historians nor disputed by the Seri. The Seri leaped to the headlines in 1894 when they stoned an American reporter to death. In 1896, four gold prospectors also were murdered. That same year, an American captain disappeared. Only his shoe was found.

The Seri no longer live on the island, having been forcibly evacuated by the Mexican government in 1956 and resettled along the coast. There are remnants of Seri villages along the shore, and occasionally the Seri use the island for vision quests and fish camps. The Mexican government returned the island to the Seri in 1976, but they now seem to prefer life on the mainland, mostly in two settlements: Punta Chueca and El Desemboque. The island is now a federal ecological reserve (you are supposed to get permission to visit it from the SEDUE office in Hermosillo).

The Seri still remain semi-nomadic, proud, and pagan. Their religion is almost unintelligible to outsiders, if not to themselves. According to some experts, they worship the god of the sea and the god of the earth, represented as a mole. Their religion has been irrigated by a flood myth in which rising waters changed people into plants.

Consequently, these plants have a spiritual life of their own. Cutting a boojum tree causes wind, a barrel cactus, rain. To calm the seas, they use ironwood (ironwood sinks). The elephant tree is the Seri "holy bush," strongly involved in their four-day vision quests. Shamans use its branches to treat the sick. Fetishes carved from the red elephant tree are messengers to the spiritual world.

The Seris are now world famous for their ironwood sculpture (there's one in the Kremlin). Previously, they carved mostly abstract pieces cut from the soft elephant tree wood. Some figures, such as the dolphin and manta rays, were the same as those now cut from ironwood.

In the early 1960s, an Arizona resident encouraged a Seri, José Astorga, to carve some figures in ironwood. Others picked up the knife, and soon half the Seris were employed carving figures, mostly simple, massive outlines of sea and desert animals. Everything they carved was scooped up by tourists. This economic windfall came at a time when there were only about 200 Seri left, attempting to survive as money-less nomads in a modern world. Now, with money, the tribe has rebounded in population to more than 500, most living in El Desemboque and the more accessible Punta Chueca.

Note: Ironwood trees are growing scarce. Most Seri, because of religious beliefs, don't cut down ironwood trees, but use wood already dead. The mestizos, who make most of the sculptures these days, are unburdened by such beliefs.

PUNTA CHUECA

A wide graded road runs north from Kino Nuevo for 18 miles to a seaside pueblo of Seri Indians. Punta Chueca is named after a

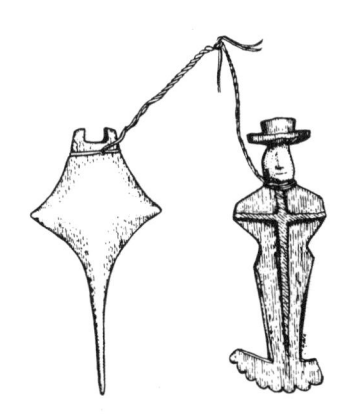

sandy hook that provides a shelter from the strong currents and choppy seas of the Canal de Infiernillo, a shallow channel separating the mainland from Isla Tiburón. The village is built of government housing. The semi-nomadic Seri are not yet accustomed to them. Some buildings stand vacant, with shacks and lean-tos built against their sides.

Park, then stand about idly. Within minutes, first one, then another, and soon a mob of colorful Seri women will descend upon you, trying to sell their crafts while clutching your clothes. The men, attracted by the turmoil, will stand off to the side, basking stoically in the confusion.

Most of the women have a rudimentary knowledge of Spanish, but prefer to keep to their own language. Other than ironwood pieces, look for the *coritas*, which are watertight baskets made from elephant trees, some of the finest basketry you will find in Mexico. They also sell inexpensive necklaces made of limpet shells and naturally dyed shark and snake vertebrae, as well as cloth dolls. Prices for carvings are high, compared to the mass-produced products in Bahía Kino. Bartering is effective, especially clothes and colored fabrics. The unbending spirit that has allowed the Seri to withstand acculturation is also seen in their bargaining stance, as hard as the ironwood they sell.

Warning: don't take photographs without permission, or you may be stoned.

Shortcut to Guaymas

If you are driving south to Guaymas from Kino Bay, you can take a short-cut to avoid backtracking to Hermosillo. From Mex. 16, turn south on Calle 4 Sur, about 38 miles from Bahía Kino (34 from Hermosillo). This paved road runs 53 miles to connect with Mex. 15, 30 miles north of Guaymas, a saving of 37 miles.

BEYOND

From Punta Chueca, the coastal road continues 24 miles to the Punta Tecopa turnoff.

Punta Tecopa (El Dolar) is reached by a 2.5 mile side road that comes to a halt at the rocky shore, with views of Patos Island offshore. At low tide, a shallow sand spit lets you to walk to Punta Sargento. From the Punta Tecopa turn-off, the dirt road continues 18 miles to El Desemboque, the main Seri settlement, before hitting the pavement of the Puerto Libertad road 14 miles beyond.

HERMOSILLO TO GUAYMAS via Hwy. 15

The highway from Hermosillo to Guaymas runs 81 miles on an easy four lane highway, passing a fine rock art site at La Pintada, and the developing beaches of San Carlos.

LA PINTADA

The finest indigenous paintings in Sonora are easily visited 3.5 miles off Mex. 15, 33 miles south of Hermosillo, 44 miles north of San Carlos. La Pintada, a national park, is found in a deep canyon of Cerro Prieto, once a refuge for Pima and Seri Indians. A dirt road leaves the highway across from a restaurant and rest area, crosses through two stock gates (close them behind you), and ends in a shady glen at the base of the canyon (ask permission to camp from nearby Rancho La Pintada).

The paintings are grouped at three sites, the first site behind the first dike, while a cement path winds up the canyon to the other two. Paintings are of geometrical shapes, deer, reptiles, birds, and a stylized eagle, wings outspread. Though the local literature claims that these painting are up to 8,000 years old, you can clearly see a picture of a man on horseback, postdating the arrival of the Spanish 400 years ago. Most of the red, ochre, and black paintings have to do with the hunt. The canyon was probably a religious retreat where the Indians sought to communicate in some way with their destiny.

Tip: most paintings are less than a foot in height, on the canyon wall opposite the path. Bring binoculars or climbing shoes.

SAN CARLOS

This is a planned resort community, dramatically set between curving beaches and the craggy peaks of the *Tetas de Cabra* (Goat Tits). Though situated 275 miles south of the border, English is spoken here as much as Spanish.

The long main road into town is lined by trailer parks, time-share condos, restaurants, hotels, numerous curio shops, a few bars, and lots of billboards ("Born in the U.S.A., living in Mexico, and drinking at Manny's"). No mortuaries or cemeteries are allowed in the master plan, which was drawn up on the assumption that tourists don't want to be reminded of anything unpleasant.

The formula works, thanks to generous helpings of sand, sea, and sun. The almost landlocked natural bay is a point-of-departure for the many islets and coves here. If you don't have a boat, there are still plenty of beaches easily at hand. If you don't have

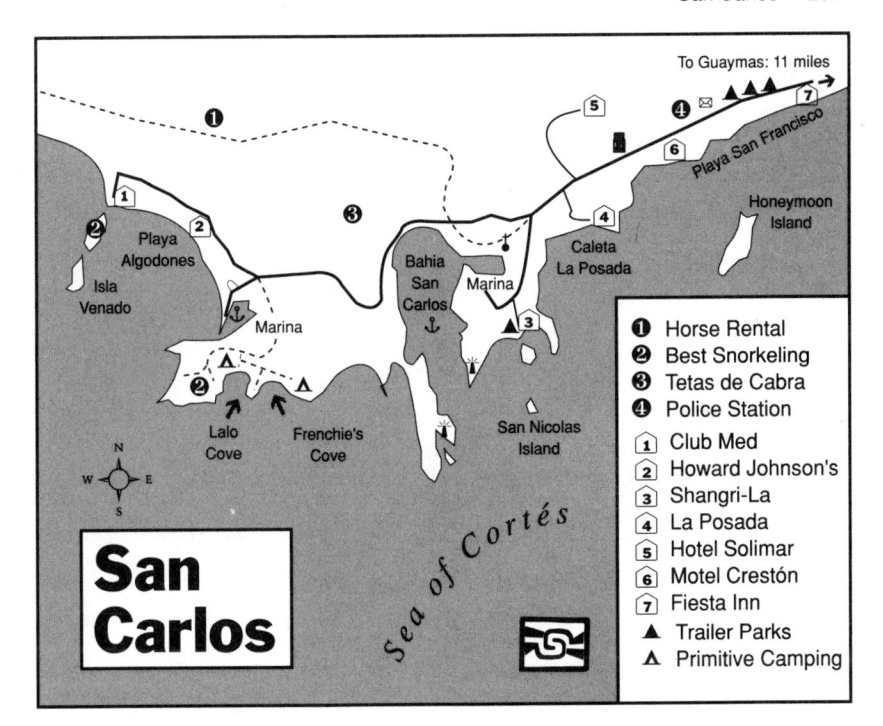

Legend (map):

❶ Horse Rental
❷ Best Snorkeling
❸ Tetas de Cabra
❹ Police Station

1 Club Med
2 Howard Johnson's
3 Shangri-La
4 La Posada
5 Hotel Solimar
6 Motel Crestón
7 Fiesta Inn
▲ Trailer Parks
▲ Primitive Camping

a car, you'll be hard put to get around; this isn't a pedestrian's town. Few southbound travelers bother to make a way-stop here, as this destination resort is designed for special interest groups, mainly snowbirds, boaters, and retirees.

BEACHES OF SAN CARLOS
Playa San Francisco

This long beach runs alongside the road to San Carlos (camping prohibited), turning into Caleta la Posada and the twin Shangri La Coves, which take their names from the hotels there. Offshore are numerous small uninhabited islets.

Caleta Lalo

An isolated cove in the shadow of the Tetas de Cabra, its pebbled shore gives way to rocky reefs that stumble into the deep, green water, making for scenic snorkeling. A sandier beach is on the other side of the point. Both are easily accessible by cars.

Playa Algodones

The sandiest beach near San Carlos (four miles away), it is also one of the more secluded, despite the new Howard Johnson Hotel. Large dunes fall down to this stretch of sand which hooks out north to Isla Venado. This picturesque arrangement was used as the setting for the movies *Catch-22* and *Lucky Lady*. Most of the old sets have been replaced by Club Med, which faces the best snorkeling reef. *Note: despite the exclusive aura, Club Med's staff cannot keep you from snorkeling around the islets, or using the beach. Park on the north side of the hotel along with all the beach vendors and walk in.*

San Carlos Addendum

There are two dive shops renting equipment and arranging dive trips. Best diving is from late May until November.

Horses can be rented near Club Med.

The San Carlos Country Club (Carretera

San Carlos; tel. 6-00-07) offers tennis courts and a mediocre 18-hole golf course.

Fishing trips can be arranged through Sociedad Cooperative Tetabampo de Pesca Deportiva (tel. 9-16-22).

PLACES TO SLEEP

The hotels and trailer parks charge honest if somewhat high rates. Common currency here is the dollar, not the peso.

Hotels

An economical motel, the **Crestón** ($$; tel. 6-00-20) is next to the San Carlos Diving Center, off the beach. For about the same price you can rent a weatherbeaten cabaña, overlooking Shangri La Cove from the **Shangri La Trailer Park** ($$; tel. 6-02-35); lots of maintenance problems, but worth it for the view and fireplaces. Some of the other trailer parks have hotel rooms ($$) built in back, but nothing with a view.

La Posada de San Carlos ($$$; tel. 6-00-15) positions itself as the deluxe hotel here, but is a haphazard arrangement of rooms with no endearing traits other than its fine beachfront. The better maintained **Fiesta Inn** ($$$) is the only other contender on the beach, a smaller clubby operation pushing time-share. Up on the browning golf course is the **Hotel Solimar** ($$$), a warren of condo-style units done in naked brick. **Club Med** is the leader here for its vast recreational facilities, though its dark rooms are small (guests aren't supposed to stay in their rooms). You can pay an expensive day, half-day, or evening rate to sample the facilities, socialize, or watch a show. Free tours are given mornings; closes winters due to the cold winds.

Camping

There is a run of three trailer parks along Carretera San Carlos (all priced the same) at the entrance to town; the best of these is the **Teta Kawi** ($$; tel. 6-02-20). Recommended: the **Shangri-La** ($$; tel. 6-02-35), at the end of the carretera, the only trailer park on the beach, and closest to the marina activity.

Much of the primitive beach camping along **Bahía Algodones** is being squeezed out by development, but there are still fine level spots back from the beach. Best beach camping, though, is on the flat bluff above **Caleta Lalo**, or on the beach next to it.

ARRIVING & DEPARTING
By Car

Take the signed turnoff six miles north of Guaymas for seven miles.

By Bus

Buses run about every half hour from downtown Guaymas, leaving from Serdán, the main boulevard; you can catch it west of where Calle 19 intersects with Serdán. The last bus leaves Guaymas around 10 p.m.

GUAYMAS

Guaymas lies squeezed between mountains and sea. Much of its shoreline is actually built on discarded oyster shells. A noisy animated port town, its streets can be a bit trashy; not much attention is directed towards city beautification.

Its beauty comes without trying. The weeping rust streaks of iron ships, the vibrant *colas* of the shrimp boats, the cry of gulls, burnt lava hills mirrored in the oil-streaked water. Historical sights are few, museums non-existent. But that is because this city turns its back on the land, looking instead to the sea for its livelihood.

The sea has always been the town's life-blood. Though discovered by Ulloa 14 years after the conquest, the port of Guaymas hardly existed before Mexican Independence in the 1820s. While under Spanish rule, all Pacific trade had to be conducted through Acapulco. After independence, a trading community quickly grew up along the bayside. The land was dry, the water brackish. In the 1820s, Lt. Hardy said of Guaymas: "the tuna (nópal) is the only thing that flourishes in the port, except rattlesnakes, scorpions, tarantulas, and other reptiles."

By 1850, 3,000 people lived here. Through this port came steel, iron, mercury, china, sugar, tea, silk, and cotton. The entire town would turn out for the unloading of ships. The last box unloaded was traditionally given to the longshoremen, after which there were celebrations. The customhouse produced the major source of revenue for the state, a prime target for rebels and freebooters who needed quick financing.

Guaymas has weathered assault from every direction. Rebellious Yaquis once forced the whole town to sleep on the piers, ready to flee to the sea. In 1852, Count Boulbon and 400 adventurers attempted a takeover of Guaymas, the first step in creating an independent Sonora. The invasion failed, and he tried again in 1854 only to be caught and executed. In 1847, U.S. warships shelled the town, then occupied it till the next year when the Mexican-American war ended. During the U.S. Civil War, supplies from San Francisco were shipped through Guaymas and Puerto Libertad to supply the Yankees stationed in Arizona. In 1862, English warships threatened the port. Two years later the French did the same. Then came the rumblings of war brought about by the Mexican Revolution in 1910.

A tough, practical town, the people are outgoing and friendly to Americans, perhaps because they don't depend on them for their jobs. Tourism is nil. But there is a good chance you will spend some time here, since it is a convenient crossroads, with connections for rail, bus, plane, and for the ferry across to Santa Rosalía. The downtown and harbor are compact, easily walked. Though specific points of interest may be lacking, color is not.

Travel Information

The state tourism office is situated behind the Municipal Palace, on Calle 22. Lots of folders, brochures, and maps.

Traveling About
By Bus

Buses roll continuously down Ave. Serdán, the main boulevard, on their way to the ferry station, the rail station at Empalme, north to San Carlos, and to the beach at Bahía Bacochibampo.

By Car

You can rent cars from Budget (tel. 2-14-50) and Hertz (tel. 2-10-00) at the airport north of town.

PLACES
Plaza de los Tres Presidentes

More a point-of-orientation than a point-of-interest, this expanse of concrete lies between the Palacio Municipal and the Muelle Municipal, which is marked by a bronze statue of a fisherman riding a porpoise. Three larger-than-life bronze statues of Adolfo de la Huerta, Plutarco Elías Calles, and Abelardo Rodríguez, three native son presidents, preside over this large bare plaza. It was here that adventurer Count Rousset of Boulbon was shot by a firing squad.

Plaza de Armas

Two blocks up from the malecón is a green oasis amid the downtown cacophony. The plaza, inaugurated in 1883, is edged by green wooden park benches that invite loitering, a comfortable place to contemplate the 18th century **Catedral de San Fernando** across the street.

Mercado Central

This market doesn't equal the vast arenas of the larger cities, but its stalls do offer some

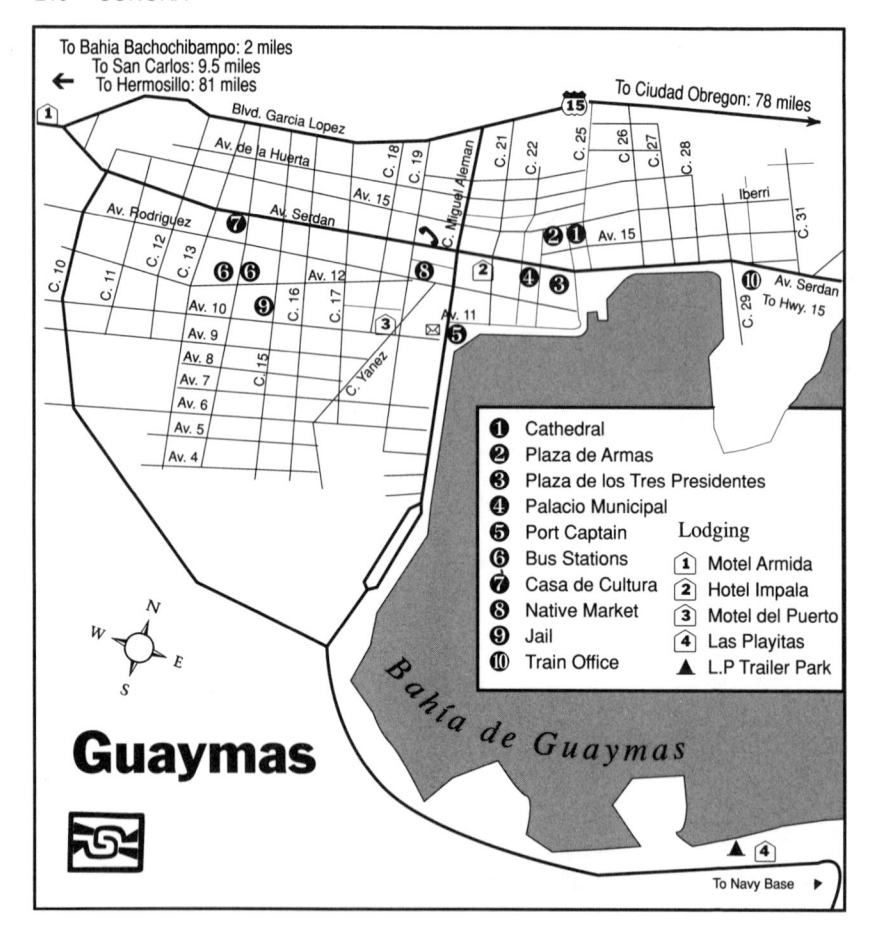

To Bahia Bachochibampo: 2 miles
To San Carlos: 9.5 miles
To Hermosillo: 81 miles
To Ciudad Obregon: 78 miles

Blvd. Garcia Lopez
Av. de la Huerta
Av. Rodriguez
Av. Serdan
Av. 15
Av. 12
Av. 11
Av. 10
Av. 9
Av. 8
Av. 7
Av. 6
Av. 5
Av. 4
Iberri
Av. Serdan
To Hwy. 15

Guaymas

Bahía de Guaymas

To Navy Base

❶ Cathedral
❷ Plaza de Armas
❸ Plaza de los Tres Presidentes
❹ Palacio Municipal
❺ Port Captain
❻ Bus Stations
❼ Casa de Cultura
❽ Native Market
❾ Jail
❿ Train Office

Lodging

[1] Motel Armida
[2] Hotel Impala
[3] Motel del Puerto
[4] Las Playitas
▲ L.P Trailer Park

artesanía brought into town by floral-dressed Indians.

Casa de la Cultura

Three blocks from the bus station on Serdán, this neo-classical building (1910) is worth visiting for the occasional art exhibit, or to find what's happening on the cultural front.

Cárcel Público

This is actually the most interesting building in town, though you wouldn't want to go inside. This crenelated castle, topped with barbed wire, is appropriately situated in an area of tough cantinas. You can see its clock tower from the two bus stations a block away.

Playa Miramar

This gray crescent of sand fringes Bahía Bacochibampo a few miles to the north. The beach is mostly taken up by homes, except at its southern end where the beach is rocky and rough, and at the northern end where it's sandier but still no match for the beaches of San Carlos farther north. A city bus runs all the way to the northern end at La Bocana, where an estero breaks through to the gulf.

San José de Guaymas

The original site of Guaymas was founded in 1701 by Father Salvatierra, refounded in 1751 by Father Lizazain, and destroyed by Apaches shortly thereafter. This mission originally was to supply the Baja California missions but was actually used later as a jail for the Sonoran Jesuits during their expulsion. A newer church now stands on the site. From the airport, there is a junction with a dirt road to the right that leads a few miles to San Jose. Along the way is the prerevolutionary Aranjuez hacienda, while four miles beyond the village is the **Selva Encantada**, a dense forest of sahuaro. The dirt road reputedly continues on to Empalme.

Fiestas

The Fiesta de la Pesca takes place sometime from May to July, depending on when the fish are passing through. Local fiestas are also celebrated March 18 and June 24, and an annual four-day carnival begins the end of the third week in February. Sometimes there are dances (Matachines and Pascolas) in the atrium of the Iglesia de San Juan Bautista on the day of this saint.

Guaymas Addendum

Unlike most cities its size, Guaymas is well endowed with phone booths; unfortunately this is such a noisy town it's hard to hear. Long distance calls are better made at Farmacia Santa Marta at Calle 19 and Ave. Serdán.

Clean clothes at Lavandería Lavamática on Calzada Moreno 96.

ARRIVING & DEPARTING
By Bus

The two terminals, one for *Tres Estrellas de Oro* (tel. 2-12-71), the other for *Pacífico* (tel. 2-05-75), face each other on Calle 14 at Rodríguez, two blocks from Serdán. Buses leave north and south every hour. *Caution: lots of drunks in this area late at night.*

By Train

The passenger station is at Empalme, less than five miles south, but there is a train information office (tel. 2-49-80) on Av. Serdán near Calle 29. Ask them what bus to

take to station. The train passes to the south evenings, to the north early mornings.

By Ferry

Tickets are bought at the Muelle Patio ferry terminal (tel. 2-33-93 or 2-23-24), off Ave. Serdán. Buses to city center leave every few minutes from near the terminal.

By Air

Only AeroMéxico flies into the Guaymas airport, which is situated just off Hwy. 15 north of town.

PLACES TO SLEEP
Hotels

The cheapest accommodations in town are a bit too rangy for most travelers. The best budget accommodations are situated in the center of town. **Motel del Puerto** ($$; Calle Yañez 92; tel. 2-34-08), one long block from the market, offers air conditioning but no other comforts other than hot water and secure parking. An alternative, **Hotel Impala** ($$; 40 Calle 21; tel. 2-13-35), one block off Serdán, has phones in rooms; first floor units are fitted with TV at no extra charge (helps block out street noise).

For a few extra dollars, you can book into one of two beachfront hotels. **Leo's Inn**, on Playa Miramar ($$; Calle 28a 133, North Playa Miramar; tel.2-94-90) has the congenial charm of cheap student housing; though beset with lots of minor defects, it catches the sea breeze on the nose. La Bocana restaurant is next door, but there are no other facilities on this dead end street. Even more isolated is **Las Playitas Motel and Trailer Park** ($$; tel. 2-27-27 or 2-27-53; P.O. Box 327, Guaymas); this rustic motel sits on a muddy bayfront, but it has a pool as consolation, as well as six pullman kitchenettes, four bungalows, and a funky restaurant and bar.

The only other accommodation on the beach is the **Hotel Playa de Cortés** ($$$; Bahía Bacochibampo; tel. 2-01-35), a sprawling resort built in 1936 on the south end of Playa Miramar. Its massive Spanish-Mediterranean architecture and dark mahogany furnishings evoke the same kind of nostalgia found in the grand train stations of old, which is not surprising, built as it was by the Southern Pacific. Despite its huge proportions, it can be distressingly empty, much of its vitality sapped by the newer resorts of San Carlos. The fanciest rooms in Guaymas are found at Hotel Armida ($$$), the busiest address in town: busy disco, three restaurants, and pool.

Camping

The only trailer parks are out at **Las Playitas Motel & Trailer Park** across the bay from Guaymas proper, and at a forlorn encampment at the end of Bahía Bacochibampo, across from Leo's Inn. For free camping, you will have to go north to San Carlos.

GUYAMAS TO NAVOJOA Via Hwy. 15

From Guaymas, the four-lane highway runs 118 miles straight through the Yaqui Republic.

EMPALME

This town lies six miles from Guaymas on the other side of the Cochofre estero, a long estuary dotted with birds (reddish egrets, grebes, mergansers). This place is best known for its rail station, where many travelers have stood lonely vigils waiting for overdue trains; only facility at the station is a small greasy spoon.

An old steam locomotive stands monument to this town's past, when it was headquarters of the defunct Sudpacífico de México. In 1908, Empalme was divided into Mexican and American zones. Southern Pacific police patrolled the American sector, where there were schools, a hospital, parks, stores, electricity and running water, all things lacking on the other side of town.

While critics complain that the Americans didn't share, they did make one important contribution to Mexico other than the railroad.

Baseball. American railroad workers formed teams and taught the Mexicans how to fill out the positions. The sport caught on and, once the railroad was built, the sport spread, as teams traveled up and down the Pacific Coast by rail to play each other. Today, Mexico's Pacific Coast League (which plays from October 8 to Jaunary 30 to avoid the heat) has overtaken soccer as the primary sport of northwestern Mexico, and has contributed such stars as Fernando Valenzuela to the United States. The winning team of this league competes for the prestigious Caribbean League Title.

Other than trains and baseball, Empalme is also a Hollywood footnote: Charles Chaplin married actress Lita Gray here in November, 1924.

BEACHES

From Empalme, the highway parallels the beach two miles away. South 2.3 miles from Empalme, a dirt road turns off Mex. 15 to a long stretch of beach, **Playa Cochori**, where there are some shade ramadas and drinking spots, a working class refuge, trashy and not particularly appealing. Another road runs 4.5 miles farther south to **Playa del Sol**, a defunct beach development of broken promises. In between these two beach turn-offs is a road inland one mile to what is left of an old NASA space tracking station.

CRUZ DE PIEDRA

This small railroad community, 15 miles south of Guaymas, marks the beginning of the Yaqui Zona Indígena, which stretches for 50 miles to the Río Yaqui, near Ciudad Obregón. The only Indian reservation of substantial size in Mexico, it was given to the Yaqui in the 1930s but it is only half of what once was the Yaqui Republic.

THE YAQUI REPUBLIC

In the early 17th century, the Jesuit missionaries segregated the Yaquis from Spanish culture, preserved the idea of communal ownership of land, and encouraged the conviction that they held exclusive rights to their land. After the Jesuits were expelled in 1767, the Yaqui refused to swear allegiance to anybody else. When the Mexicans attempted to forge a new nation after Independence, the self-sufficient Yaqui refused to take part. They were in constant rebellion through the 1830s. Between 1875-85, they actually built military forts to defend their lands. The Yaqui Republic was like a separate country.

Defeat & Diaspora

When Porfirio Díaz gained power, he crushed the Yaqui Republic, but they continued guerilla warfare until a last fatal stand in 1902. Rather than admit defeat, many Yaqui left their homeland in a massive diaspora, relocating in rural Sonora, in Pascua (near Tucson) and Guadalupe (near Phoenix). More than 15,000 were sent as slave labor to the Yucatan. They lost their traditional land.

Revolution

The Mexican Revolution brought the Yaqui together again, on the side of the revolutionaries, to fight against an old enemy, Porfirio Díaz. They were the only indigenous people in Mexico with their own battalions and leaders. In return for their help, President De la Huerta repatriated the Yaquis to their historic villages, helping them reconstruct their homes and churches, even evacuating Mexican settlers who had moved in.

Betrayal

When Obregón became president, he bought land in nearby Yaqui Valley. Water was diverted to the valley, leaving the Yaquis dry. At Vicam, the Yaqui ambushed a train Obregón was riding, and held it for five days, demanding their water. Under the pretense of negotiations, Obregón wired for troops, who arrived and would have massacred all the Indians but for a violent thunderstorm which ended the slaughter. Twenty-thousand troops were then brought in. The Yaquis again took up arms, terrorizing the region with guerila tactics.

Repatriation

When Cárdenas became president, he responded to the Yaqui rebellion by creating this Zona Indígena Yaqui. He also promised them water, but the Obregón Dam had already diverted all water south to the valley, ending the traditional natural flooding of the riverbanks which were crucial to Yaqui subsistence farming. Now water was allotted to the Yaqui only on condition that they plant cash crops. This forced them into an economic dependence on the *yori*, (the white man), away from the communal sharing and subsistence farming that had been the bedrock of Yaqui culture.

Surrender

Today the Yaqui are dependent on cash to survive, many hiring out as laborers on their own land, leased to Mexicans who have the money to plant it. They cut and haul wood, make charcoal, and fish, but do not make any arts or crafts, traditional ways for native people to earn a living (the *carrizo* once used to make mats and baskets has largely disappeared along the dry banks of the river).

It is their culture, dance, and religion that keeps Yaqui identity alive. Their ceremonial dances, which date back to the Jesuits, are a way to re-affirm their independence, even though many are as much slaves to as owners of their land.

Yaqui Ceremonies

The best time to visit these villages is during their fiestas: Año Nuevo (New Year's), Semana Santa, San Juan (June 24), la Virgen del Camino (July 2), La Virgen María, (August 15), Día de los Muertos (Nov. 1-2), and the saint days of each town.

Of the traditional prehispanic dances, the most famous is the *Venado,* the Deer Dance. A man wearing the head of a deer, rattles on his feet, dances to the rhythm of the flute and percussion instruments. He imitates the life and death of the deer. In this sacred rite, the Yaqui nation identifies with nature, symbolized by the deer. At the end, the deer goes through death throes.

The *Matachines* dance came from Africa to Spain to Mexico. This dance was taught to the Mayo and Yaqui Indians by Jesuits to replace obscene fertility rites.

THE YAQUI VILLAGES

The Jesuits organized the Yaqui around churches in eight villages that comprised their prehispanic confederation. These vil-

lages still stand. Some of the homes are traditionally built of carrizo woven between mesquite posts, religious crosses posted above the doors. The Yaquis prohibit Catholic priests or any other religion from establishing themselves here. They continue to believe in what the Jesuits taught them, which has evolved through the years into a unique form of folk Catholicism. Some very old Yaquis still believe that Christ was born in Belén, a Yaqui village named after Bethlehem.

PÓTAM

Pótam means ground moles in Yaqui, an important food source in the early days. A forest of graves lies in front of the brick church here, traditional for Yaqui villages. In 1920, President Adolfo de la Huerta funded these large brick churches, built in many Yaqui communities. During Easter week, a frightening ceremony takes place, called the *Tinieblas* (darkness); the church is shut dark, while the clank of chains rattles through the aisles, symbolic of the taking of Christ. There are also processions, the burning of Judas, and Venado and Matachine dancing. Pótam is the largest predominantly Yaqui settlement on the Río Yaqui. Turnoff is 27 miles from Cruz de Piedra.

ESTACIÓN VÍCAM

Estación Vícam is a convenient place to see the Venado, Matachines, Coyote, and Pascolas dances during Semana Santa, which take place around the church. The cemetery in front of the church is characteristic of Yaqui villages. This town also celebrates the fiesta of San Juan on the 24th of June. The village is less than five miles off Mex. 15, six miles south of Pótam.

TÓRIM

Three centuries ago, sailboats would make their way up the now barren Río Yaqui to the mission of San Ignacio de Tórim, to fill their holds with grain for the California missions. Ruins of this large stone granary—the breadbasket of California—can still be seen, along with that of the stone mission, stilted with baroque columns. Look on the hill next to the main town square and you might be able to make out the rubble of boundary stone, built in 1886 to mark the boundries of the Yaqui common lands. Yaquis celebrate the 31st of July, day of San Ignacio de Loyola, as well as Semana Santa. The village is less than two miles off Mex. 15, 5.7 miles south of Vicam.

JÓRI

Jóri lies 5.8 miles south of the turnoff to Tórim. This village has many typical waddle-weave homes visible from the highway.

BÁCUM

This village of 4,000 is centered around the Iglesia de Santa Rosa de Lima, known for its contemporary Yaqui paintings. During the Yaqui rebellion, an earlier church on this site was set fire by government troops in 1868, burning to death 120 Yaqui prisoners held inside. Major celebration: July 1, the day of Nuestra Señora del Carmen. Bácum is situated off Mex. 15, 2.1 miles past Jóri.

ESPERANZA & COCORIT

Most people in these twin towns are of Yaqui descent. Each town has indigenous governors, and is still trying to preserve old Indian customs. Numerous Yaquis make pilgrimages to Cócorit during Semana Santa, a good opportunity to see the Venado and Matachine dances. The towns are situated 10.5 miles south of Jóri, six miles north of Ciudad Obregón, where there is a paved turnoff to the dam that changed their history, Presa Obregón.

PRESA OBREGÓN

Finished in 1953, this dam holds back the waters of the Río Yaqui, now full of large-mouth bass. From Esperanza, a road travels 13 miles to the dam.

CIUDAD OBREGÓN

This is a new city, built near the fertile bottomland of the Río Yaqui. Like most farming centers, the wide streets are laid out in a neat grid, echoing the patterned fields of the countryside. Mills, gins, and grain elevators crowd the outskirts of town. Main preoccupations here are the sowing and harvesting of rice, alfalfa, corn, sesame, and wheat.

In 1921, a railroad station named Cajeme was built here. Cajeme was the Yaqui chief who 34 years earlier had led a widespread rebellion against the Mexicans. They were defeated, and Cajeme executed (his epitaph: *con cinco balas, pagó sus males*, with five bullets, he paid for his sins). In 1928, the small rail station changed its name to Obregón.

When the Río Yaqui was dammed, and 500,000 acres of valley land planted, Ciudad Obregón became Mexico's biggest agricultural boom town. To most tourists, Ciudad Obregón is 23 blocks of stop-and-go traffic before again hitting open road. But it's worth a stop in this affluent city to shop the municipal market or stretch your legs at Laguna de Nainari, an urban lake circled by a jogging path and even exercise stations.

By far, the biggest attraction for travelers is the new **Museo Yaqui** (Calle Allende and 5 de Febrero; tel. 4-32-34), next to the Palacio Municipal in the Biblioteca Pública, just a few blocks off Mex. 15. An entire floor is taken up with a complete Yaqui ethnology, including costumes, weapons, jewelry, dances, historical photos, recorded music, even a recreated Yaqui home. Yaqui jewelry and masks are sold at the door; there is a token admission charge.

The tourism office is situated on Jalisco 135 Sur; tel. 4-04-23.

Few people find reason to spend the night here, other than fatigue. Hotels are priced high, more a reflection of the general affluence of this agricultural area than of the hotels themselves.

Recommended: **Valle del Yaqui** ($$$), **Valle Grande Nainari** ($$$) or the **Costa Brava** ($$$), all on Blvd. Miguel Aleman, which turns into Mex. 15.

NAVOJOA

Much smaller and more bedraggled than Ciudad Obregón, Navojoa is situated 40 miles farther south, along the shady banks

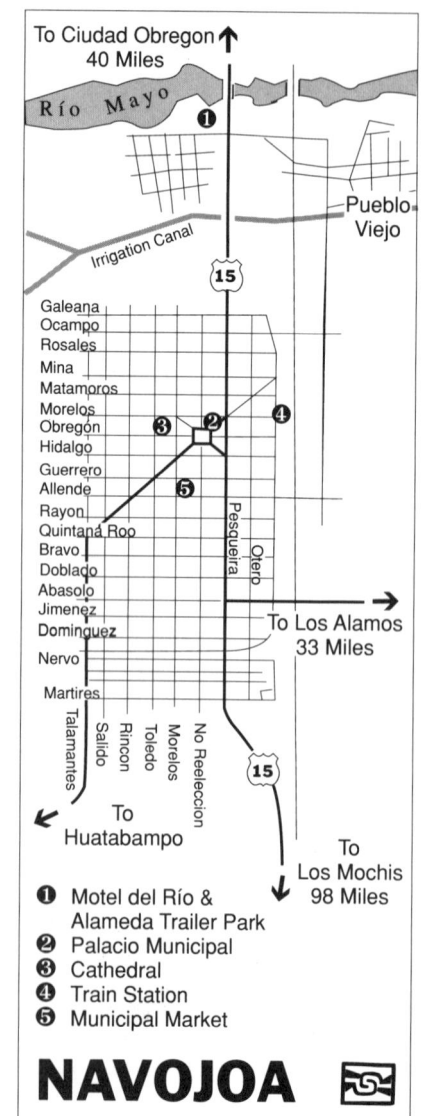

To Ciudad Obregon ↑
40 Miles

Río Mayo ❶

Pueblo Viejo

Irrigation Canal

(15)

Galeana
Ocampo
Rosales
Mina
Matamoros
Morelos
Obregón ❸ ❷ ❹
Hidalgo
Guerrero
Allende ❺
Rayon
Quintana Roo
Bravo
Doblado
Abasolo
Jimenez
Dominguez → To Los Alamos 33 Miles
Nervo
Martires

Talamantes
Salido
Rincon
Toledo
Morelos
No Reeleccion
Pesqueria
Otero

(15)

← To Huatabampo

To Los Mochis ↓ 98 Miles

❶ Motel del Río &
   Alameda Trailer Park
❷ Palacio Municipal
❸ Cathedral
❹ Train Station
❺ Municipal Market

NAVOJOA

of the Río Mayo. Mocuzari Dam holds back its muddy waters, part of an intricate network of dams and canals that irrigates this loamy bottomland.

Originally a mission site founded in 1614, the original Natividad Navojoa has since disappeared. You can still see the old bunker-styled San Juan chapel, built later by the Franciscans in the 18th century. It is situated in Pueblo Viejo (cross railroad tracks near northern Pemex station, make first left, then first right).

Pueblo Viejo is populated mainly by Mayo Indians. On June 24, Día de San Juan, large numbers of Mayos descend on Pueblo Viejo for an exuberant fiesta influenced as well by the summer solstice; lots of dancing, including the Matachines and Venado. Also heartily celebrated to a greater degree than at other Sonoran towns is Día de los Muertos (Nov. 1-2), and Día de la Virgen de Guadalupe (Dec. 12). The festivities of the latter actually begin on Dec.1, as Mayo pilgrims begin to arrive. Mayo dancers perform endlessly during these days, especially the Matachine.

Navojoa contains all the necessities: lodging, meals, auto repair, grocery stores, gas, and even a baseball team that playing in the Mexican Pacific Coast League, the "Naranjeros" (Fernando Valenzuela was born here). Also, Navojoa is the turnoff to two destinations, Alamos and Huatabampo.

*Note: if you're unable to travel the extra 30 miles for a superior hotel at Alamos, then the **Motel del Rio** and **Alameda Trailer Park**, along the south bank of the Río Mayo, are your best bet.*

THE MAYO

This delta country southwest of Navojoa is homeland of the Mayo Indians, the most numerous of the Sonoran tribes, closely related to the Yaqui in their traditions and customs. Unlike the Seri, Yaqui, and Tarahumara, the 30,000 Mayo Indians live among the Mexicans. In many cases, they can be recognized only by their poverty. In the Mayo philosophy, the world is a place of suffering and poverty, a place where a man should be poor because all good people are poor. To have too many material possessions is shameful. True to their view of the world, many of them still live in *jacales*, the one-room mud and wattle-weave huts that you see clustered in destitute villages. Most Mayos are farmers of small plots, as well as wage laborers toiling in other people's fields. Those who have taken up occupations not traditional to Mayo society are despised as *los riquitos*, the little rich ones, or *yoris revueltos*, the white turncoats. The Holy Week festivities are their most important, when passion plays are acted out. As part of the ceremonies, young males undergo initiation rites, emerging afterwards as adult members of the community.

NAVOJOA TO ALAMOS
A Sidetrip into the Sierras

The 32-mile road from Navojoa to Alamos departs Hwy. 15 and winds into the Sierra Madre, a region of miracles and mines, of fortunes made and lost.

MOCUZARI DAM

Halfway between Navojoa and Alamos, a side road goes to the dam, passing through Mocuzari, a town known for its bull semen. Bass fishing is considered excellent, and you can park and camp along the shore of reservoir.

LA ADUANA

The site of a miracle and a mine. Mayos walking by this place saw the vision of a maiden atop a cactus. To rescue her, they dislodged rocks to pile against the cactus. She vanished. When they glanced down, a rich vein of silver had been uncovered. A church, Nuestra Señora de la Balvanera, was built on this spot.

As if to verify the miracle, a cactus now grows from the side of the church, 12 feet above the ground. You can see this cactus often festooned with ceremonial ribbons. A mine was also dug, along with a smelter and reduction plant that cast Alamos silver into ingots, now in romantic ruin behind the town. In fact, the entire village is in a state of arrested ruin. But its population of 300 swells to thousands as Mayo Indians arrive every November 20th to pay homage to this vision represented by the cactus. Turn off the paved road at Minas Nuevas, 4.5 miles before reaching Los Alamos. A steeply graded road runs two miles to the village.

LA UBALAMA

This cluster of Mayo *jacales* was once known as a pottery village. Most natives have now turned their kilns to making brick. A few old *viejas* still collect clay from the arroyo to make crude pottery by hand without a wheel. Even if you don't want one, they are cheap enough to buy out of charity. The village is less than half a mile in from the paved road, at a turnoff marked "Viveros El Paraíso," just past Minas Nuevas.

ALAMOS

Alamos is a living museum, the best preserved colonial town in Mexico. Its architecture is taken from the Spanish province of Andalucía. Charles III sent the Surveyor General of Spain to lay out the manorial houses, all with adjoining walls (leaving no space for squatters). Even the trees were imported from Europe.

But the town was named for the native cottonwoods. Coronado camped in their shade in 1530 on his way north. A century

Miracle Cactus, La Aduana

so much silver it had its own mint. Baron von Humboldt wrote of passing "a drove of one thousand mules, laden with silver bars that are coming from the fortress of the Immaculate Conception of the Alamos, headed for Mexico City."

Besides building Baroque and Moorish-styled mansions, this vast wealth helped to finance the missions of California, Northern Sonora, and Arizona.

Alamos did more than fund the development of our western frontier. Captain Anza set out from Alamos to colonize upper California. In 1781, another colonizing expedition left from Alamos to settle Los Angeles. They would have left earlier, but it took a full year to convince the colonists to leave the safety of Alamos for the vast Sonoran desert and its fierce Indians. Most of those who finally left were Negroes and mulattos who had little choice but to move on.

Constant Indian attacks, disastrous floods, and spent mines finally sapped the town. The state capitol was moved to Hermosillo. The 1910 revolutionaries did not appreciate the town's ostentatious display of wealth. Large ranches were confiscated. The wealthy fled. By 1920, Alamos was a magnificent ghost town of mostly caretakers. After WWII, a few Americans stumbling into Alamos began to buy and renovate these dormant mansions.

By an act of government, the entire town is now a national monument, free of neon lights. The newest building in town is more than 100 years old.

More than 200 American families now own most of the mansions around the Plaza de Armas, stepping into the role of their former owners. Besides giving work to the locals, they also act as the town's patrons (one resident donated not just baseball mitts, but an entire stadium). Just as the wealth of Alamos laid the foundation of the American frontier, the wealth of the American frontier has returned to create new foundations for Alamos.

later, the Jesuits built an adobe mission here, and settlers moved in. Silver came after the fact, first discovered in 1683.

By the 18th century, the town produced

Plaza de Armas, Alamos

This is not bohemia. Just so you know better (according to a local welcome wagon guide): "Unlike many expatriot colonies, drinking is not done to excess. Although intimate friendships develop, flirtations between one another's husband or wife is not condoned. Conversations center around daily and world events, new books, the arts and travel. Local personalities are not discussed."

Most of the social life here is by invitation only, though you can tap into things through the hotels, which serve as social centers for the residents. Since few Mexicans live in the center, these colonial streets are unusually silent. The Plaza de Armas is empty of the vitality found in most Mexican towns. The effect is both enchanting and eerie, an ageless town slumbering in perpetual siesta.

Bearings

Entrance to Alamos is through the commercial district centered around Plaza Alameda, a long park shaded by cottonwood trees. This is the Mexican business hub, marked by curio shops, the market, and bus stop. The Plaza de Armas, two long blocks away, is the quieter center of old town, the staging area for most self-guided walking tours of town.

Travel Information

The state tourism office is next to Hotel Los Portales, to one side of church on Plaza de Armas. The Casa del Tesoro and many of the gift stores offer pamphlets and informative booklets at a price.

PLACES
Plaza de Armas

The heart of Alamos is centered on its 19th century kiosk. Porticoed mansions ring the square on three sides, marked by bulbous Doric columns supporting the arches; these pregnant columns are unique to Alamos. Its fourth side is dominated by the Cathedral.

Iglesia Parroquial de Nuestra Señora de la Concepción

Facing the Plaza de Armas, this church was built on the site of the Jesuit mission burned

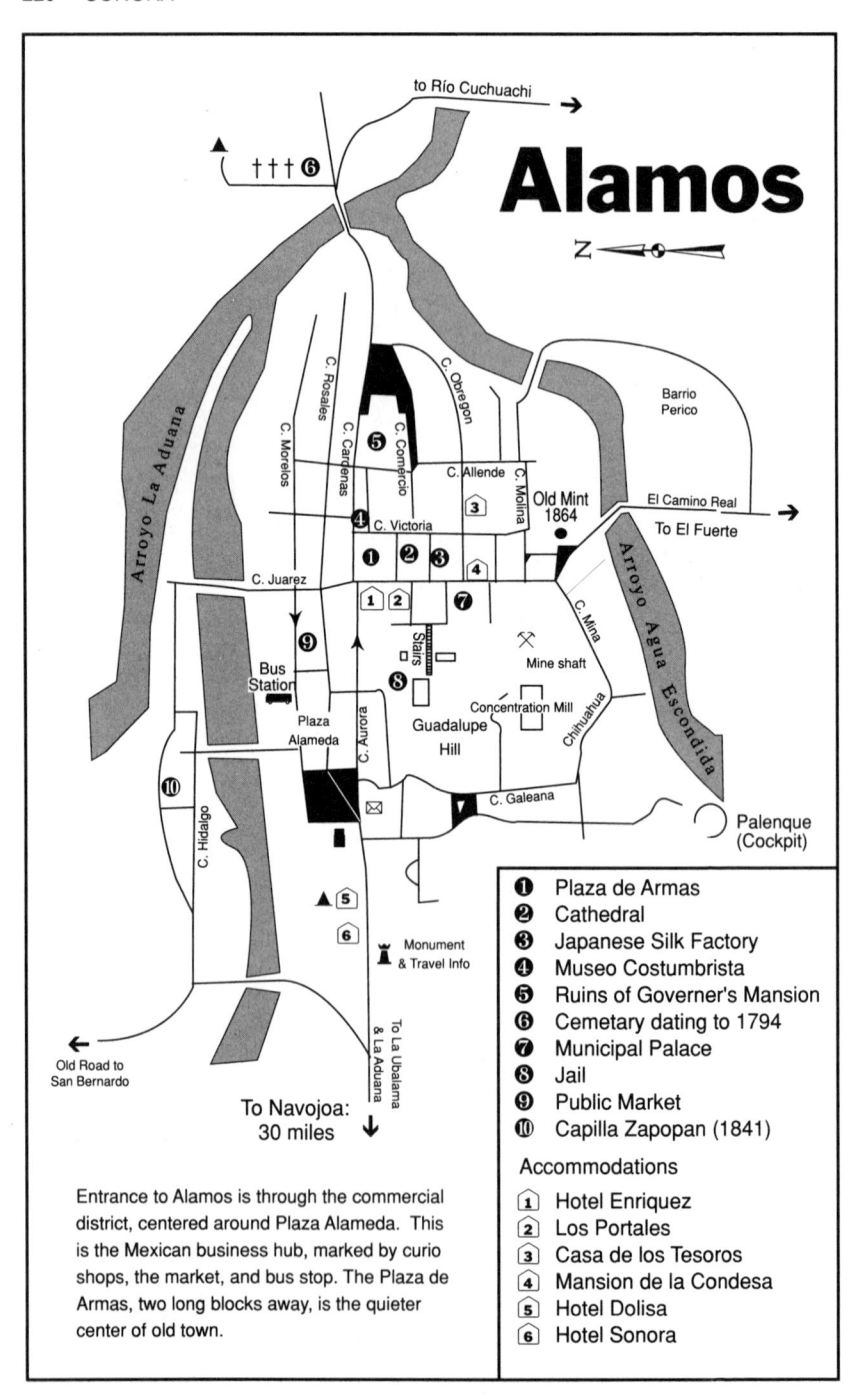

Alamos

to Río Cuchuachi →

†††❻

Barrio Perico

C. Rosales
C. Obregon
C. Morelos
C. Cardenas
C. Comercio
C. Molina

❺

C. Allende

Old Mint 1864

El Camino Real
To El Fuerte

❹ C. Victoria

③

❶ ❷ ❸

④

C. Juarez

① ②

❼

Arroyo La Aduana

Arroyo Agua Escondida

C. Mina

Stairs

Mine shaft

Bus Station

❾

❽

Concentration Mill

Plaza Alameda

C. Aurora

Guadalupe Hill

Chihuahua

❿

C. Hidalgo

✉

C. Galeana

Palenque (Cockpit)

▲ ⑤

⑥ ⚒ Monument & Travel Info

← Old Road to San Bernardo

To La Ubalama & La Aduana

To Navojoa: 30 miles ↓

❶ Plaza de Armas
❷ Cathedral
❸ Japanese Silk Factory
❹ Museo Costumbrista
❺ Ruins of Governer's Mansion
❻ Cemetary dating to 1794
❼ Municipal Palace
❽ Jail
❾ Public Market
❿ Capilla Zapopan (1841)

Accommodations

① Hotel Enriquez
② Los Portales
③ Casa de los Tesoros
④ Mansion de la Condesa
⑤ Hotel Dolisa
⑥ Hotel Sonora

Entrance to Alamos is through the commercial district, centered around Plaza Alameda. This is the Mexican business hub, marked by curio shops, the market, and bus stop. The Plaza de Armas, two long blocks away, is the quieter center of old town.

by Indians. Its baroque design was completed in 1804, cornered on a single ornate cupola tower. Fine china plates were worked into the base of the pilasters, originally donated by the doñas of Alamos. Only remnants remain, those that survived target practice by Pancho Villa's troops. The bell above rings every half hour.

Los Portales

On the west side of the Plaza de Armas is the 19th century residence of Don José María Almada, *dueño* (owner) of the richest silver mine here (it is said he laid 500 silver bars to the church so his guests wouldn't get their feet wet when attending his daughter's wedding). Now a hotel, it is worth strolling into the interior courtyard, constructed in 1720.

El Museo Costumbrista de Sonora

This museum, on the eastern side of the Plaza de Armas, brings together a visible history of Alamos, with exhibits of mining equipment, dress, and old photographs. Appearances haven't changed much. Closed Mon. and Tues.

Palacio Muncipal

One of the newer constructions in town, it dates from the turn of the century, built like a crenelated castle in contrast to the older colonial buildings. The interior courtyard has been renovated ina neo-classic vein, perhaps the only government palace in Mexico built around a stage where concerts and other performances are often held.

El Cárcel

Go down the alley on one side of the Palacio Municipal, up a flight of stairs, and along a winding path to the top of Cerro Guadalupe. Coronado made the same climb, building the first fort on top of this hill in 1531, a strategic vantage point looking out over town.

The jail is built on top of the fort's ruins, but the prisoner's have no views (there's a scenic lookout area for tourists, though). They pass their time weaving ropes, halters, hatbands, and belts from horse hair, a craft handed down for generations from prisoner to prisoner (they have about ten years to master the craft, the average length of sentence). These inexpensive items are for sale in a small guard room at the front of the jail. *Note: on returning to the U.S., don't confess where you bought them. U.S. Customs law 19USC1307 specifically prohibits importation of convict-made goods, including tourist-type items.*

Japanese Silk Factory

This was a complete factory for making silk, from mulberry trees to worms to weaving. Many Asians lived in Alamos in the mid-19th century, and this is about the only sign of their presence. They were all deported from Sonora in 1916 before their economic foothold turned into what the Mexicans feared would be a stranglehold. Across from the Palacio Municipal and behind the church, this structure now houses private homes.

Casa de los Tesoros

This hotel, two blocks behind the church, was originally built in 1789 by the Padre Quiros y Mora. Later it became a convent, which made conversion to a hotel simple. The passing public is welcome to walk right in and admire the interior portales, fountains, and courtyard shaded by palm and mango trees.

More Historic Sights

In Alamos, every other house seems to be a colonial monument. The **Mint**, established in 1864, but closed in 1896, is now a secondary school; the silver pesos minted here were used in China as the medium of exchange. The old **Governor's Palace**, at Allende and Cárdenas, awaits renovation (it was burned by Mayo Indians in 1915). Walking haphazardly through the streets, you will likely stumble across the **old hospital**, the **cock pit**, the old **tequila distillery**, and the **tannery**. The **cemetery** below town is a forest of wrought iron crosses and ancient vaults. The **Capilla de Nuestra Señora de Zapopan**, dedicated in 1841, stands on the other side of town, on the north side of Arroyo La Aduana.

Tours

In the mornings, guides can be contracted through the tourism office for a English-speaking walking tour of town, about $3 per person. But a much better **Home & Garden Tour** actually takes you into the homes, and is offered by Friends of the Library every Sat. at 10 a.m. for $5 (cookies included). Most of these homes have been faithfully reconstructed and are of one-story Roman design, with rooms built around a colonnaded courtyard. High-ceilinged reception rooms on the street side, bedrooms and kitchen in the rear.

Alamos Addendum

Jumping Beans are found in quantity in the hills surrounding Alamos, Jumping Bean Capital of the World. Called *brincadores*, these beans (actually seeds) bounce because of the moth larvae inside, which move about when the sun heats them (or when in contact with a warm hand). *Best time to look for brincadores: in June, after the first rains. They quit jumping by winter.*

Events

Alamos celebrates Día de la Purísima Concepción on December 8.

PLACES TO SLEEP
Hotels

A nice surprise in Alamos are its relatively inexpensive hotels, American standards at Mexican prices. Don't be tempted by the two modern hotels at the town's entrance until you check the colonial mansion-hotels first.

The cheapest place in town, **Hotel Enriquez** ($), is in the best location (facing Plaza de Armas) but has the worst rooms and no private baths, a time-worn mansion of charming decrepitude. Next door is the former home of a silver baron, now the **Hotel Los Portales** ($$); it still basks in the aura of its history, though the gold leaf on the Doric columns has long since flaked off. Its high-ceilinged rooms break out onto a courtyard fitted with rockers. The most active hotel, **Casa de los Tesoros** ($$$; tel. 8-00-10) is the standard group stop and the town's social center, a 200-year-old building where all rooms have fireplaces and traditional leather and mahogany furnishings, an historical landmark; unfortunately you are captive to its restaurant, since it operates on American plan only. Top hotel here, at least for individuals, is the 300-year old **Mansion de la Condesa Magdalena** ($$), across from the Silk Factory. Ask for the Magdalena Suite (rooms are named instead of numbered). This is where Mexican presidents De la Madrid and Salinas de Gortari both stayed. All rooms have big baths, and open to an interior arcaded courtyard; the restaurant and cantina are in back, along with one modern concession, a small whirlpool.

At the entrance to town are two newer hotels. The **Hotel Sonora** is a clean, comfortable budget pick, new yet built to look old; hot water mornings only. The **Dolisa** lies just down the road, an unremarkable hotel that shouldn't be considered unless you must have air conditioning.

Camping

There are two trailer parks at either end of Alamos. The **Dolisa** offers little more than some untended hook-ups behind the hotel. Better grounds are found at **Rancho Acosta** ("for clean and well-behaved people only") where there is a swimming pool. Both are a long walk into town. A third option is **El Caracol**, at the base of Cacharamba, a unique mountain meaning "pierced ear," almost eight miles before Alamos along the paved road: full hook-ups, satellite TV.

Arriving & Departing

Buses leave hourly until early evening from the station stop on Morelos, across from Plaza Alameda. Buses run to Navojoa, where you can connect with those running north and south on Mex. 15.

BEYOND ALAMOS
Río Cuchujachi

This is more a local bathing hole than the tourist attraction it is made out to be. Some deep pools are holed into the bedrock of the river, 7.5 miles from Alamos. Inquire if there is any water before leaving Alamos; this river is often dry. This road follows the Camino Real of the early Jesuits, and connects with El Fuerte to the south. *Warning: beyond the swimming holes, be on your guard. As in the old days, this rough road to El Fuerte still has reputation for robbery.*

NAVOJOA TO SINALOA STATE LINE
Via Hwy. 15

From Navojoa to the state line, a 55-mile stretch of Hwy. 15 narrows to two lanes and offers little access to the mountains. There are roads down to the beaches, rarely visited by most travelers.

HUATABAMPITO

Huatabampito (words ending with *-bampo* or *-bampito* are Indian place names) is a weatherbeaten weekend resort for Navojoa residents, a long sandy beach that rises up to undulating dunes. There are some vacation homes here, places to eat (but don't count on it), and room to camp. To reach Huatabampito, drive south from Navojoa on Mex. 15 for 17.2 miles, then turn west on a paved road, Mex. 10, for 16 miles to a junction. Turn south for Huatabampito, or continue straight two miles to Huatabampo, the principal city of this delta region.

LAS BOCAS & CAMAHUIROA

These twin beach resorts, separated by a few miles of grey sand beach, are unusually silent except on summer weekends when inlanders flee the heat. Though often uninhabited except for packs of stray dogs, these isn't much room for camping among the empty cinderblock beach shanties and wattle-weave shacks. The beaches are narrow, sandy, and gulf-like in character (no waves). The two communities are connected by a coastal road, with some threatening sandy sections in between. Las Bocas turnoff is 26 miles south of Navojoa, Camahuiroa a few miles farther south at a signed turnoff. Both access roads run about ten miles to the beach.

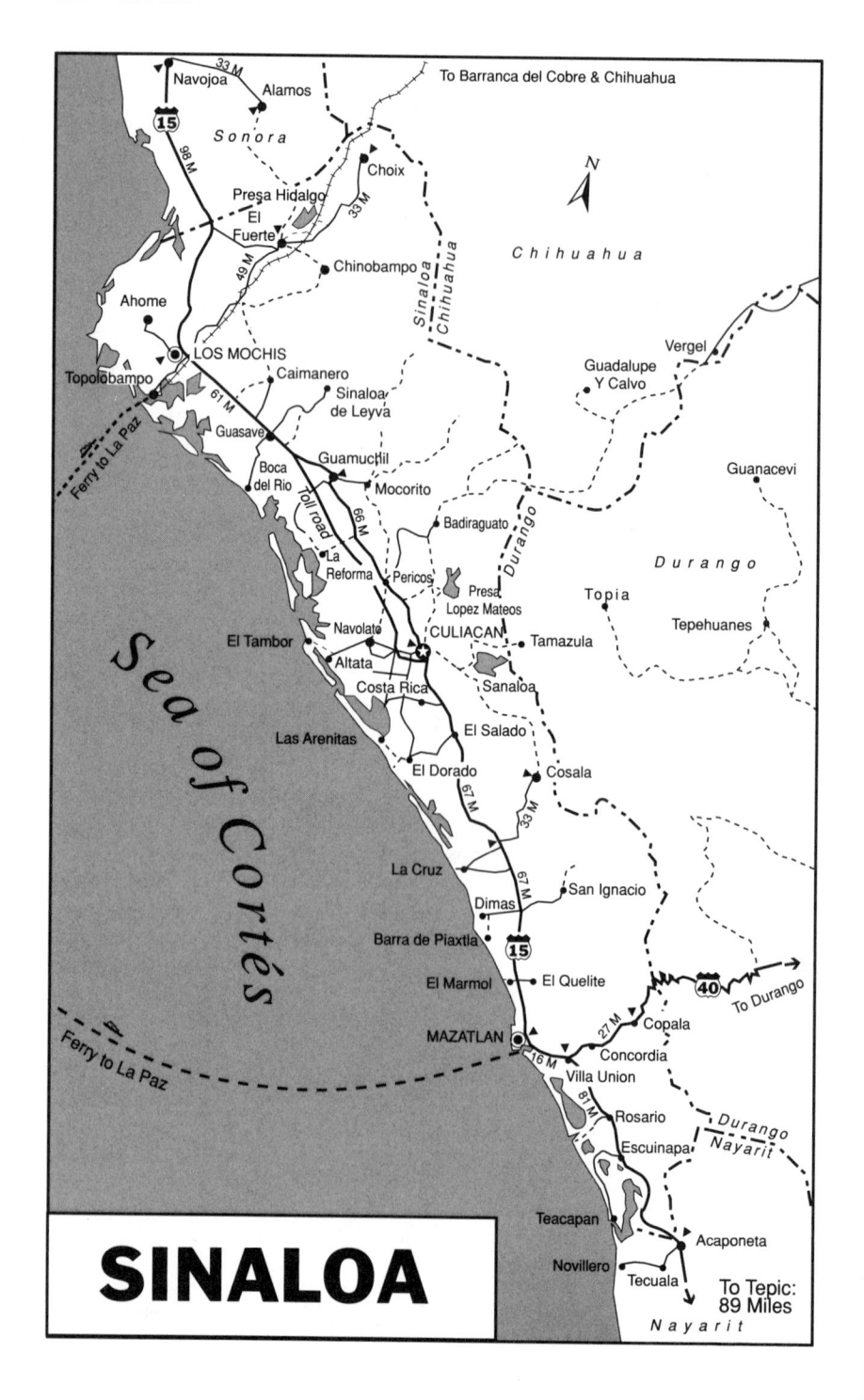

To Barranca del Cobre & Chihuahua

Navojoa · Alamos

Sonora

Choix

Presa Hidalgo
El Fuerte

Chinobampo

Ahome

LOS MOCHIS

Topolobampo

Caimanero

Sinaloa de Leyva

Guasave

Boca del Rio

Guamuchil

Mocorito

Badiraguato

La Reforma

Pericos

Presa Lopez Mateos

CULIACAN

Navolato

El Tambor

Altata

Costa Rica

Sanaloa

Las Arenitas

El Salado

El Dorado

Cosala

La Cruz

Dimas

San Ignacio

Barra de Piaxtla

El Marmol

El Quelite

MAZATLAN

Copala

Concordia

Villa Union

Rosario

Escuinapa

Teacapan

Acaponeta

Novillero

Tecuala

To Tepic: 89 Miles

Sea of Cortés

Ferry to La Paz

Chihuahua

Sinaloa / Chihuahua

Guadalupe Y Calvo

Vergel

Guanacevi

Durango

Topia

Tepehuanes

Tamazula

To Durango

Durango / Nayarit

Nayarit

SINALOA

11.

SINALOA & BARRANCA DEL COBRE

Hwy. 15 travels ten to 30 miles inland from the coast, weaving a sinuous course through svelte hills brushed with deciduous growth, a countryside as mellifluous as its name, Sinaloa. The state license plates simply abbreviate it to "Sin."

Overhead, wintertime flights of birds wing down the Pacific and Rocky Mountain flyways, heading to their breeding grounds in the vast *marismas*, or mangrove swamps, that drown most the coastline.

The water offshore warms up too much in summer for temperate-type fish. Too cold during the winter for tropical fish. The briny shallows swarm with shrimp. Most of the fishermen from the squalid villages along the inner esteros rake the bottom with nets for these crustaceans. The outer beaches are desolate, long, and sandy. Foreign travelers are an oddity, not a commodity.

Except for Mazatlán and Topolobampo, there are no major towns built along this swampy coast. One town built on the *marismas* in the 18th century, El Dorado, sank. Archaeologists are still trying to pinpoint its location (they have found parts of the church).

It is along the savannah and tucked into the foothills where the cities and towns have established themselves, waystops

along the ancient migration route now linked by pavement.

The highway crosses more than 12 rivers that drop down from the Sierra Madre, draining the state; this water is used to fertilize vast tracts of sugar cane, rice, and tomatos. Up in the foothills, colonial mining towns provide a gateway to the remote Sierras, home of Tarahumara Indians, *gambusinos* (gold prospectors), and opium growers. The Durango highway south of Mazatlan is the only paved road to cross these mountains.

OPIUM

During World War II, the United States encouraged the cultivation of opium in Sinaloa to supply much-needed morphine. Today, opium continues to be grown and exported to the United States, but illegally as heroin. Opium cultivation takes place deep in the Sierras, far from any place a prudent traveler would care to visit. But with forty years' worth of seed wafting through the sierras, you are likely to come across natural stands of opium poppies, especially along streambeds or the sides of roads. It is not a good flower to pick. It is sickly sweet to the nose, prickly to the touch. It is also likely to get you in trouble

Los Mochis exit to El Fuerte, you can turn off Hwy. 15 at the new El Carrizal exit (63 miles south of Navojoa, 35 miles north of Los Mochis), and drive 29.5 miles to a dirt road turn-off; the paved road continues on 14 miles to El Fuerte. This dirt road travels two miles to the dam, then continues 20 miles to Alamos, following the old Camino Real. *Caution: This desolate stretch beyond the dam has a reputation for robbery.*

MOCHICAHUI & SAN BLAS

On the road to El Fuerte from Los Mochis, you pass **Mochicahui**, at 9 miles. On Día de San Juan Bautista, Mayo Indians come here for a religious procession and to perform native dances. At 21.7 miles, you come to **San Blas**, where the *Chihuahua al Pacífico*, and the *Ferrocarriles del Pacífico* cross tracks at Sufragio Station.

EL FUERTE

Buried in the foothills 50 miles off the tourist track, El Fuerte is often compared to Alamos. Unlike Alamos, this town lacks both tourists and much of specific interest, except for the historical atmosphere thrown off by its old 18th and 19th century colonial buildings. The zócalo, framed by centuries-old *portales*, often seems deserted, its vitality sapped by a busy modern commercial zone a few blocks away.

The two oldest buildings face the zócalo and represent the weight of its history: an early Jesuit church and the jail, now turned into a store selling *artesanía*, most of which is brought in from other areas in Mexico. In this same building (now the Casa de La Cultura) is a small exhibition room where there are displays of arrowheads, saddles, basketry, and other regional artifacts (as well as a bathroom).

El Fuerte is laid out near the banks of the Río Fuerte, and both take their name from a fort built here in 1610 to guard against the Mayo Indians, who had destroyed the original settlement founded in 1563 (then called San Juan Bautista de Carapoa). This fort

with humorless j*udiciales federales* and *militares*, who often set up roadblocks in Sinaloa, searching for just such drugs.

SIDETRIP INTO The SIERRAS, EL FUERTE & BEYOND

From the Sinaloa state line, Hwy. 15 travels 42 miles to Los Mochis, where there is a turn-off (Son. 24) to two big dams and El Fuerte, a colonial town set back 49 miles in the Sierra Madre.

PRESA DOMINGUEZ

Largemouth bass swarm in the muddy water of this vast earth fill dam. Presa Hidalgo farther upstream is the main catchment but lacks the big fish found here. Unlike other dams, this is one of the few where primitive camping spots can be found along the shore. There are three different fishing camps here, and a few boats may be found to rent. **Alternate Access:** Instead of taking the

Panga Fishing in the Gulf

proved an important link in the Camino Real, and much silver passed through here on its way from Alamos. The original road to Alamos still remains, but there have been problems with robbery in its more remote sections. For two years (1824-26), El Fuerte was capital of Sinaloa, but its political fortunes went the way of the silver ore, and today this town exists mainly as a railstop and supply center for the Sierras.

Places to Sleep

It's foot or fathom as far as hotels go. Two of the hotels are shallow dives. The third is a pool of colonial elegance. **Hotel Posada del Hidalgo** ($$$) is a restored 19th century mansion, only half a block from the zócalo; choose room #7—President Carranza slept here. Of the other two, **Hotel El Oasis** ($) has nothing to do with its name, a cheap sleep for hardy travelers. **Hotel San Jose** ($) in front of the market is cheaper yet, and is mainly for local traders.

ARRIVING & DEPARTING :
By Rail & Bus

El Fuerte is a rail stop on the *Chihuahua al Pacífico*, which runs from Chihuahua to Los Mochis, passing by the Barranca del Cobre to Chihuahua. There are two morning trains to Chihuahua, two evening trains to Los Mochis.

Buses can be caught from Los Mochis to El Fuerte at frequent intervals.

By Car

The 49-mile paved road to El Fuerte leaves Hwy. 15 at Los Mochis. A 43-mile paved road leaves Hwy. 15 at 35 miles north of Los Mochis, a shorter route for travelers coming from or going to the north.

BEYOND EL FUERTE
PRESA HIDALGO

A graded dirt road travels 6.6 miles from El Fuerte to Hidalgo Dam, which holds back the coffee-cream waters of the Río Fuerte. Two huge monuments, one to Hidalgo, another to Tlaloc the rain god, look out on the vast expanse of silent water. Behind the reservoir, the beginnings of the barranca country rise on the horizon. Despite the advertising, there are no boating facilities here, few places to camp, and the fishing is poor; biggest draw is the shooting of doves.

JÍPAGO

Instead of backtracking from the dam to El Fuerte, you can continue on the dirt road that leaves from the dam's base for the paved highway above El Fuerte. At 3.5 miles from dam, you will pass the tiny ejido of Jípago, where some scalding hot springs (190°F) are set back 0.6 miles from the schoolhouse; you can drive to within 30 meters of the springs. From Jípago, the road tracks another 2.1 miles to the paved highway that leads either back to El Fuerte or on to Choix, gateway to the barranca country.

CHOIX

The paved road from El Fuerte ends at Choix, springboard to the Sierras. A day's travel from here puts you in the pine-forested sierras, as dirt roads radiate out to the villages of Tasajera, Nacimiento, and Potrero de Cancio up in barranca country. Little trace remains of its colonial mining days, evidenced by its zócalo, which now is taken up by a modernistic spider-like kiosk. The town itself holds scant scenic appeal, though the Río Choix, a tributary of the Río Fuerte, winds through the valley below. But on the 28th of September—Día de San Miguel Arcángel—Choix explodes with color, when an image of the saint is carried through the streets to the nearby settlement of Boca. Pilgrims from throughout the sierras attend, dancing the traditional dances.

Places to Sleep

Hermanos Gómez ($), across from the Pemex gas station, is the most familiar to foreign travelers, but a more comfortable lodging can be found at **Hotel San Luis** ($), across from the Casa de la Cultura.

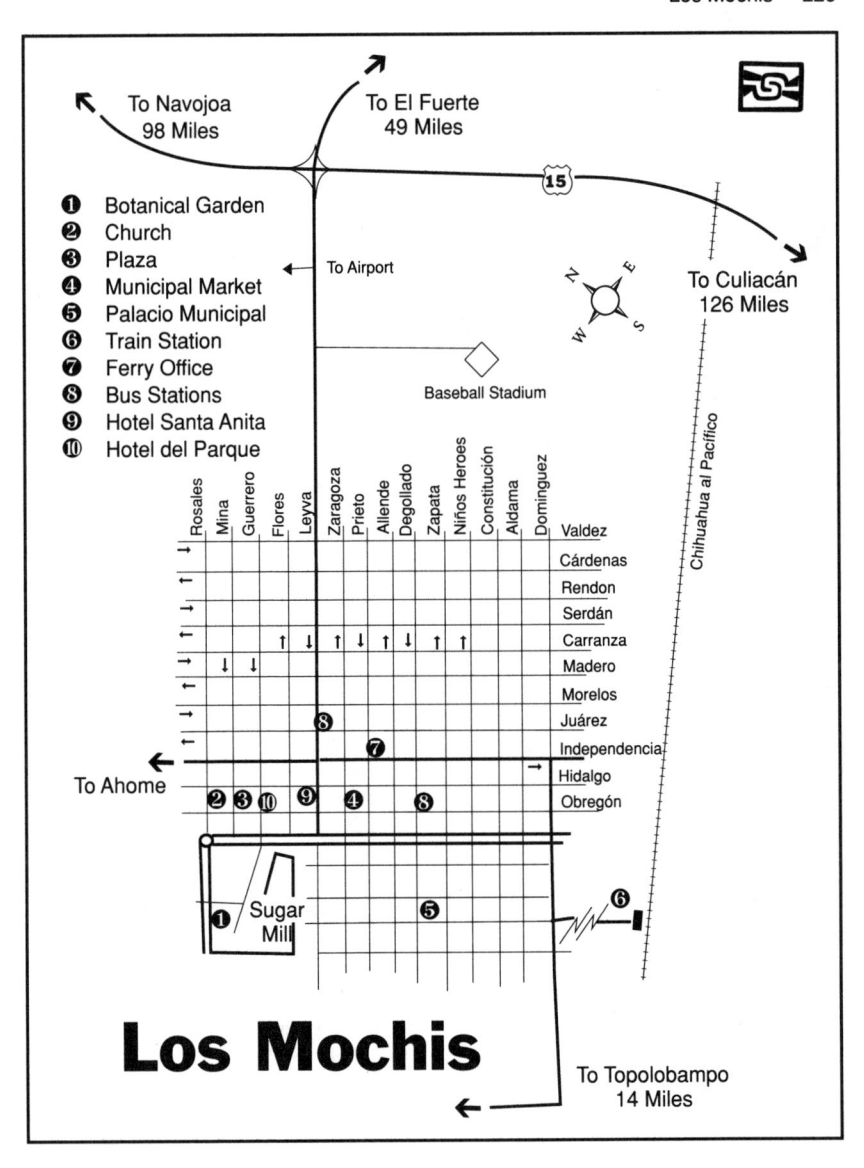

❶ Botanical Garden
❷ Church
❸ Plaza
❹ Municipal Market
❺ Palacio Municipal
❻ Train Station
❼ Ferry Office
❽ Bus Stations
❾ Hotel Santa Anita
❿ Hotel del Parque

To Navojoa
98 Miles

To El Fuerte
49 Miles

To Airport

15

To Culiacán
126 Miles

Baseball Stadium

Chihuahua al Pacifico

Rosales | Mina | Guerrero | Flores | Leyva | Zaragoza | Prieto | Allende | Degollado | Zapata | Niños Heroes | Constitución | Aldama | Dominguez

Valdez
Cárdenas
Rendon
Serdán
Carranza
Madero
Morelos
Juárez
Independencia
Hidalgo
Obregón

To Ahome

Sugar
Mill

Los Mochis

To Topolobampo
14 Miles

LOS MOCHIS

Highway 15 skirts the northwest edge of Los Mochis, one of the more interesting of the agricultural cities along the savannah. This is fortunate, since any traveler heading across the Gulf or to the Barranca del Cobre most likely will be forced to spend a night here in order to catch the early morning ferry or train.

The city is easy to understand, with its wide streets and square blocks all laid out to a grid. If Los Mochis seems faintly reminiscent of the U.S., it is because this town was founded in 1893 by Benjamin Johnston, who left Virginia in 1893 to lay this American template of order in a foreign land.

Banda Orquesta

A bully of a businessman, he maneuvered to buy vast acreage during the *Porfiriato* (the reign of Porfirio Diaz, 1876-1911), which he planted with sugar cane. He also brought workers in to cut the stalks. He built the largest sugar refinery on the west coast to crush and refine the sugar. He bought the Chihuahua-Pacífico railroad from Santa Fe, intent on extending the rails across the Sierras to Los Mochis. Though he did build a lighthouse, Mr. Johnston died in 1938 before he could realize his final vision, to turn Los Mochis into an important seaport by digging a canal 14 miles to Topolobampo (Los Mochis is only 50 feet above sea level).

You can see what is left of Johnston's palatial home, which once featured an elevator, an indoor pool, and extravagant formal gardens. Little remains of the mansion, but the gardens, planted with bushes and shrubs from around the world, make up a botanical garden of sorts, open to the public. They are located on the northwest side of town, west of the main intersection of Leyva and Obregón.

You can also visit the nearby sugar mill on weekdays. The Cía. Azucarera de Los Mochis, S.A., is Mexico's greatest producer of sugar and its potent by-product, alcohol.

The city today is lively with traffic, shaded by many large trees, aerated by big fountains, and surrounded by waving fields of sugar cane. Water from a dam on the Río Fuerte has turned this land green, except for the bright fields of marigolds, which in Mexico are the flower of the dead. But these petals have a purpose; fed to chickens, they color egg yokes a bright yellow.

Bearings

It is impossible to get lost in Los Mochis. All streets run at 90 degrees to each other, most alternating direction as one-way streets. Gabriel Leyva and Blvd. Castro are the two major arteries.

Events

Los Mochis celebrates May 31 to June 16.

Places to Sleep

The hotel zone is loosely clustered around the Leyva-Obregón intersection. Main player here is the **Hotel Santa Anita** ($$$; Av. Leyva and Calle Hidalgo; tel. 2-00-46); though expensive, it is the most rehearsed operation for travelers going into the barranca country. Other respectable choices are the **Plaza Inn**, the **Colonias Hotel** on the outskirts (a former Holiday Inn), and the **Hotel del Parque** ($$; Obregón and Javier Mina; tel. 2-02-60). Less expensive budget properties are situated near the Tres Estrellas bus terminal: **Hotel America** ($) on Allende, and **Hotel Los Arcos** ($) on Allende and Escutia.

The **Copper Canyon Trailer Park** is situated on the outskirts of town.

ARRIVING & DEPARTING
By Car

Los Mochis is situated 130 miles north of Culiacán, 270 miles from Mazatlán.

By Bus

The two bus lines operate from two different locations. *Tres Estrellas de Oro* station is situated at Degollado and Obregón, and *Transportes del Norte* is at Leyva and Juárez, both only a few blocks from the hotel zone.

By Air

Both *AeroMéxico* and *AeroCalifornia* fly out of Los Mochis international airport.

By Rail

The railroad station, 1.2 miles from city center, is for the *Chihuahua al Pacífico*, which runs past the Barranca del Cobre to Chihuahua. The closest rail stop for *Ferrocarriles del Pacífico*, which runs to Nogales and Guadalajara, is at Sufragio 23 miles away.

There are two trains that traverse the Sierras to Chihuahua: the *Vista* and the *Mixto*, which depart daily at 6 and 7 a.m., respectively. *Warning: published departure times of 7 and 8 a.m. are on Central Time; subtract an hour for local time.*

The first train, the Vista, is preferred, since it is quicker, less crowded, and provides better views. Vista tickets can be bought the day before at the Agencia Viajes Flamingo (tel. 2-19—29; or 2-16-13; Telex 53254), at Hidalgo 419, around the corner from the Hotel Santa Anita. If you must buy your ticket on the same day, plan to be at the station by 5 a.m. Don't take the bus if time is short; you will find taxis waiting in front of Hotel Santa Anita. *Tip: if you are trying to make a rail connection from Ferrocarriles del Pacífico to the Chihuahua al Pacífico, it's best to take a bus from Sufragio to Los Mochis, and buy an originating ticket to insure a seat. If you would like to leave your car in Los Mochis while you take to the rails, inquire about leaving it at the back lot of* **Hotel Santa Anita**.

TOPOLOBAMPO

Topolobampo is an unscenic town in a spectacular location, a vast bay sheltered from the sea by two long sand peninsulas. Pemex storage tanks and rusting shrimp boats are testaments to what people do here for a living (shrimp season runs from late spring to early autumn).

A workaday town, it clings to the steep hills and offers little sanctuary to the traveler. Most visitors arrive with the purpose of leaving just as quickly, either on the ferry to La Paz or on the train to the Sierras. Yet one hundred years ago, North Americans devoted entire lives to Topolobampo, then a utopian community.

Visionary Albert Kinsey Owens chose this barren bay as the site for his socialist experiment since it was "far from the evil influences of the trade and political centers of the world." A boatload of 27 colonists from the United States landed here in 1886 and, within a year, 400 idealists had joined them. Schools were established, rent and tax abolished, and in the evenings colonists were summoned to communal dinners not by bugle call but by classical music from a clarinet.

A reporter for *Harpers Weekly* wrote that "the Topolobampo colonists are a peculiar people. One cannot visit among them long without coming to the conclusion that they are an educated, steady going race of skilled craftsmen and women with a settled purpose and a fixed determination to carry it out. They are mostly persons who have positive convictions concerning religion, government, and society."

In 1893, Owens' positive convictions led him to proselytize elsewhere. The rudderless community drifted into two groups, the *saints* (the cooperationists) and *kickers* (those who wanted title to the land they worked). As they feuded among themselves over water rights, in stepped Benjamin

Johnston, recently arrived from Virginia, with a federal concession that granted him control of the water supply. No soft heart, he began court proceedings for their eviction, which effectively sunk the social experiment. At the turn of the century, about 50 American families remained in the Río Fuerte valley. Robbed of their philosophy and their land, most left before the Mexican Revolution. The few remaining families have since been absorbed into the Mexican culture.

Topolobampo Beaches

You can hire pangas at the entrance to town for excursions out to the sand islands in **Bahía Ohuira** or to the ocean beaches (most of the bay is rocky). By car, you can reach one of the better beaches in the Topolobampo area, **Playa de las Animas**, also known as **Playa Mavirí** or **Bavirí**. This long beach is shallow and calm. Access: three miles before Topolobampo (12 miles from Los Mochis), a graded road runs past rich birdwatching estuaries and over a series of low bridges to the shallow beaches.

To the south of Topolobampo, another big bay, called **San Ignacio**, can be reached on a dirt road that leaves Hwy. 15 about 17 miles south of Los Mochis.

ARRIVING & DEPARTING
By Car

Topolobampo lies 15 miles south of Los Mochis via paved road. Follow Blvd. Obregón east until it deadends, then turn right and follow the road out of town.

By Bus

City buses depart from Los Mochis along Alvaro Obregón between Leyva and Flores.

By Ferry

The ferry leaves for La Paz every day at 10 a.m., except Tuesday. The trip lasts eight hours, arriving in La Paz in the late afternoon. There are no cabins, only seats, or piles of rope to sit on. The ferry is escorted by booby birds who fish the wake as far as **Farallon Island**, a stone island that guards the bay 16 miles offshore, where there are prolific bird rookeries. You can make reservations by phoning (686) 2-01-41, or faxing (686) 2-00-35.

Accommodations

Yacht Hotel ($; tel. 2-38-62), a mile northeast of town, on a bluff overlooking a rock bound beach, is the only hotel here, a neglected operation. Primitive camping can be found out on Playa Mavirí. *Tip: if you are leaving on the ferry to La Paz the next day, you can sleep that night in your car within the secure confines of the ferry terminal, along with all the trucks.*

Events

Topolobampo celebrates Día de la Marina on June 1st, with civic ceremonies, parades and a fair.

BARRANCA DEL COBRE
Los Mochis to Chihuahua by Rail

Unlike the dry mountainous ridge of the Baja California peninsula, the Sierra Madre is full of rivers and forests. The rivers, born of the continental divide, have carved gaping canyons in the soft volcanic rock. Summer thunderstorms pour water through these *barrancas* (canyons), scouring them deeper. Their sides are ribbed with smaller ravines, also carved by the rain and winter snow runoff. These are among the deepest canyons in North America. While the highlands (averaging 7,000 to 9,000 feet above sea level) are capped with snow, banana trees grow in the canyon bottoms.

The barranca country of the Sierra Madre is cut by six major canyon systems. The early Spanish miners were drawn to these open wounds in the earth's surface. Most villages in the barrancas were either mining camps or Jesuit missions. You can still see the *arrastras* along many of the river bottoms. These massive grindstones turn in circles, grinding the ore to a powder which is then amalgamated with mercury. After the mud is washed away, the amalgam is gathered (more than $1.5 billion worth of gold and silver has been mined from the Sierra Madres in the past four centuries). The Jesuits, who entered the canyons in 1588 and were expelled in 1767, worked hard to Christianize the Tarahumara. Even today they are active in the area, but most of their missions and visitas are in ruin.

THE TARAHUMARA

Though the mining and missions are mostly relegated to the past, 50,000 Tarahumara still remain, many living as their ancestors did. The formidable canyons have sheltered them from conquest and assimilation. Though they are the second largest Indian tribe north of Mexico City (the Navajo are the largest), many of them remain semi-nomadic, summering in the highlands in their wooden cabins, retreating down into the canyons after the November harvests. They are spread throughout the barrancas, split in small family groups. They have their own dress and a language without swear words (*cuira* means hello, *ariosiba*, goodbye, *reko*, please). Some still live in caves.

Actually, anthropologists classify them into two groups, those who live like *mestizos* and those who live in the traditional way. Those of the traditional way are divided into two sub-groups. One group plants and harvests crops, raises goats, wears huaraches, and has beds, usually the only furniture in their modest homes. The other group still lives a semi-nude, nomadic lifestyle.

Tarahumara

on end, in a stuporous tesguino-induced state. Tesguino is low in alcohol content, but the Tarahumara drink a lot of it. It's an acquired taste, as many travelers to the barranca country are forced to find out.

The Tarahumara are most famous to the outside world for their long distance running. In fact, they call themselves the *Rarámuri*, the foot runners (Tarahumara is a Spanish corruption of this name). They run down deer. One of their popular games is to race through these steep mountains, kicking a wooden ball, for as long as 48 hours. Every year, the government brings a few Tarahumara to compete in the Mexico City marathon. Since their splayed feet don't fit into running shoes, they wear huaraches. Other Tarahumara help them out by handing them warm cups of *tesguino* along the way. Naturally, they never finish well, but they survive to finish, which is what their lives are all about.

Their pursuits are those of survival. They toss blasting caps obtained from miners into the river, stunning the fish long enough to dive in and grab them. To catch a squirrel, they sometimes chop down the tree. But eighty percent of their diet comes from what they grow: corn, beans, squash. Their few goats and cattle are too valuable to eat. Instead, they are kept for the manure they produce, which they use to fertilize their crops. They have disciplined themselves not to indulge in steak in order that they may survive on corn.

Corn is the mainstay in their lives. In fact, the Tarahumara claim they descended from heaven with corn and potatoes in their ears. The corn is fermented into *tesguino*, a native beer which is drunk in copious amounts and plays a large role in their religious festivals. The corn is softened with water, kept in a dark place, then mashed and boiled for up to eight hours. Catalysts are added, such as bark, lichen, or leaves. It can be drunk after 24 hours of fermentation. Many of their religious events, especially during Holy Week, are celebrated for days

BACK COUNTRY TRAVEL

Traveling by foot in the back country is a unique and inexpensive experience. Guides are both cheap and necessary. They know their way, where to camp, and what to avoid (like areas of illegal agriculture). Ask anybody of position (i.e. shopkeeper, teacher, public official) where to find a guide. Agree on a wage before setting out, and give part of the money in advance so he can leave some with his family. It is expected that you will provide the guide with food and water, apart from the wage. If you have a lot to carry, consider hiring a burro as well (cluck for go, hiss for stop).

Trust the guide, but bring a map. You can go to most any university library and copy the sections you need, or buy one through a map store. In Creel, the Tarahumara Mission Store usually has maps, but don't count on it.

Dress in layers. Temperatures in the Sierras can drop to the 30s, then warm to the 70s. The rainy season starts in June, ends in mid-September. Lots of rain sometimes falls in January. Early spring is the best time to visit, when the river level in the canyons is down from the winter storms, and before it rises again on summer rainfall. Holy Week is the peak, celebrated vigorously by the Tarahumara. Drums echo at night throughout the canyons, tesguino flows freely, the music, dancing, and wrestling go non-stop for three days.

*Caution: whenever traveling in the country, take lots of loose change, as few people have the wherewithal to change a 50,000 peso no*te.

COPPER CANYON TRAIN TRIP

The *Chihuahua al Pacífico* railway provides the main leap up into the barranca country. One of the most scenic railroads in the world, this 420-mile track goes through 86 tunnels and over 39 bridges. From Los Mochis, it makes a a sharp climb up the western slopes to El Divisadero, through pine-and-oak highlands, then down through grassy plains to the dry rainshadow desert of Chihuahua.

It took 89 years from concept to final spike. The railroad was planned in 1872 by Albert Owen, who later founded the Topolobampo colony. His plan was to connect the mid-western states of the U.S. with Bahía Topolobampo, a shortcut to the Orient. It wasn't until 1900 that the *Kansas City, Mexico, and Orient Railroad Company* began work, a project as ambitious as its name. The Mexican Revolution put a stop to construction. In 1928, another American, Benjamin F. Johnston (who founded Los Mochis), bought the line. Construction ended with his death in 1937, after which the Mexican government bought the railroad. It took another 21 years to cross the mountains. The first train from Chihuahua arrived at Los Mochis in 1961.

TRAIN NOTES

The train, which runs along the rim, does not offer a view of Barranca del Cobre. Your only opportunity to see the canyon

and the Tarahumara is the 15-minute stop at Divisadero, where there is a natural lookout. The Indians come here to sell handicrafts. To enter the canyon, plan to get off at either Bahuichivo, Divisadero, or Creel. If you are continuing on to Chihuahua, you can buy a stopover ticket for a few dollars extra.

Be one of the first to board, so you can find a place to put your things (no checked baggage) and a window that is not too scratched or dirty (right-hand "starboard" windows offer better views when heading east). Air conditioning is predictably weak, but since the train leaves the Los Mochis lowlands early in the morning, you can escape ahead of the heat. Meals can usually be bought in the dining car. The vista train leaves from both Los Mochis and Chihuahua at 7 a.m., central time. The trip takes 12 to 15 hours. The train departing from Los Mochis offers better views of the barranca country (between Temoris and Creel) than the one departing from Chihuahua, since whenever the latter is running late, it passes this area in the dusk or dark, especially during winter. Children under five travel free, under 12 for half price.

Some tour companies block seats on the regular train. Most private tours stop overnight along the way. Campers and cars can be piggybacked on flatcars.

Los Mochis to Chihuahua

The railroad is marked every kilometer by a numbered post, measuring the distance you are from Ojinaga, the railhead at the U.S. border. The train leaves Los Mochis at Km 920.

Km 882: San Blas is where the Chihuahua al Pacífico crosses tracks with the Ferrocarril del Pacífico, which runs from Nogales to Guadalajara.

Km 839: El Fuerte (see page 226).

Km 781: Río Fuerte is crossed here by the

longest bridge on this trip, 500 feet in length.

Km 748: Puente Chinipas bridges the Río Chinipas, the highest bridge you will cross, 335 feet above the river. Far below, a foot bridge also crosses the river.

Km 743: State Line divides Chihuahua and Sinaloa, as well as marks the change from Central to Mountain Time (the train schedule operates on Central Time, even in Sinaloa).

Km 708: Estación Temoris, at 3,365 feet above sea level, marks the beginning of the barranca country. The Jesuits founded the Santa María Magdalena de Temoris mission here, named after the local Indian tribe. Just beyond, at Km 705, you enter tunnel No. 49 (each tunnel is numbered on the right side as you enter), a 3,074 foot-long horseshoe.

Km 669: Bahuichivo, a small lumber town, is one of the best access points to the canyon. Here, you can find a ride seven miles down to **Cerocahui**, a mountain pueblo first established by Father Salvatierra in 1681. A later version of the Misión Cerocahui still stands, across from the **Hotel Misión**, part of the Balderrama chain that dominates the tourist circuit here ($$; reservations are made through Hotel Santa Anita in Los Mochis; P.O. Box 159; tel. 2-00-46). They send a bus to pick up guests getting off the train. The 28 rooms are warmed by wood stoves. The **Cabañas Barrancas de Uríque** also provides a taxi service to their 21 cabins, situated a remote 25 miles from Bahuichivo ($$; for reservations, write: Box 622, Chihuahua).

The Hotel Misión also offers expensive day tours, but you can arrange things freelance. Most trips are to the Cerocahui waterfall and up to Cerro de Gallego. This 7,000 ft. peak looks out over the village of Uríque, along the banks of the *Río Uríque*,

as it emerges from the maws of the Barranca del Cobre.

Uríque, a trim mining village founded in 1691, is one of the most remote canyon villages accessible by car (30 miles from Cerocahui by bus or hitching). A small hotel faces the main plaza (two others in town), a short walk away from the green river. If the hotels are full, you can always sleep by the river. Besides drinking *tesguino* in town, you can hike up into the barranca, camping shoreside, or raft downstream. From Uríque, a dirt road crosses the river and continues on to a nearby Tarahumara village. The mestizo community of Uríque comes here to watch the Holy Week ceremonies, and you can tag along with them, one of the best places in Mexico to witness these religious festivities.

Km 662: Cuiteco is a small village where Father Salvatierra built a Jesuit mission in 1684.

Km 622: Divisadero, the dividing place, at 7,200 feet, looks out over the silent breadth of the canyon. From *El Balcón* (the balcony), you can see the thin stream of the Río Uríque a mile below, the implausible creator of this giant canyon. Along the rim, Tarahumara Indians sell crafts, including their popular drums, baskets, and sometimes violins, carved from the hardwood that grows atop the canyon and glued with the pulp of lily bulbs that sprout along the river bottom. After a quick 15-minutes, the train starts to move. It is much better to let it leave without you. With the crowds gone, the canyon looms larger.

If you want to hike down the Barranca del Cobre, Divisadero is the best place to start. If "down" is your only destination, you can let gravity be your guide, but the networks of trails are confusing, and some don't reach the river. A guide is definitely recommended. The confusing trail can be steep and rocky, but unlike the Grand Canyon, the sides are sloping, and the talus soil

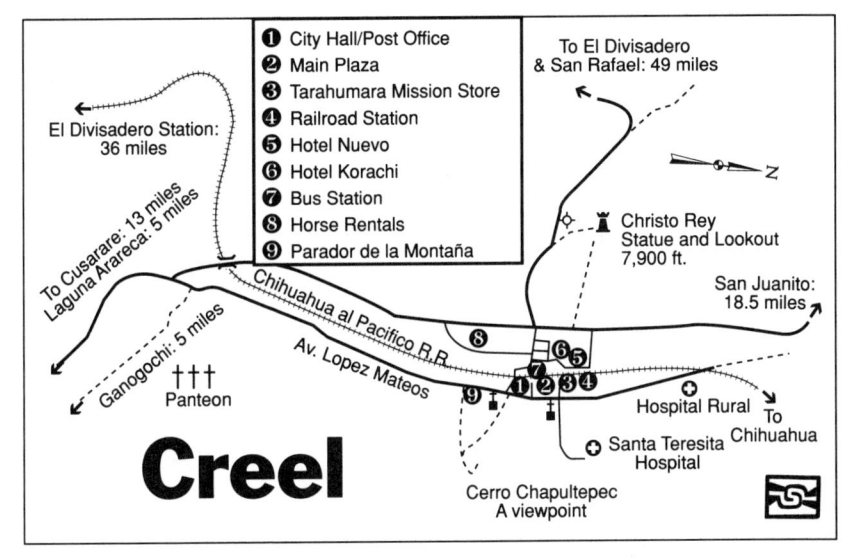

❶ City Hall/Post Office
❷ Main Plaza
❸ Tarahumara Mission Store
❹ Railroad Station
❺ Hotel Nuevo
❻ Hotel Korachi
❼ Bus Station
❽ Horse Rentals
❾ Parador de la Montaña

El Divisadero Station: 36 miles

To Cusarare: 13 miles
Arareca: 5 miles
Laguna
To

Ganogochi: 5 miles
††† Panteon

Chihuahua al Pacifico R.R.
Av. Lopez Mateos

To El Divisadero & San Rafael: 49 miles

Christo Rey Statue and Lookout 7,900 ft.

San Juanito: 18.5 miles

Hospital Rural
Santa Teresita Hospital
To Chihuahua

Cerro Chapultepec A viewpoint

Creel

allows pine and oak trees to grow at the upper levels. As you hike, you drop into another biosphere, more tropical. You will pass primitive rock houses, corn fields, perhaps a group of Tarahumara or a burro train carrying oranges and bananas, evidence of the more temperate climate below. You can make a descent in one day, but it is both pleasant and practical to spend the night on the trail.

The river, at least in spring and fall, is a tranquil place of boulders, deep green water, and rippling rapids. Downstream, the river narrows through giant boulder traps and passes through an inner gorge, where the water deepens and moves slowly. It drops out of the canyon about 28 miles from Divisadero at the the village of Uríque, a difficult voyage possible only by inflatable kayak or by swimming.

The last train to Creel passes Divisadero around 2 p.m., to Los Mochis around 4 p.m. A dirt road connects Divisadero to Creel.

Places to Sleep

There are three hotels here, all of them priced high and operating on the American Plan. The **Hotel Cabanas Divisadero Barrancas** ($$; reservations at P.O. Box 661

Chihuahua; tel. 2-33-62; 5-11-99) sits on the edge of the rim. The **Hotel Mansión Tarahumara** ($$$; P.O. Box 1416, Chihuahua; tel. 16-26-72) is styled like a medieval castle, though rooms are in individual cabins. The **Hotel Posada Barrancas**, part of the Balderrama chain ($$; reservations through Hotel Santa Anita in Los Mochis; P.O. Box 159; tel. 2-00-46) has fireplaces in its rooms and is more secluded, situated two miles west at Km. 625.5 (the train stops here also).

Km 583: Los Ojitos is the highest elevation the train reaches, 8,071 feet above sea level.

Km 593: El Lazo (The Loop) is where the tracks complete a loop as they disappear into a tunnel. Above is stone bridge that was built before the Mexican Revolution.

Km 565: Creel is the biggest settlement between Chihuahua and Los Mochis and the most important supply point for the Sierras. Creel was never a mission or Indian village. Its log houses and sawmill give it a rough frontier look. It was named after Enrique C. Creel, son of the American consul in Chihuahua, who later became governor of Chihuahua (1904-06). He was also vice president of the *Kansas City, Mexico and Orient Railroad*, which reached this spot in 1907, where it ran out of money but created a town.

The town is a functional center of operations for any exploration of the barrancas, and its 7,735 foot altitude makes for a vigorous alpine atmosphere, clear and bracing. Half a dozen stores sell Tarahumara arts and crafts. There are hotels, restaurants, a bank, stores, phones, and now even a paved road running to Chihuahua for those impatient with the train (the bus to Chihuahua takes about three hours, the train six).

From Creel, you can visit nearby lakes, waterfalls, canyons, and caves. Most popular are trips to the Basaseáchic and Cusárare waterfalls, and to Batopilas, a mining town buried in the barrancas. Other short day trips out of Creel go to the tepid hot springs of Recohuata, the Valley of the Monks, where there are interesting rock formations, and to San Ignacio, a village close to Creel where there is a centuries-old mission.

All hotels offer day trips to these sights, or you can arrange them yourself. The best resource in town is the Tarahumara Mission Store, run by Catholic missionaries. This store, which sells Tarahumara artwork and handicrafts, books, and local maps, returns its profit to the *Clínica de Santa Teresita*, a Creel hospital offering subsidized health care to the Tarahumara.

PLACES TO SLEEP

Unlike Divisadero, where the hotels are expensive, Creel offers plenty of budget rooms in keeping with the local economy.

Budget

Two hotels stand conveniently next to the rail station. The **Hotel Korachi** lies across the tracks, log cabin rooms with wood-burning stoves and hot water. More expensive but still in budget range is **Hotel Nuevo**, across the street from both the station and the Tarahumara Mission Store. Rooms are newer, more comfortable, also with wood stoves or fireplaces (necessary since wintertime snow flurries are not uncommon). On one corner of the main plaza is the friendly **Casa de Margarita**, 11 Mateos, a small house containing rooms, with cabins in back, a place where most *mochileros* (backpackers) end up. Communal meals are usually included in the price.

Moderate

Parador de las Montaña (tel. 75), on 41 Calle Mateos (reservations in Chihuahua; 114 Allende, tel. 2-2062), has TV and a phone, as well as a lounge and restaurant, making it popular with tour groups. More remote, 30 minutes away, is the **Las Cabañas del Cobre** (for reservations, write or phone 1130 E. Beaver, Troy, MI, 48084; U.S. tel. 800-543-4180), a popular departure point for backpackers. Its 23 rooms are heated by wood-burning stoves, illuminated by kerosene. It operates on American Plan only and sends a bus to meet each train.

CREEL SIDETRIPS

All the hotels listed above provide information as well as inexpensive tours to the most popular sites. The Tarahumara Mission Store is the best place to get information on more remote destinations within the canyons.

Lago Arareco

This lake is four miles from Creel along the road to Cusárare.

Cuzárare

This Tarahumara village lies to the south of Creel, reached by a 13-mile paved road. Its name means place of eagles. The original mission, built in 1740, has been recon-

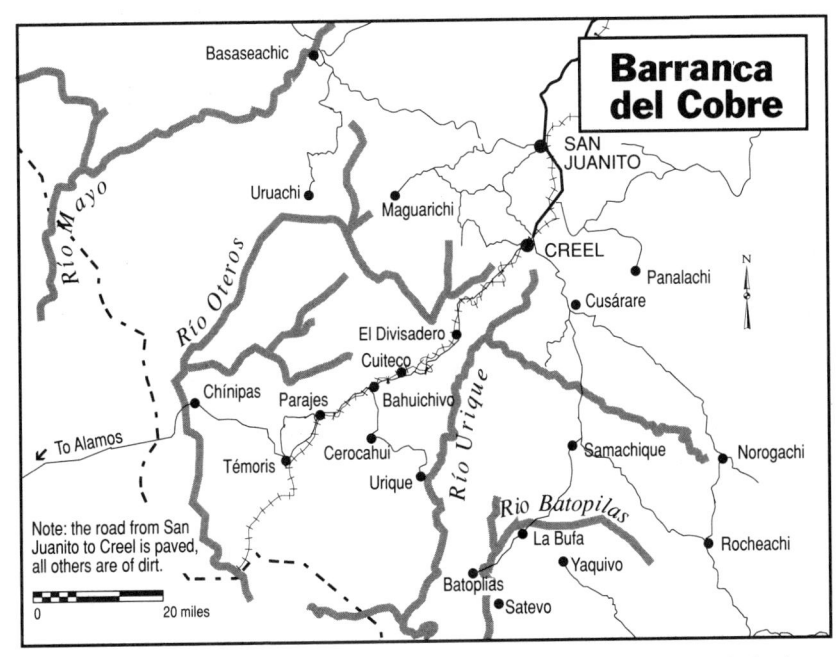

Barranca del Cobre

Basaseachic
Uruachi
Maguarichi
Río Mayo
Río Oteros
SAN JUANITO
CREEL
Panalachi
Cusárare
El Divisadero
Cuiteco
Chínipas
Parajes
Bahuichivo
To Alamos
Témoris
Cerocahui
Urique
Río Urique
Samachique
Norogachi
Note: the road from San Juanito to Creel is paved, all others are of dirt.
Río Batopilas
La Bufa
Yaquivo
Rocheachi
Batopilas
Satevo
0   20 miles

N

structed, and it is worth looking inside at the artwork and a display of local Indian handicrafts. The mission is just north of the village, down a dirt road. Nearby is the Las Cabañas del Cobre (see Creel hotels). From its parking lot, an hour-long trail leads to a waterfall, the **Cascada Cuzárare**, which plummets 95 feet. Along the road to the waterfall, ask for directions to the *pinturas rupestres*, rock paintings situated at the base of a rocky formation. Besides some older pictures of humans hunting deer with bow and arrows, there are newer ones, showing domesticated animals and a church.

Batopilas

Roughly 93 miles south of Creel, this old mining town of several thousand inhabitants serves as a secondary base camp for those launching into the primitive canyon country. Set alongside the Río Batopilas, the site was first discovered by Spanish explorers moving up through the Río Fuerte. The Batopilas mines were worked for silver as early as 1600. Most of the present town

was built between 1880 and 1910 when a North American, Alexander Shepard, based his mining operations here. You can see the adobe ruins of his Hacienda San Miguel, as well as a 90-stamp mill and reduction plant across the river just east of town. At one time 1500 miners were employed, and mules would haul the smelted silver to Chihuahua over this same road to Creel, then just a trail. Shepard even brought music to Batopilas when a grand piano was carried the length of this trail; his coffin was carried out the same way in 1902. The town's fortunes never recovered (read: *The Silver Magnet*, by Grant Shepard, Alexander's son, E.P. Dutton, New York, 1938).

There are small *fondas* (inns) where you can find a room. The **Hotel Parador de la Montaña** also runs an annex here, across from the church ($; inquire in Creel).

Day trips around Batopilas include the **Catedral de Satevo** (1750), four miles down the river from Batopilas (an easy hike), and **La Bufa**, 17 miles before Batopilas. There is a **Tarahumara Arts and Crafts Store** in town. *Note: Batopilas* *is a dry town, no alcohol.*

Access: inquire in Creel for bus schedule to Batopilas, a trip of eight to ten hours on a somewhat treacherous road that follows the path of an old Camino Real. *Warning: Batopilas has a reputation as a supply center for nearby drug cultivations. Stay on trails and travel with a guide if possible.*

Basaseáchic

The Río Basaseáchic is an innocuous stream which attains world status as it drops off a 806 foot cliff, making it Mexico's highest waterfall and one of its most soul-stirring sights. The water flairs out, then hits the canyon floor, which is enveloped in mist. Circular rainbows hang in the air. This atomized atmosphere creates a botanical garden of lichens, mosses, air plants, and ferns, along with rare plants of scientific name. A one-hour trail leads down to the small lake at the bottom of the falls. Near the bottom, at La Ventana, there is a lookout with views of the cascading water.

Access: Basaseáchic is about a four-hour trip from Creel. Take the paved road 19 miles to San Jacinto, then turn on the 60-mile graded road to Basaseáchic via Cajurichic. A better road can be taken from La Junta, 40 miles beyond San Jacinto. From La Junta, a paved road runs 68 miles to Tomóchic, then goes another 30 miles on mostly graded road to the village of Basaseáchic. From Basaseáchic, the trailhead is south of town, where there is a place to camp just past the park entrance.

Km 552: Bocoyna is a lumber town, originally founded in 1702 by Jesuit missionaries.

Km 451: La Junta, also known as Adolfo López Mateos, is the roundhouse junction, where the tracks split going east to Chihuahua and north to Ciudad Juárez, via Nuevo Casas Grandes (an interesting way to get to the ruins Casas Grandes). This is also a good place to get off the train if you are going to the Basaseáchic waterfalls.

Km 400: Cuauhtémoc is best known for its Mennonites, who arrived here in the early 1920s seeking an isolated region where they could live peacefully among themselves, unbothered by politics or government. They are easily spotted by their trademark overalls, horse-drawn wagons, and their Low German dialect (most are of German descent). The Mennonites were founded in the 16th century by Menno Simonis, during the time of Martin Luther. They live in settlements around Cuauhtémoc, marry only among themselves, refuse to vote or serve in the military, and come into town only to shop and sell their products, most notably the delicious Chihuahua cheese.

Km 268: Chihuahua is big and urban, one of the richest cities in Mexico, but not terribly exciting to most travelers. Most find time to visit the Museo de la Revolución, also known as Quinta Luz, the home of Pancho Villa. Besides weapons, maps, and photos, the bullet-punctured car in which Pancho Villa was murdered sits in back. He was assassinated in Hidalgo and buried there, but was later dug up and beheaded (Yale's Skull and Bones Society is the prime suspect). His headless body was then sent to Mexico City. The ornate mausoleum Villa built for himself in Chihuahua (now Parque Revolución) stands empty.

Other places often visited are the cathedral next to the zócalo, and Hidalgo's prison cell three blocks away on Juárez, between Carranza and Guerrero.

Chihuahua is the hub of north central Mexico, 230 miles south of Ciudad Juárez, 904 north of Mexico City. Buses leave to all parts of Mexico and trains depart for Mexico City, Ciudad Juárez, or Ojinga (across from Presidio, Texas).

LOS MOCHIS TO CULIACÁN

Hwy. 15 runs 127 miles from Los Mochis to Culiacán, mostly through flat agricultural land. Forty-one miles after leaving Los Mochis, you can forsake Hwy. 15 for a new four-lane toll road which skirts the western fringe of Culiacán. If you stay on Hwy. 15, you will enter the city directly.

GUASAVE

In Cahita, *Guasave* means "those of the planted land," a definition that still holds true. The prehispanic agricultural Indians living here were fond allies of the Jesuits, especially Padre Kino. The remains of a Jesuit mission destroyed in 1770 by flooding of the Río Sinaloa can still be seen in Nío, less than two miles to the east of Guasave (you can also see ruins of the one they were building when they were expelled). The Jesuits are long gone, but religious fervor remains, especially on November 26 and October 7, when the Día de la Virgen del Rosario is celebrated with a religious procession, and endless ritual dancing by the Yaquis and Mayos. Guasave is 36 miles south of Los Mochis.

Guasave Sidetrips

Playa Las Glorias is a getaway beach for the people of Guasave, a miles-long stretch of calm surf coming to a head where the Río Sonora breaks out onto the ocean at Boca del Río. From Guasave, Hwy. 153 travels 24 miles to the Boca del Río turnoff, which takes you to Playa Las Glorias, one of the few beaches here to face the Sea of Cortés instead of an estuary. A rougher trip goes 29 miles inland to **Sinaloa de Leyva**, another Jesuit mission town, much of it dating to the 17th and 18th century (only a tower remains of the original church). From the town you can catch a bus to **Agua Caliente de Zevada**, where a pool is fed by a natural warm spring, or to **Presa de Bacurato**, where the fishing is reputed to be excellent.

GUAMUCHIL

Sixty miles south of Los Mochis, Guamuchil is situated near Río Mocorito which feeds into the vast Estero de Altamura; the nearest ocean beach can be reached only by a 15-mile boat ride from its shore. Guamúchil is named for the local pod trees, which the Spanish uprooted and planted in the Philippines because of their usefulness; they supplied dyes, tannin, glue, lumber, and even fruit (a favorite food of parrots). A large fair is held from December 9 to 15 to celebrate the Virgen de Guadalupe, this town's patron saint.

Most people in a hurry bypass Guamuchil on the new toll road to Culiacán.

PRESA LOPEZ MATEOS

This big impoundment dam, reached by a paved 15-mile road from Hwy. 15, is an industrial showcase, but lacks any facilities for visitors other than its huge parking lot. Don't get stranded here, parking lot gates are locked at 6 p.m. (and open at 7 a.m.). Turnoff from Hwy. 15 is 16 miles north of Culiacán, 50 miles south of Guamúchil.

CULIACÁN

This city, the capital of Sinaloa, is where the tropics are first felt, a languidness drawn largely from its location alongside the confluence of two slow-moving rivers, the Humaya and the Tamazula. A *malecón*, or riverwalk, runs the length of town. Swaying footbridges, the eddying currents, and a humid wind create this feeling of oasis, but it is just a soothing backdrop to a seething stage. Culiacán often seems at war with itself.

The Spanish took the Nahuatl name for this area, *Colhuacan*, where two rivers meet. The early Toltecs were probably the first to reach this valley, 500 years before the birth of Christ. The mother tribe of the Aztecs also passed through here on their migration to central Mexico.

The town itself was founded in 1533 by Nuño de Guzmán, the cruelest of the conquistadors, excommunicated by Bishop Zumarraga for his policy of torture and enslavement. Guzmán gathered an army and carved an empire for himself, which he called Nueva Galicia. Culiacán was its northernmost outpost, the launching pad for expeditions into Sonora.

The architecture and layout of the town still hint at its colonial heritage, especially around the Plaza de la Constitución. But much has been compromised. Neon crosses glow from the top the cathedral, built in 1855. The cathedral faces Woolworths.

The best points-of-interest here are contemporary, not colonial, places like the riverside zoo, or the *Centro Cultural Difocur*, a new complex comprising indoor and outdoor theaters, an art gallery, and museum.

One block from Difocur is another interesting sight—the police station, which always seems to be in a state of continual frenzy. Culiacán is often rocked by scandal, demonstrations, and political intrigue. The PRI and PAN political parties struggle heatedly for control of the state capital. Leftists are still known to disappear, especially if involved in organizing *campesinos*. This area is one of the larger producers of crude opium in the world. Cocaine from South America moves through these same underground conduits on its way to the United States. Corruption riddles many positions of power and police are pawns in the game, which makes the political struggle much more volatile.

Most travelers on their way to Mazatlán never notice the agitation. Tourists are considered untouchable. Like sacred cows in India, you can safely wander around at will. And those that do will find this city dynamic and intriguing, Mexico's Casablanca-by-the-river.

PLACES
Cathedral and Plaza de la Constitución
This is the the central focus of the city, situated along Blvd. Obregón, which runs down to the river three blocks away.

In the other direction, Blvd. Obregón runs 20 blocks up to Colina de San Miguel, where there are fine views out over Valle Culiacán.

Malecón
The long walk along the riverfront is a social scene on a Saturday night. This riverside strip also makes for fine jogging, and there are some parks built at river's edge. At the far eastern end of the malecón is the zoo.

Parque Zoológico
This zoo is surprisingly full of exotic animals, including bears, lions, cougars, and other claw-footed animals, kept safely behind cyclone fencing. Token admission charge.

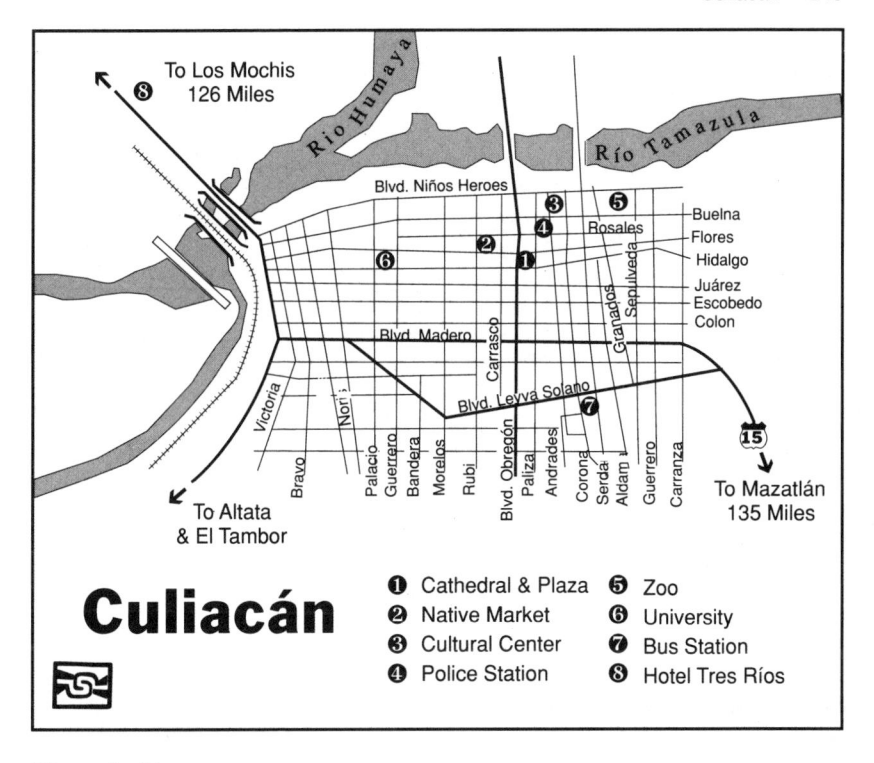

To Los Mochis
126 Miles

Río Humaya

Río Tamazula

Blvd. Niños Heroes

Rosales

Buelna
Flores
Hidalgo
Juárez
Escobedo
Colon

Blvd. Madero

Carrasco

Granados
Sepulveda

Blvd. Leyva Solano

Victoria

Nort;

Bravo

Palacio

Guerrero

Bandera

Morelos

Rubi

Blvd. Obregón

Paliza

Andrades

Corona

Serdá

Aldam

Guerrero

Carranza

To Altata
& El Tambor

To Mazatlán
135 Miles

Culiacán

❶ Cathedral & Plaza
❷ Native Market
❸ Cultural Center
❹ Police Station
❺ Zoo
❻ University
❼ Bus Station
❽ Hotel Tres Ríos

Plaza de Toros

Bullfights are held Sundays during the season. The ring lies about a mile north of the Carta Blanca beer factory, along highway 15 north out of town.

Mercado

The market, one block off of Obregón, west of the cathedral, is the typical hubbub of commerce, with little artesanía for sale.

Centro Cultural Difocur

If you have a night to kill, check out the programming here, where there always seem to be exhibits, lectures, dance, theater, or English-language movies. Facing the river, two blocks from Blvd. Obregón, the malecón offers a fine apres-movie stroll.

Universidad Autónoma de Sinaloa

Five blocks west of Blvd. Obregón, on Miguel Hidalgo y Castilla, the 19th century buildings of the University face a small plaza, across from the **Casa de la Cultura**. There is an art gallery here, where exhibits by local artists offer a glimpse into the Sinaloense mindset. The church one block away actually predates the main cathedral on Obregón.

Events

Carnival is celebrated in this city exuberantly, with parades, masked balls, amusement park rides, and a battle using flowers instead of fists.

PLACES TO SLEEP
Hotels

Hotels are numerous in Culiacán, and are on the expensive side. Only three stand out: **Hotel Los Tres Ríos** ($$$), three miles north of town on the other side of the river, is the most like a resort—a bungalow garden hotel set around a graceful pool, with restaurant and nightclub. The modern **Hotel Castel Ejecutivo** ($$$) is the most conveniently located for those who want to explore town on foot. The **Motel San Luis** ($$), atop Colina de San Miguel, offers the best views, though this is a mostly a dine-and-dance place, the rooms being little more than a natural consequence of the evening. Motorists driving through town will pass through a gauntlet of lesser-priced hotels, of which there is little difference in price, though quality seems to increase towards the eastern end of Blvd. Leyva, where the **Motel Los Caminos** ($$) and **Motel Valle Grande** ($$) are situated.

Those getting off the bus will see two hotels across Blvd. Leyva. The slothful **Hotel Salvador** ($$) should be avoided in favor of prim **Hotel del Valle** ($$), worth the few extra dollars. The cheapest hotels are situated around the central market area.

Camping

You can pitch a tent, or park a rig in the trailer park that stands to one side of Hotel Los Tres Ríos: full hook-ups, showers, and use of pool.

ARRIVING & DEPARTING
By Bus

The Camionera Central on Blvd. Leyva is well equipped with a money exchange, telegraph station, post office, guardería, phones, liquor store, and mini-mall. Buses leave every hour for Mexico and Tijuana, buses to Los Mochis every 30 minutes.

By Train

The train station lies across from the state capitol, about a quarter mile down from the giant Indian sculpture. You can catch trains north to Nogales or Mexicali, south to Mazatlán and Guadalajara.

By Air

The airport is on the road to Altata, on the town's outskirts. *AeroCalifornia*, *AeroMexico*, and *AeroSierra* fly here. The colectivo charges around $8-$10 for a ride to city center.

CULIACÁN SIDETRIPS

A dirt road from the east end of town goes 20 miles to **Presa Sanalona**, where bass fishing is reported good, but facilities are few. Also near Culiacán are the **Imala Hot Springs**, reached by a rough 15-mile road towards the Sierras. The sulfurous springs are along the bank of the Río Tamazula near Imala, where there is a 16th century church; a few miles below Imala are some **cave paintings** in a canyon; contract a guide. *Note: Imala has a reputation for skulduggery, and some Culiacán residents make a pun of its name (mala means bad).*

PLAYAS ALTATA & EL TAMBOR
A Sidetrip to the Gulf

From Culiacán, Sinaloa 30 travels for 34 miles past Navolato and across the tropical plain to the bayside beaches of Altata. These muddy beaches are protected from the open gulf by a 12-mile long sand bar. Fronting the immense Lago Pabellón, the short public beach is taken up by ramshackle restaurants set along the tideline, where you take off your shoes and let the tepid water lap your ankles while you eat estuarine seafood: clam, crab and shrimp. The other half of Altata does not fall in the public domain. Jet skiers and well-groomed children on ATVs orbit around the private homes that block access to the two-mile bay beach.

The best ocean beach in the area, **El Tambor,** is ten miles away, reached by one of three turnoffs found immediately before entering Altata; the dirt roads are easy on the car and skim along the *salitre* (salt pan) of a saltwater estero. But there are few access roads over the sandy berm to the beach and these are often clogged with cars, with few flat areas for camping (no hotels or camping in Altata either). The miles of fine gray sand are combed by straight lines of surf, and are empty except for a few homes that have been built out here. A few ramada shacks sell fish and beer. The dirt road ends within two miles at Yameto, a small shrimp fishing village on the estero.

Shrimp Pangas at Altata

CULIACÁN TO MAZATLÁN

From Culiacán to Mazatlán, Hwy. 15 weaves for 135 miles through a soft tropical landscape. Along this stretch are various side roads down to little known beaches and up to colonial towns still slumbering in the 19th century.

GULF BEACHES OF EL DORADO

Both the romantic allusion of its name and the dreamy drive through fields of sugar cane build false expectations. El Dorado is a gritty, chaotic sugar refinery town. There is little here of concern to most travelers, except how to swiftly navigate the maze of its narrow roads in order to break out on the far side of town, where a graded dirt road heads to the beaches. From El Dorado, this dirt road travels 3.8 miles to a junction. If you bear left, you will arrive after 3.7 miles at **Ponce**, a collection of abandoned buildings on a desolate stretch of flat grey beach, where workers come to drink beer and forget about sugar cane. If you bear straight at this same junction, at 7.5 miles you will

come to **Las Arenitas**, a fishing village. Its bayside beach is far removed from the "golden sands" claimed in the state tourism literature. There are two routes to get to El Dorado: directly from Culiacán (33 miles) or from the El Salado turnoff 25 miles south of Culiacán on Hwy. 15 (18 miles).

COSALÁ

This old mining town, on the flanks of the Sierra Cosalteca near the Durango state line, is a colonial jewel, easily yet rarely visited by travelers. The turn-off from Hwy. 15 is 78 miles south of Culiacán. After 33 miles of mostly paved road from Hwy. 15, you enter this town over a river and through an arch. The road runs directly to the zócalo.

The symmetry of this graceful plaza quickly gives way to the anarchy of its crooked cobbled streets. Church bells carry clearly in this clean air, measuring out the silence. There is no radio or TV reception, and the use of electricity is frugal. At night, you can throw your head back and see the

Cosalá

Iglesia de Santa Ursula facing the zócalo was built in the first half of the 19th century, a much older capilla stands a few blocks away. Its huge barrel vault, flaking plaster, and roman brick worked into the weathered stone are evidence of its 17th century construction. In an old mansion across from the main church is the **Museo de Minería e Historia**, where ore samples, old weapons, mining implements, and human bones sum up the violence and greed of its local history. Particularly interesting are a series of typewritten letters by U.S. miners of the Lluvia de Oro Mining Company depicting life here during the Mexican Revolution, as they searched for the treasure of the Sierra Madre.

Events
Cosalá celebrates June 24th, in honor of San Juan Bautista.

PLACES TO SLEEP
The cleanest hotel in town, and the only one with reliable hot water, is **Hotel Condé** ($), behind the church. The 11-room **Hotel Colonial** ($) has more character with its 30 foot ceilings and old courtyard; some rooms have big windows with views out onto the main plaza (you look out, they look in). The **Hotel Consuelo** ($) by the bus station is a poor third choice.

ARRIVING & DEPARTING
By Bus
Buses leave from the station next to the public market (1-1/2 blocks from plaza), departing four times a day for Culiacán, twice daily for Mazatlán.

COSALA SIDETRIPS
The area around Cosalá abounds in natural sights: lakes, waterfalls, hot springs, and caves. It's about 20 miles on a dirt road to **Presa El Comedero**, a bass-fishing lake with no facilities (other than a small lodge for bass fishing); the waters of the Río San Lorenzo have been impounded here to gen-

Milky Way. People here are quiet, polite, and gracious. The local economy has not been tampered with by tourists. Saddlemakers still set their saddles out on the sidewalks to cure. The general store sells many of the same dry goods it did in the 19th century. Prices are cheap.

This area was first called *Quezala* by the Indians, "where-the-Macaws-live." The Spanish kept the name when the first veins of metal were found in these hills in 1562, calling it the Royal Mine of the 11,000 Virgins of Cosalá. The original settlement was burned to the ground by Indians. The town was quickly rebuilt on its current site, and by the time it became the capital of *Occidente* (Sonora and Sinaloa), more than 20,000 people lived here.

Much of this former importance can be seen in its colonial architecture, the wooden portales, old fountains, and lichen-covered walls. One building near the church bears a plaque naming the site of the first newspaper ever published in Sinaloa; the first copies of *El Espectador Imparcial* rolled off the press in 1826. Though the neoclassic

erate electricity and irrigate fields. On the same road to El Comedero, you will pass through Carrizal, where local guides can take you to a giant cave, **La Gruta México** (purportedly 12 miles NE of town); its chambers have not been fully explored. On this same road to El Comedero you will pass the turnoff to Agua Caliente. To reach the hot springs, turn-off here and follow the dirt road about two miles to San José de las Bocas, where you can obtain a guide to take you to the hot springs. *Caution: The road beyond Presa El Comedero continues through the mountains and loops back down to Culiacán. Local authorities strongly advise against taking this road, as there are occasional problems with roadside robbery and drugs. This is the area once controlled by the notorious drug lord, Quintero.*

El Salto

Twenty-seven miles from Hwy 15, six miles before you get to Cosalá, turn off onto a dirt road at Vado Hondo (signed). After passing through the village, you will come to a cattle gate; be sure to close it after you pass. Two more miles on the dirt road brings you to the *cascadas* (waterfalls), known locally as *El Salto*, where a cool stream drops 20 feet into a pool of clear water. The bottom is sandy, angel hair grows to the rocks, and butterflies drift through the rainbow mist. Camping is possible here.

LA CRUZ DE ELOTE

Less than a mile south of the Hwy. 15 turn-off to Cosalá is the 11-mile paved road to La Cruz, where there are a few hotels, a bank, and gas station. To get to the beach, turn right at the church and follow the paved road out of town for 1.2 miles to a graded dirt road by the railroad tracks; it runs down to the beach 3.5 miles away. Plenty of flat spaces to camp, but the deserted cinderblock structures and brush shelters give a desolate cast to this long, empty beach. Summer weekends can be crowded, but during the week few people come here except to drink.

DÍMAS

Ten miles off Hwy. 15 on a paved road, and just 40 miles north of Mazatlán, this dusty town is a rail stop. Few people get off. There is little of historical or cultural importance here, though residents still spin stories of Pancho Villa riding the train through town in 1909. But it is a friendly place where travelers can tap into a tremendous amount of goodwill that has been generated by an American drifter, Ricardo Stewart, a Viet vet/merchant marine/cowboy who has been living off and on here for the last 20 years, the town's adopted son and one of the few Americans in Mexico to have an open line of credit at a cantina. As he puts it, "I don't know how people walk around here, weighed down by those 50 pound hearts."

Though the beach area close by has some of the best surfing in Mexico at the rivermouth, it is hard to reach except by foot or horseback along the river or through what has been called—true or not—one of the world's few below-ground-level jungles. Easier access to the beach is via a dirt road leaving the pavement by the *panteón* (cemetery) and traveling about eight miles to **La Barra de Piaxtla.**

Petrogylphs: spiral-shaped petroglyphs and handprints can be found along the high tide line, about two miles south of Barra de Piaxtla at Las Labradas; ask José Manuel Rosas in Dímas for a guide. About two miles before reaching Barra de Piaxtla, a rough road to these petroglyphs parallels the railroad tracks south, then runs down to the beach; walk south to find the rocks. Local residents have kept silent for years about these unusal circular petroglyphs, upon orders by some federales.

EL QUELITE

The town is named for the amaranth growing here, and a famous *corrido* (a ballad) is named for the town: "Qué bonito es El Quelite. Bien haya quién lo fundó, que en sus orillitas tiene de quién acordarme yo."

Beach at El Mármol

Three and a half miles off of Hwy. 15, 14 miles north of Mazatlán, this small village is quaint, with its wrought iron kiosk and wooden portales supporting rickety red tile roofs; next to the plazuela is a small hostel ($). At the far end of town is **El Taste**, where you can trace the ruins of a ball court where *hulama* was played. One of the oldest games of MesoAmerica, it still endures, with minor changes. The players wear *bragueros de piel* (heavy leather protection) on their thighs, and body-bat a heavy rubber ball back and forth along the narrow court, keeping it aloft without using their hands, like airborne soccer. The villages farther into the Sierras still play the game about every 15 days, but the prehispanic tradition is weakening. "The best players are dead," said the only man in Quelite who still knows how to make the special 4-kilo balls from the *árbol de hule* (rubber tree). These balls fly with amazing velocity, and have been known to kill players struck hard in the stomach, perhaps contributing to the game's decline.

EL MÁRMOL

El Mármol, "the place of marble," should be called El Cemento, as this small tidy company town lies in the shadow of a giant cement plant. The nine-mile road to the beach begins as pavement half a mile south of the Hwy. 15 turnoff for El Quelite. It then turns into hard-packed dirt before reaching the town, less than eight miles from the highway. After crossing the railroad tracks behind the town, the road becomes pocked with holes and patched with oyster shells, narrowing the closer you get to the beach. Just when you despair of reaching the ocean, it opens up before you, a wide desolate stretch of sand thrashed by surf; the road can be navigated by courageously driven sedans during the dry season. There are a few level camp sites, and the waves pealing off the point are surfable. Half a mile from the beach a turn to the north takes you through a small fishing village to an estero, where the only beach access is by foot.

MAZATLÁN

Mazatlán has the second longest malecón in the world (it stretches seven miles), the second highest lighthouse (551 feet above sea level), and is the second city ever to have been bombed from the air (during the Mexican Revolution, a bomb slipped from a pilot's hands, landing on a house).

Its true distinction lies in just this kind of diversity. It has cleaner beaches than Acapulco, more preserved history than Puerto Vallarta, and is cheaper and more convenient to ferry, train, and road than any other resort in Mexico.

Twelve miles south of the Tropic of Cancer, Mazatlán is set around a big harbor and guarded offshore by small islets and islands; its coastline is scalloped with beaches that face north, south, east and west. Three tall hills rise up from the flat plain, giving the town a frame of reference: El Crestón, Cerro de la Nevería, and La Vigía.

It was on La Vigía where 25 "jail" soldiers were posted in 1531 on Easter Sunday, sent from the original Presidio de Mazatlán at Villa Unión 16 miles to the south to keep on eye out for illegal trading. A small settlement was finally established in 1602, but the first streets weren't actually laid until 1806, when a group of German colonists moved in; the flavor of their influence is still tasted in the beer brewed here, at the Cervecería del Pacífico.

Overshadowed by Acapulco, the city never grew to its geographic potential, though in 1820 foreign trade was authorized. This made it an easy target for pirates and filibusters. U.S. warships blockaded the port in 1847 during the Mexican-American War. French warships sent by Napoleon III did the same in 1864, bombarding the town into submission.

Now large white cruise ships navigate the inner harbor and tie up to the quay, sharing space with tramp steamers. This diversity underscores the attraction here.

The largest shrimp fleet on the west coast anchors the southern end of town, while parasailers blossom in the sky along the northern beaches, the *Zona Dorada* (Golden Zone). The city economy is a happy mix of industry on one side and tourism on the other, the two linked by a long malecon along which the *pulmonías* (open-air taxis), race back and forth.

Activity is infectious here, with city tours, country treks, booze cruises, jungle boat rides, sportfishing and surfing, bullfights, late night discos, shopping, eating, and sightseeing. There is an absence of exclusive hotels and pretentious restaurants, which makes for a more egalitarian atmosphere that mixes easily with the local economy. Locals get along very well with tourists. Even the rental horses understand English.

Because of its moderate prices and convenient location, Mazatlán provides a useful hub for trips to Cosalá and Copalá in the mountains, and to beaches north and south. It's also the best place to catch a ferry or flight to La Paz across the gulf. For most purposes, Mazatlán is a practical paradise.

Travel Information

The federal tourist office (tel. 1-49-66) is on the ground floor of the Banco de México building on Olas Altas, across the street from the Siesta Hotel. The state tourism office (tel. 3-25-45) is on 100 Av. Loaiza, across the street from Los Sábalos Hotel in the Zona Dorada.

Traveling About

Most city travel is between the beaches of the Zona Dorado and city center along the malecón. Big yellow buses constantly trundle back and forth; their simple routes

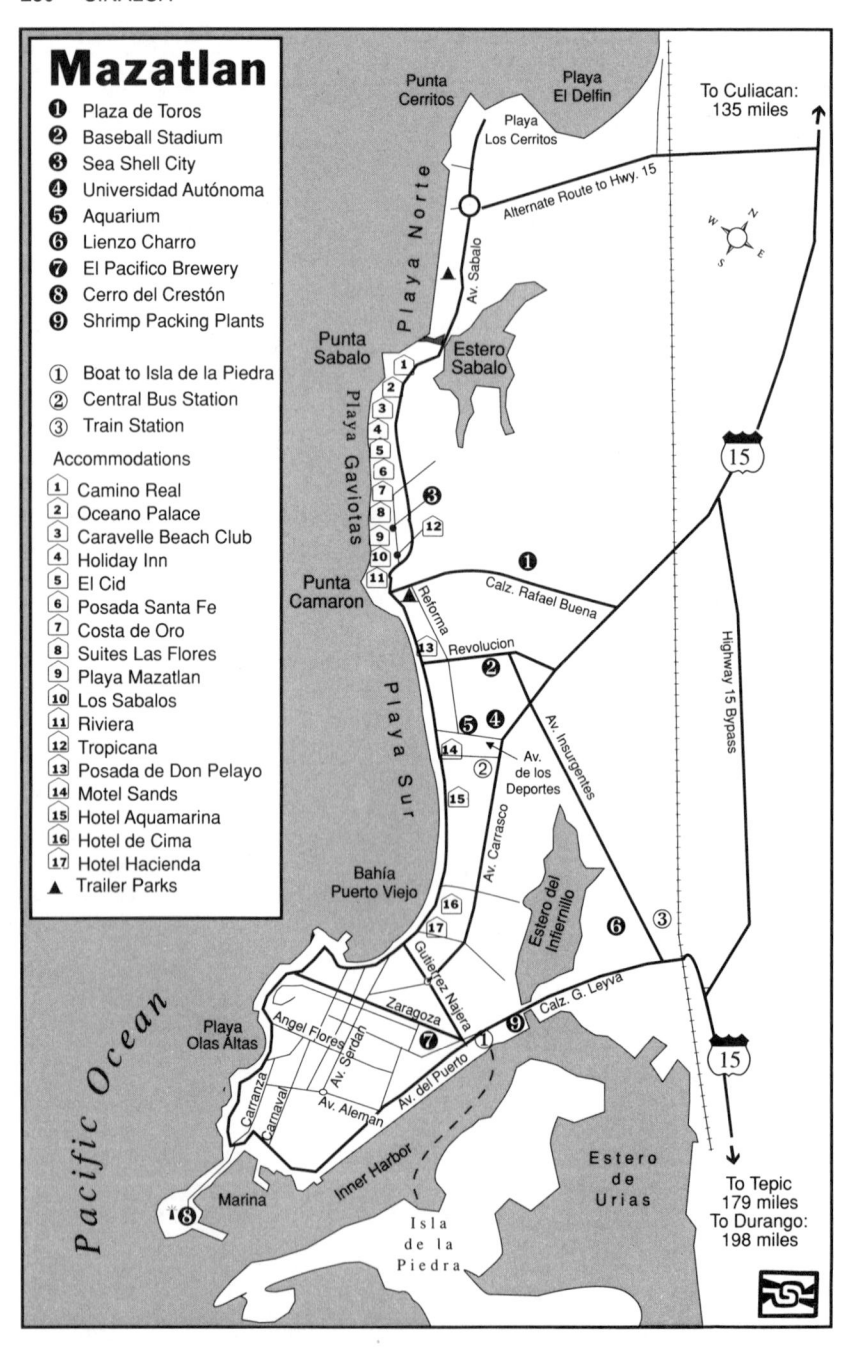

Mazatlan

❶ Plaza de Toros
❷ Baseball Stadium
❸ Sea Shell City
❹ Universidad Autónoma
❺ Aquarium
❻ Lienzo Charro
❼ El Pacifico Brewery
❽ Cerro del Crestón
❾ Shrimp Packing Plants

① Boat to Isla de la Piedra
② Central Bus Station
③ Train Station

Accommodations

1 Camino Real
2 Oceano Palace
3 Caravelle Beach Club
4 Holiday Inn
5 El Cid
6 Posada Santa Fe
7 Costa de Oro
8 Suites Las Flores
9 Playa Mazatlan
10 Los Sabalos
11 Riviera
12 Tropicana
13 Posada de Don Pelayo
14 Motel Sands
15 Hotel Aquamarina
16 Hotel de Cima
17 Hotel Hacienda
▲ Trailer Parks

Punta Cerritos
Playa El Delfin
Playa Los Cerritos
To Culiacan: 135 miles

Alternate Route to Hwy. 15

Playa Norte
Av. Sabalo

Punta Sabalo
Estero Sabalo

Playa Gaviotas

Punta Camaron

15

Calz. Rafael Buena
Reforma
Revolucion
Av. Insurgentes

Highway 15 Bypass

Playa Sur

Av. de los Deportes
Av. Carrasco

Bahía Puerto Viejo

Estero del Infiernillo

Pacific Ocean

Playa Olas Altas
Angel Flores
Zaragoza
Gutierrez Najera
Calz. G. Leyva
Carratnza
Carnaval
Av. Serdan
Av. Aleman
Av. del Puerto

Marina

Inner Harbor

Isla de la Piedra

Estero de Urias

15

To Tepic 179 miles
To Durango: 198 miles

are easily mastered by most travelers (blue buses detour into the colonias). The Sábalo-Cerritos route runs from the city market to the far northern beaches, following the *Costera*, or beach boulevard, stopping at bus stops or for groups of people waving it down. Another line, called Playa Sur, goes past the ferry station.

Taxis run fast and furious along these same two routes.

For about two-thirds the price, you can catch one of the roofless *pulmonías*, three- and four-wheeled motorized carts that dash through traffic with breezy elán.

PLACES
City Center

The shady **Plaza Republica**, overun with shoeshine boys and newspaper kiosks, is the central focus of town, flanked by the Palacio Municipal on one side, the post and telegraph offices on the other. Lots of music has been played from the bandstand since its inauguration in 1909. The **Cathedral**, which faces the bandstand, was built twenty years earlier in 1890. Its neo-gothic design is boldly tiled. The interior is worth a look, but be prepared to part with some pesos for the charity cases that congregate around the entry.

Much older and more subdued is the **Capilla de San José**, built in 1842 by Italian padres, one of the oldest buildings in town. You can reach it by walking up four blocks towards Cerro de la Nevería from behind the Church on Calle Canizales.

Close by the Cathedral in the other direction is the **Mercado Público José Mario Pino Suarez** on Av. Serdan and Calle Ocampo; this market dates to before the turn-of-the-century (1895), built on the site of the original bullring. Just follow the buses, which use one side of it as a terminal (this is where the Sábalo-Cerritos buses to the Zona Dorada originate). Its inner labyrinth is bright of color and strong of smell, full of exotic vegetables, magical herbs, fine crafts and tourist junk, pig heads, and

undefinable body organs. This is Mazatlán in microcosm, and its essence may be too concentrated for some.

Olas Altas Historical District

At Olas Atlas, history begins where the malecón ends. A new **Museo Arqeológico** is situated just one block back from Olas Altas, at Sixto Osuna No. 76. Its free exhibits include tapestries, pottery, basketry, and assorted skulls and bones. One block away, behind the Hotel Freeman, is a *peña* (a hip coffeeshop with music), called the **Amadeus Café**, where the local literati hang out. Up two blocks from the Museo on Sixto Osuna, you come to **Plazuela Machado**, at calles Belisário Domínguez and Constitución. This graceful 19th century plaza is encircled by a restored cantina, a yoga institute, a gallery where local artists are showcased, and an impressive run of 19th century wooden portales called **Los Portales de Canobio**, built by a rich Italian merchant. Half a block from the plazuela is the **Teatro Angela Peralta**, named after a celebrated opera singer who lived and died on the top floor. Even if there are no productions, it's worth a look inside at its neoclassical design, cast iron columns, and elaborate wrought iron balconies.

NORTHERN TOURIST ZONE
Acuario Mazatlán

On Av. de Los Deportes 111, is Mexico's largest aquarium, exhibiting 250 species of fish, including sharks, piranha, and even marlin. There is also a section where shells, coral, and marine artifacts are displayed. Closed Mondays.

Sea Shell Museum

On Av. Rodolpo Loaiza (tel: 3-13-01), the place claims to be the largest shell museum in the world, but is actually a come-on to get you into their emporium, where you can buy shells from all over the world; appropriately situated in the heart of the Zona Dorada.

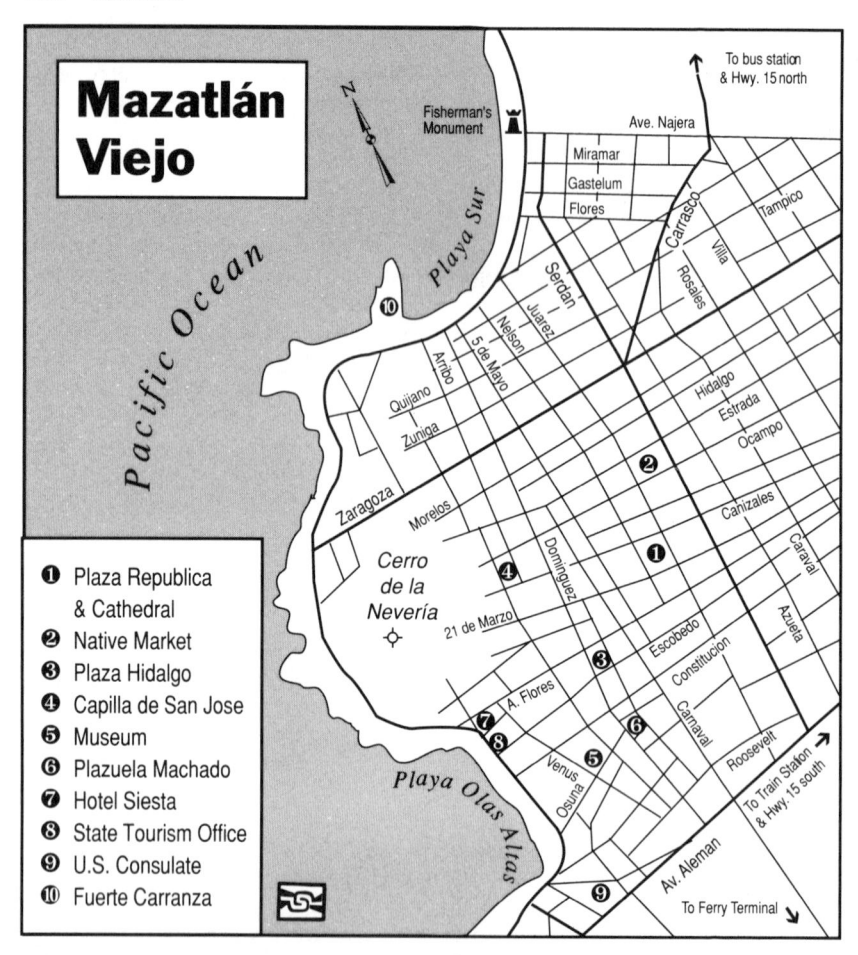

Mazatlán Viejo

To bus station
& Hwy. 15 north

Fisherman's Monument

Ave. Najera

Miramar
Gastelum
Flores

Pacific Ocean

Playa Sur

❶ Plaza Republica & Cathedral
❷ Native Market
❸ Plaza Hidalgo
❹ Capilla de San Jose
❺ Museum
❻ Plazuela Machado
❼ Hotel Siesta
❽ State Tourism Office
❾ U.S. Consulate
❿ Fuerte Carranza

Cerro
de la
Nevería
✧

21 de Marzo

Playa Olas Altas

To Train Station
& Hwy. 15 south

Av. Aleman

To Ferry Terminal

Plaza de Toros Monumental

Bullfights are held from mid-December to April. Mazatlán is passionate about bull-fighting and one of the best places to see one on the west coast of Mexico. Go in the morning to the bullring, and you will have the chance to meet with the bullfighters after they draw lots to see which bulls they fight that afternoon. The ring is situated close to the Zona Dorada on Av. Rafael Buelna.

PEAKS

Mazatlán is clearly marked by three main peaks, each with something to offer those who make it to the top.

Cerro de la Nevería

This peak, which divides the Olas Altas area from Playas del Norte, can be construed to mean Ice Cream Hill, but the name comes instead from the ice blocks, imported from San Francisco, that were stored up here in caves to keep them frozen.

With entrance just off Paseo Claussen and Av. Zaragoza, its peak offers a gull's view of the city. Down below, you can see the **High Divers Observatory Park** where they occasionally leap. Just to the north is **Fuerte Carranza**, built in 1882 for the city's defense. The waves off this point are a popular surfing spot, Cannons, named after the rusty guns that guard the bay.

Cerro del Crestón

This peak guards the harbor and is topped by a lighthouse. At 515 feet above sea level, it claims to be the highest lighthouse in the world after Gibraltar. A footpath winds up from the fishing docks built along the breakwater. El Crestón was an island until 1922, when a contract was signed with American engineers working in Manzanillo to construct this breakwater across to the mainland, turning the open roadstead into a protected anchorage. The harbor and city views are worth the climb, and you may be rewarded with a sighting of the peregrine falcons that swoop about here.

Cerro del Vigía

This hill is similar to El Crestón close by, but instead of a lighthouse it is topped by a pergola, the **Pérgola del Paseo de Centenario**. Tour buses stop here for photo opportunities, which usually include the large cannon pointed out at the harbor, which was last fired at the French during the invasion of 1864. It's aerial views of the city and the rocky southern coast of Mazatlán make this a popular picnic spot. Instead of driving to the top, you can walk up stairs that begin at the foot of the road leading to the sportfishing dock.

Harbor

Most travelers make it to the harbor for one reason or another: to charter a fishing boat, go on a bay tour or birdwatching, to take a panga over to Isla de la Piedra, catch a ferry to La Paz, buy shrimp, or just to waste time.

Inexpensive bay cruises navigate around the harbor and along the outer shoreline, where sea lions are often spotted. Fiesta Mazatlán and Bahía tour boats leave from the sportfishing docks near the ferry terminal. Booze cruises leave around sunset, while birdwatching tours to Palmito de la Virgen leave mornings. Pamphlets and brochures for these tours and trips litter the town, but it's best to go directly to the harbor to scout out times and prices.

More than 5,000 billfish are caught annually, and there are numerous sportfishing flotillas here, most leaving around 7 a.m., returning around 3 p.m.

Farther back in the harbor, past the ferry terminal, you can catch pangas across the harbor to **Isla de la Piedra** (at the dock on the end of Ave. Emilio Barragán). Nearby, at Calle Melchor Ocampo and Calzada Gabriel Leyva, is the **Cervecería del Pacífico**, which dates to 1900. Phone the Relaciones Industriales department at 2-79-66, ext. 220 if you would like a tour.

BEACHES

Mazatlán is known for the diversity of its beaches, from carnival sands to stretches of pure solitude. The only thing unchanging is the water temperature, which averages 72 degrees.

Playa Olas Altas

The shortest beach in Mazatlán, it also has some of the biggest waves, true to its name. Something of an urban beach with a narrow swath of sand fronting Blvd. Olas Altas, it does have steep enough waves for easy bodysurfing, though the rocky bottom can make for bruising exits.

Playa Sur

This beach begins near Fuerte Carranza, where there is good surf, and ends three-plus miles north at Punta Camarón (also known as Lupe's Point) where there also is good surf. In between, this long stretch of grainy sand beach is swept clean by thumping shorebreak, which drowns out the four lanes of traffic that rush nearby.

Playa Las Gaviotas

This beach claims the tamest waves along the coast, sheltered in part by the islands close offshore. This beach, narrow in places, measures the length of the Zona Dorada, where most of the resort hotels are situated. The most crowded beach in Mazatlán, it is a lucrative market for beach vendors, and

Mirador *(Look-out) on the Mazatlán Malecón*

some of the busier hotels stake out the beach with rope fences to keep them at bay. As the beach nears Punta Sábalo, it is known as **Playa Sábalo**, but the only difference is that, free of the benign influence of the offshore islands, the waves crash harder.

Playa Norte

This beach stretches from Punta Sábalo on the south to Punta Cerritos three miles to the north. **Playita El Bucanero**, at the far southern end near Hotel Camino Real, is best for families, as children can swim on the lagoon side if the waves are too threatening. This long run of shore is slowly filling in with condominiums and timeshare units, but the beach remains quite empty. The far north end is called **Playa Bruja**, where some of the best surfing and bodysurfing can be found off the point.

Playa Los Cerritos

Here ends the coastal road, more a lunch stop than a beach, A rocky outlying reef protects this short run of beach from waves. Consequently, it is used as a boat landing by commercial fishermen (good place to buy oysters). Only other facilities here are two rickety restaurants.

Playa El Delfín

Here you can find solitude among the dunes, the most private of any beach here, except for Isla de la Piedra. Just before reaching the end of the road at Playa Los Cerritos, turn inland on the only paved road, follow it for 0.9 miles to just before the railroad tracks, and turn left onto a dirt road. The road travels 1.4 miles before halting at a dune field, next by an estero, the only beach here with camping possibilities.

ISLANDS
Isla Venado

Deer Island sits close off Playa Gaviotas, and is so accessible (a ten-minute jaunt on U.S. Army surplus landing craft) that it is overrun daily with tourists. It's worth a trip, though the island has its limitations. There is a short run of beach on the calm leeward shore with another less crowded beach at the south end, but the rest of the shoreline is rocky. Beer is sold, but there are no public bathrooms. Cave paintings are reputed to have been discovered on the island, but nobody seems to know where they are located. Isla Venado offers the most visibility in Mazatlán for snorkeling, but sealife is scant. Its greatest attraction is that you have to take a boat to get to it. Amphibious vehicles leave from El Cid Hotel and, with greater frequency, from Las Flores Hotel, about every 30 minutes. Camping is allowed.

Isla de la Piedra

This Island of the Stone is not really an island, though it feels like one. Pangas transport you for a nominal price across the harbor from the dock at Av. Emilio Barragán at Av. del Puerto, a five-minute trip. But you can also drive here on a roundabout dirt road, which leaves the pavement about a mile before you reach the Mazatlán airport.

From the boat dock, it's a 15-minute walk (or ride on a unique tractor-drawn wagon) to ten miles of palm-fringed beach. The farther you walk, the more lonesome it gets. This is the main camping beach in Mazatlán, an old hippie encampment in the '70s. The villagers still have a high tolerance level. The island is named for a giant stone rising amid the agricultural fields inland.

Fiestas

The most exuberant festival in Mazatlán is Carnival, celebrated the last five days before Ash Wednesday, mostly along Av. Olas Altas. This is one of the most spirited carnivals in Mexico, rivaling Veracruz. A more pious procession is held on December 8, Día de la Inmaculada Concepción; dances in the atrium of the Iglesia are dedicated to the Virgin. On September 15, the bishop blesses the fleet in the harbor and this celebration blends into the September 16th festivities celebrating Independence Day. Mexican Fiestas held every Thursday at Hotel Playa Mazatlán (tel. 3-11-20) are gimmicky but fun nonetheless, and every Sunday the hotel shoots off fireworks over the ocean at 8 p.m.

MAZATLAN ADDENDUM

Diving is poor in Mazatlán, with little to see except sand bottom and bare rock. Visibility is generally poor, with 30 feet considered excellent, and this usually happening only in the winter and spring along the leeward shores of the offshore islands.

Tours are popular, but in most cases you can replicate the tour for less money and avoid the crowds. Besides shopping and city tours, you can take a mountain tour to Concordia and Copala, a less interesting Rosario Tour, and the San Blas jungle tour, most of which is spent in a van getting there and back. You can sign up for these in just about any hotel lobby in Mazatlán.

Horses can be rented near the Hotel Playa Mazatlán at the end of Calle Gaviotas.

Consulates: Canadian consulate is on 705 Calle Albatros (tel. 3-73-20), while U.S. consulate is on Calle Circunvalación 6 Poniente (tel. 1-26-85).

Post and Telegraph offices are in city center, facing the Plaza Republica. There are also branches of both at the bus station.

Traveler's Check refund offices: American Express Travel Services is located upstairs at Av. Camarón Sábalo 310 (tel. 3-06-00). Wagon-Lits Mexicana on Calle Angel Flores at the Plaza Principal can make refunds for Thomas Cook Travelers Checks.

PLACES TO SLEEP
Budget Hotels

The Olas Altas section of Mazatlán offers the only budget area on the beach. **Hotel Freeman**, Av. Olas Altas 200 (tel.1-34-84), is a bargain but it's also bare of character. More expensive is the **Hotel Belmar**, Av. Olas Altas 166 (tel. 2-07-99). Best budget pick is **Hotel Siesta**, Olas Altas 11 (tel. 1-23-34), with its big balconies overlooking street and ocean, but you should have a tolerance for marimbas, which are played nightly in the famous El Shrimp Bucket, a courtyard restaurant. Other budget hotels can be found by walking inland, but nothing that beats the character of the Olas Altas waterfront.

Moderate

Generally speaking, the closer to the Zona Dorada, the higher the rates and the newer the hotels. The original Playa Norte hotels are growing arthritic with age yet charge higher-than-justified prices. The **Hotel de Cima**, Av. Del Mar 30 (tel. 1-41-19) and the **Hacienda Hotel**, on Av. Del Mar at Calle Flamingos (tel. 2-70-00; fax: 4-34-77) are in a neither-here-nor-there location, across the street from the beach; their facilities are aging none too gracefully. **Hotel Sands** on Av. Del Mar 1910 (tel. 2-00-00) and **Aquamarina** on Av. Del Mar 110 (tel. 1-70-80) are second generation hotels closer to the Zona Dorada, but have no more resort facilities than a standard roadstop motel.

Posada de Don Pelayo, on 1111 Av. del Mar (tel. 3-18-88) attracts a young, cost-conscious clientele and is close enough to the Zona Dorada to walk, far enough away to enjoy moderate rates. Even closer to the epicenter is **Hotel Tropicana**, 27 Av. Loaiza (tel. 3-80-00), across street from the beach, an excellent value. The hidden **Plaza Gaviotas Hotel**, 100 Bugambilias (tel. 3-43-22; telex 6-68-98), is a block off the beach, and best avoided ever since it lowered its standards and raised its rates. **Puesta del Sol**, Av. Camarón Sábalo (tel. 3-55-44) is the only moderately priced hotel on the beach, with scant amenities; it feeds off the facilities of the mega-resort El Cid next door like a sucker fish on the belly of a shark.

Expensive

These commercial hotels are all on the beach and built to formula. The **Holiday Inn**, on Av. Camarón Sábalo 696 (tel. 3-22-22), is about as mainstream as you can get,

best for families who want no surprises and are willing to pay the price. The nearby **Oceano Palace**, on Av. Camarón Sábalo (tel. 3-06-66), is a bit frayed by the endless groups that march through, but provides a less expensive substitute for the Holiday Inn. **Caravelle Beach Club**, on Av. Camarón Sábalo (tel. 3-02-00) next door, is a slight cut in quality, compromised by the time-share aspect, but good enough to catch the overflow from the Oceano Palace. The maze-like **Costa de Oro**, on Av. Camarón Sábalo (tel. 3-58-88) is a poor third choice, better for groups than individuals. **Las Flores Hotel Suites**, on the beach at 212 Av. Loaiza (tel. 3-51-00) is an excellent choice for those who want a kitchenette, one of the best views in Mazatlán, and a location in the heart of the Zona Rosa; its adept staff is an extra. **Riviera Mazatlán Hotel**, on 51 Av. Camarón Sábalo (tel. 3-46-11), has had a checkered past, and not all guests will appreciate the shell artwork; it's the king of kitsch here, and the staff is mostly young and inexperienced. **Playa Mazatlán**, on Las Gaviotas Beach (tel. 3-44-44) remains the best known operation here, livelier than any of the others and more skilled at packaging holiday fun than the higher-priced Holiday Inn; deluxe rooms are worth the extra few dollars for the ocean views.

Only three resorts stand out as deluxe. **El Cid Resort**, on Av. Camarón Sábalo (tel. 3-33-3), is a mega-resort, meant to impress by the sheer force of its facilities, such as its $5 million disco and vast lagoon pools (one with an underwater cave where children can hide from panic-stricken parents). On Punta de Sábalo, **Camino Real**, (tel. 6-68-55) is in a geographically eminent position appropriate to its standing as the premier hotel here. Atmosphere is low-key and sophisticated. **Los Sábalos**, on 100 Av. Loaiza (tel. 3-54-09) is visually striking with its modernistic Moorish design; though unique, it lacks the facilities of El Cid and the tranquility of the Camino Real.

Camping

Trailer parks thrive in Mazatlán, but there are not enough of them (real estate value is too high). Most fill up with snowbirds, leaving little space for travelers. **Las Palmas Trailer Park**, on Camarón-Sábalo 333, in heart of Zona Dorada, is two blocks from Playa Gaviotas. **Mar Rosa Trailer Park**, on Playa Sábalo, allows tent camping when space is available. **Trailer Park Playa Escondida**, 999 Av. Sábalo Cerritos (tel. 3-25-68), is not right on the beach but close to it; discounts are also given for tent camping. **La Posta Trailer Park**, 7 Av. Rafael Buelna (tel. 3-53-10), is set back two blocks from beach on road out to Hwy. 15. Popular with caravaners.

Few free camping areas exist around Mazatlán. Some people occasionally camp out at Playa Delfín (at the road's end among the dunes), or out on Isla del Venado, but the best camping beach is on Isla de la Piedra.

ARRIVING & DEPARTING

By Air

The airport is situated 13 miles south of Mazatlán, off Hwy 15. Besides all the major car rental firms having desks here (Avis, Budget, Hertz, National), you will find baggage lockers, two restaurants, but no place to exchange money. Come prepared with pesos. *Alaska Airlines, Aeroméxico, AeroCalifornia, Mexicana,* and *Aviación de Noreste* all fly here. The *colectivo* is priced low, but four or more passengers will save time and money on a taxi.

By Bus

The Central Camionera on Blvd. de Las Americas and Calle Tamazula may be more than three miles from city center, but it's only a long block to the beach, near Hotel Sands. A major way station, buses leave hourly both north to the border and south to Guadalajara and Mexico City, as well as east to Durango and Zacatecas. You can eat here, post letters, change money, send tele-graphs, even store luggage if you want to go the beach. Phone for schedules: *Tres Estrellas de Oro* (tel. 1-49-60), *Transportes del Norte* (tel. 1-23-35), *Transportes Norte del Pacífico* (tel. 2-05-77).

By Car

Mazatlán is 750 miles from Nogales, 1197 miles from Tijuana.

By Train

Trains depart twice daily, morning and evening, to both Nogales and Guadalajara. The station for Ferrocarriles del Pacífico is on the southern fringe of town at Calle Esperanza, near Mex. 15. Though buses go from downtown to the bus station, most travelers catch a taxi. Phone 1-28-70 or 2-24-26 for exact schedule information.

By Ferry

Ferries leave from the Muelles Fiscales (tel. 2-21-59) in the harbor, easily reached by the Playa Sur bus from city center. Ferries load in the afternoon, but you must buy your ticket in the morning or your space will be given to someone else. If you don't have a reservation, be the first one at the window and ask for reservation, or failing that, ask to be put on the waitlist. Perseverance always pays.

Ferries leave every day at 5 p.m., arriving in La Paz 16 hours later. To reserve space, phone toll free (within Mexico): 91-800-696-96, or direct: (678) 4-11-98. You can also fax your reservation: (678) 1-52-35, though you will not receive an acknowledgement.

INTO THE SIERRAS
MAZATLÁN TO DURANGO

Near Mazatlán, the Sierras that run 800 miles from the border are finally crossed by pavement. Finished in 1960 after nearly 19 years of construction, Hwy. 40 is the equivalent of the Barranca del Cobre railroad, a ribbon of asphalt that winds perilously through the mountains before dropping down to Durango, a 200-mile trip that can be driven in less than six hours.

For those continuing on down the coast on Hwy. 15, a short side trip to Concordia and Copalá is called for. Hwy. 40 leaves Hwy. 15 from the southern outskirts of **Villa Union**, 16 miles south of Mazatlán.

CONCORDIA

On entering town (12 miles from Hwy. 15, 28 from Mazatlán), you can't help but notice the furniture shops here, responsible for most of the rocking chairs in Mexico. A Paul Bunyan-sized chair sits in the *plaza principal* (Main Plaza) off the highway, a tribute to this town's sustaining industry. It stands next to a cart of silver ore, symbolizing 200 hundred years of mining. The silver has been exhausted (the trees are also disappearing), but a trace of this town's former mineral wealth still can be seen in the **Iglesia de San Sebastián**, the only truly baroque-style church in Sinaloa. Begun in 1785, construction finished in 1812, but with only one tower completed. Its facade is lavishly carved and cross hatched, presided over by a stone Virgin. Many of the old buildings surrounding the plaza date to this colonial period yet offer modern conveniences: a bank, telegraph office, post office, but no hotel.

The only lodging is along the highway, **Hospedaje del Río Caliente**, a modest 14-room inn ($).

AGUA CALIENTE HOT SPRINGS

Less than a third of a mile from the highway, just before you enter Concordia from the west, voluminous hot springs well up into a series of deep basins. The water is a steamy 130 degrees, but these springs, like most rustic hot springs in Mexico, are put to practical use. Empty clorox bottles bob like ships in a fleet. When the laundry is done, the hot springs turn into a *balneario* (swimming spot). Best time to visit is in the late afternoon, unless you have laundry to do.

COPALA

Fifteen miles beyond Concordia, a cobbled road lined by electric lampposts dips down from Hwy. 40 to Copala, a grand entry to a tiny village. Except for electricity, this town seems locked in amber, preserved as a 19th century timespiece: the wooden portales and wrought iron balconies, a sea of tile roofs, narrow cobbled streets, a quaint church, a quiet people. Comfortably picturesque, Copala attracts up to 20 tour buses a day, and the villagers have grown accustomed to camcorders.

The 20th century leaves with the last tour bus, when the restaurant and cantina lock their doors, and the town closes up as if under curfew. Then it is pure tranquility for the traveler who spends the night. The tourist-hardened villagers aren't the least bit curious, which gives you the freedom to wander about absorbing the town without feeling like a thousand eyes are on you. You can thank two people for that, one a Mexican president, the other an American roughneck.

Conquistador Francisco de Ibarra discovered the site in 1566, and one of his party, Don Alonso López Portillo, stayed as one of the founders of the village.

Cobbled Streets of Copala

By 1775, tremendous wealth was mined from the silver ore, at which time the Iglesia de San José was founded. The population climbed to 10,000, but in 1850 cholera struck. The population rebounded, along with the mines. Among others, the U.S.-owned Butter Copala Mine Company set up headquarters here (now the Butter Company restaurant facing the plaza), and may have been responsible for the unique swan fountain cast in New York but standing by the church (an identical fountain is in nearby Pánuco). But the ore grew weak, and a cyclone in 1943 put an end to the swan song.

Only 100 residents were living here in the 1970s when the president of Mexico, López Portillo, arrived to visit the ancient family home (which still stands) where his father was born, and to pay homage to the many Portillo headstones here. Aghast at the deterioration, he ordered the town re-cobbled, re-tiled, and re-painted. When he returned one year later, he signed the order for the town's electrification.

The president set the stage, and another lost son brought the tourists. Daniel Garrison gave up the oil fields of Long Beach to come here where his mother was born. For 20 years he has dedicated himself singlehandedly to the bringing of travelers to Copala, mostly on the strength of the town's resurrected beauty and his wife's famous lime pie, a strange but successful combination. His restaurant at the entrance to town is impossible to miss, and he himself is a fount of local information. The tour buses now roll in daily, and the population is 1500 and climbing.

The town celebrates May 19, the day of its patron saint.

Places to Sleep

Posada de San José ($) is the only lodging in town, but you couldn't ask for more at these rates; canopied beds, a long common veranda hung with hammocks and fitted with rocking chairs overlooking the central plaza. Hotel is above the Butter Company restaurant, next to the old jail, which hasn't held a prisoner in 40 years.

Mazatlán to Durango

Mazatlán to Durango: 200 miles

Arriving & Departing

Taxis from Mazatlán charge as much as $100. A more colorful approach is to catch the *Escoba* (the Broom), a local bus that leaves Mazatlán bus terminal around 1 p.m., arriving in town about 3 p.m.

SIDETRIP FROM COPALA

Less than a mile north of Copala, a dirt road leaves Hwy. 40 for the old mining town of Pánuco, 5.5 miles away. About halfway there, near a shed where explosives were once kept, there is a dirt road which quickly turns into a footpath to **Guadalupe,** a 15-minute hike away. This is a deserted mill-and-mission site, reached by crossing a swaying suspension bridge. The impressive roofless church and old mill ruins have struck a romantic balance between man and nature, as guancaste trees, philodendron, and wild fig embrace what remains of these enduring ruins. The Río Pánuco gurgles nearby, the wild grapefruit orchard hangs heavy with yellow fruit, and usually the only human presence is a humble caretaker, Francisco Quintero. You can sit by the riverside and swim in the currents of its history.

Pánuco was once much more important than Copala but now is a somnolent colonial-styled mining village rarely visited by travelers. Situated along the side of the Río Pánuco, there are many mining relics, some still in use, and the hills around town are peppered with mine shafts. At one time there was a 40-stamp mill here, powered by a Pelton water wheel impelled by water from the dam. Nearby is a 40 foot waterfall

beyond the ancient church. Now there are few jobs and little money in town.

This area was the setting for B. Traven's famous novel, *Treasure of the Sierra Madre*.

TO DURANGO & BEYOND

About ten miles past Copala, you will pass **Motel Villa Blanca** ($$), styled like a small mountain chalet among the pine trees. But this is just a precursor of the real mountain peaks which rise up at **El Palmito**, ten miles ahead.

Just before reaching El Palmito, near the Sinaloa-Durango state line (set your clock ahead to Central Time), there is a forestry station by the side of the highway; nearby is a deep canyon reached by a mile-long hike, considered a rare birdwatching site, where eared trogons and numerous species of hummingbirds can be sighted (in this area you will find an overlap of western and eastern birds).

Twenty miles beyond El Palmito, you will cross *El Espinazo de Diablo*, The Devil's Spine. After peaking at 8,900 feet, the road falls to a 6,000 foot plateau, an easy roll into Durango, a city famous for the making of western movies, and for its giant deadly scorpions (1,608 recorded deaths between 1890 and 1925).

From Durango, it is about 160 miles down to Zacatecas, where you can either drive to Guadalajara or Guanajuato, both about 200 miles away, or loop back up to the border at Ciudad Juárez, 675 miles distant.

MAZATLÁN TO ESCUINAPA & THE NAYARIT STATE LINE

Hwy. 15 Travels 64 miles from Mazatlan to Escuinapa and another 36 miles to Río Las Cañas, which marks the border with Nayarit.

ROSARIO

From Villa Unión, Hwy 15 passes by **Agua Caliente**, where there are roadside hot springs under the second bridge north of town (usually usurped by laundry women) before reaching **Rosario**, 45 miles south of Mazatlán. Situated on the north bank of the Río Baluarte, the city's most most notable feature is the **Templo de la Señora del Rosario**. Though its ornate facade of salomonic columns and baroque design is interesting, go inside for a look at the 18th century colonial retablo, gilded in a fortune of gold.

From Rosario, a road runs towards the coast for 13 miles to **Agua Verde**, a small village; from here a dirt road in very poor condition continues six more miles to the Laguna del Caimanero and the empty ocean beaches of Agua Verde, of interest mostly to surfers.

CHAMETLA

Little more than five miles south of Rosario on Hwy 15 at K213, another side road tracks nine miles to **Chametla.** Like Rosario, it is situated along the Río Baluarte. This was the site of one of the oldest prehispanic villages in Sinaloa. It later became one of the most important ports in the 1500s. Cortés left here on April 15, 1533, on his colonization voyage to the California peninsula. Other ships left here for the the the

Orient. Today you can walk across the river. Though shown as a seaport on the nautical maps of the 16th to 18th centuries, it is actually situated about eight miles from where the Río Baluarte breaks out to the sea. The channel has become silted over the years.

A dirt road continues six miles to Playa Majahua, where a pedestrian bridge takes you over the estuary to a trashy beach and some ramshackle ramadas.

ESCUINAPA DE HIDALGO

This town, 13 miles south of Rosario, is notable not so much for the shrimp as for the women in town, who hold these by the whiskers, dangling them like handkerchiefs in front of the passing highway traffic. This area is famous for its "whiskered" tamales, made of the shrimp cultivated in farms near the coastal town of **Teacapán.** Escuinapa lies about 47 miles north of the Nayarit state line.

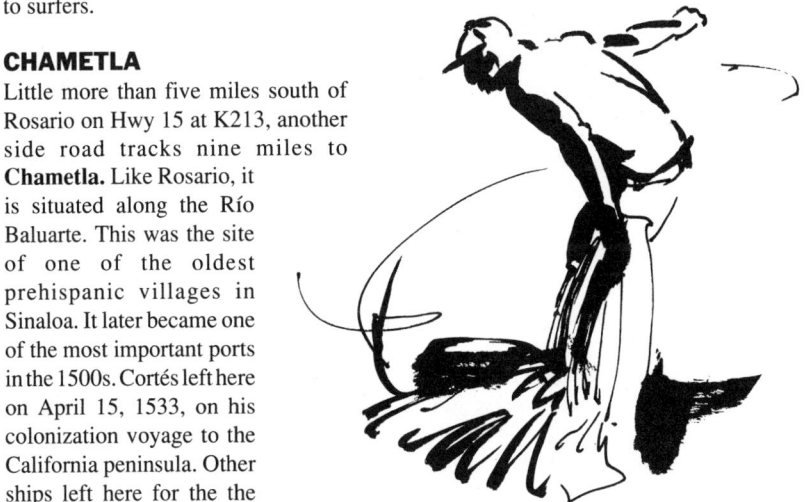

TEACAPÁN

From Hwy. 15 at Escuinapa, the 24-mile paved road to Teacapán runs flat through grassy fields, past sheets of water dotted with birds, and through mango orchards, a tropical prelude to this shrimp fishing village.

Situated almost on the state line of Nayarit, it sits on the shores of the lagoon from which it takes its name. The village itself is no great attraction, except for its groceries and bank. The only hotel in town, the **Oregon**, was famous for having more iguanas than guests. It is now closed. But a mile before town is *Lupita's Trailer Park*, set in a trim coconut grove (The gringo manager is in obsessive battle with the encroaching jungle, spraying *malathion* and shooting the iguanas to keep them from eating the coconut flowers).

From the trailer park, a dirt road runs half a mile to **La Puntilla**, which has reached a more natural state of equilibrium with the elements. The flat grass areas are embroidered with palms, fronted by a narrow swath of sand, and shaded by palapas at the water's edge. This is where the lagoon empties out to the sea. The water is calm enough for children. Farther offshore, currents race and collide with the incoming surf.

Half a mile before Lupita's Trailer Park, a pitted but paved road runs past a small North American colony 1.2 miles to the beach at **La Tambora**. Unlike La Puntilla, this is open beach with waves steep enough for bodysurfing and flat spots for primitive camping. Exotic birds flock to the surrounding swamps, including the roseate spoonbill, which is often mistaken for pink flamingos.

A second-class bus runs frequently from Escuinapa; stand roadside and flag it down.

La Puntilla, Teacapán

Tropical Water

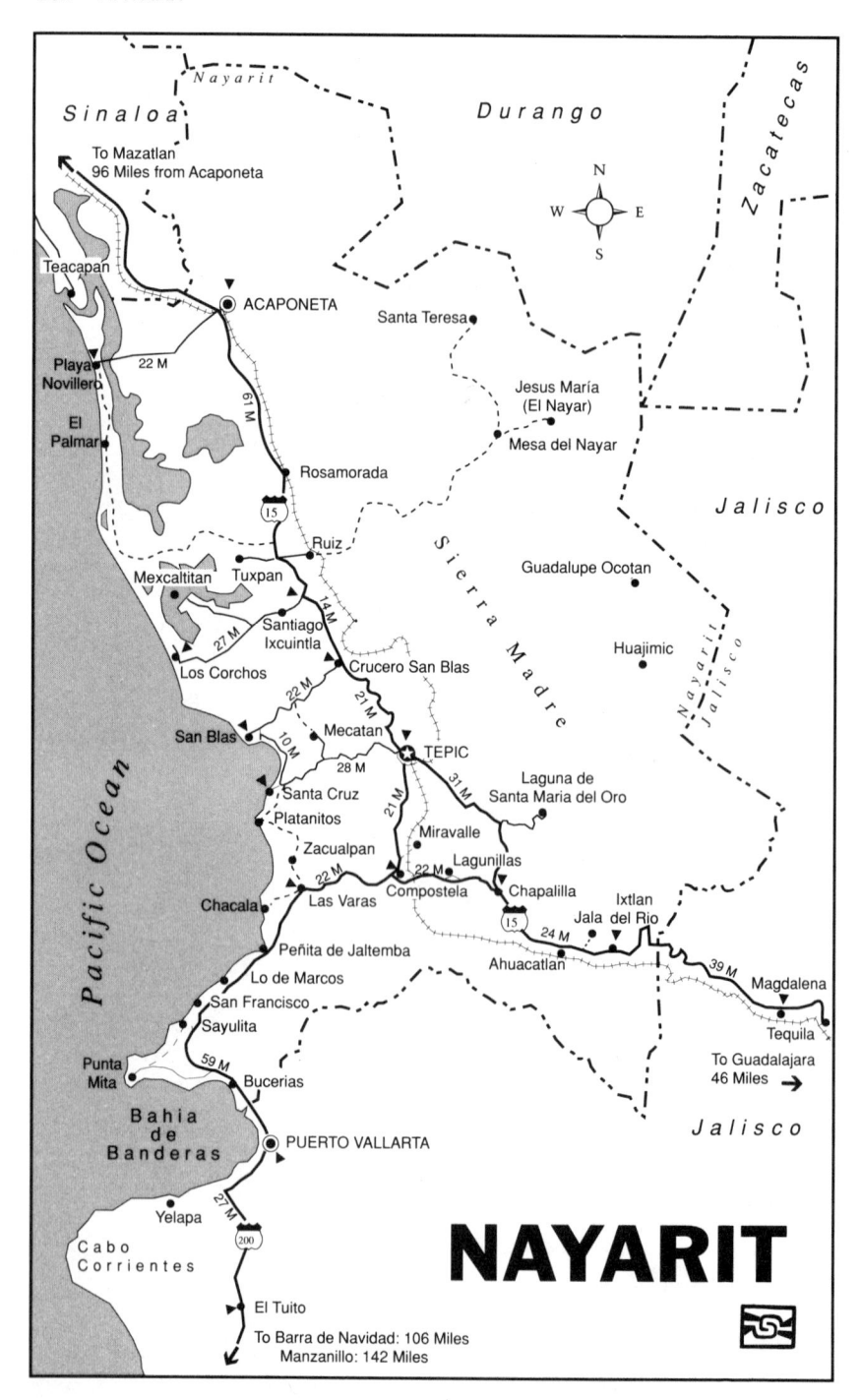

13.
NAYARIT

Nayarit is the northernmost state to lie entirely within the tropics. You wouldn't know it from the frost that sometimes laces the volcanic highlands; they reach above 9,000 feet. Three major rivers drop down from these highlands, stream through the large inland valleys, and come to rest in the *Marismas Nacionales*. This is an area of wide lagoons, maze-like channels, mangrove swamps, and sluggish deltas, an amphibious world that extends for the most part from south of Mazatlán to San Blas.

During the semi-dry season (October to May), much of *marismas* dry out, forming *salitre*, a hard salt pan. But from the middle of June till the middle of September, it rains most every day. Then you can paddle the 70 miles from Teacapán to San Blas. These marismas shelter the largest population of migratory birds in Mexico.

Along the lower elevations, the tropical evergreen forests are an exotic tangle of tuberous, leafy plants. The taller trees create an umbrella which traps the humidity on the ground, a greenhouse for the ferns and philodendrons. The names of these trees conjure up the very soul of the tropics: *zalate, tamarindo, tabachine, gumbolimbo, kapok,* and *guanacaste*.

Both these tropical forests and swampy savannahs are home to an abundant wildlife, including more migratory birds than anywhere else in Mexico.

Not all wildlife is so benign. The presence of *tigres* (jaguars), *pumas* (cougars), *escorpiónes* (similar to the gila monster of the Sonoran Desert), *boas* (boa constrictors), *cocodrilos* (crocodiles), swarms of *garrapatas* (ticks), *hormigas* (leaf-cutter ants), *cascabeles* (rattlesnakes), *coralillas* (coral snakes), and *cantiles* (water moccasins) are reason enough to step lightly on any hike through Nayarit's jungles and savannahs.

Life is more civilized in the hills and valleys of the higher elevations, along which Hwy. 15 travels. The Spanish preferred the drier, cooler, healthier climate. Here the major cities of Tepic, the capitol, and Compostela were founded.

The region was first explored in 1524. But it wasn't until Niño de Guzmán arrived in 1530 that the area was organized into the province of Nueva Galicia, which included Nayarit, Jalisco, Zacatecas and Sinaloa. A year later, the small native village of Tepic was named the capital of Nueva Galicia. But the impenetrable Sierras to the east, home to warlike Indians, isolated Nayarit from the rest of the region, and the capital was soon moved to Guadalajara. Except as a launching pad for the exploration of California, Nayarit languished, and it wasn't until 1917 that the territory was even admitted as a state.

The mountain highlands are still impenetrable, at least by car; a few dirt roads climb into these pine and oak forests, but for the most part they remain a mysterious and almost inaccessible homeland to the Cora and Huichol Indians.

CORA & HUICHOL

The Huichols, numbering around 50,000 live throughout the mountains in family rancherías. Their main village is Guadalupe Ocotán, to the northeast of Tepic. The 11,000 Cora, sometimes referred to as *Nayaritas*, also live in small rancherías. Their villages, such as Jesús María, are only assembly points for their fiestas.

Of the two tribes, the Huichol are the more accessible. The recalcitrant Cora are known for their secrecy. Though the Huichols adhere to aboriginal practices and beliefs, as well as worship a large pantheon of gods, they usually do not exclude visitors from their fiestas and religious celebrations. The Cora religion embraces more Catholic concepts, but they guard their holy spots and outsiders are never allowed to visit these pre-conquest shrines.

Huichol

The Huichol Indians have resisted modern mestizo culture, due most of all to the strength of their visionary mysticism. The peyote buttons eaten during religious ceremonies are considered a conduit to the spirit world where they can directly speak and listen to their gods. This circumvents the need for a church. Peyote is collected during the 300-mile autumn pilgrimage to Wirikuta, near Real de Catorce in San Luis Potosí, considered the birthplace of their gods. Once done on foot as a purifying

ritual, the pilgrimage is now rumored to be accomplished by bus (at ceremonies, those with yellow spots on their faces are those who took part in the pilgrimage).

Peyote is one part of their holy trilogy, which also includes corn and deer. They worship the gods of rain, fire, sun, and sea. Holy Week is the only celebration with Christian overtones, but it is merely a Catholic crust atop an ancient spring ceremony, where Christ is seen as the sun god, his death and resurrection symbolic of the old and new years. His crucifixion pertains to the traditional Mesoamerican belief in the sacred potency of blood sacrifice, which gives new life to the sun. Bulls are sacrificed instead of the sacred deer, as these are almost extinct.

The hallucinatory patterns and colors of their religion are reproduced in their artwork. *Niericas* (yarn paintings), formerly made only during hallucinatory states as an altar offering to the gods, now are sold to tourists. So are the *ojo de dios (tzicuir)* or god's eyes, which are vivid wool-woven offerings made by parents when a child is born. The highly prized gourds *(kukure)*, colored by tiny beads imbedded into beeswax, graphically represent the maker's needs and wants, a graphic prayer of sorts. Their ceremonial dress has these same visionary qualities, from their fluorescent cross-stitching to their wide brim tassled hats, full of symbolic meaning.

Principal Huichol festivals are the Change of Authority, the Petition for Rain, and a thanksgiving ceremony for the forest harvest. These are organized by the *maracámes* (spiritual wise men, a hereditary position). Visitors are tolerated and paid little attention. A good place to watch these festivities is in San Andrés, where a DC3 flies in from Tepic. Without going into the mountains, you can still spot Huichols during the winter along the coastal areas, where they come to work in the fields. Before the rainy season, they return to their mountain homes to sow their own crops.

Cora in native dress, 1915

Cora

Unlike the Huichols, the Coras are more aloof and suspicious of the outside world, of which camera-laden tourists are probably one of its more intrusive aspects. An intensely religious culture, their chief native deities are attached to Christian personages, though they still are empowered with their original powers regarding rain, health, and harvest. Tayaó (our Father) is a combination God/Jesus Christ. Tati (Our mother) is the Virgin, goddess of earth and corn. Tahás is the older brother, considered both the morning star and St. Michael, their protector against monsters. Festivities, most of which are aligned with the Christian calender, involve drinking and dancing. The more pagan aspects are held in private, at shrines where no visitors are allowed. The cave at Mesa del Nayar, for example, is one of their pre-conquest shrines, where the skeleton of their famous chief Nayarit was once kept. He died in 1624, supposedly at the age 134. When the Spanish invaded Mesa, they sent the holy skeleton to Mexico City, where it was burned in public. The Cora have reason to be reclusive.

Except during ceremonies, most of the Cora's eight traditional villages are practically empty, as most live on scattered rancherías. These *comunidades indígenas* (native communities) elect their own governors. The one non-religious ceremony that is more accessible to outside viewing is the change of authority, usually held from January 1 to 5. Cora villages include Santa Teresa, Jesús María, San Francisco, and Mesa del Nayar.

ACAPONETA TO CRUCERO SAN BLAS

From the state line at Río Las Canas, Hwy. 15 travels through flat savannah for 70 miles to a junction with the paved road down to San Blas. Along the way you pass turnoffs to Acaponeta, the flat beaches of Novillero and Los Corchos, and the island village of Mexcaltitan.

ACAPONETA

This small city, five miles south of the state line, and 40 miles south of Esquinapa, lies alongside the Río Acaponeta, a mile and a half off Hwy. 15. Few travelers bother to stop, unless interested in the **Iglesia de Nuestra Señora de la Asunción de Acaponeta**, built by the Franciscans in 1781. It faces the zócalo. There are reputed to be sulfurous hot springs at San Dieguito de Arriba, three miles to the north. All major bus lines stop at Acaponeta. This city celebrates December 12 (Nuestra Señora de Guadalupe), and August 15 (Asunción de la Virgen), where you have a good chance to see Indian dances, such as Matachines and Conquista.

Twelve miles north of Acaponeta is **Huajicori**, a small town notable for its church, the **Nuestra Señora de los Remedios**, built in 1746. Some sulfurous hot springs are reported to be only 2.4 miles from town. Less than five miles from Huajicori, along a footpath, is a petroglyph zone. To find it, you will need to contact a guide through the municipal building.

PLAYA NOVILLERO

Considered the longest beach in Mexico, it is also the most monotonous, a 45-mile-long swath of gray sand. Row after row of white surf is broken down in size by the shallow water, leaving only suds to roll up on the shore. Now reached by a bridge instead of by rustic car ferry, this typical Mexican beach resort remains a haphazard arrangement of ramada restaurants and three hotels which bloom to life during holidays but lay dormant during the week. If it is too crowded, you can drive south 11 miles on a dirt road from Playa Novillero to Palmar de Cuatla, where you'll find the same beach but fewer people. Many cars (including a coastal bus) prefer to drive on the hard-packed sand of the beach.

At the Hwy. 15 turn-off just south of the turnoff to Acaponeta, the paved road runs 22.4 miles to the beach, passing through Nayarit's fourth largest city, Tecuala, 15 miles before reaching the shore.

Places to Sleep

The mildew-ridden **Hotel Miramar** ($) at the beach claims hot water to complement the cot-style beds and bare bulb illumination. **Casablanca Hotel** ($), a block back from the beach, is cleaner but no less basic, and the rooms are cell-like. **Hotel Playa Novillero** ($$; tel. 3-03-65) charges top peso for its modern balconied rooms, but the pool is overtaken with algae, the lawn with stickers, and the barbed cyclone fence keeps guests from walking directly to the beach.

Best place to stay is in a tent on the beach.

ROSAMORADA

If you are passing by Rosamorada during Holy Week, you can see a passion play, marked by daily parades and lots of dances, mostly Matachines.

TUXPAN

Forty-two miles south of Acaponeta, you come to the turnoff to Tuxpan, 5.5 miles off the highway. The Pemex gas station at the highway junction is an impromtu trading post for stuffed iguanas and armadillos, live parrots, and exotic fruits, all of which may be thrust into your opened window.

Tuxpan is situated along the banks of the Río de San Pedro, one of the biggest rivers in Nayarit, which feeds into the Laguna de Mexcaltitán. In Tuxpan, Cora and Huichol Indians often can be spotted, down from the Sierras to buy supplies. About halfway to Tuxpan, there is a turnoff to the small village of **Coamiles**, where there is a small *Museo Arqueológico* containing prehispanic ceramic pieces found nearby, while two miles to the east by rough road is a petroglyph site (get a guide).

SANTIAGO IXCUINTLA

You must pass through this, the second largest city in Nayarit, to get to either Mexcaltitán or Playa Los Corchos. Situated five miles off Hwy. 15, the turnoff to Santiago is 9 miles south of the Tuxpan turn-off and 14 miles north of Crucero San Blas. Nothing remains of the original colonial village founded in 1570. The prehispanic petroglyphs on a hill near Calle Luis Figueroa have proven more enduring. The **Templo del Señor de la Ascención** was built in the 18th century, and the **Presidencia Municipal** fronting the plaza principal dates to the 19th century. Its clock is a reproduction of an earlier one, once considered the most impressive timepiece in Mexico. En route to Santiago, Chile, it was accidently unloaded in San Blas.

Traditionally dressed Huichol Indians are often seen in town, at the market, or around the Huichol Center for Cultural Survival and Traditional Arts, a resource center for anybody interested in this tribe. Many Indians come down from the mountains to work in the tobacco fields (Santiago is in the heart of tobacco country, where 70 percent of all Mexican tobacco is grown). Planted when the rains taper off in mid-October, the first harvest comes in December, a second one in March.

A regional fair is held after the harvests, during the last week in April and the first week in May (peaking on May 3). It is one of the biggest in the state—a spring celebration where you can see native dances such as *Doce Pares de Francia* (Twelve Peers of France), the matachines, and *sonajeros* (rattlers).

MEXCALTITÁN

This town is more interesting in concept than reality. The small island-village is considered by some to be the legendary Aztlán (the place of the herons), which the Aztecs left in the year 1111 on a 200-year-long migration to their promised land, Tenochtitlán, where Mexico City now stands.

Much like the original Tenochtitlán, Mexcaltitán is island-bound and laid out in a circle, divided into four sections, which are supposedly laid out to the cardinal points of a compass, and whose center is symbolic of the sun, the life-giver; others say the village is a template for the great Aztec calendar. Skeptics say that it is just a round island.

Other than some pre-Columbian codices

Fish Trap on way to Mexcaltitán

picturing the Aztecs leaving Atzlán in canoes, the historical evidence pointing to Mexcaltitán as this site is tenuous. (San Felipe Aztatán, a village near Tecuala, also claims to be the departure point, and even has a monument commemorating the event). Nonetheless, Mexcaltitán is called *La Cuna de la Mexicanidad*, the cradle of Mexicanality.

Which is confusing, as it is also advertised as the Venice of Mexico. The comparison is as loosely drawn as its history. At high tide during the summer rainy season, the villagers pole their canoes down the flooded streets, but there the similarities stop. Since the streets are laid out like spokes, they all lead to the tiny central plaza and bandstand, around which social life turns. Besides the modest **Iglesia de San Pedro y San Pablo**, there is a restaurant serving *tatizhuil*, shrimp with chile and corn meal, an island specialty. On one corner of the plaza is a small museum with an interesting if somewhat fragmented collection of pre-Columbian ceramics. Many of the homes bounding the narrow streets are of antique constructions using mangrove, mud, and tile. The island is only about six blocks in diameter and can easily be walked in a few minutes.

The 3,500 villagers, mestizos descended from the original Indians, pull their living from the lagoon, a hereditary monopoly passed down through the ages. On June 28 and 29 of each year, the Fiestas de San Pedro y San Pablo are held. A fleet of pangas escort the saints onto the lagoon for mass. On the 29th, a regatta is held, a race between the two saints. In older days, if San Pablo won, that predicted a poor shrimp harvest, if he lost it meant a bumper crop. These days the race is rigged.

Arriving & Departing

The 15-minute trip to the island is as interesting as the island itself. From La Batanga, pangas navigate a maze of mangroves, passing through the locks of various fish traps, atop which sit herons waiting for an easy catch. *Note: Since there are no fixed fares, you will have to negotiate a price. Try to catch the regular panga-taxi for villagers instead of arranging a private charter.*

To get to La Batanga, leave Hwy. 15 at the turnoff to Santiago Ixcuintla. After passing through town, follow the paved road to Los Corchos. At 5.5 miles south of Santiago Ixcuintla, turn north to Sentispac and follow the paved road 17 miles to the docks of La Batanga.

Alternate Route: you can also reach Mexcaltitán by turning west off Hwy. 15 one mile north of the turnoff to Tuxpan (and 10 miles north of the Santiago Ixcuintla turnoff). Follow this paved road for 23 miles (the first 19 are paved) until reaching a signed intersection. This side road travels five miles to a boat landing next to the island. *Note: as these boats can be poled directly to the island, boat fare is much cheaper than from La Batanga.*

PLAYA LOS CORCHOS

Past the turnoff to Mexcaltitán, the road continues 16 miles to Los Corchos, a small shrimp-fishing village. Three miles before entering the village, a dirt road runs a mile down to Playa Los Corchos, where you will find the same flat gray sand beach that fringes most of northern Nayarit. There are no facilities, just a blank beach, which makes it a decent if unexciting camping spot. From the village of Los Corchos (no hotels), the road splits, running 1.2 miles to **Playa Sesteo**, where there are a few restaurants, or straight to **Boca de Comachín**, where the Laguna de Mexcaltitán empties into the Pacific. Boats might be contracted here for trips out to Isla Isabela.

ISLA ISABELA

Isla Isabela is 20 miles off the coast from Boca de Camichín. Only about two-square miles, this volcanic island has a small crater lake and two beaches, Los Pescadores and the more popular Las Monas. Principal attraction are the 17 types of sea birds that nest here, including gulls, frigatebirds, pelicans, yellow- and blue-footed boobies. Because of its delicate ecology, the island was decreed a National Park in 1980 and now is managed by the Secretaría de Desarrollo Urbano y Ecología, better known as SEDUE (Say-do-ey).

Authorization to visit should be made in advance from the SEDUE office in Tepic, but you can also get authorization directly from the SEDUE officials on the island.

They supply the required guides for those who want to visit the rookeries. Though Boca de Camichín is the closest access point (about 90 minutes in calm seas), many groups hire pangas in San Blas for the four- to five-hour trip.

CRUCERO SAN BLAS

At this junction, you can either take the 22-mile paved road to San Blas on the coast, or leap up into the Sierras to Tepic, also 22 miles away.

SAN BLAS

San Blas is infamous for the invisible *jejenes* (biting gnats). You don't see them, you just feel their disembodied bites, like voodoo pins. These biting insects are prolific around San Blas, feeding off the decaying vegetation.

This ecosystem is rich in many other things besides biting insects. More than 400 species of birds make this Mexico's best wintertime birding spot. Here the steep jungled mountains of the Sierra Madre confront the coast for the first time on its 1000-mile march south. This geography interrupts the long stretch of flat beaches to the north, sculpting a scenic tropical coastline of points, rocks, reefs, and pinnacles.

San Blas was first settled in 1767 because of the sheltered harbor at the mouth of Estero El Pozo. But these colonists retreated to Tepic, complaining of the insects. Convicts were forcibly recruited to help reestablish the site in 1768. The purpose of the settlement was to supply the Baja California missions and to transport soldiers north by sea to avoid the bellicose Indians of Sonora.

The same year (1768), Father Junípero Serra left from San Blas aboard the Purísima Concepción to take over the work of the expelled Jesuits in Baja California, and to later establish the first missions of California. San Blas grew. There was timber to build ships, a harbor where they could be launched, and a customs house where tax could be collected.

But the harbor eventually filled in, the timber grew scarce, and *contrabandistas* (smugglers) used nearby bays to unload ships, avoiding customs duties. After the War of Independence in 1810, the town shrunk in size and importance.

Today, ships can no longer cross the dangerous bar and enter the shallow harbor where Philippine galleons once anchored.

Nor is there much need to. Manzanillo grew into the port that San Blas had hoped to become. San Blas has since become a backwater of tourism, attracting a large and interesting countercurrent: aging hippies, surf rats, Europeans on the cheap, binoculared birdwatchers, and dedicated beachcombers. Many end up staying for longer than anticipated; San Blas is both inexpensive and friendly. It is easy to surrender yourself to the corrosive climate, falling into a pleasant tropical lethargy that makes it difficult to summon up the energy to leave.

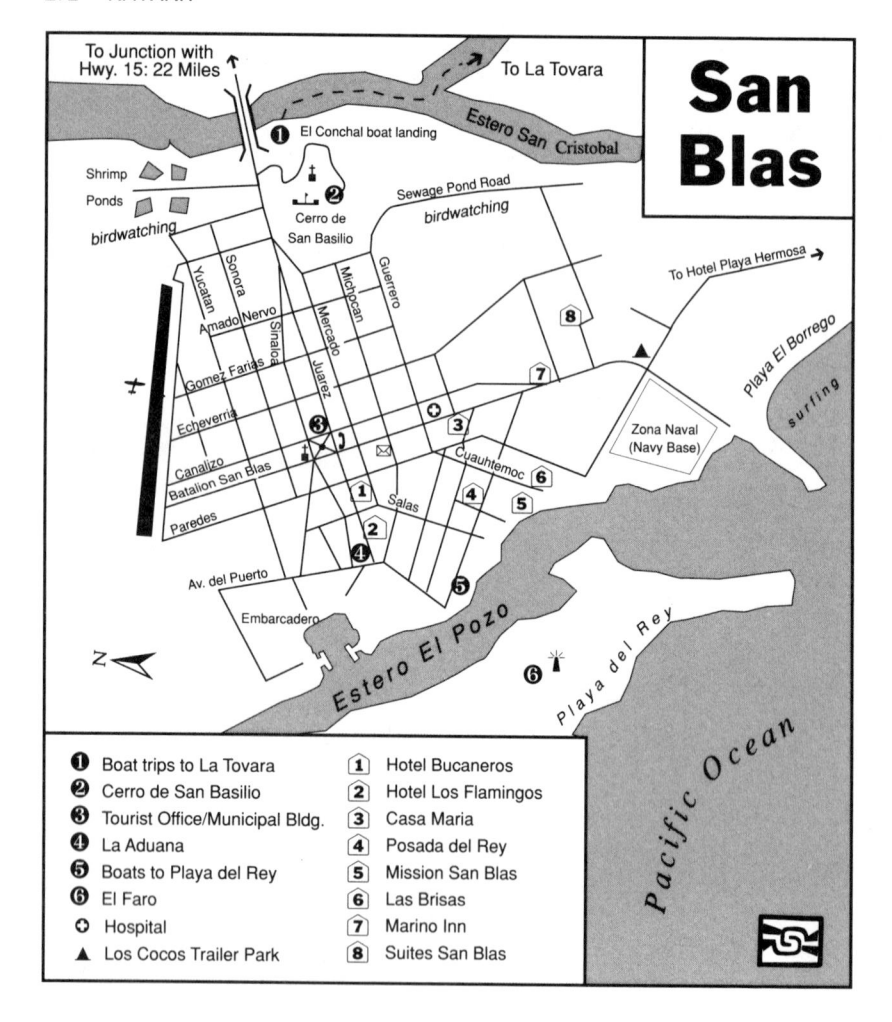

San Blas

- ❶ Boat trips to La Tovara
- ❷ Cerro de San Basilio
- ❸ Tourist Office/Municipal Bldg.
- ❹ La Aduana
- ❺ Boats to Playa del Rey
- ❻ El Faro
- ✛ Hospital
- ▲ Los Cocos Trailer Park

- ⒈ Hotel Bucaneros
- ⒉ Hotel Los Flamingos
- ⒊ Casa Maria
- ⒋ Posada del Rey
- ⒌ Mission San Blas
- ⒍ Las Brisas
- ⒎ Marino Inn
- ⒏ Suites San Blas

Bearings

Calle Juárez is the main street entering town, passing the plaza, bank, the two main hotels, and the ruins of the *aduana* (Customs) before hitting the waterfront. The other main axis is Calle Batallón, which is the main road out to Playa Borrego. At the intersection of the two is the main plaza.

Travel Information

The tourist office (tel. 5-00-05) is in the Presidencia Municipal, facing the plaza.

PLACES
La Aduana

On Av. Juárez, facing the harbor, this cavernous two-story building of eroded brick arches dates no later than the 19th century, when it was the customs house for incoming trade. As commerce tapered off (most shipping was shifted to Manzanillo), it was abandoned. In the 1930s, this building was put to use as a coconut oil factory. It is one of the few historic buildings remaining in San Blas proper.

Cerro de San Basilio

What say the Bells of San Blas
To the ships that southward pass
From the harbor of Mazatlán?
To them it is nothing more
Than the sound of surf on the shore—
Nothing more to master or man.

But to me, a dreamer of dreams,
To whom what is and what seems
Are often one and the same,—
The Bells of San Blas to me
Have a strange and wild melody,
And are something more than a name.
                    HENRY W. LONGFELLOW

Unfortunately, the bells of San Blas are now missing, along with the original townsite that was situated on this hill. Only the stone ruins of the **Iglesia de Nuestra Señora del Rosario** and the **Contaduría** still stand. The rest was built of wood. Termites ate the town, leaving no trace. The plaza is now a cornfield.

The ruins of the church date to 1792, and have been roofless since 1816. The empty belltower was immortalized by Longfellow in his poem "The Bells of San Blas," written with literary license six days before his death (he never set foot in San Blas).

More imposing is the **Contaduría**, which actually was a warehouse and administrative headquarters, not a fort which the battery of smooth-bore cannons suggest. On the edge of a steep cliff, the cannons point over the town below. In 1811, during the War of Independence, a revolutionary priest, José María Mercado, leaped from this cliff to posterity when the position was overrun by the Spanish royalists. Cerro de San Basilio is reached via a steep 0.3 mile dirt road from near El Conchal, the dam and boat landing at the entrance to town.

La Tovara

Even people not interested in the exotic birdlife can enjoy the boat trip to La Tovara

springs, the most popular tour in Nayarit. The pangas leave from El Conchal at the entrance to town. Shorter, less expensive trips can be made from La Aguada, on the road to Bahía Matanchén. They both shoot through tunnels of mangrove, passing herons, tree ducks, egrets, kingfishers, and parrots, among many others; look for mud turtles along the shoreline, iguanas in the branches above. The pangas continue up an estuary that grows progressively less brackish, arriving at a clear freshwater mineral spring, where boats dock at a palm thatch restaurant for an hour of exploring, swimming, or more birdwatching. The boats generally leave in the morning from 8 a.m until 2 p.m., though you can make arrangements for any convenient time.

Tip: catch the first boat out, your best opportunity for bird-, turtle- and iguana-watching. Tell them "despacio," as most have a tendency to gun the channels. Don't bother bargaining. Rates are regulated and are about $4 cheaper and a half-hour shorter from La Aguada. For better undisturbed wildlife viewing, you can take longer tours leaving from El Conchal, headed up the Río San Cristóbal.

BIRDWATCHING

The intricacy of the San Blas ecosystem, from its beaches, mangrove swamps and estuaries to its tropical forests, plantations, and savannahs seems to offer a niche for every species of bird. The best months for viewing are December to March, when migratory species add to the local populations, giving this area the second highest bird count in the western hemisphere. *A Field Guide of Mexican Birds*, by Peterson and Chalif is indispensable. Around San Blas, best birding sites are the sewage pond, the shrimp ponds on the north side of El Conchal, and around the ruins on Cerro de Basilio. The village of Singayata, 4.5 miles before entering San Blas, is famous for sheltering up to 300 different species, from elegant trogons to lilac-crowned parrots.

BEACHES
Playa del Rey
The longest beach in San Blas, it is the only one that must be reached by boat, a quarter-mile crossing of Estero El Pozo from the panga dock. Its common name, Isla Peso, gives an idea of the cheap fare, minus inflation. A lighthouse now stands on the site of the original fort built in 1784, which guarded the entrance to the harbor. The lighthouse separates the boat landing from the beach. These 12 miles of deserted beach are sacred to the Huichol Indians, who come here often for marriages and other ceremonies. They gather every year during Semana Santa. Usually the Huichols arrive singly or in small groups at the boat dock, and post guards during their ceremonies to keep spectators away. One of these ceremonies is in honor of *Aramara*, the goddess of the sea, and you might find some of their offerings which they launch on rafts come washing in on the incoming tide. No shade, no food, no water.

El Borrego
An easy half-mile walk from the central part of town, down Calle H. Batallón, this shallow mile-long stretch of town beach is bordered by the San Cristobál and El Pozo estuaries. During the rainy season, the water they disgorge can turn this beach brackish and brown. But during the winter months, it is a serviceable alternative to Matanchén. Much of the beach is taken up by palapa restaurants backed by coconut trees.

Matanchén
This four-mile arch of sand was discovered by Nuño de Guzmán in 1530. Guzmán used this calm bay as the main seaport for his quasi-private kingdom of Nuevo Galicia. The Jesuits also used it as a supply port for the California missions. But it was never more than a staging area, and even the muleteers carrying supplies would drop their packs and immediately return to the highlands without spending the night, fleeing the insects.

There are places to park, camp, and swim, from the surfy northern point at Las Islitas, to the calmer Rincón de Matanchén on the southern end, but there are no facilities. Bring repellent for the early morning/later afternoon bite. The turnoff for Bahía Matanchén is 2.2 miles before San Blas. After passing the village at 1.7 miles from the turnoff, you will come to a fork. Bearing left takes you to the beach of Matanchén, while to the right the road heads straight to Las Islitas. **Hotel Colon** ($) is the only hotel in Matanchén, on the road to Islitas; its concrete shell is basically no more than shelter from the rain; no hot water, but rooms do have ceiling fans to keep the mosquitoes at bay.

Las Islitas
The most scenic beach in the San Blas area, it anchors the northern end of Bahía Matanchén, where rocky pinnacles erupt from the sand. This is something of a 1960s Paradise Lost, sometimes called Stoner Beach, and not because of the stones. You can hang a hammock under a ramada, buy banana bread, and rent a surfboard. The

Las Islitas

waves here break with the precision of a zipper, and when the swell is working the legendary mile-long break radiates out across Bahia Matanchén. Bring repellent. Swarms of jejenes can be vicious here.

Playas Aticama & Los Cocos

The highway leaves the bay at Rincón de Mantenchén (the southern end of Bahía Mantenchén), humps over the hills where there is a fine river for bathing, and rolls back down to Aticama, a small village 6.7 miles from Matanchén village. The beach at Aticama turns into Los Cocos, a skinny strip of beach backed by short bluffs, shaded by the coconut trees for which it is named. Between Los Cocos and the village of Santa Cruz, is **Miramar**, a former hacienda that was also the estate of a governor in the 1960s, now a bathing spot popular with the *gente comun y corriente*, the popular classes. This area was used illegally in the 1860s to ship silver, avoiding duties at San Blas.

A stream, dammed for swimming, breaks out near here at a place called **La Manzanilla**, where there is a scenic restaurant set on a bluff overlooking this calm bay.

Santa Cruz is a smaller, tourist-less version of San Blas, a town that keeps to itself, as do the few hippies who live here, and who seem to meld naturally into the languid landscape. Just beyond Santa Cruz, the road continues to Playa La Campana, half a mile away. A bus runs three to four times a day between San Blas and Santa Cruz, a distance of about 10 miles.

Events
The Día de San Blas is celebrated on February 3. Festivities actually begin on January 31, which is the day when Padre José María Mercado leaped to his death from Cerro de San Basilio: native and popular dances, parades, and pyrotechnics.

San Blas Addendum
There is only one bank in town, Bancomer, close to Plaza Principal on Calle Juárez 26.

Telephone calls can be made from the *caseta de larga distancia* on the south side of the plaza.

The hospital is called Centro de Salud, situated on Calzada Hildago (tel. 5-02-32).

The public market is on corner of Plaza Principal.

You can arrange fishing trips or charters to Isla Isabela with the local fishermen along the inner waterfront or through a hotel.

PLACES TO SLEEP
Hotels in San Blas are cheap, but all except for Las Brisas suffer from what Neruda called "the leprous kiss of humidity." Most are within walking distance of the main plaza and the many restaurants.

Budget Hotels
Hotel Bucanero, Calle Juárez 75 (tel. 5-01-01), has a salty character but little else; lumpy beds, tepid water, loud disco. Most will feel more comfortable at the 25-room

Hotel Los Flamingos, down one block at 105 Calle Juárez. Once the German consulate, its illusion of past grandeur helps veil the reality of its leaky toilets and mildewed surfaces. **Misión San Blas** (tel. 5-00-23), formerly Casa Morales, is the only worthwhile hotel on the water (not the beach, but the estero), which means it is more likely to catch the breeze (and the bugs). Restaurant is not always open, but the pool generally is, and you can park alongside the 15 cabana-style rooms. **Hotel Playa Hermosa** faces Playa Borrego. Inaugurated by President Alemán in 1951, it has been condemned by nature, and only stays open by force of habit, probably the worse hotel in Mexico. The 13-room **Posada del Rey**, 10 Calle Campeche (tel. 5-01-23), is a trim hotel, clean and cramped, but with a pool and third-floor bar. **Casa María** is about the cheapest respectable place in town.

Moderate

What distinguishes these hotels from the competition is the air conditioning. **Hotel Suites San Blas** (tel. 5-00-47), on Calle Aticama four blocks from Playa El Borrego, features kitchenettes for self-cooking, but little else besides a pool; there is no restaurant and the disco is usually closed. The **Marino Inn Motel** (tel. 5-03-03), on Calle

H. Batallón, looks big and new, but has already surrendered to the elements; the fabrics are tatty and the pool often looks like an algae pond. By far, the best choice is **Motel Las Brisas**, 106 Cuauhtémoc Sur (tel. 5-01-12), headquarters for most birdwatchers. Rooms are clean if Spartan, though only 18 of the 42 have air conditioning. Its roundhouse restaurant is one of the best in town, and its pool is one of the few here that does not breed mosquitoes.

Camping

The **Los Cocos Trailer Park** ($; tel. 5-00-55), set in a grassy coconut grove on Calle H. Batallón at Av. Teniente Azueta, one block from Playa El Borrego, is strategically situated between town and beach, offering the only hook-ups in San Blas, as well as laundromat. If you want to park right on the beach, go to the **Playa Amore RV Resort** ($$) at Playa Los Cocos, where you can pull into a site on a grassy bluff at the ocean's edge, shaded by corozo palms, one of the most scenic spots on the coast. Other, less distinguished trailer parks are strung along Playa Los Cocos.

Because of the bugs and the low hotel rates, most travelers opt to sleep indoors. But there is lots of sand to camp on, Las Islitas being one of the more popular areas.

ARRIVING & DEPARTING
By Car & Bus
From the **Crucero de San Blas**, 14 miles south of the turnoff to Santiago Ixcuintla, the road runs 22 paved miles to San Blas. It's about a four-hour drive to Guadalajara.

Just off the main plaza, the bus station (tel. 5-00-43) offers frequent rides Tepic and less frequent trips to Guadalajara, but to Puerto Vallarta, you will have jump buses at the *central camionera* in Tepic. If you want to go to Mazatlán, get off at Crucero de San Blas, and wait for a bus there. If you want to insure yourself a seat, go to the Tepic bus station first, and then catch a bus north.

ON THE ROAD TO TEPIC
VIA HWY. 15
From Crucero San Blas, Hwy. 15 climbs the steep grades up to Tepic (belching trucks move at walking speed). To avoid the uphill crawl, you can take the new tollroad, Hwy. 15D, which begins 2.5 miles south of Crucero San Blas. About the only reason to stay on the old road is to do some birdwatching. Less than eight miles past Crucero San Blas, the old road passes Buenas Aires and **Mirador de Aguila** (Eagle Lookout, on the east side of the highway). From this lookout, 2,000 ft. in elevation, you can scan the savannah country through which the Río Santiago meanders. In the canyon below, you can usually see and hear the flamboyant military macaws, one of the few places where these rare birds still can be viewed with regularity. Twelve miles beyond, Hwy. 15 intersects with the alternate road coming up from San Blas.

SAN BLAS TO TEPIC
via SANTA CRUZ
From San Blas, you can take an alternate 37-mile long road to Tepic, which runs along Bahía Matanchén, then turns inland at Santa Cruz. Though it is four miles shorter than catching Hwy. 15 at Crucero San Blas, this winding route through the mountains is slower and subject to washouts. But it does afford a closer look at local mountain life than the toll road to Tepic.

Half a mile from Santa Cruz, a dirt road heads into the jungle, a very tough four-wheel drive road to **Platanitos**, ten miles away (easier access is from Las Varas).

At 12 miles from the Santa Cruz junction, you pass through **Jalcocotán**, a banana town. Two miles beyond, a paved road turns off to **Mecatán**, five miles away, where there is a river *balneario* a mile beyond the village, and spiral petroglyphs in Barrio del Mole nearby (this road loses its pavement but continues on to meet the paved highway running between San Blas and Crucero San Blas at a point seven miles from Hwy. 15. From the turnoff to Mecatán, the road travels 14 more miles through heavily wooded mountains to Hwy. 15 just before entering Tepic

TEPIC

The capital of Nayarit looks like a generic Mexican city, full of monuments and miracles, narrow streets and broad plazas. Resting in the Valle Matatipac, in the shadow of the sleeping volcano, Sangangüey, Tepic is a convenient place to change buses or fill up with gas on your way to Guadalajara, Puerto Vallarta, or Mazatlán.

This has been its historical role, a springboard to other places, most notably the exploration and settlement of the Californias. But even the early explorers stopped here for months at a time, long enough to enjoy the temperate climate before plunging into the pestilent lowlands. Travelers today should take similar heed. Tepic has its charms. Give it at least a few hours, if not a full day.

The original Indian village of Tepic was conquered by Francisco Cortés de San Buenaventura, sent in 1524 by his relative Hernan Cortés to search for Amazons. The notorious Niño de Guzmán established the city of Compostela here in 1531, but when Francisco Vázquez de Coronado became governor his census counted only ten Spanish houses. The capital was moved to the Compostela of today, and the village reverted to its original name, Tepic. Only 16 Spaniards lived here in 1600.

Two hundred years later, in 1811, the Spanish granted it the title "Noble and Loyal City of Tepic." After Mexican independence, it was declared the capital of the territory of Nayarit. But belligerent Cora and Huichol Indians, and the steep crags of the Sierra Madre, isolated it from the rest of Mexico. It wasn't until the first train reached here in 1912 that it became integrated with modern Mexico. In the wake of the Mexican Revolution the territory finally gained statehood.

This isolation from the rest of the nation has formed its independent character, but one entirely different from the aggressive, frontier spirit of the northern states. Just the opposite. These mountains, and the reclusive Indians that live here, have made it humble like a hermit. Tepic doesn't advertise itself, and one of the most popular guidebooks advises that "if you have to stop here, catch the next bus or train as soon as possible." Few foreigners are seen walking the narrow colonial streets. Usually those who do are glad they did.

Bearings

Mex. 15 enters Tepic from the west as Av. Insurgentes, passes the main intersection of town at Av. México, and exits east to Guadalajara. To the north of Av. Insurgentes, Av. Mexico leads to city center. To the south, it turns into Mex. 200, the road to Puerto Vallarta. A *libramiento* (highway bypass) skirts the town's southwest edge, a quick roundabout of the city.

Travel Information

The State Tourist Office is in the Exconvento de la Cruz, on Av. México Sur at Av. Ejército, on the road leaving for Puerto Vallarta, four blocks south of Av. Insurgentes Pte.

PLACES
Cathedral

The two spindly Neo-Gothic towers of the cathedral rise 130 feet, seen for miles. They were built in 1885, but the church itself dates to 1750 when it was dedicated to the Purísima Concepción de María. The towers were designed and built by Gabriel Luna Rodríguez, who also designed the Palacio de Gobierno. The cathedral faces the zócalo, eight blocks north of Insurgentes on Av.

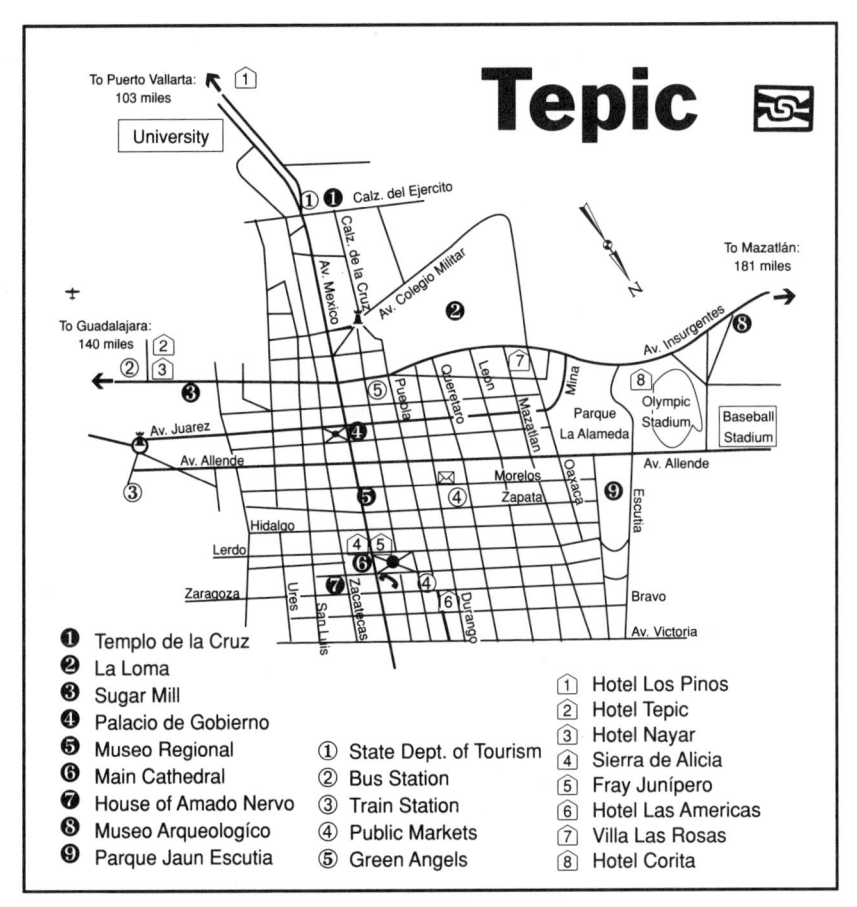

Tepic

Map legend:

- ❶ Templo de la Cruz
- ❷ La Loma
- ❸ Sugar Mill
- ❹ Palacio de Gobierno
- ❺ Museo Regional
- ❻ Main Cathedral
- ❼ House of Amado Nervo
- ❽ Museo Arqueologíco
- ❾ Parque Jaun Escutia

- ① State Dept. of Tourism
- ② Bus Station
- ③ Train Station
- ④ Public Markets
- ⑤ Green Angels

- ⊡1 Hotel Los Pinos
- ⊡2 Hotel Tepic
- ⊡3 Hotel Nayar
- ⊡4 Sierra de Alicia
- ⊡5 Fray Junípero
- ⊡6 Hotel Las Americas
- ⊡7 Villa Las Rosas
- ⊡8 Hotel Corita

Mexico, the center of the city, a pleasant spot shaded by *tabachín* (poinciana) trees.

Palacio de Gobierno

Six blocks south of the zócalo on Av. México, at Mina and Abasolo, this 19th century neo-classical edifice is the center of authority for the state. Originally designed as a penitentiary, it was found that its design was equally suited to bureaucrats. Inside on the second floor is the ubiquitous historical mural painted in 1975 by José Luis Soto.

Templo y Ex-convento de la Cruz de Zacate

This ancient chapel was built in 1744 around a patch of grass in the shape of a cross,

surrounded by bare ground. In 1540, a muleteer discovered the green patch. His mules stubbornly refused to pass over the cross, let alone eat it. Word of this strange cross spread to the King of Spain, who appointed an official to check it out. This miracle was soon surrounded by a chapel, and later adjoined by a convent in 1784.

Though it has not been cut, weeded, or watered in 450 years, the cross can still be seen today through the grilled gate of an interior chamber within the chapel. A holy spot, the cross is often crowded with worshipers (especially Christianized Huichols) seeking favors, and its interior is crowded with *retablos*, plaques thanking God for favors received; the cross is supposed to be

Retablos

Retablos are miracle paintings, striking for their primitive power and deep belief. Most are done on tin, wood, or even cardboard, though most in Tepic are commissioned in marble. These retablos are painted in honor of the person's patron saint. When a person escapes death, they often pay a village *retablero* to paint a memorial of the incident or accident, accompanied by a short narrative or other data. These are hung in churches and chapels throughout the country, spiritually compelling and unpre-tentious statements of faith.

particularly effective in curing blindness, tuberculosis, heart ailments, and leprosy.

Adjoining the chapel is the Department of Tourism, in the old convent, where historic photos hang on ancient walls. Father Serra stayed in a hospice here three different times before setting off on his various expeditions, and most likely prayed at the *Cruz de Zacate* for the success of his California missions. A bronze statue of Serra now stands in front of the church, and one of the rooms contains what are supposedly the bed and table where he slept and worked. This secularized convent also houses a museum of sorts, along with a small *artesanía* where you can buy Huichol clothes, artwork, yarn paintings and fabrics. The church and convent are conveniently situated on Av. México at Av. Ejército, on the road to Puerto Vallarta.

Museo Regional de Antropología e Historia

The museum is situated in the former colonial palace of the Counts of Miravalle. You can still see their family shield engraved in stone at the entrance (this family received the noble title for being outrageously rich and paying lots of taxes). Many fine artifacts dug up in Jalisco, Nayarit and Colima are on display here, including a 1,000-year-old stone showing an eagle clutching a snake in its talons, a historical precursor to what you see on the Mexican flag today. Many of the hollow clay figures come from around Ixtlán de Río. Sacred arrows, musical instruments and the hallucinatory artwork of the Coral and Huichol Indians are also on display, a fine ethnography of these tribes. If you plan a trip to Huichol country, this museum is considered a resource for current information on places and permits.

Museo Arqueológico

Near the baseball stadium on Av. Insurgentes, 12 blocks west of Av. México, this small museum exhibits some prehispanic ceramics, paintings and photos of Huichol dress, assorted arrowheads, metates, necklaces, pipes, rattles, and petroglyphs. Closed late afternoons and weekends.

Huichol Expeditions

To visit the Huichol tribes in the mountains, you need official permission, obtained from the Palacio de Gobierno. Planes leave from the Aeropuerto Nacional (tel. 3-31-27) to the villages of Guadalupe Ocotlán, Huajimic, Puente de Camotlán., Mesa del Nayar, and St. Teresa. The airport is reached by taking Av. Insurgentes about three miles east of Av. México to Av. Aviación. Visit the Museo Regional and the Museo Arqueológico first, for current information.

Huichol Shopping

The Huichol bring down their artwork from the mountains to sell. You can search it out around the zócalo, or near the market area. Tienda Aguira sells Huichol art exclusively, on the corner of Puebla Nte. and Zaragoza, two blocks from the zócalo. The government agency DIF supervises three stores in

Tepic: one at the Ex-convento de la Cruz, another to one side of the Municipal Palace facing the zócalo, the third at Av. Insurgentes and Gaviotas near the bullring on the east side of town on road to Guadalajara. *Note: many of the Huichol clothes are full of religious significance, and you shouldn't wear them around in Nayarit.*

Native Sons

One block east of the zócalo, along Calle Zacatecas, are two homes turned into monuments to native sons, one a poet, the other a soldier. The **Casa de Amado Nervo** on Zacatecas 281 was the birthplace of the Mexican modernist poet (1870-1919).

¿Quién será en un futuro no lejano, el Cristóbal Colón de algún planeta? ¿Quién logrará con máquina potente, sondar el oceáno del éter, y llevarnos de la mano allí donde llegaron solamente los osados ensueños del poeta?

The modest house contains photos, donated paintings, and his original manuscripts. Three blocks south on the same street is the birthplace of **Juan Escutia**, one of the legendary six Niños Heroes, young cadets who leapt to their deaths from Mexico City's Chapultepec castle rather than be defeated by General Winfield Scott's troops during the Mexican-American War in 1847. There are monuments in his memory all over the city, and, to the Niños Héroes, in every city throughout Mexico.

Events

Tepic celebrates the Fiesta de Santiago on July 25.

PLACES TO SLEEP
Budget Hotels

Budget accommodations are near the bus station, where you will find **Hotel Nayar** (tel. 3-23-22) on 403 Dr. Martinez, and **Hotel Tepic** (tel. 3-13-17) on 44 República

de Chile. Other budget hotels, such as the **Hotel Las Américas** (tel. 2-18-90) on 317 Puebla, are near the public market by the zócalo. **Hotel Los Pinos** (tel. 3-12-32), Blvd. Tepic-Xalisco, which also functions as a trailer park, offers convenient and tranquil bungalows for those with cars, as it is on the outskirts of town on the road to Puerto Vallarta.

Moderate

Hotel Corita (tel. 2-04-77) on 310 Insurgentes, next to the Olympic stadium, and **Villa las Rosas** (tel. 3-18-00), 100 Insurgentes, four blocks closer to town and across from Parque La Loma, are satisfactory for the price, a convenient stop if you are driving in from the north. **La Loma** motel just of Hwy. 15 at Parque Las Lomas is another satisfactory stop. If you want to be in the center of town, the best choices are on Av. Mexico next to the zócalo, either **Hotel Sierra de Alicia** (tel. 2-03-22) half a block from the cathedral or **Hotel Fray Junípero Serra** (tel. 2-25-25) across the street, the most expensive place in town.

Camping

There are two trailer parks in Tepic. **Los Pinos** (tel. 3-12-32), which also rents bungalows (see above) is a quiet shady repose off a busy boulevard that turns into Mex. 200 to Puerto Vallarta. The widow who runs it sells spring water to her guests. **Campamento Cora**, K899 Carr. México-Nogales (tel. 3-31-13), is not on Mex 15 as its address indicates, difficult to find, and not as atmospheric as Los Pinos, though it does have a pool.

ARRIVING & DEPARTING
By Bus
The bus station is situated off Av. Insurgentes, a long 18 blocks from the main plaza, amid a cluster of budget hotels. This is a major transfer point for travelers head-ing to Puerto Vallarta, and there is a post and telegraph office on the premises. Buses constantly leave south to Guadalajara, north Mazatlan and the border, west to Puerto Vallarta.

By Train
The train station is situated about 12 blocks from city center, at Prolongación Allende Ote. There are daily departures to Guadalajara and Nogales, but since trains don't originate here, schedules are often delayed and you may not get a seat. From Tepic to anywhere, the bus is much more efficient.

TEPIC TO GUADALAJARA

Travel on Hwy. 15 to Guadalajara can seem tortuously slow as it winds through the Sierras. As this is the main Pacific corridor to Guadalajara and Mexico City, there is little alternative to the trucks that creep along in low gear. It is 143 miles from Tepic to Guadalajara. *Note: Travelers not interested in seeing Laguna de Santa María del Oro can take Hwy. 200 heading to Puerto Vallarta and catch the toll road looping back to Hwy. 15 at Chapalilla, 31 miles south of Tepic; it's 12 miles longer, but easier to drive, once you squeeze through the narrow streets of Xalisco.*

LAGUNA DE SANTA MARIA DEL ORO
Once choked with lava, now clear with water, this tiny crater lake (only a mile and a half wide), is an oasis of spent forces. The steep hills of an ancient rim surround this pocket of tropical growth, protecting it from the winds; mountains are often mirrored in the lake, doubling its beauty. A scattering of open-air restaurants edge the shore, which serve the small hand-size fish caught from the deep lake. Springs at La Colita feed into it, and its variable temperatures are suppos-edly due to thermal waters bubbling up from the bottom. You can camp shoreside at the **Koala Campground** ($), amid grassy lawn, surrounded by mango and banana trees. Bougainvillaea climbs high into the trees and butterflies drift through the citrus-scented air. Besides a small pool, you can jump from the pier into the clear, unpolluted water. At least during the week. On week-ends, the jet skiers and drinkers from Tepic invade.

Access: A 12-mile paved road departs Hwy 15, 20 mile south of Tepic, passing the old gold-mining village of Santa María del Oro at 6.3.miles. A mile and a half farther on you pass El Mirador, a lookout over the lake, before the road drops 4.3 miles to the shoreline.

VOLCÁN CEBORUCO
About 40 miles from Tepic, to the east of Mex. 15, you can see the dormant Volcán Ceboruco rising 7,098 feet. It erupted in 1542 and again in 1870. The highway crosses through this latest lava flow, still bare of vegetation.

AHUACATLÁN

This ancient Indian town, 46 miles from Tepic, lay along the route used by all the early expeditions to the coast. There are two churches on the main plaza, one the 17th century **Ex-convento Franciscano San Juan Evangelista**, first founded in 1550. The town's name in Aztec means "place of the avocado," but more apparent are the numerous poinciana trees here. Fiesta de San Francisco is celebrated from September 25 to October 15.

IXTLAN DEL RIO

The sixth largest town in Nayarit, it is set around a 19th century plaza and a 17th century church, the **Parroquia de Santo Santiago**. On the last Sunday in October, the Día de Cristo Rey, pilgrims flock to the church atrium to watch the native dances (Pluma, Matachines, Aztec, and Quetzales). The Virgen de Guadalupe is also honored December 8 to 12.

The town itself is no great sight.. The glory years of Ixtlán came and went centuries before, when it was the site of an independent Indian chiefdom. Though there is a small **museo arqueológico** in the Presidencia Municipal, much more impressive are the only structural indigenous ruins in Nayarit, less than two miles south of town at **Los Toriles**.

Ixtlán is situated 55 miles south of Tepic on Hwy. 15.

Los Toriles

Easily reached from Hwy. 15, 1.8 miles south Ixtlán, these reconstructed Toltec ruins (900 a.d. or later) stand close by the highway. The most impressive is the Temple of Quetzalcoatl, a round platform used for sacrifices, and punctuated by dormer windows in the shape of a Latin cross, unique to prehispanic construction.

Among 13 other structures are those dedicated to the sun and the moon. But this is all supposition, and these circular ruins raise more questions than can be answered.

Underlying the mystery is a round rock, shaped like a wheel, resting on a square platform. These prehispanic Indians were familiar with the circle or wheel as a concept; in fact it plays a central role in their cosmology. Yet they never put it to functional use. They knew about about the wheel, as evidenced by a famous jaguar artifact, which rode on four wheels. They just didn't choose to employ it in a practical way. Perhaps doing so was considered sacrilegious, like asking God to do manual labor.

The prehispanic figures dug up around Ixtlán are famous for their distinctive shapes. The finest examples are exhibited in the Museo Regional in Tepic. *Caution: travelers are occasionally offered bits of clay for sale, mostly reproductions. It is illegal to leave the country with a genuine artifact, and can be a serious offense.*

Time Change

At the Nayarit-Jalisco border, set your watch one hour ahead to central time.

LA MAGDALENA

This colonial town, 39 miles east of Ixtlán, is famous for its *ópalos* (opals), which, if you stand idle for more than a few minutes along the main plaza, you will soon have the chance to buy.

Besides wandering gem dealers, there are a few stores dealing entirely in these semiprecious stones, which are mined in the nearby hills. The quality ranges widely. Beware of those displayed in water or mineral oil; the colors fade when dry. The best opals are the crimson ones called *girasoles del fuego*, or fire opals. Other opals mined here are the *arlequines*, or harlequin opals, and the *lechosos*, or milky opals, which are cloud-colored.

TEQUILA

Less than 12 miles east of Magdalena is Tequila, set amid the spiky fields of maguey. Like Tecate, it is as much a product as a place; more than 50 distilleries supply the

Maguey Plant

world with tequila. Though the town was founded in 1530 by Cristobál de Onate, it wasn't until 1873 that Don Cenobiuo Sauza laid the foundation for the modern tequila industry here. Many of the distilleries offer tours where you can follow the process as the *piñas* (agave hearts) are cooked, crushed, fermented, distilled, and then aged. Among the more popular tours are of the Sauza plant in Tequila, and the Herradura distillery in **Amatitán**, a small highway village four miles to the east on the road to Guadalajara. Tequila actually was first discovered in Amatitán, but back when the liquor was called *vinomezcal*.

The annual Feria de Tequila is held from November 30 to December 12, and the Fiesta del Tequila, on May 13. The town also celebrates May 3, Día de la Santa Cruz.

GUADALAJARA

Guadalajara is the conservative cradle of colonial tradition, the most Spanish city in Mexico. Its name is taken from a town in Spain, which in Arabic means "rocky riverbed," and the city was declared the "most loyal and noble city" by Charles V. Even today the old Spanish monarches are held in esteem, unlike elsewhere in Mexico. Many of Maximillian's troops settled here after the French intervention in the 1860s, adding to its loyalist tendencies. Eminently Catholic and highly conservative, its skyline is prickly with steeples, and there isn't much nightlife. Its attractions are mostly daytime sightseeing. Even a week would not do this city justice, let alone the outlying attractions of Tlaquepaque, Tonalá, and Lake Chapala.

Places to Sleep

Of the many hotels in Guadalajara, one of the best budget ones is **Posada Regis** ($), across the street from the **Hotel Fénix** ($$; tel. 11-57-14) on 160 Av. Corona downtown. The Fénix is the liveliest hotel at night in Guadalajara with its varied nightclubs. For historical flavor, **Hotel Francés** ($$), just off Plaza Tapatío on 35 Maestranza, is a combination hotel and national monument. For overall best value, it is hard to beat **Hotel Laffayette** ($$; tel. 13-15-29), in the garden-like Zona Chapultepec on 2005 Av. de la Paz. Though it continues to spell its name wrong, it does everything else right.

BEYOND

Guadalajara is the center of western Mexico, roughly 200 miles (a five-hour drive or bus ride) from any of the other major cities. If you are heading east, you have two basic choices. You can take the high road to the colonial towns of **Guanajuato** (187 miles) or **San Miguel de Allende** (246 miles), then drop down to Mexico City, or you can choose the low road through the heart of the old Tarascan empire, passing through **Pátzcuaro** (180 miles) and **Morelía** (199 miles), then up through the pine highlands to Mexico City. Or you can flee back to the Pacific coast, taking either Mex. 80 to **Barra de Navidad** (189 miles) or Mex. 54 via **Colima** to **Manzanillo** (194 miles).

TEPIC TO PUERTO VALLARTA

From Tepic, Hwy. 200 drops from the highlands to closely parallel the outer shore of Bahía Banderas, offering some of the easiest beach access on the coast. The distance from Tepic to Puerto Vallarta is 101 miles, a two-and-a-half hour drive for anybody foolish enough not to stop and enjoy this stretch of relatively undeveloped coast.

XALISCO

Just 4.5 miles from Tepic, Hwy. 200 runs through the middle of Xalisco, a narrow street of storefronts that once was the capital of the empire of Xalisco. Nuño de Guzmán burned down the Indian capital in 1530, but its name endured, eventually becoming the name of the state, Jalisco. This town celebrates the Fiesta de Asunción, from August 6 to 15, with fireworks and bullfights.

COMPOSTELA

Compostela, a long 23 miles from Tepic, is of more interest for what it was than what it is. The narrow main street into town is better fit for horses than cars, and both still battle for right-of-way.

The town's most striking feature is the massive **Templo del Señor de la Misericordia** that dominates the town square, a platersque fortress first built in 1539, though successive renovations have given it a patchwork look. A year after the church's founding, Coronado took his last mass here before striking off on his famous expedition of 1540, discovering the lands of Arizona, New Mexico, Texas, and the plains of Kansas 264 years before Lewis and Clark. This was formerly the capital of Nueva Galicia before it was moved to Guadalajara in 1560. In the **Presidencia Municipal** there is supposed to be a minor collection of clay figures, some arrowheads, and petroglyphs.

About a mile before entering Compostela from Tepic, a dirt road travels three miles to **Hacienda Miravalles**, one of this region's richest haciendas which dates back to a conquistador's widow taking possession of a gold and silver mine in 1543; though most of the construction dates to the 19th century, the adjoining chapel is believed to be of the 16th century. Its lands were expropriated in 1937 and given to the *campesinos*. Stripped of its fields, the hacienda fell to ruin, and is preserved today as a historical monument.

Compostela celebrates the feast of the Señor de la Misericordia on the first Friday of December, the Día de Santiago Apóstol on July 26, and the Día de Santa Cecilia, on November 22.

GUADALAJARA TOLL ROAD

Two miles south of Compostela, 25 miles south of Tepic, Hwy. 200 intersects with a toll road running 22 miles to reconnect with Hwy. 15, 31 miles south of Tepic. This route to Guadalajara is 12 miles longer than if you had stayed on Hwy. 15, yet is easier to drive.

LAS VARAS

The highway winds down from the mountains at Las Varas, 45 miles from Tepic, marking the beginning of what tourism people call the *Costa Alegre*, the Happy Coast. There is a paved turnoff here to the village of **Zacualpan**, about six miles away, where there is a museum and a archaeological rock garden comprising close to 20 stones etched with petroglyphs. The road continues from Zacualpan to the coast at **Platanitos**, roughly 12 miles away, where there are a few beach restaurants and little else. A tough 4WD road continues on 10 miles, hitting the pavement at **Santa Cruz**.

Playa Chacala

COSTA ALEGRE

This 36-mile stretch of coast breaks from Nayarit's coastwise character. Here the shoreline bends around to the southwest, forming the peninsula that guards Bahía de Banderas. Instead of silt-laden estuaries and flat gray sand beaches, you find grainier, gold-sand beaches and jungled hillsides. Hwy. 200 closely parallels the shoreline, offering easy beach access to the following bays and beaches.

PLAYA CHACALA
& PLAYA CHACALILLA

These two beaches define paradise, unsullied by development. A bumpy six mile road leaves Hwy. 200 just south of Las Varas. The road is dirt, but much of it is cobbled; some of the flat stones are believed to have come from prehispanic constructions that were destroyed to make the road.

The main half-mile-long stretch of sand is shady with coconut palms, bracketed by black stone points congested with tropical vines, hardwoods, and palms. A mild surf rolls onto the sand. Less than a mile be-yond, the road drops down into another beach, Chacalilla, which, as its name implies, is a micro-version of Chacala.

Besides a few fish-shack restaurants, the beach at each is taken up by camping areas directly on the sand, under the palms, near the surf. Both charge a token camping fee. Yachts occasionally anchor here, as did the pirates of the 17th and 18th century, most notably Thomas Cavendish, who gathered supplies here in 1587 before sailing to Baja California and successfully attacking the galleon, *Santa Ana*. Kino and Atondo also left from this idyllic beach in 1683 to colonize Loreto in Baja California. Some old storage ruins can still be seen near the northern point

About all that is left of the Indian presence here is the name, which in Nahuatl means "place of the shrimp," and petroglyphs at La Puntilla, the rocky point at the northern end of Chacala.

BAHIA DE JALTEMBA
La Peñita & Rincón de Guayabitos

These two communities have distinct personalities. One works, the other is a resort.

La Peñita, 16 miles south of la Varas, is a small commercial village, with most businesses and services on Av. Emiliano Zapata, which runs from Hwy. 200 down to the steep beach. This town is a busy congregation of bankers, mechanics, merchants, fishermen, farmers, and occasional travelers.

A mile south on Hwy. 200, Rincón de Guayabitos is a clutch of moderately priced bungalows and trailer parks, crowded around the more protected end of Bahía de Jaltemba. Guayabitos is a less expensive alternative to Puerto Vallarta. The people who stay here come for two reasons: sun and beach. More of a development than a town, there is no village backdrop to the beach scene, other than a few grocery stores and T-shirt emporiums.

Travel Information

The tourist office is in the Plaza Cívica at the entrance to Rincón de Guayabitos.

Traveling About

The only road connecting La Peñita and Rincón de Guayabitos is Hwy. 200. You can flag down the cooperativas that shuttle constantly between the two.

Beaches of Bahía de Jaltemba

The beach at **La Peñita**, situated at the head of the bay, is a bit rocky in places, and is used mainly as a launching area by fishermen. The narrow strip of sand at **Rincón de Guayabitos** may be of calmer surf but is a flurry of activity. In the high season, vendors hawk cheap jewelry. Beach strollers veer around the prone bodies basting in the sun. People cast treble-hook fishing lures out among the swimmers and snorkelers. Tour boats in from cruises to **Isla Corazón Sagrado** plow into the beach, throwing guests atumble while pelicans drop like bombs into the shallow water, chasing the sardines that swarm in the shallow water. It's a visual feast.

The long deserted northern reach of Bahía

Jaltemba, open to a thumping surf, is called **Playa Malpaso**, a long steep run of grainy sand. Two and a half miles north of La Peñita, opposite the signed turnoff to **Tonino**, a dirt road weaves down to this beach, doglegging around an airfield. An easier access is via La Peñita Trailer Park, half a mile north of La Peñita, where stairs fall down to this unsullied beach.

At the southern end of the bay, separated from Rincón de Guayabitos by a jungled point of land, is **Playa Ayala**, reached by a mile-long paved road. Palm-thatched restaurants recline along most of its length, but the beach is quieter than at Guayabitos. If you are looking for even more privacy, there is a beachlet (Caleta de Ayala) to the south of Ayala beyond the point, reached by a short foot trail.

Jaltemba Addendum

The bus station is at La Peñita, where buses pass by about every half hour to either Tepic or Puerto Vallarta. You can also flag down one of a steady stream of buses along the highway at Guayabitos.

There are two banks in La Peñita, one a Bancomer on the main street, Av. Emiliano Zapata 22.

The post office in La Peñita is situated along the main avenue, Emiliano Zapata 43. In Guayabitos the post office is in the Plaza Cívica, a plaza at the entrance to town, off Av. Sol Nuevo.

PLACES TO SLEEP
Budget Hotels

You can stay cheaper at La Peñita than at Rincón de Guayabitos. The 12 hotels here, all in the budget category, rent for two-thirds the price of what the few budget picks in Guayabitos charge. The **Miramar** on 1 Salina Cruz ($; tel. 4-02-03) is only a block from the beach. The **Rosita** is situated conveniently on the highway near the bus depot. The **Posada Russell** (tel. 4-02-02) is on the beach a few blocks from downtown.

Rincón de Guayabitos

In Rincón de Guayabitos, the **Bungalows Quintero Familiar** (tel. 4-02-48) on Sol Nuevo at Colorines Av. is about the best budget pick, across the street from the beach; rooms are supplied with *metates*, cutting boards, and sharp knifes.

Moderate & Deluxe

There are about 30 bungalow operations in Rincón de Guayabitos, most priced within a few pesos of each other, around $30-$60 a night. There are usually plenty of vacancies, allowing you to start at one end and walk to the other, comparing prices, rooms, and locations. As a general axiom, the room rates drop the farther you walk to the north. There are a few strictly hotel operations, such as **Hotel Playa de Oro** (tel. 4-03-29), but these offer little price advantage over the bungalow operations, which provide larger rooms and kitchenettes.

Camping

There are more trailer parks congregated in Rincón de Guayabitos than anywhere else between Mazatlán and Acapulco. Most are full of snowbirds roosting for the winter, with few slots available for passing travelers. The ragged **Delia's Trailer Park** ($$), a block off the beach, catches the overflow. The best choice, and the one with the most available sites, is **La Peñita Trailer Park and Campground** ($$; Apdo.. Posta #22, La Peñita de Jaltemba C.P. 633726), situated half a mile north of La Peñita, on a shady naturally landscaped bluff above Playa Malpaso; there is also a pool and an area for tent camping here. Colored by rich red soil and blue ocean, this is one of the most scenic trailer parks on the west coast.

LO DE MARCO

This small banana-and-fish village, eight miles south of Rincón de Guayabitos off Hwy. 200, lines the cobbled road that ends at the steep and surfy Playa Latracadero. There are two trailer parks here, **El Caracól** ($$$; tel. 12-49-37 in Guadalajara), and the more rustic **Pequeño Paraiso** ($$), which handles most of the transient campers; there are no other camping spots. From here a paved road continues one mile to **Las**

Minitas, a small beach that sparkles like fool's gold, the flakes coming from ore deposits here; the name comes from some small mines just south of the point. On the other side of the point, 0.2 miles from Las Minitas, is **Los Venados**. Here a freshwater stream pools into a swimming hole before breaking onto the beach, which is cornered by a black reef with tidepools. Peter O'Toole was filmed in a Robinson Carusoe movie here. These days you will find more footprints than Friday's.

SAN FRANCISCO

Just off Hwy. 200, 6.3 miles south of Lo de Marcos, the ejido of San Francisco is the sacrificial pawn of presidential politics. Former President Luis Echeverría chose San Francisco as the site of a branch of his Centro de Estudios Económicos y Sociales del Tercer Mundo, a third world leftist think-tank. He also ordered the construction of an overblown **Museo de Arte Marino** (Museum of Marine Art), and had a grand home built on the rocky southern point. For a few short years, this ejido prospered like no other.

But the radical Echeverría made enemies when he left the presidency in 1976. He had refused to give up power gracefully, leaving office amid rumors of a coup d'etat. Out of office, he continued to agitate throughout the country until banished to Australia as an ambassador. On his return, he continued to protest the conservative policies of President De la Madrid. The president annulled the $2 million annual subsidy for Echeverría's Third World Studies Center, originally given to him on the assumption that he stay out of national politics.

The jungle now strangles what is left of the overblown museum a block from the main square. The only evidence that the buildings up on the hillside were once a Third World school are the welcome signs, written in 16 languages.

The view from the school's *mirador* overlooks the steep surfy beach below, which runs the breadth of this small town. The only hotel here is the tranquil **San Francisco Club de Playa** ($$; tel. in Guadalajara 5-38-66), which borders the beach on the north side of town, below the former school.

SAYULITA

This small fishing and cattle-raising village lies three miles south of San Francisco, a mile off Hwy. 200. Other than the opportunity of its mile-long beach, there is little else for the traveler except six restaurants, two grocery stores, and a close view of rustic village life. Unfortunately, since it lies 26 miles from Puerto Vallarta, it falls within its sphere of dollar influence. The Mexican tourist-grade bungalows **Las Gaviotas** cost more than the superior ones at Rincón de Guayabitos. A mile from the center of town, the **Trailer Park Sayulita** ($$) strikes a better balance: no pool but it's on the beach, not in-town but a pleasant walk away.

BAHÍA DE BANDERAS

The largest bay in Mexico, Bahía de Banderas is a giant bite out of the coast, 20 miles long, 15 miles wide. It is sheltered from the path of tropical storms. Bad weather just skips on by, unable to turn into the bay. The weather can be monotonously wonderful, with an average of 345 sunny days a year.

When Francisco Cortés de San Buenaventura arrived here in 1524, his party was confronted by 20,000 Indians who had tied *banderas* (flags) to their quivers, and this first impression gave rise to its name. But the bay never was developed by the Spanish. The surrounding mountains were impenetrable.

Consequently, English and French pirates found the bay a sheltered retreat, and it took centuries before the coast was settled. Not until 1960 was the road to Puerto Vallarta paved, and even today the villages of Quimixto and Yelapa can only be reached by boat.

The bay has three distinct personalities. The mountainous southern shore, ending at Cabo Corrientes (Cabo San Lucas was torn from these rocks) is cut by deep coves, much of it still inaccessible by car. The head of the bay is heavily developed, from Puerto Vallarta to Bucerías. The flatter, drier northern shore to Punta Mita is scalloped with stretches of sand, mostly undeveloped.

THE NORTHERN SHORE

A 13.5-mile-long paved road parallels the northern shore, leaving Hwy. 200 at the Punta Mita junction just north of Bucerías. At the junction, there is a state tourist kiosk with lots of travel information and maps. Buses operated by Transportes Medina, run from Puerto Vallarta to Punta Mita, leaving about every two hours. You can flag them down along the highway.

Cruz de Huanacaxtle

This small village, 1.4 miles from the junction, is named after a thick-trunked native tree (also known as *Guanacaste*) with a spreading crown and ear-shaped seed pods, which you can see in the main square. The main street takes you to the harbor and beach, but better sand can be found nearby at Playa La Manzanilla.

Playas La Manzanilla & Piedra Blanca

Half a mile beyond Cruz de Huanacaxtle is La Manzanilla, also named for a tree. These Manzanilla trees grow along the beach, casting shade (their sap can raise blisters). This beach, splashed with feathery surf, joins that of Piedra Blanca, where there is an excellent oceanside trailer park ($$), managed by the Piedra Blanca Hotel ($$; tel. 2-09-12) next to it.

Playa Destiladeras

This long arc of blinding white sand is the longest beach along the north shore, 2.6 miles beyond La Manzanilla. There are a few restaurants but most of the beach is long and lonely, with waves for body surfing, and places to camp.

Playa Punta del Burro

Only a mile and a half beyond Playa Destiladeras a dirt road tracks down to this quarter-mile stretch of beach.

Playa Pontoque

This scallop of sand, also known as **Paraiso Escondido (the name of the restaurant)**, is surrounded by black rocks: good snorkeling in calm seas. The short dirt road departs the paved road 3.6 miles beyond Destiladeras near **Las Amapas**, an exotic restaurant whose menu depends on what they happen to catch in the jungle the night

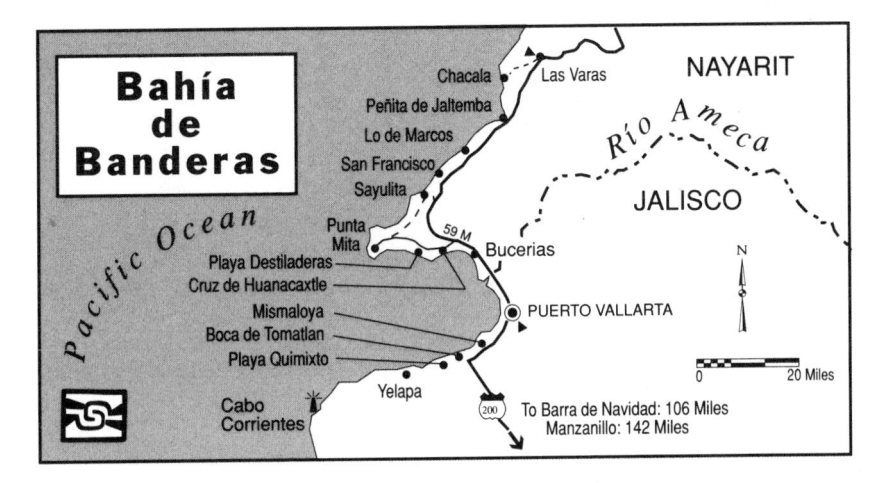

Bahía de Banderas

NAYARIT

Chacala
Peñita de Jaltemba
Lo de Marcos
San Francisco
Sayulita
Las Varas

Río Ameca

JALISCO

Pacific Ocean

Punta Mita
Playa Destiladeras
Cruz de Huanacaxtle
Mismaloya
Boca de Tomatlan
Playa Quimixto

59 M

Bucerias

PUERTO VALLARTA

N

Yelapa

Cabo Corrientes

200 To Barra de Navidad: 106 Miles
Manzanillo: 142 Miles

0   20 Miles

---

before: rattlesnake, iguana, badger, rabbit, or boar.

Punta Mita

Not to be confused with the geographical Punta Mita, or the straggly fishing village at land's end, this small village is more substantial but offers little more than cold *refrescos* to the traveler. Just beyond, less than half a mile, is **Playa El Anclote**, a surfer's beach, best during the summer when the waves come from the south. One mile beyond El Anclote you arrive at the northern point of Bahía de Banderas, also called Punta Mita. There is a big turnaround here, where the bus waits for passengers heading back to Puerto Vallarta. This is one of the better camping sites for surfers, along the northern shore facing the islets close offshore. *Note: less than a quarter mile east of the village of Punta Mita, a semi-paved road loops back through thick jungle along the outer coast of Puta Mita to Sayulita, 18 miles away.*

THE MIDDLE BAY

From the Punta Mita Junction, Hwy. 200 travels 18 miles to Puerto Vallarta, a coastal stretch under heavy development pressure.

Bucerías

This long, narrow town, about 15 miles north of Puerto Vallarta, maintains a separate identity from Puerto Vallarta. It is a moderately priced bungalow community of about a dozen operations, stretched out along the beach. The two trailer parks ($$$) are the nearest oceanside campgrounds to Puerto Vallarta. The **Bucerías Trailer Park** (tel. 37) is the larger of the two, formerly Elizabeth Taylor's beach property. Buses pass by on their way to Puerto Vallarta every half hour.

Nuevo Vallarta

Seven miles south of Bucerías is a new tourist development of exclusive private residences and the Jack Tar Hotel, an all-inclusive resort that prohibits casual visitors. Don't jump off the bus here. It's a long 2.5 mile walk to the sand.

Río Ameca

About nine miles beyond Bucerías and ten miles before Puerto Vallarta, you cross the Río Ameca, which marks the change from Mountain to Central Standard Time (turn clock ahead). This river also divides the states of Nayarit and Jalisco.

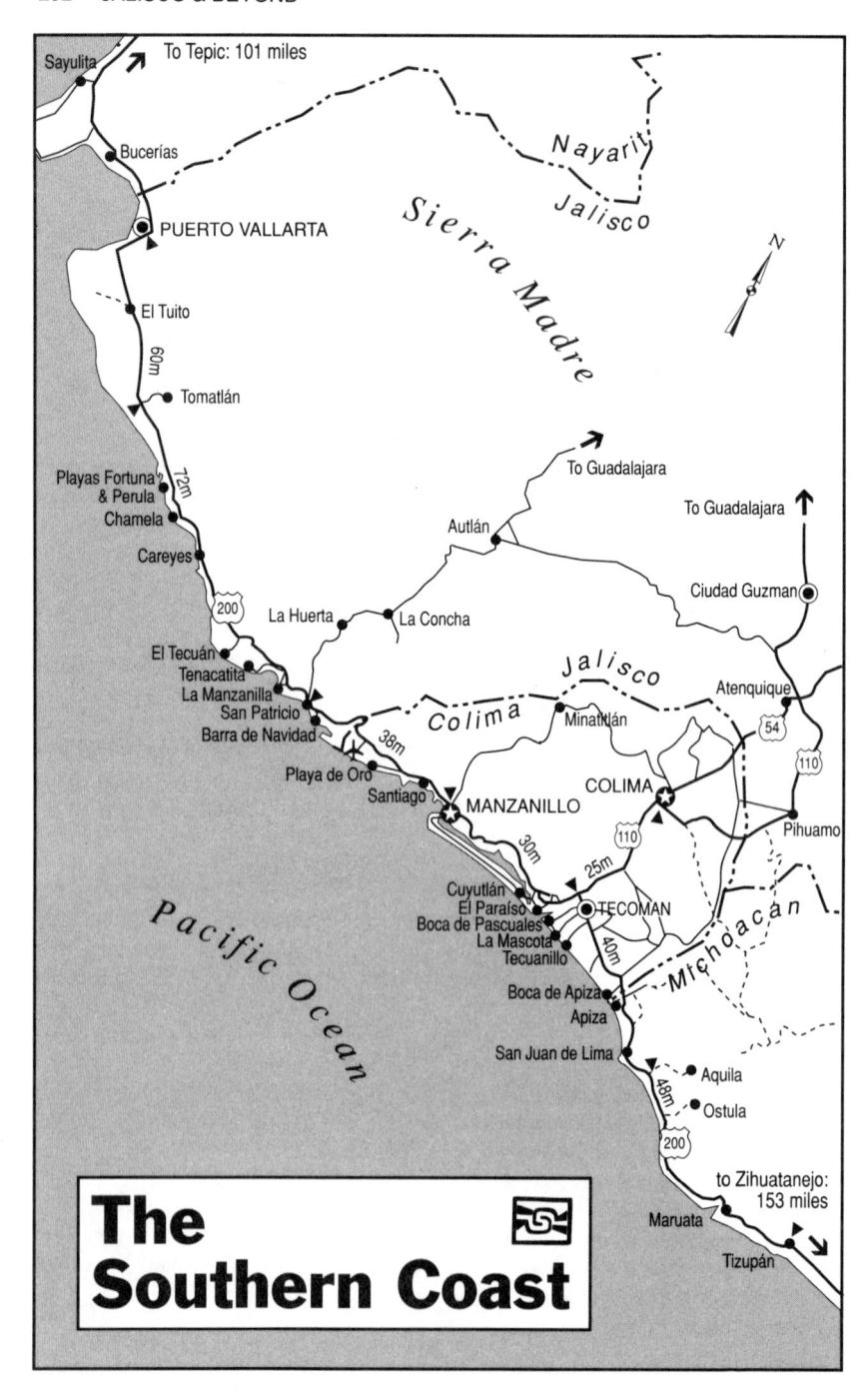

The Southern Coast

13.
Jalisco & Beyond

PUERTO VALLARTA

Puerto Vallarta has all the requisites: a jungled backdrop, a stream gurgling through the middle of town, cobblestone streets, a harbor big enough for cruise ships, golden beaches, a mild surf, sunny weather, world class resorts, and cheap hostelries. All the appearances are here, a place almost too pleasant for its own good.

Known as P.V. by anybody who stays for more than a week, this town breeds an easy familiarity in North Americans, who have done much to create the tenor of this resort. Little of Mexico's gritty side is seen, and one of the most prominent barrios is called Gringo Gulch. It is full of color and light, without the penumbra of poverty that dims the atmosphere of other cities this size. Few buildings are more than forty years old. Yet, like a well built movie set, this faux-colonial town looks as if it has existed centuries, a beguiling beauty.

It wasn't until 1851 that the first settlement, called Las Peñas, actually took root here. An agricultural town, it was renamed Puerto Vallarta in 1918 in honor of a former Jalisco governor, Ignacio L. Vallarta. The formidable Sierras kept the town isolated, and it wasn't until 1954 that regular air service began. The road from Tepic was finally paved in 1970, opening the way for tourism.

As the oft-told story goes, John Huston filmed *Night of the Iguana* here in 1963, and in this romantic jungle, Richard Burton and Elizabeth Taylor tangled in a extramarital relationship for the benefit of the world press. By association, Puerto Vallarta became a place where love flourished like the jungle around it, an eden of forbidden delight.

The myth is still alive, and two of the most visited points-of-interest are the house that Elizabeth Taylor once owned and the movie set, where the film was shot. Constant planeloads of tourists on three-day packages pump dollars into the local economy, inflating prices. For those seeking a break from reality, or the fantasy of love amid the philodendron, then P.V. may prove a perfect destination. Puerto Vallarta, after all, has been created in the image of our own wants and fantasies.

Bearings

Two main streets, both one way, run most of the city's. These streets join at either end of town, forming the exits north to Tepic or south along the coast to Manzanillo. The

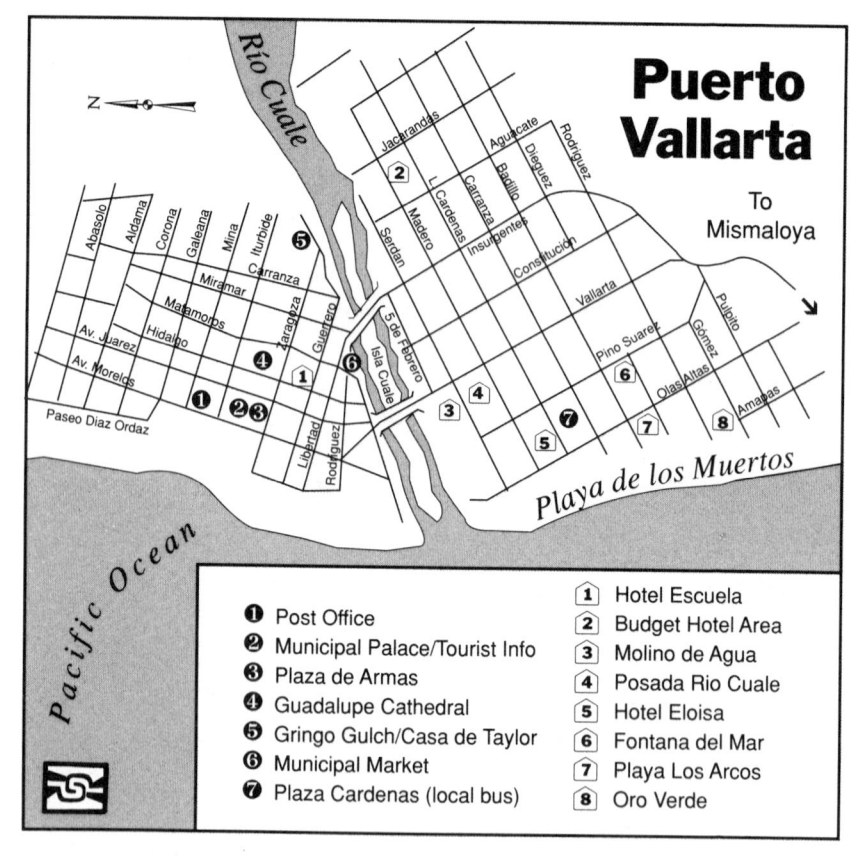

Puerto Vallarta

To Mismaloya

- ❶ Post Office
- ❷ Municipal Palace/Tourist Info
- ❸ Plaza de Armas
- ❹ Guadalupe Cathedral
- ❺ Gringo Gulch/Casa de Taylor
- ❻ Municipal Market
- ❼ Plaza Cardenas (local bus)

- ① Hotel Escuela
- ② Budget Hotel Area
- ③ Molino de Agua
- ④ Posada Rio Cuale
- ⑤ Hotel Eloisa
- ⑥ Fontana del Mar
- ⑦ Playa Los Arcos
- ⑧ Oro Verde

older commercial section is on the south side of the Río Cuale, the newer shopping-and-restaurant district on the north, where parking is scarce. A new bypass has cut down on city traffic considerably, but it still can be a slow, harrowing journey from one end of town to the other, the cobblestone streets relentlessly drumming on your nerves.

Travel Information

The city tourist information office is situated in the Presidencia Municipal, facing the Plaza de Armas between Calles Zaragoza and Iturbide one block from the malecón. Worth a visit for maps and discount coupons and to see the Manuel Lepe mural in the building's interior courtyard.

TRAVELING ABOUT
By Bus

It is easy to move about P.V. on city transportation. These comprise a fleet of buses and VW *combis*, which stop at street corners marked by bus signs, though you can often flag them down. Most leave from Plaza Lázaro Cárdenas at the corner of Calle Lázaro Cárdenas and Olas Altas, and radiate out through the city. Vans marked #1B and #03 head north through the middle of town to the big hotels and marina. You can go as far as the airport on #03 vans. Standard buses marked Pitillal go as far as the marina before turning inland. If you want to go south towards Mismaloya, you can catch a combi #02 at the Plaza Lázaro Cárdenas. Public transportation runs as late as midnight, after which you must depend on taxis or your feet.

By Taxi
Taxis are not metered, so agree on a price before getting in. Many hotel lobbies post standard tariffs.

By Car
The easiest place to compare prices is at the airport, where all major care rental companies have booths. Most travelers find they can arrange a cheaper rate from the U.S.

PLACES
Templo de Nuestra Señora de Guadalupe
This church is easily identified by its strange crown instead of a steeple. Though this church was begun during the turbulent aftermath of the Mexican Revolution, the crown was supposedly modeled on that belonging to Empress Carlotta, Maximillian's wife during the French occupation of Mexico, which would illustrate this town's ostrich-like isolation from the nationalistic fervor sweeping Mexico. The church celebrates the **Fiesta de Nuestra Señora de Guadalupe**, beginning a week before Dec. 12, when the doors remain open to welcome the processions and pilgrims. A torch, lighted at the Shrine of Guadalupe in Mexico City, is timed to arrive afoot on December 12, culminating a 570-mile relay.

Casa de Elizabeth Taylor
This house is linked to what is popularly known as the Casa de Richard Burton by a footbridge spanning the street. On 445 Calle Zaragoza, it is reached by walking up Calle Iturbide from the Plaza Municipal for five blocks, then turning right on reaching Calle Carranza. At end of the block is a fine view of the city, from what is known as Gringo Gulch. If you want a closer look at the gringo homes in P.V., check out the **Home Tours**, which are organized through the

International Friendship Club (tel. 2-54-93). These leave Sunday mornings from the plaza in front of the cathedral. This isn't cheap, but the money goes to charity.

Río Cuale
This river was once used to transport gold and silver ore from mountain mines down to the sea. Now the only thing you may see are soap bubbles, coming from the laundry ladies upstream. The river is crossed by two street bridges (Puente Viejo and Puente Nuevo by the market), and a swaying footbridge.

Just as the river divides the town, the **Isla de Río Cuale** divides the river. This long riverbed island has been made into a pleasant walkway, bordered by stores, a playground, public bathrooms, and the **Museo del Cuale**, which is a tiny one-room exhibit of Indian artifacts, this town's only acknowledgement of a prehispanic past.

Manuel Lepe House-Museum
This house-museum is the studio of Puerto Vallarta's famous native son. Run by his daughter, Marcella, on an appointment-only basis, this studio exhibits more than 60

of his paintings, including those he never finished.

Manuel Lepe died in 1984, but his popularity grows. His modern *naif* paintings are marked by a simple innocence and buoyancy, as winged children and kites float above a cavorting world. As a true naif, his technique is primitive, which means that it needs no explanation. Honored as Mexico's National Painter by President Echeverría, his "happy paintings" are far removed from the social realism of Diego Rivera. Free of ideological message, his canvases have been collected by figures as disparate as Fidel Castro, Ronald Reagan, Queen Elizabeth and Richard Nixon. Taylor and Burton bought their house on condition that the 24 Lepe paintings stayed on the walls. The pictures seem perfectly suited to the ethereal landscape of Puerto Vallarta, which can be seen below, perfectly framed by the windows of the studio where he painted.

While most Mexican cities have realistic and often tragic murals depicting their history, Puerto Vallarta chose Lepe to paint a happy mural, full of flying children. You can see the mural (his largest) in the courtyard of the **Presidencia Municipal**. It was finished by a friend after his death, and dedicated by Queen Elizabeth in 1984. The Hotel Camino Real has original Lepe paintings in most its guest rooms, and you can still buy originals at his wife's gallery, the Galeria de Laura, on 237 Lázaro Cárdenas (tel. 2-10-06) for about $2,000. Next door to the gallery, his brother, Rodrigo Lepe (tel. 2-12-77), continues the Lepe tradition, painting in a similar naif style, as does Marcella, Manuel's daughter. To visit the house-museum, inquire at the Galeria de Laura or Marcella at tel. 2-45-55). The Casa-Museo is up two blocks from Insurgentes on 485 Jacarandas at the southern end of town, and is marked by a plaque.

Art Galleries

The arts have prospered in Puerto Vallarta. Galleries are numerous. The many excellent Mexican artists indulge in technique and imagination, artistic flights of fancy supported by the dollars they earn, freeing them from the grounded monotony of more commercial work. Some of the better galleries include the **Galería Olinalá** at 268 Francisco Madero, **Galería Uno** at 561 Morelos, and the **Galería Pacífico** at 519 Juárez. For folk art, check out the **Galería de Artes Indígenas** at 274 Lázaro Cárdenas, and **La Colección** at 529 Calle Morelos. For typical mass-produced crafts, try the **Mercado Municipal**, on the north end of the Puente Viejo in a two-story building, half of which is dedicated to crafts and handiwork.

Beaches

Playa Los Muertos is the main public beach on the south side, the only sandy stretch along city center. Its name, Beach of the Dead, originates from some unrecorded massacre. The city fathers, underestimating the piratical romance of the name, have tried unsuccessfully to change it to the more innocuous Playa del Sol. This is the only close beach for those staying in the budget and moderate hotels here. It is crowded with bronzing bodies, beach vendors, and loitering gigolos—a carnival of the sands, especially during the donkey polo matches.

Note: If you want food service, the freelancers on the beach are cheaper and quicker than the hotel facilities.

The shoreline to the south is rocky, interspersed with private beaches, which you can walk as far as Concha Chinas. To the north, Los Muertos melds into **Playa Olas Altas**, where the water is a bit dirtier and brackish from Río Cuale discharge. On the north end of town, a blanket of sand stretches over most of the coastline to Bucerías.

Diving

Nobody comes to P.V. for the diving. But once here, many dive anyway, despite the often cloudy visibility. In the rainy season, when the ocean is silted with runoff from the ríos Cuale and Ameca, you might see 20 feet, a distance that increases 10 feet during the winter dry season. Best hours are before the afternoon breezes kick up wind waves. Best sites are north along the protected shore of **Punta Mita** and south around **Los Arcos**, an underwater reserve, and beyond, around **Quimixto** (some boats offer snorkeling tours). The best dive site close to town is at **Conchas Chinas**. The hotels can direct you to the various dive operations in town for advice and equipment rentals.

Harbor

The harbor three miles north of town is usually full of cruise ships and excursion boats. It is easily reached on the Pitillal bus, which makes a sharp turn inland as it passes the docks.

Fishing excursions leave from the marina, where you can go down to the docks, see what the bite is like, and make arrangements directly with the sportfishers. Smaller pangas charter off the beach at Los Muertos and in front of the Hotel Rosita, either for a few hours or the entire day.

Boat Tours also depart from the docks. Every morning, a fleet of excursion boats loads up for inexpensive trips across the bay to Los Arcos, Quimixto, Las Animas, and Yelapa, about $10 per person. These are full day cruises to small beach villages, where guests are shuttled through the surf in pangas; many cameras have been lost in the surf. In the evening, others boats such as the Sombrero (once owned by John Wayne) go on sunset booze-and-bay cruises.

Headhunters

In hotel lobbies, on the street, and in restaurants, you will be offered substantial discounts on harbor cruises and tours in return for a few minutes of your time. These people are headhunters, paid for every scalp they send to listen to a time-share sales pitch. After learning how you can invest in your vacation, you will likely end up in a

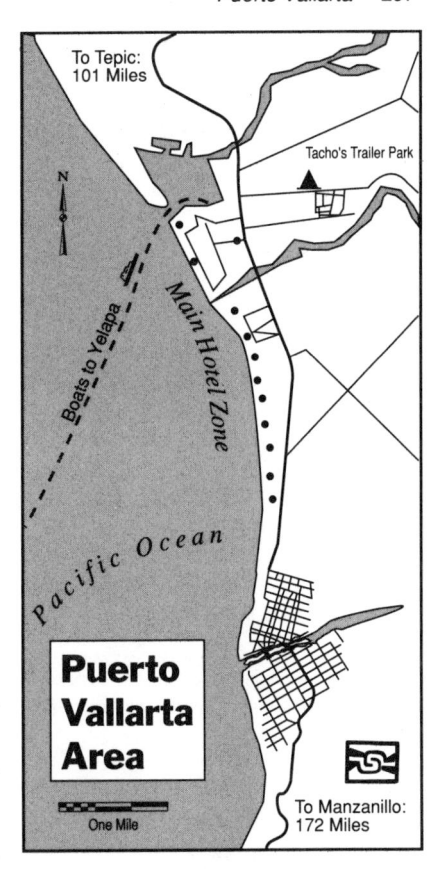

boiler room one-on-one with a pineapple-shirted salesperson imported from the U.S., who will wear down your reluctance to sign the contract in front of you, condemning you to spend two weeks of every year in a condo-hotel.

Plaza de Toros

Bullfights begin in December, run to the middle of March, and are held on Wednesdays at 5 p.m. at the **Plaza de Toros La Paloma**, across from the marina. Unlike the traditional bullfight, they usually have two instead of three matadors. According to some *aficionados*, matadors here do not work to the same life-and-death tolerances expected in the more important rings. If you want authentic atmosphere, wait until you go to Guadalajara or up to Autlán.

Puerto Vallarta Addendum

Horses can be rented from the Plaza Lázaro Cárdenas for guided tours up Río Cuale. For countryside tours, the Rancho El Ojo de Agua (tel. 2-21-65; 2-52-44) offers three-hours on horseback twice daily. Rancho White Horse (tel. 2-59-73; 2-46-16) also saddles up tourists for walks along the rustic fringe of Puerto Vallarta.

Nightlife is torrid, and the competing discos and nightclubs leaflet the city, a campaign for the tourist vote. Besides the many discos which come and go with the fashions, most of the major hotels stage Mexican fiesta nights.

Though there are no consulates, there is an acting US consular representative (tel. 2-00-69), whose office is situated above the Banco International, next to Puente Viejo, the old bridge. Office hours are morning weekdays only. A Canadian consulate can be reached at tel. 2-09-69.

If you need to get your tourist card extended, go to the Oficina de Población, on Morelos 600.

American Express traveler's services are offered at Servicios Turísticos Miller (tel. 2-11-97), at Paseo de Las Garzas in the hotel zone. For Thomas Cook traveler's checks, go to Wagons-Lit Viajes (tel. 2-00-02) at the Camino Real Hotel.

PLACES TO SLEEP

Hotels in Puerto Vallarta originally were built along Playa de los Muertos in the southern half of the city, then sprouted on the north side of town. Each year they grow bigger in size and move farther to the north. The more scenic and less developed southern coast, backed by jungled hillside, is the cognoscenti's choice, at least for those that can afford it.

Budget Hotels

If you are searching for rock bottom rates, you will find them in the southern commercial district. Most cheap hotels are on Madero, inland from Av. Insurgentes. Here you can choose among the **Hortencia** (tel. 2-24-84), the more charming **Lina** (tel. 2-16-61), the tidy **Azteca** (tel. 2-27-50), the **Cartagena**, the **Ana Liz** (tel. 2-17-57) and the superior **Villa del Mar** (tel. 2-07-85), the farthest from the beach, but the best of the bunch, which also has a TV bar.

Yazmín (tel. 2-00-87), at 168 Basilio Badillo, is the closest budget hotel to the beach, half a block away. The two-star, 52-room **Posada de Roger**, (tel. 2-08-36), nearby on 237 Basilio Badillo is on the high end of the budget scale but is so popular you generally need reservations. **Hotel Eloisa** (tel. 2-02-86), 179 Lázaro Cárdenas, is also on the high end of the budget scale, but has little to counterbalance its vacant, forlorn air except its rooftop pool, more for soaking than swimming. Its clone on the northside of town, **Hotel Rosita** (tel. 2-10-58) on 901 Paseo Díaz Ordaz, has equally little to recommend it, other than its rocky beachfront location. Centrally situated next to the cathedral on Hidalgo and Guerrero is the **Hotel Escuela CECATUR** (tel. 2-49-10), a training school for future hotel employees; it is priced higher than most budget hotels and lacks any social cachet in this town where the most frequent question is "where are you staying?"

Moderate

Hotel Playa Los Arcos (tel. 2-05-83), 380 Olas Altas, is one of the liveliest choices in this class, on the classic boy-meets-girl beach. It's less expensive adjunct, **Fontana del Mar** (tel. 20712), a block off the beach on 171 Manuel M. Diéguez, is a more tranquil alternative; some rooms here have kitchenettes (cheaper self-cooking facilities can be found at the budget Azteca). **Oro Verde Hotel** (tel. 2-15-55), next door to Hotel Playa Los Arcos, compares poorly, is hollow in spirit, and designed mostly for Canadian groups who bring their own spirit with them. Along the river at 130 Aquiles Serdán, the **Molino de Agua** (tel. 2-19-07) is a quiet oasis in a busy location; a scattering of bungalows, a bubbling whirlpool, elegant terraces, winding garden grounds, graceful pools, and gracious staff, the best choice here in this category (Warning: the caged monkey is notorious for stealing sunglasses). **Posada Río Cuale** (tel. 2-04-50), cramped on limited grounds, stands admirably on its own merits, yet falls hard when compared to Molino de Agua across the street. **Los Cuatro Vientos** (tel. 2-01-61) on 520 Calle Matamoros sits above town, looking over the rooftops; built in 1956 as one of the first hotels here, it now operates as a bed and breakfast. On the north side of town, straddling the city limits, the **Buenaventura** is more hotel-like than the out-of-town resorts, more resort-like than the in-town hotels, a fine compromise for those who can't decide where they want to stay.

Deluxe

The low end of the deluxe category is anchored by animated **Hotel Pelícanos** (tel. 2-21-07). Though hotel is off the beach, a walkway leads to a second pool overlooking the beachfront. In front of the Pelícanos, **Las Palmas Hotel** (tel. 2-04-42) continues to be plagued with maintenance glitches and lethargic staff. **Playa del Oro Hotel** (tel. 2-68-68) next to the harbor, has matured into one of the best semi-deluxe beach properties here, complete with party-size whirlpool. **Holiday Inn** (tel. 2-17-00), Av. de las Garzas, is undistinguished but reliable, a generic resort. **Bugambilias Sheraton**, (tel. 22050) looks more like an airport hotel than a tropical resort: huge, rectangular, and functional. **Krystal Vallarta** (tel. 2-14-59) is P.V.s oldest and best known resort, where you need a map to find your way to its dispersed accommodations. Challenging the Krystal complex is the Fiesta Americana triumvirate. **Fiesta Americana Puerto Vallarta** (tel. 2-20-10) is a giant dream machine, a bit contrived but standardized for the mainstream groups that congregate here. The **Fiesta Americana Plaza Vallarta Tennis & Beach Resort** (tel. 2-43-60) is pitched to tennis players with its nine-court complex, but guests still must pay up to $13 an hour to play here. **Fiesta Americana Condesa** (tel. 2-39-59), next to the Holiday Inn, is a spa resort for wealthy calorie-counters interested in anti-aging treatments.

New resorts continue to sprout to the north around the new mammoth Vallarta Marina project. **Marriott's Puerto Vallarta Resort** has followed the standard resort formula, while the **Melía Hotel** offers a bold departure with its eclectic mixture of post-modern industrial and tropical art deco.

While hotels on the north side of town are huge and commercial, those on the south side offer more character. The most unique beachfront hotel is the moderately priced **Conchas Chinas** (tel. 2-01-56), a haphazard yet ingenious arrangement of rooms that cling to the side of a cliff, falling in five flights down to a rocky beach, a place for the goat-footed (no elevators). **Camino Real** (tel. 2-55-55), on its own private beach two miles south of town, is the smoothest operation here, P.V.s premier hotel, as much for its staff as its privileged location. Two miles farther south, **Garza Blanca** (tel. 2-10-23) enjoys an exclusive position as the only luxury villa operation on the beach in P.V.; its stratospheric rates are compromised by the time share hucksterism.

Camping

There are only two trailer parks in Puerto Vallarta, neither of them on the beach. **Tacho's Trailer Park** (tel. 2-09-79), set back half a mile from the ferry terminal opposite the village of Pitillal, is a vast grassy place with a pool; the buses to P.V. pass right by, making it a more convenient spot than the other trailer park.

For on-the-beach camping you need to head to north to Bucerías, Piedra Blanca or south along the Costa Alegre.

ARRIVING & DEPARTING
By Air

The airport is five miles north of town, along the highway to Tepic. The *colectivos* running directly from the airport to the hotels are cheap, but three persons or more can save money by hiring a taxi. There are souvenir and duty-free shops (no great savings), a restaurant and bar, and seven car rental agencies here. The casa de cambio offers an equitable, convenient exchange rate, probably the best place to sell leftover pesos before flying home.

By Bus

A new *central camionera* should be open by now on the northern outskirts of town near the airport, just off the highway to Tepic; before, the five main bus lines were congregated in separate terminals along a few blocks around Calle Insurgentes south of the Río Cuale. Buses depart to Guadalajara (6 hours), Mexico City (15 hours), and Manzanillo (five hours) about every hour, and north to Mazatlan (9 hours) with less frequency. *Tres Estrellas del Oro* is the most comfortable line here, but *Transportes del Pacífico* is the main mule, running to Manzanillo hourly, and to Tepic every half hour; take this bus if you plan on going to Nuevo Vallarta, Bucerías, Crucero Cruz de Huanacaxtle, Sayulita, San Francisco, Rincón de Guayabitos, Las Varas, or Compostela.

You can catch the second class *Transportes de Cihuatlán* for coastal places to the south, like Mismaloya, Boca de Tomatlán, Bahía Chametla, and Tenacatita. Transportación Medina on Calle Brasil 1269, near the corner of Calle Honduras runs local buses out to Punta Mita.

By Car

Puerto Vallarta is about a 250-mile drive from Guadalajara, a 98-mile drive from Tepic, and a 132-mile drive from Barra de Navidad to the south, all on two-lane paved highways.

By Ferry

The ferries, once operated by the government, are no longer operating to Cabo San Lucas or La Paz. Perhaps some day they will again.

BAHÍA DE BANDERAS
THE SOUTH SHORE

Much of the south shore of Bahía Banderas can only be reached by boat. Hwy. 200 skirts Mismaloya and touches Boca de Tomatlán before heading up into the Sierras. To reach points beyond—Las Animas, Quimixto, Yelapa—most travelers take one of the tour boats leaving daily from the Puerto Vallarta harbor.

MISMALOYA

Beauty, in this case, has provoked its own destruction. About the only people who don't object to what has happened to this once-pristine bay are guests at **La Jolla de Mismaloya**, a behemoth condominium project that dominates the bayfront. It stands in curious juxtaposition to what remains of the original set of *The Night of the Iguana*, which helped spawn the tourist industry that now engulfs it. To see how striking the bay once was, you will have to go to the bar at La Jolla, where they show endless reruns of that haunting movie.

For a more primitive encounter, visit **Chino's Paradise**, a rustic restaurant hidden in the jungle alongside a boulder-strewn river; take the dirt road that follows the river up 1.2 miles to Chinos. *Note: to get to Mismaloya, you can catch the colectivo (#02) from Puerto Vallarta at Plaza Lázaro Cárdenas; these run about four times an hour.*

BOCA DE TOMATLÁN

About ten miles south of Puerto Vallarta the highway turns inland at a small bay where the Río Horcones has deposited a fine little beach. Big views of the coast can be seen before reaching the bay at Le Kliff restaurant, which was originally planned as a high dive attraction. The idea was abandoned when they couldn't find anybody willing to dive 110 feet into the surf.

John Huston anchored a boat in this protected bay to speed him to his retreat at Las Caletas. Chartering a panga from this bay remains a much quicker way to reach Quimixto, Animas, and Yelapa than riding the troop ships from Puerto Vallarta.

Farther inland, 3.5 miles from the coast, the Río Los Horcones rushes to meet Río Peña Blanca, a place called **La Junta Verano** (the summer meeting place). A restaurant, Chico's Paradise, is built here, alongside the clear water which slides over smooth granite, ripples though sluices, slams into boulders, boils, twists, falls, gurgles, bubbles and then drops into turbulent whirlpools. Enter at your own risk. Ashore is a maze of dining terraces, rickety bridges, palapas, and trails.

City buses do not go farther than Mismaloya. To get to Boca or to Chico's by bus, you will have to take the Pacífico or Cihuatlán buses from P.V., and wave them down to return to town. You shouldn't have to wait more than half an hour.

PLAYA LAS ANIMAS

This is the first sandy beach south of Boca de Tomatlán, a 400-yard stretch on which thumps a calm surf. There is a village here, but it is not developed like Yelapa. Some people ride one of the excursion boats here, camp, then return the next day, week, or month.

PLAYA QUIMIXTO

A mile beyond La Animas, this palm-thatched village, set back from an arc of sand beach, is not as well known as Yelapa, but is growing in popularity, a stop for the excursion boats. Dive boats come here for snorkeling and scuba, others for the beach. Horses can be rented for a trip up two miles

to the waterfalls which drop into a small dammed pool.

YELAPA

The most popular nautical tour from P.V., the fleet sails out of the harbor around 9 a.m., arriving two hours later at Yelapa, 25 miles away. After a sometimes precarious landing through the surf, hundreds of tourists spend four hours swimming in the surf, eating at the restaurants, and hiking to the waterfalls, returning to their boats in the early afternoon. A few always stay behind, to spend the night in this kerosene-lighted village far from civilization (but close to a liquor store).

The big attraction here is the waterfall, which can be reached by hiking about 20 minutes up from the beach along a footpath though the village. In the winter dry season, this waterfall may be little more than a drip.

In the 1970s, Yelapa was a counterculture paradise. This back-to-nature idealism still exits, with lots of expatriated Americans living in casitas, adding considerably to the population (about 600). The Hotel Nuevo Lagunita ($$; tel. 2-19-32) comprises about 45 palapas, with mosquito nets over the beds, a pool, and electricity until about 11 p.m., when the generator is turned off; reservations can be made at 62 31 de Mayo in Puerto Vallarta. There are some palapas for monthly rental. *Tip: bring a flashlight.*

🝔🝔🝔🝔🝔🝔🝔🝔🝔🝔🝔🝔🝔🝔🝔🝔

PUERTO VALLARTA TO MANZANILLO

Hwy. 200 travels 172 miles from Puerto Vallarta to Manzanillo, paralleling the coast, which is notched with four major bays—Chametla, Tenacatita, Navidad and Manzanillo—with mostly unpopulated deserted beaches, coconut plantations, and rocky headlands in-between.

EL TUITO

Seventeen miles from Boca de Tomatlán, Hwy. 200 crosses the western flanks of the Sierra Madre Occidental, passing El Tuito, set amid the *pinos* (pines). Higher up in the mountains, the campesinos tend fields of agave, which is made into a local bootleg liquor, called *raicilla*. It is considered better than tequila or mezcal, which it is, if you base your judgement on alcoholic content. Though the local product has made El Tuito famous, it is as discreetly sold as it is brewed. Just ask at one of the stores along the highway. They will direct you to a back street where you can buy old rum bottles filled with the colorless firewater, stoppered with corn husks.

TOMATLÁN

Beyond El Tuito, the road drops down 33 miles to the Tomatlán turnoff, just after crossing the Río Tomatlán which winds down out of the Sierras. This river watered the fields of the early Aztec, who cultivated the first tomatos, a vegetable unknown to the Old World. A colonial town replaced the indigenous village, but kept the name, "Place of the Tomatos." The Templo Parroquial on top of the hill was dedicated to the Virgen de la Concepción in 1775. This town celebrates July 25 and Dec. 12.

BAHIA CHAMETLA

This elongated bay stretches for more than eight miles, then reforms again as Bahia Careyes. More than nine islands dot the bay, sheltering the water and threatening navigation. The explorer Francisco Cortés died in these waters during a storm, seeking refuge and finding shipwreck. The Spanish later built a garrison here, which was attacked in 1578 by Sir Francis Drake. Nine years later, Thomas Cavendish also fired onto the fort. The dictator Porfirio Díaz built his Hacienda de Chamela here, using it as a winter refuge until the first stirrings of the Mexican Revolution in 1909.

Though the highway gives easy access to the bay, little has been developed due to its isolated location 90 miles south of Puerto Vallarta, 75 miles north of Manzanillo. The bay is divided into the northern beaches of La Fortuna and La Pérula, the central bay of Chamela (where there is a village of sorts), and the more privileged southern shore of Bahía Careyes, which is mostly blocked from public access by tourist development.

Playas La Fortuna & La Pérula

These beaches mark the northern reaches of Bahía Chameta, 84 miles south of Puerto Vallarta, seven miles from El Tuito. The point of land is called Punta Pérula. The sandy beach which hooks south changes its name from La Pérula to La Fortuna as it moves away from the rocky point. You turn off the highway at an ejido called **La Fortuna** and follow the rutted dirt road 1.3 miles to the small village called **Pérula**, an ungroomed settlement of cinderblock with little appeal beyond its long beachfront. In addition to **Playa Pérula Trailer Park**, there is a surprisingly well run hotel, **Playa Dorada Bungalows** ($$; tel. 47-53-67), offering clean kitchenettes.

Playa Chamela

This beach lies about two miles south of the

turn-off to La Fortuna. A short graded road runs down to a long stretch of sandy beach guarded by the islands of San Andrés, Pasavera, Colorado, and Cocina. The most unusual place to stay here is **Villa Polinesia Camping Club** (tel. 22-39-40 in Guadalajara), where you can pick from a trailer park, strange loft bungalows facing the ocean, or one of the 35 airless cement tents that together look more like a mausoleum than a campground (and are usually just as empty). The communal bathrooms are clean, the restaurant impressive, but rates tend to fluctuate wildly depending on who is in charge.

Next to it, there is a more conventional bungalow operation with a pool, while just to the north is the vastly overpriced **Hotel Suites Chamela** ($$), crudely built and suffering an advanced state of decrepitude. Along the highway, **Motel Chamela** ($) provides the best facilities at the cheapest rates, a three-story place of nine rooms, complete with pool. In Chamela, more a roadstop than a village, there is a supermarket and restaurant. **Access:** buses going to Manzanillo and Puerto Vallarta pass by hourly, and most stop at Chamela.

Bahía Careyes

This cloverleaf bay lies ten miles south of Chamela. On its shores sit a very private **Club Med** and the **Hotel Plaza Careyes**, through which you can gain access to the beach (just say you are going in for a drink). Hotel Plaza Careyes ($$; tel. 7-00-10) suffers as well as benefits from its stunning but obscure location, a place of high fashion and uncertain hot water. The sheltered water in the bay is clearer than elsewhere along the coast, up to 60 feet visibility at times, and the rocky shoreline is scalloped with private beaches.

The closest public beach is at **Playa Teopa**, a mile to the south, with easy short access from the highway. This steep sandy beach remains undeveloped except for a fishing hut at one end.

El Tecuán

The desolate beach stretching north from Tenacatita can be reached at El Tecuán, six miles off the highway via a winding narrow road through a bucolic landscape. Once a working cattle and mango ranch, it now struggles to attract tourists and remains blissfully unsuccessful. On the bluff is one of the Pacific Coast's more remote resorts, 36-room **Hotel El Tecuán** ($$; Desarrollos Turísticos Tecuán, Garibaldi 1676, Guadalajara, Jalisco, tel. 16-00-85; local tel. 7-01-31). From its perch you can soak up views of the coast and lagoon; modern colonial rooms are air conditioned and guests have free use of canoes, bikes, tennis court, and pool. By driving down the airfield runway (stop, look up, and listen), you come to the estero, where there is a trailer park (pay at the hotel). Unfortunately, only car camping is allowed (no tents), and there are few facilities, just an idyllic coconut grove overlooking the river as it empties into the Pacific. Long lonely beaches stretch off north and south. Nothing but solitude and surf. **Access:** turnoff to El Tecuán is 12.4 miles south of Careyes, marked by a giant landlocked lighthouse.

BAHIA TENACATITA

The coves that make up this bay are fringed by a lush landscape of palms and dark sand beaches, jungled hillsides, and primitive campgrounds. There are four access points to the bay: Playa Tenacatita, Los Locos, Boca de Iguana, and Manzanilla, each different.

Playa Tenacatita

This is the least crowded beach, reached by a 5.6 mile dirt road picked up at the southern end of the bridge over Río Purificación, about 2.5 miles south of the turn-off to El Tecuán. Halfway to the beach you pass **Rebalsito**, a small village with limited supplies.

The beach here was a way station on the

old hippie trail, and though those halcyon days are over, the beach continues to attract its share of alternative lifestyles. The beach is as wide as a freeway, and quite shallow, so the waves are gentle, the stingrays plentiful. More violent surf can be found to the north, around the rocky point, where you will find the more private **Playas La Mora** and **Gris**, exposed to the brunt of the waves.

There are some ramada restaurants where the road hits the beach. You can camp almost anywhere, though most people homestead one of the many dilapidated palapas up on the sandy berm overlooking the main beach. **Access:** no public transport runs to the beach. Once you make your way to the highway, you can usually pick up a bus by walking to Agua Caliente, a small village less than a mile north of the turn-off to Tenacatita.

Playa Los Locos

Turn off Hwy. 200 five miles south of the Tenacatita turn-off, then pound 2.4 miles over cobblestone, through thick jungle. Formerly a retreat for the sugarcane labor syndicate, it has been leased out to an international subsidiary of Holiday Inn. Access to the public has been closed. To get to this beach is almost impossible unless you are willing to pay a high day use fee at **Hotel Fiesta Americana Los Angeles Locos** (tel. 7-0220), where food, drinks and entertainment are included in the hotel rates. Even then, the security police at the gate escort you down to the hotel, where more guards with truncheons insure that your intentions are honest. Shame, because the beaches here are the most spectacular of all.

Boca de Iguanas

This place has become one of the most popular camping sites between Puerto Vallarta and Acapulco, a once desolate beach of granulated sugar, hard as a plank. A lagoon breaks out of the jungle here, opening to usually tranquil seas, calmed by its guarded location at the head of the bay.

Three trailer parks now offer camping. Of the three, the original **Boca de Iguanas** ($$) at the end of the road, across a narrow bridge, seems to blend into its exotic surroundings. Frondy shade and slung hammocks. Another trailer park is in back, filling only when the other is full; some bungalows ($$) are also for rent here. Just down the beach in a primitive campsite, multi-colored dome tents stand like mushrooms under a waving canopy of palms. The beach stretches all the way to La Manzanilla, hard enough in spots to gallop, rental horses willing. The 1.7 mile dirt access road is 2.5 miles south of the turn-off to Los Locos, 10 miles north of the junction of Hwys. 200 and 80 (the road to Guadalajara).

La Manzanilla

This village marks the southern end of Bahía Tenacatita, the only shoreside village on Bahía Tenacatita, a resort for working class *Tapatíos* (residents of Guadalajara) driving down from the city. A paved mile-long road runs from Hwy. 200 two miles south of the turnoff for Boca de Iguanas, at the K 14 marker. This is a kind of bare bones alternative to the budget resort of Barra de Navidad, a place of about 500 people, cheap fish restaurants and few hotels, such as **Posada Lusita** ($) and **Enaxxi Hotel** ($), where guests have use of a communal kitchen. Main stop for most people is **Posada del Cazador** ($), a block from the beach on the main street.

BAHIA DE NAVIDAD

This minor bay played a major role in the discovery of California. The two-mile stretch of sand is bracketed by rocky points and backed at the southern end by a lagoon. It was from here that Rodríguez Cabrillo raised canvas on June 27, 1542, his two locally built boats leaving on the first European voyage to Alta California. Three months later, on September 28, they sailed into San Diego bay, "a port, closed and very good." These were the first Europeans to set foot in Alta California. Cabrillo, who marched with Cortés during the conquest of Mexico, later slipped and broke his arm, died, and was buried on San Miguel Island. His grave has never been found, but his statue stands on Point Loma, next to the lighthouse that guards the entrance to San Diego Bay. His two ships survived tremendous storms to make it back to Navidad, completing the circle.

A much larger and more lucrative circle was drawn from Bahía de Navidad to the Orient and back, the route of the Manila Galleons. Miguel López de Legazpi left from here to conquer the Philippines. And when Urdaneta departed from Navidad on November 21, 1564, raising the coast of the Philippines three months later in record time, a trade route was established. Many crates of Oriental treasure were unloaded on the sands here. Acapulco and San Blas eventually eclipsed the importance of Navidad, and the settlement lapsed into dormancy.

The two towns, **San Patricio** and the more colorful **Barra de Navidad**, have established themselves on opposite ends of the bay, separated by a steep grainy beach swept clean by the big winter waves. The fishing economies of both have been supplanted by tourism, now that Mex. 80 to Guadalajara has cut driving time down to about five hours. A shuttle bus runs between the towns, which are connected by Hwy. 200.

SAN PATRICIO - MELAQUE

This northern part of the bay is as undefined as its name, a hyphenated marriage of overlapping interests. San Patricio is the commercial area set back from the beach, a modern Mexican village with a plaza, church, and many shops selling trade goods and beach trivia; there is a bank, post office, and a place to make phone calls. Melaque, the beach area, is mostly taken up by Mexican tourist-grade resorts, functional but sterile of character. A free shoreside campground marks the northern point, where the road ends in a bare field with no facilities.

The beach here is calmer than at Barra de Navidad, the water clearer for diving.

At the junction of Hwy. 200 and 80 there is a short dirt road to another smaller beach, **Playa Cuastecomate**, a rustic village, and lots of seafood restaurants.

San Patricio-Melaque may seem dull for much of the year, but it celebrates Saint Patrick's Day with uninhibited enthusiasm.

GUADALAJARA REDUX

The quickest way to get up to Guadalajara from Bahía de Navidad is via Hwy. 80, which climbs 66 miles up to Autlan (one of the best places to watch bullfights). From Autlan, the highway travels another 22 miles to Union de Tula, situated in a river valley and known for brewing Mezcal. The next 64 miles run through small farming towns until reaching Villa Corona, which is situated in an area full of hot springs and resorts. Another 25 miles brings you into Guadalajara, a total distance of 177 miles.

The dyed eggs cracked on your head will color your hair red for days (foreigners are fair game), and the fireworks literally can set you afire. Festivities last for a week, from March 10 to 17. Wear old clothes.

Travel Information

The tourist office (tel. 7-01-00), is of limited help but conveniently situated next to the Hotel Melaque on Av. Las Palmas.

Places to Sleep

Most of the hotels are on Calle Gómez Farías, the beachfront street, and the better choices are **Vista Hermosa** ($$; tel. 7-00-02), **Posada Las Gaviotas** ($$), **Hotel Las Brisas** ($$; tel. 7-01-08), and **Hotel Legazpi**. The main catch-all is the vacuous **Hotel Melaque** (tel. 7-00-01). Cheaper hotels can be found by walking inland.

Camping

Besides the free campground at the end of town by the rocky point, there is **La Playa Trailer Park** ($$; tel. 7-00-65), on the beach on 250 Gómez Farías, the only one alongside the bay.

Arriving & Departing

The major bus lines stop here on their way to Puerto Vallarta and Guadalajara (both about five-hour trips) or to Manzanillo. The station is a block from the beach, on the corner of the two main streets in town, López Mateos and Gómez Farías.

BARRA DE NAVIDAD

This small village of cobblestone streets long has been a hangout for North American bohemia. Known simply as Barra, this town has achieved a legendary reputation, where strange coincidences and chance meetings occur. Much of this synchronicity can be explained by its reputation in the travel underground, the friendliness and tolerance of the natives, the beauty of the bay, the tropical laissez-faire atmosphere,

free camping. A certain type of people just naturally congregate here, creating their own coincidences.

This same laid-back allure is now attracting a more mainstream tourism as people find here what other resorts lack: a vacation retreat free of commercial hype. Some people fear the consequences, since Barra itself is already built-out, with little room for growth except on the fringes. Barra has the traveler's essentials: a bank, post office, and long distance telephone service, but not much else. A new tourist development is trying to take root on the hills across the lagoon, condominiums are springing up in back, but the town itself remains a tranquil place, where watching the street vendor dip churros (batter-fried dough sticks) into a boiling vat of oil is often the evening's entertainment.

The setting is spectacular. Built on a sand bar, it is backed by a vast lagoon, and fronted by a long steep beach. The wedge-shaped town is perched like a challenge between the two. When the winter surf is particularly big, waves can sweep right into the hotels and seafood restaurants, leaving fish behind.

The town is even more exposed to summer hurricanes, which periodically threaten to erase the town. A few years ago, as a hurricane was battering the town, the villagers gathered in the only safe place, the church, to pray for relief. As they prayed, there was sharp crack, as both arms of Christ fell to his side, released from the cross. The storm suddenly abated. Stunned, the villagers declared it for what it was, a local miracle. The villagers never dared nail the arms back to the cross. If you go into the church today, you still will see the arms resting at his side, free of the the cross. Somehow, Barra is much like this, a hang-loose place of divine coincidence.

Spending the Night

With luck, you will be able to rent one of the

palm and brick bungalows that go for a few dollars a day. Otherwise, you have a raft of budget hotels to climb on. **Hotel Jalisco** ($), on Calle Jalisco 81, is a favorite of those looking for the cheapest beds.

A bit higher in price, but much higher in quality is the trim **Hotel Delfín** ($$; tel. 7-00-68) on Calle Morelos 23; run by a former German swimming star (yes, it has a pool) and his wife, it's clean, has a cafe, and draws raves from guests. Across the street, facing the lagoon is **Hotel Sands** ($$; tel. 7-00-18), on Calle Morelos 24; this is something of a party hotel, with a disco and lively happy hours around the biggest pool in Barra. On the ocean side, along Calle Legaspi, **Hotel Barra de Navidad** (tel. 7-01-22) and **Hotel Tropical** (tel. 7-00-20) are priced the same as the Sands, but the concrete bunkers lack character. **Hotel Bogavante** (tel. 7-03-84), also on Legaspi, doesn't have a pool like the other two, but the hallway opens out onto the sand, the rates are cheaper, the service better.

If you plan to stay awhile, the oceanfront **Bungalows Karelia** offers inexpensive monthly rates if you can find a room. The top hotel in town is **Hotel Cabo Blanca** ($$$; tel. 7-01-68), named after the Charles Bronson movie filmed here in 1980. A beachhead of luxury (but without a beach), it is situated on the back canals of the lagoon, a ten-minute walk to the ocean (or via shuttle). Tennis, pool, air conditioned rooms, lots of grass and flowers, all are kept in fine shape.

You can camp for free on the sand bar. Just watch out for big waves that infrequently sweep across the sand.

Arriving & Departing

Barra is 17 miles north of the Playa de Oro international airport, 38 from Manzanillo. Buses heading to Guadalajara and Puerto Vallarta (five hours) can be caught in town across from the plaza principal, as well as more frequent trips to Manzanillo. You can also catch the Melaque shuttle here.

Making Churros, Barra de Navidad

COLIMITA & LA CULEBRA

From the embarcadero at Barra, you can take a fairly expensive panga ride (prices are regulated by a *sindicato*) across the lagoon to Colimita. The attraction, other than the boat ride, is the *pescado sarandeado*, a grilled fish marinated in chile sauce, served in the waterside palapas. Behind the restaurants is a small village, Colimita, which can also be reached by road via La Culebra.

From the junction of Barra de Navidad and Hwy. 200 it is five miles to the paved turnoff to **Playa La Culebra**. The road cleaves through fields of coconut and banana trees, and *aguacate* (avocado) orchards for 4.5 miles, until reaching a long run of deserted beach and wild waves. The paved road parallels the beach north for another 2.5 miles, until it turns inland and ends at Colimita, on the other side of the lagoon from Barra de Navidad. The beach at La Culebra is edged by thorny dunes, with areas to camp.

CIHUATLÁN

This traditional Mexican town offers little to travelers who don't appreciate its rough edges and narrow streets. But passing carnivals and occasional matadors play to the locals, and the fiestas here can be a rough-and-tumble experience. This small city lies on the north bank of the Río Cihuatlán, in the state of Jalisco. Cross the bridge, and you are in the state of Colima.

PLAYA DE ORO

Similar to La Culebra, Playa de Oro is another long stretch of open beach, its primitive appeal compromised only by a few bungalows, and the flight path overhead. From the highway turnoff 17 miles south of Barra de Navidad, about four miles south of the airport turnoff, the cobbled road winds four miles to the beach. A steep surf, excellent for bodysurfing, often breaks here.

MANZANILLO

Manzanillo is a sailor's town, the most important working port on Mexico's Pacific coast. A nautical tradition of 500 years hangs over this city like a topsail. Buildings crowd along the waterfront and zócalo, a nautical raft of rickety buildings, some done in 1930s *streamline moderne*, with portholes instead of windows, and balconies that look like the bridge of a ship. Its streets often turn into stairs, climbing the steep slopes of Vigía Grande and Vigía Chica, historic lookouts where bronze bells once rang whenever ships appeared.

A few curio stores are scattered around town, but it is marine industry, not tourism, that powers this town: import and export houses, ship brokers, merchant marine flophouses, a Pemex fuel storage plant, tuna fleet, a Naval station, and a waterfront rail station where the tracks end. A tough-looking red-light district thrives along the backside of the city.

The 19th century zócalo, **Járdin Alvaro Obregón**, faces the waterfront where a web of lines moor the freighters and tramp steamers to the docks. You can sit on the wrought iron benches and watch world commerce at work.

Manzanillo belongs as much to the Pacific Rim as it does to Mexico. Though there is no historical evidence, according to common tradition, the Coliman Indians who lived here were visited by Chinese and Malaccan traders long before the arrival of the Spanish. Cortés, upon hearing of this pact of friendship between the Orientals and the Indians, sent Gonzalo de Sandoval to conquer the area.

They didn't find any Orientals but they did find great stands of trees, which were cut to build the first boats on the west coast of Mexico. These ships went on to discover the Pacific Coast and to establish trade with the Orient. Though iron freighters now replace the Manila galleons, the same trade route has been plied for four centuries, forming this town's character.

Across the bay from Manzanillo are the resorts. Because Manzanillo is no quaint colonial town, these resorts have no civic obligation to mimic the regional architecture. Instead, the Santiago peninsula is a dream flight of modern Moorish fantasy. The cupolas, spires, and arches are all painted white, in polar opposition to the colorful worldliness of Manzanillo. The two complement each other. One offers reality, the other escape. Travelers can take their pick.

Bearings

The city centers on the waterfront and zócalo. Close by you will find the post and telegraph offices, a place to make phone calls, the *Presidencia Municipal*, and a bank. The commercial center is situated five blocks inland, where Av. México and Calle Cuauhtémoc intersect. In this area are the cheap *casas de huéspedes*, the **Mexicana** and **Aeromexico** ticket offices, and some curio stores. The public market is for local consumption (of little interest to most travelers, except hungry ones), situated four blocks to the east, off Cinco de Mayo.

Travel Information

The tourism office is conveniently situated off the zócalo at 21 de Marzo and Calle Juárez. The federal tourism office is on 244 Calle Juárez, on the fourth floor (tel. 2-20-90).

Traveling About

Public buses run frequently, leaving the train station and running along Av. Niños Héroes, then north on Hwy. 200, passing all the beaches. The Ruta 1 and 2 "Miramar"

buses run to Santiago, passing by Playa Azul, the Santiago peninsula, Playa Olas Altas, and Miramar. The Ruta 3 bus that goes to Las Brisas leaves from the public market, but you can pick it up anywhere along Av. Niños Héroes. The bus marked *centro* runs from the bus station to the city center.

Beaches

The beaches of Manzanillo are much more sheltered than those at Barra de Navidad, and are cleaner the farther north you go. There are basically two beaches which rim the two bays of Manzanillo and Santiago, but they are given many names.

Playa San Pedrito is the closest beach to the city, an urban arch of sand that holds more trash than attraction. Across the estero, **Playa Las Brisas** is bordered by numerous inexpensive hotels looking out on the occasional freighters anchored offshore waiting for dock space. Unless you are staying here,

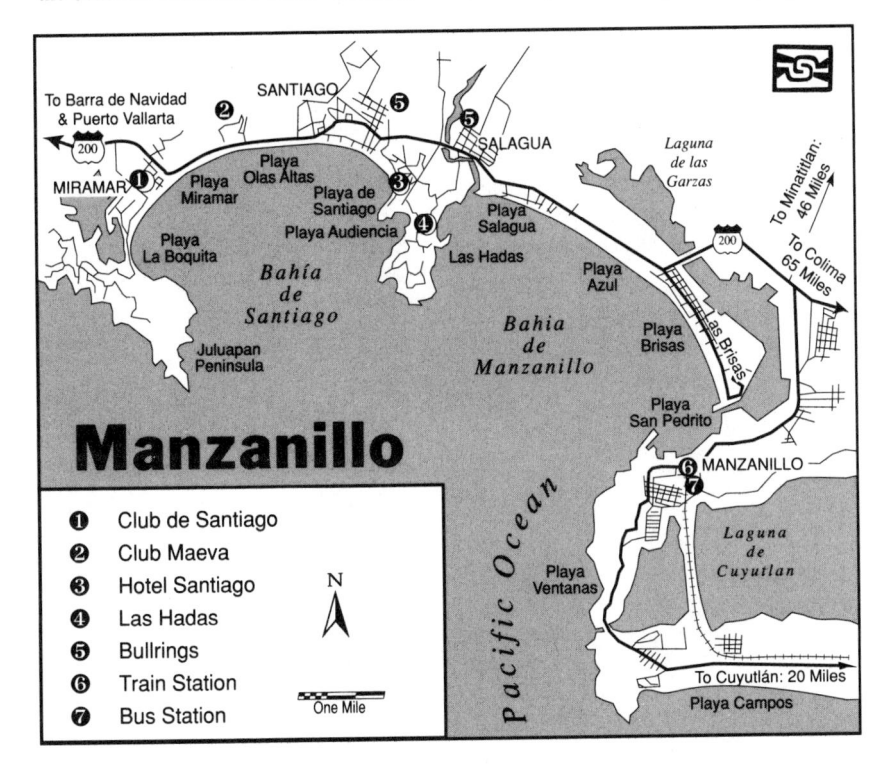

❶	Club de Santiago
❷	Club Maeva
❸	Hotel Santiago
❹	Las Hadas
❺	Bullrings
❻	Train Station
❼	Bus Station

there is little reason to visit.

Playa Las Brisas turns into **Playa Azul**, something of a misnomer, as it is still close to the discharge from the bay. But it is the longest beach here, the surf breaks mildly; it is often deserted. At its north end, it turns into **Playa Salahua**, where the sand piles into dunes. An important Indian town called Tzalahua was situated here. From Salahua, the coastline bends out to form the Santiago peninsula, a Moorish fantasy. The beach notched into its end is one of the more scenic and popular, **Playa Audiencia**, reached on a mile-long cobbled road. According to legend, Cortés met here in an *audiencia* (audience) with important Indian chiefs.

The fantasy architecture of this peninsula is worth a tour, especially **Las Hadas**, built on a preColumbian village site. Security stands at the gate; just tell them you are going in for lunch or dinner. On the north side of the Santiago peninsula, **Playa de Santiago** stretches off for about a mile: shallow, calm, streaked with dark sand. This same beach turns into **Playa Olas Altas** along the head of the bay, then becomes **Playa Miramar**, where Club Maeva operates a popular beach club which rents watersports equipment. The beach continues on, turning into the private Club de Santiago, which is not as private as its

security gates suggests (just drive on in).

From Santiago, Hwy. 200 turns inland around the Laguna Santiago and the Juluapán Peninsula. One last beach, **La Boquita** (The Little Mouth), is situated where Laguna Santiago empties into the Pacific. Access is from Hwy. 200 at **El Naranjo**, then west for about three miles, passing through a security gate.

Events

Manzanillo celebrates Carnival with particular enthusiasm, as well as the Día de Guadalupe on December 12, when the Virgen Morena is paid tribute by thousands of pilgrims.

Manzanillo Addendum

There is no great diving in the area, though better visibility and rocks can be found at the ends of the peninsulas, around the shipwrecks at Playa Boquita and in the protected waters of Playa Audiencia.

Any hotel and most waterfront restaurants can arrange fishing charters. The sailfish bite from November to December.

A volunteer U.S. consular representative can be contacted at Club Santiago mornings at tel. 3-04-13.

Tourist cards can be extended at the Oficina de Migración, on the second floor of the Edificio Federal at Playa San Pedrito.

An inexpensive sunset bay cruise leaves from the Muelle La Perlita in Manzanillo every night; tel. 2-22-62 for exact times.

PLACES TO SLEEP
Budget Hotels

The cheapest beds are found in Manzanillo's urban center, the casas *de huéspedes* clustered just east of Av. México, five blocks up from the waterfront. Hotels **Savoy** and **Miramar** on either end of the zócalo are mostly for sailors to whom an iron bunk is home. **Hotel Emperador**, set around a small atrium half a block off the zócalo is a better choice; its little cafe is locally popular. The most prestigious budget address is the more expensive **Hotel Colonial**, on 100 Av. México, a block in back of the zócalo (un-air conditioned rooms are cheapest). The only budget hotels on the beach are on the aging north side of the Santiago peninsula. The **Hotel Anita** (tel. 3-01-61) and the **Hotel Marlyn** (tel. 3-01-07) face the flat beach, which is what you pay for, as all else is haphazardly maintained, including the swimming pools.

Moderate

There are few hotels filling the gap between budget and deluxe hotels. The two main moderate hotels on the beach are **La Posada** and **Hotel Playa de Santiago**. La Posada (tel. 3-18-99), at the south end of Las Brisas, six miles from Manzanillo, advertises itself as a "passionate pink palace." Like a lady with too much rouge, it is painted a more garish shade of pink with each passing year. Owned by a U.S. expatriate, it is clubbish, casual, and faces the beach (most stick to the small pool). The less expensive Hotel Playa de Santiago (tel. 3-02-70) is a favorite with those who want a seaview balcony, a quiet location, and do not mind being on the unfashionable side of the Santiago peninsula in a hotel of faded glory.

Deluxe

The **Hotel Playa de Oro**, near the Santiago Peninsula at K15 of Hwy. 200 is a new resort that hopes to yank the low end of the deluxe market from under Club Maeva and Las Hadas. But its off-beach location (despite what its name implies), tiny dark rooms, and maze-like grounds conspire against its success. **Las Hadas** (tel. 3-00-00) remains one of the most impressive resorts around, its fantasy architecture, influenced by Gaudi and funded by a Bolivian copper magnate, has been imitated by the many buildings around it. It is worth a visit. **Club Maeva** (fax: 3-03-95) across from Playa Miramar is a middle class version of Las Hadas. Most guests never leave this 90-acre, self-contained resort because

of the constant activities and numerous facilities, including what is claimed to be Latin America's largest pool. There is also a new waterpark here, open to non-guests as well.

Camping

Despite the vast beachfront, if you can't get into one of 15 sites at **El Cid Trailer Park**, K9 on the main highway north, then the nearest beachfront trailer park is in Melaque, 36 miles away. **Miguelito Trailer Park** ($; tel. 3-25-24) at the end of the road in Las Brisas is little more than cement slabs and an often empty swimming pool; across the street is a noisy but convenient bus turnaround. **Don Felipe Trailer Park** ($$) just back from Playa Audiencia is small and usually full. **El Palmar Trailer Park** between Las Brisas and Manzanillo on the inland side of the coast highway has both a tennis court and swimming pool. The nearest camping beaches are south of Manzanillo along **Playa Campos**, or north at **Playa de Oro** or **La Culebra**.

ARRIVING & DEPARTING
By Air

The **Playa de Oro airport** is a long 26 miles from Manzanillo, 14 from Barra de Navidad. But the colectivo charges less than would be expected, and three or more people will save money on a taxi. At the terminal, you'll find car rental, a restaurant and bar, shops. On arrival, unless you have pesos, you will pay for everything at a more expensive exchange rate; there is no *casa de cambio* at the airport. Manzanillo is one of the few airports in Mexico where you can return to the airport on the colectivos; phone 2-10-86 to find out departure information. The VW vans leave from Crucero El Tajo at Av. Niños Heroes downtown.

By Bus

The central bus station is situated on Av. Hidalgo, on the highway to Colima. It's a long walk to city center, but a city bus ("centro") runs the 10 blocks into town. *Tres Estrellas* (tel. 2-01-35) is the main line here, along with *Transportes Norte de Sonora* and *Transportes del Pacífico*. Buses run to Guadalajara (six hours), Mexico City (18 hours) and Puerto Vallarta (six hours). Various lines offer second class service, with constant departures to Colima, or up the coast to Puerto Vallarta.

By Car

Manzanillo is about a four-hour drive from Puerto Vallarta (170 miles), about a five-hour drive from Guadalajara (202 miles).

By Train

The train station is situated two blocks east of main square along the waterfront. Trains depart for Guadalajara every day at 1 p.m., arriving at 8 p.m. They leave Guadalajara every morning at 9 a.m. and arrive in Manzanillo at 4 p.m. Stops en route include Cuyutlán, Tecomán, Colima, and Ciudad Guzmán. Phone *Ferrocarriles Nacionales de México* at tel. 2-00-40 to confirm the schedule. Children age 5 to 12 pay half price. The office here will also take reservations on the *Tapatío*, an express train from Guadalajara to Mexico City.

SOUTH OF MANZANILLO

CUYUTLÁN

Twenty miles south of Manzanillo, Cuyutlán is a forgotten resort. At one time, before the highway from Colima to Manzanillo, this town was a famous vacation resort, each train bringing in visitors from Guadalajara. Though the town doubles in population every winter, it is because of the campesinos, salt dealers, and their families, who come here to harvest and sell salt from the 18-mile-long Laguna de Cuyutlán. The train still passes daily, as it has since 1910, but fewer travelers get off these days.

The town is a pleasant, quiet place with a neglected plaza, a few curio shops, and a short malecón lined by some vacant 1960ish hotels that echo with the sound of better days.

The sandy beach here is almost black, and would burn your feet if it weren't for the wood-slatted walkways running down to the surf. The beach is a forest of multicolored parasols, casting shade over hundreds of empty beach chairs. Sitting in this shade, your feet sudded with surf, you can watch the vendors pull whiskers off the shrimp and scalp the coconuts. Travelers are treated well here.

The Green Wave

A mysterious attraction is the *Ola Verde* (green wave) which occurs from April to July. Some say it occurs when phosphorescent marine animals radiate in the waves, or when strange upwellings bring a greenish glow to the water. Others say this is the season when the sun strikes the waves just right, shooting green rays to the beach. Some claim it is when the seaweed in the water colors everything green, and then washes up on the beach to rot. Some swear it is a mountainous set of waves that come every year. Others declare it to be a single wave, more than 50 meters high, which the tourism department downplays into an equally impossible 15-meter wave, a glass wall that lets you see "interesting marine life of the region." One resident in town said the Ola Verde was a wave that swept through town a number of years ago, flooding the streets and breaking windows. Nobody agrees on what the Ola Verde is, except that it comes from the sea.

Places to Sleep

Most hotels here are refreshingly logical in their rates, charging half price for single

Beach at Cuyutlán

occupancy.

The big spend here is the **Hotel Los Ceballos** ($$), a 1960s-futuristic hotel; rates include meals. The **Pensión San Rafael** ($) has a surprising diversity of rooms and prices, but those facing the beach are the only ones worth the rates. **Hotel Fénix** ($) and **Hotel Colima** ($) are the cheapest of those on the beach, offering little more than a bed to sleep on. **Hotel Morelos** ($) is a block off the beach, but it compensates by offering clean rooms and the most traditional character here. Its colorful outdoor restaurant draws guests from other hotels.

ARRIVING & LEAVING
By Bus
You can catch a bus to Cuyutlán from either Armería or from the bus station in Manzanillo.

By Car
Though it is not shown on many maps, the best way to get to Cuyutlán from Manzanillo is by heading up from the west side of the zócalo on Av. Carillo Puerto. Follow this road through town. If you find yourself in a red light zone of seedy nightclubs, you are on the right road. This paved road bends around the Laguna de Cuyutlán, passes the CFE (huge electrical generating plant), and then parallels the railroad for 18 miles to Cuyutlán, along a narrow isthmus between the lagoon and Playa Campos. The deserted beach is separated from the road by a giant berm with few access points. If coming from Colima (37 miles away), turn off at Armería, and follow the paved side road five miles to Cuyutlán.

By Train
A novel way to travel is by train from Manzanillo, which gets here in the early afternoon. Check train station for exact schedules.

EL PARAÍSO
This small village, reached by way of a paved seven-mile road from Armería, is a very loose interpretation of its name. The wide beach is a fine attribute, and there is no shortage of coconuts. But the town has few facilities for travelers other than seafood

shacks, and the only hotel, **Paraiso** ($) is a big cement shell on the beach, with a swimming pool that looks full of split-pea soup.

COLIMA

From Manzanillo, it is an easy drive up to the prim capital of Colima, only a two-hour trip away via rail, or a 1-1/2 hours by toll road (65 miles). Colima is named after the only active volcano in Mexico, **Volcán de Colima**, which emits a constant plume of smoke from 20 miles away (in 1913, a huge eruption covered the area in ash).

The best place to stay is **Hotel Ceballos** ($; tel. 2-44-44) a gracefully restored traditional hotel facing zócalo at Portal Medellin 12. Across from the hotel, facing the plaza, is the **Cathedral**, on a site first established in 1527. Apart from the neon cross, the church is neoclassical in design. At the **Palacio de Gobierno**, there is a mural in honor of Hidalgo, as well as a replica of a bell he rang in 1810 to begin the War of Independence. At the **Museo de las Culturas del Occidente**, on 27 Sept. and Niños Heroes, you can view one of the most impressive collections of preColumbian pottery and artifacts in West Mexico. **Museo Nacional de la Danza, la Máscara y el Arte Popular de Occidente** is part of the *Instituto Universitario de Bellas Artes*, and offers a colorful exhibit of indigenous costumes and masks along with many unique folkloric items for sale. **Museo Arqueológico** is at the Casa de la Cultura, at Galván and Ejército Nacional. **Museo Zaragoza**, a car museum, no longer is functioning, but Sr. Zaragoza will let you in anyway if you just ask. Entrance is through the back of the Zaragoza auto-parts store, facing **Parque Núñez**. Over 350 cars, some dating to 1910, are parked in back, abandoned to their fate. Nearby is the **Parque de la Piedra Lisa**, pleasantly shady, named after a large, smooth stone. A popular legend says that any visitor who slips on the *piedra lisa* will never leave Colima, a fair warning. On February 5, during the Fiesta Brava, you can jump into the ring with a real bull, a time when aficionados are allowed to imitate the matadors.

SOUTH ALONG THE PACIFIC
Coasting down Hwy. 200

From Manzanillo, if you are headed to the lower latitudes, you will have to go inland to **Tecomán**, then take Hwy. 200 south. Around Tecomán, there are some beaches with easy access, most popular of which is **Boca de Pascuales** at the mouth of the Río Armería, popular with surfers. From Tecomán, the road winds down the desolate Michoacan coast, one of the most scenic drives in Mexico. Steep wooded hills drop into the sea, interspersed with long runs of yellow beach fringed with coconuts. The coast is undeveloped and without electricity or phones. Only a few villages here: **Maruata, Bahía Bufadero, La Peña**.

Most travelers make a day-long jump from Manzanillo to **Playa Azul**, 190 miles away, where there are half a dozen cheap hotels and bungalows. Playa Azul was once a sleepy beach town, but since the construc-

Colima artifacts are noted particularly for their wide range of zoomorphic shapes, especially dogs. The dogs are though to be emissaries of the God of Death, Xólotl, who led the dead on their journey to the underworld. It is the only animal art in Colima that wears a human face.

tion of the giant steel mill at **Lázaro Cárdenas** ten miles away, it is Pittsburgh-by-the-sea on weekends, when steel workers come to drink, carouse, and drive vehicles up and down the long, flat beach.

From Playa Azul, it is a 70-mile hop to **Ixtapa** and **Zihuatanejo**, which are completely different from each other. One is planned, the other improvised. Ixtapa is designed strictly for people on three- and four-day tour packages, and all of the the chain hotels are built to the same formula, with swim-up bars and discos, all facing the same straight beach. Zihuatanejo is much more charming, a dressed-up fishing village set around a calm bay, with budget lodgings, boutiques, and cute restaurants.

From Zihuatanejo, Hwy. 200 runs for 150 miles to **Acapulco**, best seen at night when the lights glitter on the bay. Acapulco is one of the most over-rated resorts in Mexico, plagued by severe garbage and sewage problems. Most of the middle grade hotels have been usurped by French-Canadian charter groups, making English-speaking travelers feel doubly displaced. **Pie de la Cuesta** on the north side of Acapulco is a popular alternative, at least for campers, since there are a few trailer parks here, but there are serious crime problems on the beach after dark.

From Acapulco, you can either swing back up to Mexico City, stopping at Taxco and Cuernavaca, or continue on a long 235-mile haul down Hwy. 200 to **Puerto Escondido**. This is one of the most relaxed resorts along the Pacific Coast, a haphazardly hip collection of inexpensive hotels, beautiful beaches, open air restaurants, and shops. Formerly a dedicated surfing town, it now embraces a diverse and interesting group of travelers—those who make the effort to get here. More isolated is **Puerto Angel**, 44 miles to the south. Even more remote is the beach of **Zipolito**, reached by a 2.5 mile dirt road from Puerto Angel.

From Puerto Angel, you can take one of the more torturous paved roads in Mexico

up through the jungle to **Oaxaca** (only 148 miles, but it can take five to six hours to drive) or continue on down the coast on Hwy. 200 to **Bahías Huatulco**, about 25 miles away. Despite the advertising, the resort boils down to three deluxe hotels that have been built along Bahía Tangolunga. Access to the beach is restricted to those bold enough to walk through the lobby of the Sheraton to get there. Though there are public beaches at the other bays here, this area is designed for hotel guests, not itinerant travelers.

From Bahías Huatulco, it is roughly 130 miles to the industrial port of **Salina Cruz**, and another 10 miles to the crossroads of **Tehuantepec**, the matriarchal town where women rule.

Here you can either retreat up the mountains to Oaxaca on Mex. 190 (150 miles), or continue 25 miles to the junction beyond Juchitán, where you can decide whether to take the high road or low road to the Yucatán. The quick way is by taking Mex. 185 to Villahermosa (Mexicans call it the city of two lies: it's not a villa, and it's not pretty).

Travelers Advisory

The states of Michoacán and Guerrero are rural and poor once you get into the mountains away from the resort areas. The political struggle between the entrenched PRI and the leftist parties is a very real and violent issue in the lives of the campesinos, and it wasn't too long ago that guerrillas operated in the mountains of Guerrero. This is also a marijuana producing region. Because of the pot, poverty and political struggle, travelers should take the normal precautions when traveling off Hwy. 200. In other words, don't wear your Che Guevera T-shirt up in the mountains, don't smoke pot, don't wear Rolex watches.

The more rewarding high road up into the Chiapas highlands has its hazards, including the wind-swept crossing of the isthmus (beware of trucks flipping in the wind) and the windy and washed-out mountain road to **Tuxtla Gutiérrez**. From Tuxtla, the road winds higher to **San Cristobál de las Casas**, a colonial town of Indian character, unique in Mexico. From Las Casas, it is a fantastic drop down the other side of the mountains, past the thunderous waterfalls at **Agua Azul** to the ruins of **Palenque**. From here, it is a long day's drive to the coral beaches of Quintana Roo.

Guatemala-bound travelers can reach the border crossing from Las Casas by taking Mex. 190 for 100 miles to Ciudad Cuauhtémoc. Coastal Hwy. 200 ends at Tapachula, 22 miles from the main border crossing at Ciudad Hidalgo, and 2,502 miles from the U.S. border at Tijuana.

317

Appendix

U.S. and Canadian Offices in Mexico

U.S. Embassy
Paseo de la Reforma 305
Mexico 5, DF
905-553-3333

U.S. Consulates
Ciudad Juarez, Chihuahua
Consulate General
924 Av. LopezMateos
(161) 34-048

Guadalajara, Jalisco
Consulate General
Progreso 175
(36) 25-29-28

Hermosillo, Sonora
Consulate
Issste Building, 3rd floor
Hidalgo y Costillo No. 15
(621)-38-922

Matamoros, Tamaulipas
Consulate
Avenida Primera No. 232
(891) 25-250

Mazatlan, Sinaloa
Consulate
Circunvalacion No. 6
(678) 12-905

Merida, Yucatan
Consulate
Paseo Montejo 453
(92) 25-54-09

Monterrey, Nuevo Leon
Consulate General
Av. Constitucion 411 Pon.
(83) 43-06-50

Nuevo Laredo, Tamaulipas
Consulate
Avenida Allende 3330
(871) 40-512

Tijuana, Baja California
Consulate General
Calle Tapachula 96
(706) 86 10-01

CANADA

Canadian Embassy
Schiller 529
Colonia Polanco
Mexico DF
(905) 254-3288

Canadian Consulates
Honorary Consul
Hotel Club del Sol
Mezzanine
Costera Miguel Aleman/
Reyes Catolicos
Acapulco, Guerrero
(748) 46-356

Honorary Consul
Avenida Albatros 52
Mazatlan, Sinaloa
(678) 37-320

Honorary Consul
Calle 1-F #249
Fracc. Campestre
Merida, Yucatan
(992) 70-460

Honorary Vice-Consul
German Gedovius No. 5,
Office 201
Condominio del Parque
Rio Tijuana, Baja California
Norte
(706) 84-04061

Mexican Government Tourist Offices in the United States
Chicago:
70 Eastlake St. Ste. 1413
Chicago, IL 60601
(312) 565-2786, Fax (312) 606-9012

Houston:
2707 N. Loop W., Ste. 450
Houston, TX 77008
(713) 880-5153,
Fax (713) 880-1833

Los Angeles:
10100 Santa Monica Blvd.,
Ste. 224
Los Angeles, CA 90067
(212) 203-8191,
Fax (213) 203-8316

Miami:
11522 SW 81st
Miami, FL 33156
(305) 252-1440

New York:
405 Park Ave., Ste. 1402
New York, NY 10022
(212) 755-7261,
Fax (212) 753-2874

Washington DC:
1991 Pennsylvania Ave. NW
Washington DC, 20006
(202) 728-1750,
Fax (202) 728-1758

In CANADA
Montreal:
One Place Ville Marie
Montreal, P.Q. H3B 3M9
(514) 871-1052, Fax (514) 871-3825

Toronto:
2 Bloor St. West
Toronto, Ontario M4W 3E2
(416) 925-2753, Fax (416) 926-6061

Mexican Diplomatic Offices in the U.S.

Mexican Embassy
1911 Pennsylvania Ave., NW
Washington DC, 20006
(202) 728-1600

Mexico maintains consulates in most of the principal cities in the United States, especially where there are large hispanic populations. Among these are,

Phoenix, Arizona: 602-242-7398
Los Angeles, California: 213-351-6800
San Diego, California: 619-231-0337
San Francisco, California: 415-392-5554
Denver, Colorado: 303-830-0523
Albuquerque, NM: 505-247-2139.
El Paso, Texas: 915-533-3644
Seattle, Washington: 206-682-3634

U.S. CUSTOMS
Can You Bring It Back?

Fruits & Vegetables: you can bring back bananas, blackberries, cactus fruits, dates, dewberries, grapes, lycheés, melons, papayas, pineapples and strawberries. Most vegetables are permitted except for potatoes, sweet potatoes and yams (cooked potatoes are permitted). Avocados without seeds are permitted, except in California. Many agricultural items are permitted if they pass inspection to be certain they are free of pests, soil, sand and earth. **Note:** Failure to declare agricultural items can result in fines of $25 or more (those green jacketed beagles are trained to sniff out mangos, not cocaine).

Plants & Seeds:
Special permits are required. Some plants are prohibited. Check in advance with agricultural inspectors. **Exception:** dried plant parts, such as for medicinal purposes, are permitted.

Meat: raw and cooked pork, including sausages, cold cuts, skins and pork tacos are prohibited. **Exception:** shelf-stable, canned pork and hard-cooked pork skins are permitted.

Poultry—raw meat from both domesticated and game fowl is prohibited. **Exception:** cooked poultry is permitted.

Game—check with agricultural inspectors in advance. If you are bringing back game fish, you better have a Mexican fishing license.

Other meat: imports are limited to 50 pounds per person.

Eggs: prohibited. **Exception:** boiled or cooked eggs are permitted.

Live Birds: prohibited. Wild and domesticated birds, including poultry, are prohibited. To import personally owned pet birds, contact agricultural inspectors in advance.

Straw: generally prohibited. This includes wheat straw, seeds, and all articles made from this material, including animal feed.

Nuts: permitted items are acorns, almonds, cocoa beans, chestnuts, coconuts (without husks or milk), peanuts, pecans, pinons, tamarind beans, walnuts, and waternuts.

Alcohol: you can bring back one liter of hard alcohol per adult.

Taboo

Many of more interesting trinkets bought in Mexico are not allowed in the U.S.. such as fireworks, pirated copies of tapes, narcotics and Cuban cigars. Neither can you bring in ceramics with high lead contents, steroids without a prescription, and unorthodox cures for medical problems. The law is notably hazy in some areas, such as the banning of seditious, obscene, or treasonable material. On the other hand, it can be quite succinct. Switchblades, for example, will be confiscated unless you have only one arm, in which case they are permitted. **Warning**: Mexico restricts export of gold. People have been thrown in jail for trying to leave the country with a few gold coins.

Turtle oil, lizard skin boots, or whalebone scrimshaw will probably be confiscated by U.S. Customs, along with any other products made from endangered wildlife. U.S. Customs considers all wildlife to be endangered.

If you have Customs questions while in Mexico, phone the U.S. Embassy in Mexico City at (905) 211-0042 and ask for the U.S. Customs Service.

Note: Customs allows you to bring in $400 worth of goods duty free from Mexico. A family a four can bring in $1600 worth of goods on one declaration. Enforcement is often lax, as many Mexican products are exempt from duty.

Equivalents

MEASUREMENTS

Mexico, like most of the world, measures things logically in a metric system instead of using the familiar ovoidopodul system, which can be as confusing as its name to anyone not born into it.

Distances

In Mexico, all distances are measured by kilometer. In fact, most highways are marked at two-kilometer intervals.

To translate kilometers into miles, multiply the kilometers by .62. For those without calculators, a very rough estimate can be gained by multiplying the first digit by six, and adding half of the second digit. 68 kilometers would be 36 (6 times 6) plus 4 (half of eight), or 40 miles (actually it is 42.16).

Volumes

One liter equals 0.2642 gallons, but for rough estimations, consider a liter to be the equivalent of a quart (plus a bit more). One gallon equals 3.79 liters.

Weight

Much of what is bought in Mexico, from silver jewelry to tomatoes at the market, is sold by weight, either in grams or kilograms (*kilos*). A kilogram is equal to 2.2 pounds. For a rough calculation, double the number of kilograms, then add 10 percent. For example, if you are buying 8 kilos of potatoes, multiply 8 by 2, which is 16, and add 10 percent of that sum, which is 1.6. Answer: 17.6 pounds of potatoes.

Temperature

All temperatures are given as Celsius (centigrade). Roughly, water freezes at 0 and boils at 100. Think in terms of tens.
Roughly put,

10 (50F) is jacket weather.
20 (68F) is sweater weather
30 (86F) is T-shirt weather
40 (104F) is clothes optional weather

Exact Calculations:

To calculate:	Multiply by
centimeters to inches	0.39
vice versa	2.54
meters to feet	3.28
vice versa	0.30
meters to yards	1.09
vice versa	0.91
kilometers to miles	0.62
vice versa	1.61
grams to ounces	0.035
vice versa	28.35
kilograms to pounds	2.21
vice versa	0.45

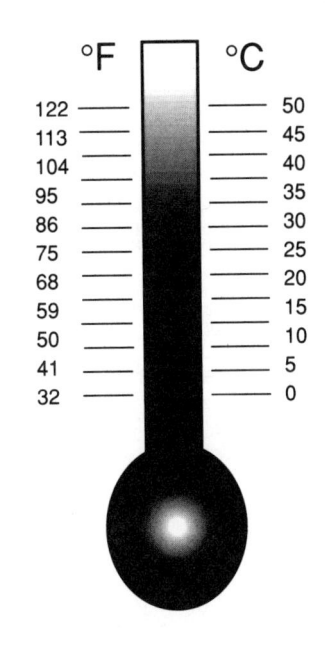

°F		°C
122		50
113		45
104		40
95		35
86		30
75		25
68		20
59		15
50		10
41		5
32		0

Acronyms, Abbreviations and a Short Glossary of Noteworthy Words

Abarrotes, a grocery store, usually small, often unrefrigerated.

Apdo., short for *Apartado Postal*, a post office box.

Av., abbrev. for *Avenida*, or Avenue.

Barrio, a neighborhood, usually of the lower class—see *colonia*

Borrachera, a drunken binge.

Borracho, a drunk person, or a state of drunkenness, as in *estoy borracho*, I am drunk. From the verb, *borrachar*.

Bruja (o), a witch. They are prevalent in rural Mexico. Some tricks of the trade: to court a girl, carry a dead hummingbird in your pocket. To seduce a person, put the leg of a beetle in their soda pop.

Bueno, means "good," but it is also used when answering the phone, instead of *Hola*.

C., abbrev. for *Calle*, or street.

Callejon, an alley or deadend street.

Casa de Cambio, a place of foreign exchange; if the rates seems too good to be true, they probably are. Beware of hidden commission charges.

Calz., abbrev. for *Calzada*, used interchangeably with *Blvd*.

Caseta Fiscal, tax collection stations along the highway for commercial trucks. Keep driving.

Caudillo, a political strongman who can deliver votes, control the unions, and maintain the peace, often with the help of his own private *pistoleros*.

Cd., abbrev. for *ciudad* (*City*).

Chilangos, a slang name for those living in Mexico City, used often in a derogatory manner by those living in *la provincia*, the provinces, or states.

CFE, the *Comisión Federal de Electricidad*, a state-owned company in charge of providing electricity.

Chile, a very hot vegetable, but also another word for penis.

Chingar, the most oft-used swear word in Mexico, literally means "to rape," a word tied to Mexico's history of conquest. Now it is part of the vernacular. What you will hear: *hijo de la chingada*, similar to S.O.B.; *vete a la chingada*, similar to "go to hell," *No chingues*, don't bother me, *me chingaron*, they screwed me. Not to be used in polite company.

C.I.A., has nothing to do with spying, instead is an abbreviation for a private company, similar to "Corporation."

CNC, the *Confederación Nacional Campesina*, a stooge union of the ruling PRI party, which busses these campesinos in from the countryside for attendance-required political rallies.

CNEP, the *Comisión Nacional de Erradicar Paludismo*, the National Commission to Eradicate Malaria. This acronym, along with a number, is painted on houses to show they have been checked for mosquitoes, a number often confused with the street address.

CNOP, the *Confederación Nacional de Organizaciones Populares*, an organization of civil servants, makes up one of the four sectors of PRI, the other three being the labor unions, campesinos, and the military.

Coca, not to be mistaken for *Coco*, which is a coconut. This is short for Coca Cola, sometimes fondly referred to as the *agua negra de imperialismo Norteamericano*, the black water of North American imperialism.

Colonia, these are distinct neighborhoods; each city is composed of different *colonias*.

CONCAMIN, a Mexican business council made up of very influential private business owners. In the political theater, they operate mostly behind the scenes, due to their poor image in this country of peasants, labor unions, and socialistic pretensions.

Con Permiso, with permission. This is a polite expression similar to "excuse me," to be used liberally when butting through lines, or working your way through a crowd.

Consupo, the National Basic Foods Corporation, operates as a retail grocery store, found in many rural villages as well as in the cities. Basic foods are subsidized by the government, making this the cheapest place to buy essential foodstuffs.

Coyote, a guide who charges high prices to escort illegal aliens across the international border to the United States.

CROC, *Confederación Revolucionaria de Obreros y Campesinos*, is another group aligned with the ruling PRI party, similar to the CNC and the CNOP.

CTM, the Confederation of Mexican Workers, is the oldest and biggest labor union, closely associated with PRI interests, but influential enough to be taken seriously by the PRI cadre.

Curandero, village healers, who use herbs and occasional incantations to cure their patients.

Depto., abbrev. for *departamento*, what is the same as an apartment.

Derecha, a direction (*a la derecha,* to the right), as well as a political persuasion (right wing), the direction Mexico is currently heading.

Derecho, straight ahead. It also means law and rights, as in human rights.

D.F., the Distrito Federal, or Federal District, another name for Mexico City.

DGN, If your tequila doesn't have these letters—a federal liquor designation—it is probably bootleg.

Distribuidora, a distributor, usually of beer or soft drinks, offering close-to-wholesale prices to the public.

Dlls., abbrev. for dollars, usually seen on price tags.

Ejidos, communal farming cooperatives, started by President Cárdenas in the wake of the Mexican Revolution. Land was expropriated from the rich landowners and distributed to the peasants, at least in theory. Meant to emulate the indigenous tradition of communal farming, these ejidos are passed from parents to children, and cannot be sold, or rented, nor can they be mortgaged for the bank loans needed to develop them. Most have proven inefficient in Mexico's new market economy, and the government is looking for a quiet way to phase them out of the national identity.

Embute, a bribe, commonly given to underpaid newspaper reporters by the government in return for favorable treatment.

Fayuca, contraband. People who illegally import items from the U.S. or abroad to sell on the mainland are called *fayuqueros,* a picaresque occupation free of the blood stain of the drug smugglers.

Federales, the plainclothes police used by the national government to keep the order in *la provincia* (the states).

FONAPAS, a cultural promotion fund.

FONATUR, the National Fund for Tourism Development, the folks who brought us Cancún and threaten similar developments at Los Cabos, Loreto, and Bahias Hualtuco.

Frontera, the borderlands adjoining both the U.S. and Guatemala are still referred to as the Frontier, a word gringos stopped using years ago.

Gachupine, originally a person born in Spain, but living in Mexico. Now used indiscriminately for gringos, light-skinned persons, or those displaying traits of arrogance and cultural superiority.

Gral., abbrev. for General.

(El) Grito, the Shout—*Viva Mexico*—roared three times on September 15th at 11 p.m. from every town and city in Mexico, in homage to Father Hidalgo's cry for freedom in 1810, which ignited the War of Independence.

Guayabera, almost a uniform for politicians and store owners. Originally from Yucatan, they are of light cotton, with waist level level pockets and applique designs, a Mexican leisure suit.

Güero, a light skinned person, often used as a name for gringos.

Hectares, a measurement of land, about two and one-half acres (multiply 2.47 to find how many acres).

Hnos., abbrev. for Hermanos, or Brothers, who often seem to go into business together.

Huarache, leather sandals, usually worn by peasants and gringos (In Mexico, a person is often judged by their shoes); walk with them new in the ocean for a custom fit.

Huevos, literally eggs, but can also mean testicles.

Huipiles, hand embroidered blouses from Yucatan and Chiapas.

INFONAVIT, the Worker's Housing Institute, which builds subsidized concrete cubicles for government workers and their families to live in.

IVA, *Impuesto al Valor Agregado*, a value added tax of six to 20 percent (the more basic the item, the less the tax); if you don't receive a receipt, you don't have to pay the tax.

Izquierda, the left, a direction as well a political persuasion.

Jefe, the boss, usually referring to the person in charge of a store, shop, yard or garage. The president is the *Jefe Máximo*.

Lana, literally wool, but also slang for money, as in *No tengo la lana*, I don't have the bread, or in this case, the wool.

Linea, the line, meaning the international border, which is considered by many to be just that, no more than a line to step across.

Llorona, a mythical weeping woman who roams throughout the night, according to some the ghost of Malinche, the mistress of Cortés.

IMSS, the *Instituto Mexicano de Seguro Social*, established in 1943, provides health and welfare benefits to workers, funded by both workers, employers, and the state.

Ing. , abbrev. for *Ingeniero*, or Engineer, a title that usually wins a bit more respect than a Licenciado.

ISSSTE, a social security institute for government workers; foreigners can usually shop in their subsidized stores.

Lic., abbrev. for *Licenciado*, technically a lawyer, but used by all college graduates as well as by anybody of social position, whether deserving or not.

Maquiladora, an assembly plant on the border. Usually owned by foreigners, they import components duty free, use cheap Mexican labor, then ship the completed product back to the U.S., paying only U.S. tax on the value added.

Machismo, the exaggerated sense of what it means to be a man, involving much bravado, a loud voice, a capacity to drink alcohol, and a proclivity to sing and fight.

Maestro, literally a teacher, but often used for a person who is a master at his craft.

Malecon, a a long ribbon of sidewalk for strolling along the edge of an ocean or river. *Maleconear* is a verb for cruising the malecon (*voy a maleconear*)

Mañana, as much a philosophy as a word. It doesn't mean tomorrow. It just means not today.

Mariachis, strolling troubadours with wide-brimmed hats, brass and string instruments, and powerful voices.

Mesero (a): a waiter. They do not bring the bill until asked. A good way to get the waiters attention is to simply say "Mesero." Some people hiss like a snake, an ungracious but effective custom.

Mestizo, the majority of the Mexican population, a mix of New and and Old World blood.

Microondas, Microwave towers that run the length of the peninsula, transmitting TV reception. These towers sit on hilltops: great vantage points, fine camp sites.

MN, abbrev. for Moneda Nacional, meaning the price is marked in pesos.

Mordida, the bite, slang for a bribe. Most any traveler who spends a stretch of time in Mexico will suffer the bite, usually at the hands of a traffic cop. Foreign travelers are prime targets, but are never taken for much. As the saying goes, they don't want to kill the goose that lays to golden egg, they just want to pluck the feathers.

Moreno, a person of dark complexion, the opposite of a güero.

N., abbrev. for *Norte*, North, considered the direction of the land of the dead by some Indian tribes.

No. , abbrev. for *Numero*, or Number.

Ote., abbrev. for *Oriente*, the East

Palacio Municipal, the municipal administrative building, usually facing a plaza.

Palapa, a open structure or hut with a palm thatch roof, a favorite roost of scorpions.

PAN, the National Action Party, a political party that stands on the right hand side of the spectrum, the Young Republicans of Mexico, popular in West Mexico.

Panga, a small open skiff powered by a big outboard. Those on the mainland are longer and narrower for use in the esteros, those on the peninsula wider and more stable for surf launching and pounding though the swells.

Panocha: a sugar candy made from cane (also an expression for the vagina).

Parada, a bus stop. Even so, you may still have to wave them to a stop.

P.B. , abbrev. for Planta Baja, the ground floor. The first floor begins one floor above.

Pemex, Petroleos Mexicanos, the petroleum monopoly owned by the national government, which controls every drop of oil, from wellhead to gas pump, from its 43-story tower in Mexico City.

Periódicos, newspapers. *Excelsior* is the main voice of the government, but international coverage is excellent. *Uno Mas Uno* and *La Jornada* are better sources of hard national news and invective left-leaning editorials, and their cable service from Havana provides one of the last communist perspectives left in the world. *Novedades* and *El Sol*, which publishes regional editions throughout Mexico, are more bland, *USA Today*-style newspapers. The *Mexico City News* is usually an excellent English language daily newspaper, depending on who the editor is of the moment.

Portillo, Lopez: the maligned president (1976-82) who held power during Mexico's spectacular economic plummet of 1982. He once said he would defend the peso like a dog. After leaving office, whenever he appeared in public people would bark at him.

Porfiriato, the reign of Porfirio Diaz, (1884-1910) during which time he opened the door to foreign investment (much like today), and tamed the country with his ruthless *rurales* (19th century counterparts to today's *federales*), who brought a violent peace to the countryside.

Pte., abbrev. for *Poniente*, the West; used on street signs.

Pulque, a poor man's beer, mildly alcoholic, brewed from the fermented sap of maguey plants, (it can't be preserved, so the only place it is sold is in *pulquerías)*.

Puros, cigars. In Mexico, you can buy famous Cuban cigars, but you must smoke them before you return to the U.S.

Rebozo, the popular woven swath worn shawl-like over the shoulders and around the arms; great for swaddling babies.

Rejas, bars that are found on almost every window that can afford it; . Decorative, even an artform, but still there for a purpose.

Retablos, miracle paintings hung in churches for answered prayers (see page 280).

S., Sur, South.

S.A., Sociedad Anónima, which means that the business is incorporated (often by anonymous investors who would rather not be in the limelight).

Sanitario: another name for the toilet, usually an outhouse or shed that is anything but sanitary.

SARH, Secretaría de Agricultura y Recursos Hidráulicos, the department of agricultural and water resources.

SCT, Secretaría de Comunicación y Transportes, in charge of both the highway and ferry systems.

SEDUE, Secretaria de Desarrollo Urbano y Ecologia, in charge of monitoring and preserving the environment, as well as overseeing parks, wildlife refuges, and federal beaches.

Se Vende, For Sale, written on cars, houses, and anything the owner wishes to sell.

Simpático, to be understanding of the beliefs, ethics and values of others.

Sr., abbrev. for Señor, Mr.

Sra., abbrev. for Señora, Mrs.

Taller: the name for a workshop, such as a Taller Mecánico (mechanic's shop), or Taller Artistico (an artist studio).

Tapatío, a person from Guadalajara.

Tarjetas: post cards.

Telmex: the national telephone company, now being sold to the public, the darling of international investors, but still damned by those who have to use it.

Tesguino, potent corn beer made by the Tarahumara. Made for immediate consumption, you won't find it in the liquor store.

Tierra y Libertad, Land and Liberty, the Zapatista battle cry still heard today. According to Article 27 of the 1917 Constitution, every campesino is entitled to a piece of land. And nobody can own more than 100 hectares of irrigated land, or 200 hectares of rain-irrigated land. Large plots were to be divided among the campesinos after the revolution. Much was, most wasn't. Vast private farms owned by *latifundistas* still exist illegally, and the struggle for land continues to provoke violence in the rural areas.

Topes, speed bumps, otherwise known as sleeping policemen.

UAG, the Autonomous University of Guadalajara, considered ultra-Catholic and right wing, a counterpart to the post-communist-oriented UNAM.

UNAM, the Autonomous National University, the central university in Mexico City, with branches all over the republic. This college is one of the largest in the world, educating close to 350,000 students per year, largely at government expense. Unlike in the U.S., ten times more money is spent on education than on the Mexican military.

Viajero, a more romantic name for travelers than *tourista*, which can be confused with diarrhea.

MEXICAN FOOD, Form and Substance

Adobo: a somewhat spicy sauce of mild chile, cloves, cinnamon, onion, and tomatoes.

Albóndigas en jitomate: meatballs stranded in tomato sauce, no noodles.

Albóndigas en Chipotle: meatballs basking in chipotle chile and tomato sauce.

Almejas: clams, best eaten raw. Often sold on the street.

Antojitos: light snacks: tacos, enchiladas, quesadillas, salsa, chips.

Arroz con leche: rice pudding, flavored with cinnamon, vanilla or raisins, often served as desert.

Atole: a bland brew of corn meal, water, and sugar, sometimes enlivened with chocolate.

Ate: a thick fruit paste.

Bistec: can be about any kind of steak, from shoe leather to T-bone.

Barbacoa: barbecued meat, often buried beneath a slow fire.

Birria: barbecued goat or mutton barbecued Mexican style.

Bolillos: tiny bread loafs rolls modeled after France's famous *petit pains* introduced during the reign of Maximillian.

Buñuelos: large round wafer-thin pastry covered with syrup.

Burritos: wheat flour tortillas filled with refried beans, green chile, cheese, and sometimes meat.

Cafe de Olla: coffee flavored with brown sugar, dusted with cinnamon. Often served in small clay mugs.

Cabrito: a milk-fed goat, usually between 45 and 70 days old, freshly killed, then cooked over open coals.

Cajeta: sauce from carmelized goat milk, a great ice cream topping.

Carnitas: a pig rendered in the pot.

Camarones con ajo: shrimp in garlic sauce.

Camarones en alambres: shish-ka-bob.

Caldo de pollo: chicken broth.

Caldo largo: a rich soup of fish and shellfish.

Caracol: conch, usually in a soup or chopped into a ceviche.

Carne Asada, thin pan-fried or broiled beef, as flavorful as it is tough.

Ceviche: raw fish (preferably a white fleshed fish, like *sierra*) and seafood chopped up with tomatoes, onions, green chile, cilantro and naturally cooked in lime juice.

Cocteles: raw oysters and cooked shrimp, lobster or shrimp, soaking in cocktail sauce, lime juice, and a dash of hot sauce.

Consomé de pollo o res: chicken or beef consommé, nothing solid to bite into.

Chicharrón: the lard under pig skin, toasted. An acquired taste.

Chilaquiles: day-old tortillas and shredded chicken, combined with cheeses, tomatoes, chiles, and cream. A hearty and inexpensive breakfast.

Chile habanero: hottest kind, can actually burn your mouth.

Chiles rellenos: Mexican stuffed peppers, made of chiles poblanos (a bit spicier but otherwise similar to bell peppers), packed with cheese or ground meat.

Chimichanga: a deep-fried burrito.

Enchilada: tortillas rolled around meat, beans, and cheese, baked with sauces, capped by cream and shredded cheese.

Enchilada Suisa: filled with chicken in milder cream-and-cheese sauce.

Filete de pescado: best fish fillets are from *huachinango* or *cabrilla*.

Flan: sweet custard, flavored with vanilla and caramel sauce.

Flautas: long deep-fried tortillas curled around fillings (they look like a flute, hence the name).

Frijoles Refritos: refried beans.

Frijoles de olla: a bean soup, often served at taco stands.

Guisados: stews of meat

Horchata: a nonalcoholic drink made from steeping rice, melon seeds or coconut in water for a few days; as popular in prehispanic times as it is today.

Huevos poché: poached eggs.

Huevos cocidos: hard-boiled eggs.

Huevos estrellados: eggs sunnyside up.

Huevos revueltos: scrambled eggs

Huevos fritos: fried eggs

Huevos tibios: soft boiled eggs

Huevos rancheros: fried eggs served on lightly fried tortilla topped with tomato- and chile-based sauce.

Huevos a la Mexicana: eggs scrambled with chopped tomatoes, onion and chile.

Huachinango: red snapper.

Jamaica: a juice of dried hibiscus (jamaica) flowers that steep in water for several hours; tastes like a cranberry drink.

Licuado: a Mexican milkshake comprising fruit, water, sugar, and sometimes milk.

Langosta: lobster

Langostina: crayfish

Lumpias: Chinese-Mexican eggrolls (most every city in Mexico has a good Chinese restaurant).

Menudo: tripe, another acquired taste, popular as an antidote for *crudo*, (hangover).

Mole: a spicy chocolate sauce of more than 40 ingredients poured over chicken or turkey. At its best, it is a heavenly blend of sesame seeds, chile, cilantro, tomatoes, raisins, and chocolate, at its worst, a cross between Kentucky Fried Chicken and a Hershey's Bar. Three main varieties are Mole Poblano, Mole Rojo, and Mole Verde.

Nopalitos: prickly pear cactus peeled, cooked and cut into chunks as a cold salad.

Ostiones en sus conchas: oyster on the half shell

Pastel: cake

Pay: a *pochismo* (English word turned into Spanish) for pie.

Picadillo: Ground beef mixed with tomatoes, garlic, zucchini, and onions.

Pescado Veracruzano: fish in a spicy yet delicate tomato sauce.

Pescado Frito: whole fried fish.

Pozole: robust soup made from a base of pork, chicken or beef. Heavily garnished with hominy.

Pulpo en su tinta: octopus drowned in its ink.

Quesadilla: tortilla filled with cheese, doubled and fried.

Queso Fundido: melted cheese, fondue-style.

Sangrita: blend of orange juice, grenadine, syrup, salt, cayenne pepper, a potent chaser for tequila.

Sincronizadas: one tortilla on the bottom, another on top, things in-between.

Sopa de ajo: fried garlic and bread cooked in chicken broth.

Sopa de lentejas: lentil soup

Sopa de verduras: vegetable soup.

Taco: a corn or flour tortilla wrapped around chicken, meat or bean filling.

Tostada, same as a taco, only hard shell and open face.

Tamales: ground corn dough spread on a corn husk, covered with a meaty sweet filling, rolled, tied, and steamed.

Tehuacan: mineral water from the same springs the Aztecs drank from. Con gas (with bubbles) or sin gas (flat).

Torta: a sandwich made of a bolillo.

BIBLIOGRAPHY

Acosta, Roberto, *Apuntes Históricos Sonorenses, La Conquista Temporal y Espiritual de Yaqui y del Mayo*. Mexico, 1949.

Alden, Peter , *Finding the Birds in Western Mexico, A Guide to the States of Sonora, Sinaloa, and Nayarit*. Tucson: University of Arizona Press, 1969.

van Andel, Tjeerd H. and G.G. Shor (eds.), *Marine Geology of the Gulf of California*. American Association of Petroleum Geologist, Memoir 3, 1964.

Andrews, Thomas F., *English Privateers at Cabo San Lucas*. Los Angeles: Dawson's Book Shop, 1979.

Aschmann, Homer, *Central Desert of Baja California*. Riverside, CA: Mannessier Pub. Co., 1967

, *Natural and Human History of Baja California*. Los Angeles: Dawson's Book Shop, 1966

, *Introduction of Date Palms into Baja California*. Economic Botony, Vol. 2, No. 2, April-June, 1957.

Ayala E., Roberto, *Sinaloa de los Destinos de México*. Mexico: 1957.

Baegert, Johann, *Observations in Lower California*. Berkeley: University of California Press, 1952.

Bancroft, Griffing, *The Flight of the Least Petrel*. New York: G.P. Putnam's and Sons, 1932.

Bancroft, Hubert H., *History of the North Mexican States and Texas. Vol. 1*. San Francisco: A. L. Bancroft, 1884.

Banks, Richard C., *Birds of Cerralvo Island*. Condor, Vol. 65, No. 4.

Bannon, John F. (ed.), *Bolton and the Spanish Borderlands*. Norman: Univ. of Oklahoma Press, 1964.

, *The Spanish Borderlands, 1513-1821*. New York: Holt, Rinehardt and Winston, 1970.

Barco, Miguel del, *The Natural History of Baja California,* trans. by Froylan Tiscareno. Los Angeles: Dawson's Book Shop, 1980.

Bates, Ken and Caroline, *Baja California*. Menlo Park, Calif.: Lane Books, 1971.

Beals, Ralph., *The Comparative Ethnology of Northern Mexico Before 1750*. Ibero-Americana, No. 2, Berkeley: Univ. of Calif., 1932.

, *The Acaxee, A Mountain Tribe of Durango and Sinaloa*. Berkeley: 1933.

Bell, P.L., *Mexican West Coast and Lower California, a Commercial and Industrial Survey*. U.S. Dept. of Commerce, Special Agent Series No. 220, Government Printing Office, 1923.

Blaisdell, Lowell, *The Desert Revolution, Baja California 1911*. Univ. of Wisconsin Press, 1962.

Blake, Dean, *West Coast Mexican Cyclones*. Monthly Weather Review, Vol. 63, 1935.

Bolton, Herbert E., *The West Coast Corridor*. Proceedings of the American Philosophical Society, Vol. 91, No. 5, 1947.

, *Rim of Christendom*. New York: MacMillan, 1936.

, *Kino's Historical Memoir of Pimería Alta.* Trans. by Herbert Bolton, 2 vols. Berkeley: University of California Press, 1919.

, *Anza's California Expeditions.* Trans. by Herbert Bolton, 2 vols., Berkeley: University of California Press, 1930.

, *Spanish Exploration in the Southwest, 1541-1706.* New York: Macmillan, 1925.

Browne, J. Ross, *A Sketch of the Settlement and Exploration of Lower California.* San Francisco, Bancroft and Co., 1868.

, *Explorations in Lower California.* Studio City, Calif.: Vaquero Books, 1966 (reprint).

Brusca, Richard, *Common Intertidal Invertebrates of the Gulf of California.* Tucson: U. of Arizona, 1980.

Buick, Harry A., *The Gringoes of Tepehuanes.* London: Longmans, 1967.

Burland, C. A., *The Gods of Mexico.* New York: G.P. Putnam's Sons, 1967.

Burrus, *Ernest J., Kino and the Cartography of Northwestern New Spain.* Tucson: Arizona Pioneer's Historical Society, 1965.

Burt, William Henry, *Unknown Animals on Islands.* San Diego Society of Natural History, Vol. 7, No. 16, October, 1932.

Cannon, Ray, *The Sea of Cortez.* Menlo Park, Calif.: Lane Mag. & Bk. Co., 1966.

Chalif, Edward and R.T. Peterson, *A Guide to Mexican Birds.* Boston: Houghton, Mifflin Company, 1973.

Chapman, Charles, *A History of California: The Spanish Period.* New York: Macmillan Company, 1921.

Clavigero, Francisco Javier, *The History of Lower California.* Transl. by Sara Lake. Palo Alto, CA: Stanford University Press, 1937.

Coolidge, Dane and Mary Roberts, *The Last of the Seris.* New York: E.P. Dutton & Co., 1939.

Cortés, Hernán, *Conquest: Dispatches of Córtes from the New World.* New York: Grosset and Dunlap, 1962.

Coyle, Jeanette, and Norman Roberts, *A Field Guide to the Common and Interesting Plants of Baja California.* La Jolla, Calif: Natural History Publishing Co., 1975.

Crosby, Harry, *The Cave Paintings of Baja California.* Salt Lake City, Utah: Copely Books, 1975.

, *The Kings Highway.* Salt Lake City, Utah: Copely Books, 1974.

, *Last of the Californios.* Salt Lake City, Utah: Copely Books, 1981.

C.T. Smith (ed.), *Guidebook of Northern Mexico-Sonoran Desert Region,* 1969.

Cudahy, John, *Mañanaland, Adventuring with Camera and Rifle Through California in Mexico.* New York, Duffield & Company, 1928

Cushing, Sumner W., *The Distribution of Population in Mexico.* Geographical Review, Vol. XI, No. 2, April 1921.

Dawson, Elmer Yale, *Cactus at the Water's Edge.* Desert Plant Life, Vol. 21, No. 4, April 1949.

Del Río, Ignacio, *A La Diestra Mano de las Indias.* La Paz: Gobierno del Estado de Baja California Sur, 1985.

Dewey, Commander, *Remarks on Baja California.* U.S. Hydrographic Office, Pub. No. 6, 1874.

Díaz del Castillo, Bernal, *The Discovery and Conquest of Mexico.* New York:

Farrar, Straus and Cudahy, 1956.

Donahue, John A., *After Kino: Jesuit Missions in Northwestern New Spain, 1711-1767*. St. Louis, Mo.: Jesuit Historical Institute, 1969.

Dozier, Craig L., *Mexico's Transformed Northwest, the Yaqui, Mayo and Fuerte Examples*. Geographical Review, Vol. 53, Oct. 1963.

Dunn, Cordon E., *Tropical Cyclones*. Compendium of Meteorology, Boston, American Meteorological Society, 1951.

Dunne, Peter M., *Pioneer Black Robes on the West Coast*. Berkeley & Los Angeles: Univ. of Calif. Press, 1940.

, *Early Jesuit Missions in Tarahumara*. Berkeley & Los Angeles: Univ. of Calif. Press, 1948.

, *Black Robes in Lower California*. Berkeley: Univ. of Calif. Press, 1952.

Durham, J. Wyatt, *Corals in the Gulf of California*. Geological Society of America, Memoir No. 20, March 26, 1947.

Ekholm, Gordon F., *Excavations at Guasave, Sinaloa, Mexico*, Anthropological Papers, Vol. 38, pt. II. New York: American Museum of Natural History, 1942)

Fierro Blanco, Antonio, *The Journey of the Flame*. Boston: Houghton Mifflin, 1933.

Forbes, Alexander, California, *A History of Upper and Lower California*. London: Smith, Elder, and Co., 1839.

Gallagher, John, *Personal Reminiscences of the War in Upper and Lower California between the American and Native Troops*. Berkeley: Manuscript at Bancroft Library.

Gamez García, Ernesto, *Historia Antigua de Sinaloa del Mocorito al Zuaque*. Culiacán: Univ. de Sinaloa, Dept. de Publicaciones, 1965.

Galbraith, F.W., *Craters of the Pinacates (in Southern Arizona Guidebook)*. Tucson: Arizona Geological Society, 1955 In Southern Arizona Guidhbook.

Gerhard, Peter, *Pirates in Baja California*. Mexico: Editorial Tlílan Tlapalon, 1963.

Gleason, Duncan, *The Islands and Ports of California*. New York: Devin-Adair Co., 1958.

Gomez, Eduardo Hernandez, *Six Little Known Prehistoric Rock Art Sites in the Municipio of Mulege*. San Diego: Baja California Symposium, 1977.

Grant, Campbell, *Rock Art of Baja California*. Los Angeles: Dawson's Book Shop, 1974.

Gulick, Howard E. *Nayarit, Mexico, A Traveler's Guidebook*. Glendale, Calif: Arthur H. Clark Company, 1965.

, and Peter Gerhard, *Lower California Guidebook, A Descriptive Traveler's Guide*. Glendale: The Arthur H. Clark Company, 1967.

Gutmann, James, *Geology of Crater Elegante, Sonora, Mexico*. Geological Society of America Bulletin 87, 1976.

Hales, Jr., John E., *Southwestern United States Summer Monsoon Source—Gulf of Mexico or Pacific Ocean?* Journal of Applied Meteorology, Vol 13, April 1974.

, *Surges of Maritime Tropical Air Northward over the Gulf of California*. Monthly Weather Review, #100, No. 4, 1972.

Hamilton, Warren, *Origin of the Gulf of California*. Bulletin of the Geological Society of America, Vol. 72, No. 9, September, 1961.

Hancock, Ralph, *Baja California*. Los Angeles: Academy Publishers, 1953.

Hallenbeck, Cleve and Juanita H. Williams, *Legends of the Spanish Southwest*. Glendale, Calif.: Arthur H. Clark Co., 1938.

Hardy, R.W.H., *Travels in the Interior of Mexico, 1825-1828*. Glorieta, NM: Rio Grande Press, reprinted in 1977.

Hastings, J. Rodney, *People of Reason and Others: The Colonization of Sonora to 1767*. Arizona and the West 3, Winter, 1961.

Hastings, James R. and R. Humphrey, *Climatological Data and Statistics for Sonora and Northern Sinaloa*. Tucson, Univ. of Arizona, Institute of Atmospheric Physics, Technical Reports on the Meteorology and Climatology of Arid Regions, No. 19, 1969.

Henderson, David, *Men and Whales at Scammon's Lagoon*. Los Angeles: Dawson's Book Shop, 1972.

Howarth, O.H., *The Western Sierra Madre of Mexico*. Geographical Journal, Vol. VI, No. 5, Nov. 1895

Hunter, Jim, *Offbeat Baja*. San Francisco: Chronicle Books, 1977.

Ives, Ronald L., *Dating of the 1746 Eruption of Tres Virgenes Volcano, Baja California Sur, Mexico*. Geological Society of America Bulletin 73, 1962. , *Lava Desert of Pinacate*. Pacific Discovery, 18, 1965.

Johnson, Paul, *A Field Guide to the Gems and Minerals of Mexico*. Mentone, CA: Gembooks, 1965.

Jones, J. Knox, Jr., Ticul Alvarez and M. Raymond Lee, *Noteworthy Mammals from Sinaloa, Mexico*. Univ. of Kansas Publ., Muc. Nat. Hist., Vol. 14, 1962.

Jones, Vern, *Baja California Cruising Notes*. Julian: Sea Breeze Publications, 1976.

Kelly, Isabel T., *Excavations at Chametla, Sinaloa*. Ibero-Americana, No. 14, Berkeley: Univ. of Calif., 1938

Kennedy, John G., *Tarahumara of the Sierra Madre; Beer, Ecology, and Social Organization*. Arlington Heights, Ill.: AHM Publishing Corp.

Kenyon, *Breeding Population of Osprey*. Condor, Vol. 49, July 1947.

Kessell, John, *Friars, Soldiers, and Reformers: Hispanic Arizona and the Sonora Mission Frontier, 1767-1856*. Tucson: University of Arizona Press, 1976.

Kirchner, John A., *Los Ferrocarriles de Baja California Sur*. La Paz: FONAPAS, 1981.

Klink, Jerry, *The Mighty Cortez Fish Trap*. New York: A.S. Barnes & Co., 1974.

Krmpotic, M.D., *Life and Works of the Reverend Ferdinand Konscak (Consag), 1703-1759, An Early Missionary in California*. Boston: Stratford Company, 1923.

Krutch, Joseph, *The Forgotten Peninsula, A Naturalist in Baja California*. New York: Sloane & Assoc., 1961. , *Invasion of Baja California*. Mexican Life, Vol. 35, No. 4, April, 1959.

Lamb, Dana, *Enchanted Vagabonds*. New York: Harper and Brothers, 1938.

Larson, Peggy, *The Deserts of the Southwest, A Sierra Club Naturalist's Guide*. San Francisco: Sierra Club Books, 1977.

Leigh, Randolph, *Forgotten Waters*. New York: J.B. Lippincott Company, 1941.

Leon-Portilla, Miguel, *Indian Place Names of Baja California Sur*. Los Angeles: Southwest Museum, Highland Park.

Leopold, A. Starker, *Wildlife of Mexico, The Game Birds and Mammals*. Berkeley:

Univ. of Calif. Press, 1959.

Lewis, Leland, *Baja Sea Guide*. Newport Beach, Calif: Sea Publications, 1971.

Lindsay, George, *Some Natural Values of Baja California*. Pacific Discovery, Vol. 23, No. 2., March-April, 1970.

Lumbier, Manuel Muñoz, *Las Islas Mexicanas*. Mexico: Secretaría de Educación Publica, 1940.

Madsen, William and Claudia, *A Guide to Mexican Witchcraft*. Mexico City: Minutiae Mexicana, 1969.

Mailliard, *Expedition of California Academy of Sciences to Gulf of California in 1921*. Proceedings of Calif. Academy of Sciences, 4th series, 12, 1921.

Martinez, Pablo L., *A History of Lower California*. Mexico: Editorial Baja California, 1960.

Massey, William C., *Tribes and Languages of Baja California*. Southwestern Journal of Anthropology, Vol. 5, No. 3, 1949.

, *Cultural History in the Cape Region of Baja California*. Berkeley: University of Calif. dissertation, June 1955.

Mathes, Michael W., *Las Misiones de Baja California, 1683-1849*. La Paz: Editorial Aristos, 1977.

, *First from the Gulf to the Pacific, The Diary of the Kino-Atondo Peninsular Expedition*. Los Angeles: Dawson's Book Shop, 1969.

, *Yenecamu: Historical Highlights of Cabo San Lucas, 1535-1822*. La Paz: Asociación Cultural de las Californias Symposium XVI.

, *A Brief History of the Land of Calafia: the Californias, 1533-1795*. La Paz: Patronato del Estudiante SudCaliforniano, 1977.

Meighan, Clement W., *Indian Art and History: A Testimony of Prehispanic Rock Paintings in Baja California*. Los Angeles: Dawson's Book Shop, 1969 , *Seven Rock Art Sites in Baja California*. Socorro, NM: Ballena Press.

McDonald, Marquis, *Baja, Land of Lost Missions*. San Antonio: Naylor Co., 1968.

McMahan, Mike, *There It Is, Baja!* Riverside, Calif.: Manessier Publishing, 1973.

Moran, R., *Cardon*. Pacific Discovery, Calif. Academy of Sciences, Vol. 21, No. 2, March-April, 1968.

Murray, Spencer, *Cruising the Sea of Cortez*. Palm Desert, Calif: Desert-South west, 1963.

Napoli, Father Ignacio Maria (trans. by James Moriarty & Benjamin Smith), *The Cora Indians of Baja California*. Los Angeles: Dawson's Book Shop, 1970.

Nabhan, Gary, P., *Gathering the Desert*. Tucson: Univ. of Arizona Press, 1985.

Nelson, Edward W., *Lower California and its Natural Resources*. Riverside, Calif.: Manessier Publishing Co., 1966 (reprint of 1921 edition)

North, Arthur, *Camp and Camino in Lower California*. New York: Baker and Taylor Co., 1910.

Olea, Hector R., *Breve Historia de la Revolución en Sinaloa, 1910-1917*. México: Biblioteca del Instituto Nacional de Estudios Históricos de la Revolución Mexicana, 36, 1964.

Orr, Robert, *Expedition to the Sea of Cortez*. Animals, Vol. 6, No. 4, London, 1965.

Pas, van der, *In Search of the Original Californian, Herman ten Kate's Expedition to Baja California 1883-1884*. Copy of typescript in Bancroft Library.

Paz, Octavio, *The Other Mexico, Critique of the Pyramid*, trans. by Lysander Kemp. New York: Grove Press, 1972.

, *The Labyrinth of Solitude*. New York: Grove Press, 1961.

Pfefferkorn, Ignaz, *Sonora, a Description of the Province*. Tucson: University of Arizona Press, 1989.

Pennington, Campbell W., *The Tarahumar of Mexico*. Salt Lake City: Univ. of Utah Press, 1963.

Peyrot, G., *Un Viaje a Baja California*. Mexico: Editorial Litorales, 1968.

Prospectus of the Trust Company of Guaymas and Mulege Ferry and Sugar Culture and Refining Company. Bacon & Company, 1880; Manuscript at Bancroft Library.

Polzer, *A Kino Guide*. Tucson: Southwestern Mission Research Center, 1968.

Purcell, Susan Kaufman, et. al., *Mexico-United States Relations*, New York: Academy of Political Science, 1981.

Reed, John, *Insurgent Mexico*. New York: Simon and Schuster, 1969.

Reid, *Pearling in the Americas*. Bulletin of the Pan American Union, Vol. 40, No. 3, March 1915.

Riding, Alan, *Vecinos Distantes, Un Retrato de los Mexicanos*. Mexico City: Planeta, 1985.

Robertson, Thomas A., *A Southwestern Utopia*. Los Angeles: Ritchie Press, 1964.

Robinson, John W., *Camping and Climbing in Baja*. Glendale, Calif: La Siesta Press, 1979.

Roca, Paul, *Paths of the Padres through Sonora: An Illustrated History & Guide to its Spanish Churches*. Tucson, Ariz: Arizona Pioneers Historical Society, 1967.

Roden, Gunnar I., *Oceanographic and Meteorological Aspects of the Gulf of California*. Pacific Science, Vol. 7, Jan. 1958.

Rogers, Woodes, *A Cruising Voyage Round the World*. London, 1708-1711.

Rosendal, Hans E., *Mexican West Coast Tropical Cyclones*. Weatherwise, Vol. 16, 1963.

Salvatierra, Juan María de, *Selected Letters about Lower California*, translated by Ernest Burrus. Los Angeles, Calif.: Dawson's Book Shop, 1971.

Sanford, Paul, *Where the Old West Never Died, Sage of Meling Guest Ranch*. San Antonio: Naylor Co., 1968.

Sauer, Carl O., *The Road to Cibola*. Ibero-Americana, No. 3, Berkeley: Univ. of Calif., 1932.

, and D.D. Brand, *Atzlán: Prehistoric Mexican Frontier on the Pacific Coast*. IberoAmericana, No. 1, Berkeley: Univ. of Calif., 1932.

, *The Personality of Mexico*. Geographical Review, American Geographical Society, Vol. 31, 1941.

Serra, Junipero, Ben Dixon (ed.), *The Journal of Padre Junipero Serra, Loreto to San Diego*. Manuscript, Junipero Serra Museum, San Diego, 1955.

Shepard, Francis P., *Submarine Topography of the Gulf of California*, 1940 E. W. Scripps Cruise to the Gulf of California, Geological Society of America, Memoir 43, Part III, 1950.

Shreve, Forrest, *Vegetation of the Northwestern Coast of Mexico*. Bulletin, Torrey Botanical Club, Vol. 61, 1934.

, *Lowland Vegetation of Sinaloa*. Bulletin, Torrey Botanical Club, Vol. 64, 1937.

, *The Vegetation of the Cape Region of Baja California*. Madroño, Vol. 4, No. 4, Oct. 1937.

, and Ira L. Wiggins, *Vegetation and Flora of the Sonoran Desert*. Palo Alto: Stanford Univ. Press, Calif, 1964.

Sluiter, Engel, *The Word Pechelingue, Its Derivation and Meaning*. Hispanic American Historical Review, Vol. XXIV, 1944.

Spicer, Edward, *Cycles of Conquest, The Impact of Spain, Mexico, and the United States on the Indians of the Southwest, 1533-1960*. Tucson, Ariz: University of Arizona Press, 1962.

Steinbeck, John, and Edward R. Ricketts, *The Log from the Sea of Cortez*. New York: Viking Press, 1941.

Sykes, Godfrey, *The Camino del Diablo: With Notes on a Journey in 1925*. Geographical Review, 17, 1927

, *The Colorado Delta*. American Geographical Society, Special Publication No. 19, 1937.

, *Summer Journey on the Devil's Road*. Desert Magazine, April, 1951.

Taraval, Father Sigismundo, *The Indian Uprising in Lower California 1734-1737*, trans. by Marguerite Wilbur. Los Angeles: The Quivara Society, 1931.

Taylor, Alexander, *A Historical Summary of Baja California, 1532-1867*. Pasadena, Calif.: Socio-Technical Books, 1971.

Thompson, Donald, and Nonie McKibben, *Gulf of California Fishwatcher's Guide*. Tucson: Golden Puffer Press, 1976.

, Lloyd T. Finely, and Alex N. Kerstitch, *Reef Fishes of the Sea of Cortez*. John Wiley & Sons, Inc. 1979.

Timberman, O.W., *Mexico's Diamond in the Rough, a Lower California Adventure*. Los Angeles: Westernlore Press, 1959.

Tinker, Ben, *Mexican Wilderness and Wildlife*. Austin: University of Texas Press.

Toor, Frances, *A Treasury of Mexican Folkways*. New York: Crown Publishers, 1947.

Violetti, Paul E., *Shelling in the Sea of Cortez*. Tucson: Dale Stuart King Publisher, 1964.

Wagner, Henry, *Spanish Voyages to the Northwest Coast of America in the Sixteenth Century*. San Francisco: California Historical Society, 1929.

, *The Discovery of California*. California Historical Society Quarterly, Vol. 1, No. 1, July 1922.

, *The Voyage of Francisco de Ulloa*. Calif. Historical Society Quarterly, Vol. 3, No. 4, December 1924.

, *Pearl Fishing Enterprises in the Gulf of California*. The Hispanic American Historical Review, Vol. 10, No. 2, May, 1930.

Wampler, Joseph C. *New Rails to Old Towns: The Region and Story of the Ferrocarriles Chihuahua al Pacífico*. Berkeley: 1969.

Weed, W.H., *Notes on Certain Mines in the States of Chihuahua, Sinaloa, and Sonora, Mexico*. Transactions, American Institute of Mining Engineers, vol. 32, 1902.

Werner, David, *Donde No Hay Doctor*. Palo Alto: The Hesperian Foundation.

Wilbur, Stanford, *Birds of Baja California*. Berkeley: University of California Press, 1987.

Wiggins, Ira L., *Flora of Baja California*. Palo Alto, Calif: Stanford University Press, 1980.

Wilbur, Sanford, *Birds of Baja California*. Berkeley: Univ. of California, 1987.

INDEX

NOTES

FREE NEWSLETTER

We are constantly trying to keep pace with the rapid political, social and economic changes in Mexico. If you would like to receive a free newsletter update to this book, please fill in the form below and send it to:
 La Paz Publishing
P.O. Box 1889
Ramona, CA, 92065

_____

Name

_____

Address

_____

City, State & Zip

ADDITIONAL BOOKS

If you would like an additional copy of
WEST MEXICO, From Sea to Sierra,
please send $16.95, plus $2.00 shipping. If
you have a California address, please add
7% sales tax ($1.20). Send check or money
order to:
La Paz Publishing
P.O. Box 1889
Ramona, CA, 92065

AGRADECIMIENTOS

My indebtedness for completing this book extends to more people than can be named, or even remembered, companions of the road. In particular, though, I give a sorrowful *abrazo* to the late Anita Walker, who shared her love and insight into the Mexican mystique; may the mariachis sing in the hereafter. And to my dear friends in La Paz, who contributed countless hours to this book without ever knowing it. To my brother-in-law, Peter Cole, whose talent for bringing ink to life with the Zen of a brush stroke is pure alchemy. To the imperturbable librarians at the University of San Francisco, University of Arizona, the Mission Santa Barbara, the Bancroft Library in Berkeley, and the Biblioteca Pablo Martinez in La Paz. To Ana Rosshandler for correcting the Spanish text. To Cris Featherweed, for her editorial torque, and to Mat Marcus for his computer problem-solving. To Bruce Proctor, for his darkroom skills in printing the unprintable photo on the cover. And to Eric and Lyndal Cole, for letting me not just work in their studio, but live for a quite a few moons in their house as well, along with my entire family, and to Eric particularly for his after-hours help in photostating the illustrations. To Gwen and Gary Pellecchia at La Paz Publishing, Gary for his careful reading of the first part of the book, Gwen for never refusing the least favor asked; she has helped greatly in getting this book produced and on the bookshelf.

Most of all, I want to thank my wife Jil, for her intuition and frank advice, her patient support, her willingness to go to places only so others wouldn't have to. And of course thanks to my irrepressible children, Olivia and Dashiel; their smiles have more power than a diplomatic passport, opening hearts that would otherwise remain closed.

Above all, to my father and in memory of my mother. They never failed to support the wayward direction of their son. To them, I dedicate this book.

After graduating from U.C.S.B. in 1978, Charles Kulander left for Mexico, solo-sailing a 25 ft. boat down from San Francisco, a portable Smith-Corona stowed under his bunk. He has lived in Mexico for 10 years—La Paz, Loreto, Manzanillo, Cuernavaca, and Mexico City—working as a freelance writer, associate editor of Baja California Magazine, and as a section editor for the Mexico City News. He has traveled to every region in Mexico, spent four years sailing the Sea of Cortés, made the first solo descent by boat of the Barranca del Cobre (from Divisadero to Urique), and continues to explore the geographies of the Mexican mystique.

Peter Jon Cole is an internationally renowned sculptor who lives in La Paz, Baja California Sur. He has an M.F.A. from Boston University, and has shown his work in Salt Lake City, Boston, Mexico City and La Paz. He is the recipient of a Ford Foundation Grant, the prestigious Kahn Award, and a Fulbright Grant for study in Mexico.